^{THE} BEST

HOSPITALS

^{IN}AMERICA

THE BEST
HOSPITALS
IN AMERICA

Second Edition

JOHN W. WRIGHT *&* LINDA SUNSHINE

 **Gale Research Inc.**

An International Thomson Publishing Company

I(T)P

NEW YORK • LONDON • BONN • BOSTON • DETROIT • MADRID
MELBOURNE • MEXICO CITY • PARIS • SINGAPORE • TOKYO
TORONTO • WASHINGTON • ALBANY NY • BELMONT CA • CINCINNATI OH

John W. Wright and Linda Sunshine
Edward J. Dwyer, *Principal Writer and Researcher*
John Kryk, *Principal Writer and Researcher (Canada)*
John Rosenthal and Mary Quigley, *Senior Writers and Researchers*
Maureen Chiofalo, *Research Associate*
Ashe Typing (Ridge, NY), *Data Entry*

Gale Research Inc. Staff
Karen Boyden, *Coordinating Editor*
Sheila Dow, Jim Edwards, Christine B. Jeryan, Paul Lewon, Kyung-Sun Lim, Jacqueline L.
Longe, Zoran Minderovic, Donna Olendorf, and Robyn Young, *Assisting Editors*
Jeffrey Muhr, *Editorial Technical Support*
Cynthia Baldwin, *Product Design Manager*
Mark Howell and Pamela A.E. Galbreath, *Cover Design*
Mark Howell and Tracey Rowens, *Page Design*

Cover photo of hospital courtesy of the University of Michigan Medical Center.

♾" The paper used in this publication meets the minimum requirements of American National Standard for Information Sciences—Permanence Paper for Printed Library Materials, ANSI Z39.48-1984.

♻ This book is printed on recycled paper that meets Environmental Protection Agency standards.

This publication is a creative work fully protected by all applicable copyright laws, as well as by misappropriation, trade secret, unfair competition, and other applicable laws. The authors and editors of this work have added value to the underlying factual material herein through one or more of the following: unique and original selection, coordination, expression, arrangement, and classification of the information.

Library of Congress Cataloging-in-Publication Data
Wright, John W., 1941-
    The best hospitals in America / John W. Wright & Linda Sunshine. — 2nd ed.
        p.   cm.
    Sunshine's name appears first on the earlier ed.
    Includes index.
    ISBN 0-8103-9874-5
    1. Hospitals—United States—Directories. 2. Medicine—Specialties and specialists—United States—Directories. 3. Medicine—Research—United States—Directories. 4. Hospitals—Canada—Directories. 5. Medicine—Specialties and specialists—Canada—Directories. 6. Medicine—Research—Canada—Directories. 7. Consumer education.   I. Sunshine, Linda.   II. Title.
RA981.A2S86   1995
362.1'025'73—dc20   94-37062
                                                                                  CIP

Printed in the United States of America

10 9 8 7 6 5 4 3 2 1

 I⟨T⟩P™   Gale Research Inc., an International Thomson Publishing Company.
                ITP logo is a trademark under license.

CONTENTS

UNITED STATES

APPENDIXES

INDEXES

NOTE TO READERS

Because the practice of medicine and the administration of hospital care is conducted by fallible human beings, we cannot and do not in any way guarantee that you will receive flawless medical treatment at the hospitals, clinics, and medical centers described in this book. While this book describes some of the finest medical institutions in the world, errors in judgment can happen even at the best hospitals. We cannot, therefore, be held responsible for any medical mishap or malpractice that might occur if you choose one of these institutions as a result of reading this book.

Please note, too, that all of the facts and figures in the book have been provided by the hospitals we've included and are based on material gathered through June 1994. Some of the information will no doubt change—doctors can and often do switch their affiliations, and room charges usually go up each year—so we recommend that you call the hospital directly if you have any questions. This is especially true regarding admissions policies and financial requirements, which, in today's volatile hospital environment, could change suddenly at some institutions.

ACKNOWLEDGMENTS

Over the last decade or so, several magazines have regularly run lists of "best hospitals," but, as far as we know, this is the first book of its kind ever published. Although our Introduction makes it clear that the results are based on extensive research, we do not claim to be professionals in the health care field. We are writers—journalists, if you prefer—who have searched for reliable information on behalf of prospective patients, who in today's dramatically changing hospital world need all the help and advice they can get. We, of course, had a great deal of assistance.

From inception, this book has had the solid underpinning of continuous consultation with physicians in various regions of the country. We need to offer a special word of thanks to the many physicians who helped us, some of them at every stage of the book's development. At the very beginning of our research, our discussions with Drs. Frank Harford and Robert Leupold helped us develop our first set of criteria and compile our initial list of hospitals. We consulted further with physicians around the country, both about our criteria for determining excellence in hospital care and about specific hospitals in their regions and specialties. They included Drs. Najib Bouz, Melvin Britton, Peter Buckley, Thomas Bunch, Harris Burstin, William Conway, Roger Enlow, John Ervin, Thomas Ferguson, Irving Fox, Charles Goldberg, Francis Goldstein, Stewart Greisman, George Griffin, Glen Hait, James Halper, John Hurley, David Martin, Ellen Millis, Desmond O'Duffy, Martin Oster, George Paxton, Marc Rubinstein, Irwin Steiger, Steven Tay, Robert Treat, and Michael Wise. A number of other physicians spoke to us—and quite candidly, too—but only on the condition that they remain anonymous. As our list of hospitals continued to take shape, we went back to several of these doctors for further advice. Of course, not all of them would comment on every hospital and not every hospital they recommended was included, though we frequently mention those institutions in the introductory remarks to hospitals in the same area. In Canada, we received advice from Drs. Andre Lalonde, George Wyse, Gord Jaycee, and Judith Sharnian. Several nursing professionals, including Jeanette Pick, Barbara Burke, and Valerie Shannon, were also very helpful. In the end, the final choices were ours.

We also learned a great deal from the published articles and books about hospitals written by physicians, including Arnold Relman, the editor of the prestigious *New England Journal of Medicine;* Joyce Craddick; Herbert Dietrich; Steven Jones; William Schwartz; and John Wennberg; though we wish to make clear that none of these doctors specifically recommended hospitals to us.

Throughout the project, we received help and advice from numerous other sources. We would like to thank the people at the Health Care Financing Administration, especially Phillip Cotterill and Karen Beebe, for their patience and cooperation in obtaining and explaining the complexity of care lists compiled for Medicare purposes. We also wish to acknowledge Alice Brown at the Joint Commission on Accreditation of Healthcare Organizations for her help in explaining the procedures for hospital evaluation. (See Appendix 1 for more information on this most important group and their first public listing of first-rate hospitals around the country.) In addition, numerous people in various parts of the National Institutes of Health gave us information on a continuing basis, always courteously and efficiently.

A special word of thanks must be given to the more than 150 people in public affairs and communications departments at all of the hospitals we contacted. Their patience in dealing with our questions and their cooperation in trying to obtain detailed facts and figures from doctors and administrators— even when they met strong resistance—have made this a much better book.

We'd also like to express our appreciation to the University of Michigan Medical Center. The hospital building photograph on the book's cover is courtesy of their Department of Public Relations.

Finally, to the people at Gale Research Inc., especially Karen Boyden, our sincerest thanks for all your help and for believing in this project.

INTRODUCTION

When you or someone you love becomes seriously ill and needs special medical attention, how do you go about finding the best possible hospital to treat that illness? Unless you need immediate emergency room services—when the closest place may be the best place—you probably select a hospital because of its location or because of the recommendation of a single doctor. More frequently today, you go where your health plan says you must go. Yet, hospital care can vary greatly from one institution to another, and in a medical crisis you want to find the best hospital—one capable of delivering the most advanced care. This book can help.

The Best Hospitals in America is the only comprehensive guide to the services offered at the most prestigious medical institutions in the United States and Canada. Based on the recommendations of physicians from around the country, and supported by information from government sources, professional and popular publications, and surveys or interviews with about 150 hospitals, this book provides the kind of authoritative information you need to choose the right hospital. For while our research has convinced us that there are hundreds of first-rate hospitals in the United States and Canada, we also discovered that it is difficult for the general public to find out which ones are providing the most up-to-date treatments and doing so with care and concern for their patients. Our intention is to help remedy that situation by identifying hospitals and medical centers whose special qualities have earned them the highest standing in the medical community.

At these institutions can be found many of the world's leading physicians; the most up-to-date, state-of-the-art medical technology; and, in almost every instance, the most prestigious medical research programs. Most important, these hospitals are known within the medical community for their ability to treat the most complicated types of illness in a wide range of specialties or, for a few of the hospitals included, in specific areas, such as cancer or orthopedics. All of these hospitals are regional referral centers, and, in a few cases, national and international referral centers, offering the most advanced forms of medical practice available today. In other words, these are places to which physicians in other hospitals often send their sickest patients—and with good reason.

The hospitals profiled in this book are home to many of the most highly regarded medical programs in the nation. Included here are such extraordinary services as the Cleveland Clinic's program in cardiac surgery, the cancer treatment center at the Mayo Clinic, stroke rehabilitation at Columbia-Presbyterian Medical Center in New York, heart transplantation at the University of Alabama, and neonatology at Brigham and Women's in Boston. Other programs, such as the liver transplant program at Presbyterian University Hospital in Pittsburgh, or the bone marrow transplant program at the Fred Hutchinson Cancer Research Center in Seattle, are known throughout the world for their pioneering efforts in these relatively new areas.

Until recently, such knowledge was the special province of those in the medical profession and the hospital industry. With the information in this book, however, you will be able to find outstanding treatment centers for just about any serious illness. The institutions included here are listed by U.S. state or Canadian province, so you will be able to select a hospital in your geographic area. For certain serious conditions, however, you may be willing to travel to receive the most advanced care. This book can help you pinpoint the particular hospital or hospitals throughout the country that specialize in the condition you, a family member, or a friend is suffering from.

To this edition, we've added several helpful appendixes. One presents the well-known *U.S. News & World Report* rankings of the best U.S. hospitals according to medical specialty. Another identifies federally funded cancer centers, where all of the latest treatments and therapies are being developed. Finally, to demonstrate that many fine hospitals exist across the country, we've included a listing of 274 U.S. hospitals that have received a special citation of commendation from the Joint Commission on Accreditation of Healthcare Organizations (JCAHO). Most of these institutions are community hospitals or VA medical centers that rarely attract attention, but provide the kind of superb medical care that demands recognition.

First created in 1951 by four major medical associations, including the AMA, the Joint Commission was charged with establishing basic national standards of hospital care. It quickly became a vital agency for hospitals across the country, as state government licensing boards and major insurance companies all came to rely on the on-site surveys the commission conducted.

In recent years, the commission has expanded its coverage to include HMOs, hospices, and clinics. It has also recently decided to transform the way it carries out its mission of improving the standards of health care. Under the banner of an "Agenda for Change," the JCAHO has announced plans to publish much of the data it collects and to issue "report cards" on every hospital it surveys. In addition, it plans to make random, unannounced visits to hospitals to help assure continuous adherence to basic standards. These policies should take effect in 1995, and information on all surveyed hospitals and health care organizations should be available within three years.

Just what will result from these major changes in the accreditation process is hard to predict, since we don't know what kinds of information will be made public. Many observers believe that all data relevant to judging a hospital's performance should be released, since taxpayers fund so much of the costs of hospitalization.

THE CRITERIA FOR SELECTION

The criteria we developed for selecting the hospitals and medical centers described in this book were based entirely on the needs and concerns of patients. We sought hospitals that deliver quality care in a wide range of medical categories (in a few cases, in special areas, such as cancer or rehabilitation) and that do so in well-kept facilities, employing the most up-to-date medical technology. We especially looked for hospitals with high-powered staffs of senior physicians who have national reputations in their fields; with excellent nursing staffs whose quality is maintained through rigorous requirements for acceptance; and with a concern for working conditions.

With these criteria in mind, we began to solicit recommendations from physicians in all parts of the country. Not surprisingly—at least not to many people in the hospital and health care fields—these physicians led us directly to the large teaching hospitals in their areas. A teaching hospital is attached to, or affiliated with, a well-known medical school. They are called teaching hospitals because they provide new doctors with continuing education programs and settings in which to cultivate the practice of medicine. In earlier days, teaching hospitals most often treated indigent patients, whose poverty consigned them to the role of medical guinea pigs. By the 1950s and 1960s, however, many of these hospitals had emerged as prestigious institutions where research and clinical practice were combined, resulting in unprecedented breakthroughs in every area of medical science. Consequently, enormous financial grants from the federal government, corporations, foundations, and wealthy individuals helped place teaching hospitals at the center of American medicine.

All of the hospitals and medical centers described in this book have highly respected clinical research programs—the kind that lead to new and better forms of patient care. Many of them, for example, have been specially designated by the National Cancer Institute as regional Comprehensive Cancer Centers or Clinical Cancer Centers and, as such, receive funding for research, patient care, and, in the case of comprehensive centers, even community education projects. (See Appendix 3 for the complete list of cancer centers.) In addition, most of the hospitals in this book are the leading recipients of research grants from the National Institutes of Health (NIH).

Surprisingly, at least to us, we discovered that the impact of a strong research program on the quality of a hospital's care goes far beyond the laboratory. The commitment to support research for finding cures or improving treatments for a broad range of illnesses is a major reason that so many first-rate medical specialists are attracted to the most prestigious teaching hospitals. These men and women frequently pass up the certain financial rewards of a private practice to gain a place in the vanguard of medical exploration. This is not to say that these doctors are not involved in the care and treatment of patients on a daily basis. Every magazine survey, as well as the highly successful, comprehensive book *The Best Doctors in America*, certifies that they are, as the names of doctors from these hospitals always dominate such lists of respected medical professionals.

Despite the fine reputation of most teaching hospitals among many doctors and nurses, some people are uncomfortable with the notion that they and their illnesses will be scrutinized by neophytes and made the subject of academic discussion. However, for those who value sophisticated medical care, these are inconveniences worth enduring. It is precisely this commitment to advancing medical knowledge that accounts for the special place teaching hospitals have in our health care system.

The combination of high-powered research programs and superb medical staffs has made teaching hospitals the repositories of the most advanced styles of medical practice. For this reason, they are frequently asked to treat very sick patients—the ones local community hospitals are simply not equipped to deal with. These are the hospitals where doctors refer their patients when sophisticated specialized care is required.

Known as tertiary care hospitals (your physician gives primary care, the local hospital secondary), these hospitals are recognized by the medical community for their expertise in specific areas. (Of course, we should note that all the general hospitals described here also offer basic medical services, such as simple obstetrics and general surgery, but that's not the reason they were selected.) These are the hospitals, for example, that perform most organ transplants, utilize the latest experimental cancer drugs, or employ the most up-to-date techniques for treating heart disease. Simply put, they deal with the sickest patients and offer the most complex care.

In investigating each of the hospitals included in this book, we also paid close attention to the quality of the nursing staff. Most patients regard nursing care as only slightly less important than the abilities of their physicians. After all, patients spend more time with their nurses than with their doctors. The hospitals in this book demonstrated that they have created environments that allow nurses a meaningful role in the care and treatment of their patients, and that the hospitals encourage them to pursue nursing as a career. These are essential components in nursing excellence, according to the American Nursing

Association. For this reason, we have included the number of nurses who have B.S. degrees, a sure sign that a professional career track exists at the hospital and that nursing staff turnover will be reduced.

Since most hospitals now do patient surveys to determine the level of patient satisfaction, we were often able to discover whether patients were pleased with the care they received and whether they would return if they required hospitalization in the future. In the few cases where institutions refused to share this information with us, we've noted that fact; prospective patients might want to investigate those institutions more closely on their own.

Finally, we invited each hospital to tell us about their quality assurance program. While every accredited hospital must have a system of peer review of doctors' performances, we discovered that there is a great deal of variation in the effectiveness of these systems. We've taken note of the hospitals in our survey that seem to pay more attention to this increasingly important dimension of quality control, but we were disappointed to discover that many hospitals remain unwilling to share such information with the public.

HOW TO USE THIS BOOK

Most of the hospitals we've selected offer a broad array of services, and every entry contains an extensive list of medical specialties available at each hospital. Whenever possible, we also provide a list of special clinics and programs. The main body of text for each entry, however, contains a detailed description of each hospital's best-known specialties. These are often in fields where the hospital is a major referral center for the region, or even for the nation, because it has the sophisticated technology and medical expertise to handle the most complex kinds of cases. Very few hospitals offer organ transplants, and fewer still do bone marrow transplants, so we always note when these and other similarly advanced and difficult-to-find services are available. We also describe the more common medical services—for cancer, diabetes, heart disease, kidney disease, stroke rehabilitation, and so forth—which have an impact on so many lives. In many of the hospitals included here, the programs for these illnesses are among the most highly regarded in the country.

A separate section in each entry describes special areas of research. Almost every hospital in this book has a major research program, usually connected to the institution's strengths in clinical medicine. We describe the most important research projects to help you find those places that will have the very latest treatment or even experimental programs.

In addition to this information, we include lists of well-known medical specialists for most hospitals. The purpose of these lists is to help you connect your medical needs to a real person, not just a faceless institution. We were surprised to learn that many of these physicians are easily accessible to any sick person needing their help.

The Best Hospitals in America   **xix**

And so, too, are all the hospitals in this book. Early in our research, we discovered that many people think it's necessary to "know someone" to gain entry to these high-powered hospitals, or that one needs to be under the care of a physician directly affiliated with the hospital. Others think you must have full medical insurance coverage or you won't be admitted. All of these assumptions are false, as you will discover in the sections on admissions policy that we provide for each hospital. You can easily become a patient in these hospitals, if need be, and can do so even if you are one of the 35 million Americans not covered by a health insurance plan. To demonstrate this, we noted, whenever possible, hospitals' willingness to help make alternative financial arrangements, as well as the amount of free care each hospital provides annually (including charity cases and uncollectible debts). You will be both shocked and impressed by the amount of uncompensated care most of these institutions provide.

New to this edition is an entry section on patient satisfaction. Every hospital surveyed was asked to provide information on how patients responded to the care they received. Almost every hospital included in the book was able to show that more than 90% of former patients rated their care as good to excellent.

Finally, we include some basic statistics to show the size of the hospital (number of beds) and how difficult it may be to get in (occupancy rate). The number of doctors, residents, and nurses will allow you to see just how many staff members there are in relation to the number of patients. In addition, we include the number of board-certified physicians and the number of nurses with B.S. degrees to show how accomplished the staffs at these top-flight hospitals are. Basic room charges are provided to help you make comparisons among various regions of the country (compare, for example, the Cleveland Clinic and the Mayo Clinic, or any New York City hospital with any midwestern institution).

In short, more information from more hospitals has been gathered for the second edition of *The Best Hospitals in America*—more than has ever before been collected for any book or magazine article on this subject. We hope our efforts will stimulate others who seek quality care to take the same steps we did, to ask the hard questions, and to urge hospitals and doctors to demonstrate that they can meet the tests of demanding patients. We know that there are hundreds of other first-rate hospitals in the United States, and we hope that this book will be the first of many to provide the public with information about such institutions.

UNITED STATES

UNIVERSITY OF

ALABAMA HOSPITAL

Although its origins date back to 1888, when a group of Birmingham citizens opened a one-story hospital for charity patients, it is only over the last fifteen years or so that this now vast complex has taken a place alongside the nation's very best medical institutions. An international leader in both basic and clinical research, the University of Alabama Hospital is one of America's most highly regarded settings for the diagnosis and treatment of all kinds of illnesses. It is one of the world's leading organ transplantation centers and a renowned center for congenital heart surgery. It is also noted for treatment programs in arthritis, cancer, heart disease, kidney disease, liver disease, and neurological injuries and illnesses. For the physicians and the people of Alabama and the surrounding areas, UAB, as it is usually called, serves as a regional referral center for neonatal intensive care and for trauma, especially burns.

UAB enjoys an excellent reputation in the medical community. Seventy-four UAB physicians are listed in *The Best Doctors in America*. In addition, University Hospital ranked third among the 25 best hospitals in the nation in the physician survey by Dietrich and Biddle published as *The Best Medicine in America*. It was also recently named an outstanding treatment center for arthritis, cancer, and heart disease in a survey by *New Choices for Retirement Living*. The only other medical center named in all three

UNIVERSITY OF ALABAMA AT BIRMINGHAM

BIRMINGHAM, ALABAMA

AN INTERNATIONAL LEADER IN BOTH BASIC AND CLINICAL RESEARCH, THE UNIVERSITY OF ALABAMA HOSPITAL IS ONE OF AMERICA'S MOST HIGHLY REGARDED SETTINGS FOR THE DIAGNOSIS AND TREATMENT OF ALL KINDS OF ILLNESSES.

categories was the Mayo Clinic. The UAB Comprehensive Cancer Center is one of only 12 centers nationwide recently awarded a five-year regional grant from the National Cancer Institute (NCI) to fund its Cancer Information Service.

Compared with other hospitals in Birmingham, UAB handles the most complex cases. Patients are drawn from other areas by the reputation of UAB for its advanced care capabilities. More than 3,000 people from outside the state are admitted as patients each year and more than half of all patients are from outside Jefferson County, where UAB is located. Several hundred of these come from outside the U.S.

Two services make University of Alabama Hospital attractive to referring physicians outside the Birmingham area. One is the Medical Information Service by Telephone (MIST), which has served as a model for several similar systems around the country. MIST is composed of specially trained telephone operators who can put calling physicians quickly in touch with UAB faculty physicians to answer specific clinical questions, at no cost to the caller. The second service is the Critical Care Transport Service, which includes a small jet and three ground vehicles, all led by teams of physicians, nurses, and respiratory therapists. These specially outfitted land and air vehicles make nearly obsolete the phrase "too sick to transfer."

University Hospital is one of seven units comprising UAB's Academic Health Center in Birmingham. Other clinical components of the urban campus include the Smolian Psychiatric Clinic, the Engel Psychiatric Day Treatment Center, and the Lurleen Wallace Tumor Institute and Radiation Therapy Building. There are strong ties to other governmental and private, non-profit patient care institutions adjacent to the campus, including the Birmingham VA Hospital, Children's Hospital, Eye Foundation Hospital, and Cooper Green Hospital.

SPECIAL FACILITIES AND PROGRAMS

There are 70 centers of specialization at UAB. The most noteworthy are described below.

UAB has one of the largest dialysis programs in the country, with almost 45,000 treatments a year. For those needing kidney transplants, UAB in recent years has performed more than any other program in the U.S.—322 in 1993 alone, including nine combined kidney/pancreas transplants.

Organ transplantation has played a significant part in solidifying UAB's image as a major referral center in the Southeast. With almost 350 heart transplants performed since 1981, and 38 in 1993 alone, UAB ranks among the top institutions in the nation. Pediatric patients are a specialty of this service. Forty-one liver transplants were performed in 1993 and a pediatric program is underway.

The Alabama Organ Center (AOC) is the federally approved organ procurement organization for the entire state of Alabama. The center works closely with all hospitals in Alabama as well as those from other states throughout the southeastern region and the nation to procure and share organs for transplantation.

Since its inception in 1979, the AOC has provided more than 3,000 organs for transplantation. The Organ Donor Hotline is (800) 252-3677.

For cancer, the newest treatment options available are offered by the UAB Comprehensive Cancer Center, one of 27 institutions nationwide designated as comprehensive by the National Cancer Institute. These include clinical trials using immunotherapeutic approaches such as monoclonal antibodies and vaccines, as well as bone marrow transplantation and a developing gene therapy program. The most advanced standard therapies are also available at the UAB Cancer Center. Each year the center diagnoses, treats, and counsels more than 12,000 patients from around the world. A staff of more than 500 cancer physicians, nurses, and support specialists is recognized both for its expertise and its compassion and concern.

A unique program for breast cancer patients allows already-diagnosed women to consult with a team of three specialists in one visit to explore appropriate treatment options. Called the Interdisciplinary Breast Cancer Unit, it is staffed by a surgical oncologist, radiation oncologist, and medical oncologist, as well as a full range of support personnel.

The Bone Marrow Transplant (BMT) Program, established in 1991, operates at full capacity. The most common transplants performed are for the leukemias and breast cancer—the latter accounting for about half the patient load. By the end of 1994, the BMT unit will occupy expanded facilities which will allow increased inpatient capacity from 60 to 200 procedures a year; outpatient services also will be expanded.

Initial patient trials in the gene therapy of colon and breast cancer are expected to begin at UAB by early 1995. Cancer vaccine therapy is another emphasis, and patient trials using this novel treatment are under way. A gene therapy vaccine trial is expected to begin by early 1995.

Hospitals that have extensive heart transplant programs invariably offer a full range of cardiology services. At UAB, more than 1,500 open heart procedures are performed each year. The number of

AT A GLANCE

Beds: 908
Occupancy Rate: 74%
Average Patient Count: 708
Average Patient Stay: 5.9 days
Annual Admissions: 43,597
Births: 3,833
Outpatient Clinic Visits: 350,000
Emergency Room/Trauma Center Visits: 37,398

HOSPITAL PERSONNEL
Physicians: 850
Residents: 481
Registered Nurses: 1,300

ROOM CHARGES (PER DIEM)
Private: $485–$519
Semiprivate: $477–$483
ICUs: $1,102–$1,975

ADDRESS
619 South 19th Street
Birmingham, Alabama 35233

TELEPHONE
Hospital: (205) 934-4011

cardiac catheterizations in the hospital alone totaled almost 5,000 in 1993, and included 2,383 diagnostic procedures and 1,632 balloon angioplasties. The insertion of cardiac stents—thin coils of special alloys to support the vessel walls—is a specialty. In addition, the UAB specialists conducted 174 electrophysiology studies and performed 450 radiofrequency ablations. They also implanted almost 150 pacemakers and more than 25 defibrillators.

One of the latest developments in cardiac diagnosis is magnetic resonance imaging (MRI). UAB is one of the world leaders in developing the MRI for this purpose. Not only is a 1.5 tesla machine dedicated to clinical studies of the heart, but one of the largest magnets in the world (4.1 tesla) is in use for research protocols.

In recent years, the university has seen its neurosciences program begin to benefit Alabama citizens, as more treatments for injuries and diseases of the brain and spinal cord system become available. A special four-bed seizure monitoring unit is just one aspect of one of the largest epilepsy research centers in the nation. And one of the country's largest combined neurosurgery-neurology intensive care units saves lives that previously would have been lost to head and spinal cord injuries, brain tumors, and viruses affecting the central nervous system. A new brain angiography suite allows sub-specialists to perform intricate procedures inside the skull. Automated operating arms, coupled with computer mapping of brain tumor sites, allow surgeons to remove only the necessary tissue in these delicate operations.

The UAB Spain Rehabilitation Center is the site of the nation's Statistical Center for Spinal Cord Injury Care Systems, as well as a Comprehensive Head Injury Center, and is a leader in urological research and in stroke and arthritis rehabilitation. It includes a community pool therapy program. UAB's expertise in orthopedic surgery—from joint replacement and reconstruction to acetabular fracture repair—is complemented by its rehabilitation program.

The UAB Multipurpose Arthritis Center is one of only a handful of such federally designated sites. It offers the most clinically advanced treatment available in rheumatology, including diagnostic arthroscopy, joint scans, reconstructive joint surgery, and monitoring of joint injury with single-fiber arthroscopy.

The newest clinical building at UAB's academic health center is the Center for Psychiatric Medicine. It houses extensive programs in geriatric psychiatry, child and adolescent psychiatry (with the adjacent Children's Hospital of Alabama), alcohol and substance addiction programs, and others. It also includes the Community Mental Health Center.

Additional specialty centers include the Cardiovascular Research and Training Center, the Nutrition Sciences Center, and one of the original federal Centers for AIDS Research.

In the summer of 1992, UAB's 600-plus clinical physicians strengthened the services available to patients visiting the Medical Center by combining outpatient services into the Kirklin Clinic, a $125 million, 430,000-square-foot structure designed by world-renowned architect I. M. Pei. Named for UAB's pioneering cardiac surgeon, Dr. John Kirklin, the multispecialty clinic makes it easier for the projected 500,000 annual patients to benefit from the University's health care programs.

A special 20-bed hotel-style nursing unit occupying an entire hospital floor is especially popular. Called the Camellia Pavilion after the state flower, it incorporates special amenities, including VCRs, sleeper sofas for family, in-room refrigerators, whirlpool and exercise equipment in a fitness center maintained by an exercise physiologist, and a specially recruited staff. Meals are served bedside or in the dining room, with fine china, crystal, and silver. Reservations are made by admitting physicians, and most non-ICU patients can be accommodated by a nursing staff cross-trained in several nursing specialties. Providing patients with pleasant surroundings and the best of care reduces the stress and anxiety of their illness and hospitalization.

University Hospital's patient-focused care incorporates a work-redesign program. A patient sees fewer staff, because staff is trained in multiple tasks; more procedures are performed in the unit, reducing travel time to other departments; and a team concept with decentralized authority is built into what the hospital calls "Patient Care 200." The teams consist of a registered nurse, a patient care technician, and a unit support specialist.

MEDICAL SPECIALTIES

Adolescent Medicine, Allergy, Anesthesiology, Cardiology, Cardiothoracic Surgery, Dermatology, Ear, Nose and Throat, Endocrinology, Family Medicine, Gastroenterology, General Surgery, Genetics, Geriatric Medicine, Hematology/Oncology, Infectious Diseases, Internal Medicine, Nephrology, Neurology, Neurosurgery, Obstetrics/Gynecology, Oral and Maxillofacial Surgery, Orthopedic Surgery, Pathology, Pediatrics, Perinatology, Plastic Surgery, Preventive Medicine, Psychiatry, Pulmonary Medicine, Radiation Oncology, Radiation (Diagnostic), Rehabilitation Medicine, Rheumatology, and Urology.

WELL-KNOWN SPECIALISTS

- Dr. Claude Bennett *Clinical immunology and rheumatology*
- Dr. John Cuckler *Orthopedics; specialist in total joint replacement*
- Dr. Arnold Diethelm *General surgery; specialist in kidney transplants*
- Dr. John Hauth *Maternal-fetal medicine; specialist in high-risk obstetrics*
- Dr. James Kirklin *Cardiothoracic surgery; specialist in cardiac transplants*
- Dr. William Koopman *Clinical immunology and rheumatology; director, Multipurpose Arthritis Center*
- Dr. Albert Lobuglio *Hematology/oncology; director, Comprehensive Cancer Center*
- Dr. Albert Pacifico *Cardiothoracic surgery; specialist in congenital heart disease*

- Dr. Gerald Pohost   *Cardiovascular disease; specialist in nuclear magnetic resonance imaging of the heart and metabolic studies*
- Dr. Gary Roubin   *Cardiovascular disease; specialist in angioplasty and stenting procedures*
- Dr. Sergio Stagno   *Pediatric virology*
- Dr. David Warnock   *Nephrology*
- Dr. John Whitaker   *Neurology; specialist in multiple sclerosis*
- Dr. Richard Whitley   *Virology*

PATIENT SATISFACTION

The hospital has attained a high level of patient satisfaction. Surveys are conducted continuously to make sure the needs and desires of the patients are being considered.

Nurses and physicians have consistently received very high scores in the following areas: skill and knowledge, courtesy and respect, friendliness, and communication. On a 0 - 100 scale, all these items score 90 or above. The highest-scoring survey item is skill and knowledge of physicians, which has a score of 95.

According to the latest survey, 95% of respondents would recommend UAB to others; 90% would use UAB again. (The reason for future non-use is the distance the patient lives from UAB.)

RESEARCH

Research at UAB receives an impressive amount of funding—more than $175 million in 1,000-plus contracts and grants. By far, the majority of all the federal money for research coming into Alabama goes to UAB. The university is in the top four southeastern universities receiving support from the National Institutes of Health (NIH) and is in the top 20 in the nation in NIH funding. In terms of external funding, UAB ranks in the top 40 nationally in federal research and development funding. The hospital is the site of an NIH-funded General Clinical Research Center.

The largest research unit at UAB is the Comprehensive Cancer Center, which receives over $25 million per year. UAB has built this and many of its other programs on the foundation of an internationally recognized program in immunology. The Cancer Center has a major commitment to vaccine research, gene therapy, and the use of monoclonal antibodies for delivery of radiation and for radioimmunoguided surgery, as well as bone marrow transplantation and other therapies.

Major research projects are also in place to combat conditions such as rheumatoid disease, cystic fibrosis, diabetes, gastrointestinal system disorders, heart disease, herpes and other viruses, hypertension, immunodeficiency in children and transplant patients, and the damaging effects of burns and head injuries.

UAB's Arthritis Research Center has undertaken a massive attack on rheumatic diseases. It is evaluating more new biologic drugs than almost any other center in the United States. Gene therapy for autoimmune diseases is in the animal research phase at the myriad UAB science laboratories. One development is that a lupus-type disease was corrected in mice with the insertion of a normal gene.

UAB research was enhanced by its leadership role in studying the growth of scientific crystals in space by one of its scientists who was a payload specialist on the shuttle *Columbia*. That specialist now directs the university's X-ray crystallography program, which is integral in designing drugs for such conditions as cancer, AIDS, hypertension, and organ rejection.

Recently, the university became the designated center for Civitan International's worldwide program of research and training for mental retardation and developmental disabilities. A $20 million pledge from the civic organization resulted in a striking new building and top level staff. It is the headquarters for several initiatives, including a new $5 million grant from the Robert Wood Johnson Foundation, which targets the effects of smoking and environmental smoke on the development of children.

Since 1987, almost 400 disclosures of discoveries and inventions have been reported to the UAB Research Foundation. Option and license agreements now exceed $500,000 annually.

ADMISSIONS POLICY

Patients can be admitted to the hospital without a doctor's referral through the emergency room or one of the clinics. Anyone can make an appointment by calling (205) 934-9999. There is a special number for doctors to call for either referral or for consultation: 1-800-452-9860.

Patients are required to show proof of insurance coverage or other means of fulfilling their financial obligation to the hospital, although special arrangements can be made on a case-by-case basis. In recent years, UAB has provided $50 million worth of uncompensated care annually.

PATIENT/FAMILY ACCOMMODATIONS

The University Inn offers 169 rooms for overnight stays. Some rooms are equipped with microwaves and refrigerators. The inn provides shuttle service to the hospital and clinics as well as the airport and train station. Room charges at University Inn are $39 per day for patients and visitors of inpatients. (Call: 205-933-7700.)

UNIVERSITY

MEDICAL CENTER

The University Medical Center (UMC) of the University of Arizona Health Sciences Center first received national attention in 1985 when surgeons there implanted the Jarvik-7 artificial heart. This was the first federally authorized use of the artificial heart as a bridge to transplantation. UMC recently continued that tradition by performing the first transplant of the CardioWest device for 186 days, until a human donor heart was available. To date, UMC has performed two other transplants of the CardioWest.

University Medical Center, a private non-profit hospital located on the campus of the Arizona Health Sciences Center, was established in 1971 as an acute care center for the Southwest. UMC offers heart, liver, kidney, bone marrow and corneal transplantation services; a comprehensive epilepsy program; the bone-stretching Ilizarov program; a movement disorders program for Parkinson's disease patients; stereotactic radiosurgery; and an assisted reproductive technology program for reproductive endocrinology and infertility.

UMC also has a number of specialized services for women and children: child and adolescent care, infant and toddler care, pediatric intensive care, postpartum and gynecological care, birth care, and neonatal intensive care. Special adult care services include psychiatric care; neurology, neurosurgery and orthopedics; cardiac intensive care; cardiac immediate care and telemetry; medical oncology and bone marrow transplantation; medical/surgical care; and medical/surgical intensive care.

SPECIAL FACILITIES AND PROGRAMS

The Cardiac Disease Service includes both medical cardiology and cardiac surgery. Patient services in medical cardiology include primary care; coronary intensive care; electrocardiology; cardiac catheterization services, including angiography and myocardial biopsy; and interventional cardiology, including percutaneous coronary angioplasty and shock ablation of arrhythmias. At present, UMC offers the only pediatric cardiology service in Southern Arizona. While cardiac surgery is offered at other Tucson hospitals, UMC is the only hospital in Southern Arizona at which heart and heart-lung transplant surgeries are regularly performed.

UMC offers a wide range of cancer diagnostic and treatment services, unique in Southern Arizona, in conjunction with the cancer research activities of the Arizona Cancer Center. While the Arizona Cancer Center is not itself a part of UMC, the Cancer Center relies upon the Medical Center for a variety of inpatient and outpatient services. The center is housed in a five-story building that opened in 1986, and is adjacent and connected by walkways to the Medical Center. The Oncology Program at UMC accommodates medical oncology, surgical oncology, and radiation oncology, which includes external beam therapy, hypothermia, interstitial radiation implant therapy and stereotactic radiosurgery. The Medical Center's oncology program serves patients throughout Arizona and the Southwest. During fiscal year 1992-1993, over half of new Cancer Center patients were from outside the Tucson metropolitan area.

In 1989, the Medical Center began a program in Interoperative Radiation Therapy (IORT). The therapy is typically performed on patients with a solid malignancy. While in surgery, radiation therapy is delivered by special equipment that allows radiation to be directed precisely at the tumor and at a much higher dosage than would be possible with other

AT A GLANCE

Beds: 312
Occupancy Rate: 72%
Average Patient Count: 224
Average Patient Stay: 5.2 days
Annual Admissions: 15,811
Births: 3,514
Outpatient Clinic Visits:
    293,887
Emergency Room/Trauma
    Center Visits: 34,387

HOSPITAL PERSONNEL
Physicians: 665
    Board Certified: 539
Residents: 416
Registered Nurses: 867
    BS Degree: 217

ROOM CHARGES (PER DIEM)
Private: $600
Semiprivate: $540
Ward: $500

ADDRESS
1501 North Campbell
    Avenue
Tucson, AZ 85724

TELEPHONE
(602) 626-0111

conventional methods. The Medical Center has equipped a special operating room with an orthovoltage machine and the necessary support equipment used in IORT. UMC has been perfecting new methods to employ stereotactic techniques and linear accelerators to treat brain tumors without surgery.

Women's and Children's Services serves as the clinical environment for the Department of Pediatrics and the Department of Obstetrics and Gynecology of the University of Arizona College of Medicine. Both departments work closely together in this program.

UMC is the only designated tertiary care center for high-risk maternity patients in Southern Arizona. Obstetrics services provide 24-hour anesthesia coverage and a wide range of fetal monitoring, maternal care, labor, delivery, and postpartum care services. In addition, special care is provided for complicated labors, such as toxemia premature labor, diabetics in labor, and patients with cardiac problems in labor.

A comprehensive range of pediatric services are offered as well, including pediatric and neonatal intensive care, pediatric cardiovascular and pulmonary surgery, pediatric hematology/oncology and newborn transport. Significant numbers of the Neonatal Intensive Care Unit patients have been born elsewhere and transported to UMC.

UMC has a nationally recognized heart transplantation program. Since inception in 1979, 370 hearts have been transplanted. In addition, 24 heart-lung, 16 single-lung and one double-lung transplants have occurred. UMC is one of the limited number of cardiac implant centers nationwide. The use of the artificial heart implant as an emergency bridge to transplant was pioneered at the Medical Center. Other implant devices, such as the left ventricular assist device, also have been employed in the implantation program.

In 1989, UMC began a Bone Marrow Transplantation program in conjunction with the University of Arizona College of Medicine and the Arizona Cancer Center. The program provides multidisciplinary holistic care for cancer patients over the age of eight who require bone marrow transplant. The program is the only one in Arizona to offer both related and matched unrelated allogenic transplants. UMC is also a fully accredited marrow collection center for the National Marrow Donor Program. Patient origin data for this program show that approximately 75% of bone marrow transplantation patients come from outside the Tucson metropolitan area, including 10% who come from outside Arizona. Since inception, 208 transplants have been performed.

In conjunction with the Department of Surgery of the University of Arizona College of Medicine, the Medical Center initiated a kidney transplantation program in March 1991, and a liver transplant program in July 1991. The Kidney Program has been developed to serve a broad spectrum of adult and pediatric patients throughout Arizona who have end-stage renal disease and are maintained on dialysis. It is anticipated that the Kidney Transplant Program will also serve diabetic patients who can benefit from a combined kidney and pancreas transplant. Approximately 16% of the referrals to the kidney transplant program have come from outside Tucson. Thirty-seven patients have received kidney transplants to date. Recipients of liver transplants may include patients with biliary cirrhosis, cholangitis, liver cirrhosis, metabolic disorders or deficiencies, and fulminant hepatic failure. The Liver Transplant Program has performed 23 transplants.

The Arizona Arthritis Center studies the many causes of arthritis, as well as the best treatments for current arthritis patients. Current research features innovative surgery, including artificial joint techniques; the use of drugs, such as cyclosporine and cortisone; and reduction of the financial costs of arthritis care.

In 1985, UMC established a multidisciplinary Trauma Center as part of a joint trauma program with Tucson Medical Center. In 1986, the American College of Surgeons verified that UMC is able to provide Level I Trauma Care. The Trauma Center is one of the only two such centers in Southern Arizona, and is complemented by the capabilities of UMC's aerotransport program. In fiscal year 1993, UMC had 800 trauma cases.

MEDICAL SPECIALTIES

Anesthesiology, Cardiology, Cardiovascular and Thoracic Surgery, Dermatology, Endocrinology, Family and Community Medicine, Gastroenterology, General Medicine, General Surgery, Geriatrics, Hematology/Oncology, Infectious Disease, Neurosurgery, Obstetrics and Gynecology, Ophthalmalogy, Orthopedics, Psychiatry, Pulmonary/Critical Care, Radiation Oncology, Radiology, Renal Disease, Rheumatology/Immunology, Urology and Vascular Surgery.

Pediatric Specialties: Allergy and Immunology, Cardiology, Gastroenterology/Nutrition, Pediatrics/Adolescent Medicine, Genetics/Dysmorphology, Hematology/Oncology, Infectious Disease, Neonatology/Nutritional Sciences, Neurology and Pulmonary Diseases.

WELL-KNOWN SPECIALISTS

- Dr. Geoffrey Ahern   *Neurology*
- Dr. Frederick Ahmann   *Oncology/hematology*
- Dr. David Alberts   *Oncology/hematology*
- Dr. Victor Bernhard   *General surgery*
- Dr. Burnell Brown, Jr.   *Anesthesiology*
- Dr. J. Robert Cassady   *Radiation oncology*
- Dr. Jack Copeland   *Thoracic surgery; specialist in transplantation*
- Dr. William Dalton   *Oncology/hematology*
- Dr. George Drach   *Urology*
- Dr. Gordon Ewy   *Cardiovascular disease*
- Dr. William Feinburg   *Neurology*
- Dr. Alan Gelenberg   *Psychiatry*
- Dr. Stanley Goldberg   *Pediatric cardiology*

- Dr. Thomas Grogan *Pathology*
- Dr. Ronald Hansen *Dermatology*
- Dr. Kenneth Hatch *Obstetrics/gynecology*
- Dr. Richard Leman *Pediatric pulmonology*
- Dr. Thomas Miller *Oncology/hematology*
- Dr. Wayne Morgan *Pediatrics*
- Dr. Charles Otto *Anesthesiology*
- Dr. Dennis Patton *Nuclear medicine*
- Dr. Stuart Quan *Pulmonary and critical care medicine*
- Dr. Kathryn Reed *Obstetrics/gynecology*
- Dr. Stuart Salasche *Dermatology*
- Dr. Sydney Salmon *Oncology/hematology*
- Dr. Jose Santiago *Psychiatry, schizophrenia*
- Dr. David Shimm *Radiation oncology; specialist in head and neck cancer*
- Dr. William Sibley *Neurology*

PATIENT SATISFACTION

Inpatients are surveyed three times per year by mail. The full spectrum of concerns addressed in this survey include admitting, nursing and medical care, billing, discharge planning, and overall satisfaction. Results have always been very positive. In the most recently completed survey, 97% of patients expressed satisfaction with the nursing response to calls for assistance; 97% were satisfied with the clinical skills of the nurses; 98% were satisfied with the clinical skills of their physician; and 97% were satisfied overall with the care they received at UMC.

RESEARCH

The Arizona Cancer Center undertakes fundamental molecular and cellular studies and offers clinical trials of advanced treatment methods, including biological response modifiers, improved drug delivery systems, new anticancer drugs, drug combinations, hypothermia, and computer-enhanced radiation therapy.

The Steele Memorial Children's Research Center has internationally recognized research programs in cancer; cardiac abnormalities; child abuse; hemophilia; infectious diseases; lung disorders, such as asthma and cystic fibrosis; molecular genetics; nutritional disorders of the newborn; school health; and sudden infant death syndrome (SIDS).

The University Heart Center has a newly emerging program in bypass, perfusion, and transplantation science, and long-established programs in the molecular and cellular pharmacology and physiology of the adult and developing heart. Also studied are the effects of various cardiac medicines on clotting mechanisms and clinical trials for patients under treatment for heart failure and for patients with heart arryhthmias who may have had unsatisfactory responses to presently available drugs.

The Respiratory Sciences Center has a special focus on airway obstructive diseases, including asthma. Cellular, epidemiological, immunological, genetic and molecular approaches to research are featured in the center.

Also significant is the research on gerontology, restorative medicine, and geriatrics included in the Arizona Center on Aging. Clinical research is being conducted in management of arthritis, depression, disease prevention, pain, sleep disorders, and many other areas relating to the elderly.

The Arizona Emergency Medicine Research Center, which opened in 1990, is the newest Arizona Health Sciences Center (AHSC). Its personnel study fundamental and clinical aspects of trauma biology, with a particular interest in improved health delivery systems. This latter focus is particularly prominent in new AHSC research ventures in areas like health and medical informatics, including image management and communication systems, health and medical decision support systems, medical library science, health and medical information systems, and health care policy and management.

ADMISSIONS POLICY

Any person who comes through UMC's emergency department will be admitted if the attending physician deems it appropriate, regardless of ability to pay.

There is a policy regarding ability to pay, but the hospital says that no one in need of medical care for an illness or injury that would threaten life or limb is denied admission. Noninsured patients seeking elective procedures are required to make a deposit before admission. However, if such patients cannot meet the financial requirements, their cases are referred to the medical director, who will work with the physicians in charge of the cases to determine whether admission can be delayed until financial questions are resolved. If the medical director feels that medical reasons preclude delay, the patients are admitted.

CEDARS-SINAI

MEDICAL CENTER

In southern California, the level of concern about health care/wellness is probably higher than in any other part of the country. The large number of first-rate hospitals in the Los Angeles area is striking evidence of this. Therefore, the number one rating Cedars-Sinai Medical Center (CSMC) received in a recent survey of the Los Angeles community can be viewed as a strong endorsement from knowledgeable consumers. The survey respondents gave Cedars-Sinai the highest rating of any Los Angeles community hospital in all seven of the categories used to measure quality—best image and reputation, best overall quality, best doctors, best nurses, most services, most personalized care, and most modern equipment. In addition, Cedars-Sinai was the highest rated in all 15 categories related to specific services, including general surgery, heart care, cancer treatment, maternity, pediatrics, and physical therapy. These results testify in dramatic fashion to the extraordinary reputation of Cedars-Sinai as one of the finest hospitals in the country.

CEDARS-SINAI IS TRULY ONE OF THE WORLD'S MOST SOPHISTICATED AND DIVERSIFIED MEDICAL CENTERS, DELIVERING HIGH-QUALITY MEDICAL AND SURGICAL CARE.

Cedars-Sinai traces its origins back to Cedars of Lebanon Hospital, founded in 1902 as Kaspare Chon Hospital, and Mount Sinai Hospital, founded in 1921. The hospitals merged in 1961 to form Cedars-Sinai Medical Center. In 1976, a facility to house both operations was opened. Today, on more than 24 acres of land, eight-story twin towers for inpatients rise above the several other buildings that comprise the Cedars-Sinai complex.

Cedars-Sinai is more than "the hospital to the stars," as it has often been called. Patients seeking care for virtually any kind of health care problem can find a complete spectrum of medical and surgical services. Through a 1,700-member medical staff, the medical center provides the latest state-of-the-art diagnostic and treatment technologies. Inpatients receive impressive attention with a higher number of nursing hours delivered per patient than in many other hospitals. Life-saving treatment is also emphasized, with more than 15% of all beds devoted to 14 specialized intensive care units. Cedars-Sinai is truly one of the world's most sophisticated and diversified medical centers, delivering high-quality medical and surgical care.

While patient care is certainly a large component of its program, Cedars-Sinai also has strong programs in research, medical education, and community service. In biomedical and clinical research, CSMC ranks among the top 20 voluntary hospitals in the nation with about 286 projects underway at any given time. In affiliation with the School of Medicine of UCLA, Cedars-Sinai offers residency training in seven specialties as well as specialized education for medical students. Training programs are also available in nursing, pharmacy, and medical technology. CSMC also offers programs in continuing medical education for physicians both locally and nationwide. The Medical Center offers a wide range of community programs as well.

AT A GLANCE

Beds: 1,012
Occupancy Rate: 75%
Average Patient Count: 694
Average Patient Stay: 6.3 days
Annual Admissions: 40,265
Outpatient Clinic Visits:
    49,126
Emergency Room/Trauma
    Center Visits: 50,342

HOSPITAL PERSONNEL
Physicians: 1,756
Residents: 296
Registered Nurses: 1,160

ROOM CHARGES (PER DIEM)
Private: $864
ICU: $3,835–$5,802

ADDRESS
8700 Beverly Blvd.
Los Angeles, CA 90048

TELEPHONE
(310) 855-5000

SPECIAL FACILITIES AND PROGRAMS

Cedars-Sinai provides patient care in all specialties of medicine, surgery, psychiatry, obstetrics and gynecology, and pediatrics. Numerous departments have won national and international recognition for patient care. A few are highlighted below.

In cardiology, Cedars-Sinai is noted for both cardiologic care and research. Facilities include intensive care unit beds for surgical and/or medical cardiology; "step-down" beds, where patients are continuously monitored after heart attack or any cardiac procedure; beds for patients who do not require continuous cardiac monitoring; and the Cardiovascular Intervention Center, one of the most innovative and active catheterization laboratories in the country. These facilities contain state-of-the-art equipment for monitoring heart patients and performing highly technical procedures. The Cardiac Stress Laboratory performs treadmill stress testing and exercise echocardiography. The Cardiac Non-Invasive Laboratory performs very sophisticated cardiovascular imaging. Also part of the Division of Cardiology is the Cardiac Preventive and Rehabilitation Center, which offers an extensive program of cardiac rehabilitation for patients recovering from heart attacks or bypass surgery.

Standardized treatments throughout the world, first researched and pioneered through the achievements of the Division of Cardiology's professional staff, have gained stature for the Medical Center. Among major achievements are development of the Swan-Ganz catheter for monitoring the condition of critically ill patients and the use of the drug Streptokinase for dissolving clots in heart attack victims. In ground-breaking work that has received national attention, CSMC physicians have pioneered the excimer laser for nonsurgical treatment of arterial blockages.

From treatment of congenital birth defects to the most complex open heart procedures, Cedars-Sinai is prominent in the West for cardiovascular and thoracic surgery. Special expertise in valve repair and replacement also has helped put Cedars-Sinai at the forefront of internationally recognized centers for heart surgery. Problems involving arrhythmias (irregular heart beats) also are a specialty at Cedars-Sinai. In addition, surgeons perform complex surgical charting of arrhythmias and removal of the areas associated with arrhythmias. Cedars-Sinai has one of the few lung-only transplant facilities in North America. Thoracic surgery is performed on lesions of the lung and esophagus. These areas are supported by hospital-wide consultative services.

Cedars-Sinai is one of the West's leading transplantation centers. Currently, transplantation of hearts, lungs, kidneys, livers, and bone marrow are provided for both adult and pediatric patients. Pioneering work is also being done in xenographic transplantation and the maintenance of patients suffering liver failure with a unique liver support system, which, in some cases, may preclude the need for transplantation. Transplantation programs for the pancreas and the small intestine are expected to be introduced soon.

The Comprehensive Cancer Center at Cedars-Sinai is one of the first centers in the nation to offer round-the-clock outpatient care exclusively for cancer patients. The center delivers a full range of state-of-the-art treatments for rapid detection, diagnosis, therapy and emergency care crucial to successful management of the disease. These services make it possible to eliminate many inpatient days formerly associated with cancer treatment.

At the Cedars-Sinai multidisciplinary Laser Research Center, physicians work to develop and apply new electro-optic technologies in the treatment of disease. A primary focus has been on applying laser energy power to cardiovascular disease. The center, a collaborative effort between the Departments of Surgery and Medicine and the Division of Cardiology, was the site of the first medical center use of the excimer laser for clearing blocked coronary arteries and peripheral vessels of the leg. A procedure for fragmenting biliary stones with a pulsed dye laser has been refined here. Laser research is underway for removing tumors of the lungs and brain; for removing secondary cataracts and sealing leaking blood vessels behind the eyes of patients with cataracts; and for gynecologic, and head and neck applications.

Pulmonary Medicine specialists diagnose and treat lung disease, including emphysema, chronic bronchitis, asthma, pneumonia, and lung cancer. They also give pulmonary function tests, blood gas analysis, and respiratory therapy treatments. Staffed by a team of health care professionals, the Pulmonary Rehabilitation Center provides education, breathing treatments, breathing exercises, and individually tailored exercise programs for patients with chronic obstructive lung disease. In addition to researching the prevention and treatment of the major lung diseases, the physicians also study respiratory failure, pulmonary hypertension, and respiratory muscle physiology.

The Cedars-Sinai Department of Pediatrics provides complete inpatient and outpatient medical/surgical services for newborns through adolescents, supported by the resources of the entire Medical Center. Pediatricians, nurses, and related specialists are trained and experienced in responding to the special needs of children. All rooms in the pediatric suite contain fold-out beds, enabling parents to stay with their children through the night. Flexible visiting hours also help make the hospital experience as anxiety-free and pleasant as possible for children and family alike. A play therapy program helps lessen children's fears and anxieties about illness and the hospital. Under supervision, play therapy allows children to express their feelings and act out anxieties using safe, creative outlets such as dolls and art.

Specialized pediatric services include cardiology and cardiac surgery, endocrinology, gastroenterology, hematology-oncology, neonatal intensive care, nephrology, pediatric intensive care, treatment of pulmonary diseases including cystic fibrosis and asthma, and all surgical procedures.

The Department of Nuclear Medicine provides sophisticated cameras, nuclear scanners, and computerized technology to help physicians evaluate the function of internal organs such as the heart, liver, lungs, and bones. The Department is a national and international leader in nuclear imaging—with major achievements in nuclear cardiology, pulmonary medicine, oncology, and endocrinology. Significant clinical research activities into diseases of the heart, cancer, and many other important clinical disorders are ongoing.

The Department of Obstetrics and Gynecology at Cedars-Sinai functions as a comprehensive women's hospital. An ultramodern obstetrical suite ensures the greatest available safety and comfort for patients. Obstetric services range from the homelike comfort of Labor-Delivery-Recovery rooms for patients with normal pregnancies to facilities for high-risk mothers and their babies.

Cedars-Sinai has achieved a national reputation in identifying and treating high-risk mothers. Services include pre-pregnancy genetics counseling and advanced maternal-fetal surveillance procedures, such as chorionic villus sampling, a technique that detects some genetic abnormalities during the first trimester of pregnancy. This procedure, which is now used nationally, was perfected for clinical use by a CSMC researcher. Women at risk for premature delivery are carefully monitored through close examination and state-of-the-art technology. Maternal-fetal medicine specialists are prepared to provide intensive maternity care at all times. Neonatal intensive care units are available when needed.

An interdisciplinary team of internationally renowned physicians and other reproductive health specialists provides complete care for couples seeking treatment for infertility. Fertility testing and procedures for men and women are performed in a modern, custom-designed facility. Psychological and sexual counseling is available to couples dealing with stress related to infertility treatment.

The Ambulatory Care Center delivers extensive outpatient care through a group of clinics in primary and subspecialty areas, including internal medicine, surgery, obstetrics/gynecology, pediatrics, and many consultative specialties. Patients may receive a variety of diagnostic treatment services, including laboratory and radiology testing, radiation therapy, electrocardiogram, dietetic consultation, and social services counseling.

Patients who have suffered the loss of physical function through illness, injury or amputation are assisted by the Department of Physical Medicine and Rehabilitation. A multidisciplinary team approach—including physical and occupational therapy, social services and psychiatric liaison services—helps patients become as self-sufficient as possible, while helping patients and their families also adjust to new limitations. Programs include an amputee program, chronic pain management, head and spinal cord injury treatment, and stroke rehabilitation.

The Department of Emergency Medicine is a major point of entry for patients admitted to Cedars-Sinai. It provides comprehensive emergency care to patients in the Cedars-Sinai service area, as well as to those involved in trauma cases. As a certified Paramedic Base Hospital, the Medical Center directs treatment by two-way radio with paramedic ambulances while patients are being transported. It is also certified as an Emergency Department Approved for the Care of Pediatrics and meets Emergency Cardiac Care Standards set by the American Heart Association. Cedars-Sinai operates a Level I Trauma Center and heliport. In addition to a heliport, a hospital must have an extensive emergency medicine department, general surgeons on 24-hour duty, and a fully accredited general surgery residency program to qualify as a trauma center.

The Department of Patient Care Services coordinates Nursing Services (including Nursing Research and Development, and Patient and Community Education),

Medical Social Work, Home Care, and the Hospice. These areas are linked for the delivery of exceptional bedside care. Social Work and Nursing cooperate in the discharge process to return patients to their homes as quickly and conveniently and in the best medical condition possible.

The approximately 1,500 nurses at Cedars-Sinai Medical Center are an essential part of the health care team. They have the knowledge and expertise needed to provide the patient with the highest quality nursing care 24 hours a day. Nursing care includes working closely with patients, their families, and other members of the health care team to both determine and assist in meeting individual needs. In addition, nurses provide the patient and family with information about hospital procedures and nursing care to assure access to necessary emotional support.

MEDICAL SPECIALTIES

Anesthesiology, Cardiology, Cardiovascular Surgery, Dentistry, Diagnostic Radiology, Emergency Medicine, Endocrinology, Gastroenterology, General Medicine, Gynecologic Oncology, Hematology/Oncology, Infectious Diseases, Infertility, Internal Medicine, Maternal-Fetal Medicine, Neonatology, Nephrology, Neurology, Obstetrics/Gynecology, Ophthalmology, Pathology, Pediatrics, Physical Medicine and Rehabilitation, Pulmonary Medicine, Radiation Therapy, Rheumatology, Surgery, and Urology.

WELL-KNOWN SPECIALISTS

All doctors listed below are directors of their respective departments.
- Dr. Harold Amer   *Pediatrics; specialist in pediatric intensive care*
- Dr. Michael Bush   *Endocrinology; Diabetes Outpatient Training and Education Center*
- Dr. Mayer Davidson   *Endocrinology; specialist in diabetes*
- Dr. Burton Fink   *Pediatrics; specialist in pediatric cardiology*
- Dr. Calvin Hobel   *Obstetrics/gynecology; specialist in maternal-fetal medicine*
- Dr. Carol Hurvitz   *Pediatrics; specialist in pediatric hematology/oncology*
- Dr. Leo Lagrasse   *Obstetrics/gynecology; specialist in gynecologic oncology*
- Dr. Frank Litvack   *Cardiology*
- Dr. Jack Matloff   *Surgery; specialist in thoracic and cardiovascular surgery*
- Dr. Philomenia McAndrew   *Hematology/oncology*
- Dr. Richard Meyer   *Medicine; specialist in infectious diseases*
- Dr. Andrea Morrison   *Pediatrics; specialist in pediatric neurology*
- Dr. Jeffrey Pomerance   *Pediatrics; specialist in neonatology*
- Dr. Judith Rachman   *Obstetrics/gynecology*
- Dr. Eugene Richards   *Physical medicine and rehabilitation*
- Dr. David Rimoin   *Pediatrics; specialist in medical genetics/birth defects*
- Dr. Steven Simons   *Medicine; specialist in pulmonary disease*
- Dr. H. J. Swan   *Cardiology*

- Dr. Stephen Targan   *Gastroenterology*
- Dr. Ronald Thompson   *Radiation therapy; specialist in radiation oncology*
- Dr. Alfredo Trento   *Surgery; specialist in heart transplantation*
- Dr. Frank Williams   *Psychiatry; specialist in family and child psychiatry*

PATIENT SATISFACTION

Patient satisfaction surveys are sent to patients after discharge. The patients are asked to rate admissions, hospital personnel, housekeeping, facilities, diet and meals, etc. The results are analyzed by an outside analytical and reporting agency quarterly.

Cedars-Sinai Medical Center receives a 95% positive evaluation from former patients indicating that they would recommend the hospital for patient care.

RESEARCH

Investigations and studies carried out by Cedars-Sinai researchers have made significant contributions to modern medicine. Medical advances developed at Cedars-Sinai have been adopted throughout the general medicine community to assist all patients.

More than 132 principal investigators and 300 employees work at any given time on some 286 basic biomedical and clinical research projects through the Cedars-Sinai Research Institute. A $23 million annual budget receives 60% of its funding from research grants and contracts awarded by federal government sources. The remaining 40% of funding comes from state, corporate, and private foundation sources.

The activities are widely varied. Significant research is conducted on pituitary tumors, growth disorders, and infertility. Cedars-Sinai surgeons are developing innovative approaches with lasers and television endoscopy to treat diverse conditions such as biliary or bile-conveying disease, blocked arteries, and infertility. Rheumatologists engage in research including x-ray and drug studies for rheumatoid arthritis. In gynecologic oncology, physicians have undertaken ground-breaking research including the use of photodynamics therapy, the use of lasers to destroy tumor cells previously sensitized to light. Other areas of inquiry include surgical endoscopy, otolaryngological surgery, and cystic fibrosis.

ADMISSIONS POLICY

Patients may be admitted through their personal staff physician, the Emergency Room (ER), or the Ambulatory Care Clinic. If the patient is admitted through the ER, he or she is assigned a physician. If admitted through Ambulatory Care, the patient makes an appointment, is screened, and gets assigned a physician from Ambulatory Care.

There is a financial requirement for admission to Cedars-Sinai. Patients are expected to provide proof of insurance or pay a deposit. In 1993, Cedars-Sinai committed $25 million to uncompensated care.

PATIENT/FAMILY ACCOMMODATIONS

For outpatients and families of inpatients, accommodations can be arranged at various nearby hotels with rates from $60 to $125 per day.

SCRIPPS CLINIC

AND RESEARCH

FOUNDATION

LA JOLLA, CALIFORNIA

Scripps Clinic and Research Foundation is one of the oldest and largest non-profit, private medical centers in the United States. Its name is often mentioned by medical professionals, along with the Mayo Clinic and several others, as one of the best private research institutions. Scripps Clinic physicians provide comprehensive medical care for the entire family, treating the simple and common, as well as complex and life-threatening health problems. Combining sophisticated technical expertise with excellent patient care, Scripps is a leader in areas as diverse as cancer treatment, neurologic disorders, organ transplantation, cardiovascular disease, kidney disorders, the use of laser technology, and the management of orthopedic disorders.

Founded by Miss Ellen Browning Scripps, operations of the Scripps Clinic began almost 60 years ago, on December 11, 1924, as the Scripps Metabolic Clinic, functioning as part of the Scripps Memorial Hospital. In the beginning, the clinic specialized in diagnostic services and research, primarily of diabetes. The clinic separated from the hospital in 1951 and its present name, Scripps Clinic and Research Foundation, was adopted in 1956.

Today, the Scripps Health Network provides comprehensive care throughout San Diego County, California. The Scripps Clinic complex in La Jolla includes the Anderson Outpatient Facility, where

SCRIPPS CLINIC AND RESEARCH FOUNDATION IS ONE OF THE OLDEST AND LARGEST NON-PROFIT, PRIVATE MEDICAL CENTERS IN THE UNITED STATES. ITS NAME IS OFTEN MENTIONED BY MEDICAL PROFESSIONALS, ALONG WITH THE MAYO CLINIC AND SEVERAL OTHERS, AS ONE OF THE BEST PRIVATE RESEARCH INSTITUTIONS.

there are more than 600,000 patient visits each year. The facility also includes the 173-bed Green Hospital of Scripps Clinic, to which Scripps Clinic physicians admit their patients. Scripps also has regional clinics located in Del Mar, Rancho Bernardo, Rancho San Diego, San Diego, and San Marcos. In addition, Scripps operates four community hospitals located in the communities of La Jolla, Encinitas, Chula Vista, and El Cajon. The hospitals also provide convalescent and home health care services.

The Scripps Clinic Medical Group, under the presidency of Dr. Thomas Waltz, has 300 members offering services in over 50 fields of medicine and surgery, together with specialized centers. In medicine and surgery, Scripps has distinguished itself in allergy and immunology treatment; cardiovascular diseases and surgery, including interventional cardiology and open heart surgery; the treatment of liver diseases; organ transplants, particularly liver, kidney and pancreas; rheumatology; and sleep disorders. It has also established 16 specialty centers recognized for their excellence. The services and treatments provided by some of these centers are described below.

Scripps offers many educational opportunities. Scripps Clinic provides an internal medicine residency, as well as clinical fellowships in allergy and clinical immunology, dermatology and Mohs surgery, endocrinology, gastroenterology, hematology and medical oncology, orthopedic surgery, rheumatology, sleep disorder medicine, and vascular surgery. In addition, the Scripps Research Institute has graduate programs in chemistry and in macromolecular and cellular structure chemistry; the Department of Pathology has a clinical laboratory training program in medical technology; and the Sleep Disorders Center offers a polysomnographic training course, one of only seven in the U.S.

SPECIAL FACILITIES AND PROGRAMS

The Ida M. and Cecil H. Green Cancer Center offers a comprehensive and multidisciplinary approach to cancer treatment, research, and education. The center is recognized internationally for its specialized programs in bone marrow transplantation, limb salvage

AT A GLANCE

Beds: 173
Occupancy Rate: 64%
Average Patient Count: 110
Average Patient Stay: 4.9 days
Annual Admissions: 8,218
Outpatient Clinic Visits:
　600,000
Urgent Care Center Visits:
　49,000

HOSPITAL PERSONNEL
Physicians: 300+
　Board Certified: 100%
Registered Nurses: 370
　BS Degree: 178

ROOM CHARGES (PER DIEM)
Private: $653
Semiprivate: $551
ICU: $2,011

ADDRESS
10666 N. Torrey Pines Road
La Jolla, CA 92037

TELEPHONE
(619) 455-9100

cancer surgery, skin cancer, monoclonal antibody therapy, and breast and gynecological cancer, to name a few.

The Heart, Lung, and Vascular Center includes an award-winning interdisciplinary medical team that utilizes the latest technological developments and techniques in diagnosing and treating ailments such as high blood pressure, stroke, vascular diseases, lung cancer, emphysema, other pulmonary diseases, coronary artery disease, rheumatic heart disease, and other heart diseases.

The Asthma and Allergic Diseases Center, offering evaluation, treatment, education, and research, is one of only 11 centers with a national designation from the National Institutes of Health.

The Brain and Stroke Research and Treatment Center pursues the causes of and cures for diseases and disorders of the brain and peripheral nervous system.

The Shiley Sports and Health Center includes a fitness center open to the public, a Sports Medicine Center available by physician referral, and a Health Resource Center, which offers free consultation with registered dieticians and programs for the public, such as smoking cessation, weight management, and stress reduction.

Patients who come to the Liver Disease Center have access to the latest diagnostic and treatment approaches that are not generally available outside a specialized center. Scripps Clinic's liver transplant program, one of the most successful in the United States, is part of this center. Also available at the Green Hospital of Scripps Clinic are kidney and combination kidney/pancreas transplant. About 90 transplants in all are performed each year.

The Diabetes Center offers complete medical services, as well as extensive ongoing educational, counseling, and behavior modification programs designed to help patients live with diabetes as easily and comfortably as possible. The American Diabetes Association has awarded the center a Certificate of Recognition for its patient education programs.

The Fertility Center, which was one of the first in the United States, has a success rate for pregnancies that has equaled and often surpassed the national average of 20%. The In Vitro Fertilization Laboratory at Scripps Clinic is the only one in San Diego certified by the College of American Pathologists/American Fertility Society.

The Musculoskeletal Center includes the disciplines of rheumatology, orthopaedic surgery, neurology, endocrinology, and radiology. Coordination of care in these complicated areas helps ensure the best possible outcome for the patient.

The Pain Treatment Center at Scripps Clinic is coordinated by the Division of Medical Psychology. The center's laboratories concentrate on pain technologies—combinations of devices and equipment specifically intended for use in the evaluation, treatment and management of chronic pain—as well as on behavioral modification programs.

The Sleep Disorders Center provides diagnosis and treatment of all sleep-related disorders and is staffed by the largest and most experienced group of full-time sleep specialists in California.

Among the many additional programs and services are an arthritis treatment program, comprehensive cardiac therapy, epilepsy surgery, Mohs surgery for skin cancer, speech therapy, a travel clinic, and urgent care centers at the La Jolla, San Diego, and Rancho Bernardo clinics.

MEDICAL SPECIALTIES

Allergy and Immunology, Anatomic Pathology, Cardiac Surgery, Cardiovascular Diseases, Chest and Critical Care Medicine, Community Medicine, Cutaneous and Mohs Surgery, Dermatology, Diabetes, Endocrinology and Nephrology, Family and General Practice, Gastroenterology, General Surgery, Head and Neck Surgery and Otology, Hematology and Medical Oncology, Infectious Diseases, Internal Medicine, Interventional Radiology, Medical Psychology, Nephrology, Neurology, Neuroradiology, Neurosurgery, Obstetrics and Gynecology, Occupational and Environmental Medicine, Oral Medicine and Stomatology, Ophthalmology, Optometry, Organ Transplantation, Orthopedic Surgery, Pathology, Pediatric and Adolescent Medicine, Plastic and Reconstructive Surgery, Podiatry, Psychiatry, Radiation Oncology, Radiology, Rheumatology, Sleep Disorders, Ultrasound and Computerized Tomography, Urgent Care and Emergency Medicine, Thoracic and Vascular Surgery, and Urology.

WELL-KNOWN SPECIALISTS

- Dr. Eugene F. Bernstein   *Specialist in vascular and thoracic surgery*
- Dr. Clifford W. Colwell, Jr.   *Specialist in orthopaedic surgery*
- Dr. Donald J. Dalessio   *Specialist in neurology*
- Dr. Mitchell H. Friedlaender   *Specialist in ophthalmology*
- Dr. Hubert T. Greenway   *Specialist in dermatology and cutaneous surgery*
- Dr. Ruth H. Grobstein   *Specialist in radiation oncology*
- Dr. P. Kahler Hench   *Specialist in rheumatology*
- Dr. Franklin Kozin   *Specialist in rheumatology*
- Dr. David A. Mathison   *Specialist in allergy*
- Dr. Robert McMillan   *Specialist in hematology and medical oncology*
- Dr. Joseph B. Michelson   *Specialist in ophthalmology*
- Dr. Jack C. Sipe   *Specialist in neurology*
- Dr. Donald D. Stevenson   *Specialist in allergy*
- Dr. Paul S. Teirstein   *Specialist in interventional cardiology*

PATIENT SATISFACTION

Scripps Hospital patients are asked about their overall satisfaction with their stay, whether or not the patient "bragged" about the hospital, would he/she return to the hospital, would he/she recommend the hospital, any surprises during their hospital stay, the outcome of the stay, and the hospital image. In the most recent surveys, 93% to 95% of the respondents gave Scripps high marks on satisfaction with their overall care and the hospital's services; 93% said they would recommend Scripps to others.

RESEARCH

The Scripps Clinic and Research Foundation receives about $80 million annually in grants for clinical research in many specialties. The Stein Clinical Research Center, a 116,000-square-foot, four-story facility, houses research in molecular and experimental medicine, neuropharmacology, and neurobiology. Other research facilities include the Scripps Research Institute, with more than 1,200 staff members conducting advanced research, and the Immunology Laboratory, which receives more than 100,000 samples per year for testing to detect major and often rare disorders.

At the Scripps Research Institute, researchers delve into ways of understanding, controlling, treating, and ultimately eliminating diseases. Major areas of inquiry include heart disease and stroke; cancer; arthritis and other autoimmune diseases; viral disorders, including hepatitis, herpes and AIDS; various forms of kidney dysfunction; alcoholism and chemical abuse problems; and multiple sclerosis.

Since 1974, Scripps has operated a General Clinical Research Facility within Green Hospital. It is one of only 74 such facilities in the nation designated by the National Institutes of Health, and the only one affiliated with a medical school. A small number of beds are set aside in this facility for the development and evaluation of new and experimental procedures, especially for autoimmune diseases and systemic lupus erythematosus.

Perhaps the best known recent research involves the drug 2-CdA, now marketed as LEUSTATIN. Developed and tested at Scripps, 2-CdA is highly effective in providing total remission for hairy-cell leukemia, a previously fatal form of cancer.

ADMISSIONS POLICY

Scripps Clinic doctors admit patients to the Green Hospital of the Scripps Clinic. Appointments with Scripps Clinic physicians can be made by contacting the clinic directly or by recommendation of one's personal physician.

If the doctor deems it necessary, the hospital admits the patient. An estimate of charges is provided. If the patient cannot pay a deposit, the hospital collects whatever the patient can pay, then sets up a payment arrangement through the billing department. Approximately $2.5 million of indigent care is provided annually.

STANFORD UNIVERSITY

HOSPITAL AND CLINIC

We doubt that any best-hospital list compiled over the last 30 years would have excluded this extraordinary medical institution. In fact, almost every department at Stanford is consistently rated among the best in the country. The most basic and perhaps obvious reason is the very high caliber of people who come to work, to study, to do research, and to practice medicine here. Several Stanford researchers have won prestigious international awards, including the Nobel Prize and the Lasker Award, for their work in cancer. Physicians such as Norman Shumway, the world famous heart transplant surgeon, Halstead Holman, an expert in the treatment of arthritis, and Phillip Sunshine, a neonatalogist, have won extensive professional and public acclaim. In recent years, 19 members of the Stanford faculty have been elected to the National Academy of Sciences and 25 to the Institute of Medicine, numbers very few institutions can match. Ninety-seven Stanford physicians are listed in *The Best Doctors in America*.

The spirit of excellence that distinguishes the senior medical staff affects the way people are admitted or hired on every other level, too. The struggle to secure a place in Stanford's residency programs is legendary among young doctors, and the medical school annually receives 6,000 applications for less than 100 openings. From the patient's perspective, however, a perhaps more important

STANFORD UNIVERSITY
MEDICAL CENTER

STANFORD, CALIFORNIA

WE DOUBT THAT ANY
BEST-HOSPITAL LIST
COMPILED OVER THE LAST
30 YEARS WOULD HAVE
EXCLUDED THIS EXTRA-
ORDINARY MEDICAL
INSTITUTION. IN FACT,
ALMOST EVERY DEPARTMENT
AT STANFORD IS
CONSISTENTLY RATED
AMONG THE BEST IN
THE COUNTRY.

measure of Stanford's commitment to employing the best people can be found by reviewing some facts and statistics about the nursing staff, certainly among the most impressive we discovered while researching this book.

Qualifications for nurses are high. Almost 58% of Stanford's registered nurses hold baccalaureate degrees, far above the national average. Stanford is nationally famous for conducting seminars on many aspects of nursing research and nursing management (several staff members have written a book on this topic), as well as in specialized medical areas where the hospital has led the way in developing patient-care techniques, especially cardiovascular and perinatal nursing.

The Medical Center has four components: the Stanford University School of Medicine; Stanford University Hospital, a teaching and research facility with patients from Palo Alto, nearby communities, and around the world; the Stanford University Clinic, a collection of more than 100 outpatient clinics staffed by medical school faculty members; and the Lucile Salter Packard Children's Hospital at Stanford, an independent, non-profit pediatric teaching hospital providing general acute and tertiary care exclusively for children.

The clinic serves as "doctor's office" for faculty members. The clinic group practice for Stanford's full-time faculty physicians is called the Faculty Practice Program, and is governed by a faculty committee. It offers medical students, residents, and postdoctoral fellows an opportunity to become familiar with outpatient problems under faculty supervision. Clinic revenue is a source for faculty salaries and general operating costs of the medical school.

The Stanford University Medical School, founded in 1858, is the oldest medical school in the West. The medical school was started in San Francisco as the medical department of the University of the Pacific. Stanford University was opened in 1891. In 1959, the medical school moved from San Francisco to new quarters, including classrooms, laboratories, hospital, and clinics, on the Stanford University campus. The hospital was co-owned by the city of Palo Alto and known as the Palo Alto-Stanford Hospital Center. Each year, the medical school accepts 86 students from over 5,500 applicants.

In 1968, Palo Alto-Stanford Hospital Center was purchased by Stanford University and incorporated as Stanford University Hospital. In 1983, the outpatient clinics were renamed Stanford University Clinic.

Stanford University Hospital is a university-owned subsidiary corporation. Like the medical school and clinic, the hospital is a non-profit organization operated without tax support or subsidy from the university.

SPECIAL FACILITIES AND PROGRAMS

Organ transplantation, cancer diagnosis and treatment, cardiovascular medicine and surgery, neurosciences, and high-risk maternal care are noted clinical specialties of Stanford University Hospital.

The transplantation programs at Stanford have compiled some impressive firsts. The first adult cardiac transplant in the U.S. was performed at Stanford, as was the first successful lung transplant. The programs have grown in capabilities and activity each year. Annually an average of 38 heart transplants, seven heart-lung transplants, and nine lung transplants are performed. Other organ transplant procedures provided at University Hospital are kidney (32 annually), liver (12 annually), and pancreas-kidney (10 annually). The Stanford Bone Marrow Transplant Program is internationally known for its clinical and scientific achievements. In all, 719 transplant procedures had been completed through August of 1993, with 195 performed in FY 1993 alone.

The medicine practiced at Stanford University Hospital is usually leading-edge. The cardiovascular medicine program is well-known for its cardiothoracic surgery capabilities and is developing medical and genetic therapies to prevent restenosis following angioplasty. Stanford's work in oncology is recognized internationally. By combining radiation and chemotherapy, Stanford physicians developed the first successful treatment of lymphoma. The Department of Endocrinology was the first to propose the theory linking insulin resistance to hypertension. In urology, Stanford is a pioneer in developing endoscopic laser and other less invasive surgery techniques. Stanford is also a leader in treating immune disorders and connective tissue diseases.

Specialty clinics and facilities at the Stanford University Clinic include the Stroke Center, the Epilepsy Center, a comprehensive rehabilitation center, a hand clinic, the Peterson cancer center, a trauma center, a cardiac catheter lab, a video laparoscopy surgery suite, a sleep center, and a Marfan syndrome clinic.

Lucile Salter Packard Children's Hospital at Stanford is a regional tertiary care facility providing all pediatric medical and surgical services associated with Stanford University Medical Center. The hospital is staffed and equipped to address the entire spectrum of children's health care needs, from preventive care to intensive treatment of injury or illness.

AT A GLANCE

Beds: 663
Occupancy Rate: 72%
Average Patient Count: 477
Average Patient Stay: 5.3 days
Annual Admissions: 22,308
Outpatient Clinic Visits:
   262,437
Emergency Room/Trauma
   Center Visits: 37,576

HOSPITAL PERSONNEL
Physicians: 1,674
Residents: 521
Registered Nurses: 1,043
   BS Degree: 58%

ROOM CHARGES (PER DIEM)
Private: $895
Semiprivate: $838
ICU: $895–$5,651

ADDRESS
300 Pasteur Drive
Stanford, CA 94305

TELEPHONE
(415) 723-4000

Among the pediatric services offered by the hospital and its medical staff are a variety of nationally recognized programs, including cancer diagnosis and treatment, bone marrow transplantation, heart and heart-lung transplantation, treatment of cardiovascular disorders, liver transplantation, and services offered by the Mothers and Infants Center (jointly operated with Stanford University Hospital) encompassing high-risk maternal and neonatal care.

Through its role as a teaching hospital and research center affiliated with Stanford University School of Medicine, Lucile Packard Children's Hospital brings the benefits of pediatric medicine advances to the service of its young patients. Ronald McDonald House offers low-cost housing for patients and families.

The Ambulatory Care Center, which augments inpatient care, offers a comprehensive primary care clinic, as well as more than 40 subspecialty clinics. The Rehabilitation Engineering Center provides custom seating and wheelchair systems, and orthotic, prosthetic, and communication devices for children and adults with disabilities.

MEDICAL SPECIALTIES

Alcohol and Drug, Allergy, Anesthesia, Arthritis, Behavioral Medicine, Bone Marrow Transplantation, Cardiac Transplants, Cardiovascular Medicine, Cardiovascular Surgery, Chemotherapy, Dermatology, Diagnostic Radiology and Nuclear Medicine, Ear, Nose, and Throat, Emergency Services, Endocrinology, Epilepsy, Family and Community Medicine, Gastroenterology, General Surgery, Geriatric Medicine, Gynecology and Obstetrics, Gynecological Oncology, Hand Surgery, Hematology, Immunology, Infectious Diseases, Internal Medicine, Kidney, Liver and Pancreas Transplantation, Mammography, Marfan Syndrome, Multiple Sclerosis, Nephrology, Neurology, Neurosurgery, Oncology (Medical), Ophthalmalogy, Orthopedic Surgery, Pain Management, Pathology, Pediatric Surgery, Pediatrics, Perinatology, Plastic and Reconstructive Surgery, Primary Care, Psychiatry, Radiation Oncology, Reproductive Endocrinology and Infertility, Respiratory Medicine, Sleep Disorders, Stroke, Thoracic Surgery, Trauma, and Urology.

Within these specialties are more than 100 subspecialties, each with its own clinic. For specific information call (415) 723-5631.

WELL-KNOWN SPECIALISTS

- Dr. Stewart W. Agras *Psychiatry; specialist in eating disorders*
- Dr. Michael David Amylon *Pediatrics; specialist in pediatric hematology-oncology*
- Dr. Daniel Bernstein *Pediatrics; specialist in pediatric cardiology*
- Dr. Karl G. Blume *Medical oncology-hematology; specialist in bone marrow transplant*
- Dr. Mark S. Blumenkranz *Ophthalmology; specialist in vitreo-retinal surgery*

- Dr. Robert F. DeBusk   *Cardiovascular disease; specialist in cardiac rehabilitation*
- Dr. James F. Fries   *Rheumatology; specialist in lupus*
- Dr. Charles B. Gerson   *Rheumatology; specialist in general rheumatology*
- Dr. Sandra J. Horning   *Medical oncology-hematology; specialist in lymphomas*
- Dr. Neil Olcott IV   *General surgery; specialist in general vascular surgery*
- Dr. Jack Remington   *Infectious disease; specialist in AIDS, toxoplasmosis*
- Dr. Mansfield F. W. Smith   *Otolaryngology; specialist in otology*
- Dr. Roger A. Winkle   *Cardiovascular disease; specialist in electrophysiology*
- Dr. Carol H. Winograd   *Geriatric medicine; specialist in general geriatric medicine*

PATIENT SATISFACTION

On a scale from 1 to 10 (with 10 being excellent) the average response from about 500 inpatients was 8.5 in the latest survey results available. Courtesy and service were rated at 8.7 and nursing also drew an 8.7 response. Stanford physicians have been consistently rated above 9.0.

RESEARCH

Stanford received almost $105 million in government grants in 1993, most from the National Institutes of Health (NIH). Among the significant recent accomplishments of the research program are the discovery in 1990 of the "off-switch" for genetic production in bacteria; development of a treatment to enhance patients' immunological response against B-cell lymphoma with genetically engineered vaccine from their own tumors; and the discovery in 1993 of a protein that appears to be a root cause of type I diabetes, and prevention in mouse experiments.

Other ongoing research includes the following:

Investigation of potential drug treatments and immunization strategies against AIDS, as well as a collaborative research effort with industry to devise new approaches to AIDS therapy, are underway.

Molecular studies are focusing on how the immune system orchestrates the body's defenses against disease and how the myriad components of the immune system develop.

Studies are being conducted to determine the structure of fundamental biological molecules and efforts are underway to engineer proteins with clinical significance. Work is also being done on identification of genes or genetic markers that determine an individual's susceptibility to specific diseases.

Cardiovascular researchers are studying drugs and devices for treating heart disease, including atherectomy to restore occluded arteries, agents for preventing heart attack and treating arrhythmias, drugs to dissolve blood clots, and implantable devices to shock ailing hearts into normal function.

Concerning radiation therapy and chemotherapy to treat Hodgkin's disease, refinement is continuing of the techniques developed at Stanford that have made this once-fatal form of lymphatic cancer more than 80% curable.

New approaches to cancer treatment include hyperthermia, the use of heat to kill tumors; radiosensitizers, chemicals that can increase cancer cells' susceptibility to radiation bombardment; and new approaches to solid tumors of the head and neck and to tumors of the genitourinary system.

Clinical testing of new methods, including magnetic resonance imaging, computer-generated images from x-rays of different wavelengths, and synchroton radiation produced by the Stanford Linear Accelerator, is done.

ADMISSIONS POLICY

Strictly speaking, nonemergency patients are admitted only by the hospital's medical staff. But since anyone can make an appointment for consultation or treatment through the Stanford University Clinic, admission to the hospital is not difficult for anyone who is really sick. In fact, patients admitted through the clinic make up more than half of the 153,000 patient-days of care at Stanford University Hospital. For information call Clinic Patient Relations at (415) 723-6903.

Proof of adequate coverage through private or public insurance or third party or a cash deposit are required prior to admission except in cases of emergency, transfer or free care programs.

PATIENT/FAMILY ACOMMODATIONS

Ronald McDonald House offers low-cost housing for patients and families.

UC DAVIS

MEDICAL CENTER

The University of California, Davis Medical Center (UCDMC) is the sole Level I Trauma Center serving the Sacramento-Sierra area of California and is the primary tertiary care referral center for a 32-county area covering more than five million residents. With over 300,000 inpatient and outpatient visits per year, the Medical Center is the busiest in the region, despite having only 18% of the licensed hospital beds. Nationally recognized in many of its specialties, including cancer care, cardiology, endocrinology, gynecology, neurology, orthopedics, rheumatology, and urology, it is also known as a leader in high technology applications to patient care, offering the most modern treatment procedures. UCDMC has also been designated a Children's Hospital within a Hospital by the National Association of Children's Hospitals and Related Institutions, the only hospital in the region to meet the rigorous criteria required for membership.

The University of California established the UCDMC campus in 1973 to support the clinical training and research needs of the Cal-Davis Medical School, and to provide inland Northern California with expanded patient care. Since then, the facility has evolved into a major health sciences campus, consisting of 82 separate buildings, including 40 off-site facilities. The campus is located on 120 acres in central Sacramento, three miles from the state Capitol.

The University of California, Davis Medical School (UCDMS) is known for its emphasis on primary care training. Over the years, 46% of all graduates have chosen to specialize in primary care and the UCDMS ranked ninth in the nation in the number of graduates matched to primary-care residencies for the period from 1981 through 1991. Also, UCDMS ranks among the top 10% in the nation for students choosing family medicine.

The reputation of the University of California, Davis Medical Center as a prestigious medical facility has been strengthened through a number of affiliations, partnerships, and relationships. For example, the Shriners' Hospital for Crippled Children is building a $65 million, 300,000-square-foot hospital on a site adjacent to the medical center to replace its facility in San Francisco and serve as the flagship for all 23 Shriners' hospitals, bringing together for the first time an orthopedic service, a burn care unit, and a spinal cord injury rehabilitation unit. A joint venture with Continental Medical Systems, Inc. will establish the region's only dedicated state-of-the-art center for acute rehabilitation patients. In a new affiliation with Mercy Health Care Sacramento, UCDMC residents in family practice are doing rotations at Mercy General Hospital, effectively expanding the services available for all Sacramento residents.

SPECIAL FACILITIES AND PROGRAMS

The Multi-Organ Transplant Center of the University of California, Davis Medical Center provides a broad spectrum of transplantation programs, including kidney, liver, kidney/pancreas, pancreas, heart, and bone marrow. In 1986, UCDMC joined together with Sutter Memorial Hospital to form the Northern California Regional Renal Program. To date, over 500 kidney and other organ transplants have been performed. Recent patient survival outcome data indicates that the Multi-Organ Transplant Center consistently meets or exceeds national norms. Through UCDMC's Regional Trauma Center, Cal-Davis obtains the largest number of transplantable organs in northern California. The rapid access to these organs improves the outcomes by minimizing the time between organ donation and transplantation. An added bonus of this organ availability is that transplant candidates wait a shorter period of time for a matching donor organ.

UCDMC brings a very highly trained and skilled transplant team to each procedure; these are headed by experienced transplant surgeons who are prominent teachers and researchers in their respective fields. Other physician team members include immunologists, anesthesiologists, pathologists, nephrologists, cardiologists, pulmonologists, hepatologists, gastroenterologists, infectious disease specialists, and oncologists. These doctors are joined by other transplant professionals including clinical nurses, pharmacists, social workers, and dieticians. A financial counselor is also part of the team. Together, this team meets the special needs of transplant candidates, living donors, and transplant recipients in their evaluation, surgery, and post-operative treatment. Referring physicians are regularly involved through consultation and notification of their patient's progress and the transplant team remains a permanent, 24-hour resource to these physicians in the ongoing management of their transplanted patients.

The cancer program at the UC Davis Cancer Center encompasses all cancer treatment activities, including medical and surgical oncology, as well as radiation oncology. The radiation oncology center includes two advanced linear accelerators, a treatment simulator, and a three-dimensional treatment planning computer. UC Davis Cancer Center is a leading center for advanced treatment techniques such as photodynamic laser therapy, radioimmunotherapy, and limb salvage. Other services include a cancer pain clinic, a fine-needle aspiration biopsy clinic, a full-service 12-bed infusion center, a pharmacy and clinical laboratory, diagnostic radiology and mammography, and a bone marrow laboratory.

UC Davis has an active clinical trials program that studies new drugs and new drug combinations. This program enables patients treated at UCDMC to have immediate access to the most current treatment regimens for different types of cancer. These studies are done in cooperation with the Southwestern Oncology Group, the National Surgical Adjuvant Breast and Bowel Project, and the Radiation Therapy Oncology group. The UCDMC Cancer Center is nationally recognized for its advanced technology and treatment techniques.

In late 1991, the UC Davis Medical Center and School of Medicine formally established the UC Davis Heart Center as an interdisciplinary clinical program of the divisions of cardiovascular medicine, cardiac surgery, and pediatric cardiology. The Heart Center offers referring physicians and their patients streamlined access to full range of cardiac services available at UC Davis. The cardiac program offers comprehensive, advanced services responsive to the needs of the referring physician. The UC Davis Heart Center adult and pediatric services include cardiac surgery; complex aortic surgery, including bypass; the heart transplantation program; interventional procedures; electophysiologic studies and ablation procedures; pediatric cardiology; pediatric cardiac surgery; a cardiac rehabilitation program; cardiac risk

AT A GLANCE

Beds: 485
Occupancy Rate: 80%
Average Patient Count: 378
Average Patient Stay: 6.4 days
Annual Admissions: 21,000
Births: 1,300
Outpatient Clinic Visits:
    248,500
Emergency Room/Trauma
    Center Visits: 48,400

HOSPITAL PERSONNEL
Physicians: 893
Residents: 440
Registered Nurses: 1,500

ROOM CHARGES (PER DIEM)
Levels I–V Care:
    $713–$2,200
Level VI Care: $2,200–$5,900

ADDRESS
2315 Stockton Boulevard
Sacramento, CA 95817

TELEPHONE
(916) 734-2784

reduction; a coronary heart disease reversal program; an arrhythmia/pacemaker clinic; a heart failure clinic; and the women's heart care network.

The Division of Cardiovascular Medicine offers state-of-the-art services to patients at risk for cardiovascular disease, as well as those needing definitive diagnosis or treatment for myocardial infarction, coronary artery disease, heart valve problems, and congenital heart disease in adults. Services include exercise testing, echocardiography—including transesophageal echocardiography, arrhythmia monitoring, pacemaker placement, diagnostic cardiac catheterization and angiography, percutaneous transluminal coronary angioplasty, atherectomy, and percutaneous balloon valvuplasty. Special programs of the Division of Cardiovascular Medicine include intravascular ultrasound assessment of coronary lesions; direct intracoronary Doppler measurement of coronary flow; a broad-based, multispecialty approach to atherosclerosis prevention, particularly in patients with hyperlipidemia and hypertension; a cardiac services program integrating the clinical services of adult cardiology, pediatric cardiology, and cardiothoracic surgery; endomyocardial biopsy; vena cava filter placement; a chest pain emergency program; and electrophysiology inpatient service, including pacemaker and defibrillator.

The faculty and staff of the UCDMC Department of Orthopaedic Surgery provide the full spectrum of operative and nonoperative care for medical and surgical disorders of the musculosketal system. Specialty services consist of trauma and trauma reconstruction, musculoskeletal tumors, pediatric orthopaedics, sports medicine and arthroscopy, upper extremity, hand and microvascular surgery, children's spinal deformities, spine trauma adult reconstructive spine surgery, total joint arthroplasty and general adult reconstructive surgery, and surgery of the foot and ankle. The Department of Orthopaedic Surgery offers one of the largest trauma programs in the nation; the only multidisciplinary clinic for the treatment of bone and joint infections in Northern California; and reconstructive surgery of the brachial plexus (the only center offering this service in central Northern California). Other specialty interests and capabilities of the staff include Ilizarov techniques, closed intramedullary surgery, reconstruction of complex fractures and problems of the acetabulum and pelvis, knee ligament reconstruction, limb preservation surgery for malignant tumors of the extremities, custom and specialized total joint replacement surgery, allograft surgery, specialized fixation techniques for spinal disorders in children and adults, gait analysis with special interest in cerebral palsy, specialized interest in pediatric disorders of the foot and hip, total joint replacement of the upper extremity, brachial plexus reconstructive surgery, microsurgery, and peripheral nerve surgery.

The UC Davis Medical Center's Department of Urology is a comprehensive diagnostic and treatment center for adult and pediatric urological conditions. Urinary incontinence is treated through pharmacologic and surgical means. Male infertility is addressed through testicular biopsy, vasograms, seminal vesiculograms, vasovasostomy, and vasoepididymostomy. Expert surgeons, medical oncologists, and radiation therapists cooperate in the treatment of urological cancers. Special treatment services include percutaneous nephrolithotripsy (antegrade and retrograde percutaneous intrarenal lithotripsy and intrarenal surgery); endoinfundibilotomy, endopyelotomy, endoureterotomy, endoureteroenterotomy, and diagnostic and therapeutic ureteroscopy; microsurgical vasoepididymostomy; metabolic evaluation clinic for recurrent stone formers, offering every advanced surgical procedure for urolithiasis, from complex open to complex endoscopic; and reconstructive urologic surgery for children.

The UCDMC Department of Pediatrics comprises a team of pediatric specialists practicing the latest in ambulatory pediatrics, hematology/oncology, cardiology, child development and behavior, endocrinology, gastroenterology, genetics, infectious diseases, neonatology, nephrology, pulmonary medicine, rheumatology, and immunology. Specialists are available 24 hours a day for the acceptance of pediatric referrals, while also conducting related clinics throughout the week. Superior diagnostic capabilities are available for identification of a full range of pediatric conditions. In addition to excellence in patient care and active research programs, UCDMC pediatricians subscribe to a philosophy of teamwork, personalized care, patient and family education, prevention, and clinical and community support. Special features include a Pediatric Acute Care Clinic for emergency care; a private practice office, University Pediatrics Associates; a Genetics Clinic, providing prenatal diagnosis to children and their families; a Developmental Support Clinic where premature children or those prenatally exposed to substances receive specialized support services; a Pediatric Critical Care Unit that is a referral center for Central and Northern California; a designated trauma center for children; a Child Protection Center that treats more than 2,000 abused children each year, working with law enforcement and child protection agencies; innovative programs to allow the use of the latest endocrine therapies on children; and age-specific support groups for children with diabetes and their families. Pediatric care also includes a specialized center for gastrointestinal and nutritional disorders; a Hemostatis Diagnostic Laboratory for coagulation and platelet function studies; a Pulmonary Clinic for children with cystic fibrosis, asthma or other pulmonary conditions; a highly specialized Neonatal Intensive Care Unit that treats newborns throughout Central and Northern California, offering a full range of subspecialty consultation; a high-frequency ventilation program using oscillator and jet respirators with neonates; a Dialysis and Renal Transplantation Center for children with renal disease; a preventive cardiology program; a Pediatric Infectious Disease Clinic, including the only Center for Pediatric AIDS in central Northern California; and a Pediatric Rheumatology Clinic. A Pediatric Oncology Center with a strong affiliation with the Pediatric Oncology Group, one of two federally funded groups in the nation for the study of cancer in children, is located at UCDMC.

Hemodialysis has been offered at UCDMC for treatment of both acute and chronic renal failure since 1970. Peritoneal dialysis for treatment of acute renal failure antedated that of hemodialysis and an ambulatory dialysis program for treatment of chronic renal failure was inaugurated in 1979. At the present time dialysis services are offered to University patients in three locations. Services are available for patients with acute renal failure and those with chronic renal failure requiring hospitalization at the University Medical Center. Outpatient services are provided in two community-based centers, University Dialysis Clinic in the Sacramental Medical Foundation Blood Center, and the other at Southgate Dialysis Clinic in south Sacramento. University Dialysis Clinic has 20 stations and Southgate Dialysis Clinic, a satellite of the University outpatient clinic, has 22 stations. University Dialysis Clinic also offers peritoneal dialysis either intermittent or continuous for treatment of chronic renal failure. At the present time University Dialysis Clinic is managing 122 end-stage renal disease patients with hemodialysis and an additional 52 patients with peritoneal dialysis. The Southgate Clinic currently manages 62 patients with maintenance hemodialysis including high-flux biocompatible membranes, highly purified water treated with reverse osmosis, bicarbonate dialysate, and volumetric controlled ultrafiltration.

UCDMC offers an abundance of other patient care services, laboratory procedures, diagnostic radiology procedures, and specialized surgical procedures. In concert with academic program requirements, advances in technology, and changes in the health care needs of UCDMC's population, the hospital has developed several services/programs unique to the region. These include the Level I Trauma Center, Life Flight Emergency Helicopter Transport, the Northern Central California Hemophilia Program, the Regional Poison Control Center, the Sierra Regional Eye and Tissue Bank, the Skull Base Surgery Program, Limb Salvaging/Lengthening, Radiation/Pesticide/Toxic Exposure Decontamination, the Alzheimer's Disease Diagnostic and Treatment Center, the AIDS Research Center (one of 11 centers nationwide), the Center for Aging and Health, a Nutrition Support Service (for transplant, intestinal malabsorption, anorexia, bulimia, tube-fed, and intravenous patients), a Vitamin and Mineral Core Laboratory, and the Regional Burn Center.

MEDICAL SPECIALTIES

Cancer Care, Cardiology, Cardiovascular Medicine, Clinical Nutrition and Metabolism, Emergency Medicine and Toxicology, Endocrinology and Metabolism, Gastroenterology, General Internal Medicine, Hematology and Oncology, Infectious and Immunological Diseases, Nephrology, Neurology, Obstetrics/Gynecology, Occupational and Environmental Medicine, Ophthalmology, Orthopedics, Physical Medicine, and Rehabilitation, Pulmonary and Critical Care Medicine, Radiology, Rheumatology/Allergy/Clinical Immunology, Surgery, Transplantation Surgery, Trauma Medicine, and Urology.

WELL-KNOWN SPECIALISTS

- Dr. Thomas F. Anders *Psychiatry; specialist in child psychology*
- Dr. F. William Blaisdell *Surgery; specialist in vascular surgery*

- Dr. Timothy J. Bray   *Orthopedics; specialist in orthopedic trauma surgery*
- Dr. R. Jeffrey Chang   *Obstetrics/gynecology; specialist in gynecology*
- Dr. Thomas A. Depner   *Nephrology; medical director of the University Dialysis Clinic*
- Dr. Paul J. Donald   *Otolaryngology; director of the Center for Skull Base Surgery*
- Dr. William J. Jagust   *Neurology; director of the UC Davis Northern California Alzheimer's Disease Center*
- Dr. Mark J. Mannis   *Ophthalmology; medical director of the Cornea and External Disease Service*
- Dr. John Jay McCann   *Pediatrics; medical director of the UCDMC Child Protection Center*
- Dr. Frederick J. Meyers   *Medical oncology; chief of the Division of Hematology and Oncology*
- Dr. Saul Schaefer   *Cardiology; medical director of interventional cardiology*
- Dr. Dennis M. Styne   *Pediatrics; specialist in pediatric endocrinology*

PATIENT SATISFACTION

In the latest patient satisfaction survey, telephone calls were made randomly to inpatients who had been recently discharged. Patients expressed a high level of satisfaction with the overall care they received while at UCDMC. The patients were most highly satisfied with the quality of care provided and the courtesy of the staff. They were similarly satisfied with the overall performance of physicians and nurses. Electively admitted patients were more satisfied than those admitted under emergency conditions. A vast majority of the patients interviewed indicated they would recommend UCDMC to a friend or relative and would return themselves if they needed further medical care.

RESEARCH

Research is a major emphasis, with UC Davis scientists and physicians conducting more than 300 simultaneous projects at any given time. UC Davis enjoys a reputation for a collaborative, multidepartmental approach to research. To accommodate the rapidly expanding research programs, two research buildings, Research I and Research II, were completed at the Sacramental campus in 1993.

The UC Davis Center for Neuroscience is a multidisciplinary center designed for sophisticated neurophysiological research. It is considered a major institution for the study of human neurosciences. Many faculty members are world leaders in brain research, dealing with structure, function, learning, and memory in aging and disease. School of Medicine researchers, including those in neurology, neurosurgery, geriatrics, general medicine, physical medicine and rehabilitation, and at the Alzheimer's Center, collaborate with other campus researchers at the center.

With $42 million in research grants and contracts, UC Davis has the highest number of research dollars per square foot of research space. Also, UC Davis ranks in the top 15% for the number of clinical science grants per clinical faculty.

Established with a $4 million federal grant, the Agricultural Health and Safety Center conducts research and outreach programs aimed at controlling and preventing farm-related accidents and illnesses. One of only two such programs in the nation, the center is a collaborative effort among university medical, agricultural, and extension specialists.

A five-year, $2.8 million federal grant established a regional Alzheimer's disease center at UC Davis. The center promotes collaborative studies among Alzheimer's researchers and clinicians at Highland General Hospital in Oakland, the VA Medical Clinic in Martinez and UC Davis Alzheimer's diagnostic and treatment centers in Berkeley and Sacramento.

The Department of Orthopaedic Surgery is working in three major areas relating to bone growth and biomechanics: bone growth factors; biomechanics of bones and joints; and fatigue damage in bones, which appears to be an important factor in bone metabolism and osteoporosis.

Joining the ambitious five-year, $70 million National Cancer Institute breast cancer prevention study in the 1991-92 fiscal year, UCDMC is participating in a study of 16,000 women nationwide. Researchers are testing whether the anti-cancer drug tamoxifen, known to prevent recurrences and the development of new tumors in the opposite breast, is effective in preventing this disease.

Ophthalmology researchers developed a simple blood test that detects early stages of some cancers occurring elsewhere in the body. Called the cancer-associated retinopathy assay, the new test detects a rare form of retinal degeneration that occurs in association with certain forms of cancer, such as tobacco-caused lung cancer.

Cancer researchers continue to show progress in clinical trials using radioactive monoclonal antibodies to treat advanced breast cancer and lymphoma. Scientists from the UC Davis Cancer Center also are conducting a wide range of clinical trials of cancer therapeutics.

The Center for Aging and Health focuses on research, teaching, patient care, and public service in geriatrics and gerontology. In the 1992-93 fiscal year, researchers at the center launched a three-year National Institutes of Health (NIH) study to determine the well-being and assess the needs of people over age 60.

UC Davis is one of 11 NIH-designated AIDS research centers in the U.S. More than 30 UC Davis researchers, including physicians, veterinarians, and basic scientists, are collaborating on studies of potential AIDS vaccines and therapies.

Through collaboration with neurobiologists on campus, UC Davis School of Medicine and Medical Center neuroscientists are expanding their research in the areas of cognitive, molecular, and pediatric neuroscience. They continue their focus on myasthenia gravis, the autoimmune diseases that affects eye, facial, chewing, swallowing, and breathing muscles.

Researchers in the Division of Occupational and Environmental Medicine published the results of a three-year study that showed that pregnant women who make computer chips experience a rate of miscarriage that is nearly twice the average for all women. The study also found that fabricators have a higher average infertility rate. Results from the $3.5 million study, funded by the Semiconductors Industry Association, led to the new health and safety recommendations this year for the industry.

National Cancer Institute grants will help urology researchers identify which patients with prostate cancer are to be treated, when treatment should be started and which treatment is most effective. Looking at genetic abnormalities that appear with prostate cancer, the research is aimed at identifying and assessing the prevalence of the abnormalities and how they manifest in benign, premalignant, and malignant prostate tissue samples.

UC Davis was named one of the 16 vanguard clinical centers—one of only two in California—to participate in the largest and most ambitious clinical medical trial in the nation's history. Named the Women's Health Initiative, it is a 15-year, $625 million National Institutes of Health study that will target heart disease, cancer and osteoporosis.

In recent animal studies conducted in the Department of Medical Microbiology, a pathogenic strain of *Nocardia asteriodes*, a bacteria commonly found in the soil, has been implicated as a possible cause of Parkinson's disease. The finding could be very important to developing methods for prevention, early diagnosis, and improved treatment of this neurological disease.

ADMISSIONS POLICY

Patient admission is arranged by the UC Davis Medical Center physician responsible for the patient's care. Emergency or direct-referral admissions may be made by calling the specific applicable medical services at the Medical Center.

Payment or insurance arrangements must be made prior to admission unless an emergency exists. If the patient is not covered by insurance, cash payment equal to the estimated cost of care is required.

Indigent care provided in the 1993-94 fiscal year totaled $52 million.

Special phone number for admissions information: (916) 734-2450.

UCLA MEDICAL

CENTER

UNIVERSITY OF CALIFORNIA

LOS ANGELES, CALIFORNIA

UCLA Medical Center is recognized by physicians as one of the best hospitals in the U.S. and quite possibly the best in the western United States. Since opening its doors in 1955, the Medical Center has grown rapidly in terms of size and expertise. It ranks among the top hospitals in the country in a dozen medical specialties and the volume of daily activities makes it among the busiest. Yet despite its size and specialization, UCLA Medical Center has built a reputation for humanistic patient care spearheaded by an emphasis on primary care medicine and by a dedicated and highly educated nursing staff.

UCLA Medical Center is the primary teaching hospital for the School of Medicine at UCLA. The center provides inpatient and outpatient services in nearly all medical specialties. Top rate medical care is furnished by an impressively large medical staff of more than 2,000 physicians. With experts in nearly all health care fields, UCLA physicians provide primary and tertiary care for adults and children.

UCLA Medical Center is a non-profit academic medical center that offers a full spectrum of medical and surgical care. It was built in conjunction with the UCLA Schools of Medicine and Nursing on the southern portion of the UCLA campus. The Medical Center is one component of UCLA's Center for the Health Sciences, which includes the Schools of Medicine, Nursing, Dentistry, and Public Health; the

Neuropsychiatric Institute and Hospital; the Jules Stein Eye Institute and Doris Stein Eye Research Center; the Clarence E. Reed Neurological Research Institute; the Brain Research Institute; the Jerry Lewis Neuromuscular Research Center; and the Jonsson Comprehensive Cancer Center. The Medical Center houses the Hazel E. Wilson Pavilion, more than 80 subspecialty clinics, and a complete Emergency Medical Center. Most of the Medical Center's outpatient services are located in the UCLA Medical Plaza which opened in 1990.

In keeping with its patient orientation, UCLA runs a strong community outreach program. It provides educational seminars and publications to members of the local community. The Medical Center also gives free health screenings to members of the public several times each year. Through its Continuing Medical Education efforts, the center shares with community physicians the expertise of its leading researchers and clinicians. Its Home Health program provides nursing, medical equipment, and rehabilitation services and other therapies to patients in their homes. And, in this age of managed care, UCLA has been working with managed care organizations to give their members access to the Medical Center's treatment resources.

As a result of its reputation for patient-centered care, specialized medicine, and top-notch research and education facilities, UCLA draws more than 3,800 patients per year from outside the Southern California area for treatment of severe illnesses. In fiscal year 1993, 110 patients were admitted from other countries and 761 from states other than California and Nevada.

SPECIAL FACILITIES AND PROGRAMS

The UCLA Transplantation Programs maintain a cohesive surgical, medical, and support staff, which forms an experienced and committed team to face the challenges of organ transplantation. Physicians in many subspecialties act as consultants to multiple transplant disciplines, and their breadth of experience enhances the clinical success of all of the UCLA Organ Transplant Programs.

AT A GLANCE

Beds: 691
Occupancy Rate: 59%
Average Patient Count: 357
Average Patient Stay: 6.1 days
Annual Admissions: 21,555
Births: 1,555
Outpatient Clinic Visits:
   343,284
Emergency Room/Trauma
   Center Visits: 34,877

HOSPITAL PERSONNEL
Physicians: 600
   Board Certified: 100%
Residents: 800
Registered Nurses: 1,052
   BS Degree: 634

ROOM CHARGES (PER DIEM)
Private: $675
Semiprivate: $585
ICU: $1,760

ADDRESS
10833 Le Conte Avenue
Los Angeles, CA 90024

TELEPHONE
(310) 825-9111

UCLA was among the pioneers in human organ transplantation, performing some of the earliest transplant procedures in the United States. In 1965, the first accredited transplantation program was initiated at UCLA in renal transplantation, followed by pediatric and adult bone marrow transplantation in 1973. The introduction in 1984 of a new specific immunosuppressive drug, Cyclosporine, revolutionized the field of organ transplantation. Only months after Cyclosporine became commercially available, UCLA initiated successful programs in liver and heart transplantation. Heart-lung transplantation followed in 1988, and lung transplantation in 1990. By now, UCLA Medical Center has performed over 1,400 kidney transplants, 375 heart transplants, 1,300 bone marrow transplants, and 1,100 liver transplants. Its success rates for all these procedures are among the best in the nation.

UCLA's Cancer Center has been recognized as comprehensive by the National Cancer Institute since 1976. Patients who come to UCLA for cancer care benefit from the most advanced forms of current therapy and supportive services. They also have access to the latest protocols for investigative treatments on the frontier of oncology through the Jonsson Comprehensive Cancer Center's clinical research unit. Patients also have access to Phase I and II trials of biologic response modifiers (interleukins, interferous growth factors, etc.) as well as Phase III NCI-sponsored clinical trials through the Southwest Oncology Group for breast, lung, and gastrointestinal malignancies, lymphomas, melanomas, and meningiomas.

Patient care is provided by a team of specialists who work together to help the cancer patient and his or her family contend with the immediate and long-term effects of the disease. Convenient, service-oriented, state-of-the-art care for cancer patients who do not require hospitalization is provided in the Bowyer and Surgical Oncology centers as well as in the UCLA Breast Center. Facilities for radiation therapy; for outpatient care of pediatric, urologic, gynecologic, neurosurgical, skin, and head and neck cancer patients; as well as for hospitalization if necessary, are within or adjacent to the UCLA Medical Plaza complex.

Heart disease in its many forms receives special attention at UCLA Medical Center. Patients with cardiomyopathies or acute myocarditis, and ventricular dysfunction from valvular or coronary artery disease are evaluated at the Ahmanson-UCLA Cardiomyopathy Center to establish etiology of disease, possible reversibility of left ventricular dysfunction, optimal design of medical therapy, and in a small number of patients, eligibility for cardiac transplantation. The Center offers all levels of subsequent follow-up care in collaboration with referring primary physicians according to their preference. Invasive studies and therapies are provided at the Adult Cardiac Catheterization Laboratory. The lab offers a wide array of services: treatment of adult congenital heart disease; cardiac catheterization (including coronary arteriography); exercise hemodynamic studies; clinical electrophysiological studies; percutaneous endomyocardial biopsy; angioscopy, laser angioplasty, atherectomy, and percutaneous transluminal coronary angioplasty; balloon valvuloplasty; and thrombolytic therapy of acute coronary thrombosis. Cardio-vascular diagnostic studies are provided to the Adult Cardiac Imaging and Hemodynamics Laboratory. The UCLA Arrhythmia Consultation Service offers inpatient and outpatient evaluation of patients with cardiac arrhythmias. Other special heart facilities include the Cholesterol and Lipid Management Center, the Congenital Heart Disease Center, and the Pacemaker Clinic.

The Division of Cardiothoracic Surgery provides consultative and therapeutic services for surgical treatment of cardiac, pulmonary, and esophageal disease. The Division offers a full complement of cardiac services for acquired heart disease, congenital heart disease, and transplantation. For acquired heart disease there are programs in coronary artery bypass grafting, valve repair and replacement, treatment of thoracic aneurysms, and the insertion of pacemakers and electrical defribrillators. The department has extensive experience in the treatment of congenital cardiac lesions including the arterial switch procedure, use of homografts, and the Fontan procedure.

Comprehensive diagnostic, treatment, and consultation services are provided by the faculty in Neurology at UCLA. Disorders of the brain, spinal cord, peripheral nerve, and muscle, together with neurobehavioral problems, are diagnosed and treated through a variety of specialized outpatient and inpatient services.

The Jules Stein Eye Institute, the Doris Stein Eye Research Center, and the Department of Ophthalmology constitute a comprehensive center dedicated to the preservation of vision and prevention of blindness through patient care, research, and education. A world-recognized center for vision science, the Jules Stein Eye Institute each year registers more than 60,000 visits from patients with all categories of eye disorders and visual system diseases. An alliance with prominent ophthalmologists extends patient consultation and care services throughout Southern California.

The Department of Orthopaedic Surgery provides consultation and treatment for disorders of the musculoskeletal system. Its faculty members provide comprehensive services or orthopaedic specialties including joint replacement and reconstructive surgery, hand and microvascular surgery, sports medicine, arthroscopy, foot and ankle surgery, pediatric orthopaedics, spinal diseases, orthopaedic trauma and orthopaedic oncology, and metabolic bone disease.

In the Department of Radiation Oncology, patients with cancer and other selected diseases are managed through the use of ionizing radiations. This patient management includes diagnosis or its confirmation, pretreatment evaluation, treatment applications, evaluation of results, and periodic assessment of the patient's status, usually for many years. Radiation therapy has been successful in the curative and palliative management of a wide range of cancers involving nearly every anatomic site, including the skin, eye, brain and spinal cord, oral cavity, upper aerodigestive tract, lung, breast, rectum, anus, prostate, testis, bladder, soft tissues, bone, lymphoid tissues, and female genital tract. Ionizing radiations may be used alone or in combinations with surgery and/or chemotherapy.

UCLA Radiological Sciences provides the full range of diagnostic imaging services, as well as selected therapeutic techniques, on both an inpatient and outpatient basis. Using the full range of diagnostic modalities—radiography, fluoroscopy, ultrasound (including color Doppler), CT, MRI, and SPECT—the 42 radiologists of the department offer specialized services in the following areas: breast imaging; cardiovascular radiology; endovascular therapy; gastrointestinal radiology; genitourinary radiology; head and neck radiology; musculoskeletal radiology; neuroradiology; neurosciences imaging; nuclear medicine; pediatric radiology; and thoracic radiology.

The UCLA Rehabilitation Program includes both physician-based and hospital-based components. Physician-directed services are designed to meet the needs of patients with disabilities related to neurologic, cardiovascular, and joint disease. Hospital-based rehabilitation services include physical therapy, occupational therapy, speech pathology, functional assessment (gait analysis), prosthetics, and orthotics.

The Department of Psychiatry and Biobehavioral Sciences of the UCLA School of Medicine is located within the Neuropsychiatric Institute. Faculty of the Department work in the Neuropsychiatric Hospital to provide patient care through outpatient, inpatient, and partial hospital programs for children, adults, and the elderly. Highly trained professionals evaluate each patient and then develop and implement an individually designed treatment plan using all available forms of appropriate medical and psychosocial treatments. The Access Center is the admission, evaluation, and referral center for all clinical programs at the Neuropsychiatric Hospital.

The Surgery Center was designed to provide a comfortable, state-of-the-art outpatient operating room setting in which patient friendliness is an important concern. Family members are encouraged to be present in the pre-operative and recovery areas, and all efforts are made to minimize waiting periods for patients and their families. Anesthetic techniques are employed that will shorten recovery time yet provide appropriate post-operative pain control. All age groups, from infants to the elderly, are accommodated.

The UCLA Pain Medicine Center provides a multidisciplinary program dedicated to treatment of anatomically and physiologically based pain. The Pain Medicine Center prefers to work with referring physicians rather than treating self-referred patients. After initial consultation, the referring physician promptly receives a comprehensive report summarizing findings and therapies. Problems treated include cancer pain, back and neck pain, post-herpetic neuralgia, reflex sympathetic dystrophy, headaches, myofacial pain, pancreatic pain, and neuropathic pain.

The pediatric services provided at UCLA range from well-child care to the treatment of the most difficult and life-threatening illnesses. Among the many programs that bring infants and children to UCLA Medical Center are those in gastroenterology and nutritional disorders, kidney diseases, cardiology, diabetes, HIV infections, intensive newborn care, childhood cancer, neurological disorders, adolescent medicine, cystic fibrosis, and the special care areas of bone marrow, heart, liver, and kidney transplantation. Play and educational therapy as well as counseling for infants, children, and families are provided through Child Development. In addition, children may be referred for evaluation of school and learning problems. Services are available for longitudinal well-child care and health maintenance.

The General Pediatric Faculty are available, if requested, to case manage any referral by a physician in private practice that results in an inpatient stay. A designated faculty member will coordinate consultations and provide direct feedback and progress reports to the referring physician.

MEDICAL SPECIALTIES

Anesthesiology, Cardiology, Dentistry, Dermatology, Emergency Medicine, Endocrinology and Metabolism, Geriatrics, Hematology/Oncology, Immunology, Infectious Diseases, Internal Medicine, Medical Genetics, Neonatal Intensive Care, Nephrology, Neurology, Obstetrics/Gynecology, Ophthalmology, Organ Transplantation, Orthopedics, Pediatrics, Psychiatry, Pulmonary and Critical Care Medicine, Radiation Oncology, Radiology, Rehabilitation, Rheumatology, Sports Medicine, Surgery, and Urology.

WELL-KNOWN SPECIALISTS

- Dr. Donald P. Becker *Neurosurgery*
- Dr. Ronald W. Busuttel *Liver transplantation*
- Dr. Stephen A. Feig *Pediatric cancers*
- Dr. Alan M. Fogelman *Cardiology*
- Dr. E. Carmecle Holmes *Surgery*
- Dr. Susan Love *Breast cancer*
- Dr. Wesley S. Moore *Vascular surgery*
- Dr. Joseph K. Perloff *Cardiology*
- Dr. J. Thomas Rosenthal *Kidney transplantation*
- Dr. Dennis J. Slamon *Breast and ovarian cancers*
- Dr. Bradley R. Straatsma *Ophthalmology*
- Dr. Roberta Williams *Pediatric cardiology*

PATIENT SATISFACTION

Results of a survey in January, 1994, showed 100% of the patients responding to the survey were satisfied or very satisfied with physician services. Ninety-five percent were satisfied or very satisfied with nursing services. Eighty-nine percent rated their overall experiences at UCLA Medical Center as good or very good.

RESEARCH

The total annual research budget is approximately $178 million. Researchers at UCLA are credited with a number of significant new developments in the past few years. Among these are the following:

Dr. Ernest Noble, Thomas P. and Katherine K. Pike Professor of Alcohol Studies at the UCLA School of Medicine, first identified a gene associated with severe alcoholism in 1990. This marked the first time a genetic link to alcoholism was clearly established, although it had been suspected for years. Noble also linked the same gene, the A1 allele of the D2 dopamine receptor, to other addictive behavior, such as the use of cocaine and other drugs.

In 1991, researchers at the UCLA School of Medicine and UCLA Brain Research Institute found that the brains of people who receive an education and continue to challenge themselves intellectually exhibit certain anatomical changes from those who do not, and these people may experience better mental functioning throughout life as a result. The researchers found that the total length of dendrites, the stimulus-receiving structures of nerve cells, were longer in more educated people.

In a major step toward understanding opiate drug action, Drs. Chris Evans and Robert Edwards were the first to clone a cellular receptor that recognizes opiate drugs and allows them to take effect on the body in 1992. The finding is essential to the understanding of opiate drugs' role in pain perception and euphoria, as well as to elucidating the biological processes involved in opiate tolerance and dependence.

In 1992, Drs. Laura Allen and Roger Gorski, both of the UCLA School of Medicine Department of Anatomy and Cell Biology, identified an important anatomical difference between the brains of homosexual men, heterosexual men, and heterosexual women. A structure connecting the cortex of the left and right sides of the brain, called the anterior commissure, was found to be 18% larger in homosexual men than in heterosexual women, and 34% larger than in heterosexual men.

In 1992, researchers at the UCLA Jules Stein Eye Institute prevented retinal degeneration in a strain of mice using an artificial gene called a transgene. Retinitis pigmentosa is a group of hereditary, progressive diseases causing retinal degeneration and eventual blindness in humans.

In 1992, researchers at the UCLA School of Medicine showed for the first time that brain metabolism and function change as a result of behavior therapy just as they do with drug therapy for the treatment of obsessive-compulsive disorder. Obsessive-compulsive disorder is characterized by unwanted, uncontrollable thoughts that may cause a person to behave compulsively.

A team of UCLA surgeons and other transplant specialists performed the first combined small bowel/liver transplant in the western United States. Until January 1992, that type of transplant had only been performed successfully 14 times worldwide. The 20-year-old patient has since recovered and resumed a normal life.

A team of UCLA researchers headed by Dr. Gerald Berke performed the first successful laryngeal transplant in a canine model in 1992. The UCLA team's success in this goal is a significant step in the science of solid organ transplantation.

Dr. Daniel Kaufman and colleagues identified the cause and developed a preventive therapy for insulin-dependent diabetes mellitus in laboratory mice in 1993. Such interventions in humans may be as little as five years away.

UCLA neurologist Dr. Dale Bredesen has made significant strides toward the understanding of the pathology of neurodegenerative diseases such as Alzheimer's disease and Parkinson's disease. His 1993 studies of certain genes in the brain have shown how neurons are killed in these diseases, and how cell death can be prevented.

ADMISSIONS POLICY

Patients must have a medical need to require hospital admission. A physician must request and direct the patient's admission and must be a member of the medical staff of the hospital. Patients may be admitted by their own physician, a clinic doctor, or through the emergency department where a physician will be assigned to them.

Patients are expected to have appropriate medical insurance. However, some patients do provide the expected deposit by credit card, cash or check. Patients are assisted in many instances by financial counselors to obtain the benefits that they may be eligible for. They may also be referred to other health care facilities for medical care. The dollar value of uncompensated care provided exceeds $66 million per year.

A special phone number for admission information is available: (310) 825-8911.

UC SAN DIEGO

MEDICAL CENTER

UNIVERSITY OF CALIFORNIA

SAN DIEGO, CALIFORNIA

UCSD Medical Center, founded in 1966, is one of five academic health centers in the University of California system. It serves as the primary teaching and research facility for the UCSD School of Medicine. The Medical Center includes two hospital sites—UCSD Medical Center, Hillcrest, and UCSD Medical Center, La Jolla. The Hillcrest facility, located 13 miles from the UCSD campus, served as the clinical hospital for the educational and research facilities until 1993, when the John M. and Sally B. Thornton Hospital and Perlman Ambulatory Care Facility opened on the UCSD campus in La Jolla and assumed these functions.

Thornton Hospital is a medical/surgical facility designed to incorporate the newest technology into a comfortable, patient-centered environment. Specialty practices are based at the adjacent Perlman Ambulatory Care Center. The Shiley Eye Center is also a part of the UCSD Medical Center in La Jolla, providing patients with advanced eye care, and also housing research laboratories for the department of ophthalmology. Thornton Hospital is the location of UCSD's centers for cardiology, oncology, and orthopedics. The Medical Center complex in Hillside includes the Outpatient Center, an Ambulatory Care Center, and the Theodore Gildred Cancer Facility, as well as research and teaching facilities. In addition to the two hospitals, outpatient services are also

THE UCSD MEDICAL CENTER MAINTAINS A BROAD SPECTRUM OF PRIMARY, SECONDARY, AND TERTIARY SERVICES IN AN ENVIRONMENT WHERE THE LATEST ADVANCES IN HEALTH CARE AND TECHNOLOGY ARE MADE AVAILABLE TO THE PATIENT.

provided by UCSD physicians in medical offices in Miramesa.

UCSD has received a number of special designations because of its excellence. It is the only general acute care institution in San Diego and Imperial Counties. It has been designated a research center by the National Institute on Aging and is also one of 14 medical centers nationwide named as a Multipurpose Arthritis and Musculoskeletal Diseases Center. The National Institute of Mental Health has established the nation's first Research Center for Late Life Psychosis here. It is one of 16 Vanguard Centers for the Women's Health Initiative of the National Institutes of Health. Further, UCSD Medical Center was selected by UNICEF to participate in the global Baby Friendly Hospital Initiative to establish a standard of excellence for teaching and encouraging pregnant women and new mothers to breastfeed.

The UCSD Healthcare Network is a growing system of primary care practices throughout the community, with well-respected community hospitals and physician groups entering into partnerships with UCSD Medical Center to create a comprehensive, university-based network of healthcare services.

The UCSD School of Medicine has more than 500 physicians and scientists on its faculty, and the highly regarded teaching program accepts 120 new students each year and approximately 540 residents and fellows, who receive post-graduate training in the research laboratories and the patient care setting.

SPECIAL FACILITIES AND PROGRAMS

The UCSD Medical Center maintains a broad spectrum of primary, secondary, and tertiary services in an environment where the latest advances in health care and technology are made available to the patient.

The UCSD Center for Transplantation performs heart, lung, heart-lung, liver, kidney, and kidney-pancreas transplants as well as bone marrow stem cell transplantations. In 1993, the 1,000th transplant was completed in the country's oldest and most successful kidney transplant program. Also in 1993, UCSD surgeons performed San Diego's first living

AT A GLANCE

Beds: 562
Occupancy Rate: 55%
Average Patient Count: 308
Average Patient Stay: 5.3 days
Annual Admissions: 22,170
Births: 3,777
Outpatient Clinic Visits:
 388,456
Emergency Room/Trauma
 Center Visits: 46,000

HOSPITAL PERSONNEL
Physicians (Salaried): 550
Physicians (Attending): 1,200
Residents: 400
Registered Nurses: 1,162

ROOM CHARGES (PER DIEM)
Private: $745
Semiprivate: $695
ICU: $1,200–$2,900

ADDRESS
200 W. Arbor Drive
San Diego, CA 92103-9981

TELEPHONE
(619) 543-6222

related donor lung transplant, replacing the lungs of a 16-year-old cystic fibrosis patient with sections of each of his parent's lungs. In addition, skin, bone, joint, and cornea transplant capabilities support the burn, orthopedic, and ophthalmology programs.

The UCSD Cancer Center, a National Cancer Institute designated cancer center, serves San Diego and surrounding counties. It brings together experts on the genetics and the basic biology of cancer with clinicians who are developing new approaches to diagnosing and treating malignancies.

UCSD Medical Center was instrumental in developing San Diego County's trauma system. The hospital's emergency services designation includes the County's only Level I Trauma Center, Life Flight Aeromedical Services, the Regional Poison Information Center and the Regional Burn Center for San Diego and Imperial Counties.

UCSD's high risk pregnancy program and infant special care center are regional referral resources. UCSD also offers the Assisted Reproductive Technologies program to help women with fertility problems achieve pregnancy.

The Medical Center complex in Hillcrest includes the Center for Women's Health, an Outpatient Center, an Ambulatory Care Center, and the Theodore Gildred Cancer Facility, as well as research and teaching facilities surrounding the hospital. Opening near the complex in 1994 is the Bannister Family House, providing convenient and affordable lodging to families of patients from outside the area.

The Shiley Eye Center provides patients with advanced eye care and vision services, and also houses research laboratories of the faculty in the department of ophthalmology. Physicians at the center specialize in cornea transplants, glaucoma, pediatric ophthalmology, and general ophthalmology.

MEDICAL SPECIALTIES

Adolescent Medicine, AIDS, Allergy/Immunology, Alzheimer's Disease, Anesthesiology, Burn Medicine, Cardiology, Community and Family Medicine, Diabetes, Endocrinology, Epilepsy, Gastroenterology, Genetics, Geriatrics, Neonatalogy, Neurology, Neurosurgery, Nuclear Medicine, Obstetrics/Gynecology, Oncology, Ophthalmalogy, Orthopedics, Pathology, Pediatrics, Plastic and Reconstructive Surgery, Psychiatry, Pulmonary Rehabilitation, Radiology, Rehabilitation Medicine, Reproductive Medicine, Rheumatology, Surgery, Transplantation Surgery, and Trauma Medicine.

WELL-KNOWN SPECIALISTS

- Dr. William Ashburn   *Anesthesiology*
- Dr. Antonino Catanzaro   *Medicine*
- Dr. Anthony DeMaria   *Cardiology*
- Dr. Robert Goltz   *Dermatology*
- Dr. Mark Green   *Cancer*

- Dr. James Harrell *Pulmonary medicine*
- Dr. Stephen Howell   *Cancer*
- Dr. John Isenberg   *Gastroenterology*
- Dr. Dilip Jeste   *Psychiatry*
- Dr. Robert Katzman   *Neurosciences*
- Dr. Kenneth Moser   *Pulmonary medicine*
- Dr. William Nyhan   *Pediatrics*
- Dr. Robert Resnik   *Reproductive medicine*
- Dr. Douglas Richman   *Infectious disease*
- Dr. Robert Weinreb   *Ophthalmology*
- Dr. Michael Weisman   *Rheumatology*

PATIENT SATISFACTION

From December 1993 through March 1994, a patient satisfaction survey was conducted at Thornton Hospital, UCSD Medical Center's newest facility. Approximately 599 inpatient and outpatient discharges were contacted by phone, and 11% responded. Thornton Hospital's focus is on excellent quality care. Patients were asked to rate their satisfaction on a scale of 1 to 6. Patient satisfaction rates for the areas surveyed—physician care, care team, amenities, discharge and general questions—were 90% or more in all areas. There was a 93.2% positive response to the question, "Would you return to the hospital?" There was a 91.5% positive response to the question, "Would you recommend the hospital?" There was a 93% positive satisfaction rating on overall satisfaction.

UCSD's Hillcrest facility is currently developing its own surveys based on Thornton's. UCSD Medical Center is also designing and installing computerized systems to capture and analyze customer feedback at all sites.

RESEARCH

Research at UCSD encompasses more than 500 projects totalling more than $100 million. Research centers established by the NIH include the AIDS Treatment Evaluation Unit, the Alzheimer's Disease Research Center, the UCSD Cancer Center, and the Diabetes Control and Complications Trial. The NIH has also committed millions of dollars in funding to specialized research projects at UCSD. These include: the Alzheimer's Disease Cooperative Study Unit ($3.7 million), the Vanguard Clinical Center for Clinical Trial and Observation Study of Women's Health ($2.8 million), the Specialized Center of Research in Arteriosclerosis ($2.1 million), the HIV Neurobehavioral Research Center ($8.6 million), the AIDS Clinical Trials Group ($4 million), and the Child and Adolescent Trial for Cardiovascular Health ($1.3 million). Some examples of the work being done follow:

UCSD Medical Center researchers developed a new compound that dissolves gallstones, and first applications show great promise for patients who, because of other health problems, cannot undergo gallbladder surgery.

Researchers have received approval from the federal Recombinant DNA Advisory Board for Phase I human trials of gene therapy for HIV infection.

UCSD neurologist Leon Thal is coordinating a national consortium of medical centers to test promising drugs for Alzheimer's disease.

ADMISSIONS POLICY

Patient are admitted by UCSD Medical Center physicians through clinics and the emergency room as well as by private community physicians.

Patients are required to pay 50% of their estimated bill upon admission, but this payment is not a condition of admission for emergency cases.

UC SAN FRANCISCO

MEDICAL CENTER

The East Coast medical schools usually dominate the standard lists of the nation's best training grounds for new physicians. However, for almost two decades, the Medical Center at the University of California, San Francisco has been listed in the top five, due to its reputation for research, excellence in teaching and outstanding patient care. The school's continuing efforts for excellence were rewarded when the most recent survey of U.S. graduate schools as published by *U.S. News and World Report* ranked UCSF number one, tied with Johns Hopkins and Harvard. And, in training for specialty care, UCSF topped the list for AIDS, a sign of its commitment and work in the San Francisco community, which has one of the country's highest concentration of AIDS cases. UCSF researchers at the medical center and the affiliated San Francisco General Hospital—the foremost AIDS treatment center in the West—have been leaders in classifying the AIDS virus, evaluating treatment, and identifying risk factors. The school also placed in the top five for research, primary care, women's health, geriatric care, and drug and alcohol abuse care. The benefit for patients is the access to more than 2,200 physicians, all of whom are on the faculty of the School of Medicine; many are authors of authoritative textbooks in their various fields and editors of the most prestigious journals.

UNIVERSITY OF CALIFORNIA

**SAN FRANCISCO,
CALIFORNIA**

SOME 75 MEDICAL SPECIALTIES AND SUBSPECIALTIES ARE PRACTICED AT UCSF— SEVERAL OF THEM AT SUCH A HIGH LEVEL OF SOPHISTICATION AND COMPLEXITY THAT THE HOSPITAL HAS BECOME THE MAJOR REFERRAL CENTER FOR NORTHERN CALIFORNIA AND PARTS OF IDAHO AND NEVADA.

UCSF includes Mount Zion Medical Center, Moffitt and Long Hospitals, the UCSF Children's Medical Center, Langley Porter Psychiatric Institute, and the UCSF Ambulatory Care Service. The School of Medicine at UCSF is responsible for patient care, teaching and research at the justly famous San Francisco General Hospital, owned by the city, which handles 260,000 patients every year. More than 80,000 patients are served annually in the hospital's emergency room, one of the finest trauma services in the country.

Some 75 medical specialties and subspecialties are practiced at UCSF—several of them at such a high level of sophistication and complexity that the hospital has become the major referral center for northern California and parts of Idaho and Nevada. About one-third of all patients come here from outside the five-county Bay Area, many from across the country and some from overseas.

Over 4,200 kidney transplants have been performed at UCSF, more than at any other hospital in the world; presently over 200 are done here each year, many of them on children. The center also has a national reputation for liver transplant, for both children and adults, including the new procedure of using a partial liver from a living relative for transplant.

UCSF is also an international leader in the fields of pediatric cardiology; more than one-half of all newborns in this area requiring heart surgery are brought to UCSF. The Congenital Heart Surgery Program uses an innovative and aggressive approach to repair defects by performing multiple procedures during a single admission. Facilities include a special pediatric intensive care unit for cardiac cases. In fact, according to the hospital, of the 5,000 patients admitted each year to the 72-bed pediatric unit, less than 10% have what could be considered a common condition or ailment. Cancer, cystic fibrosis, hemophilia, neurological tumors, puberty disorders, growth disorders, and so-called craniofacial anomalies all have special treatment centers at UCSF.

In addition, for some 700 or more newborns each year who may be at risk or whose mothers may be, the Center is a leading referral institution in neonatology and high-risk pregnancy, and it offers both in-utero treatment and fetal surgery as well.

The quality of the staff, both physicians and nurses, is one of the major reasons UCSF is considered one of the best medical facilities in the country. Every national survey published in the past decade has listed many UCSF physicians as among "the best." In the most recent survey asking physicians to rate their peers, 187 UCSF doctors were ranked among the top in the nation.

In addition, the hospital employs 1,177 full-time nurses. These superbly trained nurses have helped assure the quality of patient care at the Center. In a nationwide survey undertaken by the American Academy of Nursing, UCSF was cited (with only 40 others) as a "magnet" hospital, one that attracts and retains professional nurses in a manner far above the average. The study found that these hospitals were superior places to work because they involved nurses in patient care in a meaningful way.

The physical facilities at UCSF are relatively new or have been modernized. The Joseph M. Long Hospital was completed in 1983, and more recently a surgical pavilion, a radiation oncology pavilion, an ambulatory care center, an emergency service pavilion, and an emergency service pavilion were opened.

SPECIAL FACILITIES AND PROGRAMS

For the treatment of cancer, UCSF is a regional referral center for leukemia, gynecological cancers, brain tumors, and the latest therapies such as bone marrow transplantation, including procedures where the donor and the recipient are not related. In 1997, UCSF will become a Comprehensive Cancer Center, designated by the National Cancer Institute, making it the first such center in northern California.

In cardiology, UCSF's physicians and surgeons have access to the most up-to-date clinical research through the Cardiovascular Research Institute. Every form of treatment is available, including those which make use of the most advanced techniques in surgery, electrophysiology, and cardiac catheterization, as well as the latest drug therapies.

UCSF pioneered the latest diagnostic equipment—including magnetic resonance imaging—and developed the most advanced cochlear implant for aiding the deaf, a bladder pacemaker, the use of lasers for surgery, and lithotripters for dissolving kidney stones. While every medical center in this book provides access to this kind of technology, only a few have a medical staff with such an outstanding reputation as UCSF.

The Department of Neurological Surgery runs well-known programs for the treatment of brain tumors, pituitary tumors, and cerebral and spinal malformations, for both children and adults.

A selected listing of clinics and centers include: Allergy, Adult Immunodeficiencies, Alzheimer's Center, Arthritis Clinic, Breast Screening Clinic, Children's Renal Center, Diabetes Center, Ear, Nose and Throat Clinic, Comprehensive Epilepsy Center, Eye Clinic, Gastrointestinal Clinic, Infectious Disease and Tropical Medicine Clinic, General Internal Medicine,

AT A GLANCE

Beds: 797
Occupancy Rate: 66%
Average Patient Count: 520
Average Patient Stay: 7 days
Annual Admissions: 26,936
Births: 1,637
Outpatient Clinic Visits: 338,267
Emergency Room/Trauma Center Visits: 52,991

HOSPITAL PERSONNEL
Physicians: 1,200
Residents: 890
Registered Nurses: 1,357

ROOM CHARGES (PER DIEM)
Private: $1,025
Semiprivate: $1,015
ICU: $1,985–$5,440

ADDRESS
505 Parnassus Avenue
San Francisco, CA 94143

TELEPHONE
(415) 476-1000

Hematology-Oncology Clinic, Gynecology Clinic, Lipid Clinic, Male Infertility Clinic, Multiple Sclerosis, Obstetrics Clinic, General Pediatrics, Pediatric Specialties Clinic, Plastic and Reconstructive Surgery Clinic, Psychiatric Clinic (Adults), Renal Clinic, Screening and Acute Care Clinic, Thyroid Clinic.

MEDICAL SPECIALTIES

Ambulatory Care, Anesthesiology, Cardiology, Chronic Illness, Dermatology, Dentistry, Emergency Medicine, Endocrinology, Gastroenterology, Genetics, Hematology, Infectious Diseases, Internal Medicine, Kidney, Heart, Lung, Liver, Pancreas, and Bone Marrow Transplantation, Neonatal and Perinatal Medicine, Nephrology, Neurology and Neurological Surgery, Nuclear Medicine, Obstetrics/Gynecology, Oncology, Ophthalmology, Orthopaedics, Orthopedic Surgery, Otolaryngology, Pathology, Pediatrics, Plastic Surgery, Psychiatry, Pulmonary Medicine, Radiation Oncology, Radiology, Replantation Surgery, Rheumatology, Surgery, Tropical Medicine, Urology, and Vascular Surgery.

WELL-KNOWN SPECIALISTS

- Dr. Nancy Ascher   *Transplant surgeon*
- Dr. Kanu Chatterjee   *Cardiology*
- Dr. Morton Cowan   *Director of the Pediatric Bone Marrow Transplant Unit*
- Dr. Haile Debas   *Surgery*
- Dr. Donald Goodkin   *Multiple sclerosis*
- Dr. Melvin Grumbach   *Pediatric endocrinologist*
- Dr. Michael Harrison   *Codirector of the Fetal Treatment Program*
- Dr. I. Craig Henderson   *Breast cancer specialist*
- Dr. Creig Hoyt   *Pediatric ophthalmologist*
- Dr. Robert Jaffe   *Chief of obstetrics/gynecology and reproductive sciences*
- Dr. Steven Kramer   *Chairman of ophthalmology; director of the Beckman Vision Center*
- Dr. Roderic Phibbs   *Chief of neonatology*
- Dr. Abraham Rudolph   *Pediatric cardiology*
- Dr. Emil Tanagho   *Chairman of urology*
- Dr. Charles Wilson   *Chairman of neurosurgery*

PATIENT SATISFACTION

In a survey sent to all discharged patients, more than 90% of the respondents reported that they were satisfied with their treatment.

RESEARCH

The UCSF School of Medicine research budget exceeds $250 million annually, and in eight of the past 21 years, the school has been awarded more funds from the National Institutes of Health than any other medical school in the country.

In 1993 UCSF research projects received $188 million from NIH, second only to Johns Hopkins.

UCSF is one of the world's major centers for the study of biomedical research. Several discoveries have had widespread effects.

UCSF microbiologists won the Nobel Prize in 1989 for their discovery of "cancer genes" known as oncogenes. UCSF researchers also developed an artificial surfactant, which is used worldwide to help premature infants with underdeveloped lungs breathe. It saves thousands of lives yearly. The groundbreaking work to provide a basis for a successful vaccine against hepatitis B was also conducted at UCSF. Molecular geneticists have developed safe and accurate methods for the prenatal identification of sickle cell anemia. Other basic research programs exist in neurobiology, developmental and cell biology, immunology, parasitic disease, human development and aging, behavioral sciences, reproductive sciences, and psychiatry.

In the past two decades several major breakthroughs have involved UCSF staff, both in the basic research and in the transfer of that knowledge to patient care. In recent years, for example, the new multichannel cochlear implant, which gives hearing-impaired individuals the ability to hear, was developed by UCSF physicians and scientists. Inhibition of the immune reaction which causes transplanted kidneys to be rejected by the body was started in a process developed at UCSF. The millisecond Cine CT scanner, which makes it possible to scan the beating heart, and one of the most advanced versions of magnetic resonance imaging were also developed at UCSF.

Currently, an experimental bladder pacemaker, which gives "normal" function to paraplegics and quadriplegics was invented by UCSF staff. So too was a method of treating ocular cancer without removing the eye, new surgical techniques for formerly inoperative retinal detachments, and a dozen different ways of using lasers, microsurgery, and ultrasound.

UCSF clinicians and investigators have made an enormous, multi-disciplinary contribution to the fight against AIDS, both locally and nationally. There are now about 150 investigators conducting research through the UCSF AIDS Clinical Research Center. Their research encompasses the epidemiology of how AIDS is spread, development of a model for care that is both humane and cost effective, preventive public health education, and basic studies of AIDS, the immune system, and the HIV virus.

Many clinical research grants from NIH are given to physician-researchers at UCSF, including major grants to plastic surgery, pulmonary medicine, malignant brain tumor treatment, cardiovascular responses to stress, arteriosclerosis, and sickle cell disease research. The hospital is also the site of two NIH-funded Clinical Research Centers, one for adults and one for children.

Among the many special research facilities at UCSF are the Rosalind Russell Research Center for Arthritis, the Cardiovascular Research Institute, the Cystic Fibrosis Research Center, the Koret Vision Center, the Brain Tumor Research

Center, the Cancer Research Institute, the Center for Neuroscience Research on Analysis of Long-Term Changes in the Mammalian Brain, the Gene Therapy Core Center, and the Keck Center for Integrative Neurosciences.

ADMISSIONS POLICY

Most patients here are referred by their physicians, usually for advanced diagnostic or surgical procedures. Most outpatient specialty practices do not require a physician referral. Patients seeking a UCSF physician can call the referral line, (415) 885-7777. Patients without insurance must place a 50% deposit at time of admission.

CRAIG HOSPITAL

A serious spinal cord or brain injury often requires the most extensive rehabilitation program of any disabling condition. A spinal cord injury can affect the whole body, and a brain injury can alter a person's reasoning and emotional responses.

ENGLEWOOD, COLORADO

Located in a Denver suburb, Craig Hospital is world renowned for its care and rehabilitation of patients with spinal cord and brain injuries. Since 1956, the Hospital has used its specialized approach to help educate, adapt and rehabilitate patients so they can resume normal lives as soon as possible. More than 9,600 patients have been treated at Craig for initial and ongoing rehabilitation. Last year alone, patients from 37 states and three foreign countries came to Craig; 1,322 had spinal cord injuries and 275 had traumatic brain injuries.

Patients usually stay from two to four months in Craig's 80-bed facility, often continuing treatment on an out-patient basis from the hospital's wheelchair accessible apartments. Craig reports that 92% of its spinal cord injury patients and 63% of its brain injury patients return home, rather than to long-term care facilities.

SPECIAL FACILITIES AND PROGRAMS

The goals of Craig's spinal injury program include understanding altered body physiology, mobility

LOCATED IN A DENVER SUBURB, CRAIG HOSPITAL IS WORLD RENOWNED FOR ITS CARE AND REHABILITATION OF PATIENTS WITH SPINAL CORD AND BRAIN INJURIES.

skills, adaptive living, vocational assessment, and family and psychological issues.

The brain injury program focuses on reaching functioning goals and re-learning cognitive skills, including memory. Since the majority of patients are young men, peer support is an important component of the rehabilitation process.

Each patient works with a team consisting of nurses, physical therapists, a family service counselor, a therapeutic recreation specialist, and when necessary, a respiratory therapist, a speech and language therapist, as well as a psychologist or neuropsychologist. The team is directed by the patient's Craig physician.

Craig's therapy programs include counseling, teaching daily living skills and personal care, patient and family education, personalized equipment coordination, neuropsychology, rehabilitation nursing, occupational therapy, physical therapy, psychological counseling, respiratory therapy, rehabilitation engineering, school tutoring, speech and language therapy, therapeutic recreation, and vocational counseling.

Other specialized programs include the Reconstructive Hand Surgery program, which helps patients increase hand functions. The Spinal Cord Injury Neurosurgical Clinics treat problems like spasticity, chronic spinal pain, and late deterioration of neurological function.

A Fertility Clinic helps spinal cord patients assess their potential for having children. A Neuroscience Laboratory uses the latest equipment and technology for functional electrical stimulation, biofeedback, evoked potentials, and brain mapping. The Ventilator Dependent program helps wean patients, if possible, from the ventilator and trains family members in home care techniques. Outpatients Services coordinates the care of patients who return to Craig for re-evaluation and follow-up services, including problems associated with aging.

WELL-KNOWN SPECIALISTS

- Dr. Mark P. Cilo *Traumatic brain injury*
- Dr. Robert Edgar *Neurosurgical management of spinal cord pain, myelopathy, and spasticity*
- Dr. Scott Falci *Neurosurgical management of spinal cord pain, myelopathy, and spasticity*
- Dr. Daniel P. Lammertse *Spinal cord injuries, especially aging problems and high quadriplegia*
- Dr. Robert R. Menter *Spinal cord injuries, especially aging problems and high quadriplegia*
- Dr. Peter Peterson *Pulmonary management of traumatic spinal cord injury*
- Dr. Alan H. Weintraub *Rehabilitation of traumatic brain injury*

PATIENT SATISFACTION

Craig conducts a quarterly Patient Satisfaction Survey of all discharged in-patients and out-patients. All patients who indicate dissatisfaction with any aspect of the services are contacted for follow-up and clarification of issues. As part of the hospital's quality improvement process, the results of the survey are regularly shared with management and staff.

In the most recent survey, over 95% of the patients surveyed rated their overall experience "good to excellent."

RESEARCH

Craig receives more than $1.5 million annually in funding, primarily from the Department of Education's National Institute on Disability and Rehabilitation Research and from the Centers for Disease Control.

A federally designated Model Spinal Injury System for more than two decades, Craig was also recently designated a Rehabilitation Research and Training Center in Aging with a Spinal Cord Injury.

All research focuses on both the early and rehabilitative care and post-hospital outcomes of patients with spinal cord and brain injuries.

An instrument used to measure the extent of handicap following injury has been developed at Craig and is used throughout the field. The research staff has written two widely used texts, one on the treatment of high quadriplegia, and the other on aging with a spinal cord injury.

ADMISSIONS POLICY

Craig prefers to receive patients as soon as possible after injury, often within a few days. However, most patients arrive two to four weeks after their injury. For patients outside the Denver area, Craig's air transport team, with a specially equipped air-ambulance Lear jet, can arrange a flight.

The patient's attending physician is required to contact Craig prior to admission. A Craig primary care physician will discuss the specific medical conditions with the patient's attending physician to determine if the patient can benefit from the services and treatment program at Craig. Craig accepts many insurance plans. Patients who do not have health insurance are frequently eligible for state Medicaid

AT A GLANCE

Beds: 70
Occupancy Rate: 84.1 %
Average Patient Count: 58.9
Average Patient Stay: 20–72
    days
Annual Admissions: 573
Outpatients: 1,396

HOSPITAL PERSONNEL
Physicians: 207
Residents: 1
Registered Nurses: 48.9
    (FTE)

ROOM CHARGES (PER DIEM)
Private: $556.50
Semiprivate: $556.50

ADDRESS
3425 South Clarkson
Englewood, CO 80110

TELEPHONE
(303) 789-8000

benefits because of the seriousness of their injuries. Craig provides free care assistance to offset medical costs not covered by insurance, based on financial eligibility.

PATIENT/FAMILY ACCOMMODATIONS

Craig strongly encourages families to be involved in a patient's rehabilitation and provides free housing for up to 30 days (usually the first two weeks of admission and the last two weeks before discharge) to encourage involvement. During their stay at Craig, families learn specialized care and training the patient will require at home. Families wishing to stay longer than 30 days may rent housing for $25 per night. The family housing consists of one- and two-bedroom furnished apartments, many wheelchair accessible.

Craig is located on the campus of Swedish Medical Center, a 325-bed acute care facility, with which it shares some services.

UNIVERSITY HOSPITAL

UNIVERSITY OF COLORADO
HEALTH SCIENCES CENTER

DENVER, COLORADO

Although the city of Denver ranks only 26th in the nation in terms of population, its half-million inhabitants have ready access to some of the best medical services available anywhere. "Ninety-nine percent of problems people have, can be treated in Denver," claims Dr. Alden Harken, chairman of the department of surgery at University Hospital. "I've worked in Washington, Philadelphia, and Boston and I don't think any of those centers offer the breadth of specialized medical treatment available here. There tend to be areas in the country where everyone seems to be asking new questions and doing new things at once. I think Denver is one of those places right now."

There are seventeen acute care hospitals in the Denver area—most of them very highly regarded. Several have nationally known programs in specialized fields; for example, Craig Hospital for spinal cord injuries, and the National Jewish Center for Immunology and Respiratory Medicine. Denver's major tertiary and quaternary care hospital, however, is clearly University Hospital located at the University of Colorado. As one doctor from Denver told us, "When you talk about a major referral center for the region, every hospital is a junior partner compared to University Hospital." Of the 122 doctors listed in *The Best Doctors in America* for the state of Colorado, 112 are associated with the University of Colorado Health Sciences Center—55 specifically with University Hospital.

AS ONE DOCTOR FROM DENVER TOLD US, "WHEN YOU TALK ABOUT A MAJOR REFERRAL CENTER FOR THE REGION, EVERY HOSPITAL IS A JUNIOR PARTNER COMPARED TO UNIVERSITY HOSPITAL."

About 92% of all patients come from metropolitan Denver, which includes seven counties and encompasses a large geographic area, and much of the state's entire population. So 8% are actually coming from quite a distance to avail themselves of University Hospital's broad range of medical services. The Adult Burn Center, for example, serves a five-state region and attracts patients with its specially designed ICU; the hospital is also a designated Level I Trauma Center. It is also a regional referral center for a neonatal problems as more than half of the 2,600 births that take place here each year are considered the result of high-risk pregnancies. In addition, over 300 low-weight or extremely ill babies are cared for annually in the neonatal intensive care unit. Out-of-state patients received $245 million worth of services in 1991. Sizable numbers came for highly specialized treatment. Forty percent of all bone marrow transplants in 1992 were performed on out-of-state patients; 24% of all liver transplants; 17% of all craniotomies; and 11% of all angioplasties and related procedures.

SPECIAL FACILITIES AND PROGRAMS

University Hospital performs organ transplantation services for the region; heart transplantation was begun in the mid-1980s, but kidneys have been transplanted at University Hospital for over 15 years, and today more than 60 a year are transplanted. This should not be surprising since kidney disease in both adults and children is one of the hospital's more active areas. Over 1,600 kidney transplant patients have been treated at University Hospital.

Liver, pancreas, limb, and bone marrow transplants are also performed. In March of 1994, University Hospital completed the Rocky Mountain region's first double-lung transplant into a Cystic Fibrosis patient. The hospital boasts markedly higher survival rates on its transplants than the national average—99% survival on kidney transplants versus 93% nationally; 92% on liver transplants versus 74%; and 95% on heart transplants versus 82%.

In 1988, the University of Colorado Cancer Center (UCCC) received National Cancer Institute designation and began service to the six million people of the Rocky Mountain region. UCCC members conduct basic research, patient care, education, and prevention and control. The Cancer Center treats brain, gastrointestinal tract, gynecologic, head and neck, heart, liver, lung, and prostate cancers.

The Temple Hoyne Buell Heart Center was established in 1991 to provide a complete array of heart services. Hundreds of patients who have had a portion of their heart muscle damaged are treated in the Heart Failure Treatment Program with drug therapy designed to stave off the need for a heart transplant. The Heart Transplant Program operates in a dedicated, state-of-the-art unit for solid organ transplant patients that opened in 1991. The Cardiac Care Inpatient Unit provides up-to-date forms of therapy for patients with heart failure and abnormal heart rhythms. The Unit for Cardiovascular Interventions is a new program designed to provide comprehensive, advanced care for patients with cardiovascular disease. The Cardiac Catherization Laboratory permits definitive evaluation of heart muscle mechanics, cardiac and pulmonary physiology, and coronary and valvular anatomy. University Hospital was the first in the region to develop a complete non-invasive peripheral vascular diagnostic laboratory and also offers individualized education, counseling, and medically supervised exercise for people with cardiac disease.

The C. Henry Kempe National Center for the Prevention and Treatment of Child Abuse provides a wide array of educational, research, and clinical programs. Services range from a therapeutic preschool for sexually abused children (ages three to six) to Hope for the Children, an evaluation and treatment program for families in which physical abuse, sexual abuse, and other problems have been documented or evaluated for courts. The center's Child Protection Team was started in 1958; now there are more than 900 such teams in the country. The team includes a pediatrician, a child health associate, a social worker, and a coordinator. It evaluates and provides intervention for 400+ suspected victims of child abuse per year.

The Colorado Psychiatric Hospital treats patients who are mentally ill or have sleep disorders or neurophysiological dysfunctions. Programs include addiction research and treatment, an anxiety and phobic disorders clinic, and psychiatric emergency services. A mother and child clinic for schizophrenic mothers and their preschool children is the only such facility in the region. The Denver Institute of Psychoanalysis maintains an analytic clinic providing low-cost psychoanalysis for Colorado residents.

Other special clinics treat almost every kind of ailment, including allergies, arthritis, cleft palate, cystic fibrosis, diabetes, epilepsy, infertility, liver disease, chronic lung disease, lung tumors, osteoporosis, pain, sickle-cell anemia, spina bifida, and venereal disease. All the specialty departments have clinics as well. In addition, University Hospital has developed a number of specialized programs and is affiliated with the Webb-Waring Lung Institute, the Barbara Davis Institute for the Treatment and Research of

AT A GLANCE

Beds: 393
Occupancy Rate: 72%
Average Patient Count: 283
Average Patient Stay: 5.7 days
Births: 2,560
Annual Admissions: 14,000
Outpatient Clinic Visits:
    184,000
Emergency Room/Trauma
    Center Visits: 50,700

HOSPITAL PERSONNEL
Physicians: 514
    Board Certified: 409
Residents: 750
Registered Nurses: 800
    BS Degree: 50%+

ROOM CHARGES (PER DIEM)
Private: $456
Semiprivate: $412
ICU: $1,283

ADDRESS
4200 East Ninth Avenue
Denver, Colorado 80262

TELEPHONE
(303) 399-1211

Childhood Diabetes, the Eleanor Roosevelt Institute for Cancer Research, and the John F. Kennedy Child Development Center, which offers help for dyslexic, emotionally disturbed, and physically handicapped children.

MEDICAL SPECIALTIES

AIDS, Allergy/Clinical Immunology, Ambulatory Services and Surgery, Anesthesiology, Bloodless Surgery and Medicine, Bone Marrow Transplantation, Burn Medicine, Cancer Care, Cardiology/Cardiac Surgery, Cardiac Transplantation, Clinical Pharmacology, Cryosurgery, Dermatology, Diabetes, Electrophysiology, Emergency Medicine, Endocrinology, Epilepsy, Family Medicine, Fetal Cell Transplantation, Gastroenterology, General Surgery, Geriatric Medicine, Hand Surgery, Hematology, High-risk Obstetrics, Infectious Diseases, Infertility, Internal Medicine, Neonatalogy, Neurology, Neurosurgery, Obstetrics/Gynecology, Occupational Medicine, Ophthalmology, Orthopedics, Otolaryngology, Pain Management, Pathology, Perinatal Medicine, Plastic and Reconstructive Surgery, Psychiatry, Pulmonology, Radiology, Rehabilitation Medicine, Rheumatology, Sports Medicine, Transplant Surgery, Trauma Medicine, Urology and Vascular Surgery.

WELL-KNOWN SPECIALISTS

- Dr. Michael Bristow   *Cardiology, specialist in heart failure, molecular cardiology*
- Dr. Paul A. Bunn Jr.   *Medical oncologist, specialist in lung cancer*
- Dr. Peter Chase   *Expert in pediatric diabetes*
- Dr. David Clarke   *Pediatric cardiothoracic surgery*
- Dr. E. David Crawford   *Prostate cancer surgeon*
- Dr. Alden N. Harken   *Cardiac surgeon, specialist in arrhythmia surgery*
- Dr. Mark Bernard Hazuka   *Radiation oncology, lung cancer specialist*
- Dr. Bruce Jafek   *Otolaryngologist, expert in head and neck surgery*
- Dr. Igal Kam   *Liver and kidney transplant surgeon*
- Dr. Marilyn J. Manco-Johnson   *Medical oncology, hematology*
- Dr. William A. Robinson   *Oncologist, specialist in malignant melanoma*
- Dr. Robert Rutherford   *Vascular surgeon; author of standard textbooks in general vascular surgery*
- Dr. Robert Schrier   *Chairman, department of medicine, well-known expert in kidney disease*
- Dr. Ronald J. Sokol   *Gastroenterology*

PATIENT SATISFACTION

Results of outpatient surveys for 1993-94 show that 90% of those responding would recommend University Hospital to family and friends. The latest available inpatient results are for 1991-1992. These show 93% of patients surveyed were satisfied with their University Hospital experience. Ninety percent said they would recommend the hospital to family and friends.

RESEARCH

Each year the faculty and staff of the CU School of Medicine and University Hospital receive approximately $120 million in research grants. The NIH funds a Clinical Research Center at the Hospital. Among the major areas of investigation are genetics, AIDS, Alzheimer's disease, genetic cardiology, cancer, vascular disease, Parkinson's disease, various neonatal problems, adults with diabetes, hypertension, lupus, chronic obstructive pulmonary disease, and scleroderma.

Other areas of investigation are funded by the American Heart Association, the American Cancer Society, the Leukemia Society, several major pharmaceutical companies, the NIH, and other well-known foundations. Aging, immunology, kidney disease, lupus, metabolism, and oncology are just a few of the subjects under study. A Hepatobiliary Research Center, funded by the NIH, studies and treats diseases of the liver and biliary tract.

The CU School of Medicine has moved ahead dramatically this year in the national rankings on research productivity. National Institutes of Health (NIH) grants alone brought CU from 13th to eighth among all U.S. public medical schools, and from 28th place to 21st among all U.S. medical schools. CU moved ahead of other notable research institutions such as Iowa, New York University, Wisconsin, and Texas (Dallas).

A fetal neural transplant program developed by physicians at University Hospital and the CU Health Sciences Center (HSC) is the first program in the country to receive a federal grant to study human fetal brain tissue transplants as a treatment for Parkinson's disease. Curt Freed, M.D., and his neurological colleague Robert Breeze, M.D., received a four-year, $4.5 million grant from the National Institutes of Health (NIH) in conjunction with Columbia-Presbyterian Medical Center in New York and North Shore University Hospital at Cornell University Medical College, Long Island.

HSC physicians performed the first fetal neural transplant in the United States in 1988. At that time, a Reagan administration moratorium was in place that prohibited the use of federal funds for fetal tissue research. This grant is the first NIH-funded grant for human fetal tissue research since the lifting of the ban.

ADMISSIONS POLICY

A patient can be admitted to the hospital without a physician's referral. Admission to the hospital through a clinic or emergency room is also possible.

Clinic admissions can be made by calling the referral center at (303) 329-3066. A referral coordinator will direct the caller to the appropriate clinic and possibly set up an appointment.

All patients are expected to provide evidence of insurance or personal resources upon admittance to University Hospital. Emergency patients are accepted. Colorado citizens can be admitted if medically indigent, but elective procedures are permitted only when medically indigent funds are adequate. Over $16 million worth of indigent care is provided annually.

YALE-NEW HAVEN

HOSPITAL

NEW HAVEN, CONNECTICUT

Founded in 1826 as a 15-bed charitable institution, Yale-New Haven was Connecticut's first hospital, serving the local community. While the 900-bed facility still draws the majority of its patients from Connecticut, it has become one of the nation's premier medical centers because of the research and treatments carried out in 90 specialty clinics.

Yale has been recognized nationally for clinical excellence in almost every specialty area. *U.S. News & World Report* identified Yale as one of the best hospitals for endocrinology, gastroenterology, geriatrics, gynecology, psychiatry, and rheumatology. Among its best-known programs are craniofacial reconstruction, organ transplantation, and epilepsy surgery. With a sophisticated range of diagnostic and therapeutic techniques, the hospital also provides psychiatric treatment for both children and adults.

Facilities include specialized centers for cancer, geriatric assessment, liver study, sports medicine, gastrointestinal procedures, pain management, primary care and women's health.

WHILE THE 900-BED FACILITY STILL DRAWS THE MAJORITY OF ITS PATIENTS FROM CONNECTICUT, IT HAS BECOME ONE OF THE NATION'S PREMIER MEDICAL CENTERS BECAUSE OF THE RESEARCH AND TREATMENTS CARRIED OUT IN 90 SPECIALTY CLINICS.

SPECIAL FACILITIES AND PROGRAMS

Yale-New Haven is Connecticut's largest children's hospital and historically the state's largest maternity hospital. In 1993, a new 11-story Children's Hospital opened, bringing about a unique collaboration between obstetric and pediatric specialists. Known as the West Pavilion, the Children's Hospital features an all-new inpatient gynecology unit to serve the gynecology/oncology needs of women of all ages. It is also the only hospital in the area with neonatal and pediatric intensive care units.

YNHH is also one of 28 NCI-designated Comprehensive Cancer Centers, offering the newest therapies, such as stem cell transplantation. Similar to bone marrow transplants, which permit extremely high doses of radiation and chemotherapy, stem cell procedures are far easier for patients to tolerate and less risky, with shorter hospitalizations.

Yale-New Haven's Dorothy Adler Geriatric Center is an outpatient consultative service that provides a comprehensive assessment of older persons who have medical, psychological, cognitive or social problems. The center evaluates between 30 and 50 new patients and their families each month.

The comprehensive transplant center offers heart, heart lung, single lung, bi-lateral lung, liver, pancreas, kidney, allogenic bone marrow, and autologous bone marrow transplants. Transplant patients are housed in dedicated areas with specially trained staff. All heart and heart-lung transplant recipients are cared for in a special 18-bed Cardiothoracic Intensive Care unit.

Two special units offer a unique, multi-specialist approach to treating epilepsy and facial deformities. The Epilepsy Surgery Program incorporates a multidisciplinary team in the care of epilepsy patients, including neurologists, neurosurgeons, neuropsychologists, clinical coordinators, and technicians. The team's work consists of identifying the area in which seizures originate, localizing the area, and then safely removing it. In treating facial conditions and deformities, the craniofacial surgery program also uses a multidisciplinary team of experts which can include plastic, neuro and oral surgeons, otolaryngologists, opthamologists, speech therapists, orthodontists, and geneticists.

YNHH is the only hospital in the state to offer a number of highly specialized treatments. Stereotactic radiosurgery is a non-invasive procedure for the

AT A GLANCE

Beds: 900
Occupancy Rate: 78%
Average Patient Count: 646
Average Patient Stay: 6.7 days
Annual Admissions: 35,579
Births: 5,016
Outpatient Clinic Visits:
    243,219
Emergency Room/Trauma
    Center Visits: 69,081

HOSPITAL PERSONNEL
Physicians: 1,914
    Board Certified: 1,235
Residents: 432
Registered Nurses: 1,155

ROOM CHARGES (PER DIEM)
Private: $877
Semiprivate: $877
ICU: $2,179

ADDRESS
20 York Street
New Haven, CT 06504

TELEPHONE
(203) 785-4242

treatment of brain tumors, which directs a highly precise dose of radiation at the tumor with minimal damage to the surrounding tissue.

Photopheresis uses an ultraviolet light in the treatment of cutaneous T cell lymphoma, scleroderma, and rheumatoid arthritis. Future applications of this therapy include treatment for lupus, multiple sclerosis, organ transplant rejection, and AIDS.

Extracorporeal Membrane Oxygenation (ECMO) is a technology used to treat neonatal patients suffering from pulmonary insufficiency, usually due to prematurity and low birth weight. The Yale ECMO machine is the only one in the state.

The hospital also uses a device called a Left Ventricular Assist Device (LVAD), which is used in end-stage heart disease cases to sustain life through an acute crisis or until definitive therapy can be started.

Other unique programs at YNHH include the state's only inpatient Dermatology Unit, the Liver Study Center and pain implants available at the Pain Management unit.

A private, non-profit institution, YNHH operates a Level I trauma center, offering the highest level of emergency care. In addition, the hospital maintains programs in the following areas: newborn special care, neurosurgical intensive care, high risk pregnancies, burn treatment, interventional radiology, inpatient dermatology, dental services for impaired children, and child psychiatry.

MEDICAL SPECIALTIES

Dermatology, Diagnostic Imaging, Internal Medicine, Laboratory Medicine, Neurology, Obstetrics and Gynocology, Ophthalmology, Orthopedics and Rehabilitation, Pediatrics, Surgery, and Therapeutic Radiology.

WELL-KNOWN SPECIALISTS

- Dr. John C. Baldwin   *Cardiothoracic surgery; specialist in adult heart and lung transplantation*
- Dr. Lawrence S. Cohen   *General cardiovascular disease*
- Dr. Donald J. Cohen   *Child and adolescent psychiatry*
- Dr. Richard L. Edelson   *Dermatology; specialist in cutaneous lymphomas and immunologic diseases of the skin*
- Dr. James Fisher   *Radiation oncology*
- Dr. Mark Robert Fouloukian   *Psychiatric surgery*
- Dr. Gerald H. Friedland   *Infectious diseases; specialist in AIDS*
- Dr. Richard A. Matthay   *Pulmonary and critical care medicine; specialist in asthma, chronic obstructive pulmonary disease, and lung cancer*
- Dr. John A. Persirig   *Craniofacial plastic surgery*
- Dr. Clarence H. Sasaku   *Otolaryngology; specialist in laryngology*

PATIENT SATISFACTION

In a survey of about 10,000 discharged patients, about 90% responded that they would describe YNHH as a "good" or "model" hospital and 96% would recommend it to a friend or relative in need of hospitalization.

RESEARCH

Nationally recognized for its outstanding research programs, Yale University School of Medicine received more than $203 million in grants in 1993. In NIH funding, the school ranks third in the nation. The medical school has been singled out for its work in drug and alcohol dependency, geriatric care, pediatrics and women's health. While laboratory and clinical studies are conducted by virtually every department, the highest funded research is in internal medicine, psychiatry, pediatrics, surgery, dermatology, genetics, and the Child Study Center.

The school is in the forefront of research into Lyme disease, a condition caused by infected ticks. Work is being conducted in both treatment of the disease and the development of a vaccine.

Yale was among the first to perform clinical trials using fetal tissue transplants for the treatment of Parkinson's disease.

The school is also noted for the research and treatment of male and female infertility.

ADMISSIONS POLICY

Any patient requiring hospitalization will be admitted. The patient's attending physician must have admitting privileges. All patients are accepted regardless of ability to pay. Free and uncompensated care totaled more than $21 million in 1993.

GEORGETOWN

UNIVERSITY

MEDICAL CENTER

**WASHINGTON,
DISTRICT OF COLUMBIA**

No compendium of great medical centers in the United States would be complete without Georgetown University Medical Center. Georgetown has united research and patient care in a particularly effective manner, combining both laboratory and clinical discoveries with patient care directly at the bedside. There is hardly a major medical specialty here that has not been singled out for national recognition.

The Georgetown University Medical Center complex includes the Georgetown University Hospital, the Pasquerilla Healthcare Center, the Vincent T. Lombardi Cancer Research Center, the Schools of Medicine and Nursing, and the FIDIA-Georgetown Institute for the Neurosciences. Georgetown University Hospital is a level I trauma center. It also serves as the primary training site for the Georgetown University Medical School, hosting post-graduate education in 21 specialty areas. Each year, more than 300 physicians receive residency training through Georgetown programs. The hospital offers a full range of acute inpatient services, including a significant number of tertiary care programs. The clinical facility of the School of Medicine provides outpatient services. The Pasquerilla Healthcare Center, completed in 1987, is the latest addition to the Medical Center complex. It houses the Departments of Medicine, Obstetrics and Gynecology, Ophthalmology, Orthopedic Surgery, Pediatrics, and Surgery. The Lombardi Cancer

NO COMPENDIUM
OF GREAT MEDICAL
CENTERS IN THE UNITED
STATES WOULD BE COMPLETE
WITHOUT GEORGETOWN
UNIVERSITY MEDICAL CENTER.

Research Center, dedicated to the great football coach, contains outpatient care facilities, research laboratories and administrative offices. The School of Medicine, founded in 1851, graduates over 50 new doctors annually. The FIDIA-Georgetown Institute conducts research in the neurosciences.

Research is a major activity at Georgetown. During the 1980s, research funding increased threefold. This included multi-million dollar funding for interdisciplinary investigations in neuropharmacology, cardiovascular physiology, and radiation medicine. In addition, research funding has contributed to a multi-million dollar expansion of facilities, which has enabled Georgetown to maintain a leadership position in the treatment of cardiovascular diseases, cancer, perinatal special needs, and the neurosciences. Other Georgetown specialties frequently cited for excellence include AIDS, endocrinology, gastroenterology, geriatrics, gynecology, neurology, orthopedics, rheumatology, and urology.

SPECIAL FACILITIES AND PROGRAMS

Georgetown provides a full range of inpatient and outpatient treatment services, including hematology, pediatric, gynecologic, immunologic, medical, and surgical oncology. The Lombardi Cancer Research Center is an integral part of Georgetown's oncology programs. Founded in 1970, it offers a multispecialty approach to cancer treatment. An outstanding group of clinicians and scientists constitutes a sophisticated local, regional, and national resource for programs and protocols in cancer diagnosis and treatment. Basic and clinical studies are performed in many specialties. The Nina Hyde Center for Breast Cancer Research in the Lombardi Cancer Research Center offers the most up-to-date treatments and research protocols available for breast cancer.

Georgetown cardiologists are nationally recognized in their specific areas of expertise, and physical facilities for inpatient and outpatient care are state-of-the-art and comprehensive. A cardiovascular transport program coordinates the transfer of patients from referring hospitals to Georgetown for tertiary cardiac services. Cardiovascular-thoracic surgeons

AT A GLANCE

Beds: 452
Occupancy Rate: 78%
Average Patient Count: 3,534
Average Patient Stay: 7.1 days
Annual Admissions: 18,103
Births: 1,600
Outpatient Clinic Visits:
    146,876
Emergency Room/Trauma
    Center Visits: 22,542

HOSPITAL PERSONNEL
Physicians: 898
    Board Certified: 800
Residents: 443
Registered Nurses: 855
    BS Degree: 690

ROOM CHARGES (PER DIEM)
Level 1 Care: $145
Level 2 Care: $198
Level 3 Care: $283
Level 4 Care: $424
Level 5 Care: $810
Level 6 Care: $1,320
Level 7 Care: $1,860

ADDRESS
3800 Reservoir Road, N.W.
Washington, DC 20007

TELEPHONE
(202) 784-3000

provide comprehensive services in areas ranging from cardiac transplantation to extracorporeal membrane oxygenation (ECMO).

Diagnostic catheterizations have been performed since the early 1950s, coronary artery bypass graft surgery since 1972, and angioplasties since the procedure was developed. Cardiac catheterization and angioplasty continue to be central elements of the hospital's overall cardiac care service.

The Cardiac Arrhythmia Service at Georgetown provides the latest diagnostic and therapeutic services for cardiac arrhythmia patients. Therapeutic approaches include standard and research anti-arrhythmic drugs, the automatic implantable cardioverter defibrillator for selected patients, and cardiac surgery for selected arrhythmia patients, in conjunction with the Division of Cardiovascular Surgery. Pacemaker evaluation, implantation, and follow-up services also are available.

Georgetown University Hospital, nationally renowned for its cardiac education, is the primary training center for the largest cardiology fellowship in the Washington metropolitan area.

Georgetown also provides comprehensive adult and pediatric neurology and clinical neurophysiology services, including diagnosis and management of epilepsy; Parkinson's disease and other movement disorders; multiple sclerosis; stroke; headache; muscular dystrophy; motor neuron disease; peripheral neuropathies; chronic pain disorders; sleep disorders; Lyme disease; and neuropsychological disorders, including Alzheimer's disease.

General and specialty neurosurgery includes treatment of malignant and benign brain tumors; surgery for pituitary tumors and aneurysms; surgical treatment of disc diseases (cervical, thoracic, and lumbar); head and spine trauma; and surgical treatment of pain (malignant and benign).

The FIDIA-Georgetown Institute for the Neurosciences conducts fundamental research and related scholarly activities in neurosciences, including neuroanatomy, neurophysiology, and neuropharmacology. Created in 1985, it is the most significant partnership established at Georgetown and one of the largest in the United States.

Georgetown offers sophisticated care for all mothers and infants, particularly those with serious complications related to pregnancy and birth. High-risk patient care involves preconception counseling, prenatal testing using high level ultrasonographic imaging, electronic fetal heart monitoring, fetal blood sampling, and management of delivery and postpartum care.

The Division of Neonatology in the Department of Pediatrics provides comprehensive care for critically ill newborns delivered at Georgetown or transferred to the nationally acclaimed hospital's neonatal intensive care and intermediate care units. Services include Extracorporeal Membrane Oxygenation (ECMO); high frequency jet ventilation; administration of surfactant for babies with underdeveloped lungs; and comprehensive delivery room management for all infants at risk. A neonatal intensive care unit was recently opened.

The Department of Obstetrics and Gynecology offers a comprehensive range of services accommodating to women's special medical needs. The Division of Gynecologic Oncology takes an interdisciplinary approach to the treatment of ovarian, cervical, and other gynecologic cancers. The Division of Reproductive Endocrinology and Infertility is expert in detecting and treating the endocrine abnormalities and anatomical malformations that make conception difficult for one out of every six couples. Along with operative endoscopy, microsurgery, and laser surgery, this division offers gamete intrafallopian transfer. The Division of Maternal-Fetal Medicine and Genetics is renowned throughout the Mid-Atlantic region for expert, comprehensive care for mothers and fetuses during "high-risk" pregnancies, including the treatment of eyrthroblastosis fetalis with intrauterine transfusions. In addition, the division's members are uniquely skilled in the use of ultrasonography for the evaluation of fetal health and in such advanced genetic diagnostic techniques as cordocentesis, amniocentesis, and chorionic villus sampling. The National Institutes of Health (NIH) Perinatology Research Branch is the first branch the NIH has relocated to a private institution. This multidisciplinary project provides an integrated approach to research into the causes of perinatal and infant mortality, and is the first of its kind in the United States. The National Capital Lactation Center and Human Milk Bank ensure that babies get the nutrition they need and help mothers successfully provide that nutrition.

In the Department of Pediatrics, the Division of Pediatric Cardiology is regionally and nationally renowned for the diagnosis and treatment of congenital heart disease, including pediatric cardiac arrhythmias, using interventional catheterization and other advanced techniques. The division includes specialists in fetal cardiology as well. The Department of Pediatrics also operates the Pediatric Mobile Van, which serves medically underserved neighborhoods in the District of Columbia that are located east of the Anacostia River. Residents, medical students, and attending physicians provide primary pediatric care without cost to the patients. Pediatric residents provide primary pediatric care under the supervision of an attending physician at Community of Hope Health Service in the Columbia Heights neighborhood of D.C. This is a clinic serving as a homeless shelter for families and the surrounding area.

Other services available include cardiac transplantation and organ tissue donation and placement. Available programs include the Impotence Treatment Program, the Lipid Disorders Center, and the National Capital Lactation Center.

MEDICAL SPECIALTIES

Adolescent Medicine, Anesthesia, Audiology, Cardiology, Cardiovascular Surgery, Clinical Pharmacology, Critical Care Medicine, Dental Oncology and Maxillofacial Prosthetics, Dermatology, Diabetes and Metabolism, Emergency Medicine, Endocrinology, Gastroenterology, General Surgery, Genetics, Gynecologic Oncology, Hematology/Oncology, Immunology and Allergy, Infectious Diseases, Internal Medicine, Laboratory Medicine, Medical Oncology, Neonatology,

Nephrology, Neurology, Neurosurgery, Obstetrics/Gynecology, Ophthalmology, Oral and Maxillofacial Surgery, Orthopaedic Surgery, Otolaryngology, Pathology, Pediatrics, Pediatric Hematology/Oncology, Pediatric Surgery, Plastic Surgery, Psychiatry, Pulmonary and Critical Care, Radiology, Radiation Medicine, Reproductive Endocrinology and Infertility, Rheumatology, Speech-Language Pathology, Surgical Oncology, Thoracic Surgery, and Urology.

WELL-KNOWN SPECIALISTS

- Dr. Marc E. Lippman   *Director of Lombardi Cancer Research Center*
- Dr. Robert Marcuvza   *Chairman of Department of Neurosurgery*
- Dr. Edmund Pellegrino   *Director of Georgetown Center for the Advanced Study of Ethics; director of Center for Clinical Bioethics*
- Dr. Owen M. Rennert   *Pediatrics*
- Dr. John Queenan   *Obstetrics/gynecology*

PATIENT SATISFACTION

A survey taken by the University Hospital consortium in early 1994 reported that 58% of all inpatients rated their overall care as excellent, while 61% rated their overall care as better than expected. Eighty percent of all inpatients indicated that they would definitely return for future treatments and would recommend Georgetown University Medical Center to others.

RESEARCH

The research enterprise at Georgetown University Medical Center has experienced remarkable growth in the past seven to eight years. In 1986, for example, Georgetown was in the top half of the nation's 120-some academic health centers in terms of National Institutes of Health funding; since that time, Georgetown's increasingly competitive stature in biomedical research has moved it into the top third of such institutions. In 1986, sponsored research awards totaled approximately $36 million; in April 1994 that total surpassed the $100 million mark.

Georgetown has a rich history of discovery, innovation, and teaching in the biomedical sciences and technologies. In the early 1950s, largely due to the accomplishments of cardiologists like Proctor Harvey, M.D., and cardiovascular surgeons like Charles Hufnagel, M.D., Georgetown became a leading center for the diagnosis and treatment of heart disease. In 1952 at Georgetown, Hufnagel implanted the first artificial heart valve in a patient. At the same time, much of the early, groundbreaking work on hemodialysis was conducted at Georgetown in the laboratories of George E. Schreiner, M.D. In the 1970s, the National Biomedical Research Foundation at Georgetown pioneered the development of the first whole-body computerized axial tomography (CAT) scanner.

Although Georgetown continued to extend its clinical and scientific expertise through key faculty recruitments, it was not until the latter half of the 1980s that it formulated and activated plans for increased emphasis on research at all levels. In 1989, the leadership of the institution designated four interdisciplinary areas as priorities for this express purpose: cancer research and treatment; cardiovascular biology, medicine, and surgery; perinatal biology and medicine; and the neurosciences. Many of Georgetown's recent achievements in research reflect this new emphasis in these areas.

The National Cancer Institute has designated Georgetown's Lombardi Cancer Center as the site for two "Specialized Programs of Research Excellence" (SPOREs), one in breast cancer and the other, prostate cancer. The Lombardi Center is one of the nation's leading centers for the investigation of breast cancer and for the development of novel diagnostic and therapeutic modalities based on the molecular biology of the disease.

The National Institute of Child Health and Human Development (NICHD) recently awarded Georgetown a five-year, $58 million grant to establish, at the Medical Center, a Perinatal Research Branch. This branch is an intramural program of the NICHD and is dedicated to "translational" research aimed at identifying and solving the problems associated with infant mortality.

With $20 million in federal funding, Georgetown has also recently established a Program in Cognitive and Computational Sciences as a major component of neuroscience research at the Medical Center. Under the aegis of this program, investigators will study pattern recognition and, among other practical applications, seek to develop new modes of imaging the nervous system for diagnostic and therapeutic benefits.

Georgetown has won funding as well for six prestigious NIH program project grants: neuropharmacology of excitatory amino acids; the vascular biology of coronary artery disease; the molecular basis of tumor resistance to radiation; the cell biology of the male reproductive system; pediatric immunology; and the molecular targeting of therapy for tumors of the nervous system.

Moreover, the National Institute for Allergic and Infectious Disease (NIAID) has designated Georgetown as one of the 20-some AIDS Clinical Trials Units in the country. Specialists in the treatment of individuals infected with the human immunodeficiency virus are working in conjunction with NIAID and others to test new pharmacologic therapies for the disease. As for the immediate future, Georgetown is now laying the foundations for a Molecular Cardiology Institute, which will focus on the fundamental mechanisms of heart function and dysfunction and seek clinical applications for this basic knowledge. Also, Georgetown's Hospital-based Clinical Research Center is increasingly focused on testing clinical applications of molecular medicine and gene therapy.

ADMISSIONS POLICY

Patients are admitted as routine, urgent, or emergent admissions. They can be admitted via the Admissions Office, ER, doctor's office, clinics, or can be transferred in. All patients must have a physician with admitting privileges as their attending physician of record. ER patients will be assigned an admitting physician as necessary. Outside physicians without admitting privileges may obtain temporary admitting privileges through the Medical Director's Office or transfer the responsibility to an accepting physician with admitting privileges.

If patients lack insurance or other means to pay, Georgetown refers them to its Social Work department to review the possibility of Medicaid eligibility, as well assess the potential for charity aid. Georgetown renders approximately 2.5% to 3% free care.

Special phone number for admissions information: (202) 784-3179.

PATIENT/FAMILY ACCOMMODATIONS

The Leavy Center Hotel and Conference Center provides discount accommodations at the rate of $65.00 per night + tax per occupancy. Two area hotels, the Holiday Inn and the Savoy Suites are nearby and also extend discount rates ranging from $60.00 to $99.00 per night.

The Leavy Center and Conference Center accommodations are comparable to those at other hotels such as the Marriot. The patient's families find them very comfortable and accommodating to their needs.

GEORGE WASHINGTON

UNIVERSITY MEDICAL

CENTER

George Washington University Medical Center (GWUMC) is a nationally recognized, interdisciplinary health care facility. The Medical Center includes the University Hospital, a top-ranked School of Medicine and Health Sciences, a comprehensive basic and clinical research program, and a 22-year-old health maintenance organization serving more than 70,000 members. It provides clinical services through the University Hospital and Medical Faculty Associates, which houses the specialty practices of the medical faculty. It is especially known for is Neurological Institute, Cancer Center, cardiovascular research and treatment, and Emergency Department.

The George Washington University Hospital is a unique center-city facility that serves a diverse group of patients, from area residents to visiting dignitaries and heads of state. A designated tertiary care institution, the University Hospital provides area physicians and patients with the latest technological innovations in diagnosis and treatment for the most acute clinical conditions. The University Hospital is also a certified Level-I Trauma Center, having met the American College of Surgeon's requirements for medical staff training and clinical research on trauma care and community education. More than 1,000 physicians are affiliated with the Hospital, 300 as full-time faculty. Fifty-eight George Washington University physicians were named in the 1994-95 edition

WASHINGTON, DISTRICT OF COLUMBIA

GEORGE WASHINGTON UNIVERSITY MEDICAL CENTER (GWUMC) IS A NATIONALLY RECOGNIZED, INTERDISCIPLINARY HEALTH CARE FACILITY.

of *The Best Doctors in America*. The Emergency Department sees approximately 48,000 patients annually, including many of the homeless and working poor of the nation's capital. More than 17,000 patients are admitted to the Hospital every year.

U.S. News & World Report's annual guide to the best graduate schools ranks the George Washington University School of Medicine and Health Sciences as one of the top five in the nation for training generalist physicians. The "Practice of Medicine" curriculum places students in clinical settings from the start of their medical school experience. Among the clinical rotations for medical students are tours of duty at Children's National Medical Center, home for the GW Department of Pediatrics and St. Elizabeth's Hospital of Psychiatry. In addition to the medical doctor degree, the GW School of Medicine and Health Sciences offers degrees in associated health professions, including a Physician's Assistant program, ranked sixth in the country, and a rapidly expanding Master of Public Health (M.P.H.) program that offers an M.P.H. degree, a joint M.D./M.P.H. degree, a joint J.D./M.P.H. degree, and a Physician Assistant M.P.H. program. GWUMC also coordinates the consortium for training District of Columbia emergency medical personnel.

The Medical Faculty Associates (MFA) is the faculty practice of clinicians who teach full-time at the George Washington University School of Medicine and Health Sciences. All MFA physicians are Board Certified or Board Eligible in their specialties and are a valuable resource to the community for treatment and for graduate medical education.

The Ronald Reagan Institute for Emergency Medicine (RRIEM) was established at GWUMC in 1991, ten years after President Ronald Reagan was treated at the George Washington University Medical Center following the attempt on his life. The mission of the RRIEM is "to foster the development of the finest emergency medical care—locally, nationally, and internationally—through research, training and education." RRIEM programs focus on five areas: international emergency medicine, disaster medicine, violence, informatics/new technologies, and resuscitation/reanimation research.

SPECIAL FACILITIES AND PROGRAMS

GWU Medical Center has a national reputation in many specialties. A few of them are highlighted below.

The GWU Medical Center's Division of Endocrinology is widely known for its broad range of clinical experience in the diagnosis and treatment of disorders of the endocrine system and body metabolism. The Diabetes Center treats a considerable number of patients with type I and type II diabetes, as well as pregnant patients with diabetes. Physicians, diabetes educators, dieticians, and a podiatrist offer a multidisciplinary approach to patient care.

The Division of Cardiology delivers secondary and tertiary care to a diverse patient population. Recognized for innovation in a variety of fields—including ischemic and valvular heart disease, clinical electrophysiology, and cardiac arrhythmia—the division supports active and ongoing research. The GW Institute for Cardiology Research was established this year. Its first program is a $5 million study to evaluate the benefits of a combination of angioplasty and thrombolytic therapy, two therapies usually viewed as being in competition with one another.

The Division of Gastroenterology and Nutrition provides primary and tertiary care to patients with a variety of gastrointestinal and nutrition disorders. Research includes new therapies for cholesterol gallstones, inflammatory bowel disease, and peptic ulcer. The division has an extensive specialty service that was just expanded in the areas of interventional pancreatic and biliary endoscopy. Division Director Hans Fromm, M.D., was recently awarded the Ismar Boas Medal of the German Society for Digestive and Metabolic Diseases, and has been elected Vice Chairman Elect of the Biliary Section of the American Gastroenterological Association.

The Division of Infectious Diseases is well recognized for the active role of its faculty in the care and treatment of patients with a variety of infectious diseases, including HIV infection and its complications. Besides a very active inpatient program, the division maintains an outpatient clinic for individuals with infectious disease problems. As part of the infectious disease division, the outpatient AIDS research unit provides HIV-infected patients with the opportunity to participate in a variety of clinical trials, including the use of new antiretroviral agents to prevent the progression of HIV infection and new antimicrobial drugs to prevent and/or treat opportunistic infections in this population. The division recently received funding through a Ryan White grant to provide additional case management services to HIV-infected individuals. Dr. Gary L. Simon, Director of the Division, is expanding the basic research activities of the division through collaborative research with basic scientists in other departments within the medical center. Expansion of clinical activities is also envisioned with the development of new clinics both within and outside of the medical center.

AT A GLANCE

Beds: 501
Occupancy Rate: 83.6%
Average Patient Count: 419
Average Patient Stay: 6.6 days
Annual Admissions: 17,500
Births: 1,411
Outpatient Clinic Visits:
  30,174
Emergency Room/Trauma
  Center Visits: 48,000

HOSPITAL PERSONNEL
Physicians (Permanent): 259
Physicians (Affiliated): 1,000+
Registered Nurses: 629

ROOM CHARGES (PER DIEM)
Private: $1,091
Semiprivate: $581
ICU: $1,345

ADDRESS
901 23rd Street, N.W.
Washington, DC 20036

TELEPHONE
(202) 994-1000

Other specialty centers within the University Hospital include the Center for Vascular Medicine and Surgery, the Endoscopy Center, the Center for Wound Care, the Breast Care Center, the Center for Cancer Treatment and Research, the Center for Blood Disorders, the In Vitro Fertilization Program, the Lipid Research Center, and the Neurological Institute.

MEDICAL SPECIALTIES

Allergy and Immunology, Anesthesiology, Cardiology, Dermatology, Endocrinology, Gastroenterology, Geriatrics, Infectious Diseases, Obstetrics/Gynecology, Oncology/Hematology, Ophthalmology, Orthopedics, Otolaryngology, Nephrology, Neurology, Neurosurgery, Nuclear Medicine, Pediatrics, Plastic Surgery, Psychiatry, Radiology, Rheumatology, Surgery, Urology, and Vascular Surgery.

WELL-KNOWN SPECIALISTS

- Dr. Elwyn James Anthony *Psychiatry*
- Dr. A. Barry Belman *Pediatric urology*
- Dr. William M. Chadduck *Pediatric neurological surgery*
- Dr. Ralph G. DePalma *Vascular surgery*
- Dr. David N. F. Fairbanks *Otolaryngology*
- Dr. Arthur Frank *Eating disorders*
- Dr. Paul T. Gavaris *Ophthalmology; specialist in oculoplastics*
- Dr. Jeanne E. Hicks *Rheumatology*
- Dr. Thomas Joel Hougen *Pediatric cardiology*
- Dr. John J. Kelly, Jr. *Neurology*
- Dr. Craig M. Kessler *Hematology/oncology*
- Dr. Herbert L. Kotz *Obstetrics/gynecology*
- Dr. John G. McAfee *Nuclear medicine*
- Dr. L. Gregory Pawlsen *Geriatrics*
- Dr. Michael R. Pranzatelli *Pediatric neurology*
- Dr. Laligam N. Sekhar *Neurological surgery*
- Dr. Robert J. Stillman *Reproductive endocrinology*
- Dr. Martin S. Wolfe *Infectious diseases*

PATIENT SATISFACTION

George Washington is currently developing a new patient satisfaction questionnaire. First results are expected in late 1995.

RESEARCH

GWUMC researchers oversee more than $42 million in funded and sponsored research. This research is conducted, among others, by leaders in the fields of cardiovascular research, cholesterol and lipid research, pharmacology, kidney disease, molecular biology, cancer, neurological disease, and health care sciences. The Medical Center offers opportunities to community physicians and their patients to participate in pharmacological trials and research protocols conducted here for the National Institutes of Health and government research agencies, as well as protocols that are privately funded.

Among several projects, such as the use of growth hormone in patients with pituitary deficiency, the research accomplishments of the endocrinology faculty include the internationally acclaimed discovery of the lung as an endocrine organ. Division Director Kenneth L. Becker, M.D., has recently received a three-year merit review award for $400,000 to support his research on the lung's production of hormones, which serve as diagnostic and prognostic markers for the presence and severity of pulmonary injury (such as pneumonia, emphysema, inhalational burn injury, and lung cancer).

Research projects in cardiology include a five-year National Heart, Lung, and Blood Institute grant for five overlapping studies to investigate the relationship between insulin and the pathogenesis of atherosclerosis in African Americans. The study incorporates techniques developed at GW for assessing blood flow, and for probing insulin receptors as well as other immunochemistry and hematologic measures. These will be assessed to determine the mechanism for coronary heart disease. This study will end in 1997.

ADMISSIONS POLICY

A patient can be admitted through the Emergency Room for an illness or a medical emergency. Patients can also be admitted for scheduled care or surgery by having their primary doctor phone the admitting office.

GWU does not turn any patient away because of lack of insurance. If the care is scheduled through the admitting office, the patient would have to bring a percentage of the cost for the procedure that is to be performed. If the percentage requirement cannot be met, payment arrangements can be made.

Special phone number for admissions information: (202) 994-2825.

SHANDS HOSPITAL

UNIVERSITY OF FLORIDA
HEALTH SCIENCE CENTER

GAINESVILLE, FLORIDA

Since its opening in 1958, Shands Hospital has been a pacesetter in the field of health care and has evolved into a leading tertiary care referral center for the state of Florida and the southeastern U.S. The relationship between Shands and the University of Florida Health Science Center results in a wide variety of health care services, ranging from the routine to the highly specialized across the entire spectrum of medical, surgical, pediatric, obstetrical and psychiatric services. Forty-nine Shands physicians were named in the second edition of *The Best Doctors in America.*

Shands Hospital is the patient care and clinical education unit of the Health Science Center. It is also a federally-funded clinical research center, one of 75 nationwide and the only one in the state of Florida. By virtue of its relationship with the health center, Shands has at its disposal the basic science and clinical research capabilities that allow it to remain in the forefront of health care in the Southeast. Patients from throughout Florida are referred to Shands for its many special clinical and diagnostic services. About 5% of patients come from other states.

The University of Florida Shands Clinic is an outpatient facility managed by the University of Florida College of Medicine. The clinic is primarily located at the Health Science Center adjacent to Shands Hospital, with satellite clinics throughout

SINCE ITS OPENING IN 1958, SHANDS HOSPITAL HAS BEEN A PACESETTER IN THE FIELD OF HEALTH CARE AND HAS EVOLVED INTO A LEADING TERTIARY CARE REFERRAL CENTER FOR THE STATE OF FLORIDA AND THE SOUTHEASTERN U.S.

Gainesville and elsewhere. At the Clinic, multispeciality diagnostics and treatment are provided by the College of Medicine's faculty physicians representing more than 110 medical specialties.

Shands Hospital opened as a state agency and was incorporated in 1980. Facilities and capabilities at Shands have grown throughout its history in keeping with the advancement of modern medicine. The growth has continued in the 1990s with a new MRI facility and a new four-story cancer center. In 1992, the bone marrow transplant program doubled in size, and lung and neonatal heart transplant programs were commissioned. Also in 1992, plans for a $226 million expansion of ambulatory and inpatient facilities were approved with implementation currently underway.

SPECIAL FACILITIES AND PROGRAMS

Cancer patients from throughout Florida are referred to the Shands Cancer Center, where a full range of oncology services is available. University of Florida physicians at Shands Hospital representing every subspecialty area of medicine participate on multidisciplinary teams to coordinate comprehensive screening, diagnosis, and treatment services for cancer patients. The cancer center has taken a leadership role in research aimed at finding cures for the disease. Major research funding has been awarded to cancer researchers working at the center to support a broad range of research. A freestanding complex for the cancer center has recently been constructed and was opened in May 1991. The Shands Cancer Center is one of Florida's eight regional childhood cancer centers.

New transplantation surgical techniques and discoveries in immunology, biochemistry, pharmacology, and bioengineering are applied at the University of Florida. Shands' transplantation program, which includes heart, liver, kidney, bone marrow, cornea and bone transplants, has become the state's leading program in the field. Since 1985, Shands physicians have performed 160 heart transplants. Shands has also been the site of more than 1,600 kidney transplants since the program began in 1966.

AT A GLANCE

Beds: 576
Occupancy Rate: 77%
Average Patient Count: 420
Average Patient Stay: 6.5 days
Births: 3,766
Annual Admissions: 23,627
Outpatient Clinic Visits:
    257,865
Emergency Room/Trauma
    Center Visits: 37,185

HOSPITAL PERSONNEL
Physicians: 440
    Board Certified: 360
Residents: 600
Registered Nurses: 1,101
    BS Degree: 327

ROOM CHARGES (PER DIEM)
Private: $465
Semiprivate: $450
ICU: $700–$995

ADDRESS
1600 S.W. Archer Road
Gainesville, FL 32610

TELEPHONE
(904) 395-0111

The Hospital has one of 10 programs in the country specializing in bone transplants and is world renowned for its achievements. The first lung transplant program in the state of Florida opens in 1994.

The latest advances in the diagnosis and treatment of heart disease are available at the Shands Cardiovascular Center owing to the pioneering research efforts of University of Florida physicians. The Center includes cardiologists, cardio-thoracic surgeons, vascular surgeons, basic scientists and a comprehensive health care team dedicated to the diagnosis, treatment and prevention of heart disease. The adult and pediatric cardiology departments are advancing cardiology through state-of-the-art procedures including laser angioplasty and the angioscope, digital angioplasty, balloon valvuloplasty, esophageal echocardiology, fetal echocardiography, outpatient cardiac catheterization, and electrophysiology testing. Florida's first open-heart surgery was performed in 1959 by cardio-thoracic surgeons at the Shands Cardiovascular Center. Sophisticated new procedures are pioneered by researchers and scientists specializing in mitral valve replacement, human heart transplantation, and artificial heart transplantation.

The Shands Neurological Center encompasses neurologists, neurosurgeons, basic neuroscience researchers and a comprehensive health care team dedicated to the diagnosis and treatment of neurological disease.

Wounds that heal too slowly or incompletely, internal organ damage that fails to heal properly after surgery or injury, and unwanted scar formations resulting from abnormal wound healing are major challenges facing scientists in multiple medical fields. The newly established Wound Research Center at the UF Health Science Center provides a focal point for collaborative research to advance the frontiers of wound healing. Physicians practicing at Shands Hospital are involved in some of today's most significant areas of medical research, including the testing of growth factors to speed wound-healing, the addition of glutamine to surgical patient's diets to enhance recovery of the intestinal lining and other body tissues, and the use of drugs in treating keloid scars and preventing the growth of scars that sometimes develop around implanted artificial joints, breast implants and pacemakers. The Wound Research Center is the collaborative effort of physicians within the Department of Obstetrics and Gynecology and the Department of Surgery at the University of Florida and Shands Hospital.

Patients with severe burns are referred to Shands for highly specialized treatment. The Burn Intensive Care Center at Shands is a self-contained intensive care facility with adjoining rooms for physical therapy and other forms of rehabilitative care. University of Florida physicians at Shands are studying the skin's ability to regenerate itself in cultures. By growing skin, patients in the burn intensive care unit, who may otherwise be scarred for life, possibly suffer less serious scarring and adhesions.

Shands is also a major referral center for patients needing total hip replacement, as well as for surgical removal of bone cancers; reimplantation surgery for severed fingers, hands or limbs; and for treatment of a wide range of bone injuries. Additionally, the orthopaedic center specializes in certain areas of childhood bone deformities. Patients who have bone tumors, have lost bone due to trauma, or have special reconstructive problems often benefit from bone transplantation performed by orthopaedic physicians. The Human Motion Laboratory is one of only nine in the United States. This laboratory treats patients suffering from cerebral palsy, stroke, muscular dystrophy, major joint injuries, spine disorders, or any illness that causes an abnormal walk or motion pattern.

In the category of unique care, Shands' Hyperbaric Chamber accommodates as many as three patients simultaneously and has been used in treating victims of diving accidents as well as patients with chronic bone infections, gas gangrene, radionecrosis, and carbon monoxide poisoning. The hyperbaric chamber is provided by a long-term loan to Shands by the National Aeronautics and Space Administration (NASA). Additionally, Shands is affiliated with NASA as the designated backup hospital for space shuttle launches.

Children's health care in much of Florida has always been linked to Shands Hospital. Some of the many comprehensive services and outreach programs available at Shands include a 24-bed Pediatric Intensive Care Unit (including a special six-bed unit for children with heart disease); one of only seven Children's Lung Centers in the nation; one of three Genetic and Diabetes Units in Florida; and the first camp for children with cancer in Florida.

The University of Florida is one of three institutions selected as a state-supported regional diabetes center in Florida. The three centers provide the latest means of treatment, as well as education and research programs on diabetes. Shands also houses several regional medical centers for pediatric patients, including the Children's Lung Center, the Regional Pediatric Pulmonary Center, the Spina Bifida Center, a Regional Perinatal Center and Neonatal Intensive Care Units. It is one of four major referral centers in Florida for infants and children needing complicated cardiovascular surgery. The first infant heart transplant was performed at Shands Hospital in November 1993 as part of the Neonatal and Infant Heart Transplant program. The first lung transplant was performed at Shands Hospital in March of 1994.

MEDICAL SPECIALTIES

Allergy, Anesthesiology, Cardiology, Community Health and Family Medicine, Dermatology, Endocrinology and Metabolism, Gastroenterology, General Medicine, Immunology, Infectious Diseases, Nephrology, Neurology, Neurosurgery, Obstetrics/Gynecology, Oncology, Ophthalmalogy, Orthopedics, Otolaryngology, Pathology, Pediatrics, Psychiatry, Radiation Oncology, Radiology, Rheumatology, and Surgery.

WELL-KNOWN SPECIALISTS

- Dr. James A. Alexander   *Thoracic surgery; specialist in pediatric cardiac surgery*

- Dr. A. Jay Block *Pulmonary and critical care medicine*
- Dr. C. Richard Conti *Cardiovascular disease*
- Dr. Richard G. Fessler *Neurological surgery; specialist in spinal surgery*
- Dr. William A. Friedman *Neurological surgery; specialist in stereotactic radiosurgery*
- Dr. John R. Graham-Pole *Pediatrics; specialist in pediatric hematology-oncology*
- Dr. Pamela Hawks-Ann *Pediatrics; specialist in metabolic diseases*
- Dr. Craig S. Kitchens *Medical oncology/hematology; specialist in disorders of bleeding thrombosis*
- Dr. Robert B. Marcus, Jr. *Radiation oncology; specialist in sarcomas*
- Dr. Nancy P. Mendenhall *Radiation oncology; specialist in lymphomas, breast cancer and other cancers*
- Dr. Carl J. Pepine *Cardiovascular disease; specialist in cardiac catheterization*
- Dr. Albert L. Rhoton, Jr. *Neurological surgery; specialist in cranial nerve and tumor surgery*
- Dr. Janet Silverstein *Pediatrics; specialist in pediatric endocrinology*
- Dr. Mary H. Wagner *Pediatrics; pediatric pulmonology*
- Dr. Ralph C. Williams, Jr. *Rheumatology; specialist in lupus*

PATIENT SATISFACTION

A total of 3,032 patients were surveyed during FY 1993. The two services areas that received the highest scoring ratings were Quality of Medical Care and Quality of Nursing Care. The questions within the Medical Service Area that received the most favorable responses (a score of strongly agree or agree) regarded physician courtesy to patients and understanding physicians' explanations. The questions within Nursing Care that received highly favorable responses were nursing courtesy to patients and nursing concern for patient needs. More than 90% of all patients surveyed rated these questions favorably. Almost 90% of patients indicated that they would recommend Shands Hospital to family and friends. Overall Quality of Service was rated favorably (a score of strongly agree or agree) by almost 90% of the patients who responded.

RESEARCH

Shands Hospital is the major teaching hospital affiliated with the University of Florida Health Science Center, the most comprehensive academic medical center in the Southeast. The Health Science Center encompasses six colleges that garnered more than $73 million in competitive external research grants during fiscal year 1992-1993. In addition, the Health Science Center and Shands Hospital received $10.1 million in private gifts for research during fiscal year 1992 - 1993. Major subjects of research include cancer, diabetes, drug design and development, brain and spinal cord disease, genetics and organ transplantation.

A sampling of current research programs includes the following:

Preventing diabetes is the primary goal of diabetes researchers. UF researchers are studying the use of insulin therapies in preventing diabetes in people who have the antibody markers for the disease but have not yet developed diabetes. Studies into how and why diabetes occurs are ongoing.

UF professors are conducting research on designing new drugs to combat Alzheimer's disease. Funded by a $3.5 million grant from the National Institute on Aging, researchers from the colleges of Pharmacy and Medicine are synthesizing new drugs and drug delivery systems in an all-out assault on the disease.

An expanded program of cancer research, education and patient care is being developed with the aid of a $525,000 planning grant from the National Cancer Institute.

The Neuroscience Clinical Research Center is an inpatient nursing and intensive care unit where volunteer patients with severe neurological problems participate in the testing of promising but unproven diagnostic techniques, therapies, and surgical procedures. Shands neurosurgeons are also studying ways to adapt magnetic resonance imaging to the operating room.

Genetic research projects span a wide spectrum of life sciences and life problems aimed at profiling the genetic flaws that contribute to AIDS, albinism, rheumatic heart disease, degenerative eye diseases, malaria, nervous system disorders, and rare mental/physical disorders such as Angelman and Prader Willi Syndromes. Other genetic projects are aimed at ensuring healthy offspring for couples who carry the genes for certain diseases, and at improving tissue matching for organ transplantation.

ADMISSIONS POLICY

The patient can "self refer" to any primary care clinic such as General Pediatrics, General Internal Medicine, Family Practice, Gastroenterology, and sometimes Ophthalmology, Orthopaedics, and Otolaryngology (ENT), depending on the problem. For the more specialized areas, such as Neurosurgery, Pulmonary, Hematology/Oncology, Endocrinology, or any of the pediatric subspecialties, a referral from the patient's general physician or specialist is required.

Sometimes patients will call the hospital directly because their own doctors will not refer them to Shands. These patients are referred directly to the most appropriate service to make arrangements to be seen in one of the physician clinics.

If a patient lacks insurance, he or she must complete a financial screening form to try to obtain appropriate sponsorship, such as Medicaid, SSI, County Indigent, State Indigent, or Health Care Responsibility Act.

If a patient needs care and Shands is the closest, most appropriate facility to provide the care, it will be provided. If the patient is in an emergency situation, financial questions are not asked until after the patient has received treatment.

Shands Hospital provided over $70 million in uncompensated care to patients who did not pay their hospital bills during FY 1993.

UM/JACKSON

MEMORIAL MEDICAL

CENTER

UNIVERSITY OF MIAMI

MIAMI, FLORIDA

Outside of Florida, most people recognize the University of Miami-Jackson Memorial Medical Center as an excellent research and tertiary treatment center. But within the Sunshine state, this reputation has often been overshadowed by the hospital's role as the primary health care provider for Dade County residents, many of whom cannot afford to pay their hospital bills. Therefore, in 1991, Dade County residents voted to remedy Jackson's chronic financial problems by imposing upon themselves an additional one-half cent sales tax. An overwhelming 57% of Dade residents approved the tax increase, which provided $12.6 million toward expanding hospital programs and services in 1992 alone.

The sales tax will also allow the medical center to remain on the cutting edge of modern medicine while remaining true to its mission to provide excellent care to all patients regardless of their ability to pay. A public hospital, UM/Jackson annually provides an astounding $214 million in indigent care and handles 12% of Florida's Medicaid patients.

The hospital's commitment to providing care for the needy dates back to its founding in 1899 as Miami's first charity hospital. Funded first by private donors and later by the city of Miami, it was renamed in 1924 after James Jackson, the first president of the hospital's medical staff. Dade County took over governance from the City in 1949; in 1954, the hospital

OUTSIDE OF FLORIDA, MOST PEOPLE RECOGNIZE THE UNIVERSITY OF MIAMI-JACKSON MEMORIAL MEDICAL CENTER AS AN EXCELLENT RESEARCH AND TERTIARY TREATMENT CENTER.

became affiliated with the University of Miami School of Medicine, which had opened two years earlier.

Today, Jackson has a budget of $660 million, making it the fifth largest hospital in the country, according to the *American Hospital Association Guide to the Health Care Field*. More than 700 physicians serve the needs of over 60,000 patients per year. Only the University of Southern California Hospital admits more patients. The AHA Guide ranks Jackson fourth in its number of beds and the number of births each year, and 15th in its 84.4% occupancy rate.

Jackson Memorial Hospital is the teaching hospital for the University of Miami School of Medicine, a private institution. One of the youngest medical schools in the country—it celebrated its 40th birthday in 1992—UM has won worldwide acclaim. From its humble beginnings in 1952 with a mere 28 students and four faculty members, the school has grown into Florida's largest medical school, and one of the largest health care centers in the nation. Its annual budget of $400 million pays the salaries of 983 full-time faculty members (of whom more than 600 are doctors), who train close to 600 students.

SPECIAL FACILITIES AND PROGRAMS

The hospital provides first class medical care. Virtually every medical specialty and subspecialty is covered in one of the medical center's many components, which include the world-renowned Bascom Palmer Eye Institute/Anne Bates Leach Eye Hospital, the Papanicolaou Comprehensive Cancer Center, the Mailman Center for Child Development, National Parkinson Foundation, the University of Miami Hospitals and Clinics/National Children's Cardiac Hospital, the Lewis Calder Memorial Library and other medical libraries, and the JMH Ambulatory Care Center. Approximately one-third of the hospital's 1,500 beds are devoted specifically to specialties such as trauma, burns, cancer, newborn special care, rehabilitation, psychiatry, neurological and spinal cord injuries, and organ transplants.

AT A GLANCE

Beds: 1,517
Occupancy Rate: 89%
Average Patient Count: 1,148
Average Patient Stay: 7.3 days
Annual Admissions: 62,261
Births: 10,845
Outpatient Clinic Visits:
    290,823
Emergency Room/Trauma
    Center Visits: 103,728

HOSPITAL PERSONNEL
Physicians (Admitting): 1,300
Physicians (Attending): 700
Residents: 550
Registered Nurses: 2,000+

ROOM CHARGES (PER DIEM)
Private: $295–$315
Semiprivate: $265–$295
ICU: $800

ADDRESS
1611 N.W. 12 Avenue
Miami, FL 33136

TELEPHONE
(305) 325-7429

The most recent addition to this list is perhaps the most impressive. The Ryder Trauma Center opened its doors on August 3, 1992, exactly three weeks before Hurricane Andrew battered south Florida. The largest and most comprehensive trauma center in the world, and a "hospital of choice" for anyone protected by the Secret Service, Ryder was ready to handle the patients injured by the storm, and prevented further loss of life and injury. Its four operating rooms are only a 15-second elevator ride away from a rooftop helipad capable of supporting helicopters up to 22,000 pounds. It is one of the few hospitals in the world that can accommodate the 20,000-pound U.S. Army Blackhawk helicopters that were used as rescue units during the hurricane.

Equally outstanding is the Bascom Palmer Eye Institute/Anne Bates Leach Eye Hospital, recognized as one of the finest ophthalmological institutes in the world. As a part of the University of Miami School of Medicine, it provides education, patient care, and research, particularly in the area of vitreo-retinal diseases. The Laser Research Center, one of the few experimental research laboratories in the United States, investigates laser use for a variety of ophthalmologic conditions. It would take almost a whole separate section to describe in detail all of the services offered by this institute alone. A major referral center for the southeast U.S. and Central and South America, the eye hospital treats over 115,000 inpatients and outpatients annually. Outpatient clinics provide specialists in the areas of retina, vitreous, glaucoma, macula, external diseases, pediatric and neuro-ophthalmology. All of the latest diagnostic and therapeutic equipment is available to treat any kind of eye problem. The Children's Eye Clinic, the Low Vision Clinic, the Contact Lens Clinic and the Florida Lions Eye Bank are all part of the institute.

Jackson's Comprehensive AIDS Program puts it in the forefront of the battle against AIDS. As the main hospital for the South Florida AIDS Network, Jackson is a leader in the research, prevention, and treatment of HIV and AIDS. The program's director, Margaret Fischl, and Gordon Dickinson, associate professor of medicine at the University of Miami Medical School, were the first doctors to discover the effectiveness of AZT in treating AIDS patients.

The hospital's Newborn Special Care Center includes the largest Intensive Care Neonatal Unit in the U.S., with more than 1,700 admissions annually. The hospital has just completed an expansion of its Intermediate Care Neonatal Unit, increasing it to 60 beds.

In addition, Jackson is highly regarded for its transplant units. The kidney transplant center boasts the nation's most successful long-term survival rate.

The Center for Neurological Diseases has earned international acclaim for its work in stroke, Parkinson's disease, Alzheimer's disease, multiple sclerosis, and disease of peripheral nerves and muscles. CND handles a broad spectrum of neurological diseases ranging from sleep disorders and headache to Lou Gehrig's disease, and treats 13,000 patients a year.

The Rehabilitation Center is a designated regional spinal cord injury center, one of 17 in the nation, providing acute and rehabilitative care for persons with spinal cord injuries. It has been accredited in four areas: hospital-based rehabilitation; vocational education; job placement; and the spinal cord injury program.

Jackson is also a designated Comprehensive Cancer Center, providing a multidisciplinary team approach to various aspects of a patient's treatment. Recently merged with the Papanicolaou Cancer Research Institute, the center is one of 28 federally designated centers nationwide. Patients benefit from the center's basic research into the causes and prevention of cancer by having access to new drugs and clinical tests. Services are offered in breast cancer, dermatological oncology, gastrointestinal oncology, gynecologic oncology, head and neck cancers, hematologic oncology, lung cancer, medical oncology, neurosurgical oncology, (brain and spinal cord tumors), oncological intractable pain, ophthalmic oncology, orthopaedic oncology, pathology, pediatric cancer, radiation therapy, surgical oncology, and urologic malignancies.

The Women's Hospital Center services are equally comprehensive. Women with pelvic cancers and benign gynecologic disorders are attended by a wide array of medical and surgical specialists. In fact, the center is the largest gynecologic oncology facility in the southeastern United States. More than 10,000 babies are delivered every year at the hospital; more than 50% are high risk cases. The state of Florida's first in vitro fertilization program is located at the Women's Hospital Center, as a service of the Department of Obstetrics and Gynecology's Division of Endocrinology.

MEDICAL SPECIALTIES

Adolescent Medicine, Allergy, Burn Medicine, Cardiology, Cardiothoracic Surgery, Dermatology, Endocrinology, Emergency and Trauma Care, Family Medicine, Gastroenterology, Genetics, Gynecology, Hematology, Intensive Care, Juvenile Diabetes, Neonatal Intensive Care, Nephrology, Neurology, Neurosurgery, Obstetrics, Oncology, Ophthalmology, Orthopedics/Rehabilitation, Pediatrics, Pediatric Cardiology, Plastic Surgery, Psychiatry, Radiology, Transplantation, and Urology.

WELL-KNOWN SPECIALISTS

- Dr. Hervy E. Averette   *Gynecologic oncology*
- Dr. Mark D. Brown   *Orthopaedics*
- Dr. Barth A. Green   *Spinal cord injury*
- Dr. William H. Harrington   *Internal medicine; specialist in hematology*
- Dr. Alfred S. Ketchum   *Oncology*
- Dr. J. Maxwell McKenzie   *Thyroid disease*
- Dr. Ralph Millard   *Plastic surgery*
- Dr. Daniel H. Mintz   *Juvenile diabetes*
- Dr. Edward W.D. Norton   *Ophthalmology*
- Dr. Victor A. Politano   *Urology*
- Dr. Peritz Scheinberg   *Neurology*

- Dr. Eugene R. Schiff *Liver disease*
- Dr. Robert Zeppa *Surgery; specialist in Miami shunt*
- Dr. C. Gordon Zubrod *Oncology*

PATIENT SATISFACTION

According to a survey given to every patient discharged from the medical center, about 90% replied that they were satisfied with their care and would recommend the hospital to a friend or relative.

RESEARCH

The University of Miami School of Medicine received a total of $60 million in research grants in 1993 with about 70% from federal agencies like NIH.

More than three-quarters of the research is in clinical and psychosocial studies on aging, AIDS, cancer, immunology, neuroscience, epidemiology, drug dependency, and dysfunctional families. Pediatric research, especially neonatal projects, are currently underway (over 10,000 babies were delivered at Jackson this year). The National Institute of Child Health and Human Development has provided a five-year base grant of $1.3 million to the medical center as one of seven centers to participate in a clinical research network of neonatal medicine. One of eight participating centers in the Infant Health and Development Program, the medical center was awarded a $2.6 million grant to continue its study of the effectiveness of services designed to reduce the health and developmental problems often experienced by low birthweight babies.

The internationally renowned University of Miami Blood Research Center is headed by Dr. William Harrington, one of the heroes of the book *Human Guinea Pigs*, who inoculated himself with a mystery blood disease called ITP to prove his theory that it was caused by the body rejecting its own blood platelets.

The medical center is also known for the pioneering work of Dr. Daniel Mintz in transplanting the cells of the pancreas that produce insulin, and the success of Dr. Hubert Rosomoff with back pain in the UM Comprehensive Pain Center.

Experimental laser research work is conducted in the departments of otolaryngology, obstetrics/gynecology, neurosurgery, and ophthalmology. Other areas of research conducted at Jackson include stress testing, wound healing, radiologic studies, triaging trauma patients, hematologic diseases, and dermatological studies, among others. The medical school also runs the world's largest tissue bank.

The William Lehman Study Center at the Ryder Trauma Center is conducting the largest program in existence to find connections between types of automobile accidents and the types and severity of injuries they cause. In addition to a medical team to repair their injuries, every automobile accident patient is met by a Crash Team that videotapes the patient's injuries and studies the cause of the accident. The crash team pieces together photographs of car damage, eyewitness reports, medical observations, and computer animation, to help engineers design safer cars. The unit's current efforts focus on injuries sustained in head-on collisions by patients who were protected by safety belts or air bags. The unit is funded by a $6 million grant from the U.S. Department of Transportation.

Finally, the Touch Research Institute, the only one of its kind in the world for research on the sense of touch, aims to investigate the role of this sense in medicine and disease.

ADMISSIONS POLICY

Patients can be admitted without a referral through a clinic or emergency room, at which time an attending physician is assigned. Once emergency care is given, patients are responsible for their charges.

A deposit towards full charges is required without any insurance or third-party payer. Self-pay patients are required to pay an estimate of full charges based on medical or surgical stay. Any waiver of deposit must be approved by Director or Vice President of Finance.

$214 million in indigent care is provided annually.

EMORY UNIVERSITY

HOSPITAL / EMORY

CLINIC

ATLANTA, GEORGIA

Patients come to Emory Clinic from all over the world for diagnosis of a medical problem, consultation with a particular clinical specialist, or for medical or surgical treatment. After examination, patients who need hospitalization are referred to Emory University Hospital. A university-owned, not-for-profit hospital, Emory University Hospital provides care, including highly specialized medical and surgical services, to acutely ill adults through its staff of physicians and the faculty of the Emory University School of Medicine. Sixty Emory physicians are listed in *The Best Doctors in America*.

Emory University Hospital provides a full range of advanced specialized patient care, bringing into play the results of research and teaching. A major center for advanced tertiary medical care and research, Emory is one of the nation's largest centers for heart surgery and angioplasty, and has become a noted referral center for the most difficult cardiac cases. Emory also receives special recognition for its programs in multiple organ and tissue transplants, oncology, neurology, and neurosurgery.

PATIENTS COME TO EMORY CLINIC FROM ALL OVER THE WORLD FOR DIAGNOSIS OF A MEDICAL PROBLEM, CONSULTATION WITH A PARTICULAR CLINICAL SPECIALIST, OR FOR MEDICAL OR SURGICAL TREATMENT.

In keeping with its historical origins, Emory Clinic is a partnership of physicians, all of whom are members of the Emory University School of Medicine. The hospital has been closely associated with Emory University since 1922, when Welsey

Memorial Hospital, Emory Hospital's predecessor, moved onto the Emory campus.

Both Emory Clinic and Emory University Hospital are part of the Woodruff Medical Center of Emory University. Other divisions of the Medical Center include the Crawford Long Memorial Hospital; the Schools of Medicine, Nursing, and Dentistry; and the Yerkes Regional Private Research Center. In addition, there are seven independent agencies affiliated with Woodruff Medical Center: Henrietta Eagleson Memorial Hospital, Wesley Homes Health Services, Atlanta Veterans Administration Hospital, the U.S. Public Health Service Center for Disease Control, and the Georgia Mental Health Institute. These institutions are an integral part of the teaching, research, and patient care services of the Woodruff Medical Center.

SPECIAL FACILITIES AND PROGRAMS

Cardiac surgery is an important specialty at Emory University Hospital, with more than 1,000 operations performed every year. Emory was one of the first institutions to offer heart valve replacement, and it remains a leader in this field. Emory also trains approximately 800 cardiologists, radiologists, and other physicians each year in special angioplasty courses taught at the Gruentzig Center, named for the developer of this procedure, Dr. Andreas Gruentzig, who practiced at Emory.

Emory also provides an array of other heart services. The Emory Heart Center provides prevention, diagnosis, and treatment of adult cardiac problems. In the Cardiac Transplant Program, specialists evaluate heart transplantation candidates, perform transplant surgery and care for patients after transplantation. In 1993, 31 adult and six pediatric heart transplants were performed by Emory surgeons. The Emory Center for Heart Failure specializes in diagnostic and therapeutic services for all degrees of cardiomyopathy, ranging from silent ventricular enlargement to advanced congestive heart failure. Designed to decrease the amount of time that a heart attack victim waits before receiving life-saving intervention, the Chest Pain Center provides

AT A GLANCE

Beds: 604
Occupancy Rate: 78%
Average Patient Count: 415
Average Patient Stay: 8.1 days
Annual Admissions: 35,997
Outpatient Clinic Visits:
    54,416

HOSPITAL PERSONNEL
Physicians: 313
    Board Certified: 251
Residents: 212
Registered Nurses: 939

ROOM CHARGES (PER DIEM)
Private: $399
Semiprivate: $394
ICU: $1,475–$1,705

ADDRESS
1364 Clifton Road, N.E.
Atlanta, GA 30322

TELEPHONE
(404) 321-0111

around-the-clock care and immediate access to Emory cardiologists for patients who have known or suspected heart problems.

In transplantation, Emory has grown to be one of only a handful of medical centers in the U.S. with a multiple organ and tissue transplantation program. The program includes heart, heart-lung, lung, heart-kidney, liver, kidney, kidney-pancreas, bone, bone marrow, cornea, and sclera transplantation. It is the only hospital in Georgia performing lung transplantation.

Emory Hospital has the largest number of beds dedicated to bone marrow transplant patients on the East Coast, and it will soon have the capacity to perform more transplantations than any other center in the region. It will then be one of the top five centers in the nation. The hospital performs autologous and unrelated and related donor allogeneic transplantation. It is the only center in Georgia approved to perform matched unrelated donor bone marrow transplantation.

Emory is one of the nation's leaders in the neurosciences, especially in the surgical treatment of aneurysms and brain tumors, as well as movement disorders, such as Parkinson's disease. Several surgical procedures to alleviate the debilitating symptoms of Parkinson's are presently being investigated, including clinical studies with microelectrode-guided pallidotomy, the results of which are showing tremendous promise.

The latest diagnostic technology is available, including echocardiography, cardiac imaging, magnetic resonance imaging (MRI), computed tomography (CAT), ultrasonography, and nuclear medicine. Emory Hospital is the only medical center in Georgia with a cyclotron and radiophysics laboratory, including a positron emission tomography (PET) scanner. The cyclotron and lab make it possible for researchers to create the radionuclides needed to image the heart's metabolism, the brain, and various types of tumors. These imaging capabilities are only possible with an onsite cyclotron.

The Winship Cancer Center of Emory University is a cancer research center, which coordinates multidisciplinary and translational research activities. The center, through its outreach efforts and by increasing access of state-of-the-art cancer research, participates in prevention, diagnosis, education, and treatment of cancer. More than 100 active clinical research trials are currently available to patients through the Winship Cancer Center's Clinical Research Facility, including some open only to National Cancer Institute-designated centers. In addition to Emory-sponsored trials, patients may participate in trials sponsored by national cooperative groups made up of the country's leading research institutions.

The Emory Breast Health Center offers women a comprehensive service that includes disease prevention, education, early detection, diagnosis, treatment, and reconstruction. In addition to screening mammography, the center provides complex diagnostic mammographic evaluation of breast lesions. Fine needle aspiration is commonly performed in the Breast Health Center, with or without stereotactic imaging, for diagnosing a wide range of breast problems.

The Emory Eye Center offers a broad range of consultative services, including medical and surgical management of anterior segment diseases and trauma, corneal and external diseases, glaucoma, neuro-ophthalmic and neurologic diseases, oculoplastic diseases, and vitreoretinal diseases. Emory ophthalmologists have been leaders in the use of ophthalmic lasers, corneal transplants, modern cataract surgery with intraocular lens implantation, anterior segment reconstruction, and vitreous surgery.

Outpatient services include a pharmacy for patients, visitors and staff; outpatient transplant clinics; a heart failure center; a urinary and fecal incontinence center; physical, recreational and occupational therapy; and day programs for head injury and stroke patients. An outpatient surgery center is located at the Emory Clinic, where almost all of the physicians who practice at Emory Hospital have their exam rooms and offices.

Although the hospital is considered a general acute care hospital, it does not provide maternity, pediatric, or major emergency services; facilities for these services are available at Crawford Long Hospital of Emory University or Egleston Hospital for Children at Emory University.

MEDICAL SPECIALTIES

Anesthesiology, Cardiology, Dentistry, Dermatology, Endocrinology, Gastroenterology, General Surgery, Gynecology/Obstetrics, Hematology, Infectious Diseases, Internal Medicine, Medical Oncology, Nephrology, Neurology, Neurosurgery, Ophthalmology, Orthopedic Surgery, Orthoptics, Otolaryngology, Pathology, Pediatrics, Plastic Surgery, Psychiatry, Pulmonary Disease, Radiation Therapy, Rehabilitation Medicine, Rheumatology, Thoracic Surgery, and Urology.

WELL-KNOWN SPECIALISTS

- Dr. Wayne Alexander   *Chairman, Department of Cardiology*
- Dr. Virgil Brown   *Director, Division of Arteriosclerosis, Lipid Metabolism*
- Dr. Mahlon DeLong   *Chairman, Department of Neurology*
- Dr. Robert Gordon   *Chief Liver Transplant Surgeon*
- Dr. Kirk Kanter   *Chief Heart Transplant Surgeon*
- Dr. Spencer King   *Director, Gruentzig Center*
- Dr. Charles Nemeroff   *Chairman, Department of Psychiatry*
- Dr. Howard Ozer   *Director, The Winship Cancer Center (of which Emory Hospital is a component)*
- Dr. Rein Saral   *Director, The Emory Clinic (formerly, Director, Bone Marrow Transplant Program)*
- Dr. William Wood   *Chairman, Department of Surgery*

PATIENT SATISFACTION

Emory's results are among the best we have seen. In the latest survey, 96% rated the quality of their physician care as very good or excellent. 98% said they would return if further hospitalization were required. 98% rated the overall care as good to excellent. 97% found the nursing care good or better.

RESEARCH

Emory University Hospital is the clinical site for much of the research conducted by the Emory University School of Medicine, which received more than $40 million in grants for the 1993-1994 fiscal year. Much of the work is focused on the clinical environment.

Emory's researchers are doing pioneering work in the analysis and treatment of Parkinson's disease. In December of 1992, a patient was treated using a technique called pallidotomy, which involves surgically inactivating a small portion of the brain. The Emory procedure allows for precisely recording, mapping and analyzing the activity of cells in the part of the brain where aberrant cell activity causes Parkinsonian motor deficits.

Research physicians at Emory University Hospital are evaluating a new type of bone marrow transplant that may be used extensively in the future to treat advanced-stage breast cancer.

An Emory neurosurgeon, Dr. Dan Barrow, is using a new procedure that permits surgeons to operate on previously inoperable brain aneurysms.

In the W. Dean Warren Clinical Research Center, Emory researchers have one of the most advanced centers for investigating the latest medical and surgical therapies, including gene therapy to treat inherited diseases.

In the past two years, Emory has expanded its liver transplantation research activities in testing graft tolerance and the effectiveness of immunosuppressant drugs. The use of portal stents, which can prolong the life of patients awaiting a liver transplant, is also being researched and developed further.

Major areas of cancer-related research include immunotherapy, bone marrow transplantation, cancer prevention and control, and breast cancer research.

ADMISSIONS POLICY

Physicians may refer patients to Emory Clinic by phone or mail for diagnosis or treatment of an already diagnosed problem.

Only faculty members of the Emory University School of Medicine can admit patients to Emory University Hospital.

There are no financial requirements. Emory Hospital provides financial evaluations for patients who cannot pay and will help them find assistance. Charity cases made up 3.4% of Emory Hospital's revenue in 1993.

NORTHWESTERN

MEMORIAL HOSPITAL

Northwestern Memorial Hospital (NMH) is a comprehensive tertiary-care facility receiving referrals from throughout the Midwest, as well as the entire United States, and offering a full range of adult, geriatric, maternal, fetal, and perinatal medicine. Pediatric care is provided by the related Children's Memorial Hospital. Northwestern Memorial is a private, nonprofit institution that serves as the principal teaching hospital of Northwestern University Medical School.

Despite its name, NMH is not connected to Northwestern University in the same way that UCLA and Columbia are to their universities. The hospital and the school are both members of the McGaw Medical Center of the university, a charitable, research, and educational consortium that also includes Northwestern University Dental School and three other private teaching hospitals: Evanston Hospital Corporation, Children's Memorial Hospital, and Rehabilitation Institute of Chicago.

Northwestern Memorial and the medical school are on adjacent campuses along Chicago's downtown lakefront and share a number of facilities and resources. All NMH's attending physicians hold appointments in the medical school. Approximately one-third of the hospital's physicians are full-time faculty in the medical school; the remaining two-thirds have part-time teaching responsibilities and

CHICAGO, ILLINOIS

NORTHWESTERN
MEMORIAL HOSPITAL
(NMH) IS A COMPREHENSIVE
TERTIARY-CARE FACILITY
RECEIVING REFERRALS FROM
THROUGHOUT THE MIDWEST,
AS WELL AS THE ENTIRE
UNITED STATES, AND
OFFERING A FULL RANGE
OF ADULT, GERIATRIC,
MATERNAL, FETAL, AND
PERINATAL MEDICINE.

practice privately in the community. Fifty-nine NMH staff physicians were named in *The Best Doctors in America*. Another 49 physicians whose main affiliation is with NMH were also cited.

After a three-year trial period, the Northwestern Healthcare Network—a collaboration among NMH, Children's Memorial Medical Center, Evanston Hospital Corporation and Highland Park Hospital—was founded in 1993. Together, they serve 91,000 inpatients a year in a 1,667-bed system geared to meet the needs of a managed care environment.

SPECIAL FACILITIES AND PROGRAMS

With nearly every modern medical and surgical specialty represented, NMH is one of the major academic medical centers in the Midwest. A few of its more prominent departments are detailed in the following paragraphs.

Northwestern Memorial Hospital provides comprehensive care in cardiology and cardiothoracic and vascular surgery, treating more than 3,000 cardiovascular patients each year. In addition to such advanced diagnostic capabilities as echocardiography, nuclear cardiology, treatment advances in interventional cardiology, and endovascular surgery, Northwestern Memorial offers services related to heart disease prevention, early detection, and state-of-the-art diagnostic testing. NMH also has special programs in arrhythmia and heart failure, and heart disease in women. In addition, NMH vascular surgeons have recently been granted an academic award from the NIH to develop a vascular center devoted to research, education, and clinical care in vascular disease.

With one of the Chicago area's largest programs, NMH provides a full range of diagnostic, treatment, rehabilitation, and support services for cancer patients and their families. NMH is a leader in the use of advanced techniques such as biologic therapies, bone marrow transplantation, and hyperthermia. Facilities include a 33-bed inpatient oncology unit, comprehensive hospice program, and a Radiation Oncology Center that is among the largest and best equipped in the region. In addition to mammography and breast surgery, the breast cancer center provides a range of services unique to the Chicago metro area: risk appraisal, genetic counseling, and personalized screening recommendations for women concerned about their breast cancer risk.

Prentice Women's Hospital and Maternity Center of Northwestern Memorial Hospital is the only hospital in Chicago devoted entirely to women's health care. Almost 5,000 babies are born here every year. Prentice has 20 labor, delivery and recovery rooms; four Cesarean section rooms; and six operating rooms. The neonatal intensive care unit has been designated Level III by the state. The hospital has a program for high-risk pregnancies and for women having multiple pregnancies or pregnancies with multiple risk factors. The Active Management of Labor program is designed to reduce the rate of Cesarean sections.

While Prentice is particularly noted for comprehensive maternity services, including pre- and post-natal health education and support programs for mothers and families, it addresses the widest spectrum of healthcare needs of women of all ages, providing comprehensive genetics testing and infertility services, inpatient and outpatient gynecology surgery and care, gynecologic cancer services, and osteoporosis and menopause programs.

Northwestern Memorial provides a spectrum of care in digestive diseases, including diseases of the esophagus, stomach, liver, kidneys, intestines, gall bladder, and pancreas. It currently operates the largest kidney transplantation program in the state of Illinois, and has recently started liver and pancreas transplants.

The NMH HIV Center is a leading multi-disciplinary outpatient facility providing comprehensive care and support services. In addition to providing patient care, the center is a training site for physicians and other healthcare professionals, as well as a nationally recognized center for AIDS research.

With state-of-the-art capabilities, including arthroscopic, endoscopic, and micro-surgery, NMH is a leader in hand and wrist surgery, and joint reconstruction and replacement surgery. Widely regarded as the premier center of its type in the Midwest, Northwestern Memorial Hospital's Regional Spinal Cord Injury Center has conducted extensive research on the best forms of early intervention and treatment for these injuries. The hospital also has an active sports medicine program, and its orthopedic surgeons serve as team doctors for Chicago's professional sports teams.

The Neurosciences program at NMH, which includes neurology, neurosurgery, otolaryngology, and neuro-ophthalmology, has been recognized by the National Institutes for Health as a major research center. It was among the first in the country to treat brain cancer and other neurological problems with advanced medical and surgical techniques, and performs over 2,500 inpatient procedures each year. Other special programs include a carpal tunnel syndrome clinic; a cochlear implant program; a neurological testing center; and a Muscular Dystrophy Association clinic.

Northwestern Memorial Hospital serves the city's senior population by providing multi-disciplinary care

AT A GLANCE

Beds: 740
Occupancy Rate: 71%
Average Patient Count: 525
Average Patient Stay: 6.1 days
Annual Admissions: 35,997
Births: 4,867
Outpatient Clinic Visits:
    181,345
Emergency Room/Trauma
    Center Visits: 47,389

HOSPITAL PERSONNEL
Physicians: 1,103
    Board Certified: 972
Residents: 300
Registered Nurses: 1,140
    BS Degree: 740

ROOM CHARGES (PER DIEM)
Private: $800
Semiprivate: $780

ADDRESS
Superior Street and Fairbanks
    Court
Chicago, IL 60611

TELEPHONE
(312) 908-2000

and community outreach services. A Geriatric Evaluation Service provides a comprehensive evaluation of medical condition, psychological state, social functioning, and daily living activities by staff members including an internist, a nurse practitioner, and a social worker who may draw on backup services from many other departments.

MEDICAL SPECIALTIES

Allergies, Ambulatory Care, Anesthesia, Arthritis, Cardiology, Cardiothoracic Surgery, Clinical Pharmacology, Community Health, Critical Care Medicine, Dentistry, Dermatology, Emergency Medicine, Endocrinology, GI, General Medicine, Head and Neck Tumors, Hematology, Human Genetics, Infectious Diseases, Nephrology, Neurology, Neurosurgery, Obstetrics/Gynecology, Oncology, Ophthalmology, Orthopedic Surgery, Otolaryngology, Pathology, Pediatrics, Plastic Surgery, Psychiatry, Pulmonary Medicine, Radiology, Rehabilitation Medicine, Surgery, Transplantation Surgery, Urology, and Vascular Surgery.

WELL-KNOWN SPECIALISTS

- Dr. John Grayhack   *Urology*
- Dr. Peter Hurst   *Dentistry*
- Dr. Lee Jampol   *Ophthalmology*
- Dr. David Nahrwold   *Surgery*
- Dr. Roy Patterson   *Medicine*
- Dr. Henry Roenigk   *Dermatology*
- Dr. Lee Rogers   *Radiology*
- Dr. Dante G. Scarpelli   *Pathology*
- Dr. Michael Schafer   *Orthopedic surgery*
- Dr. John Sciarra   *Obstetrics/gynecology*
- Dr. George Sisson   *Otolaryngology*
- Dr. Harold Visotsky   *Psychiatry*

PATIENT SATISFACTION

Northwestern Memorial receives very high marks from its patients. Overall satisfaction with the care received by inpatients has registered at least 96% over the past two years. Ambulatory surgery patients recorded 98% to 99% satisfaction in their surveys. Ninety-eight to ninety-nine percent of those surveyed indicated that they would recommend Northwestern to a relative or friend.

A high number of respondents to the hospital's surveys have made pointed remarks about the personal level of care received. Many came to Northwestern becasue of its technological capabilities and were surprised at the attentive, personalized care they received—a service they did not expect from a large teaching hospital.

RESEARCH

Research is conducted at Northwestern Memorial Hospital in partnership with Northwestern University Medical School.

NMH houses the Clinical Research Center, one of the original centers of its kind in the U.S. It is a specialized mini-hospital that admits 200 patients a year to participate in research on diseases and new treatments. A few of the research accomplishments of NMH in 1993 are noted below.

A team of Northwestern University Medical School and Massachusetts General Hospital researchers, led by NMH neurologist Dr. Teepu Siddique, found the genetic mutation that causes the inherited form of Lou Gehrig's disease. NMH's cardiology division was the first in Chicago and among the first in the country to study the advantages of placing a metallic stent within the coronary arteries to prevent reclosing following balloon angioplasty.

Researchers, led by NMH endocrinologist Dr. Mark Molitch, participated in a nine-year study which concluded that the frequency of diabetes-related eye, kidney and nerve disease could be greatly reduced by keeping blood glucose levels under better control.

The clinical leukemia program at Northwestern University, headed by NMH hematologist/oncologist Dr. Martin S. Tallman, reported dramatic success in treating hairy-cell leukemia.

ADMISSIONS POLICY

Patients may be admitted to NMH through several routes. A patient may already have an established relationship with an internist or specialist on NMH's staff or be referred to an NMH physician, often a specialist, by another physician in the community. Patients may also refer themselves to NMH physicians. The hospital maintains the Telephone Referral Service, (312)908-8400, to assist patients in identifying an appropriate physician. Finally, patients may enter the hospital through the Emergency Room, a designated Level I Trauma Center.

Patients who come through the Emergency Room will be treated regardless of their ability to pay. Uncompensated care for fiscal year 1993 was $42,859,000.

REHABILITATION

INSTITUTE OF

CHICAGO

For nearly 40 years, the Rehabilitation Institute of Chicago has been a front-runner in comprehensive patient care and treatment, research into disabling conditions, and the training of rehabilitation professionals. With a 176-bed facility designed exclusively for rehabilitation, RIC is widely recognized as a national leader in the field, offering a wide range of specialized programs.

Founded in 1954 by Paul B. Magnuson, a prominent orthopedic surgeon, RIC began in an old converted warehouse as an outpatient clinic with a staff of six. Today, the institute is located in an attractive 20-story tower with 176 beds and almost 1,000 employees. More than 6,000 people are treated annually on an inpatient and outpatient basis.

The doctors, nurses and therapists are all specially trained in rehabilitation medicine and operate with a team approach to care. Guided by a physician, the treatment team for each patient consists of physical and occupational therapists, nurses, social workers, therapeutic and recreational specialists, psychologists, vocational rehabilitation specialists, speech/language pathologists, audiologists, and chaplains. Family support and participation is integral in the recovery process, with relatives encouraged to attend therapy sessions, team meetings and physician consultations.

FOR NEARLY 40 YEARS,
THE REHABILITATION
INSTITUTE OF CHICAGO
HAS BEEN A FRONT-
RUNNER IN COMPREHENSIVE
PATIENT CARE AND
TREATMENT, RESEARCH INTO
DISABLING CONDITIONS,
AND THE TRAINING
OF REHABILITATION
PROFESSIONALS.

The Best Hospitals in America

SPECIAL FACILITIES AND PROGRAMS

RIC offers specialized programs with the most innovative and advanced treatment available, on both an inpatient and outpatient basis. The programs are Amputee, Arthritis, Brain Injury, Pain, Pediatric/Adolescent, Post-Polio, Orthopedics, Spinal Cord Injury, Stroke, Sports Medicine, and a Medical Program for Performing Artists.

The institute also runs specialized clinics not available at many other rehabilitation facilities. For example, RIC offers a gynecological clinic for disabled women, driver's education services, in-house orthotics and prosthetics production, and a center for technology-assisted communication and environmental control.

Other clinics include electromyography testing, foot and gait, neuropsychological evaluations, postpolio, pulmonary rehabilitation, rehabilitation engineering, seating and positioning center, sexual dysfunction clinic for men with spinal cord injury, sports and conditioning program, therapeutic recreation, vestibular testing and balance training, vocational evaluation, counseling and placement, and work hardening.

Six satellite clinics in the Chicago area treat patients with spine and sports injuries, offer a comprehensive day program for brain-injured patients, provide physical and occupational therapy for geriatric patients, and fit prosthetic and orthotic devices.

Community outreach activities include a sports program for disabled athletes, a support group for the families of patients with head injuries, and a stroke club.

WELL-KNOWN SPECIALISTS

- Dr. Henry B. Betts *Medical director*
- Dr. Kristi Kirschner *Stroke rehabilitation and women's disabilities*
- Dr. Joel Press *Sports medicine*
- Dr. Elliot Roth *Stroke*
- Dr. James Sliwa *General rehabilitation*
- Dr. Yeongchi Wu *Amputations*

AT A GLANCE

Beds: 176
Occupancy Rate: 85 %
Average Patient Stay: 25 days
Annual admissions: 2,208
Outpatient Clinic Visits: 65,000

HOSPITAL PERSONNEL
Physicians (Attending): 38
Physicians (Consulting): 126
Residents: 40
Registered Nurses: 141

ROOM CHARGES (PER DIEM)
General Rehabilitation: $515
Brain Trauma: $590
Ventilator: $800

ADDRESS
345 E. Superior St.
Chicago, Illinois 60611

TELEPHONE
(312) 908-6000

PATIENT SATISFACTION

Inpatient Satisfaction Survey data is collected on an ongoing basis. The questionnaire is conducted one month after an inpatient is discharged from the hospital. The Inpatient Satisfaction Report has recently switched from a quarterly to a semi-annual format. Comments logged by telephone interviewers, however, are still distributed quarterly to department managers.

In the October 1993 (fourth quarter) Report, satisfaction ratings in all clinical departments topped 90%. The percentage of patients who would recommend RIC was 92% at the beginning of 1993 and rose to 96% by the fourth quarter. Following is a summary of hospital functions receiving 90% or greater satisfaction ratings for both 1992 and 1993:

Function	1993 Rating
Patient/family involvement	92%
Explanations of schedules, procedures and therapies	94%
Patience and consideration of staff	94%
Staff response to questions	95%
Explanation of follow-up	95%
Overall care received	95%
Patient/family teaching	96%
Staff encouragement, but not pushy	96%
Staff's skill in providing treatment	96%

RESEARCH

Research falls into three broad categories: applied clinical research is directed towards diagnosis and management of patients' disabilities; outcomes research evaluates the benefits of rehabilitation treatments; and basic research studies neurologic and musculo-skeletal disorders.

The institute averages about $3.3 million directly in research funds annually and another $2.7 million in collaborative research with Northwestern University.

The federal National Institute on Disability and Rehabilitation Research awarded RIC a $3 million grant in 1993 to evaluate and develop methods to enhance the quality of life for stroke survivors. A center for improving the recovery of brain-injured patients through vocational training and community re-integration is funded by the Rehabilitation Service Administration.

Studies are underway to evaluate the role of substance abuse in causing adverse reactions in brain-injured patients. Researchers are also studying the fundamental mechanisms underlying motor disability in stroke and spinal cord injuries.

ADMISSIONS POLICY

Admission is based upon the patient's need for a comprehensive, interdisciplinary, coordinated team approach. Patients may be referred by health care professionals, insurance representatives or by themselves. They do not need a doctor on staff. RIC admits patients with Medicare, Medicaid and private insurance coverage. It is the hospital's policy that no patient requiring medical care will be refused solely due to lack of financial resources. The hospital provides about $1.7 million in free care annually.

RUSH - PRESBYTERIAN - ST. LUKE'S MEDICAL CENTER

For more than 150 years, Rush-Presbyterian-St. Luke's Medical Center has been a leader in health care in Chicago and the Midwest. Located just minutes from The Loop on Chicago's West Side, Rush is the largest private hospital in Illinois and home to one of the nation's oldest medical schools west of the Alleghenies. As one of the nation's leading academic medical centers, Rush maintains strong education and research functions. Rush physicians and scientists are involved in nearly 1,500 research projects, including studies promising new techniques and therapies, as well as laboratory studies aimed at achieving a better understanding of various illnesses. As a result, Rush patients benefit from the newest treatments, including those not widely available at other hospitals.

Rush-Presbyterian-St. Luke's Medical Center is the hub of a comprehensive health care system that serves approximately 1.5 million people in the greater Chicago area and northwest Indiana. The Rush System for Health offers a full range of health care services, from office-based physician care to complex care in hospital settings. In addition to Rush University, Presbyterian-St. Luke's Hospital and the Johnston R. Bowman Health Center for the Elderly, the Rush system includes three affiliated hospitals—in Skokie, Aurora and Chicago's North Side; three joint venture hospitals in Des Plaines, Oak Park, and Melrose Park;

FOR MORE THAN 150 YEARS, RUSH-PRESBYTERIAN-ST. LUKE'S MEDICAL CENTER HAS BEEN A LEADER IN HEALTH CARE IN CHICAGO AND THE MIDWEST.

the Rush Corporate Health Center in downtown Chicago; Rush Prudential Health Plans, a joint venture of the Medical Center and Prudential Insurance Company providing managed care; Rush Occupational Health; and the Rush Home Care Network.

Rush-Presbyterian-St. Luke's traces its origins back to the founding of Rush Medical College in 1837. In 1969, Rush Medical College merged with Presbyterian-St. Luke's Hospital to form the Medical Center. The institution then quickly upgraded its educational and research capabilities with the establishment of Rush University in 1972 along with the College of Nursing. The College of Health Sciences opened in 1975, and the Graduate College in 1981. In total, Rush has built on this base to achieve national fame as a medical center of international repute. Rush has been named the nation's Virology Quality Assurance Laboratory, which makes Rush scientists responsible for monitoring results from all clinical virology laboratories conducting NIH-funded AIDS research. Rush's Alzheimer's Disease Center was named a National Alzheimer's Disease Center by the National Institute on Aging of the National Institutes of Health. Rush is among eight hospitals nationwide to be designated an Adult Liver Transplant Center by Medicare. In addition, the World Health Organization named the Department of Biochemistry at Rush a Collaborating Center for the Field of Osteoarthritis.

Presbyterian-St. Luke's Hospital, which also dates its antecedents in the nineteenth century, is a major referral center providing primary care to its immediate community, and secondary and tertiary care to patients from across the country. State-of-the-art facilities include 34 operating rooms where more than 20,000 procedures are performed annually. The Rush Surgicenter has four operating rooms for the broad range of outpatient procedures. The Rush Perinatal Center is licensed by the state of Illinois as a level III facility with a 40-bed neonatal intensive care unit. The Center for Critical Care Medicine includes a 14-bed medical intensive care unit, a seven-bed non-invasive respiratory care unit, a 10-bed coronary care unit, and a 24-bed coronary stepdown unit.

AT A GLANCE

Beds: 912
Occupancy Rate: 74%
Average Patient Count: 620
Average Patient Stay: 7.6 days
Annual Admissions: 28,568
Births: 2,400
Outpatient Clinic Visits:
    233,380
Emergency Room/Trauma
    Center Visits: 36,245

HOSPITAL PERSONNEL
Physicians: 1,084
    Board Certified: 881
Residents: 620
Registered Nurses: 1,069
    BS Degree: 802

ROOM CHARGES (PER DIEM)
Private: $800
Semiprivate: $792
ICU: $1,424

ADDRESS
1653 West Corners Parkway
Chicago, IL 60612-3833

TELEPHONE
(312) 942-5488

The seven Rush Institutes encompass the Medical Center's largest clinical services and combine patient care and research to address such health problems as cancer, heart disease, aging, mental illness and neurological diseases. Building on the strengths of the Medical Center, the Institutes offer primary health care services, as well as up-to-date treatments for these diseases and others. The Institutes are designed for the patient's convenience by locating laboratory, consultation and workups in one place. The Institutes also support cutting-edge research, seeking out new treatments, improved surgical procedures, and the underlying causes of various diseases. Physicians and technicians at the Rush Institutes work together to speed up the transfer of knowledge to the hospital bed.

SPECIAL FACILITIES AND PROGRAMS

The Rush Cancer Institute builds on Rush's long-standing reputation for excellence in multidisciplinary cancer care. Programs are staffed by teams of oncologists, surgeons, nurses, psychologists, nutritionists, and other cancer specialists who design treatment plans to match each patient's medical and emotional needs. Comprehensive care is available for breast cancer, chest tumors, gastrointestinal malignancies, gynecologic cancer, head and neck cancer, leukemia, lymphoma, and pigmented lesions (skin cancer).

Medical treatment may include surgery, radiation, chemotherapy, or a combination of approaches. Bone marrow transplantation is also available. Innovative treatments include neutron therapy, a specialized radiation therapy for certain inoperable tumors. The treatment is offered by Rush in cooperation with Fermi National Accelerator Laboratory in Batavia, Illinois.

Special services—including a weekly support group—are available to help patients and families cope with the emotional consequences of cancer. Psychologists offer individual and family counseling, as well as instruction in stress management, pain control, and cancer prevention. The Wellness Resource Center offers a full range of free information and support.

The Rush Heart Institute combines all aspects of heart disease diagnosis, treatment, preventive care and research in one program. Staff includes specialists in cardiology, cardiovascular/thoracic surgery, critical care medicine, pulmonary medicine, and preventive medicine, who devise an individualized treatment plan for each patient. More than 200 research projects are under way, focusing on high blood pressure, cholesterol and lipid disorders, heart failure, cardiogenic shock, and new techniques for clearing blocked arteries and diagnosing heart problems. The Institute also conducts laboratory research to gain a better understanding of heart disease and how to reverse—or prevent—its effects.

There are patient care and research programs in the five major areas. Comprehensive treatment is available for all types of heart problems, including medication and nonsurgical procedures, such as angioplasty, for clearing blocked arteries. The institute also has special services for people who experience irregular heart rhythms and people who have pacemakers. Diagnostic testing includes stress testing, electrocardiography, echocardiography, intravascular ultrasound, and other techniques for evaluating the heart and cardiovascular system. When necessary, cardiac catheterization is conducted in a special laboratory. Cardiovascular/thoracic surgeries, including coronary bypass surgery, heart valve replacement and heart transplant, are also performed here. For less advanced cases, heart specialists design one-year plans to reduce cardiac risk factors such as high blood pressure, obesity and smoking.

For critical care, the Rush Center for Critical Care Medicine includes a 14-bed medical intensive care unit, a 7-bed noninvasive respiratory care unit, a 10-bed coronary care unit, and a 24-bed coronary stepdown unit.

The Rush Arthritis and Orthopedics Institute provides comprehensive research, diagnosis and treatment for all forms of arthritis and musculoskeletal problems. The Institute pools the talents of physicians and scientists in orthopedic surgery, rheumatology, and biochemistry. Patient care and research are intertwined as physicians and scientists work together to refine diagnostic, surgical and therapeutic techniques. There are patient care and research programs in joint replacement surgery, back pain and injuries, spine surgery, foot and ankle problems, arthritis, hand and elbow disorders, sports medicine, and bone cancer.

The Rush Institute for Mental Well-Being offers comprehensive treatment for a variety of psychiatric conditions, including depression, obsessive-compulsive disorder, panic disorder, anxiety disorder, schizophrenia, and chemical dependency. Staff includes psychiatrists, psychologists, social workers, and psychiatric nurse specialists, who tailor treatment to each patient's unique needs. Research focuses on suicide prevention, alcohol and drug dependency, winter depression, violence prevention, psychiatric trauma, and child and adolescent mental health.

Specialized inpatient psychiatric care is offered in five units: a 31-bed general psychiatric unit, a 19-bed acute care unit, an 11-bed adult stress unit, a 15-bed child and adolescent unit and a 22-bed geriatric unit. There is also a full range of outpatient services, including evaluation and diagnosis, pharmacologic therapy, medication management, and psychotherapy. Special facilities include the Rush Day Hospital, offering intensive treatment during the day and allowing patients to live at home, as well as the Rush Residential Center, a supervised living environment for outpatients.

Rush Behavioral Health provides inpatient and outpatient services for people suffering from alcohol or drug dependency, and includes extended care and a family program. A full range of inpatient and outpatient services for patients age 3 to 18 is available, including the Rush Day School, a private, not-for-profit therapeutic school for emotionally disturbed children, ages 5 to 12.

The Geriatric Psychiatry Program offers comprehensive inpatient and outpatient psychiatric treatment for adults age 65 and older. Treatment may also include physical rehabilitation and medical care.

The Rush Neuroscience Institute provides comprehensive, innovative care—medical and neurosurgical treatment, as well as emotional support—for people with various neurological diseases. The institute conducts nationally renowned research, including studies of new medical and surgical treatments, as well as laboratory studies exploring the cause and progression of neurological disease.

The institute also provides diagnostic services for people with signs and symptoms of Alzheimer's disease, in coordination with the Rush Alzheimer's Disease Center. Comprehensive epilepsy evaluation and treatment, including innovative diagnostic and surgical techniques, were pioneered at Rush. Treatment for Parkinson's disease, dystonia, Gilles de la Tourette's syndrome, Huntington's disease, and other disorders that limit freedom of movement is also available. Multidisciplinary care, focusing on psychological as well as physical effects, is offered to those suffering from multiple sclerosis. Neuromuscular disorders, comprehensive stroke care, and headache treatment are among other services.

The focus of the Rush Institute for Primary Care is to improve primary patient care in the metropolitan Chicago area by designing education and research programs to increase the supply of generalist physicians, nurse practitioners and nurse midwives, and to expand the knowledge base of the primary care field. Another key component of the Institute is an information network, which links primary care providers within the Rush System for Health to promote integrated patient care, education, and research.

The Rush Institute on Aging specializes in medical, psychiatric and rehabilitation care for older adults, with the goal of returning patients to their highest level of independent living. The staff is made up of physicians and nurses, therapists in a variety of specialties, psychiatrists, psychologists, and social workers—all dedicated to the care of older adults. The Center of Research on Health and Aging studies the needs of older adults and trains health professionals to meet them.

Rush's transplant programs are among the most active and successful in Chicago and the region. Multidisciplinary teams include surgeons, medical specialists, clinical nurses, social workers, and psychologists. Education and support services are available for patients and families. Ongoing research focuses on new anti-rejection drugs, organ preservation and surgical techniques.

Rush has a nationally ranked program offering both living donor and cadaver kidney transplants; the pediatric kidney transplant program is one of the largest in the city, and one of the few in the state offering dialysis and transplantation for infants. One of the most experienced liver transplant teams in the country, Rush handles technically complex and high-risk cases. Transplants are available for both adults and children with end-stage liver disease. Hospital services include a Liver Intensive Care Unit for patients with acute or chronic liver failure. Heart transplants are available for patients with untreatable heart disease. Bone marrow transplants are performed for the treatment of leukemia, lymphoma, and selected solid tumors, including breast, ovarian and brain cancer. Treatment is also available for rare blood disorders such as aplastic anemia. Limb-sparing bone surgery is provided for patients with cancers of the bone or cartilage. Rush surgeons perform one of every 10 long-segment bone transplants performed in the U.S. annually. Eyesight-saving cornea transplant surgery is performed on both children and adults. Rush is one of the Chicago area's major referral sites for cornea transplant.

At the Rush Center for Women's Medicine, emphasis is placed on patient education and disease prevention, keeping in mind women's unique health concerns. Special care is available for women seeking help for premenstrual tension, physical and emotional aspects of menopause, sexual problems, and spouse abuse, and for women who have had miscarriages or whose infants have died. Labor and delivery suites in the Rush Perinatal Center offer homelike settings for childbirth. The center has two operating rooms equipped for cesarean section births and for emergency procedures. Rush has been designated by the state to serve as the regional center for a network of Chicago-area hospitals providing care to high-risk obstetrical and neonatal patients. General obstetrical and gynecologic services are provided by clinicians based at the Medical Center and throughout the greater Chicago area.

Specialized care is available for infertility, including in vitro fertilization. Counseling and medical care for women with high risk pregnancies, including women expecting multiple births and those with diabetes, heart problems and high blood pressure, is provided. Gynecologic cancer services offer the latest in chemotherapy, radiation and surgical treatments. Psychotherapeutic support is also available. Evaluation and treatment for problems such as incontinence including surgical and nonsurgical therapies is available. Counseling for patients with postpartum depression and their families is provided in cooperation with the Rush Institute for Mental Well-Being.

Rush also offers specialized treatment for HIV infection and complications caused by AIDS, kidney disorders, digestive disorders, blood disorders, neurological problems, and respiratory problems.

Other special facilities include the Liver Intensive Care Unit, the Rush Comprehensive Functional Assessment Program for adults 60 and older, and the Rush Poison Control Center.

MEDICAL SPECIALTIES

Adolescent Medicine, AIDS Medicine, Allergies, Arthritis, Cardiology, Cardiovascular Surgery, Dermatology, Dentistry and Oral Surgery, Emergency Medicine, Endocrinology, Gastroenterology, Geriatrics, Hematology, Infectious Diseases, Nephrology, Neurology, Neurosurgery, Nuclear Medicine, Obstetrics/Gynecology, Oncology, Ophthalmology, Orthopedics and Rehabilitation Medicine, Otolaryngology, Pediatrics, Psychiatry, Pulmonary and Intensive Care Medicine, Surgery, Transplantation Surgery, Urology, and Vascular Surgery.

WELL-KNOWN SPECIALISTS

- Dr. Philip D. Bonomi   *Medical oncology/hematology; specialist in breast and lung cancers*
- Dr. James L. Cavanaugh   *Psychiatry; specialist in forensic psychiatry*
- Dr. Maria R. Costanzo   *Cardiology; specialist in heart transplantation*
- Dr. Floyd A. Davis   *Neurology; specialist in adult infectious and demyelinating diseases*
- Dr. Ernest W. Fordham   *Nuclear medicine*
- Dr. Jorge O. Galante   *Orthopaedic surgery; specialist in reconstructive surgery*
- Dr. Steven Gitelis   *Orthopaedic surgery; specialist in tumor surgery*
- Dr. Christopher G. Goetz   *Neurology; specialist in adult movement disorders*
- Dr. Harold A. Kessler   *Infectious disease; specialist in AIDS and herpes virus infections*
- Dr. Stephen Korbet   *Nephrology; specialist in dialysis*
- Dr. Laurence A. Levine   *Urology; specialist in impotence*
- Dr. Howard B. Levy   *Pediatrics; specialist in abused children*
- Dr. Sara T. Lincoln   *Medical oncology/hematology; specialist in gynecologic cancer*
- Dr. Hassan Najafi   *Thoracic surgery; specialist in adult cardiothoracic surgery*
- Dr. Kirk H. Packo   *Ophthalmology; specialist in vitreo-retinal surgery*
- Dr. Harvey D. Preisler   *Medical oncology/hematology; specialist in leukemia*
- Dr. Jeffrey B. Robin   *Ophthalmology; specialist in corneal diseases and transplantation*
- Dr. Will Ryan   *Endocrinology and metabolism; specialist in Paget's disease*
- Dr. Thomas J. Schnitzer   *Rheumatology; specialist in osteoarthritis*
- Dr. George D. Wilbanks   *Obstetrics/gynecology; specialist in gynecologic oncology*

PATIENT SATISFACTION

According to a recent survey, patient satisfaction with Rush is high. This hospital survey reported that 90% of former patients rated the overall quality of nursing care as good or very good; 90% also gave a good/very good rating to the quality of their physician care. Ninety-five percent said they would recommend the center to their family and friends.

RESEARCH

For the period of July 1993 - June 1994, Rush received $30,317,098 in grant and foundation money to fund research. The top five areas that received the most grant and foundation money are: Internal Medicine, Neurological Sciences, Psychiatry, the Center for Research on Health and Aging, and the Rush Alzheimer's Disease Center.

At Rush, Dr. Denis A. Evans, a nationally known expert on Alzheimer's disease, is leading research on the epidemiology of the disease, with particular attention to the progress of the disease in individual cases. He collaborates with 15 researchers whose specialties include neurology, psychiatry, and biostatistics. A $1 million grant was recently awarded to Dr. Evans and his co-researchers by the National Institute on Aging. Under this grant, they will investigate differing rates of cognitive decline among Alzheimer's patients by assessing their mental functions at yearly intervals. By testing 350 patients, Dr. Evans hopes to identify factors, such as age or education level, that may influence the rate of cognitive decline.

Rush neurologist Dr. Cynthia L. Comella is looking for ways to prevent sleep disorders associated with Parkinson's disease. In an effort to prevent these disorders, she is studying the sleep patterns of patients who agree to spend two nights in a sleep laboratory. In addition to sleep problems, 30% of these patients suffer from daytime hallucinations. Her research has led her to the conclusion that by identifying distinct types of sleep patterns, scientists may develop strategies to block or prevent these hallucinations.

Rush cardiologists are investigating a nonsurgical technique to remove scar tissue left by heart attacks. This tissue can trigger irregular heart rhythms—a common problem called ventricular tachycardia, which can, in turn, lead to sudden death. During the procedure, called catheter ablation, a thin tube tipped with an electric probe is threaded up through a patient's artery to the heart, where the scar tissue is burned away with a charge of electricity. Catheter ablation is standard for treating irregular heart rhythms caused by a congenital defect. Rush cardiologist Raman L. Mitra, M.D., Ph.D., was the first to perform it on people with ventricular tachycardia as a result of heart attack. Five such patients have had the procedure at Rush so far, the first of whom was symptom-free 14 months after the ablation. The only alternatives to catheter ablation are open-heart surgery or a device called a defibrillator, which is implanted in a patient's chest to regulate the heart beat.

ADMISSIONS POLICY

Patients can be admitted only if their physician is on staff. To obtain an appointment with a Rush physician, patients may call for a referral at (312) 942-5555.

Admitting needs to know what benefits the patient has. If the patient is not insured, admitting assists him/her in applying for public aid. In certain situations, a patient can be treated on a charity care basis. In fiscal year 1994, $15 million in indigent care was provided.

The special phone number for admissions information is (312) 942-5700.

PATIENT/FAMILY ACCOMMODATIONS

The Inn at University Village serves as the medical center's 113-room guest house on campus. The Inn offers patients and their families rooms at $63 per night versus the regular rates of $145 for a single and $155 for a double. Call (312) 243-7200 for information and reservations.

UNIVERSITY OF

CHICAGO MEDICAL

CENTER

To measure the distinction of the University of Chicago Hospitals, one need just consider that 11 of the 63 Nobel Prize winners from the University of Chicago were faculty members or former students at the Medical Center. Furthermore, University of Chicago faculty have dominated research in certain areas, among them the relationship between cancer and hormones; diabetes and insulin production; gastroenterology; and evolutionary biology. The University has also made major contributions in transplantation, infectious diseases, heart disease, pharmacology, and sleep research.

The University of Chicago Medical Center is more than a great research center, however. Forty-eight of its physicians are listed in *The Best Doctors in America*—more than any other Illinois hospital. The scope, quality, and accessibility of its patient services also make it a vital medical resource for Chicago-area people and others. The hub of patient care lies in the University of Chicago Hospitals, an 865-bed modern medical center consisting of 20 buildings with more than 12 miles of corridors and 20 acres of space for research, based in Hyde Park, on the campus of the University of Chicago. The hospitals include Bernard Mitchell Hospital, the primary adult patient care facility; Wyler Children's Hospital; Chicago Lying-in Hospital, a maternity and women's hospital; Weiss Memorial Hospital, a 225-bed acute

TO MEASURE THE DISTINCTION OF THE UNIVERSITY OF CHICAGO HOSPITALS, ONE NEED JUST CONSIDER THAT 11 OF THE 63 NOBEL PRIZE WINNERS FROM THE UNIVERSITY OF CHICAGO WERE FACULTY MEMBERS OR FORMER STUDENTS AT THE MEDICAL CENTER.

care hospital on Chicago's North Side; and more than 125 specialty clinics. The hospitals comprise a tertiary care facility and also are a major provider of primary care to Chicago's South Side.

In 1993, about 40% of UCH inpatients came from outside the hospital's South Side primary serving area. About 12% came from outside the Chicago metro area, and about 3% from distant states or foreign countries, particularly for the transplant, cancer, neurosurgery and genito-intestinal programs. UCMC has received a delegation from Byelorussia in connection with pediatric cancer cases resulting from the Chernobyl nuclear incident and has provided care to several victims of the Bosnian war.

SPECIAL FACILITIES AND PROGRAMS

The University of Chicago Hospitals form the clinical arm of the University of Chicago Division of Biological Sciences. Only a few departments are highlighted here.

The hospitals offer transplantation programs in several areas. The liver transplantation program is one of the largest in the country and is a leader in innovative procedures for transplantation in small children. The hospitals also transplant kidney, pancreas, bone marrow, bone, and other tissues and conduct research in transplant immunology. In fiscal 1994, over 150 organ transplants and 125 bone marrow transplants were performed.

A National Cancer Institute clinical center since 1973, the University of Chicago Medical Center is one of six NCI sponsored "phase-I" centers in the U.S. for clinical trials of new anti-cancer drugs. Chicago has particular expertise in the study and treatment of leukemia, lymphoma, lung cancer, breast cancer, gastrointestinal cancer, head and neck cancer, genito-urinary cancers, sarcomas and melanomas. Other expertise exists in cancer cytogenetics and molecular biology; immunotherapies including use of interferons, interleukins and growth factors; high-dose chemotherapy with autologous bone marrow transplantation for breast cancer; and the medical and surgical treatment of

AT A GLANCE

Beds: 665
Occupancy Rate: 78%
Average Patient Count: 519
Average Patient Stay: 7.3 days
Annual Admissions: 32,000
Births: 3,500
Outpatient Clinic Visits:
    492,000
Emergency Department
    Visits: 81,000

HOSPITAL PERSONNEL
Physicians: 596
    Board Certified: 483
Residents: 620
Registered Nurses: 961

ROOM CHARGES (PER DIEM)
Private: $795
Semiprivate: $750
ICU: $1,615

ADDRESS
5841 S. Maryland Avenue
Chicago, IL 60637

TELEPHONE
(312) 702-1000

bone cancers, limb-salvage surgery for osteosarcoma, and complex joint replacement.

The University of Chicago Hospitals are also leaders in development of techniques for interventional cardiology, particularly for valvuloplasty, new angioplasty techniques, and rotoblator for clogged coronary arteries. Modern echocardiographic techniques for the evaluation of heart disease, such as contrast echocardiography and nuclear angiography, are also available. Chicago physicians are also experts in the diagnosis and treatment of arrhythmias.

In endocrinology, Chicago is one of seven NIH Diabetes Research and Training Centers in the U.S. and its doctors have an in-depth understanding of the treatment of Cushing's disease, hirsutism, polycystic ovary syndrome, pediatric endocrine disorders, thyroid disorders, and osteoporosis. The medical center is also one of five NIH sponsored Clinical Nutrition Research Units for the treatment of complicated nutritional problems, such as inflammatory bowel disease. The Joseph B. Kirsner Center for Digestive Diseases offers expertise in the diagnosis and treatment for the full range of gastrointestinal disorders.

Chicago has had a strong reputation in neurology for many years. Today, programs cover the full range of neurological disorders, including autoimmune disease, ALS, brain tumors, dementia, epilepsy, and myasthenia gravis. Chicago physicians have been pioneers in the treatment of multiple sclerosis, particularly beta-interferon therapy.

As is often the case at major medical centers, the strengths of Chicago's other departments are reflected in pediatrics.

Wyler Children's Hospital is a tertiary-care teaching hospital and a major referral center operating 149 beds. Wyler annually admits nearly 4,000 patients from the Chicago area, the Midwest, and around the world. Nearly 50,000 visits a year are handled through outpatient clinics and the emergency room.

The pediatric liver transplantation program is the second-largest in the country and was the first living-donor program in the world. In 1993, Wyler performed the first liver transplant from an unrelated living donor. Wyler has performed more bone marrow transplants in children than any other center in Illinois.

The cancer program at Wyler offers every available form of therapy, both conventional and investigational, for a child afflicted with cancer. The program is a principal member of the Children's Cancer Study Group, an international consortium of cancer research hospitals that participate in trials and exchange information on the latest advances in diagnosis and treatment.

The Frankel Pediatric Intensive Care Unit at Wyler has a 22-bed facility for treating children with multiple traumas; complex medical problems, including cardiac and neurosurgery; renal failure; and transplants. In addition, a 45-bassinet neonatal intensive care unit provides premature and critically ill infants with advanced medical care and life support systems. As a pediatric level-I trauma center—one of only three in the city—Wyler receives more than 500 children with severe injuries each year.

The Bernard Mitchell Hospital is one of the most technologically advanced inpatient structures in the country. It includes the Arthur Rubloff Intensive Care Tower, which houses the University of Chicago Hospitals Burn and Electrical Trauma Units as well as intensive care units for transplantation, neurosurgery, and cardiac and general surgery patients.

Chicago Lying-in Hospital, with quarters within the Mitchell Hospital, includes one of the country's most advanced newborn intensive-care units, as well as state-of-the-art obstetrical and gynecological facilities and a leading program in endocrinology and infertility. The Regional Perinatal Network provides 11 area hospitals with consultation and transport services for 18,000 births, more than one-third of them considered high-risk, per year. The network is committed to reducing fetal and infant mortality throughout the surrounding urban, suburban, and rural communities, covering nearly 3,200 square miles.

MEDICAL SPECIALTIES

Allergy, Anesthesiology, Cancer, Cardiac Surgery, Cardiology, Dentistry, Dermatology, Emergency Medicine, Endocrinology, Gastroenterology, Genetics and Genetic Counseling, Geriatrics, Hematology/Oncology, Infectious Diseases, Internal Medicine, Neonatology, Nephrology, Neurology, Neurosurgery, Obstetrics/ Gynecology, Ophthalmology, Organ Transplantation, Orthopedics, Otolaryngology, Pathology, Pediatrics, Plastic and Reconstructive Surgery, Psychiatry, Pulmonary Medicine, Radiology, Rheumatology, Surgery, Thoracic Surgery, Transplantation Surgery, Trauma, Urology, and Vascular Surgery.

WELL-KNOWN SPECIALISTS

- Dr. Dana K. Anderson   *Surgery; specialist in general surgery, endocrine surgery*
- Dr. Barry G. W. Arnason   *Neurology; specialist in infectious and demyelinating diseases, especially multiple sclerosis*
- Dr. Alfred L. Baker   *Specialist in gastroenterology, especially liver disease*
- Dr. George Edward Block   *Specialist in gastroenterologic surgery, especially for gastrointestinal cancers*
- Dr. Christine Cassel   *General internal medicine; specialist in geriatric medicine and medical ethics*
- Dr. Leslie DeGroot   *Medicine and radiology; specialist in endocrinology and metabolism, especially diseases of the thyroid*
- Dr. Bruce L. Gewertz   *Surgery; specialist in vascular surgery*
- Dr. Harvey M. Golomb   *Hematology/oncology; specialist in medical oncology, especially leukemia and lung cancer*
- Dr. Samuel Hellman   *Oncology; specialist in radiation oncology, Hodgkin's disease and breast cancer*

- Dr. Arthur L. Herbst   *Obstetrics and gynecology; specialist in gynecologic oncology, especially cervical and ovarian cancers*
- Dr. Peter R. Huttenlocher   *Specialist in pediatric neurology, child development*
- Dr. F. Leonard Johnson   *Pediatric; specialist in pediatric hematology/oncology*
- Dr. Kwang Sun Lee   *Specialist in neonatal-perinatal medicine*
- Dr. Bennett Leventhal   *Psychiatry; specialist in child and adolescent psychiatry, especially autism*
- Dr. Kenneth Polonsky   *Specialist in endocrinology, especially diabetes*
- Dr. Mark Jeffrey Ratain   *Clinical pharmacology; specialist in medical oncology/hematology, clinical pharmacology, especially analysis of new anti-cancer drugs*
- Dr. Samuel Refetoff   *Specialist in endocrinology, especially diseases of the thyroid*
- Dr. Richard L. Schilsky   *Director of the University of Chicago Cancer Research Center; specialist in medical oncology/hematology, especially clinical pharmacology*
- Dr. Everett E. Vokes   *Specialist in medical oncology/hematology, especially head and neck, lung and brain cancers*
- Dr. Bryce K. A. Weir   *Neurological surgery; specialist in vascular neurological surgery*
- Dr. David James Wilber   *Specialist in cardiovascular disease, especially cardiac electrophysiology*
- Dr. Stephanie Williams   *Specialist in medical oncology/hematology, especially high-dose chemotherapy and autologous bone marrow transplantation for breast cancer*

PATIENT SATISFACTION

The University of Chicago Hospitals have long been leaders in patient satisfaction analysis. The hospitals have worked closely with both the Picker Institute and the University Hospitals Consortium to develop, refine, and test accurate methods of measuring satisfaction, comparing the results obtained from different hospitals, and using these findings to improve patient care.

For example, although the initial Picker survey, completed in 1990, found that the hospitals had the highest overall satisfaction rating of any of the 17 academic hospitals surveyed, the hospitals did not score as well as some others on pain control. After comparing their responses with other institutions, the UCH pain-control team found that hospitals with better pain ratings used patient-controlled analgesia more frequently. The team quickly increased their supply of PCA pumps; a short time later an internal survey showed that patients were far more satisfied and a subsequent survey by the University Hospitals Consortium found that the hospitals had one of the better pain-control scores.

Data on inpatient satisfaction from the most recent surveys is kept confidential to encourage the spread of more candid surveying techniques and information sharing between hospitals. However, outpatient responses are available and UCH patients have expressed a high degree of satisfaction with their care here.

More than 95% of patients reported that they were satisfied with their care at the University of Chicago Hospitals and that they would recommend the Hospitals to a friend.

RESEARCH

The University of Chicago received $116 million in research funding in 1993. Major areas of research include cancer, heart disease, GI tract diseases, endocrinology, neuroscience, and immunology. Chicago physicians have a long history of research accomplishments extending back to the early 1900s. These efforts are greatly aided by the close involvement of the Pritzker School of Medicine. Over 90% of the students at Pritzker engage in research prior to completing their M.D. degree, and nearly 20% pursue combined M.D./Ph.D. degrees. Nearly 30% of the graduates become faculty members, a higher percentage than in any other university.

Current areas of clinical research that are particularly exciting include:

1. Development of new anti-cancer drugs. In 1990, the National Cancer Institute selected the University of Chicago Cancer Research Center as one of only six research centers in the United States to win a coveted phase-I contract to carry out National Cancer Institute-sponsored clinical trials of new anti-cancer drugs. In 1994, the University of Chicago Cancer Research Center also secured one of six cooperative agreements with the NCI to conduct phase-II clinical trials of these new drugs. These phase-I and phase-II trials are the first steps in the evaluation of promising new medications. This research program has concentrates on treatment of refractory solid tumors—cancers of the breast, lung, prostate, colon, kidney, brain or head, and neck that do not readily respond to standard therapies.

2. Transplantation. The University of Chicago remains the country's leading center in the use of living donors for liver transplantation. The use of living donors has become the treatment of choice for pediatric patients and the technique is being evaluated for use in adults. Researchers at the University are also in the forefront of fields such as pancreatic transplantation, research in the use of pancreatic islets for transplantation, and investigation of new forms of regulating the immune response to transplanted tissue.

3. Diabetes. Researchers at the University of Chicago continue to make valuable contributions to the understanding and treatment of diabetes, leading the search for defective genes associated with the different forms of diabetes, and shedding light on the production, secretion, and functioning of insulin. The medical center includes one of seven National Institutes of Health Diabetes Research and Training Centers in the United States.

4. Cardiology. Researchers at the University of Chicago Medical Center have been pioneers in research in areas such as heart-muscle biology, gene therapy, and interventional techniques such as valvuloplasty and rotablation. They are leaders in the understanding and treatment of heart-rhythm disorders and in

the study of lipoprotein (a), a common but poorly understood form of cholesterol that can predispose patients to coronary artery disease.

5. Gastroenterology. The university has just opened a new center for the clinical and basic study of inflammatory bowel disease—concentrating on genetics, immunology, and novel therapeutic approaches. This is the largest such center in the world. Among the subjects studied by the Center's GI researchers are genetic markers for a predisposition for colon cancer; the absorption and metabolism of calcium, vitamin D, and trace minerals and their relationship to human diseases; and the prevention of fibrosis that leads to scarring and cirrhosis of the liver.

ADMISSIONS POLICY

Admission is through a doctor on staff. Prospective patients can also be admitted through the emergency room or through one of the many specialty or regional clinics. Admissions information can be obtained by calling (312) 702-6233.

Financial arrangements are made on a case-by-case basis. For patients without the means to pay, the hospital will seek to arrange state or federal benefits.

Uncompensated care, including charity care, bad debts and costs exceeding reimbursement for Medicaid patients, is about $90 million.

UNIVERSITY OF

ILLINOIS HOSPITAL

AND CLINICS

The University of Illinois Hospital is the largest academic health center, and part of the largest health sciences center, in the world. Its resources include a 400-plus bed facility with access to more than 45 specialty outpatient offices. UIH&C's eight-story hospital is one of the newest and best equipped in the Midwest and is the focal point of the University of Illinois at Chicago Health Sciences Center. The University of Illinois Hospital and Clinics provide the full spectrum of advanced health care services at one facility located on the near west side of Chicago.

The University of Illinois Hospital opened its doors as a 50-bed facility in 1925. The current building opened in 1980 at the cost of $60 million and replaced the 55-year-old original hospital. In the 1980s, as did most inner city hospitals, UIH experienced a financial crisis. While the poor had traditionally constituted the hospital and its traditional patient base, nobody worried about their ability to pay their bills as long as virtually the entire hospital's budget was covered by the state. During the early and mid-1980s, the state reduced its financial support, and Medicare started limiting its payments. By 1987, a quarter of its patients having no way to pay their bills, the hospital had to absorb $33 million in unreimbursed care costs, more than twice what it received in state subsidies. This created a crisis that threatened the survival of the hospital. However, in 1989 the

UNIVERSITY OF ILLINOIS AT CHICAGO HEALTH SCIENCES CENTER

CHICAGO, ILLINOIS

THE UNIVERSITY OF ILLINOIS HOSPITAL IS THE LARGEST ACADEMIC HEALTH CENTER, AND PART OF THE LARGEST HEALTH SCIENCES CENTER, IN THE WORLD.

Illinois Legislature voted additional annual subsidies and took additional steps to insure the hospital's future.

Today, the University of Illinois Hospital and Clinics is recognized as a leader in health care in the United States. *U.S. News & World Report* ranked University of Illinois Hospital in the top 3% of the nation's 1488 academic medical centers in 10 of the 16 medical specialties surveyed. In a survey of Chicago doctors and nurses published in the January 1993 issue of *Chicago* magazine, the UIC Health Sciences Center was listed as one of seven centers of health care excellence in the Chicago area. The hospital is a referral center for thousands of seriously ill patients from the Midwest, the United States, and overseas. Its outpatient specialty clinics concentrate on medical areas including pain control, sickle cell anemia, arthritis, teen obstetrics, diabetes, nutrition, rehabilitation, and women's health. Throughout the hospital are several specialized intensive care units where highly trained staff use some of the most advanced medical equipment available to care for surgery patients, respiratory and critical care patients, heart attack patients, critically ill children, premature babies, and transplant recipients.

The hospital and clinics are staffed by faculty members of the University of Illinois College of Medicine. Many are recognized by their peers as leaders in their specialties. Each year, the hospital is a training site for more than 800 resident physicians. The hospital and medical staff also rely on the professors and resources in four other UI colleges—Nursing, Pharmacy, Dentistry and Associated Health professions—to handle the most complex and difficult medical cases. This allows UIHC to offer a broad range of state-of-the-art diagnostic and therapeutic services in each of 19 clinical departments.

SPECIAL FACILITIES AND PROGRAMS

The Department of Neurosurgery, under the direction of world-renowned Dr. James Ausman, treats a full spectrum of neurosurgical problems. The department specializes in providing treatment for complex diseases involving the nervous system, such as cerebral aneurysms, including giant and posterior circulation aneurysms and arteriovenous malformations (AVMs). A LINEAC radiosurgical unit is available to treat AVMs and selected tumors. Brain tumors of all types (e.g., skull base tumors, pituitary tumors and acoustic neuromas) are also treated. Stereotactic and endoscopic surgery are available as well. Complex spine surgery, peripheral nerve surgery, epilepsy surgery, and stroke surgery are additional areas of special interest.

The transplantation program of the University of Illinois Hospital transplants kidneys, pancreas and livers. The program coordinates the collaborative efforts of a multidisciplinary team consisting of surgeons, transplant physicians, and clinical nurse specialists. Support staff includes a psychologist, a social worker, a patient services representative, a nutritionist, and a clinical pharmacologist, as well as transplant nurses, residents and fellows. UIH performs 21% of all kidney transplants in the state, completing its 1,000th procedure in 1992. Its survival rates are exemplary—100% survival on kidney transplants from a living related donor after two years and 93% on graft cadaver procedures. Transplantation surgery is conducted in a modern dedicated transplant unit that provides intensive care and sophisticated technological support to transplant recipients.

In cardiology, UIH manages patients with all types of diseases affecting the cardiovascular system. A full range of services in diagnostic, interventional and preventive cardiology is provided. UIH physicians are recognized by the National Institutes of Health as leaders in the treatment of advanced cardiovascular diseases. Special services include exercise testing, noninvasive imaging, Ultrafast computed tomography to detect calcium in coronary arteries, electrophysiology, cardiac catheterization, and outpatient consultation.

Special clinical programs in cancer care include the NCI-sponsored minority-based Community Clinical Oncology Program and multi-clinical NCI trials on cancer prevention and treatment. UIH is also an NCI-designated National Breast Cancer Prevention Trial study center.

The University of Illinois Hospital offers nationally-recognized diagnostic and therapeutic services in endocrinology and metabolism for patients with diabetes, thyroid disorders, osteoporosis, hirsutism, lipid disorders and other diseases of the endocrine glands. Programs include comprehensive management of patients with diseases of the pituitary, adrenals, and parathyroid, as well as fine needle aspiration of the thyroid. Additional areas of special interest are neuroendocrinology and the effects of radiation on the endocrine glands.

UIH is also noted for its practice in gastroenterology. Services include a hepatic transplant program, the Digestive Disease and Liver Center, and a Gallstone Center. An outpatient clinic evaluates patients with gallstones, acute and chronic hepatitis, anal incontinence, inflammatory bowel nutritional disorders, and swallowing problems. Specialized endoscopic procedures are performed in the GI laboratory.

In rheumatology, treatment is provided for the full spectrum of rheumatic diseases, including arthritis

AT A GLANCE

Beds: 424
Occupancy Rate: 74%
Average Patient Count: 309
Average Patient Stay: 6.4 days
Annual Admissions: 17,444
Births: 3,649
Outpatient Clinic Visits:
 341,418
Emergency Room/Trauma
 Center Visits: 45,255

HOSPITAL PERSONNEL
Physicians: 700
 Board Certified: 558
Residents: 849
Registered Nurses: 855
 BS Degree: 415

ROOM CHARGES (PER DIEM)
Private: $610
Semiprivate: $570
ICU: $1,210

ADDRESS
1740 West Taylor Street
Chicago, IL 60612

TELEPHONE
(312) 996-7000

and allied conditions as well as disorders of connective tissue. UIH physicians have special expertise in the areas of rheumatoid arthritis; osteoarthritis; rheumatic disease in the geriatric patient; systemic lupus erythematosus; other diffusive connective diseases, such as scleroderma, dermato (poly) myostis and arthritis, fibromyalgia, and various forms of soft-tissue rheumatism; and osteoporosis.

UIH&C also includes the internationally recognized Eye and Ear Infirmary, which provides specialized inpatient and outpatient care, including an Eye Trauma Center. Physicians at the Eye Center offer care based on 11 subspecialties, treating retinal disease, corneal disease, and pediatric eye conditions.

The Department of Respiratory and Critical Care Medicine diagnoses and treats patients with diseases of the lung and other respiratory disorders as well as patients that require critical care in the intensive care setting. Among the conditions treated are difficult asthma, severe COPD, interstitial lung disease, problematic tuberculosis, and respiratory failure. A major area of special interest and recognized expertise are sleep disorders such as apnea and other sleep-related respiratory diseases. Among the other services offered are the Asthma Center, the Pulmonary Function Laboratory, the Fiber Optic Bronchoscopy Laboratory, the Pulmonary Rehabilitation Program, the Sleep and Ventilatory Disorders Center, and the Pulmonary Center.

AIDS research and care is a major focus of specialists in infectious diseases. Research concentrates on AIDS-related opportunistic infections, tuberculosis, toxoplasmosis, and human host-defense mechanism.

The department of Otolaryngology provides a complete range of nationally recognized services, including otology/neurotology, head and neck surgery for benign conditions as well as for head and neck cancer, facial plastic and reconstructive surgery, nasal and sinus surgery, pediatric otolaryngology, laryngology and voice disorders, speech pathology, audiology, and hearing aid dispensing. In addition, the department has a cochlear implant program.

Specialists in Urology at UIH provide diagnosis and treatment of all forms of urologic disease. The department of Urology has well-known expertise in urologic cancers, female urology, male infertility, stone disease and urologic microsurgery.

Pediatric services range from general and emergency care to a full range of subspecialty pediatric care for infants, children, and adolescents in both outpatient and inpatient settings. Neonatal and pediatric intensive care are also available. UIH is a designated perinatal center. The Neonatal Intensive Care unit is equipped with advanced technology and provides care for extremely small babies born to high-risk mothers. It has facilities for mechanical ventilation, pediatric cardiology, pediatric surgery, cardiac surgery, endocrinology, genetics and hematology/oncology, to name a few. The Neonatology service is recognized both nationally and internationally for its clinical support, advanced technology, and research.

MEDICAL SPECIALTIES

Allergy, Anesthesiology, Cancer Care, Cardiology, Dentistry, Dermatology, Emergency Medicine, Endocrinology, Environmental and Occupational Medicine, Family Practice, Gastroenterology, General Internal Medicine, Geriatric Medicine, Hematology, Infectious Disease, Medical Oncology, Nephrology, Neurology, Neurosurgery, Obstetrics/Gynecology, Ophthalmology, Orthopedics, Otolaryngology, Pathology, Pediatrics, Physical Medicine and Rehabilitation, Psychiatry, Radiology, Respiratory and Critical Care Medicine, Rheumatology, Surgery and Urology.

WELL-KNOWN SPECIALISTS

- Dr. Herand Abcarian   *Surgery and surgical oncology; specialist in colon and rectal cancer*
- Dr. Carlos Beckerman   *General nuclear medicine*
- Dr. Barbara Kay Burton   *Pediatrics; specialist in metabolic diseases*
- Dr. John Chandler   *ophthalmology; Specialist in corneal diseases and transplantation*
- Dr. Ira Chasnoff   *Neonatal-perinatal medicine*
- Dr. Gerald Fishman   *Ophthalmology; specialist in ophthalmic genetics*
- Dr. Cathy Helgason   *Neurology; specialist in stroke treatment*
- Dr. Songya Pang   *Pediatrics; specialist in pediatric endocrinology*
- Dr. Allen Putterman   *Ophthamology; specialist in oculoplastic and orbital surgery*
- Dr. Kenneth Rich   *Allergy and immunodeficiency*
- Dr. Joyce Schild   *Otolaryngology; specialist in laryngology and pediatric otolaryngology*
- Dr. Antonio Scommegna   *Obstetrics/gynecology; specialist in reproductive endocrinology*
- Dr. M. Eugene Tardy, Jr.   *Otolaryngology; specialist in facial plastic surgery*
- Dr. Robert Weinstein   *Infectious diseases; specialist in hospital-acquired infections*
- Dr. Alon Winnie   *Anesthesiology; specialist in pain management*
- Dr. Joyce Elizabeth Wise   *Pediatrics; specialist in pediatric endocrinology*

PATIENT SATISFACTION

Patients are surveyed across 30 satisfaction factors. UIH&C achieved a mean score of 6.1 across all factors, on a scale of 1 to 7. Ninety-six percent said they would return if further hospitalization were required; 95% would recommend UIH&C.

RESEARCH

For the 1993 fiscal year, the UIC College of Medicine received 358 grants totalling almost $30 million. More than half of these were awarded to clinical departments.

Major grants in excess of $1 million included the areas of cancer research, medicine, obstetrics and gynecology, ophthalmology, pediatrics and psychiatry.

A $46 million, 225,000-square-foot center for research in molecular biology is scheduled to open in 1995. The building will allow University of Illinois—Chicago to build on its already strong reputation in genetic research, which includes recombinant DNA and gene cloning. The center will accommodate 500 researchers and 50 faculty members in the areas of biology, chemistry, medicine, microbiology and immunology, pediatrics, surgery, ophthalmology, urology, and pharmacy.

The university's Neuropsychiatric Institute is undergoing a $12 million renovation. Built in 1941, the NPI was the first facility of its kind in North America devoted to the integrated study of the neurosciences, including neurology, neurosurgery, and psychiatry.

Among important recent accomplishments and studies conducted at UIC are the following:

UIH neurologists and neurosurgeons have devoted years of research to discovering new techniques for treating epilepsy, brain tumors, and other neurological disorders. Dr. Cathy Helgason, a neurologist and expert in the treatment of acute stroke, coordinates five national studies in stroke prevention and directs a major investigation of the potential of aspirin to prevent strokes.

Tapas Das Gupta, director of the specialized Cancer Center, has developed state-of-the-art surgical, chemotherapy, and immunotherapy techniques for the treatment of sarcoma and melanoma.

Renee Hartz, chief of cardiothoracic surgery, is studying why bypass surgeries cause more complications in women than in men.

ADMISSIONS POLICY

Over 50% of the UIH patient population comes from its clinic system. All other admissions are physician accepted via emergency room, transfers, or referrals.

Patients who have no third party coverage are asked for a deposit prior to or at the time of admission. If they cannot meet this amount, UIH submits paperwork for approval by the Chief of Staff (elective) and, for urgent or emergency care, the hospital attempts to apply for medical assistance from the Illinois Department of Public Aid. UIH does not have a policy for free care. However, as a state facility partially supported by state dollars, it meets the health care needs of its citizens.

More than $30 million of indigent care is provided annually.

The special phone number for admissions information is: (312) 996-0341.

INDIANA UNIVERSITY

MEDICAL CENTER

Located in downtown Indianapolis, Indiana University (IU) Medical Center consists of University Hospital & Outpatient Center, a highly specialized adult hospital; the James Whitcomb Riley Hospital for Children, the state's only comprehensive pediatric hospital; IU Health Care, primary care physician offices located throughout the metropolitan area; and IU School of Medicine, the state's only medical school. In addition, more than 90 outpatient clinics on campus diagnose and treat patients from every county in Indiana and beyond.

Since 1914, IU Medical Center has served as a major regional referral center for the treatment of complex health problems. University Hospital and Riley Hospital are respected and renowned as two of the nation's most sophisticated and specialized teaching hospital facilities. Some 75% of patients have complex illnesses, with multiple health problems in addition to their primary diagnosis. Specialized care, advanced technology, and superior clinical skills represent the character of IU Medical Center and its commitment to individualized, patient-centered care. IU School of Medicine, a part of IU Medical Center, educates two-thirds of all physicians in Indiana. Over 50 Medical Center physicians were recognized in the latest edition of *The Best Doctors in America*.

INDIANAPOLIS, INDIANA

UNIVERSITY HOSPITAL AND
RILEY HOSPITAL ARE
RESPECTED AND RENOWNED
AS TWO OF THE NATION'S
MOST SOPHISTICATED AND
SPECIALIZED TEACHING
HOSPITAL FACILITIES.

More than one-quarter of the beds at University and Riley hospitals are devoted to critical, intensive care, so neurology, cardiology, medical, surgical, pediatric, and burn patients can be continually and carefully monitored and appropriately treated in special state-of-the-art units.

During 1993, over 300,000 patients came to Indiana University Medical Center for diagnosis and treatment from every county in Indiana. The most recent data show that 94% of all patients came from Indiana; the other 6% from other states and countries.

Indiana University Medical Center was cited as having Medicare patient mortality rates significantly lower than predicted for 1988, 1989, and 1990, the most recent three years for which the government issued these statistics. Of the nearly 6,000 hospitals in the U.S. and its territories, only 59 had statistically significant lower than expected mortality rates in 1990. A 1992 *Wall Street Journal* article noted that IU Medical Center was the only hospital with significantly lower than expected mortality rates for all three years.

The Medical Television Network beams eight hours of programming weekly to 75 hospitals and health care facilities throughout Indiana. Educational outreach programs allow medical specialists to share valuable knowledge and teach important skills to physicians and nurses at other health care facilities and to private practitioners in Indiana. The Medical Center's presence is felt throughout the state and in many areas of the U.S. In return, patients are referred here from every Indiana county and beyond.

A study conducted by HCIA, Inc., a health care information company that provides information and analytical services, and Mercer Management Consultants identified IU Medical Center as one of the 100 best performing, general acute care hospitals in the country. Performance was assessed from a number of financial, efficiency, and clinical measures that reflect use of resources, provision of care, and quality of outcome, a balance that HCIA believes best measures the long-term stability of an institution. According to the report, "benchmark" hospitals not only provide high value to their customers, but also operate efficiently and invest in their facilities.

SPECIAL FACILITIES AND PROGRAMS

The James Whitcomb Riley Hospital for Children is the only comprehensive children's hospital in Indiana and a major referral center for infants, children, and adolescents from across Indiana and surrounding states. Riley operates one of the largest pediatric intensive care units anywhere; more than 700 critically ill infants are admitted each year to the hospital's newborn intensive care unit. Riley provides services not generally available in hospitals throughout the state for management of unusual, complex or therapeutic problems. Riley established the first "nurture center"—a special care unit for chronically ill infants—as well as the first inpatient units in the country where parents may stay with their children during hospitalization. Other special facilities include a pediatric burn center, the only one of its type in Indiana. Riley also is the only hospital in the state to provide pediatric renal dialysis, as well as an advanced technique called extracorporeal membrane oxygenation (ECMO), a support system that "breathes" for children with serious lung disorders so their lungs can heal.

Because of the number and variety of pediatric cancer patients cared for at Riley Hospital, a new pediatric bone marrow transplant unit is presently under construction. In addition, a new pediatric outpatient center, adjacent and connected to Riley Hospital, has been designed to better meet patient and parent needs, and will be constructed in the next two years.

In 1992, Indiana University Medical Center received a National Cancer Institute (NCI) grant to fund planning for a comprehensive cancer center on campus. This three-year grant marks the first step in IU Medical Center's efforts to become an NCI-designated comprehensive cancer center. A basic cancer research building as well as a patient treatment center are being built to centralize research projects relating to cancer, and to provide all outpatient cancer care in one location.

IU Medical Center completed construction of a high-technology imaging center housing nearly $7.5 million worth of equipment within University Hospital & Outpatient Center in 1993. This facility is the only one in Indiana which offers all high-tech modalities (PET, CT, MRI, etc.) in one location and it is one of only several in the United States. It includes Indiana's first and only Positron Emission Tomography (PET) system, whose effectiveness is strengthened by proximity to other modalities; a fully certified technician staff in ultrasound; two Magnetic Resonance Imaging (MRI) scanners; the latest generation of CT technology that offers faster service, better quality, and dyes with fewer side effects; and sophisticated breast imaging equipment.

The imaging center includes a patient-focused design that enables more than one procedure to be completed in a single day and a physical layout that facilitates staff collaboration and results in enhanced information sharing. One of IU Medical Center's MRIs has the largest bore in Indianapolis

AT A GLANCE

Beds: 692
  University Hospital: 428
  Riley Hospital: 264
Occupancy Rate: 72%
Average Patient Count: 500
Average Patient Stay: 7.7
  days
Births: 1,094
Annual Admissions: 20,700
Outpatient Clinic Visits:
  294,843
Emergency Room/Trauma
  Center Visits: 1,500

HOSPITAL PERSONNEL
Physicians: 698
  Board Certified: 620
Residents: 694
Registered Nurses: 955
  BS Degree: 105

ROOM CHARGES (PER DIEM)
University Hospital
Private: $359
Semiprivate: $338
ICU: $973
Riley Hospital
Private: $518
Semiprivate: $496
ICU: $1149–$1264

ADDRESS
1100 West Michigan Street
Indianapolis, IN 46223

TELEPHONE
University Hospital
(317) 274-4751
Riley Hospital
(317) 274-7793

for particularly obese patients, allows spectroscopy to investigate tumor bio-chemistry, and is uniquely used to image and evaluate silicone implant leakage and as a non-invasive alternative to angiography. Other MRI distinctions include faculty specifically trained in neuroradiology, and an orthopedic radiologist.

In 1993, IU Medical Center completed work on a proton beam therapy patient treatment room at the IU Cyclotron in Bloomington. This treatment room is one of only three nationwide. Because it can target treatment to a very precise site, proton beam therapy is more effective against tumors with minimal damage to surrounding healthy tissue. Consequently, proton beam therapy is very useful in treating certain tumors of the eye, brain, spinal cord, and pituitary gland in adults and children.

Indiana University Medical Center transplant teams perform more trans-plants than any other Indiana hospital, and IU Medical Center was the first in the state to perform a wide variety of procedures: kidney transplant, liver trans-plant, cornea transplant, bone marrow transplant, pancreas transplant, and in-fant and newborn heart transplants. IU Medical Center has been performing transplants for more than 30 years and performed more than 300 procedures in 1992 alone. The Medical Center now offers seven transplantation programs for adults and six for children.

Indiana University Medical Center meets the needs of bone marrow trans-plant patients with a dedicated 14-bed adult bone marrow transplantation unit in University Hospital & Outpatient Center. The adult bone marrow transplant program will be expanded in a new $20 million clinical cancer building sched-uled to open in 1994.

The pediatric bone marrow transplant program will be enhanced with ten dedicated beds in the privately funded $7.1 million Riley Children's Cancer Center, currently under construction. Dr. David Emanuel, nationally known for his work in preventing complications among bone marrow transplant patients, joined Riley Hospital earlier this year to direct this program.

The kidney programs at Indiana University Medical Center are designed to handle all forms of congenital and acquired renal disease. The comprehensive adult program includes special services for hypertension, metabolic stone dis-ease, renal failure, and end-stage renal disease, and hypertensive manifestations of systemic problems such as collagen vascular disease and diabetes. The pro-gram is well known for its innovative home dialysis services as well as more complex hospital-based dialysis programs. The pediatric program is the only pediatric renal-dialysis unit in Indiana, and handles all forms of childhood kidney disease and emphasizes home dialysis.

The Indiana Diabetes Center was developed to help patients successfully control and manage diabetes. The center provides expert medical care, as well as the latest information in diabetes care, assisting patients in coping with the complex tasks of managing diabetes day to day and assessing and treating complications when they develop. Patients also have access to the latest in diabetes research through close collaboration of the Indiana Diabetes Center with the Diabetes Research and Training Center, located at IU Medical Center. Opportunities for patients to participate in diabetes research projects and the latest in diabetes therapy and technology are available. The comprehensive diabetes care center is the only one in Indiana offering education, research, exercise, and obstetric and treatment programs for diabetes patients of all ages.

The IU Breast Care and Research Center, the first of its kind in Indiana, was established to help detect breast cancer, conduct research, and encourage collaboration among all breast care specialists with a multidisciplinary approach to diagnosis and treatment.

The IU-Wishard Trauma Center is a Level I trauma center, the first such certified facility in the state. It is particularly strong in burn care and pediatric care. Pediatric subspecialty care is provided in operating rooms (ORs) and intensive care units (ICUs) designed specially for children at Riley Hospital for Children. The center is staffed by a complete trauma team 24 hours a day. Three IU Medical Center faculty are dedicated to trauma. The EMS service based at Wishard Hospital (on the IU Medical Center campus) is staffed by ALS-certified personnel.

MEDICAL SPECIALTIES

Allergy and Immunology, Anesthesia, Arthritis, Bone Marrow Transplantation, Burn Treatment, Cancer, Cardiology and Cardiac Care, Cardiac Transplants, Child Psychiatry, Cerebral Palsy, Clinical Pharmacology, Corneal Transplants, Dentistry, Dermatology, Diabetes, Eating Disorders, Endocrinology, Epilepsy, Family Practice, Gastroenterology, Genetic Testing, Growth Anomalies, Heart Transplants, Hematology, Hemophilia, Internal Medicine, Infectious Diseases, Kidney Transplantation, Liver Transplants, Lung Transplants, Muscular Dystrophy, Myelomeningocele, Nephrology, Neurology, Obstetrics/Gynecology, Oncology, Ophthalmology, Orthopedics, Otolaryngology, Pathology, Psychiatry, Radiology, Surgery, and Urology.

WELL-KNOWN SPECIALISTS

- Dr. Deborah I. Allen   *Family medicine*
- Dr. Kenneth D. Brandt   *Rheumatology, osteoarthritis*
- Dr. D. Craig Brater   *Clinical pharmacology*
- Dr. John P. Donahue   *Urology; specialist in cancer of the genitourinary tract, renovascular hypertension and adrenal disease*
- Dr. Mark L. Dyken   *Neurology; special interest in cerebral vascular disease, strokes, and diagnostic problems in neurology; co-author of* Cerebrovascular Diseases, *a physician's reference*
- Dr. Lawrence Einhorn   *Medical oncology/hematology, lung cancer, testicular cancer; internationally renowned for work with genitourinary tumors*

- Dr. Harvey Feigenbaum   *Internal medicine and cardiovascular disease; expert in cardiology and echocardiology*
- Dr. Jay Grosfeld   *General and pediatric surgery, neonatal surgery, pediatric surgical oncology, and pediatric trauma*
- Dr. C. Conrad Johnston   *Internal medicine and endocrinology, metabolic bone disease, osteoporosis*
- Dr. Frederick B. Stehman   *Gynocologic oncology*
- Dr. David Williams   *Clinical care of children with immune system and blood disorders such as leukemia and aplastic anemia*
- Dr. Douglas P. Zipes   *Cardiology, cardiovascular disease, electrophysiology*

PATIENT SATISFACTION

To monitor the quality of its care from the patients' eyes, IUMC mails a survey to each discharged patient within 14 days of discharge. Among the key findings for 1993 are that 91% of the respondents rated University Hospital's physicians as "good" or "very good"; 90% of Riley Hospital's physicians fell into the same categories. The responses about the nursing care at both hospitals mirrored those on the doctors. An annual telephone survey is also conducted and recently 94% of those questioned said they would recommend University Hospital to friends and family and 98% would recommend Riley Hospital.

RESEARCH

Research funding at Indiana University Medical Center totaled $72,794,829 in 1993. Nearly 160 new and competing renewal grants were sponsored, and more than 637 active investigative and research studies were reported. In addition, IU Medical Center faculty were responsible for more than 1,300 publications last year.

One of the most important initiatives underway is research by physicians at the Krannert Institute of Cardiology to prevent arterial restenosis. Researchers have pioneered two means of local drug delivery to coronary arteries, one using microparticle delivery and the other involving photodynamics. In both procedures, drugs are delivered directly to the injured artery site to stop heavy scarring of the smooth muscle wall following angioplasty. Once the microparticle and photodynamic therapies are approved for human use, they could become a standard treatment following angioplasties. In addition, they could be applied to the treatment of plaque-blocked peripheral arteries as well.

In addition, IU Medical Center cardiologists have been at the forefront of echocardiography since its inception. Over the last three decades, they have worked to perfect the technique, expand its applications, and instruct other physicians on it use through preceptorships, extensive publishing in medical texts and journals, and lectures throughout the world.

The IU School of Medicine established the world's first DNA bank to store tissue cells of individuals with inherited disorders for future research and diagnosis. IU Medical Center researchers with colleagues at Harvard were among the first to apply the DNA marker technique that launched the global search for the chromosomal location of defective genes. Research initiatives have uncovered the Huntington's disease gene; pinpointed the location of the aberrant genes in two types of familial Alzheimer's and nearly 40 other inherited disorders; identified 30 new genetic syndromes, including a rare kidney disorder that is often misdiagnosed; and are presently examining the genetic and biological bases of alcoholism.

Another IU Medical Center geneticist, Lei Yu, Ph.D., Associate Professor of Medical and Molecular Genetics, has performed important research in the area of pain control. Dr. Yu and his team successfully cloned the gene for one of three types of opiate receptors found on the surface of the brain and spinal cord cells.

In one of IU Medical Center's best-known contributions to medicine, Lawrence Einhorn, M.D., Distinguished Professor of Medicine, developed the protocol for treatment of testicular cancer. Dr. Einhorn's treatment regimen has turned a 90% mortality rate into a 90% cure rate. His innovative platinum drug combination became the first in the world to cure cancer where previous chemotherapy failed.

In a related innovation, John Donohue, M.D., Chairman of Urology, created a nerve-sparing surgical technique that permits continued function after removal of testicular and prostate cancers. Physicians from around the world are on a long waiting list to obtain fellowships to learn the procedures used at IU.

In pediatrics, IU Medical Center investigators contributed to research that virtually defeated childhood leukemia, and continue to develop services for children with learning disabilities, cranial facial anomalies, cerebral palsy, cancer, and heart and kidney disease. David Williams, M.D., Director of the Herman B. Wells Center for Pediatric Research and a researcher in the prestigious Howard Hughes Medical Institute, leads a team of scientists and clinicians fighting children's cancer and blood diseases, and investigating gene transfer therapy.

ADMISSIONS POLICY

Patients must be admitted to University Hospital or Riley Hospital for Children by a physician on the Indiana University Medical Center medical staff. The majority of the hospital's patients are referred by their physicians to IU Medical Center, although a growing percentage refer themselves to IU Medical Center physicians and clinics.

There are no financial requirements for admission. Most IU Medical Center physicians, as well as the hospitals, provide care to patients regardless of their ability to pay. IU Medical Center hospitals are state-owned. IU provided $3,801,232 in charity care during the fiscal year that ended June 30, 1993.

PATIENT/FAMILY ACCOMMODATIONS

Lodging for patients and family members is available at the University Place Conference Center and Hotel at a discounted rate of $59.

UNIVERSITY OF IOWA

HOSPITALS AND

CLINICS

IOWA CITY, IOWA

Americans living in rural areas have often found it difficult to obtain quality medical care beyond the primary level. Today continuing changes in the farm economy with the attendant drop in farm population—over a million people left between 1980 and 1990 alone—have joined forces with the recent changes in the way Medicare payments are dispersed to play havoc with the economic stability of hospitals throughout the farm belt region. As the hospital system is forced to restructure itself, the vital services offered by the major, heavily subsidized academic medical centers are bound to grow in importance.

The University of Iowa Hospitals and Clinics (UIHC) have long been the primary providers of secondary and tertiary care services in this region. Opened in 1870 as a clinical training area for the medical school, the first University Hospital was built in 1898; by 1914, it had 250 beds and a growing reputation. Today, University Hospital is the largest university-owned teaching hospital in the country, employing over 1,000 doctors in more than 100 specialties. Fifty-one of UIHC's physicians are listed in *The Best Doctors in America.*

TODAY, UNIVERSITY HOSPITAL IS THE LARGEST UNIVERSITY-OWNED TEACHING HOSPITAL IN THE COUNTRY, EMPLOYING OVER 1,000 DOCTORS IN MORE THAN 100 SPECIALTIES.

While there are only 200,000 people in Iowa City and nearby Cedar Rapids combined, the University of Iowa Hospitals and Clinics register close to half a million patients per year. Most come from Iowa and

Illinois, though there are patients here from almost every other state and from 20 countries outside the U.S.

SPECIAL FACILITIES AND PROGRAMS

During 1994, the University of Iowa Hospitals and Clinics celebrated 25 years of solid organ transplantation. From three corneal transplants performed in 1955-56, the transplantation programs have grown to national recognition. The hospitals perform over 500 organ and tissue transplants each year, with bone, bone marrow, and corneal transplants accounting for more than half of that total. UIHC's transplantation service has performed over 1,500 kidney transplants and more than 140 pancreas transplants. In the past year, transplant surgeons successfully performed 42 liver transplants and have plans to establish an Islet Cell Transplant program to treat diabetes. About 66 kidney transplants are conducted each year. The Bone Marrow Transplant Program holds special expertise in non-related donor transplants. Now in its 12th year, the program transplants healthy bone marrow into some 100 patients each year who come from all areas of the U.S. and overseas.

Iowa's Department of Otolaryngology is nationally known for its work with cochlear implants for restoring hearing. The hospital performed 28 such implants in 1993 alone. In addition, it is beginning to have success using multichannel implants to restore hearing for the profoundly deaf.

The John and Mary Pappajohn Clinical Cancer Center opened its doors in the winter of 1993 with 88 inpatient beds and an ambulatory clinic. Radiology, ultrasound, flouroscopy services, and a diagnostic mammography suite are all located within the center. The Cancer Center also includes hematology and cytology laboratories, as well as an oncology pharmacy and a chemotherapy suite with 19 private patient stations.

Several other new clinics were opened in 1993. The Asthma Clinic provides specialized consultation for patients with asthma who require steroids. The Primary Care General Medicine Clinic was opened to provide easy access to primary medical care.

AT A GLANCE

Beds: 891
Occupancy Rate: 78%
Average Patient Count: 649
Average Patient Stay: 7.5 days
Births: 1,573
Annual Admissions: 34,060
Outpatient Clinic Visits:
    466,429
Emergency Room/Trauma
    Center Visits: 23,342

HOSPITAL PERSONNEL
Physicians/Dentists: 597
Residents: 499
Fellows: 182
Registered Nurses: 1,562

ROOM CHARGES (PER DIEM):
Semiprivate: $192–$633
ICU: $497–$665

ADDRESS
200 Hawkins Drive
Iowa City, IA 52242-1009

TELEPHONE
(319) 356-1616

As the list below makes clear, every major specialty and subspecialty is practiced at the University of Iowa Hospitals and Clinics. Ophthalmology, for example, runs a statewide screening program for glaucoma and is also the leading referral center for corneal transplants (137 performed in 1992-93); Internal Medicine sponsors the Renal Dialysis Network which, through a network of hospitals around the state, administered almost 9,500 renal dialysis treatments last year; Genetics provides a complete range of diagnostic, therapeutic, and educational services through 15 regional clinics.

One of the most active departments in terms of statewide programs is pediatrics. Children with cancer, from all parts of Iowa, are given an examination and initial treatment, but most of them are then returned to their home communities for continued therapy. Physicians here are very active in the prenatal and neonatal fields; the Neonatal Intensive Care Unit is a 32-bassinet center annually treating over 500 critically ill infants from all parts of Iowa.

A new General Pediatrics Clinic provides an interdisciplinary approach for infants and children under age four who are referred to UIHC for "failure to thrive." Patients include children with weight less than the fifth percentile and others with growth concerns.

The University of Iowa Hospitals and Clinics is also home of the state's Poison Control Center and its most active Burn Center, where most of the major burn victims in Iowa are treated each year. The Emergency Treatment Center is Iowa's only comprehensive emergency treatment center. At the Iowa Psychiatric Hospital, which has 58 adult and 12 pediatric beds, more than 900 inpatients and 1,700 outpatients are treated annually, making it the largest such facility in the state.

MEDICAL SPECIALTIES

Anesthesiology, Dermatology, Family Practice, Hospital Dentistry, Internal Medicine, Neurology, Obstetrics/Gynecology, Ophthalmology, Orthopaedics, Otolaryngology-Head and Neck Surgery, Pathology, Pediatrics, Psychiatry, Radiology, Surgery, and Urology.

WELL-KNOWN SPECIALISTS

- Dr. Barrie Anderson   *Obstetrics and gynecology; cancer specialist*
- Dr. Nancy Andreasen   *Psychiatry*
- Dr. Antonio Damasio   *Specialist in human brain mapping*
- Dr. Hanna Damasio   *Specialist in human brain mapping*
- Dr. Bruce Gantz   *Otolaryngology; pioneer in cochlear implants*
- Dr. Ken Kimura   *Pediatric surgery; specialist in repairing inherited abnormalities of the esophagus and stomach*
- Dr. Maureen Martin   *Transplant surgery; specialist in kidney and liver transplantation*

- Dr. Arnold Menzes   *Neurosurgery; specialist in repairs to the craniovertebral junction*
- Dr. Michael Trigg   *Pediatric bone marrow transplantation*
- Dr. Richard Wenzel   *Epidemiology*
- Dr. Richard Williams   *Urology; cancer specialist*
- Dr. George Winokur   *Psychiatry; specialist in schizophrenia*

PATIENT SATISFACTION

The University of Iowa Hospitals and Clinics score exceptionally high in patient satisfaction. An extraordinary 99% of the respondents to UIHC's patient satisfaction questionnaire said they would return if in need of further health care services.

RESEARCH

The University of Iowa Hospitals and Clinics supports research projects of the University's College of Medicine and the other health science colleges. Those research endeavors totalled slightly more than $100 million in 1993.

More than 150 trials are under way at University Hospitals to determine the best methods for preventing and treating cancers. These projects range from the study of promising anti-tumor agents to bone marrow transplantation to new surgical and radiotherapy techniques.

The first large-scale preventive trial for prostate cancer began in 1993 at University Hospitals and 221 other sites across the U.S. In all, some 18,000 men aged 55 and older will participate in the Prostate Cancer Prevention Trial, a seven-year, $60 million intergroup study designed to test whether taking the drug finasteride will prevent prostate cancer.

A recently completed study at UIHC showed that the heart medication captopril delayed the need for dialysis and reduced the risk of death in diabetes patients with kidney disease. The significant findings gave physicians world-wide an effective way to manage kidney disease.

Cystic fibrosis patients will benefit from research currently underway at UIHC. Researchers are examining the transfer of healthy cells into the lungs through a virus injected into the nasal passages.

The UIHC participates with 16 other U.S. medical centers in the Women's Health Initiative—a $625 million National Institutes of Health study that will investigate how to prevent heart disease, cancer, and bone fractures, the major causes of poor health and death in women.

A five-year study of carotid arteries conducted at the UIHC and three other centers proved that both men and women with moderately elevated cholesterol and early hardening of the arteries can be safely treated with cholesterol-lowering medication and diet modification to slow atherosclerotic changes in the arteries.

The UIHC has a major role in the nation's first large-scale breast cancer prevention study along with 270 other sites in the United States and Canada.

The study will determine whether the drug tamoxifen prevents breast cancer in women who are at an increased risk for the disease.

In addition to these projects, important research is also being conducted on Alzheimer's disease, infant nutrition, and schizophrenia.

ADMISSIONS POLICY

Patients are admitted and/or transferred to the UIHC as follows:

Through the Emergency Treatment Center as an emergency patient—UIHC physicians evaluate an emergency patient and, if required, will admit the patient to the appropriate inpatient unit.

After evaluation in a UIHC clinic—a patient can be immediately admitted to the UIHC, or a determination can be made that a future admission is necessary, for which arrangements are made.

Direct admission—a UIHC physician can accept a patient for admission to the UIHC without a clinic or ETC evaluation. Also, the Internal Medicine Department allows referring physicians admitting privileges to the UIHC. (That is, an outside physician can refer a patient to the UIHC for admission without evaluation by a UIHC physician prior to admission.) The Department of Family Practice admits a patient to the UIHC without an evaluation by a UIHC physician prior to admission.

If a patient lacks insurance, this is usually identified by registration staff. The registration staff member will then query the patient to determine if they need assistance in applying for state or county aid. If the patient requests assistance, the registration staff member contacts Social Services and indicates what action or information is needed. Social Services then follows up with the patient. The State of Iowa provides health care to indigent residents through an appropriation to the University of Iowa Hospitals and Clinics. University Hospitals bills against that appropriation of state funds when care is provided to a resident of Iowa who has been certified by the resident's county to receive state supported care. Each year the hospital provides over $79 million of indigent care.

THE MENNINGER

FOUNDATION

"No greater illusion prevails than that mental illness is usually hopeless or has at best a bad outlook," wrote Dr. Karl Menninger. "Precisely the reverse is true. Most of its victims recover."

The Menninger Foundation was established in 1925 when Dr. Charles Menninger and his two sons, Drs. Karl and Will Menninger, bought 20 acres of land on the outskirts of Topeka and remodeled an existing farmhouse to serve as a 13-bed psychiatric hospital. Although it was not the first psychiatric hospital in the United States, it was the first to use a "total environment" approach involving a family atmosphere, physical exercise and a team of multidisciplinary doctors. "Often called 'The Mayo Clinic of psychiatric hospitals,' The Menninger Foundation is regarded as one of the major psychiatric treatment and teaching facilities in the world," according to *The New York Times*. More than 100,000 patients have been seen at The Menninger Foundation over the past 58 years.

The Menninger Foundation is a national mental health center for the diagnosis and treatment of severe mental illness; a major source for the education of mental health professionals; a research center for the development of basic knowledge about human behavior; and a pioneer in the prevention of mental illness, particularly in business and industry.

TOPEKA, KANSAS

"OFTEN CALLED 'THE MAYO CLINIC OF PSYCHIATRIC HOSPITALS,' THE MENNINGER FOUNDATION IS REGARDED AS ONE OF THE MAJOR PSYCHIATRIC TREATMENT AND TEACHING FACILITIES IN THE WORLD," ACCORDING TO *THE NEW YORK TIMES.*

Management consultants Boox Allen & Hamilton reported at the time of the first edition of this book on two important findings. First, The Menninger Foundation is regarded by professionals and lay public alike as an institution of high quality and innovation. Second, no other institution offers the breadth of services available there in treatment, education, research and prevention. We do not believe that this has changed in the interim.

The Menninger Foundation is an internationally recognized training center for mental health professionals. More than 170 active faculty members work with students in many disciplines. "We like to think (our students) have learned what limits to place on their expectation .... But their hope should remain unextinguished and inextinguishable. They should believe steadfastly that there is no patient for whom something helpful cannot be done," wrote Dr. Karl Menninger in *The Vital Balance*.

The Karl Menninger School of Psychiatry trains physicians in general and child psychiatry. The school offers postdoctoral training in clinical psychology; post-master's training in psychiatric social work; and training for clergy focusing on marriage and family counseling. The Topeka Institute for Psychoanalysis provides training in psychoanalysis.

In the past 60 years, The Menninger Foundation has demonstrated that timely and skillful therapeutic intervention in the lives of troubled patients, in an atmosphere of optimistic expectation and caring, can lead to improved health.

Today, as proof of its success, most of the 500 public and private psychiatric hospitals in America use the Menninger Foundation as a guidepost for treating mental illness.

SPECIAL FACILITIES AND PROGRAMS

Superior psychiatric and neurological services for both children and adults include comprehensive diagnosis, individualized treatment plan, treatment by a team of skilled professionals, family involvement throughout the treatment process, and consultative services provided by a multidisciplinary staff.

A brief listing of some of the services shows the broad range of both inpatient and outpatient clinical services available at the Menninger Foundation. They include hospitals for adults and children offering comprehensive psychiatric evaluation, diagnosis and consultation, as well as psychoeducational evaluation, neurological evaluation, neurosurgery, and neuropsychological testing.

In the Eating Disorders Program, a full range of services from least to most intensive is offered. The program serves patients, both men and women, from across the country, also offering services to family members. It is one of the components of the Women's Program recognized as one of the nation's best in 1993 by *Mirabella*.

The Trauma Recovery Program focuses on illnesses related to trauma such as childhood abuse, rape, and post-traumatic stress. It also provides special service for cases of self-mutilation. This program also is a part of the Women's Program at Menninger.

Professionals in Crisis is a program offering a broad range of confidential services from telephone consultation and outpatient evaluation and treatment to thorough evaluation and treatment in an inpatient setting among peers. Family involvement is strongly encouraged. It is designed for executives and other high-functioning professionals experiencing depression, alcohol or drug abuse, problems in relationships, difficulty making decisions, impaired memory, agitation, fatigue, sleep problems, and severe anxiety or panic attacks.

A full range of services from outpatient treatment to inpatient evaluation and treatment is available in the Alcohol and Drug Abuse Recovery Program. A day hospital program and aftercare follow-up are among the services. Family involvement, wellness, 12-step programs, and education about physical and psychological facts about chemical dependency are stressed in the program.

The HOPE Program treats schizophrenic, schizoaffective and other psychotic disorders. Long an expert in treatment of schizophrenia, Menninger offers one of the country's best treatment and diagnostic services. Every effort is made to provide an opportunity for patients to live more rewarding, meaningful, and productive lives, and to help families with support and education.

Menninger started partial hospitalization programs more than 40 years ago. One of the programs in highest demand is the Community Residence Program, a transitional living program with family-style living. Residents work cooperatively to prepare meals, complete household chores, and operate income-producing activities for themselves. Staff provide transportation and other assistance as needed and teach residents skills. A treatment team oversees residents' medical care and works with families.

Menninger offers an urgent admission service for youth in crisis. Designed to meet the special needs of children and adolescents, ages 5 to 17, the program offers rapid-response, same-day admissions for young people in psychiatric crisis. Help is

AT A GLANCE

Beds: 143
Occupancy Rate: 77%
Average Patient Count: 130
Average Patient Stay: 19 days
Annual Admissions: 885
Outpatient Clinic Visits:
  30,000

HOSPITAL PERSONNEL
Physicians: 61
  Board Certified: 57
Residents: 46
Psychologists: 35
Registered Nurses: 110
  BS Degree or Higher: 95
Social Workers: 43

ROOM CHARGES (PER DIEM)
Critical Care: $1,005–$1,080
  Medical Service Fee: $105
Intensive Care: $750–$950
  Medical Service Fee: $105
Extended Care: $585–$795
  Medical Service Fee: $75
Transitional Care: $585–$650
  Medical Service Fee: $75
Residential Care: $425
  Medical Service Fee: $55

ADDRESS
5800 SW Sixth Avenue
Topeka, KS 66601-0829

TELEPHONE
(800) 351-9058

available for youth who are experiencing one or more of these behaviors: suicidal behavior or thoughts; aggressive behavior; extreme withdrawal; impaired view of reality; oppositional, defiant behavior; severe noncompliance with needed medical treatment; or other behavior that puts themselves or others at extreme risk.

The Residential Treatment Program for Adolescents is designed for adolescents, ages 13-18, with emotional and behavioral difficulties, who require intensive treatment in a structured setting, but not in a secured and more intensive hospital unit. Adolescents participate in the development of their treatment program, establishing goals and directions for treatment. Components of the program are therapeutic living, activities and therapeutic groups, therapy, academic program, and partnership with family.

Outpatient services include psychiatric evaluation, diagnosis, and consultation for patients of all ages; integrated psychopharmacology and psychotherapy treatment modalities; neurology and internal medicine services; individual and group psychotherapy, hypnosis and hypnotherapy, and psychoanalysis; family therapy, marriage counseling, and sex therapy; the Headache Center; the Sleep Disorders Clinic; biofeedback; psychoeducational services; speech and hearing services; the Preschool Day Treatment Center; and outpatient offices in Kansas City and St. Louis.

PSYCHIATRIC SPECIALTIES

Alcohol Abuse Treatment, Biofeedback, Child and Adolescent Psychiatry, Personality Disorders, Eating Disorders Treatment, Family Therapy, Forensic Psychiatry, Geriatric Psychiatry, Headache Treatment, Hypnotherapy, Individual and Group Psychotherapy, Marriage Counseling, Neurology and Neurosurgery, Pain Management, Personality Disorders, Preventive Psychiatry, Psychopharmacotherapy, Psychosomatic Medicine, Psychosocial Services, Schizophrenia, Sex Therapy, Stress Management.

WELL-KNOWN SPECIALISTS

- Michele Berg, Ph.D. *Director of the Menninger Center for Learning Disabilities*
- Dr. Efrain Bleiberg *Child psychology and psychoanalysis; specialist in personality disorders*
- Bonnie Buchele, Ph.D. *Specialist in problems related to incest and other sex crimes*
- Dr. Glen O. Gabbard *Specialist in borderline personality disorder, sexual misconduct, medical marriages, psychodynamic psychiatry and psychoanalysis*
- Harriet Lerner, Ph.D. *Specialist in psychology of women*
- Flynn O'Malley, Ph.D. *Specialist in adolescent depression*
- Dr. Don Rosen *Director of the Professionals in Crisis Program*
- Linda Sebastian, MN, ARNP *Director of the Women's Program*

- Meredith Titus, Ph.D. *Specialist in eating disorders, trauma, chronic illness, mother-daughter relationships, and other women's topics*
- Dr. Kathryn Zerbe *Specialist in eating disorders and women's health*

PATIENT SATISFACTION

Menninger routinely surveys patients and tabulates results semi-annually. Adult patients, parents of juvenile patients and the young patients themselves are surveyed separately. Results for the first half of 1994 showed that 87% of the adults responding felt that their treatment at Menninger had definitely helped them in coping with their conditions. Parents of children being treated are usually the toughest group for a psychiatric hospital to satisfy; interestingly, over 90% of the parents surveyed felt that their children had definitely been helped by their treatment at Menninger. More than 80% of the young patients themselves recorded similar sentiments. Staff expertise and professionalism as well as the nurturing care were highly praised as well.

RESEARCH

Through grants from pharmaceutical companies, the Center for Clinical Pharmacology Research offers Midwesterners innovative medications that are still undergoing the research process required by the FDA. A variety of studies of new medications such as sumatriptan for migraines, the "fat pill" for obesity, and medications for Alzheimer's disease and generalized anxiety disorder have been researched at the center. Pharmaceutical representatives who have monitored the Menninger facility are consistently impressed with the center's high degree of sophistication.

Activity in the area of outcomes research on clinical services focuses on the effectiveness of treatment programs and modalities at Menninger.

Menninger has made significant contributions in the research of schizophrenia, psychotherapy, psychodynamic psychiatry, biofeedback, hypertension, suicide, infants, and preschoolers.

ADMISSIONS POLICY

Menninger has an open admissions policy. It accepts referrals from individuals, family members, and referring mental health professionals—regardless of discipline.

Room charges at Menninger are set according to the level/intensity of care required for the individual patients. Rates are also different for adults and children/adolescents. Medical services and psychotherapy services are additional charges.

Concerning payment, each case is assessed individually. Menninger wholly relies on the fees it receives for the services it provides. Menninger is unable to provide grants or scholarships for diagnostic evaluations or treatment. Some services offer a sliding fee scale based on income.

Menninger has established policies defining charity services as those services for which no payment is anticipated. In assessing a patient's ability or inability to pay, Menninger utilizes generally recognized minimum income guidelines relevant to the communities in which services are provided, but also considers individual cases where incurred charges are significant when compared to income. Charity care provided in 1992 and 1993, measured at established rates, was approximately $1,583,000 and $1,425,000, respectively.

Special phone number for admissions information: (800) 351-9058 (available 24 hours a day; emergency admissions accepted).

OCHSNER CLINIC

AND HOSPITAL

We received some idea of how highly regarded the **NEW ORLEANS, LOUISIANA** Ochsner Clinic is when doctors kept referring to it in the same context as the Mayo Clinic and the Cleveland Clinic. While not nearly as large or as famous as those two institutions, about 200,000 people visit the Ochsner Clinic and Hospital each year. Patients come to Ochsner from throughout the U.S., particularly the Gulf South, and also from Latin America. Ochsner's regional reputation is so strong that it provides 24-hour emergency helicopter transport service that serves a 200-mile radius. Ochsner also provides family medical care in 11 neighborhood clinics throughout the greater New Orleans metropolitan area and four clinics in Baton Rouge. In all, the Ochsner physicians see over 670,000 patients annually. About 45,000 of these are out-of-state patients including about 7,000 from other countries.

Ochsner's tradition of fine medical care dates back almost half a century. Founded in 1941 by five surgeons, the Ochsner Clinic was named after one of them—Dr. Alton Ochsner, a world-renowned surgeon and teacher as well as the first physician to draw a connection between cigarette smoking and lung cancer. Today the Ochsner Clinic is a private partnership of physicians and surgeons who practice in over 50 specialties and subspecialties. Its professional staff also serves as the attending medical staff of the adjoining Ochsner Foundation Hospital.

WE RECEIVED SOME
IDEA OF HOW HIGHLY
REGARDED THE OCHSNER
CLINIC IS WHEN DOCTORS
KEPT REFERRING TO IT IN
THE SAME CONTEXT AS
THE MAYO CLINIC AND
THE CLEVELAND CLINIC.

While Ochsner is a tertiary care facility for the most seriously ill, it also provides excellent diagnostic services. Many people come to the Ochsner Clinic for a thorough diagnostic evaluation, officially called a Clinic Check, or for one of the specific medical services described in the following paragraphs. If a patient's condition warrants hospitalization, a clinic physician will admit him or her to the Ochsner Foundation Hospital, which is adjacent to the clinic. Or patients may choose to return to their referring physicians for admission to a hometown hospital.

In 1944, partners of the Ochsner Clinic established the Alton Ochsner Medical Foundation to carry out patient care, medical education, and clinical research activities. It has become one of the nation's largest non-university-affiliated graduate medical education programs. Approximately 250 residents and fellows participate in 24 training programs. The Foundation also offers 10 professional education programs in its school of Allied Health Sciences.

The Ochsner Foundation Hospital recently received Accreditation with Commendation from the Joint Commission on Accreditation of Health Care Organizations. This top level of accreditation is received by only about 4% of all hospitals in the country.

SPECIAL FACILITIES AND PROGRAMS

The Ochsner Transplant Center was started in 1984 as the Gulf South's only multi-organ transplant center. This was the official start of combined transplant efforts, even though Ochsner specialists had been performing kidney transplants since the 1960s and Dr. John Ochsner performed the Gulf South's first heart transplant in 1970. The Ochsner Transplant Center's cardiac transplant program was cited last summer in the *Washington Post* as the fifth busiest heart transplant program in the country. Also, Ochsner lung transplant specialists performed a double lung transplant for cystic fibrosis on a seven-year-old girl, the youngest patient in the U.S. to ever undergo the procedure.

The Cardiovascular Health Center (CHC) is open to anyone looking for a healthy lifestyle, whether they be cardiac rehabiliatation patients or aspiring athletes. Through this medically-supervised program, physicians, nurses, and therapists from the Ochsner Medical Institutions help people focus on healthy lifestyles and work on efforts toward that goal. Quickly becoming one of the nation's most comprehensive cardiovascular health centers, the CHC provides a range of services for the general public. Services such as fitness assessments, diagnosis, prevention, intervention, and rehabilitation are all available at the center. Using tests like body composition analysis, blood cholesterol counts, pulmonary function, and others, the staff at the CHC can provide additional health and fitness support to people whether they are healthy or have heart disease or other risk factors.

The Extra-Corporeal Membrane Oxygenation (ECMO) program at Ochsner has been a lifesaver for hundreds of newborns, infants, and young children from around the country. The ECMO program provides life support to infants and young children who have a reversible lung disease. The 10-year-old Ochsner program is the leading center for pediatric ECMO in the Southern region of the U.S. and continues its prominence among 85 such centers nationwide.

The Ochsner Hematology/Oncology department is currently involved in several chemoprevention trials and is the coordinating site for these studies in a two-state area. The Obstetrics/Gynecology and Neonatology departments are recognized regionally as the first choice for high-risk pregnancies and critically ill newborns. Other departments with high referral rates are Urology and Gastroenterology.

The Ochsner Kidney Dialysis Program has grown and reached out to the regional community. The dialysis program is available in New Orleans and in the south Louisana communities of Thibodeaux and Houma.

Ochsner On Call is a telephone triage service that lets callers speak to registered nurses trained to answer medical questions 24 hours a day, 365 days a year. Ochsner On Call lets people discuss their medical questions with registered nurses over the phone. The program is a free tool that people can use in making health care decisions. The registered nurses answering the phones are specially trained in responding to a wide variety of medical questions.

Programs are also available for communicative disorders, psychiatric testing services, diabetes, the health of international travelers, cardiac rehabilitation, smoking elimination, home health services, breast screening, organ transplants, and weight control.

MEDICAL SPECIALTIES

Anesthesiology, Colon and Rectal Surgery, Dermatology, Emergency Medicine, Gynecology and Obstetrics, General Internal Medicine, Allergy and Clinical Immunology, Cardiology, Endocrinology and Metabolic Diseases, Gastroenterology, Hematology and Oncology, Hypertensive Diseases, Infectious Diseases, Nephrology, Prospective Medicine, Pulmonary Diseases, Rhematology, Family Medicine, Neurology,

AT A GLANCE

Beds: 532
Occupancy Rate: 51%
Average Patient Count: 270
Average Patient Stay: 5.3 days
Annual Admissions: 18,000
Births: 1,200
Outpatient Clinic Visits:
  150,000
Emergency Room Visits:
  30,000

HOSPITAL PERSONNEL
Physicians: 300
  Board Certified: 275
Residents: 200
Registered Nurses: 454

ROOM CHARGES (PER DIEM)
Private: $310
Semiprivate: $270
ICU: $650

ADDRESS
1516 Jefferson Highway
New Orleans, LA 70121

TELEPHONE
Hospital
(504) 842-3000
Clinic
(504) 842-4000

Neurosurgery, Nuclear Medicine, Occupational Health, Ophthalmology, Orthopedic Surgery, Otorhinolaryngology, Pathology, General Pediatrics, Pediatric Anesthesiology, Neonatology, Pediatric Surgery, Physical Medicine and Rehabilitation, Psychiatry, Radiation Oncology, Diagnostic Radiology, Surgery, and Urology.

WELL-KNOWN SPECIALISTS

- Dr. David E. Beck   *Colon and rectal surgery*
- Dr. Lawrence Blonde   *Endocrinology; specialist in diabetes treatment*
- Dr. Edward S. Connolly   *Neurological surgery; specialist in spinal surgery*
- Dr. J. Byron Gathright   *Colon and rectal surgery; specialist in colon/rectal cancer treatment*
- Dr. Richard J. Gralla   *Medical oncology; specialist in lung cancer treatment*
- Dr. Robert R. Kuske   *Radiation oncology; specialist in breast cancer treatment*
- Dr. John Ochsner   *Thoracic surgery; specialist in heart and lung transplantation*
- Dr. George A. Pankey   *Infectious disease*
- Dr. Robert Perrillo   *Gastroenterology; specialist in hepatitis treatment and research*
- Dr. Robert L. Rietschel   *Dermatology; specialist in contact dermatitis and hair treatment*
- Dr. Alfred G. Robichaux III   *Obstetrics/gynecology; specialist in maternal and fetal medicine*
- Dr. Robert E. Sonnemaker   *Nuclear medicine*
- Dr. Charles M. Stedman   *Obstetrics/gynecology; specialist in maternal and fetal medicine*
- Dr. Hector O. Ventura   *Cardiology; specialist in transplantation medicine*

PATIENT SATISFACTION

Patient satisfaction at Ochsner consistently ranks above 90% in several areas over time, with nine out of ten patients saying that they would recommend Ochsner to other people.

RESEARCH

The total Ochsner research budget is about $7 million. About $3 million of that total figure is raised internally by the Alton Ochsner Medical Foundation.

In January 1993, the new Ochsner Biomedical Research Building was dedicated. This new five-story facility is physically connected to the hospital, and it allows several different research laboratories to be brought together from throughout the institutions.

A major focus of Ochsner research is on molecular genetics and cellular immunology, areas that can have a tremendous impact on public health issues such as heart disease, cancer, AIDS, and other infectious diseases.

In the Transgenic Laboratory, scientists are studying the effect of sunlight on activation of the AIDS virus, the development of transgenic models expressing various HIV proteins, and the development of models of neurodegenerative disease and models which potentially could shed light on nervous system growth factors. Work in the Polymerase Chain Reaction Clinical Laboratory will permit Ochsner physicians to detect various forms of hepatitis which are not now easily diagnosed, to perform HLA typing for transplantation, and to detect AIDS in patients more accurately than is now possible.

An important part of Ochsner research efforts are the activities conducted by the Ochsner Community Clinical Oncology Program (CCOP). The Ochsner CCOP has been highly rated in the past by the National Cancer Institute (NCI). Through this program, community physicians work with scientists conducting NCI-supported clinical trials. The Ochsner CCOP allows Ochsner physicians to work with physicians and patients in several sites across Louisana and Mississippi. The Ochsner CCOP is coordinating several cancer studies, two of which have been heavily publicized in the national media. The Breast Cancer Prevention Trial and the Prostate Cancer Prevention Trial are NCI-sponsored studies to determine if those cancers can be prevented in people at risk for those diseases.

ADMISSIONS POLICY

Patients at Ochsner Foundation Hospital must be admitted by an Ochsner Clinic-affiliated physician. Appointments with an Ochsner physician can be made by calling (504) 842-4111.

If a patient does not have health coverage, he/she will be asked to make a deposit by cash, check or credit card. If total charges for services exceed that deposit, the difference is due upon discharge.

PATIENT/FAMILY ACCOMMODATIONS

Lodging is available at the Brent House Hotel. A 150-room, full-service hotel, Brent House is physically connected to the patient care facilities at Ochsner. Charges for Brent House run from $78–$93 per day. Rates are lower for patients at Ochsner or family members.

JOHNS HOPKINS

MEDICAL

INSTITUTIONS

BALTIMORE, MARYLAND

The Johns Hopkins Hospital is the central patient facility of one of the most prestigious and most influential medical centers in the country today. Staffed by physicians from a medical school that is among the best in the world, the hospital provides care in almost every area of modern medicine, from AIDS treatment to urology. While every department is highly regarded, several have international reputations—particularly cancer care, cardiology, endocrinology, gastroenterology, geriatrics, gynecology, neurology, orthopedics, otolaryngology, urology, ophthalmology, pediatrics, and psychiatry—so patients are referred here literally from around the world as well as from around the country and surrounding region. Almost half of Johns Hopkins' patients are from outside the Baltimore area. In recent years, patients from almost sixty different countries have been referred here.

At the center of Hopkins' renown within the medical community is one of the world's largest and most respected medical research programs, a program whose clinical impact is especially strong, as a few examples will illustrate. The first implantable insulin pump was developed at Hopkins and first used on a patient in 1986. Hopkins is also credited with the first use of a PET Scanner to image neuroreceptors in the living brain. It also pioneered the use of genetically engineered t-PA, a human protein that stops

THE JOHNS HOPKINS HOSPITAL IS THE CENTRAL PATIENT FACILITY OF ONE OF THE MOST PRESTIGIOUS AND MOST INFLUENTIAL MEDICAL CENTERS IN THE COUNTRY TODAY.

heart attacks. Hopkins orthopedic surgeon David S. Hungerford helped develop a new artificial knee which he successfully implanted. Hopkins basic scientists Daniel Nathans and Hamilton Smith won the Nobel Prize in 1978 for their discovery of the body's own chemical scissors for cutting DNA.

The melding of research and patient care at Hopkins is part of a long tradition dating back to 1889 when the hospital first opened, and followed four years later by the medical school. Both were outright gifts of a Quaker merchant whose name—Hopkins—these institutions still bear, along with several other hospitals and medical schools at that time. They helped to usher in the era of modern medical training by bringing students from the classroom to the hospital, from the laboratory and lecture hall directly to the patient's side.

Throughout the twentieth century the physicians and scientists at Hopkins continued to play a prominent role in the evolution of modern medicine. The discovery of mercurochrome, dramamine, adrenalin, and vitamin D all happened here as did the development of CPR. The cutting edge combination of research and clinical application has continued to this day. In 1992, for example, Hopkins neuroscientists pinpointed the role of nitric oxide as a messenger in the brain which has implications for the treatment of stroke, Alzheimer's disease, and Huntington's disease.

It would, however, be a mistake to leave the impression that research is the predominant activity at Hopkins. With over 38,000 admissions to the hospital and over 400,000 office and clinic visits recorded each year, this is obviously an exceptional health care resource. Only a handful of hospitals can match Hopkins in terms of the number of services offered; fewer still can equal its reputation for excellence in so many areas.

SPECIAL FACILITIES AND PROGRAMS

Johns Hopkins was rated among the top hospitals in America by *U.S. News and World Report* in 15 specialties, more than any other hospital in America. As

AT A GLANCE

Beds: 961
Occupancy Rate: 81%
Average Patient Count: 782
Average Patient Stay: 7.4 days
Annual Admissions: 38,760
Births: 3,027
Outpatient Clinic Visits: 408,172
Emergency Room/Trauma Center Visits: 79,209

HOSPITAL PERSONNEL
Physicians: 1,640
  Board Certified: 1,225
Residents: 608
Registered Nurses: 1,956
  BS Degree: 1,000

ROOM CHARGES (PER DIEM)
Semiprivate: $539.21
ICU: $1,348.42

ADDRESS
600 N. Wolfe Street
Baltimore, MD 21287

TELEPHONE
(410) 955-5000

Hopkins has evolved, it has taken on the look of a dozen or so mini-hospitals which reflect its physicians' preference for specialization in a single disease or anatomical category. Its programs and facilities are designed to bring together doctors with common interests so patients and interdisciplinary research benefit from their pooled knowledge. Listed here are some of Hopkins' outstanding centers.

The Adolf Meyer Center for Psychiatry and the Neurosciences, founded in 1982, was the first in the country to bring patient care, teaching, and research in psychiatry, neurology, and neurosurgery together under one roof, in this case a nine-story tower. Together, Meyer specialists treat pain, stroke, seizures, depression, and diseases such as Parkinson's, Huntington's, multiple sclerosis, and Alzheimer's. Advances in neuroradiology allow quicker, more precise diagnosis and localization of brain tumors, giving surgeons needed information to plot their delicate approaches. Among the more recent advances in the Meyer Center: scientists have devised tiny timed-release drug capsules that can kill tumor cells with steady doses; they have come up with a new treatment regimen that keeps boys with Duchenne's muscular dystrophy on their feet longer; they have pooled the talent of behaviorists and neurosurgeons who can help restore patients with chronic pain to productive lives even if physical distress cannot be rooted out completely.

The Harvey M. and Lyn P. Meyerhoff Center for Digestive Diseases opened in 1986 as a facility dedicated to the treatment of diseases of the digestive tract. Digestive diseases, including ileitis and colitis, afflict as many as two million Americans and often lead to lifetimes of repeated hospitalization, surgery, and pain. Here, gastroenterologists, surgeons, pathologists, radiologists, researchers, nurses, and nutritionists all collaborate on studying and treating disorders of the bowel, liver, stomach, and pancreas.

The Wilmer Eye Institute is widely considered one of the top places in the world for eye care. Wilmer eye specialists pioneered in laser surgery and have taken a leading role in blindness prevention programs around the world, especially in developing countries plagued by avoidable causes of blindness. Wilmer serves as the leading referral center in the country for diagnosis, treatment, and research on the principal causes of "low" or impaired vision.

Wilmer scientists now use the laser technique to treat such leading causes of blindness as glaucoma, macular degeneration—the primary cause of vision loss in those over 60—and diabetic retinopathy, which threatens the sight of thousands with diabetes. Wilmer physicians coordinate the largest number of clinical studies supported by the National Eye Institute. In the last five years alone, their research has yielded an impressive list of advances. Included are development of tissue-matching methods that have improved the success of corneal transplants; improved surgical techniques for vitreous and retinal diseases, such as detached retinas; perfection of surgery for lens implants; perfection of extended-wear contact lenses; and the development of new techniques to evaluate the extent of disease in the inner eye. Currently, Wilmer scientists are leading the way in a $5 million, five-year program to adapt space-age technology to produce aids for patients with reduced vision.

The Johns Hopkins Oncology Center, according to the National Cancer Institute, is one of the country's "centers of excellence," a place where patients can turn for state-of-the-art intensive treatment not available at most hospitals. World-renowned for the treatment of aplastic anemia and leukemia and other cancers of the blood, the regional center's doctors specialize in aggressive approaches that can include a combination of surgery, radiation therapy, bone marrow transplantation, and immunotherapy. They are particularly renowned for pioneering in the fields of bone marrow transplantation for leukemia and aplastic anemia, and radioimmunotherapy for primary liver cancer.

The center's layout was designed with two goals in mind: to make it easier for physicians to be involved in patient care, research, and education at the same time, by placing labs and conference rooms within a short walk from patient rooms; and to make waiting and treatment areas as airy, non-threatening, and relaxing as possible for patients. Disrupting lives as little as possible has always been one of the Oncology Center's highest priorities, spurring creation of two federal-style homes nearby, where out-of-town families can stay while one member is treated, rather than try to set up housekeeping for weeks at a time in hotels.

The Clayton Heart Center has a novel design; it sprawls across the fifth floor of five adjoining buildings and is planned so patients need not travel far from their beds for tests and treatment. Many of Hopkins' cardiac surgeons are as adept at operating on the tiny hearts of children as they are on adults, and no artificial division has forced the creation of completely separate programs. Part of the Heart Center is located right in the adjoining Children's Center.

Medicare has singled out the Clayton Center's heart transplant program as one of only eight in the country approved for reimbursement; more than 25 heart and heart-lung transplants are performed at Hopkins each year. More than 1,100 Clayton Center patients each year undergo open-heart surgery in the program headed by Bruce Reitz, who performed the world's first heart-lung transplant.

Medical intervention and prevention are just as highly stressed as surgical approaches. The Lipid Research Clinic, for instance, screens families of patients with high levels of cholesterol and triglycerides to help reduce their risk of developing irreversible cardiovascular disease. The Johns Hopkins Preventive Cardiology Program, established in 1983, seeks to cut the death toll from heart disease by identifying high-risk people early, and applying interventions, such as stress reduction, smoking cessation, and dietary programs.

The Children's Center also includes a Neonatal Intensive Care Unit with a 114-member staff to take care of high-risk, mostly premature babies. The unit is next to the obstetrics area, so tiny babies, some weighing less than two pounds, can be whisked immediately into the nurturing environment of an incubator.

The Children's Center's Pediatric Intensive Care Unit (PICU) is Maryland's trauma center for children, who are brought in by ambulance or by helicopter to the center's rooftop. More than 320 children are treated each year in the PICU.

The Brady Urological Institute was dedicated in 1915 in honor of James Buchanan Brady, famed philanthropist who gave the money following his successful treatment of prostate problems. From its founding until today, it has been considered one of the nation's foremost centers for patient care and research in urology. Patrick Walsh, the current director, is noted for his pioneering work establishing new surgical approaches for the management of prostate cancer, particularly for his surgical approach that removes the prostate gland without damaging crucial nerves.

In 1987, more than 10,000 patients were treated in the Brady Institute, drawn to it for its in-depth specialization in pediatric urology; urologic cancers, including neoplasms of the bladder, kidney, prostate, and testes; neurological dysfunction of the urinary tract; and treatment of kidney stones.

The research laboratories have active programs in the study of benign and malignant neoplasms of the prostate, innovative techniques for predicting the biological behavior of cancers, and disorders of sexual and reproductive functions in men.

A selected list of other clinics and services includes: Adolescent Medicine, Adolescent Pregnancy Program, Adult Seizures, Affective Disorders, Allergy, Anxiety, Behavioral Medicine, Birth Defects, Burn Treatment, Breast Reconstruction, Cardiac Arrhythmia, Cornea and Anterior Segment Surgery Center, Dementia Research, Dermatology Ambulatory Care Unit, Diabetes, Eating Disorders, Emergency Services, Endocrine Clinic, Epilepsy, Eye Consultation, Facial Nerve, Facial Rehabilitation, Fertility Control Center, Foot Clinic, Fractures, Genetics, Glaucoma, Gynecological Oncology, Hand Clinic, Head Injuries, Head and Neck Trauma, Hearing and Speech, Hematology, High Risk Obstetrical, Immunodeficiency, Infectious Diseases, In Vitro Fertilization, Lipid Clinic, Low Vision, Male Infertility, Medical Genetics, Movement Disorder, Multiple Sclerosis, Neuromuscular Clinic, Occupational Medicine, Ocular Oncology, Oncology (Pediatrics), Ophthalmologic Surgery, Orthopedics, Pain Treatment, Plastic Surgery, Prenatal Birth Defects, Prenatal Diagnostics, Preventive Cardiology, Psychogeriatric, Retinal Consultations, Retinal Degenerations, Sarcoidosis Consultation Service, Scoliosis, Sexual Behavior Consultation, Schizophrenia, Sleep Disorders, Spine Clinic, Surgical Diagnostic and Consultation, Swallowing, Thyroid, Urology, Urological Oncology, Voice Disorders, and the Women's Health Center.

Comprehensive outpatient services are available at the newly built 420,000-square-foot Outpatient Center.

MEDICAL SPECIALTIES

Hopkins directory of referrals lists over 200 clinical services, covering just about every medical specialty and subspecialty. Major divisions include Allergy and

Immunology, Anesthesiology, Cardiology, Dermatology, Endocrinology, Gastroenterology, Gynecology and Obstetrics, Laboratory Medicine, Medicine, Neurology, Neurosurgery, Oncology, Ophthalmology, Orthopedic Surgery, Otolaryngology, Pathology, Pediatrics, Psychiatry and Behavioral Sciences, Radiology and Radiological Science, Rehabilitation Medicine, Rheumatology, Surgery, and Urology.

WELL-KNOWN SPECIALISTS

- Dr. John G. Bartlett *AIDS and infectious diseases*
- Dr. William Baumgartner *Cardiac surgery; leader in heart and heart/lung transplants*
- Dr. John Cameron *Developed Whipple procedure*
- Dr. Benjamin S. Carson, Sr. *Pediatric neurosurgeon*
- Dr. Charles Cummings *Otolaryngology; developed hydroxylapaptite implant for paralyzed vocal chords*
- Dr. John Freeman *Pediatric neurology; specialist in epilepsy and ketogenic diet*
- Dr. David Guyton *Pediatric ophthalmology*
- Dr. Peter O. Kwiterovick *Lipid specialist*
- Dr. Paul W. Ladenson *Endocrinologist*
- Dr. Donlin Long *Neurosurgeon; expert in skull base surgery*
- Dr. Paul McHugh *Psychiatry; specialist in repressed memory theories*
- Dr. Victor A. McKusick *Genetics; director Human Genome Database*
- Dr. George W. Santos *Specialist in bone marrow transplant*
- Dr. Walter Stark *Ophthalmologist; specialist in treating cataracts*
- Dr. Richard Stauffer *Orthopedic surgery*
- Dr. Edward Wallach *Gynecology; specialist in reproductive endocrinology*
- Dr. Patrick C. Walsh *Urology; specialist in prostate cancer*
- Dr. David Zee *Neurology*

PATIENT SATISFACTION

The Johns Hopkins Hospital is committed to measuring the satisfaction of its patients with all aspects of the care and services provided to patients and families. Hopkins has contracted with an independent research firm to conduct periodic patient satisfaction surveys of its inpatient and outpatient populations. The survey firm also provides data about patient satisfaction at other hospitals using the same survey instruments, thus allowing Hopkins to compare itself with other community and academic teaching hospitals. In terms of recent results, 95% of patients rated the overall quality of services between good and excellent; 95% definitely or probably would recommend the hospital; and 91% rated the outcome of their hospital stay between good and excellent.

RESEARCH

In recognition of its highest caliber research capabilities, Johns Hopkins ranks first in the amount of research funding by the National Institutes of Health. In 1993 it was the only institution to receive over 4% of NIH's total funding pool. That distinction brought Johns Hopkins' total NIH funding to $187 million for the year. Total research expenditures amounted to $239 million.

The quality of research at Hopkins is reflected in the recognition its most well-known researchers have received. Among the best known on current staff are the following. Solomon Snyder, a researcher in neurosciences, has received the Lasker Award for his discoveries including nitric oxide as a neurotransmitter. Daniel Nathans and Hamilton Smith, molecular biologists and Nobel prize winners as noted previously, have continued to do pioneering work. Most notably, Nathans has developed a technique of gene mapping using restriction enzymes, while Smith has discovered the usefulness of restriction enzymes to genetic studies. Bert Vogelstein, a specialist in oncology and genetics, has won the Passano award. Murray Sachs has blazed new paths in biomedical engineering. Guy McKhann, a neurologist and director of the Kreeger Mind/Brain Institute, is a recognized expert in memory and cognition. Thomas Pollard, director of the department of Cell Biology and Anatomy, is a leading expert in myosin and other motion molecules in cells.

AIDS research is a large area of interest at Hopkins. Researchers at the John Hopkins Medical Institutions and one other medical center are participating in tests on volunteers of the first oral AIDS vaccine, designed to specifically block sexual transmission of HIV-1, the virus that causes AIDS. Hopkins researchers have recently completed a study of the effects of the drug AZT on 2,000 AIDS-infected men. Researchers have also found that moderate to large doses of vitamins A, C, B1, and niacin are associated with a slower onset of full-blown AIDS in HIV-positive men. In the same study, high levels of dietary zinc were associated with faster progression of the virus. This is the first epidemiologic evidence to clearly link nutrient intake and the progression of HIV-1 infection to AIDS.

Led by Johns Hopkins molecular geneticists, an international team from the U.S. and Japan has reported a new approach for isolating human chromosomes. According to the researchers' report, this discovery will allow scientists in any laboratory to isolate human chromosomes cheaply and in quantities previously unavailable. It will also help scientists extract specific genes for study more quickly, in a direct physical way that is currently impractical.

Hopkins researchers have also taken a significant step in explaining the genetic basis of allergic diseases such as asthma and hay fever. Their findings help to explain why some people are more likely than others to suffer from these disorders and may help develop finely targeted treatments. Asthma is the number one reason for pediatric admissions to emergency rooms. The death toll nationwide due to asthma has risen 43% in the last 15 years.

A number of studies focus on cancer prevention, detection, and treatment. For example, using cells from the late senator and vice president Hubert H. Humphrey, Johns Hopkins researchers have developed a molecular technique that has the potential to diagnose cancers years before they become invasive and cause death based on detecting cancer-specific mutations. Such cell mutations were detectable in specimens taken from Humphrey nine years before he underwent bladder removal and six years before he received any therapy. The mutation is of the p53 gene, a gene which in its mutated state is well-known for its involvement in a variety of cancers including breast and colon cancer. Hopkins scientists have also weighed in on the great broccoli debate, having found that a chemical found in the vegetable protects animals against the development of cancer. A Hopkins research team recently reported finding a marker in prostate cancer tissues that correlates extremely well, in initial studies, with the virulence of the cancer. This could be a key to the selection of the most appropriate treatment avenue to follow.

ADMISSIONS POLICY

·All patients admitted to Johns Hopkins are interviewed to determine financial responsibility. It is the policy of the hospital to establish with each patient, or the individual assuming responsibility for the patient's bill, a reasonable arrangement for payment. Patients without hospitalization insurance are expected to deposit, on admission, a sum based on their estimated charges. A deposit may be reduced or waived based on the patient's financial situation and the urgency of their need for medical care.

In recent years, Hopkins has absorbed over $30 million in unreimbursed care.

For an elective admission, where the patient or responsible party does not comply with the hospital's requirements, admission is postponed until they pay the estimated charges or insurance coverage is obtained. It is also the policy of Johns Hopkins that uninsured foreign nationals must pay 100% of their estimated hospital bill before admission.

Most of the patients at Johns Hopkins have been referred by their physician or by a local hospital, but anyone can make an appointment at one of the many clinics there, and if hospitalization is required they will be admitted by a Hopkins physician. The phone number for admissions information is (410) 955-5464 for adults and (410) 955-2000 for children.

PATIENT/FAMILY ACCOMMODATIONS

Uniglobe Harborside Travel offers one-stop shopping for services, including airline, train, and hotel reservations, as well as ground transportation. The agency guarantees the lowest applicable rates for all travel service. Out-of-town patients can call Uniglobe directly at 1-800-353-2121.

BETH ISRAEL

HOSPITAL

BOSTON, MASSACHUSETTS If a hospital is to be judged on the quality of its nursing program, then Beth Israel will certainly be rated one of the best in the country. Its nursing department has been cited as a model for nursing practice by the *New York Times*, the *Boston Globe*, and many professional journals. Nurses at Beth Israel have averaged more than 30 publications a year since 1980 and four times that many presentations. Beth Israel was selected by the American Academy of Nursing as one of 41 magnet hospitals in the United States and was asked to participate in three national studies examining nursing care, which were sponsored by the Division of Nursing Health and Human Services, the National Commission on Nursing, and the Institute of Medicine. In addition, nurses from more than 20 countries and 20 states have requested either a field placement or observation experience at Beth Israel during the last five years, and some have returned for second visits.

The primary-care nursing program at Beth Israel, developed in 1974, has one of the longest and most successful histories in the country and has served as a model for many other hospitals. Each patient is assigned a registered nurse, who is responsible for developing a coordinated individual care plan. The primary nurse accepts 24-hour accountability for maintaining continuity of care from admission to discharge or transfer and provides direct nursing care to

IF A HOSPITAL IS TO BE
JUDGED ON THE QUALITY
OF ITS NURSING PROGRAM,
THEN BETH ISRAEL WILL
CERTAINLY BE RATED ONE OF
THE BEST IN THE COUNTRY.

primary patients and other assigned patients while on duty. The primary nurse leaves clear directions to other staff when not on duty. This hospital-wide system allows nurses to give more personalized care and helps ensure that competent care is maintained throughout hospitalization.

SPECIAL FACILITIES AND PROGRAMS

Inpatient medical services cover cardiology, medicine, neurosurgery, neuromedicine, obstetrics/gynecology, orthopedics, psychiatry, surgery, and medical and surgical intensive care units.

Beth Israel is one of the major teaching facilities for Harvard Medical School, and most of its physicians hold faculty appointments at the school. There are over 675 interns and residents each year in medicine, pathology, surgery, and other medical specialties and over 675 interns, residents, and postgraduate fellows continue in training for medicine, surgery, pathology, and other medical specialties. Beth Israel has led the country in providing innovative training programs in geriatrics and primary-care medicine.

Nursing students from 15 area schools, social work students from two colleges, and dietary intern students in medical technology, pharmacy, physical and occupational therapy, respiratory therapy, and radiological technology all receive part of their clinical education at Beth Israel.

Nursing research is an integral part of the professional practice model of the Division of Nursing. Nurse researchers with doctoral degrees conduct studies and publish their findings.

Biomedical research at Beth Israel is conducted at the Charles A. Dana Research Institute in all areas of adult medicine, including cardiology, computer sciences, dermatology, endocrinology, gastroenterology, hematology, infectious disease, nephrology, neurology, nutrition, obstetrics, oncology, orthopedics, psychiatry, pulmonary diseases, rheumatology, surgery, and other fields related to clinical medicine and its underlying scientific basis. The nation's oldest clinical research facility, the Harvard Thorndike Laboratories has been located at Beth Israel since 1973.

AT A GLANCE

Beds: 452
Occupancy Rate: 83%
Average Patient Count: 362
Average Patient Stay: 5.5 days
Annual Admissions: 29,000
Births: 5,456
Outpatient Clinic Visits:
    181,000
Emergency Room/Trauma
    Center Visits: 36,000

HOSPITAL PERSONNEL
Physicians: 518
Residents: 300
Registered Nurses: 917

ROOM CHARGES (PER DIEM)
Private: $770
Semiprivate: $730
ICU: $2,000

ADDRESS
330 Brookline Avenue
Boston, MA 02215

TELEPHONE
(617) 735-2000

Beth Israel was established in 1916 by the Boston Jewish community to meet the needs of the growing immigrant population. The hospital moved to its current location in 1928, when its affiliation with Harvard Medical School began.

In 1972 Beth Israel was the first hospital in the nation to issue a written statement on the rights of patients, including the rights to be treated with privacy, personal dignity, and respect and to receive full and detailed information about their cases. The statement is distributed to each patient admitted and to each new employee. It has served as a model for similar statements issued by other hospitals and enacted as legislation in various states.

The Beth Israel Dental Unit is a private group practice covering all areas from routine checkups to oral surgery. The Walk-in Center provides prompt medical care for minor emergencies. Beth Israel's Berenson Emergency Unit is part of the Longwood Area Trauma Center, which handles the most difficult emergencies from the Greater Boston region and beyond. The unit treats more than 35,000 patients a year.

Since 1983 and in collaboration with the neighboring Dana-Farber Cancer Institute, Beth Israel has performed about 50 bone marrow transplant procedures a year. This program includes one of the oldest solid tumor programs in the country and is a major center for treatment of Hodgkins and non-Hodgkins lymphoma.

Beth Israel also performed 30 kidney transplants and six pancreas transplants last year. Caring for the area's most complicated cases for over 20 years, the Kidney Dialysis Program cares for 45 exceptionally complex patient cases at any time. It also provides continuous and overnight home dialysis.

Beth Israel maintains an innovative general medicine center for ambulatory care (BI Healthcare Associates) and outpatient specialty units. The Home Care Program provides more than 7,000 visits to homebound, chronically ill patients by nurse practitioners, physicians, or social workers acting as a team.

Other facilities at Beth Israel include a neonatal intensive care unit with 15 Level II and five Level III bassinets. The Breast Care Center conducts a comprehensive interdisciplinary program to prevent, diagnose, and treat breast cancer and other breast disorders. The Menopause Wellness Center provides a comprehensive program for treatment of menopause. Treatment provided at the Cardiac Center includes electrophysiology and interventional cardiology services.

Beth Israel offers many preventive, informational, and health-promotion programs, such as smoking cessation, weight loss, and treatment of stress-related illnesses, including allergies, chronic illness, high blood pressure, and hypertension, through behavioral medicine techniques. The Men's Program for the Treatment of Sexual Dysfunction offers a comprehensive approach to impotence.

MEDICAL SPECIALTIES

Anesthesia, Bone/Mineral Metabolism, Cardiology, Dermatology, Endocrinology, Gastroenterology, General Surgery, Gerontology, Hematology/Oncology,

Infectious Disease, Infertility, Nephrology, Neurology, Neurosurgery, Obstetrics/Gynecology, Orthopedics, Pathology, Psychiatry, Pulmonary Care, Radiology, Rheumatology, and Surgery.

WELL-KNOWN SPECIALISTS

- Dr. Kenneth A. Arndt *Chief of Dermatology; specialist in laser surgeries*
- Dr. Clyde Crumpacker *Virology; specialist in infectious diseases, such as AIDS and herpes*
- Dr. Rosemary Duda *Chief of Oncologic Surgery*
- Dr. Albert Galaburda *Specialist in the relation between brain structure and dyslexia*
- Dr. Robert M. Glickman *Chief of Medicine; specialist in gastroenterology*
- Dr. Robert Goldwyn *Specialist in reconstructive plastic surgery*
- Dr. Mary Jane Houlihan *Surgery; specialist in breast diseases*
- Dr. Steven Lipson *Orthopedic surgeon*
- Dr. Edward Lowenstein *Chief of Anesthesiology*
- Dr. Mitchell T. Rabkin *President of Beth Israel; leader in development of innovative systems of health care, such as primary nursing practice and a hospital-based ambulatory care center*
- Dr. Steven Robinson *Chief of Hematology*
- Dr. Lowell Schnipper *Chief of Oncology*
- Dr. William Silen *Chief of Surgery; specialist in gastrointestinal surgery*
- Dr. Larry H. Strasburger *Psychiatry; specialist in forensic psychiatry*

PATIENT SATISFACTION

A study of patients surveyed during the last six months of 1993 shows that 88.3% of respondents would recommend Beth Israel to their friends and families. Particular praise was given to the nursing staff.

RESEARCH

Beth Israel is the eighth largest recipient of National Institutes of Health (NIH) grants among independent hospitals in the United States. In 1993, the hospital was awarded $44,220,000 in research funding. Of that, $26 million was from federal sources. Research grants at the hospital increase at an average of about 15% annually.

The NIH-funded Clinical Research Center with ten beds provides researchers the opportunity to bring their theories and treatments to patients and volunteers. Achievements at Beth Israel include development of the first implantable pacemaker, significant advances in balloon angioplasty, and a nasal insulin spray. There are currently 410 studies underway in the hospital's ten medical departments in areas such as asthma, gastroenterology, gene therapy, infectious disease, orthopedics, immunology, tumor growth, trauma research, diabetes, clotting, rheumatoid arthritis, and obesity.

Several Beth Israel projects have recently been the focus of international press coverage. Among them are the first study of the prevalence, cost, and use of alternative medicine in the United States; the first national report on the quality of patient care from the patient's perspective; pioneering work in noninvasive magnetic resonance angiography and magnetic resonance imaging of the onset of stroke; oral tolerance and fusion toxin proteins as treatments for rheumatoid arthritis; new drug therapies for asthma; strategies to avoid hip fractures in the elderly; and new noninvasive techniques to clear coronary arteries.

ADMISSIONS POLICY

Patients can be admitted to Beth Israel without a physician's referral through the emergency room or clinic. However, it is important for patients in managed care networks to comply with the requirements of their specific plan, in terms of referral pathway.

There is no financial requirement for emergency medical treatment. In cases of scheduled admissions, if the patient lacks insurance and is not eligible for free care or Medicaid, or is unwilling to work out appropriate arrangements with respect to payments, a deposit is required.

Beth Israel provides $17,572,000 in charity/free care per annum and incurs another $9,318,000 in bad debt.

BRIGHAM AND WOMEN'S

HOSPITAL

Through the Boston area's network of first rate hospitals, one can trace the history of modern medicine and also peer into the future of medical miracles still being developed. Perhaps the best example of this is Brigham and Women's Hospital (BWH). It is a world-famous tertiary care center, a teaching affiliate of the Harvard Medical School, and one of Boston's most popular hospitals. Almost 70 BWH doctors are listed in the current edition of *The Best Doctors in America*.

The Brigham, as it is often called, is actually the result of a 1980 merger of three of Boston's oldest and most prestigious hospitals: the Peter Bent Brigham Hospital, the Robert B. Brigham Hospital and the Boston Hospital for Women. For decades the Boston Hospital for Women set the standard in obstetrics and gynecology, while doctors at Peter Bent Brigham Hospital achieved international recognition for initiating what became modern neurosurgery, for developing the artificial kidney machine, and for performing the first successful kidney transplant in 1954.

Brigham and Women's is one of five major teaching hospitals of the Harvard Medical School. All members of the hospital's active staff hold teaching appointments at Harvard. BWH provides clinical rotations for about one-third of the more than 300 third- and fourth-year medical school students. Thousands of graduate medical students compete each year for openings in 35 different accredited training programs

BOSTON, MASSACHUSETTS

IT IS A WORLD-FAMOUS
TERTIARY CARE CENTER, A
TEACHING AFFILIATE OF THE
HARVARD MEDICAL SCHOOL,
AND ONE OF BOSTON'S
MOST POPULAR HOSPITALS.

in which 662 residents and 727 fellows were enrolled in FY 1993. The hospital also participates in exchange programs wherein residents rotate through programs at 12 other Harvard teaching hospitals. Brigham and Women's is also the clinical affiliate for nursing students in more than 10 nursing schools in the area, with as many as 200 students on site on any given day.

The nursing program at Brigham and Women's Hospital espouses theory-based practice, planning care that is unique to each patient's physical and emotional needs. The overarching philosophy is to teach nurses how to put themselves in the patient's place, and to respond as if their roles were reversed. The hospital also supports 25 to 50 nurses in advanced education each year. Clinical nurse specialists consult with primary nurses in improving patient education and outcomes.

Brigham and Women's long history of medical milestones dates back to the 19th century. In 1847, the first anesthesia administered in an American maternity ward was administered at the Boston Lying-In Hospital. In 1929, Peter Bent Brigham and Women's physicians recorded the first use of the Iron Lung to save a polio victim's life. The first artificial kidney machine was introduced here in 1947. In the 1980s, Brigham researchers developed the use of electrocardiography for abdominal fetal monitoring. And the first heart-lung transplant in Massachusetts was completed at Brigham and Women's in 1992.

Today Brigham and Women's is a leading provider of women's health services, New England's largest birthing center, and a designated regional center for high-risk obstetrics and neonatology. The Menopause Center is one of the first established in the country.

Brigham and Women's is also nationally recognized for its transplant programs and is one of the country's foremost centers for joint replacement and orthopedic surgery, and for the treatment of arthritis, rheumatic disorders, and cardiovascular disease.

The hospital's preeminence in all aspects of clinical care is coupled with its strength in medical research. For six of the last seven years, Brigham and Women's has led independent hospitals nationwide in National Institutes of Health funding. These funds help Brigham and Women's conduct internationally acclaimed clinical, basic, and epidemiologic studies.

In March 1994, Brigham and Women's and Massachusetts General Hospital announced plans to merge the two medical centers to form Partners Health Care System Inc., a hub for an integrated health care delivery system. Despite the merger, both hospitals will continue to operate independently and maintain their own identities. However, it will be a cornerstone in the building of a high quality, efficient, health care delivery system in partnership with community-based, primary care providers.

SPECIAL FACILITIES AND PROGRAMS

Brigham and Women's is nationally recognized for its transplant programs, including heart (40 in FY 1993), lung (11), kidney (54), and heart-lung transplant surgery (1), and bone marrow transplantation (82). More than 1,200 kidney transplants have been performed here. The hospital is also one of the country's foremost centers for joint replacement and orthopedic surgery, with 750 joint replacement operations performed in fiscal year 1993.

The Department of Rheumatology and Immunology is one of the nation's oldest and largest. Its staff includes more than 30 physicians, as well as nurses with special training in arthritis problems and access to physical therapists, occupational therapists, and psychologists. The Robert B. Brigham Arthritis Center accepts about 20,000 patient visits a year, with 3,000 of these being new patients. Components of the department include an asthma and allergic disease center, a center for pediatric rheumatology that sees about 300 patients each year, a lupus center, a spine center which specializes in the evaluation and management of lower back problems, and an active clinical pharmacology unit.

In cardiothoracic surgery, Brigham and Women's is considered a major heart transplant center (40 heart transplants were performed here in 1993). It is also one of the leading facilities for bypass surgery with more than 1,400 procedures performed in 1993. Brigham and Women's is also internationally known for its cardiac care and cardiovascular services. It offers acute coronary care, angioplasty, and treatment of heart rhythm disturbances.

The expertise of the radiation therapy department attracts thousands of patients from all over the United States as well as from Europe. Over 20,000 treatments for leukemia, tumors, and genetic disorders are performed each year.

BWH also houses one of the few Level I trauma centers and burn centers in the region. There are also special facilities there for the treatment of lupus, multiple sclerosis, and stroke, as well as an occupational medical service, a pain treatment unit, and a thyroid diagnostic service.

The latest *U.S News & World Report* survey listed the following specialties (top ten rankings noted in parentheses) at Brigham and Women's as being among the 40 best in the United States: AIDS, Cancer,

AT A GLANCE

Beds: 751
Occupancy Rate: 80%
Average Patient Count: 598
Average Patient Stay: 5.8 days
Annual Admissions: 37,816
Births: 8,693
Ambulatory Visits: 599,654
Emergency Room/Trauma
  Center Visits: 49,011

HOSPITAL PERSONNEL
Physicians: 1,950
Residents: 662
Fellows: 727
Registered Nurses: 1,200

ROOM CHARGES (PER DIEM)
Private: $750
Semiprivate: $700
ICUs: $1750–$1850

ADDRESS
75 Francis Street
Boston, MA 02115

TELEPHONE
(617) 732-5500

Cardiology (ranked 6th best), Endocrinology, Gastroenterology (9th), Geriatrics, Gynecology (4th), Neurology, Orthopedics, Otolaryngology, Rheumatology (3rd), and Urology.

MEDICAL SPECIALTIES

Asthma and Allergic Diseases, Bone Marrow Transplantation, Cardiology and Cardiothoracic Surgery (including heart transplantation), Gynecologic Cancer, Kidney Dialysis and Transplantation, Microsurgery, Neurology, Neurosurgery, High-Risk Obstetrics and Newborn Medicine, Orthopedic Surgery, Psychiatry, Radiation Therapy and Diagnostic Imaging, Rehabilitative Medicine, Rheumatology and Immunology, and Trauma.

WELL-KNOWN SPECIALISTS

- Dr. K. Frank Austen   *Professor of medicine*
- Dr. Menton R. Bernfield   *Chairman, department of newborn medicine*
- Dr. Eugene Braunwald   *Professor of medicine*
- Dr. G. Norman Coleman   *Chairman, department of radiation oncology*
- Dr. Sanjay Datla   *Professor of anesthesia*
- Dr. Simon Gelman   *Professor of anesthesiology*
- Dr. P. Reed Larsen   *Professor of medicine*
- Dr. John A. Mannick   *Professor of surgery*
- Dr. Gerard W. Ostheimer   *Professor of anesthesia*
- Dr. Albert L. Sheffer   *Clinical professor of medicine*
- Dr. Thomas Smith   *Professor of medicine*
- Dr. Nicholas L. Tilney   *Professor of surgery; specialist in kidney transplant surgery*

PATIENT SATISFACTION

Brigham and Women's is currently launching a comprehensive patient satisfaction survey program. Results will not be available for some time.

RESEARCH

Brigham and Women's is an NIH-sponsored Clinical Research Center, where studies in arrhythmias, cancer, juvenile diabetes, and metabolic bone disease, among other ailments, are conducted. Other major grants come from the American Heart Association and the American Cancer Society.

Brigham and Women's Hospital set an institutional record of $100.4 million in fiscal year 1993 for the receipt of new awards from all outside funding sources. This figure, which is for direct costs only, and for the life of the awards, is up nearly $15 million over fiscal year 1992 and reflects the hospital's standing as one of the world's most productive centers of medical research. It includes almost $92 million from NIH, putting Brigham & Women's first in the nation in NIH grants.

Of particular note was an $11.5 million NIH award as one of 16 Vanguard Centers for the Women's Health Initiative, the most far-reaching women's health study undertaken in the United States. Also noteworthy was a $5 million grant for a study of HIV transmission from mother to child, as well as a $7.8 million award from Ciba-Geigy for a study of the formation of blood clots during heart attacks.

Virtually every week, news media chronicle yet another research finding from Brigham and Women's Hospital. In the past year, the hospital has been in the news for stories ranging from clinical trials of captopril, a new drug shown to vastly improve the long-term outcome for heart attack victims; to the discovery of a gene responsible for a form of hypertension—for the first time proving that hypertension may be genetic in origin; to new research findings that may help elucidate the causes of Alzheimer's disease.

The scientific community, as well as the public, relies heavily on such findings. In fact, a recent survey by the Institute for Scientific Information found that over a five-year period, research conducted at Brigham and Women's generated more citations in scientific papers than any other hospital in the world.

A prime example is the Nurse's Health Study, conducted through the hospital's Channing Laboratory. For 16 years, this pioneering epidemiological women's health study has been collecting information from more than 120,000 female nurses across the country. Originally launched to assess risk factors for cancer and cardiovascular disease (with particular emphasis on oral contraceptives), it has yielded information critical to helping women make basic life-style decisions.

Research findings can also provide unexpected opportunities, as was proven when the hospital's high-tech SPECT (Single Proton Emission Computer Tomography) imaging capability was used to show that blood flow in the brain is severely altered by cocaine use. Striking images show a cocaine user's brain looking like Swiss cheese. With funding from the DuPont Merck Pharmaceutical Company, the hospital developed an educational video which has been distributed, free of charge, to schools nationwide.

ADMISSIONS POLICY

Patients are admitted by a physician on staff, through the hospital's Emergency Department or an outpatient service, or by physician referral. Appointments with Brigham and Women's physicians may be made by contacting the hospital's physician referral service at 800-622-2252.

Prospective nonemergency patients are expected to have insurance coverage, prove their ability to pay, or demonstrate eligibility for subsidized or free care. Brigham and Women's has a longstanding record as one of the state's most generous private hospitals, providing more than $28 million of free care in FY 1993.

DANA-FARBER

CANCER INSTITUTE

BOSTON, MASSACHUSETTS Dana-Farber Cancer Institute (DFCI) was ranked as "one of the premier cancer centers in the world" by the National Cancer Institute, which recently redesignated Dana-Farber as one of its 27 comprehensive cancer centers. The Institute's focus is a marriage between basic and clinical cancer research and the use of research discoveries to develop treatments for patients with cancer. Its commitment is to prevent, treat, and eliminate cancer in children and adults. Many of the Institute's clinical and basic programs reflect this commitment—the development of more effective drugs and drug combinations; new measures to reduce the side effects of chemotherapy and radiotherapy; and the continual introduction of new treatment technologies for forms of cancer resistant to standard measures.

The Institute began in 1947 as the Children's Cancer Research Foundation, one of the world's first research and treatment centers devoted exclusively to pediatric cancer. Its programs in patient care, clinical investigation, and basic research grew to such an extent that in 1969 the Institute expanded to provide services to all cancer patients, regardless of age. As a comprehensive cancer center, Dana-Farber conducts basic and clinical research and provides pediatric and adult patient care, training and education of future cancer specialists, and outreach programs to disseminate cancer treatment information to laypeople

DANA-FARBER CANCER INSTITUTE (DFCI) WAS RANKED AS "ONE OF THE PREMIER CANCER CENTERS IN THE WORLD" BY THE NATIONAL CANCER INSTITUTE, WHICH RECENTLY REDESIGNATED DANA-FARBER AS ONE OF ITS 27 COMPREHENSIVE CANCER CENTERS.

and to affiliated community hospitals and physicians throughout northern New England. Dana-Farber is also the only cancer center to be designated as a Center for AIDS Research by the National Institute of Allergy and Infectious Diseases.

Dana-Farber is basically an outpatient adult bone marrow transplantation and chemotherapy facility with a capacity of 57 beds, 16 of which are devoted to bone marrow transplantation. Any major surgery or radiation therapy required by patients of the Institute is performed at Beth Israel Hospital, Brigham and Women's Hospital, or the New England Deaconess Hospital. Pediatric patients are treated on an outpatient basis at Dana-Farber through its world-famous Jimmy Fund Clinic. Children requiring overnight care are treated at The Children's Hospital.

Dana-Farber is a teaching affiliate of Harvard Medical School and maintains alliances with other Harvard teaching hospitals. Institute professional staff hold faculty appointments at Harvard Medical School or on one of the other Harvard faculties. An oncology fellowship program is provided annually for young pediatricians and internists.

The Institute is named for Dr. Sidney Farber, whose pioneering work with chemotherapy in 1947 enabled him to produce the first complete remissions in children with leukemia, and for the Charles A. Dana Foundation, which has helped support the Institute for three decades.

Dana-Farber is recognized internationally for its excellence in cancer treatment. Two out of three children who enter the Jimmy Fund Clinic walk out cured. More than half of all people with cancer treated at Dana-Farber are cured.

SPECIAL FACILITIES AND PROGRAMS

Dana-Farber has 18 distinct clinical divisions and 12 specialty clinics. A number of these are described below.

Dana-Farber is a noted bone marrow transplantation center for both autologous and allogenic transplants. Institute researchers helped introduce the use

---

AT A GLANCE

Beds: 57
Occupancy Rate: 81%
Average Patient Count: 46
Average Patient Stay: 7 days
Annual Admissions: 2,446
Outpatient Clinic Visits:
  56,523

HOSPITAL PERSONNEL
Physicians: 147
  Board Certified: 213
Residents: 37
Registered Nurses: 158
  BS Degree: 118

ROOM CHARGES (PER DIEM)
Private: $725
Semiprivate: $725
Bone Marrow Transplant:
  $990

ADDRESS
44 Binney Street
Boston, MA 02115

TELEPHONE
(617) 632-3000

---

of naturally occurring growth factors to spur recovery of patients' bone marrow after high-dose chemotherapy. To make bone marrow transplantation safer and more effective, doctors substitute a potent combination of young bone marrow cells (stem cells) and growth factors that spur their maturation. The Cancer Risk and Prevention Clinic was created in 1992 to advance the early detection and prevention of breast cancer in women at high risk for the disease. In 1993, the Women's Cancers Program was launched. This initiative aims to reduce the incidence of cancers of the breast, lung, and gynecological and reproductive systems by bridging the gap between research and patient.

Dana-Farber offers the Predictive Genetic Testing program, one of the nation's first programs for testing members of families with an inherited susceptibility to cancer. The program aims to identify individuals at risk and provide genetic and psychological counseling.

The Institute's Division of Biostatistics and Epidemiology is considered one of the world's outstanding statistical centers and serves the Eastern Cooperative Oncology Group, one of the leading clinical cooperative groups in the United States. More than 200 treatment centers throughout the world, participating in approximately 100 studies, send their clinical data to the division for analysis.

Among the other areas of special interest are specialties in dermatology, genito-urinary cancers, gynecological oncology, lung cancer, myelodysplasia, and sarcoma. The Brain Tumor Clinic targets brain cancers in children and adults. Half of the patients with head and neck cancers with a poor prognosis have proven responsive to an aggressive program of chemotherapy, radiation and/or surgery developed by Institute researchers.

The Institute's Communication Office operates the Cancer Information Service to provide cancer patients and their families, health professionals, and the public with up-to-date information on the detection, diagnosis, and treatment of cancer. Its toll-free number, serving Massachusetts, Maine, New Hampshire, and Vermont, is (800) 422-6237.

Laboratories at Dana-Farber include Eukaryotic Transcription, Gene Regulation, Immunopathology, Membrane Immunochemistry, Molecular Biology, Molecular Carcinogenesis, Molecular Genetics, Molecular Immunobiology, Molecular Immunochemistry, Molecular Immunology, Neoplastic Disease Mechanisms, Structural Molecular Biology, and Tumor Virus Genetics. Other laboratories are dedicated to Biochemical Pharmacology, Clinical Pharmacology, and Infectious Diseases.

MEDICAL SPECIALTIES

Biostatistics and Epidemiology, Blood Component Laboratory, Cancer Control, Cancer Genetics, Cancer Pharmacology, Cell Growth and Regulation, Gynecologic Oncology, Human Retrovirology, Immunogenetics, Lymphocyte Biology, Medical Oncology, Medicine, Oncodiagnostic Radiology and Nuclear Medicine,

Pediatric Oncology, Radiotherapy, Respiratory Therapy, Social Work, Surgical Oncology, Tumor Immunology, and Tumor Virology.

WELL-KNOWN SPECIALISTS

- Dr. Kenneth C. Anderson   *Medical oncology/hematology; specialist in myeloma*
- Dr. George P. Canellos   *Medical oncology/hematology; specialist in lymphomas and breast cancer*
- Dr. John R. Clark   *Medical oncology/hematology; specialist in head and neck cancer*
- Dr. C. Norman Coleman   *Radiation oncology; specialist in lymphomas and general radiation oncology*
- Dr. Timothy Joseph Eberlein   *Surgical oncology; specialist in colon and rectal cancer*
- Dr. Emil Frei III   *Medical oncology/hematology; physician-in-chief emeritus*
- Dr. Marc B. Garnick   *Medical oncology/hematology; specialist in genito-urinary cancer*
- Dr. Holcombe Edwin Grier   *Pediatrics; specialist in pediatric hematology/oncology*
- Dr. Dan Hayes   *Medical oncology/hematology; specialist in breast cancer*
- Dr. Philip W. Kantoff   *Medical oncology/hematology; specialist in genito-urinary cancer*
- Dr. Donald Kufe   *Medical oncology/hematology; specialist in clinical pharmacology*
- Dr. Peter M. Mauch   *Radiation oncology; specialist in lymphomas*
- Dr. Robert J. Mayer   *Medical oncology/hematology; specialist in gastrointestinal oncology and leukemia*
- Dr. Lee M. Nadler   *Medical oncology/hematology; specialist in immunotherapy, lymphomas, and cancer biotherapy*
- Dr. Stephen E. Sallan   *Pediatrics; specialist in pediatric hematology/oncology*
- Dr. Margaret A. Shipp   *Medical oncology/hematology; specialist in lymphomas*
- Dr. Arthur Skarin   *Medical oncology/hematology; specialist in lung cancer and lymphomas*
- Dr. Howard Weinstein   *Pediatrics; specialist in pediatric hematology/oncology*

PATIENT SATISFACTION

The Institute routinely surveys its patients. The surveys are processed through Press, Ganey Associates Inc. in Indiana. The feedback from the patients is highly favorable and positive. The Institute scored in the highest category by its patients when they were asked of their "likelihood of recommending DFCI to others." Ratings of the doctors and nurses were among the highest in the country in the Press, Ganey database, which includes 355 hospitals nationwide.

RESEARCH

At Dana-Farber, more than 300 technicians and research fellows and almost 500 MDs and PhDs staff nearly 30 separate divisions and laboratories, addressing two central questions concerning cancer—what causes normal cells to transform into malignant or destructive cells, and what is the best way to destroy each type of cancer cell?

Total annual research funding is over $52 million. Areas of research include cancer, cancer pharmacology, tumor immunology, cell growth and regulation, cellular and molecular biology, human retrovirology, immunogenetics, infectious diseases, neoplastic disease mechanisms, tumor virology, immunobiology, immunochemistry, immunopathology, molecular genetics, radiation biology, structural molecular biology, cellular genetics, cancer genetics, lymphocyte biology, AIDS, obesity, multiple sclerosis, and more.

Recent discoveries and clinical applications in cancer research at Dana-Farber include the following: Pointing to a flaw in a gene known as p53, researchers have demonstrated that susceptibility to developing cancer can be passed from one generation to the next. The gene is discovered in families afflicted by the rare Li-Fraumeni syndrome, in which members are at very high risk for developing tumors of the adrenal gland, breast, brain, and soft tissues.

Dana-Farber and Sandoz Pharmaceutical Corp. entered into a novel long-term collaboration to develop a new generation of potent anti-tumor agents based on scientists' understanding of the molecular missteps that lead to cancer.

Dana-Farber scientists discovered a group of genes that raise susceptibility to a common inherited form of colon cancer and several other malignancies. The finding reveals an entirely new mechanism for cancer's development. It also raises hopes for saving thousands of lives by screening individuals at high risk for the disease to detect budding tumors.

Dana-Farber established the nation's first Division of Human Retrovirology in 1989 and was designated New England's only Center for AIDS Research by the National Institute of Allergy and Infectious Diseases.

The AIDS virus, HIV-1, has yielded many secrets to laboratory researchers at Dana-Farber, including aspects of its structure, genetic makeup, and the means by which it enters a host cell, co-opts its genetic machinery, and replicates hundreds of times. Studies of maternal-fetal AIDS transmission and of anti-AIDS drugs in laboratory animals form the basis for patient trials at health centers across the U.S.

ADMISSIONS POLICY

Patients may be referred to Dana-Farber by their primary physicians, or they may inquire directly about admittance to consultation or treatment programs. For further information call the appropriate number listed below.

Adult: (617) 632-3476

Breast Evaluation Center: (617) 632-3666
Head and Neck Clinic: (617) 632-3090
Lung Cancer Clinic: (617) 632-3468
Pediatric: (617) 632-3270
Sarcoma Clinic: (617) 632-3986

Every effort is made to provide care for those families unable to pay. Dana-Farber has established a formal process that evaluates each case on an individual basis. The goal is to ensure that every patient receives the best available treatment. Patients without sufficient funds are provided for whenever possible.

LAHEY CLINIC

**BURLINGTON,
MASSACHUSETTS**

Like those at the Mayo and Cleveland Clinics, physicians at Lahey Clinic work on salary, not a fee-for-service basis, and treat patients through the team approach of consultation and coordinated care. This approach has wide-reaching effects. The clinic is staffed and governed by full-time physicians whose control over quality, the clinic believes, is much more effectual than in other hospital organizations. The Lahey Clinic's quality assurance program is unusually impressive, as exemplified by its receiving a rare "accreditation with commendation" during its 1993 review by the Joint Commission on Accreditation of Healthcare Organizations.

At the Lahey Clinic, 300 physicians work with a staff of 3,000 to provide care in virtually every specialty and subspeciality of medicine to more than 2,000 patients each day, almost 25% of whom come from beyond Massachusetts.

Lahey, located 12 miles north of Boston, is a not-for-profit institution dedicated to providing coordinated medical care. In this environment, while a patient's care is managed by his or her principal physician, he or she has access to physicians in more than 30 specialties. Lahey is also the centerpiece of the Lahey Health Care Network, a system covering eastern Massachusetts with community-based physician group practices to ensure patients accessibility to Lahey services at all levels—primary, secondary,

THE LAHEY CLINIC'S QUALITY ASSURANCE PROGRAM IS UNUSUALLY IMPRESSIVE, AS EXEMPLIFIED BY ITS RECEIVING A RARE "ACCREDITATION WITH COMMENDATION" DURING ITS 1993 REVIEW BY THE JOINT COMMISSION ON ACCREDITATION OF HEALTHCARE ORGANIZATIONS.

and tertiary. Lahey Clinic North, a regional medical center located in Peabody, Massachusetts, opened in the fall of 1993.

Lahey Clinic is a center of expertise in areas such as the treatment of brain tumors, diagnostic imaging, management of hypertension, treatment of kidney disorders, laser surgery, pancreatic autotransplants, and use of radiation therapy for cancer. In gastroenterology, the Clinic treats the full range of digestive problems, with particular experience in inflammatory bowel disorders, diseases of the pancreas, motor disorders of the esophagus, and hyperalimentation. Lahey also has expertise in the full range of general surgical procedures.

As a means of minimizing hospitalization and reducing the cost of health care, the Lahey clinic stresses the development and use of testing and treatment techniques on an ambulatory basis. For this reason it has long undertaken diagnostic tests related to an approaching hospital stay on an outpatient basis, days in advance of hospital admission. With clinical departments and self-contained ambulatory surgery facilities, the clinic is designed to accommodate a large outpatient population. Physicians for the clinical departments have their offices and examining rooms within the medical center's Charles A. Dana Ambulatory Care Center. The Mary and Arthur Clapman Hospital provides inpatient care.

Lahey's social services department provides professionally trained social workers and continuing care nurses to hospitalized patients and their families. This staff helps in planning for discharge from the hospital or transfer to another facility and in counseling for emotional or social problems related to illness or hospitalization.

Prospective members of the medical staff undergo rigorous screening before being invited to become part of the Clinic. All new staff members remain on a probationary status for a period of three years. Ninety-eight percent of Clinic physicians are either board-certified or board-eligible, and all who are appointed to the senior staff must be board-certified.

The Lahey Clinic was established in 1923 as a small, private clinic operated by Dr. Frank H. Lahey,

AT A GLANCE

Beds: 272
Occupancy Rate: 80%
Average Patient Count: 190
Average Patient Stay: 6.6 days
Annual Admissions: 12,112
Outpatient Clinic Visits:
    483,201
Emergency Room/Trauma
    Center Visits: 58,357

HOSPITAL PERSONNEL
Physicians: 300
    Board Certified: 95%
Residents: 80
Registered Nurses: 566
    BS Degree: 233

ROOM CHARGES (PER DIEM)
Private: $750
ICU: $1,440–$1,920

ADDRESS
41 Mall Road
Burlington, MA 01805

TELEPHONE
(617) 273-5100

a prominent Boston surgeon, in his apartment in the city. The initial staff consisted of four surgeons. From it quarters in the Back Bay area of Boston, the Lahey medical staff achieved an international reputation. Lahey physicians pioneered such areas as thyroid, liver, and biliary surgery; radiation therapy; and neurosurgery, urology, and diagnostic imaging. By the mid-1970s the staff had grown to approximately 70 physicians, and the Clinic was housed in buildings spread over several city blocks. Inpatient services were provided at city hospitals more than a mile away. To consolidate the Clinic's diverse activities in one location, the Lahey Clinic Medical Center was opened in Burlington in 1980. The seven-story Lahey Medical Center contains in one complex the outpatient resources of the Charles A. Dana Ambulatory Care Center and the inpatient resources of the 272-bed Mary and Arthur R. Clapman Hospital.

SPECIAL FACILITIES AND PROGRAMS

Complete diagnosis and treatment is available to adults and children with all types of heart disease. Special interests include coronary artery disease, exercise physiology, disordered lipid and lipoprotein metabolism, cardiac electrophysiology, cardiac pacemakers, automatic inplantable cardioverter defibrillators, valvular heart disease, coronary bypass surgery, and coronary angioplasty. The Cardiac Rehabilitation Program brings together cardiac specialists, physical therapists, a nutritionist, a psychologist, a pharmacologist, and others to provide comprehensive rehabilitation training to those who have had heart attacks or other cardiac disorders and return them to active lives as quickly as possible.

Approximately one-third of Lahey patients are cancer patients. Lahey's multispecialty approach facilitates the diagnosis and treatment of all forms of cancer. For example, the Brain Tumor Clinic brings together neurologists, neurosurgeons, diagnostic radiologists, radiation oncologists, neuropathologists, and other specialists to provide comprehensive care of patients with brain tumor disorders, including techniques of radiosurgery—the pinpoint use of radiation therapy to treat deep-seated tumors. The Breast Cancer Center utilizes the skills of medical, surgical and radiation oncologists, plastic surgeons, diagnostic radiologists, and other specialists to diagnose and treat breast cancer. Treatment options include chemical, radiation, and surgical therapies, including lumpectomy with breast conservation, mastectomy, and simultaneous breast reconstruction. A breast cancer support group is available to provide emotional and educational support. In therapy coordinated with pulmonary medicine specialists, the Gamma Med 1.2i system for high intensity brachytherapy enables a powerful radioactive "seed" to be placed, by remote control rather than by the physician, directly adjacent to cancerous tissue in a patient's lung, allowing a much more powerful dosage to be used and shortening the therapy to minutes rather than days.

The Center for Diseases of the Gallbladder, Biliary Tree, Pancreas and Liver brings together gastroenterologists, general surgeons, and physicians from many other specialties to focus on problems of these complex organs, with capabilities ranging from outpatient endoscopic procedures to major liver surgery.

Lahey's Institute of Urology coordinates the skills of urologists, nephrologists, endocrinologists, diagnostic radiologists, and others to deal with the full range of disorders of the upper and lower genitourinary tract. Lahey physicians are leaders in such areas as surgery to preserve or restore kidney function, bladder reconstruction, and treatment of infertility and impotence problems.

The Department of Ophthalmology provides the full range of eye services, including cataract removal and lens implantation; diseases of the cornea and the conjunctiva, including corneal transplantation; disorders of the retina; and detection and treatment of glaucoma, including argon laser therapy. The department carries on an active vision examination and contact lens practice.

Lahey's Department of Diagnostic Radiology utilizes a full range of imaging techniques, including magnetic resonance imaging (MRI), computerized tomographic (CT) scanning, nuclear medicine, and ultrasound, as well as traditional x-ray systems. The department maintains an ongoing research partnership with several high technology companies for the development of systems that apply computer technology to imaging processes. Special interests of department members include interventional radiology techniques, such as renal artery angioplasty and fine needle biopsy.

Lahey's colon and rectal staff is known for its skills in this field, and has the most experience in New England—more than 500 cases—with the procedure underway to preserve bowel function for ulcerative colitis and polyposis patients who must have their colons removed.

The Lahey Clinic Section of Nephrology provides comprehensive, diagnostic, and therapeutic services for all forms of kidney disease and hypertension. Multifaceted dialysis care is offered to both hospitalized and ambulatory patients with acute or chronic renal failure. Hemodialysis, continuous ambulatory peritoneal dialysis, or night-time cycler dialysis can be utilized depending on the individual patient's medical status and preferences. Whenever possible, renal transplantation is considered as a therapeutic option for end-stage renal disease; 12 kidney transplants were performed in 1993. Patient education plus nutrition and social service counseling are available.

Other special facilities/services include pulmonary rehabilitation, an epilepsy center, a sexual dysfunction center, and a Lipid Clinic. Subspecialties of particular excellence and reputation at Lahey include cardiac surgery, where the first one-stage aortic replacement was performed; electrocardiology; inflammatory bowel disease, particularly ulcerative colitis and Crohn's disease; urinary bladder reconstruction; and laser prostate surgery.

MEDICAL SPECIALTIES

Allergy and Dermatology, Cardiology, Colon and Rectal Surgery, Endocrinology and Metabolism, Gastroenterology, General Internal Medicine, General Surgery,

Gynecology, Hand Surgery, Hematology, Infectious Diseases, Nephrology, Neurology, Neurosurgery, Oncology, Ophthalmalogy, Orthopedic Surgery, Otolaryngology/Head and Neck Surgery, Pediatric and Adolescent Medicine, Plastic and Reconstructive Surgery, Psychiatry and Behavioral Medicine, Pulmonary and Critical Care Medicine, Radiotherapy, Rheumatology, Thoracic and Vascular Surgery, Urology, and Vascular Medicine and Surgery.

WELL-KNOWN SPECIALISTS

- Dr. John W. Braasch   *Surgery; specialist in biliary, liver, and pancreatic surgery*
- Dr. Eugene P. Clerkin   *Internal medicine; specialist in endocrinology and hypertension*
- Dr. Charles A. Fager   *Neurosurgery; specialist in cranial, nerve, and spinal surgery*
- Dr. John A. Libertino   *Urology; pioneer in renal artery surgery and laser treatment of bladder cancer*
- Dr. Richard MacDermott   *Gastroenterology; leader in clinical research on new drug therapies for ulcerative colitis and Crohn's disease*
- Dr. Samuel Moschella   *Allergy and dermatology; specialist in skin cancer and leprosy*
- Dr. F. Warren Nugent   *Gastroenterology; specialist in Crohn's disease*
- Dr. Lars Svenson   *Cardiothoracic surgery; performed the first one-step aortic replacement ever done*
- Dr. Ferdinand Venditte   *Cardiology; a leading authority in cardiac electrophysiology and AICD*
- Dr. Leonard Zinman   *Urology; specialist in reconstructive surgery of the upper and lower urinary tracts*

PATIENT SATISFACTION

Overall patient satisfaction scores range between 92 and 95 on a scale of 1 to 100, with 100 being excellent.

RESEARCH

Research at Lahey Clinic is principally clinically oriented. Lahey staff concentrate on ways to improve the technology and techniques of care. Among significant developments in 1993—the Section of Cardiology gained recognition for its work with new transvenous implantable defibrillators and a new translumenal extraction catheter, and John A. Coller, M.D., Department of Colon and Rectal Surgery, became the first surgeon in the northeast to use a new robotic device for controlling the laparoscope during noninvasive surgery.

Ongoing research includes clinical research by Richard P. MacDermott, M.D., head of the Section of Gastroenterology, on new drug therapies for ulcerative colitis and Crohn's disease, and continuing basic research by Brooke R.

Seckel, M.D., chairman of the Department of Plastic Surgery and Reconstructive Surgery, on nerve regeneration.

The Clinic participates in numerous national studies, including the tamoxifen study for breast cancer prevention. Total research funding in 1993 was approximately $8.7 million.

ADMISSIONS POLICY

Anyone with a health concern can come to the Lahey Clinic for diagnosis and treatment. Appointments may be made either by the patient directly or through referral by a physician. Individuals can make appointments for themselves by calling the Appointment Office at (617) 273-8000.

Appointment coordinators are specially trained to match patients with physicians based on their health-care needs and preferences. Prospective patients may also request appointments with specific physicians. Physicians referring patients can do so with ease by calling the Physicians Referral Office at (617) 273-8899.

A patient can be admitted as an inpatient only by a member of the Lahey Clinic medical staff. Patients are required, at the time of admission, to indicate their method of payment, which may include private insurance, Medicare, Medicaid, or welfare. Patients with insurance issues are referred to a financial counselor. If indicated, special arrangements are made.

More than $11.2 million in free care was provided in 1993.

MASSACHUSETTS

GENERAL HOSPITAL

BOSTON, MASSACHUSETTS There are three cities in the United States that enjoy an overabundance of excellent medical care centers—New York, Chicago, and Boston. Boston enjoys three of the best-known medical schools and more than ten fine teaching hospitals. With so many fine medical facilities clustered together in such a small area, it is difficult to believe that one institution could emerge as the dominant hospital of the region. But in the minds of many doctors and hospital administrators, Massachusetts General is not only Boston's most important hospital but also one of the best in the world. Mass General, as it is called, delivers primary care to hundreds of thousands of Bostonians while also serving as one of the major tertiary care centers of New England. It is by far the largest of the Harvard-affiliated hospitals, and it is also the oldest and arguably the most influential.

Chartered in 1811 and opened in 1821, Massachusetts General Hospital (MGH) perhaps has been the single most important American setting in the evolution of modern medicine. The use of an anesthetic (ether) during surgery, for example, was first publicly demonstrated at Mass General in 1846, and in 1866 the first description of appendicitis and the recommendation of a surgical treatment were made by Massachusetts General physicians. In 1926, doctors at the MGH were instrumental in finding the causes of lead poisoning and developing a treatment

MASSACHUSETTS GENERAL
ENJOYS A WELL-EARNED
REPUTATION IN THE WORLD
MEDICAL COMMUNITY FOR
BEING AMONG THE VERY
BEST IN ALMOST EVERY
MEDICAL SPECIALTY.

for it. MGH researchers also discovered a surgical cure for hyperparathyroidism, a common endocrine disorder, in 1929 and pioneered work in nuclear medicine as early as 1937.

Following World War II, Massachusetts General's reputation as an important research institution continued to grow, especially after one of its physicians shared the Nobel Prize for discovering coenzyme A and describing its role in metabolism. During the 1960s two important breakthroughs—the first successful reattachment of a human arm and the discovery of practical means to freeze blood—brought MGH enormous national media attention. And, MGH's importance as a research hospital has only increased, as has its national and international influence.

Today, Massachusetts General Hospital is an enormous medical facility, with an operating budget of over $1 billion, that records more than 700,000 patient visits and admissions each year. MGH is the largest non-government employer in the city of Boston, employing more than 10,000 people, of whom more than 3,500 work in research.

Massachusetts General enjoys a well-earned reputation in the world medical community for being among the very best in almost every medical specialty. In fact, more than 100 of the hospital's physicians are listed in the current edition of *The Best Doctors in America*. Many MGH patients have been referred from all over the United States and from more than 90 countries by their physicians because the medical staff of MGH has earned an excellent reputation for diagnosing difficult cases. Most people who travel here come for one of the many specialized care services in areas such as arthritis, dermatology, diabetes, neurosurgery, thyroid disease, and recently developed techniques such as the use of magnetic resonance imaging (MRI) for the diagnosis of lesions of the brain and other organs. Massachusetts General also has leading-edge capabilities in noninvasive diagnostic modalities for heart diseases, applications of the laser for diagnosis and treatment of various diseases, diagnostic tests using monoclonal antibodies for cancer of the

AT A GLANCE

Beds: 933
Occupancy Rate: 79%
Average Patient Count: 783
Average Patient Stay: 7.8 days
Annual Admissions: 36,821
Outpatient Clinic Visits:
    558,446
Emergency Room/Trauma
    Center Visits: 83,355

HOSPITAL PERSONNEL
Physicians: 1,896
Residents: 527
Registered Nurses: 1,842

ROOM CHARGES (PER DIEM)
Private: $753
Semiprivate: $710
ICU: $1,290–$1,900

ADDRESS
32 Fruit Street
Boston, MA 02114

TELEPHONE
(617) 726-2000

gastrointestinal tract and liver diseases, and the use of the proton beam to treat brain and eye tumors.

The complex medical services and the research programs are the main reasons for Massachusetts General's widespread fame, but to the people of Greater Boston it is the easy access to doctors in a host of fields that make the hospital vital. Clinical services include children's services, dermatology, gynecology, neurology, neurosurgery, obstetrics, oral and maxillofacial surgery, orthopedic surgery, psychiatry, radiation medicine, radiology, surgery, and urology.

In March 1994, Massachusetts General Hospital joined with Brigham and Women's Hospital to form Partners Healthcare System, Inc., an affiliation established to create an integrated health care delivery system, while preserving each hospital's dedication to teaching and research. In addition to the two founding hospitals, the network will include physician practices and community hospitals, as well as the McLean Hospital, a psychiatric facility in Belmont, Mass., and Spaulding Rehabilitation Hospital in Boston.

SPECIAL FACILITIES AND PROGRAMS

Physicians at Massachusetts General were concerned with the treatment of cancer patients long before they opened their first so-called Tumor Clinic in 1925. Today, the hospital's cancer center is the largest facility for oncological treatment and research in New England. Over 3,500 new cancer patients come here every year, and more than 11,000 are treated annually, most on an outpatient basis. About 120 physicians from a variety of departments—including the special Pediatric Hematology Oncology Unit—are involved in treating patients with the most up-to-date therapies and advanced technology.

Long-term rehabilitation medicine is provided at Spaulding Rehabilitation Hospital, the largest facility of its kind in the world. Spaulding's 127 physicians sustain 16 comprehensive programs to prepare patients to return to families and communities at their highest possible level of independence. Renowned for its ability to provide intensive rehabilitation while managing complex medical problems, Spaulding treats more than 2,800 inpatients and 2,600 outpatients annually.

In recent years, there have been extraordinary advances in orthopedics, many of which have taken place at MGH. The MGH Orthopaedic Service is an international leader in the management of musculoskeletal disease. Each year, the service treats thousands of patients suffering from arthritic or broken hips, severe skeletal trauma, bone cancer, spinal disorders, disk disease, hand disabilities, sports injuries, and other serious problems. The Orthopaedic Service is also a major training center for resident physicians and Harvard Medical School students, and its laboratories are counted among the most productive in the world.

MGH orthopaedic service is well-recognized for its accomplishments. The Orthopaedic Service's bone allograft surgery program has been remarkably successful in freeing patients of bone cancer while preserving their limbs. Its surgeons are world leaders in hip replacement surgery. The Sports Medicine Unit has made significant contributions to the diagnosis and treatment of knee injuries.

The MGH Urologic Service has 54 dedicated urologic beds, and a four-bed urologic intensive care unit is located on the eleventh floor of the hospital's White and Bigelow Buildings. Additional private beds and pediatric urology beds are available in the new Ellison Building. The Urologic Service has four dedicated operating rooms in which more than 3,000 operative procedures are performed yearly. In addition, more than 4,100 adult patients are seen each year in the service's outpatient clinic. Cystoscopies and other minor surgical procedures are performed in the outpatient clinic. The service also has specialty clinics in oncology, urinary calculi, and urinary diversion, and is part of the hospital's infertility clinic and pediatric urology clinic. The urologic stone treatment center includes a lithotriptor, laser lithotripsy, and an active research effort. The Urologic Laboratory is equipped for molecular biology, tissue culture, transport, histology, laser and renal and gut physiology studies.

Clinicians and researchers of the MGH stroke service are seeking to improve stroke treatment at every stage. A primary focus is on prevention. In collaboration with the radiology department, the Stroke Service is using new technologies to identify patients with reduced blood flow to the brain. With MGH cardiologists, neurologists are developing and applying new therapies to reduce atherosclerosis. The Neurological Intensive Care Unit is equipped with eight beds for intensive monitoring of critically ill stroke patients.

For patients with diseased or damaged hearts, Massachusetts General offers a complete range of services, from prevention to transplantation. This hospital has recently established a program in preventive cardiology that includes behavioral medicine, stress reduction, nutrition counseling, exercise, smoking cessation, and weight loss, as well as research into cardiac risk factors and new agents to lower cholesterol.

MGH houses a large and very active transplantation program. It was the first hospital in New England to perform a simultaneous heart and liver transplant. New anti-rejection drugs developed at MGH dramatically improve the success rates of transplants performed at the hospital.

The Vincent Memorial Service (the Women's Care Division of Massachusetts General) has a long-standing tradition of providing women with excellent medical and gynecologic care for a wide spectrum of gynecologic problems. General gynecologic care includes general and specialized physical examination; screening for infections; and screening for cancer, including Pap smears, breast examination with regular mammography, and patient health education. Its in vitro fertilization (IVF) unit offers new services in the area of assisted reproductive technology. An obstetric unit has recently been added to the services available.

The MGH Center for Risk Analysis has been established to identify women at risk of developing breast cancer, while the MGH Comprehensive Breast Health Center coordinates every aspect of breast cancer detection and patient care.

Just about every department has offices in the Ambulatory Care Center, where over 550,000 patients a year are treated in more than 70 specialized outpatient clinics. Here is a brief alphabetical listing of some of them: Adolescent Gynecology, Allergy, Arthritis/Rheumatology, the Cancer Center Unit (includes nine clinics), Cardiac Ambulatory Care, Child Psychiatry, Cystic Fibrosis, Diabetes, Eating Disorders, Huntington's Disease, Infectious Disease (the Traveler's Advice Center), Infertility, Learning Disorders, Movement Disorders, Muscular Dystrophy, Neurovisual Disorders, Occupational Health, the Pain Group, Plastic and Reconstructive Surgery, Psychiatry (Acute and General), Radiation Medicine, Reproductive Endocrinology, Scoliosis (Adult and child), Sleep Disorders, and the Thyroid Unit.

The latest listing of top hospitals in the U.S. from *U.S. News and World Report* listed 12 MGH specialties among the top 40 in 16 categories. Eleven of these specialties were ranked within the top 12 of their categories. AIDS (ranked 6th), Cancer (12th), Cardiology (3rd), Endocrinology (2nd), Gastroenterology (3rd), Geriatrics (6th), Gynecology (5th), Neurology (2nd), Orthopedics (3rd), Rheumatology (6th), Urology (9th) and Psychology (7th).

MEDICAL SPECIALTIES

Allergy and Immunology, Anesthesiology, Cardiac Surgery, Cardiology, Dermatology, Endocrinology, Gastroenterology, Genetics, Gerontology, Gynecology, Hypertension, Infectious Diseases, Neonatology, Nephrology, Neurology, Neurosurgery, Obstetrics, Oncology and Hematology, Oral and Maxillofacial Surgery, Organ Transplantation, Orthopedic Surgery, Pathology, Pediatrics, Pediatric Surgery, Plastic and Reconstructive Surgery, Psychiatry, Pulmonary Medicine, Radiation Medicine, Rehabilitation Medicine, Replantation of Limbs, Rheumatology, Thoracic Surgery, Urology and Vascular Surgery.

WELL-KNOWN SPECIALISTS

- Dr. R. Rex Anderson   *Dermatologist; specialist in vascular birthmarks*
- Dr. Lloyd Axelrod   *Endocrinology and metabolism; specialist in diabetes*
- Dr. Lawrence F. Borgea   *Neurosurgery; specialist in spinal surgery*
- Dr. Deborah J. Colton   *Infectious disease; specialist in AIDS*
- Dr. Randall David Gay   *Endocrinology and metabolism; specialist in endocrine surgery*
- Dr. Donald S. Kaufman   *Medical oncology/hematology; specialist in genito-urinary cancer*
- Dr. Allen Lapey   *Pediatric allergy; specialist in cystic fibrosis*
- Dr. Richard Leplick   *Anesthesia; specialist in critical care medicine*
- Dr. Robert H. Shapiro   *Endoscopy; specialist in biliary endoscopy*
- Dr. Arthur E. Weyman   *Cardiology; specialist in electrocardiography*

PATIENT SATISFACTION

MGH is currently launching a comprehensive patient satisfaction survey program. Results will not be available for some time.

The anecdotal evidence from newspapers and magazines, and from doctor recommendations, gives us great confidence that doctors and staff are attentive to patient needs.

RESEARCH

Massachusetts General Hospital conducts the largest hospital-based research program in the United States, with a 1993 research budget exceeding $175 million.

MGH has established a number of multidisciplinary centers in which researchers and clinicians from all over the world grapple with some of the most difficult problems in medicine. The Cardiovascular Center concentrates on means of detecting myocardial infarction and preventing coronary thrombosis. The Neuroscience Center is dedicated to neuroendocrinology—central nervous system growth factor research. Cancer research encompasses work in immunogenetics, molecular genetics, molecular hematology, and molecular biology. Studying basic aspects of the skin, infections, immunology, bioengineering, and neurobiology is the focus of the Cutaneous Biology Research Center. The Transplantation Biology Research Center is carrying out laboratory investigations in transplantation immunology focusing on the largest problem in transplantation medicine—the rejection of transplanted organs.

In the past few years, MGH researchers and clinicians have registered an impressive list of milestones. A few of the many highlights are described below.

In cancer research, MGH scientists have identified a tumor-suppressor gene that has been associated with inherited and noninherited forms of cancer. They have also developed a new way to treat invasive bladder cancer that preserves the patient's bladder function.

Massachusetts General has been the site of pioneering work on AIDS, including studies of anti-HIV therapies.

Accomplishments in genetics research include the discovery, in 1993, of the long-sought genes for Huntington's and Lou Gehrig's disease, in collaboration with scientists from other institutions. Also in 1993, the gene for neurofibromatosis Type 2 was discovered.

Cardiovascular research achievements have included the extraction and analysis of a substance suspected of causing many cases of high blood pressure.

The Wellman Laboratory of Photomedicine is the world's largest basic and applied biomedical laser facility.

The Center for Imaging and Pharmaceutical Research explores the relationship between modern imaging technology and drug development.

ADMISSIONS POLICY

Although this is one of America's best-known hospitals—a place where famous people such as John Wayne, Henry Kissinger, and Yelena Bonner were treated—Massachusetts General treats far more people whose names are not household words. The hospital's doors are open to people from all walks of society. Patients can be referred by their doctors to a specialist on staff, or they can inquire about doctors through a special patient referral number: (617) 726-3400. Patients calling this number will most likely be directed to a doctor in the Wang Ambulatory Care Center. Of course, those needing immediate help will be treated and, if need be, admitted through Emergency Services or the Medical Walk-in Unit—in fact, a surprising 40% of all admissions enter the hospital this way.

MCLEAN HOSPITAL

BELMONT,
MASSACHUSETTS

Located on a 240-acre, 300-bed campus just outside Boston, McLean Hospital has the look of a small New England College. Yet in this setting, important work is carried on at this private, nonprofit psychiatric hospital affiliated with Massachusetts General Hospital and the Harvard Medical School. Each day it treats up to 180 to 190 people in its inpatient services and almost twice as many in its outpatient and aftercare programs. A national center for psychiatric and chemical dependency treatment, research, and teaching, McLean was ranked as the best psychiatric hospital in the country in the latest listing by *U.S. News and World Report.*

The third oldest psychiatric hospital in the United States and the first to open in Massachusetts, McLean was founded in 1811 as part of Massachusetts General Hospital. Today, as a free-standing hospital, it is a network of inpatient and partial hospital units, community residences, outpatient clinics, and other facilities located in Belmont, 10 miles west of Boston. McLean is also home to the largest research program of any private psychiatric hospital in the United States and is a teaching facility of Harvard Medical School.

Every patient at McLean is approached with the expectation that no matter what the diagnosis and the severity of the emotional illness, he or she can be treated. Therapies range from traditional psychoanalysis

A NATIONAL CENTER FOR PSYCHIATRIC AND CHEMICAL DEPENDENCY TREATMENT, RESEARCH, AND TEACHING, MCLEAN WAS RANKED AS THE BEST PSYCHIATRIC HOSPITAL IN THE COUNTRY IN THE LATEST LISTING BY *U.S. NEWS AND WORLD REPORT.*

to such newer techniques as behavior and family therapy, but the goal is always to return the patient to the community as soon as possible. To make this goal of return to the community more achievable, McLean recently put into effect a complete revamping of its approach to patient care, minimizing hospitalization and emphasizing quicker discharge times for those admitted as inpatients.

In order to meet the unique needs of each patient in today's environment, McLean offers five levels of treatment. The first level is rapid evaluation and stabilization of patients through McLean's Clinical Evaluation Center. More than 20 specialty clinics are available at McLean for patients that do not require a hospital stay. Community residential care services are provided for patients who do not require inpatient hospitalization, but can benefit from supervised, overnight care in a variety of settings. Partial hospital care is provided on a day, evening or weekend basis in a highly structured therapeutic setting. On-grounds, intensive inpatient services, including assessment, diagnosis, acute crisis intervention, stabilization, and aftercare planning are also available. At each of these levels, treatment programs are designed around the individual problems patients face. Some of the areas McLean programs focus on are alcohol and drug abuse, bipolar and psychotic disorders, child and adolescent care, geriatric care, and mood, anxiety, and trauma.

This vertically integrated system of patient care was introduced in 1993 and has radically affected McLean's methods of delivering patient services. Five years prior, McLean Hospital's treatment of individuals with acute psychiatric disorders focused largely on inpatient programs. The average length of patient stay statistics illustrate the impact of the change. In 1988 the average patient who came to McLean for treatment stayed for 64 days; in 1993, that patient remained hospitalized for only 16 days. In fact, only a small minority of McLean patients are treated on an inpatient basis today. In 1993, there were about 4,200 inpatient admissions, as compared with 785 treated in the free-standing Community Residential and Treatment Program; a little over 40,000 treated through partial hospital visits; and more than 65,000 treatments provided through outpatient visits.

This innovative system of care at McLean is seen as laying the groundwork for a new system of care that will enable McLean to reach out over greater distances and to new constituencies by playing an important role in emerging networks of health care providers. For example, McLean has recently joined other members of the Mass General family of affiliations and Brigham and Women's Hospital in the Partners Healthcare System, Inc.

McLean has always educated psychiatric professionals. Today over 400 students annually train at McLean for careers in nursing, social work, psychology, psychiatry, and other human service professions. An even larger number of practicing professionals come to McLean for continuing education programs that cover subjects as diverse as neurochemistry and couples therapy. In addition, McLean staff members frequently serve as faculty for programs offered by the American Psychiatric Association and other national professional societies.

Through contractual arrangements, the staff also work with people in schools, prisons, and other community settings.

SPECIAL FACILITIES AND PROGRAMS

Access to care at McLean is through the Clinical Evaluation Center (CEC), which gives patients and referring professionals a single, convenient "doorway" to all of the hospital's services. The CEC provides rapid evaluation and stabilization of new patients, short-term observation and respite care, and a streamlined process that quickly moves patients to the most appropriate program. The CEC is staffed with experienced staff 24 hours-a-day, 7 days-a-week.

The McLean Behavioral Medicine Practice is located at the unaffiliated Pediatric and Adolescent Referral Center in Waltham, Massachusetts. Families bring their children to the practice in order to receive expert assessments from some of New England's finest medical and surgical specialists. The Behavioral Medicine Practice specializes in dealing with the psychological and emotional disorders that may accompany a medical condition and interfere with emotional and social adjustment. The Practice works closely with the child's medical providers to help him or her deal with these emotional problems. Specialists provide comprehensive evaluations and treatment to the child and family for such problems as sleep disturbances, eating difficulties, school problems, overanxiousness, fears, and medical noncompliance.

Other evaluation and treatment services available at the Behavioral Medicine Practice include developmental assessment, psychological testing, behavior modification, biofeedback, psychopharmacology, individual psychotherapy, group therapy for children and adolescents, and parent support groups. Specialized problems treated on an outpatient basis focus on developmental delays, infant and early childhood feeding problems, hyperactivity, attention deficit disorder, behavioral problems, phobias, withdrawal and/or depression, eating disorders, and sexual and physical trauma, among others.

AT A GLANCE

Beds: 309
Occupancy Rate: 88%
Average Patient Count: 180
Average Patient Stay: 16 days
Annual Admissions: 4,190
Partial Hospital Visits: 40,072
Outpatient Clinic Visits:
　65,159
Residential Care Patients
　Served: 785

HOSPITAL PERSONNEL
Psychiatrists: 240
Psychologists: 173
Nursing Staff: 221
Social Workers: 70
Rehabilitation Professionals:
　26

ROOM CHARGES (PER DIEM)
Child/Adolescent Services:
　$898
Geriatric Services: $620
Bipolar/Psychotic Disorders
　Services: $868
Mood/Anxiety/Trauma
　Services: $758
Short-Term Services: $1,093

ADDRESS
115 Mill Street
Belmont, MA 02178

TELEPHONE
(617) 855-2000

The McLean Institute for Couples and Families is an adult outpatient program that provides services to people who are experiencing life transitions or more serious stresses in their primary relationships. Using an integrated framework of psychodynamic and systems approaches, the Institute offers couples therapy, family therapy, and the treatment of sexual dysfunction. Couples and families are helped to understand and improve their interpersonal relationships, while developing a deeper understanding of themselves as individuals. The Institute's multidisciplinary staff includes psychiatrists, psychologists, social workers, and psychiatric nurses. Five separate programs are offered.

Couples therapy is for married or unmarried heterosexual or homosexual couples who want to improve their relationships. Therapy focuses on enhancing communication, understanding the roots of current problems, developing mutual empathy, and changing problematic patterns of interaction. Family Therapy addresses families with troubled relationships and problems associated with life stages such as adolescent turmoil, mid-life crisis, or other family stresses. The special difficulties of stepfamilies and single parent families are also addressed. In the Human Sexuality Program, individuals or couples work with a therapist to assess possible causes of sexual difficulties. Therapy is provided using interpersonal, behavioral, psychodynamic, and cognitive techniques. Couples Therapy for the Sexually Abused and Their Partners, Divorce Counseling and Couple Group Therapy are among the other programs offered at the Institute for Couples and Families.

Inpatient services include the following programs: the Alcohol and Drug Abuse Treatment Center; the Hall-Mercer Children's Center; the Depression Treatment Unit; Clinical Evaluation Units; and Generic Units.

McLean also markets high quality psychiatric treatment programs and services in diverse settings throughout the United States. These efforts focus on psychiatric services in acute care hospitals, community residential treatment services, and employee assistance programs.

PSYCHIATRIC SPECIALTIES

Modes of treatment include individual, couples, family, group and behavior therapy; psychopharmacology; rehabilitation therapies; psychological testing; medical pediatric, and neurological evaluation and care; and detoxification and other therapies related to chemical dependency.

WELL-KNOWN SPECIALISTS

- Dr. Rose J. Baidasearini   *Specialist in psychopharmacology*
- Dr. Joseph Biederman   *Specialist in child and adolescent psychiatry*
- Dr. James A. Chu   *Specialist in dissociative disorders*
- Dr. Barbara J. Coffey   *Specialist in child and adolescent psychology*
- Dr. Jonathan Q. Cole   *Specialist in psychopharmacology*
- Dr. Shervert H. Fraiser, Jr.   *Specialist in general psychology*

- Dr. James J. Hudson   *Specialist in eating disorders*
- Dr. John Terry Maltsberger   *Specialist in suicidology*
- Dr. Steven M. Mirin   *Specialist in addiction psychology*
- Dr. Andrew Alan Nierenberg   *Specialist in mood and anxiety disorders*
- Dr. Larry H. Strasburger   *Specialist in forensic psychiatry*
- Dr. Arthur F. Valenstein   *Specialist in psychoanalysis*
- Dr. Anna K. Wolff   *Specialist in psychoanalysis*

PATIENT SATISFACTION

Due to the difficulty in receiving valid feedback, patient satisfaction surveys are not taken. Surveys of referring physicians show that the overwhelming majority are very satisfied with the treatment their patients have received at McLean and the improvements patients have experienced.

RESEARCH

McLean has a rich history of research dating back to 1888. The Mailman Research Center, long recognized as one of the world's most comprehensive facilities for basic scientific research into mental illness, integrates the physiological and the psychological in its approaches to psychiatric research. Recently, the hospital launched a $30 million capital campaign to expand and update the existing facilities. During the 1993 fiscal year, McLean received a record $16.6 million in external funding to support research.

The scientific program at McLean Hospital continues to be at the forefront of psychiatric research in its size, productivity, and technological sophistication. McLean maintains the largest research program in any psychiatric hospital and the largest neuroscience research program at any hospital, department, or school affiliated with Harvard. Currently, 120 investigators and 162 support staff work on 376 research projects at McLean. While these projects range in focus from basic neurochemistry to clinical pharmacology, most of the research there is dedicated to the study of the major psychiatric disorders, including schizophrenia, bipolar disorder, major depression, Alzheimer's disease, and alcohol and drug abuse.

A hallmark of McLean research is its integration of scientific and clinical expertise. Research studies are performed in all of the clinical programs and address psychiatric illness in all age groups, from childhood to old age. Research requiring laboratory facilities or special procedures is also performed on the hospital's campus at the Mailman Research Center, the Alcohol and Drug Abuse Research Center, the Brain Imaging Center, and the Sleep Disorders Center.

In Alzheimer's research, investigators at the Mailman Research Center have made continuing progress in identifying the enzymes that produce a small protein called beta amyloid that is suspected as a cause of the disease. These McLean scientists are now designing drugs to stop the progression of Alzheimer's disease by preventing production of beta amyloid.

The nutrient choline is essential for the normal structure and function of nerve cells in the brain. At the Brain Imaging Center, investigators, using magnetic resonance imaging (MRI), have observed that older adults may increasingly be unable to absorb choline from their food for distribution to the brain. This nutritional failure may be an important factor contributing to the development of Alzheimer's and other degenerative disorders of the brain associated with age.

McLean was among the first research facilities to use functional magnetic imaging in the study of schizophrenia. Researchers have discovered abnormalities of blood flow occurring in response to local activation of the brain. These abnormalities suggest that metabolic anomalies or anomalous development of the vascular system in the brain may contribute to the symptoms of schizophrenia.

For the treatment of schizophrenia and bipolar disorder, McLean scientists are developing agents that act only at sites felt to be important in producing therapeutic effects, rather than throughout the entire brain and body. In addition, as opposed to the effects of standard antipsychotic drugs, these agents are designed to modulate, rather than block, normal cellular functions, producing greater benefits with fewer side effects.

Investigators at the Brain Imaging Center (BIC) are performing the first systematic study of magnetic resonance imaging (MRI) scans of the brain in normal children. The data obtained will be a valuable resource for comparison to scans from children with psychiatric disorders, to identify abnormalities that may explain early onset mental illnesses.

In other studies at the BIC, abnormalities in the chemicals known to be involved in the metabolism of nerve cells have been observed deep in the brain in patients with bipolar disorder and major depression. Additional studies are underway to determine whether these findings are specific to mood disorders, how these abnormalities may change with treatment, and what they suggest about the alterations in brain function which underlie or characterize depression.

ADMISSIONS POLICY

Generally, admissions to McLean are scheduled through the Clinical Evaluation Center. To make a referral or to access McLean's system of care, call (800) 955-9005.

Before admission, families are asked to call the hospital's Patient Accounts Office to discuss financial arrangements. Room charges vary with the needs of individual patients and their insurance coverages. The hospital does provide a limited amount of free care.

NEW ENGLAND

MEDICAL CENTER

Even with all the competition in Greater Boston, New England Medical Center (NEMC) stands out— for many reasons. First, the medical center, the primary teaching hospital of Tufts University School of Medicine, provides excellent services that are enhanced by its numerous and varied research projects and educational programs. The Medical Center is also widely known for its innovations in health care management. Extensive research, leading to the promotion of health and improvement of the health care system, is conducted, particularly through the Health Institute, a social science research and development unit established in 1988. NEMC has a distinguished history of achievement in scientific research, including the development of an infant formula (today known as Similac) used to nourish millions of infants worldwide; discovery of the link between obesity and heart disease; research leading to the discovery of drugs to prevent the body's rejection of a transplanted organ; the first laser heart surgery performed in the world; and the use of Interleukin-2 with anti-tumor lymphocytes as an experimental treatment for cancer.

In terms of medical services, the New England Medical Center offers comprehensive inpatient care for both adults and children. It provides all levels of health care—from the most basic health maintenance and primary care to the most complex, such as brain

BOSTON, MASSACHUSETTS

EVEN WITH ALL
THE COMPETITION IN
GREATER BOSTON, NEW
ENGLAND MEDICAL CENTER
(NEMC) STANDS OUT—
FOR MANY REASONS.

surgery, cancer treatment, heart bypass surgery, organ transplants, and stroke management. NEMC Hospital is a not-for-profit tertiary referral facility for the treatment of acutely ill adults. The Floating Hospital for Infants and Children provides both inpatient and outpatient care for newborns to teenagers.

New England Medical Center began with the establishment of the Boston Dispensary, created in 1796 by a group of Boston citizens to ensure that the poor of the city had access to health care. Over the years, other institutions have become part of the medical center—The Floating Hospital for Infants and Children (1894), Pratt Diagnostic Clinic (1930), New England Center Hospital (1948), and the Rehabilitation Institute (1958).

Nursing care at New England Medical Center is based on the primary nursing model—each patient has a primary nurse who coordinates nursing care, educates the patient and family about the patient's care, and assists with discharge planning. All full-time physicians at the Medical Center hold faculty appointments at Tufts University School of Medicine.

The Medical Center is located near the Boston Common, next to Boston's Theater District and Chinatown and a few blocks from the Downtown Crossing shopping area. In recent years, its facilities have been extensively replaced and renovated.

Indicative of its tertiary care services and strong referring physician base is NEMC's relatively wide geographic area from which the hospital draws its patients. In 1993, approximately 33.8% of NEMC's discharges were from the City of Boston, 26.0% were from the rest of Greater Boston, 28.0% were from other eastern Massachusetts cities and towns (the South Shore, Cape Cod, and the islands) and 12.2% were from the rest of Massachusetts and other states. Pediatric discharges draw from an even wider area.

SPECIAL FACILITIES AND PROGRAMS

NEMC is especially recognized for its practices in AIDS, Cancer, Cardiology, Endocrinology, Gastroenterology, Gynecology, Neurology, Orthopedics, Otolaryngology, and Urology. Specialists in these areas and others have modern facilities and equipment in specialty centers to draw on. NEMC Hospital is a member of four collaborative transplantation programs: the Boston Center for Liver Transplantation, the Boston Center for Heart Transplantation, the Massachusetts Center for Lung Transplantation, and the Massachusetts Center for Pancreas Transplantation. NEMC Hospital is also in three clinical trials to determine whether autologous bone marrow transplantation improves the survival rate or quality of life for breast cancer patients. In 1993, 33 transplant patients received new livers; 53 received bone marrow transplants; 25 had new kidneys transplanted; and seven received donor hearts. NEMC is one of the few hospitals in the nation performing stem cell transplantation, which is used to treat cancer patients for whom traditional bone marrow transplantation is no longer possible. Stem cells are withdrawn from the bloodstream, preserved, and then returned to the patient following chemotherapy.

NEMC has a number of specialized centers for the treatment of cancer including the Breast Health Center, one of the first multi-disciplinary diagnosis and treatment centers to be established for breast cancer patients. Beginning in 1992, the Center became a participant in a ten-year nationwide clinical trial to determine whether breast cancer can be prevented among high-risk women through long-term use of the drug tamoxifen.

Diagnostic and treatment services, primarily for patients with three types of skin cancer—basal cell carcinoma, squamous cell carcinoma, and malignant melanoma—are provided by the Skin Cancer Center. Treatment modalities include Moh's micrographic surgery, curettage and electrodesiccation, cryosurgery, topical chemotherapy, and surgical excision. The center works closely with surgeons in Plastic Surgery and Otolaryngology for patients who require extensive repair. A multidisciplinary service designed to screen and treat patients with suspicious pigmented lesions, dysplastic nevi, lentigo maligna, and melanoma is available at the Pigmented Lesion Center. The center's unique personalized approach helps patients recognize potential problems. It also offers same day excisional biopsies, photographic evaluation of developing lesions, skin self-exam training, and individual identification of risk factors.

The Lung Tumor Evaluation Center provides a comprehensive multidisciplinary approach to the treatment of thoracic pathology. It specializes in the evaluation and treatment of cancer of the lung, esophagus, chest wall, mediastinum, and pleura. It is staffed by thoracic surgeons, pulmonary specialists, oncologists, and radiation therapists who are available to see each patient in a single visit. Treatment options for all patients are discussed at a weekly conference immediately after the clinic.

Patients with both primary and recurrent disease are evaluated and entered in one of several ongoing national or local cancer research trials by the Colorectal Cancer Center.

AT A GLANCE

Beds: 527
Occupancy Rate: 80%
Average Patient Count: 511
Average Patient Stay: 7 days
Annual Admissions: 21,683
Births: 2,000
Outpatient Clinic Visits:
    353,204
Emergency Room/Trauma
    Center Visits: 27,567

HOSPITAL PERSONNEL
Physicians: 490
    Board Certified: 100%
Residents: 465
Registered Nurses: 1,249
    BS Degree: 788

ROOM CHARGES (PER DIEM)
Private: $647
Semiprivate: $560
ICU: $1,436–$1,578

ADDRESS
750 Washington Street
Boston, MA 02111

TELEPHONE
(617) 956-5000

The Cardiovascular Center offers a full complement of diagnostic facilities for the evaluation and treatment of cardiac disease. Available technologies include cardiac catheterization, clinical electrophysiology, Doppler echocardiography, electrocardiography, loop monitoring, myocardial biopsies, radionuclide angiography, SPECT thallium stress testing, stress testing, tilt table testing, transesophageal echocardiography, and 24-hour Holter monitoring. In cardiac arrhythmia treatment, NEMC is one of the few hospitals nationally using radio frequency to treat ventricular fibrillation, a common form of cardiac arrhythmia which causes over 700,000 deaths annually in the U.S.

The Kidney Disease and Hypertension Center specializes in the diagnosis and treatment of hypertension and kidney disease, from early onset through the entire course of illness. In one location, the center provides the services of the Nephrology and Hypertension Clinics, the DCI Dialysis Unit, the outpatient services of the Kidney Transplantation Program, the Kidney Function Diagnostic Laboratory, and the Nephrology Clinic Research Center.

A full-service clinical program for couples who have been unable to conceive is available at the Fertility Center. Staffed by a multidisciplinary team of infertility specialists, the center offers comprehensive diagnostic, therapeutic, educational, and support services. Available therapies include artificial insemination, assisted reproductive technologies (such as in vitro fertilization), laser surgery, microsurgery, ovulation induction, and pelviscopic surgery. The In Vitro Fertilization (IVF) Center offers a specialized state-of-the-art IVF and GIFT programs. Embryo cryopreservation is available.

The New England Eye Center was established in 1991 as a tertiary referral center for eye disorders, with a particular focus on the use of lasers in eye treatment.

The Pratt Diagnostic Clinic, founded in 1938, is a nationally recognized specialty referral center, providing second opinions and expert diagnostic evaluations for difficult medical problems. It also offers the Executive Health Program, a health management service designed to detect and treat conditions associated with corporate lifestyles.

Other specialty adult facilities include the Francis Stern Nutrition Center, the Syncope Evaluation Center, and the Day Surgery Center. A wide range of outpatient clinics also exists.

The Floating Hospital for Children, which celebrated its 100th anniversary in 1994, is the pediatric hospital of New England Medical Center. It provides care to children, from newborns to young adults, in an environment specially designed to meet their needs. It also serves the community as a pediatric teaching institution and a pediatric research center.

Some of the specialized pediatric services and centers include neonatology, the Affiliated Children's Arthritis Centers of New England, the Pediatric Fibrosis Center, the Children's Cancer Center, the Center for Children with Special Needs, pediatric rheumatology, and pediatric cardiology. Special rooms throughout the inpatient floors are designated for parent-physician conferences, family waiting, and parent quiet time. In addition, there is a limited number of "rooming-in" or Family Participation rooms, each accommodating a child and an adult.

MEDICAL SPECIALTIES

Allergy, Anesthesiology, Cardiology, Clinical Decision Making, Dentistry, Dermatology, Endocrinology, Gastroenterology, General Internal Medicine, Geographic Medicine and Infectious Disease, Health Services Research, Hematology/Oncology, Nephrology, Neurology, Neurosurgery, Nutrition Services, Obstetrics/Gynecology, Ophthalmology, Orthopaedics, Otolaryngology, Pathology, Physical and Rehabilitation Medicine, Psychiatry, Pulmonology and Critical Care, Radiation Oncology, Radiology, Rheumatology/Immunology, Surgery, and Urology.

Pediatric specialties include: Arthritis and Rheumatic Disease, Birth Defects/Genetic Counseling, Cardiology, Endocrinology, Gastroenterology/Nutrition, General Pediatrics, Hematology/Oncology, Infectious Disease, Neonatology, Nephrology, Neurology, Pulmonary/Allergy, Surgery, Trauma, and Urology.

WELL-KNOWN SPECIALISTS

- Dr. Michael Atkins   *Hematology/oncology; specialist in research with Interleukin-2, treatment for kidney cancer and melanoma and other cytokines*
- Dr. Diana Bianchi   *Newborn medicine; developed an innovative prenatal maternal blood test for serious genetic abnormalities*
- Dr. Clifford L. Craig   *Orthopaedist*
- Dr. Tim Crombleholme   *Pediatric surgery*
- Dr. William Dietz   *Gastroenterology and nutrition; director, Growth and Nutrition Clinic (failure to thrive); director, Weight Control Program*
- Dr. Charles Dinarello   *Geographic medicine and infectious diseases; researcher of Interleukin-2 for treatment of kidney cancer, melanoma, and cytokine*
- Dr. John Erban   *Hematology/oncology; leader of studies with tamoxifen, research in bone marrow transplantation trials*
- Dr. N. A. Mark Estes, III   *Cardiology; director, Cardiac Arrhythmia Service, Cardiac Electrophysiology Laboratory*
- Dr. Martha Hutchinson   *Director, Cytology Laboratory; developed new Pap Smear procedure*
- Dr. Sherrie Kaplan   *Health Institute; studies MD-patient relationships*
- Dr. Joseph Lau   *Health Service Research; specialist in HIV infection of babies with infected mothers*
- Dr. Judy Lieberman   *Hematology/oncology; specialist in AIDS research*
- Dr. James Mier   *Hematology/oncology; originally purified Interleukin-2 for treatment of cancer*
- Dr. Kenneth B. Miller   *Director, Bone Marrow Transplantation; specialist in stem cell transplantation*

- Dr. Carmen Puliafito   *Director, New England Eye Center; specialist in laser eye surgery*
- Dr. Barton Sachs   *Orthopaedics; Center for Spine Care, specialist in laser back surgery*
- Dr. Grannum Sant   *Urology; specialist in incontinence*
- Dr. Robert Sege   *General pediatrics and adolescent medicine; specialist in infants with AIDS, violence on children*
- Dr. Harry P. Selker   *Director, Center for Cardiovascular Health Services*

PATIENT SATISFACTION

Patient satisfaction is assessed using a mail-out/mail-back paper and pencil self-report questionnaire. The survey is sent annually to all patients discharged during a target period—usually three to four months. Non-respondents are recontacted; final overall response rates average around 57% in the most recent survey. Reports are prepared for individual patient care units in addition to division-level and hospital-wide aggregate statistics. Ratings of New England Medical Center were very favorable, as were levels of overall satisfaction with the hospital stay. Satisfaction continues to increase throughout the years.

RESEARCH

NEMC has consistently engaged in a large and diverse program of medical research. In 1992, the Hospital received the sixth largest share of hospital-based research funds awarded by the National Institutes of Health (NIH). In fiscal year 1993, NEMC received $44 million in research grants; $31.4 million from the federal government and $13 million from the state, industry, or foundations. NEMC is committed to the further expansion of research activities and believes these activities to be crucial in the framework of a large teaching institute.

The Health Institute (THI) does patient-outcomes research. In 1990 THI received a $17 million grant from the Kaiser Family Foundation to train researchers and develop a comprehensive research program to measure patient outcomes and to determine the factors (medical and social) that contribute to these outcomes. The Clinical Study Unit of NEMC was awarded a five-year, $10 million NIH grant to support inpatient and outpatient research on promising clinical therapies. The grant funds bed costs, ambulatory visits, and personnel costs. NEMC has received several grants to fund basic research on the synthesis, structure, and function of cessation of bleeding. In nutrition research, NEMC and several cooperating Boston institutions were awarded a five-year grant from the NIH to study such issues as the development of obesity and regulation of energy metabolism. NEMC has been provided with $5.1 million to support research on the digestive tract, where the results will be useful in developing drugs to treat digestive and possibly central nervous system disorders, such as ulcers. NEMC researchers have developed a method which may lead to earlier detection and treatment of T-cell leukemia. They are also studying the viruses that cause cervical warts and the mechanism by which such warts can become cancerous. Funding is provided by the NIH. Researchers have also developed a technique, using high-resolution video cameras and computer imaging, that records detailed color images of electrical activity in the brain. This may have important implications in the diagnosis and treatment of Alzheimer's, epilepsy, brain tumors, and degenerative neuromuscular disorders. A procedure to develop more precise images of brain tissue, using MRI and a complex computer program, has also been made available. The New England Eye Center Vision Research Laboratory is scheduled to open in 1994. This laboratory is designed for specialized research in the molecular genetics of ocular disorders and retinal and corneal cell biology and physiology.

Other major research is being conducted in such areas as adult hematology/oncology, primary care, domestic violence, newborn medicine, and AIDS.

ADMISSIONS POLICY

Patients can be admitted to the New England Medical Center through the clinics or emergency rooms, referred by their physician, self-referred or transferred from another hospital.

The medical center accepts all major forms of insurance. There is no financial requirement to be admitted to the hospital, and financial assistance is available. Like all Massachusetts hospitals, NEMC participates in the states' free care pool; $26 million in free and uncompensated care was provided in FY 1993.

For information on adult admissions, call (617) 956-6000; for pediatric admissions, call (617) 956-5081.

HENRY FORD

HOSPITAL

For more than 77 years, Henry Ford Hospital (HFH) has been as vitally important to the people of Detroit as the motor company with the same name. The first Henry Ford founded this hospital at just about the same time he shocked the young automobile industry by offering workers the unheard of sum of $5 a day—twice the going rate—to assemble his Model T. Intense care and concern for the working man and his family were the hallmarks of Ford's labor policies during these early years and, when the small, 48-bed hospital opened in 1915, it quickly became a symbol of Ford's commitment to the people who were building a powerful industry and a great city.

Now, eight decades later, just as the automotive industry has been forced to retool to meet the foreign competition, hospitals are being challenged to meet the demands of government, insurance companies, and patients for better, cost-efficient care. Henry Ford Hospital has been at the forefront of the move by medical centers to use business management techniques to reduce costs while improving the quality of patient care. More than 1,000 employees have taken a special six-day course in quality management to improve care. For example, a medical team recently devised a plan for a common chemotherapy treatment that allows the patient to shorten the hospital stay by a full day while getting more effective medication and cutting the hospital's expenses. The

FOR MORE THAN 77 YEARS, HENRY FORD HOSPITAL (HFH) HAS BEEN AS VITALLY IMPORTANT TO · THE PEOPLE OF DETROIT AS THE MOTOR COMPANY WITH THE SAME NAME.

hospital's management techniques are so highly regarded that its president and CEO, Gail L. Warden, has been elected chairman of the powerful American Hospital Association at a crucial time for the industry. For the patient, these innovative management techniques often translate into shorter hospital stays, fewer unessential procedures and tests, and more effective treatments.

Henry Ford Hospital is a 903-bed specialty referral center where more than 800 doctors pool their talents in a group practice similar to the Mayo, Lahey, and Cleveland Clinics. Affiliated with Case Western Reserve Medical School, the teaching and research hospital is part of the Henry Ford Health System, which includes a 17-story outpatient center, a regional trauma center, and a network of suburban medical clinics, offering primary and specialty care in neighborhood settings. The hospital logged more than 10,000 visits last year from patients from 30 states and overseas who came to Detroit to obtain high-powered, sophisticated medical care in over 40 specialties.

The transformation of Henry Ford from a tiny facility for auto workers to a nationally recognized medical complex should not blur the fact that it remains an essential resource for the people of Detroit and its suburbs. More than 5,000 physicians in this area use HFH as a referral care center for their most critically ill patients. Each year more than 35,000 patients are admitted to the hospital and an incredible 2.3 million are seen in the 35 ambulatory care centers in the city and surrounding suburbs. Opened in the early and mid-seventies, these centers are staffed with HFH specialists who have access to many of the same testing facilities as the main hospital. HFH is also in the forefront of managed care with Michigan's largest HMO, serving more than 400,000 people from 3,000 employers.

In the city itself, HFH employs almost 16,000 full- and part-time employees. It also contributes more than $38 million a year in hospital care for the indigent, the poor, and those without adequate health insurance. The hospital also runs an extensive Geriatric Outreach program and provides community training

AT A GLANCE

Beds: 903
Occupancy Rate: 84%
Average Patient Count: 604
Average Patient Stay: 6.2 days
Annual Admissions: 35,355
Births: 2,735
Outpatient Clinic Visits:
    2,300,000
Emergency Room/Trauma
    Center Visits: 86,568

HOSPITAL PERSONNEL
Physicians: 1,400+
    Detroit Campus: 523
    System-Wide: 900+
Residents: 6,000
Registered Nurses: 1,427

ROOM CHARGES (PER DIEM)
Private: $595
Semiprivate: $572
ICU: $1,655

ADDRESS
2799 West Grand Blvd.
Detroit, MI 48202

TELEPHONE
(313) 876-3400

in CPR. HFH is a major educational resource for the allied health professions offering 25 programs to over 450 students. A school of nursing, a graduate program for residents in other area hospitals, and a continuing education program enrolling 2,000 doctors a year are all indicative of Ford's crucial role in keeping Detroit's medical population superbly trained and well-informed.

HFH is understandably Detroit's most popular hospital. While it is very large, and some people complain about the irritating inconveniences sheer size can cause, patient responses are, on the whole, very positive. One important reason for this is the presence of more than 1,400 registered nurses, an extraordinary number in a hospital with fewer than 1,000 beds.

SPECIAL FACILITIES AND PROGRAMS

HFH is well known for several of its specialties, including cardiovascular medicine and surgery. The HF Vascular Institute is noted for the diagnosis, treatment, prevention, and research of diseases of the heart and vascular system. Current offerings include angioplasty as an alternative to open heart surgery for some patients; heart transplant; and electrophysiology for diagnosis of arrhythmias. In vascular surgery, HFH is recognized for work in replacing diseased arteries with a prosthesis.

The Bone and Joint Center is the only such bone center in Michigan and one of ten in the U.S. where histologic structure of the bone is studied. The division serves as a regional referral center and sees more than 1,000 new patients annually with metabolic diseases pertaining to the skeletal system, kidney stones, and parathyroid glands.

HFH serves as a regional center for the diagnosis and treatment of kidney disease and is one of the largest hemodialysis centers in Michigan, with 37 dialysis stations. It is also one of the state's major kidney transplant facilities, with a transplant being done every week on the average; in 1993, 61 kidney transplants were performed. The HFH has the second largest multi-organ transplant program in the state.

The hospital has long been recognized for diagnosis and treatment of metabolic disease, including diabetes. In neurology, the department's cerebral blood flow system, one of only about 50 in the U.S., is used to noninvasively study illnesses such as hydrocephalus, epilepsy, stroke, and migraine that involve the rate of blood flow to the brain.

Specialists in neurosurgery are well recognized for innovations in the development of microneurosurgical techniques and advance of surgical treatment of disorders of the brain and spinal cord. HFH is one of the 14 Stroke Centers in the U.S. and one of only 16 Neuromagnetometer Labs in the world for the study of migraines, as well as epilepsy, stroke, and head trauma. It is one of 11 sites nationwide testing a viewing wand and computer system that surgeons can use to display different parts of their patient's anatomy in 3-D on color video monitors.

The oncology department is a coordinated, cooperative effort by specialists in 20 different fields who share their expertise. The team includes more than 30 specialists. Research projects include human-tumor cloning, immunizing tumor patients with healthy human-donor tissue, developing monoclonal antibodies to cancer, new drug development, and the study of heredity's role in cancer.

Orthopaedics and Sports Medicine is staffed by surgeons with extensive training in subspecialties including pediatric orthopedics. HFH's Center for Athletic Medicine addresses the unique health needs of competitive and recreational sports and is one of only a few comprehensive diagnostic, treatment, and preventative centers to be housed within a hospital complex.

Specialty "centers of excellence" include neurosurgery and neurology for the treatment and study of the brain and spinal cord; cardiovascular medicine for heart surgery and rehabilitation; nephrology for the treatment of kidney disease, including dialysis and transplantation; bone and mineral disease; orthopaedics and sports medicine; oncology for cancer treatment; and sleep disorders. In addition, HFH offers special programs, such as those for high-risk pregnancy, kidney stones, lung cancer, and other conditions benefiting from the multispecialty approach to care.

Other special programs at HFH include the Chemical Dependency Program, for both inpatient and outpatient adults and teenagers, at four sites in the city.

MEDICAL SPECIALTIES

Anesthesiology, Chemical/Alcohol Dependency, Dentistry, Dermatology, Diagnostic Radiology, Gynecology/Obstetrics, Internal Medicine, Neurological Surgery, Neurology, Neonatal Intensive Care, Ophthalmology, Orthopaedic Surgery, Otolaryngology, Pediatrics, Psychiatry, Surgery, Therapeutic Radiology and Urology.

WELL-KNOWN SPECIALISTS

- Dr. John Anderson   *Allergy and immunology*
- Dr. Henry Bone III   *Paget's disease*
- Dr. Beth Ann Brooks   *Child and adolescent psychiatry*
- Dr. Calvin Ernst   *General vascular surgery*
- Dr. Sidney Goldstein   *Heart disease*
- Dr. Edward Krull   *Mucous membrane disease*
- Dr. Edwin Monsell   *Otology/neurotology*
- Dr. Robert Narins   *Kidney disease*
- Dr. Gary Talpos   *Endocrine surgery*
- Dr. K. Michael Welch   *Headache and stroke*

PATIENT SATISFACTION

Surveys found that 92% of the patients would recommend the hospital to a friend or relative. Almost 89% were either satisfied or very satisfied with the care provided.

RESEARCH

In the last eight years, the amount of research has grown dramatically, with more than $27 million in annual funding for 1,200 basic and clinical research projects in such areas as stroke, hypertension, heart disease, cancer, osteoporosis, arthritis, sleep disorders, diabetes, and lung diseases. HFH receives $14 million from NIH alone to study stress fractures, effects of cocaine, and sleep disorders.

Its largest grant is for a 16-year study, begun in 1992, to determine the effectiveness of screening for prostate, lung, colorectal, and ovarian cancers.

The National Cancer Institute recently selected HFH as one of only three sites in the midwest to research new therapies and treatments for brain tumors in adults and children.

Sleep research at HFH's Sleep Research and Disorders Center has resulted in findings pertaining to jet lag and sleep-inducing medication. The Center was one of the first in the U.S. accredited by the American Sleep Disorders Association.

ADMISSIONS POLICY

Most appointments can be made directly by calling the HFH facility nearest you and asking for the Appointment Desk of the specialty clinic you need to see. If the specialty is not available at the HFH center nearest you, you will be given information about the closest site where it is available.

If you prefer to have your family physician refer you to an HFH specialist, the physician can make the call and appointment for you. In such a case, your family physician will be kept informed of your status and care while you are seen at HFH. If your physician has any problem or question, he/she may call the Referring Physician Office at 1-800-888-4340, 24 hours-a-day.

A hospital spokesperson said that anyone who was ill and required hospitalization could be admitted whether or not they could pay, and even if they lacked insurance. Almost all of these admissions are made through the Emergency Room of the main hospital.

UNIVERSITY

OF MICHIGAN

MEDICAL CENTER

To put it simply, what the University of Michigan Medical Center (UMMC) practices is high-technology medicine at its very best. The chief indications of the excellence of the University of Michigan Medical Center lie in the state-of-the-art equipment in every area of medicine, the most advanced treatments (including one of the nation's leading organ transplantation programs), and a research program whose many achievements over the years have brought its funding to one of the highest levels in the country. Moreover, a recent study by HCIA, a leading healthcare information company, ranked the University of Michigan in its list of 100 top hospitals providing high value and efficient patient care. In addition, 92 of the physicians associated with UMMC are listed in *The Best Doctors in America*.

The U-M Medical Center provides health care to more than 750,000 people each year through more than 110 outpatient clinics, and another 35,000 people on an inpatient basis. The Medical Center includes seven hospitals—University Hospital, C. S. Mott Children's Hospital, Women's Hospital, Holden Perinatal Hospital, Child and Adolescent Psychiatric Hospital, Adult Psychiatric Hospital, and the W. K. Kellogg Eye Center—and the University of Michigan Medical School.

Growth of UMMC's clinical and research facilities has continued from the mid-1980s into the 1990s,

ANN ARBOR, MICHIGAN

TO PUT IT SIMPLY, WHAT
THE UNIVERSITY OF
MICHIGAN MEDICAL CENTER
(UMMC) PRACTICES IS HIGH-
TECHNOLOGY MEDICINE
AT ITS VERY BEST.

as does renovation of existing facilities. Plans call for a nearby off-site ambulatory care facility on more than 180 acres—five times the square footage of the Medical Center—to address the growing need for outpatient space. Currently under construction is the $88 million Cancer and Geriatrics Center, which is slated to open in mid-1996. Construction of a third research building (Medical Sciences Research Building III) was to be completed in the Summer of 1994. The facility includes biomedical research laboratories and lab support space to meet the needs of the University of Michigan Medical School's growing research activities.

Renovation continues on C. S. Mott Children's Hospital. The Mott renovation will cap an extensive Maternal and Child Health Center project designed to replace and renovate four of the Medical Center's seven hospitals and expand the existing A. Alfred Taubman Health Care Center outpatient facility. The Taubman Center and University Hospital was opened in 1986 to replace existing facilities. When the renovation project is completed in 1995, it will mark a decade in which every inch of clinical space at the U-M Medical Center was either rebuilt, renovated or replaced.

SPECIAL FACILITIES AND PROGRAMS

The U-M Medical Center is one of the leading transplant centers in the United States. Over 200 heart transplants have been performed since the start of the program, with an 83% survival rate. Six heart and lung transplants have also been completed. More than 1,600 kidney transplants (95% survival rate) and 500-plus liver transplants (75% survival) have been done. Other activities include over 200 bone marrow and 40 pancreas transplants.

The departments of neurology, neurosurgery, and psychiatry stand among the best programs in the state. The Department of Neurology provides diagnostic and therapeutic services for patients with movement disorders, neuromuscular diseases, seizure disorders, dementia, and cancer affecting the nervous system. It also has many research projects underway in these areas.

The Section of Neurosurgery has recently established a new program in surgical management of pain and movement disorders, the only one in the state. At the hospital and in satellite clinics, chronic pain management is treated through a combination of exercise, medication regimes, nerve blocks, and nerve stimulations.

The Department of Psychiatry offers programs in anxiety disorders, grief survival, and substance abuse; it also has programs for children with borderline personality disorders. The Adolescent Psychiatry Service focuses on depression, eating disorders, personality disorders, and suicide.

Approximately 450 newborns were treated at Holden Perinatal Hospital last year; 315 of them were premature. Holden provides care for newborns who need intensive care or surgery, or who have a life-threatening disease. Pediatrics is another well-known specialty of the U-M Medical Center, which treats over

6,000 children a year as inpatients. Pediatric specialties include birth defects, cardiology, cystic fibrosis, endocrinology, hematology/oncology, surgery, and many others.

The U-M Medical Center is one of the world's leading centers for the study of rheumatic diseases and diabetes. In addition, the medical center has been a pioneer in nuclear medicine and in the intraoperative use of ultrasound in neurosurgery, the use of angioplasty during emergency treatment of heart attacks, and the use of TPA (tissue plasminogen activator), a drug that dissolves blood clots and helps keep heart attacks from damaging the heart.

The Spinal Cord Injury Center at U-M is designated a Model Spinal Cord Injury Center by the National Institute on Disability and Rehabilitation Research. It provides care from the accident site through hospitalization, rehabilitation, and follow-up.

Among other services available are the Nurse-Midwifery Program for both obstetrics and well-woman care, the Breast Care Center and the Breast Cancer Detection Center, the Sleep Disorders Center, an in vitro fertilization program, a comprehensive hearing center, and the Osteoporosis Test Center. MedSport is a center for the treatment of sports injuries and the prevention of injuries and disease through proper training and lifestyle habits. Treatment for melanoma patients is conducted at the newly established Multidisciplinary Melanoma Clinic. Emergency services include a full trauma center support, a replantation and microvascular reconstruction team on 24-hour call, a nationally recognized burn unit, and the Survival Flight helicopter and emergency jet service.

The U-M Comprehensive Cancer Center is one of only 28 National Cancer Institute-designated cancer centers in the country. More than 250 physicians specialize in cancer treatment and research.

The Breast Care Center and Breast Cancer Detection Center offers "one-stop shopping" for women diagnosed with breast cancer. Patients come to one facility and specialists in such areas as oncology, surgery, radiation oncology, social work, and psychiatry see the patient in a one-day visit. The detection center

AT A GLANCE

Beds: 860
Occupancy Rate: 82%
Average Patient Count: 706
Average Patient Stay: 7.6 days
Annual Admissions: 34,124
Births: 2,162
Outpatient Clinic Visits:
   714,758
Emergency Room/Trauma
   Center Visits: 57,166

HOSPITAL PERSONNEL
Physicians: 814
Residents: 642
Registered Nurses: 1,597
   BS Degree: 1,161

ROOM CHARGES (PER DIEM)
Private: $530
Semiprivate: $525
ICU: $1,747

ADDRESS
1500 East Medical Center
   Drive
Ann Arbor, MI 48109

TELEPHONE
(313) 936-4000

offers special low-dose mammography and same-day results. The director of the Cancer Center and the chairman of radiation oncology are world-renown breast cancer specialists.

The Radiation Oncology department is the home of one of only two race-track microtons in clinical use in the country. With multilead collimators controlled directly by a computer, the microtron is able to focus radiation onto a treatment field that conforms more closely to the shape of the tumor, thus sparing adjacent normal tissues better than previously possible. The technology at UMMC also can treat more types of cancer than the equipment available anywhere else.

The Human Genome Center was the site of the nation's first human gene therapy performed outside the NIH. It houses one of the only human disease oriented genome centers in America.

The Turner Geriatric Clinic is the state of Michigan's largest primary care facility for the elderly. It provides hospital and outpatient medical and nursing care, home visits, and social work and psychiatric services for about 2,500 men and women each year.

One of the first burn centers established in the country, and still viewed today as one of the best in the United States, the Trauma Burn Center offers a complete range of care, including surgery, long-term outpatient services, and burn prevention services. The unit now also treats trauma patients.

The Cognitive Disorders Clinic evaluates patients for symptoms of Alzheimer's disease and other dementias by using PET, MRI, and SPECT. In addition, investigational drugs are being used to treat the conditions, and drug therapy is being used to allay the symptoms of depression that often accompany the disease.

Among the more specialized programs are the Post-Polio Program , which focuses on those who had polio 30-40 years ago and again are suffering physical "aftershocks" of the crippling virus; the Multipurpose Arthritis Center, the only such center in the state, and one of only a handful in the country, which offers a multidisciplinary approach to patient care, research, and education; and the Chelsea Arbor Treatment Center, established in 1987, which targets alcoholism and substance abuse from both a clinical and research standpoint.

Other specialty clinics include: Allergy, Ambulatory Care Services, Asthma, Cardiac Rehabilitation, Cleft Palate, Hyperlipidemia, Hypertension, Immunization, Nutrition, Occupational Therapy, Osteoporosis Testing, Pain Management, Retina Service, Thyroid, and many others.

MEDICAL SPECIALTIES

Allergy/Asthma, Anesthesiology, Burns, Cardiology, Clinical Research, Critical Care Medicine, Dentistry, Dermatology, Endocrinology and Metabolism, Emergency Services, Gastroenterology, General Medicine, Geriatrics, Gynecology, Hematology, Infectious Diseases, Infertility, Internal Medicine, Neonatology, Nephrology,

Neurology, Neurosurgery, Nuclear Medicine, Obstetrics, Ophthalmology, Orthopedics, Otolaryngology, Pathology, Pediatrics, Physical Medicine and Rehabilitation, Physical Therapy, Plastic Surgery, Psychiatry, Pulmonary Medicine,
Radiation Therapy, Radiology, Rheumatology, Surgery, Thoracic Surgery, and
Urology.

WELL-KNOWN SPECIALISTS

- Dr. James W. Albers   *Neurology; specialist in neuromuscular disease*
- Dr. Arnold G. Coran   *Pediatric surgery*
- Dr. John E. Freitas   *Nuclear medicine; specialist in thyroid diseases*
- Dr. Harry S. Greenberg   *Medical oncology/hematology; specialist in neuro-oncology*
- Dr. Eve J. Higginbotham   *Ophthalmology; specialist in glaucoma*
- Dr. Nancy Hopwood   *Pediatrics; specialist in pediatric endocrinology*
- Dr. Allen Lichter   *Radiation oncology; specialist in lung cancer*
- Dr. Roger F. Meyer   *Ophthalmology; specialist in corneal diseases and transplantation*
- Dr. George W. Morley   *Specialist in gynecological cancer*
- Dr. Mark Orringer   *Thoracic surgery; specialist in thoracic oncological surgery*
- Dr. Aileen B. Sedman   *Pediatrics; specialist in pediatric nephrology*

PATIENT SATISFACTION

Patient satisfaction surveys are conducted biannually. On a five-point scale, with
five being high, the overall satisfaction rating for inpatient care across the Medical
Center is 4.45. UMMC scored particularly well with regard to patients obtaining
the medical results they expected, and the way the staff treats the patients.

The outpatient rating was recently 4.35. High scores were obtained in meeting patient's expectations for medical care, the staff treating patients with respect, and how efficiently the service was coordinated.

RESEARCH

The University of Michigan Medical Center receives more than $100 million in
research grants each year and its research expenditures exceed more than $200
million annually. It ranks tenth in NIH funding among all universities and
second among public universities. An NIH-supported Clinical Research Center
is located in University Hospital and a unit of the Howard Hughes Medical
Research Institute has been established there, with a core group in molecular
genetics. Top research areas are described below.

The Kresge Hearing Research Institute is the country's number one recipient
of NIH hearing research grant awards. Researchers in genetics have discovered
the genes responsible for cystic fibrosis and Huntington's disease, and, through
gene therapy, have cured muscular dystrophy in mice. UMMC has also received

funding for major efforts in research on Alzheimer's disease, arthritis, diabetes, geriatrics, and dermatology.

The W. K. Kellogg Eye Center received more than $4 million in grants in 1993-94 and ranks fourth in the country among departments of ophthalmology in research money received from the National Eye Institute. Researchers are participating in eight national multicenter trials sponsored by the NEI, and retinal dystrophies and glaucoma are among its chief areas of research interest. Recently, Kellogg Eye Center researchers have located a gene responsible for juvenile onset primary open-angle glaucoma and a gene responsible for early onset x-linked macular degeneration.

The Medical Center has been awarded a $10.5 million, five-year grant from the National Institute on Aging to continue the work of the Michigan Alzheimer's Disease Research Center. The grant will expand both research and clinical activities at the Medical Center and throughout the state. Clinical services will be enhanced for patients with Alzheimer's disease, while gathering large amounts of data on the disease and other forms of dementia. The Medical Center also has a $6.1 million grant from the National Institute on Aging to create a Geriatric Research and Training Center—the first of its kind in the country—to enhance current research and training in geriatrics and aging.

U-M researchers are investigating a new method of detecting breast cancer that may prove to be more sensitive than mammography. The new diagnostic method involves ultrasound and color-flow imaging to monitor blood flow, as abnormal blood flow is often associated with cancerous tumors. Meanwhile, a new protocol in which chemotherapy is administered prior to surgery is causing cancerous breast tumors to shrink in women with advanced cancer. In one-fourth of the cases, the cancer has completely disappeared. And U-M researchers, led by Max Wicha, M.D., director of U-M Cancer Center, discovered a protein that inhibits breast cancer growth—a breakthrough that may lead to a new treatment method and help prevent this disease.

ADMISSIONS POLICY

A patient must be admitted by a doctor on staff, unless it is a life-threatening situation. Emergency patients are admitted through the emergency room. In the future, admissions through affiliated groups/hospitals will be permitted.

Patients admitted through the emergency room are admitted without regard to financial resources. For non-emergent admissions, UMMC staff work very closely with physicians and patients to secure some form of financial resources.

UMMC provided $1.9 million of charity care services in fiscal year 1993 and also incurred $26.6 million in bad debt. In addition, some physicians are allowed a set number of free admissions each year; the dollar amount involved is not known.

PATIENT/FAMILY ACCOMMODATIONS

As an integral part of the University of Michigan Medical Center, Med-Inn offers 90 guest rooms. The hotel is directly connected to the University Hospitals and offers affordable accommodations to hospital visitors. Med-Inn discounted rate for patients and visitors is $51 per night. An additional charge of $10 per night is made for a suite.

MAYO CLINIC

AND HOSPITALS

The Mayo Clinic is one of the few medical institutions in the United States whose status can legitimately be called legendary. In health circles, the Mayo name has been synonymous with excellence in medical diagnosis and treatment for over a century. First opened by Dr. William Worall Mayo and his two sons, who were also physicians, the Mayo Clinic evolved into the first so-called group practice, whereby doctors pooled their knowledge and skills in treating all kinds of illness. By the early years of the turn of century, the brilliant medical achievements (especially in surgery) of the Mayos and their growing number of associates had spread far beyond the surrounding area. People were already coming from long distances to help swell the patient rolls which, by 1912, had reached 15,000. In 1915, the success of the Clinic was clearly demonstrated when the Mayo family donated $1.5 million to found the now world-famous Mayo Graduate School of Medicine.

Mayo's reputation for excellence continued to grow over the ensuing decades. Well-known statesmen, socialites, athletes, and movie stars made the trek to Minnesota with the hope of finding treatment for ailments other doctors proclaimed incurable. A few novels and movies of the 1940s and 1950s helped to popularize the notion that Mayo doctors had answers that others did not. Then again, so many medical discoveries happened at Mayo that those hopes,

THE MAYO CLINIC IS
ONE OF THE FEW MEDICAL
INSTITUTIONS IN THE
UNITED STATES WHOSE
STATUS CAN LEGITIMATELY
BE CALLED LEGENDARY.

both the real and the fictional, were not without some foundation. In 1922, for example, doctors at Mayo first used iodine to successfully treat goiters; in 1933, the first blood bank was established; and just after World War II, two Mayo doctors discovered the drug cortisone, which won them the Nobel Prize and brought relief to millions of people suffering from arthritis and many other ailments. And in 1943, Mayo doctors developed an anti-blackout suit and an oxygen mask that helped prevent fighter pilots from blacking out at high altitudes.

Today, more than 1,000 physicians and scientists are continuing the long Mayo tradition of finding new answers to all kinds of medical problems. Still at the core of the Mayo approach is the idea of group practice. As always, every single case is studied by several specialists who review the patient's records and tests with the primary physician and jointly decide on diagnosis and treatment. Severity and complexity of the illness determine the number of specialists needed, but in almost every area of specialization the Clinic staff has achieved a high degree of recognition. So widespread is its fame that every year close to 300,000 people come to Mayo for evaluation and treatment; 60,000 of them travel over 500 miles to do so. They come from literally every state in the nation and from dozens of foreign countries, and they are rarely disappointed with the quality of care they receive for their travels.

Only a handful of medical centers can provide more than 2,000 hospital beds and 81 operating rooms, but those are the combined totals at Rochester Methodist and Saint Mary's, both of which officially became part of the Mayo Clinic in May of 1986. Saint Mary's was actually the first small hospital used by the Mayos before the turn of the century. Today it is a 15-building modern medical complex staffed by very highly-trained nurses, some of whom are members of the same religious order that founded the hospital a century ago and which is still actively involved in the administration of the hospital. Rochester Methodist, which first opened in 1954, has been cited by the American Nursing Association (ANA) as a superior place for

AT A GLANCE

Beds: 2,071
Occupancy Rate: 71%
Average Patient Count: 1,470
Average Patient Stay: 7.1 days
Annual Admissions: 65,624

HOSPITAL PERSONNEL
Physicians: 1,374
Residents: 1,418
Registered Nurses: 2,600

ROOM CHARGES (PER DIEM):
Private: $409
Semiprivate: $378
ICU: $979

ADDRESS
200 First St. SW
Rochester, MN 55905

TELEPHONE
(507) 284-2511

nurses to work. In its study, the ANA found Rochester Methodist to be among the top hospitals in the country in terms of its concern for quality nursing care.

Mayo is without question a large, complex organization dispensing medical services in a precise, almost military fashion in order to handle the large numbers of people who come there every year. On a typical day at Mayo Rochester, 1,200 new patients arrive; 212 surgical procedures are performed; 16,150 lab tests are performed; 2,906 radiology procedures are completed; and 550 electrocardiograms are conducted. Still, there can be no doubt that most patients there sense they are in the hands of very caring people whose medical knowledge is second to none.

One measure of that knowledge is the extensive educational programs conducted by Mayo and budgeted at over $54 million. Each year, about 800 residents and more than 150 research fellows attend the Mayo Graduate School of Medicine, where more than 100 specialties and subspecialties are taught by staff members from the Clinic and from the research facility. There is also a Continuing Medical Education Program for experienced practicing physicians. At the Mayo Medical School, which first opened in 1972, and accepts only 40 students a year out of 1,600 applicants, the teaching staff is made up exclusively of physicians from the Clinic. In addition, about 250 medical students from other medical schools come to Mayo each year for intensive short-term training. Finally, the Mayo School of Health Related Sciences trains about 200 students a year in 12 allied health programs, including physical therapy, laboratory technology and nurse anesthesia.

The Clinic employs upwards of 16,000 staff members and doctors to dispense treatment to nearly 400,000 patients annually, almost all of whom take the legendary Mayo Clinic "checkup." Since only about 20% of Mayo patients are referred by a primary care physician, "the checkup," which can take an hour or longer, is necessary to familiarize the Clinic doctor with the patient's medical history and health status. Despite this requirement, Mayo Clinic charges are some of the lowest in the country. The comprehensive exam runs from $1,200 to $1,600, and the average cost per stay is still under $500 per day.

In an effort to bring "The Mayo Way" to people in other parts of the country (and the world), Mayo opened a satellite clinic in Jacksonville, Florida in 1986, and another in Scottsdale, Arizona in 1987. The two sun-belt clinics employ Mayo-trained physicians and have access to all of Mayo's resources through a direct telecommunications link to Rochester, Minnesota. The Jacksonville clinic has more than doubled in size since its opening to accommodate the more than 26,000 patients who register there annually. The Scottsdale clinic has been even busier, with 130 doctors and 900 administrative and support staff members handling the nearly 33,000 patients who registered in 1992.

Each clinic shares in the discoveries made in Minnesota, but also performs its own research and medical education. Doctors at the Jacksonville clinic have completed more than 350 clinical research studies since the clinic's opening, most notably in Alzheimer's disease, urology, and sleep disorders. The Scottsdale clinic's research has focused on molecular genetics, and cell and molecular biology. It is one of only a handful of hospitals in the country equipped for both gene deletion and gene insertion, which allows investigators to copy (and therefore study) human disease in the laboratory.

SPECIAL FACILITIES AND PROGRAMS

Mayo's multispecialty team approach to medicine gives each patient the opportunity to consult with specialists from virtually every medical field. Among the specialties in which Mayo enjoys a top rating are cancer, cardiology, endocrinology, gastroenterology, geriatrics, gynecology, neurology, orthopedics, ophthalmology, otolaryngology, psychology, rehabilitation, rheumatology and urology. A few highlights follow.

Mayo is the federally designated Comprehensive Cancer Center for its region. Every year, an average of 27,000 cancer patients come to the Clinic for treatment. About 6,000 are new patients, making Mayo the largest cancer practice for new patients in the country. Two major departments, oncology and radiation oncology, are concerned with the diagnosis and treatment of cancer, but over 100 physicians from throughout the Clinic are also involved in particular types of cancer, including colon/rectal, gastroenterologic, neurologic and pulmonary. There are also separate pediatric and rehabilitation oncology units. In addition to the standard therapeutic options of radiation and chemotherapy, patients can also participate in an extensive clinical trials program in new therapies still in the experimental stage.

The Mayo Clinic is also a major center for kidney and liver transplantation. Over 1,000 kidney transplants have been performed since the program began in 1963, and over 80% have been successful. Liver transplantation was begun there only in 1985, but Mayo is already considered one of the leading institutions for this very difficult operation. Under the leadership of Dr. Rudd Krom, whom the Clinic recruited from the Netherlands, more than 56 transplants have taken place, with a success rate of 85%.

Other kinds of transplantation are also available at Mayo. Corneal transplants have been performed since 1950 and today about 100 a year are done, with a success rate approaching 95%. Bone marrow transplantation, on the other hand, was just started in 1982 and as of March 1986, 50% of the transplants have been successful. Finally, while bone grafts from bone banks have been done for many years, only recently have doctors been using long bones from donors to replace bones destroyed by tumors (15 were transplanted in 1985).

Computer-assisted stereotactic neurosurgery allows Mayo surgeons to remove tumors deep within the brain. With this advanced technique, surgeons use computer-guided lasers to locate and vaporize tumors. It offers treatment for some problems that would otherwise be inoperable.

MEDICAL SPECIALTIES

Allergic Diseases, Anesthesiology, Audiology, Cardiovascular Diseases, Cardiovascular Surgery, Child and Adolescent Psychiatry, Colon and Rectal Surgery,

Community and Area Medicine, Dentistry, Dermatology, Dialysis, Emergency Medicine, Endocrinology, Family Medicine, Gastroenterology, Gastrointestinal Surgery, General Surgery, Gynecologic Surgery, Gynecology, Hematology, Hemophilia, Hypertension, Immunology, Infectious Diseases, Internal Medicine, Laboratory Medicine and Pathology, Medical Genetics, Nephrology, Neurologic Surgery, Neurology, Neuro-Oncology, Obstetrics, Oncology, Ophthalmology, Oral Surgery, Orthopedics, Otolaryngology, Outpatient Surgery, Pediatrics (including Pediatric Cardiology, Oncology and Rheumatology), Plastic Surgery, Physical Medicine and Rehabilitation, Preventive Medicine, Psychiatry and Psychology, Radiology, Reproductive Endocrinology, Rheumatology, Sleep Disorders, Surgical Oncology, Thoracic Diseases, Thoracic Surgery, Transplantation Surgery, Urology, Vascular Surgery.

WELL-KNOWN SPECIALISTS

- Dr. Richard Bryan   *Orthopedic surgery*
- Dr. Philip Bernatz   *Thoracic surgery*
- Dr. Thomas Bunch   *Rheumatology; specialist in arthritis treatment*
- Dr. Robert Frye   *Cardiology*
- Dr. William Furlow   *Urology; specialist in impotence and incontinence*
- Dr. Clark Hoagland   *Hematology; head of bone marrow transplant unit*
- Dr. Keith Kelly   *Surgery; gastroenterologist*
- Dr. Patrick Kelly   *Neurosurgery; specialist in brain tumors*
- Dr. Rudd Krom   *Head of liver transplant program*
- Dr. Robert Kyle   *Oncology; specialist in myeloma*
- Dr. Edward Laws   *Neurosurgery*
- Dr. Charles Moertel   *Director of Comprehensive Cancer Center; specialist in colon cancer*
- Dr. J. Desmond O'Duffy   *Rheumatology*
- Dr. W. Spencer Payne   *Thoracic surgery*
- Dr. Harold Perry   *Dermatology; specialist in psoriasis*
- Dr. Mark Pittelkow   *Dermatology; specialist in skin-growth for burn victims*
- Dr. Douglas Pritchard   *Orthopedic surgery*
- Dr. Charles Reed   *Chairman of Allergic Diseases program*
- Dr. David Utz   *Urologist; specialist in prostate cancer*
- Dr. Jack Whisant   *Neurology; specialist in cerebrovascular disorders*
- Dr. John Woods   *Plastic surgery*

PATIENT SATISFACTION

Mayo Clinic patients report high overall satisfaction with their medical care. Patients consistently say that Mayo caregivers provide the most thorough and accurate exams and the most detailed explanations of their medical condition. In recent surveys, 96% of Mayo patients said they would recommend Mayo to others.

RESEARCH

Because so much energy is given to patient care at the Clinic, most people do not think of Mayo as one of the nation's leading research institutions. But the very special brand of medicine practiced there is actually based on intense teamwork among a tightly-knit group of first-rate physicians who are supported by an extensive research program. In fact, 150 physicians and medical scientists, over 300 associates and almost 900 allied health personnel are engaged in full-time research; in addition, just about every doctor on staff is involved in some form of research. Supported by a budget of over $125 million, physicians are constantly finding new ways to treat disease, as well as contributing to basic research.

Historically, the best known medical discovery made by Mayo scientists is probably the isolation and first clinical use of cortisone in the treatment of rheumatoid arthritis. Drs. Edward Kendall and Philip Hench received the Nobel Prize for this accomplishment in 1950.

Current research programs span the entire gamut of medicine. The largest amount of money is spent on a broad array of basic and clinical research projects in cancer. Other areas of intense public concern are also under investigation, including diabetes, osteoporosis, fertility and sterility, heart disease, and myasthenia gravis. Mayo is also a designated Clinical Research Center funded by the National Institutes of Health (NIH).

Two pioneering studies at Mayo illustrate how Mayo pursues connections between diseases to identify new treatment pathways. Both have grown from a major study of osteoporosis. The first on arteriosclerosis looks at coronary arteries as if they were bone tissue. Mayo scientists have discovered that the plaque that plugs up the coronary arteries has the same proteins that are found in bones. Learning how to regulate bone so it stays in the right places may eventually contribute to controlling hardening of the arteries. In the other study, understanding the mechanism by which prostate cancer spreads to bone may eventually bring about controlling the spread of the disease.

ADMISSIONS POLICY

Admission to the Mayo Clinic may be gained in several ways. Direct arrangements can be made through a Mayo physician, if the patient is already under Mayo care. Local physicians can call the Clinic and arrange the appointment, or the patient can call for himself or herself. The number for the appointment information desk is (507) 284-2111. Patients may also write for an appointment: Mayo Clinic, Appointment Information, Rochester, MN 55905.

Mayo holds each patient personally responsible for his or her account. At the end of a medical center visit, the patient is presented with a bill and will be asked to pay in full or make financial arrangements. If hospitalized, the patient is asked to pay an estimated balance of hospital charges not covered by insurance. If this is not possible, a satisfactory payment plan will be established.

Mayo provided $36 million in charity care in 1993.

UNIVERSITY OF

MINNESOTA HOSPITAL

AND CLINIC

MINNEAPOLIS, MINNESOTA

Hospital consultants consider the Twin Cities area one of the most competitive hospital markets in the country. There are 27 hospitals there, many of them offering excellent care and a few (Hennepin County Medical Center and St. Paul-Ramsay, for example) that have national reputations in several fields. Only one, however, offers the variety and depth of service that one looks for in a truly extraordinary medical center of more than local importance. Although it is only up the road, quite literally, from the world-famous Mayo Clinic, the University of Minnesota Hospital and Clinic (UMHC) has succeeded in maintaining its place as a leading regional referral center and arguably the most influential medical institution in the state. More than half of the UMHC patients come from outside the Twin Cities and almost one-quarter from other states and countries. Best known to the general public for its outstanding work in organ transplantation, UMHC is also very highly regarded in medical circles for many programs, including those in neurosurgery, ophthalmology, oncology, endocrinology, gastroenterology, nephrology, neurology, orthopedics, otolaryngology, rheumatology, pediatrics and urology.

ALTHOUGH IT IS ONLY UP THE ROAD, QUITE LITERALLY, FROM THE WORLD-FAMOUS MAYO CLINIC, THE UNIVERSITY OF MINNESOTA HOSPITAL AND CLINIC (UMHC) HAS SUCCEEDED IN MAINTAINING ITS PLACE AS A LEADING REGIONAL REFERRAL CENTER AND ARGUABLY THE MOST INFLUENTIAL MEDICAL INSTITUTION IN THE STATE.

Since 1911, patient care, education and research have been the cornerstones of the University of Minnesota Hospital and Clinic. For 82 years, the hospital has served as the State of Minnesota's academic medical center. Its physicians have made pioneering advances in many specialty areas, including heart and lung care, transplantation, neurological care, orthopedics, and oncology. UMHC's survival rates for certain types of women's cancer are among the highest in the United States; survival rates for pediatric cancer are also among the best. UMHC is also nationally noted for its neonatal care capabilities. University of Minnesota Hospital and Clinic houses the world's largest pancreas transplant program and one of the largest adult and pediatric kidney transplant programs. It also provides specialized bone marrow procedures available at only a few, if any, hospitals in the world.

Variety Club Children's Hospital is a pediatric "hospital within a hospital" at UMHC. It serves as a national and regional referral center for children needing specialized medical care. Variety Club Children's Hospital excels in the treatment of premature infants, congenital anomalies, pediatric heart and kidney problems, cancer, cystic fibrosis, central nervous system disorders, and infectious diseases.

UMHC is consistently a regional leader in the application of new technology to medical care. It currently has two MRI units and three linear accelerators. Its Thermotron-RF hyperthermia machine is the only hyperthermia device available in the U.S. Other equipment includes an array of lasers to help diagnose and treat patients in many specialties, including ophthalmology, gynecology, cardiology, dermatology, and otolaryngology.

All full-time physicians at the University of Minnesota Hospital and Clinic are also teachers and researchers. They provide services in over 150 specialties and subspecialties that offer the latest diagnostic and treatment methods for the most simple to the most complex medical concerns. Eighty-two UMHC physicians are listed in the latest edition of *The Best Doctors in America*. About 20% of patients are out-of-state residents. In addition to the adult and children's hospitals, the facilities include the Minnesota Heart and Lung Institute, the Transplant Center, and the University of Minnesota Cancer Center. The University of Minnesota Medical School was one of

AT A GLANCE

Beds: 565
Occupancy Rate: 65%
Average Patient Count: 365
Average Patient Stay: 7.4 days
Annual Admissions: 17,819
Births: 450
Outpatient Clinic Visits:
    390,023
Emergency Room/Trauma
    Center Visits: 18,562

HOSPITAL PERSONNEL
Physicians (Full-Time
    Attending): 520
    Board Certified: 411
Physicians (Part-Time Clinical
    Staff): 223
    Board Certified: 193
Residents: 922
Registered Nurses: 720

ROOM CHARGES (PER DIEM)
Private: $530–$790
Semiprivate: $530–$790
ICU: $790–$810

ADDRESS
Box 604
420 Delaware St., SE
Minneapolis, MN 55455

TELEPHONE
(612) 626-3000

16 medical programs selected to launch the Women's Health Initiative, the largest clinical trial ever undertaken in the U.S. for the study of the causes of death in women.

UMHC has extended its services to the community in many ways. The Community-University Health Care Center and Variety Club Children's Clinic in south Minneapolis bring health care to people who might not otherwise receive it. Home Health Care provides services to discharged patients who live within 30 minutes of UMHC. Under the High Rise Program, UMHC nurses visit three Twin Cities senior high rises each week to review medications, monitor progress, and provide consultation and education, free of charge. University physicians and nurses also participate in outreach programs in communities around Minnesota and neighboring states.

SPECIAL FACILITIES AND PROGRAMS

The University of Minnesota has acquired an international reputation for its expertise in transplantation. The world's first open-heart surgery, performed at the University in 1952, led to its current status as a major heart transplant center. The University has renowned programs in lung, kidney, and pancreas transplantation as well. For the 12 months ending on June 30, 1994, 376 organ transplants were performed. These included 183 kidney procedures, 61 combined kidney and pancreas transplants, and 44 pancreas transplantations, as well as 34 lung, 33 liver and 21 heart transplantations. Since 1963, more than 6,000 solid organ transplants have been completed, including over 4,000 kidney procedures and more than 300 heart transplants.

UMHC is also an internationally respected pioneer in the area of bone marrow transplantation. The University of Minnesota performed the first successful bone marrow transplant in 1968. To date, more than 2,000 bone marrow transplants have been performed there, making UMHC one of the largest bone marrow transplantation centers in the world. Both autologous and allogenic procedures are available. These are performed in the UMHC Bone Marrow Transplant Inpatient Unit, which consists of 32 rooms designed to meet the special needs of patients recovering from this procedure. Patient care is provided by a staff of some 30 attending physicians who are board-certified hematologists, oncologists, pediatric hematologists/oncologists and immunologists. It is coordinated by specially trained nurse coordinators who provide case management and ensure continuity of care.

Specialized medical services for women are provided by the Women's Health Center, the Mature Women's Clinic, the Women's Cancer Center, and a unique clinic dedicated to adolescent gynecology. The Women's Health Center provides gynecologic care, and specialized treatment for cancer or infertility. The Mature Women's Clinic meets the complex medical and informational needs of women who are approaching or experiencing menopause. Individualized medical services include hormonal evaluation; hormone replacement therapy;

mammography; screening for cancer and osteoporosis; and counseling on sexuality, nutrition, and exercise. The Women's Cancer Center treats women with cancers of the reproductive system and screens healthy women at risk for cancer. The Center boasts the highest survival rates in the nation for women with ovarian cancer and it is among the top four in the country for overall survival rates for all gynecological cancers.

The University of Minnesota Hospital has long been at the forefront of heart and lung medicine. In addition to performing the first successful open heart surgery, it is credited with developing the first successful heart-lung machine which made longer, more complex surgery possible. This led to the first replacement of a heart valve with an artificial valve in 1958 and the creation of one of the nation's first post-surgery intensive care units. Cardiovascular and thoracic services at UMHC are provided through the Minnesota Heart and Lung Institute. On an outpatient basis, the Cardiology Clinic diagnoses and treats a variety of cardiac problems, including clinical cardiology, heart rhythm disturbances, coronary artery disease, and heart failure. The Heart Catheterization Clinic evaluates patients in need of coronary angiography, angioplasty, or other cardiac catherization laboratory procedures. A Heart Disease Prevention Clinic is available to diagnose and treat high blood cholesterol, other lipid disorders, and heart disease risk factors, including high blood pressure, diabetes and smoking. Procedures not available everywhere, such as valve repair, coronary endarterectomy, and electrical surgery to treat ventricular arrhythmias are also offered.

Up-to-date treatments of cancer are available at UMHC in the areas of surgery, radiotherapy, immunotherapy, and chemotherapy. Cancer diagnoses and treatments are provided through the University of Minnesota Cancer Center. Specific diagnosis and treatment is provided by specialists in breast cancer, bone tumors, colorectal cancer, eye retinoblastoma, cancer of the central nervous system, head and neck cancers, leukemias and other hematologic malignancies, lung cancer, malignant melanomas, and urologic and male genital cancers. Treatment specialties include total body or total nodal irradiation for bone marrow transplantation, stereotactic radiosurgery, use of local hypothermia in conjunction with radiation therapy, and treatment of children's tumors.

The University of Minnesota Hospital and Clinic provides a comprehensive range of services, both surgical and nonsurgical, for the treatment of neurological diseases and disorders. Interdisciplinary programs in neurosciences include stroke and cerebral diseases, neuro-oncology, spine surgery, the Multiple Sclerosis Clinic, craniofacial anomalies and skull base surgery, the Intestinal Implant for Brain Tumors Program, the Alzheimer's Disease Clinic, neuromuscular disease, neurofibromatosis, neuro-ophthalmology, myelodysplasia, and the Headache Management Program.

Pediatric Services, housed in the Variety Club Children's Hospital, takes a multidisciplinary approach to its work. The hospital is known for its success with kidney dialysis, childhood cancers, cystic fibrosis, neonatal and pediatric intensive care, organ transplantation, birth defects, genetic disorders, gastrointestinal disease, and other diseases of infants, children and adolescents.

The University of Minnesota Hospital and Clinic operates several other notable specialty clinics. UMHC houses one of the country's largest cystic fibrosis centers, treating nearly 400 patients each year. The center has achieved an average patient survival rate of nearly 40 years, one of the highest in the world. UMHC has also broken new ground in healing chronic wounds that can lead to amputation. Only a handful of such specialized programs exists and UMHC's Wound Healing and Limb Salvage System has served as a model for most of the others. The hospital and clinics provide specialized as well as general care for diabetics of all ages. Long term eye, kidney and nerve complications of diabetes are of particular interest.

UMHC also has access to one of the most sophisticated, well-equipped medical helicopters in the country. It is provided by Life Link III, a critical-care transport service owned by UMHC and two other local hospitals. The emergency room is staffed by physicians trained in emergency medicine and supported by in-house specialists representing all subspecialties.

MEDICAL SPECIALTIES

Allergy, Anesthesiology, Cardiology, Cardiovascular Surgery, Dermatology, Endocrinology and Metabolism, Gastroenterology, General Surgery, Infectious Diseases, Medical Oncology/Hematology, Nephrology, Neurology, Neurosurgery, Nuclear Medicine, Obstetrics/Gynecology, Ophthalmology, Orthopedics, Pediatrics, Psychiatry, Radiation Oncology, Rheumatology, Thoracic Surgery, and Urology.

WELL-KNOWN SPECIALISTS

- Dr. Joseph R. Bloomer   *Gastroenterology; hepatology*
- Dr. Paula J. Clayton   *Psychiatry; mood and anxiety disorders*
- Dr. Jay N. Cohn   *Cardiovascular disease; heart failure*
- Dr. Donald J. Doughman   *Ophthalmology; corneal diseases and transplantation*
- Dr. Ann C. Dunnigan   *Pediatrics; pediatric cardiology*
- Dr. Alexandra H. Filipovich   *Allergy and immunology; immunodeficiency*
- Dr. Margaret Kendrick Hostetter   *Pediatrics; pediatric infectious disease*
- Dr. James H. House   *Hand surgery; paralytic disorders*
- Dr. Joseph M. Keenan   *Geriatric medicine*
- Dr. John H. Kersey   *Medical oncology/hematology; bone marrow transplantation*
- Dr. Samuel C. Levine   *Otolaryngology; otology*
- Dr. Seymour Levitt   *Radiation oncology; breast cancer*
- Dr. John S. Majarian   *General surgery; transplantation*
- Dr. James E. Mitchell   *Psychiatry; eating disorders*
- Dr. Jonathan D. Mulschafter   *Ophthalmology; neuro-ophthalmology*
- Dr. Bruce A. Peterson   *Medical oncology/hematology; lymphomas*

- Dr. Norma K. C. Ramsay   *Pediatrics; pediatric hematology/oncology*
- Dr. Pratap K. Reddy   *Urology; endocrinology*
- Dr. R. Paul Robertson   *Endocrinology and metabolism; diabetes*
- Dr. David A. Rothenberger   *Colon and rectal surgery*
- Dr. Kenneth F. Swanson   *Child neurology; inherited biochemical disorders*
- Dr. Roby Calvin Thompson, Jr.   *Orthopedic surgery; tumor surgery*
- Dr. Leo B. Twiggs   *Obstetrics/gynecology; gynecologic oncology*

PATIENT SATISFACTION

Ninety-five percent of respondents rate the inpatient care provided at UMHC as "good", "very good" or "excellent." The number of "very good" and "excellent" ratings has risen consistently in surveys conducted since 1992, indicating effective analysis of the returns and elimination of problems identified in the surveys. An outpatient survey was being developed for introduction by the Fall of 1994.

RESEARCH

More than $50 million in research funds is awarded annually to UMHC.

The University and its Virginia Piper Cancer Institute have been designated by the National Cancer Institute (NCI) as one of ten U.S. sites to study whether widespread use of screening tests for prostate, lung, colorectal, and ovarian cancer saves lives. The NCI is also supporting a national study of 25,000 long-term survivors of childhood cancer.

In neurosurgery, the National Institutes of Health (NIH) has funded studies of neuromotor control and training of young neuroscientists. A four-year NIH grant has also been received to research neuron transplantation for Alzheimer's disease.

A wide variety of other research efforts are also underway at UMHC. The Diabetes Center was one of ten selected to take part in a national study to prevent insulin-dependent diabetes. The Department of Orthopaedic Surgery is conducting NIH-funded research into osteoclasts and tumor osteolysis. Work is continuing on a study of blunt trauma and articular cartilage damage. Ashkey Haase, a UMHC microbiologist, has discovered that HIV is active in lymph tissue long before it can be detected by blood tests, a discovery that could affect timing and aggressiveness of therapy for HIV infection and early symptoms of AIDS. Kamil Ugurbil, a professor of biochemistry, scored a scientific first for his participation in developing a new application of magnetic resonance imaging that shows the brain at work. Robert Vince, professor of medicinal chemistry, has received an NCI grant to support ongoing research in the design of new drugs for cancer and infectious diseases, including AIDS.

ADMISSIONS POLICY

An inpatient must be admitted by either a full time attending UMHC physician or a community physician with admitting privileges. An outpatient does not need a referral.

The University of Minnesota Hospital and Clinic attempts to obtain registration information, identify third-party payer requirements, and handle financial concerns before a patient is treated.

Payment for services received at the University of Minnesota Hospital and Clinic is the responsibility of each individual patient or the agency that authorized the patient's care. UMHC is a self-supporting institution; state appropriations are not available for free care. Deposits may be required for patients with inadequate third-party resources or under specific deposit protocols or policies.

If a patient is unable to pay for services at UMHC, he or she may seek advice in securing aid from the county welfare department. In 1992-93, more than $20 million in uncompensated care was provided.

Special phone number for admissions information: (612) 626-6685.

BARNES HOSPITAL

Most physicians in the Midwest believe Barnes Hospital is one of the premier teaching and research hospitals in this part of the country. As one measure of the excellent reputation that Barnes Hospital enjoys, Barnes received almost 35,000 referrals from across the United States in 1993, as well as numerous patients from overseas. Patients are referred to Barnes because it is recognized as one of the most technologically advanced hospitals in the country.

Founded in 1914 through a bequest from a wealthy St. Louis businessman, Barnes is today the primary teaching hospital of the Washington University School of Medicine and the central facility in a 26-building medical complex that includes another first rate teaching hospital (Jewish Hospital) and the highly regarded St. Louis Children's Hospital. Barnes affiliated with Jewish Hospital in 1992. The affiliation maintains the unique identities of each institution, while providing an opportunity to enhance medical care and eliminate redundancies. In 1993, Barnes-Jewish merged with community-based Christian Health Services, adding the two Christian Health hospitals to form a healthcare network that comprises 4,400 licensed beds, 4,200 medical staff members, 18,000 full- and part-time employees, and 7,200 auxiliary members and volunteers. This makes the BJC Health System the second largest secular not-for-profit system in the United

ST. LOUIS, MISSOURI

PATIENTS ARE REFERRED TO BARNES BECAUSE IT IS RECOGNIZED AS ONE OF THE MOST TECHNOLOGICALLY ADVANCED HOSPITALS IN THE COUNTRY.

States. More than half of the 177 Missouri physicians listed in the second edition of *The Best Doctors in America* are on staff at BJC hospitals.

Barnes has traditionally had a reputation for technology leadership. Having performed almost 2,000 transplants, Barnes Hospital is considered one of the nation's premier transplant hospitals. Barnes has been involved in a number of transplant breakthroughs, performing one of the first lung transplants for emphysema and the first bilateral lung transplant. In October 1993, Barnes was the site of the first nerve transplant in the U.S. Barnes surgeons are also pioneering new noninvasive/minimally invasive surgery techniques. Barnes is a U.S. trial site for a device called the Pryotech which directs energy into the body to destroy a tumor. Barnes also uses stereotactic neurosurgery to treat certain types of tumors and malformations between the brain's arteries and veins, and is pioneering the use of cryotherapy (the freezing of tumorous tissue) for use in patients with prostate cancer.

Barnes also prides itself on the professionalism of its nursing staff. All newly hired nurses go through an intensive six-week orientation session; formal classroom work and additional preceptor training are required for intensive care duty. Many nurses there have bachelor's degrees, and the hospital encourages further education by providing tuition reimbursement. Barnes has adopted the primary nursing delivery of care model, whereby a patient has the right to have an individual caregiver accountable for his or her care throughout the stay. The hospital is also a national model for "critical pathways", which is a multidisciplinary treatment plan that improves the coordination and organization of the caregiving process.

SPECIAL FACILITIES AND PROGRAMS

Transplantation surgery is an important part of Barnes Hospital's special services. Barnes doctors performed 221 solid organ transplants in 1993. These included 115 kidney transplants, 19 heart transplants, 39 liver transplantations, and 48 lung procedures. In addition, 30 autologous and 13 allogenic bone marrow transplants were completed. Barnes Hospital and Washington University School of Medicine have made significant contributions in the field of islet cell transplantation; four of these procedures were carried out in 1993. Dr. Susan Mackinnon, considered to be the world's foremost authority on nerve transplantation, directs the Barnes Hospital nerve transplant program.

The Barnes success rates in transplantation surgery are noteworthy. The success rate for kidney and kidney/pancreas transplants is in the range of 90 to 95%. Over 85% of heart transplant recipients survived for at least one year and 73% were still living after five years. Liver transplant survival rates are 76% one year post-transplant. Lung transplant recipients survived at least one year in 82% of cases and 73% survived for at least three years. Survival rates with autologous bone marrow transplants are 80%, but only 46% with allogenic transplants.

Barnes also offers a host of important medical specialties. Patients come from all over the world for cardiology services and cardiothoracic surgery, especially surgery for Wolff-Parkinson-White syndrome, heart malformations, difficult coronary artery bypass, and esophageal cancer. Barnes's 15-bed Cardiac Care Unit is the only one anywhere with a PET scanner within the unit.

Ophthalmologists at Barnes have pioneered treatments for diabetic retinopathy, glaucoma, and other conditions. Barnes has received recent national recognition for research into treatment for macular degeneration and ocular histoplasmosis. All kinds of ophthalmologic laser surgery are performed there, and Barnes is the home of the St. Louis Eye Bank.

Specialists in otolaryngology have done important work in dizziness, extracochlear implants, neck and throat cancer, sclera tympanoplasty, sleep apnea, and tongue cancer.

The Burn Center at Barnes was one of the first in the country to develop techniques that have since become standard procedure at other hospitals.

Plastic and reconstructive surgery is a pioneered specialty at Barnes, with national referrals for reimplantation of severed body parts, facial reconstruction necessitated by both congenital and accidental causes, sex reassignment, and hand surgery.

In neurology and neurosurgery, Barnes' specialties include Alzheimer's disease, brain surgery, epilepsy (including mapping the brain to detect and eliminate errant electrical activity centers that cause seizures), immunology and rheumatology (at the Howard Hughes Center), multiple sclerosis, and muscular dystrophy (at the Jerry Lewis Center). In conjunction with ophthalmology, orbital and other eye area tumors receive attention.

The Cromalloy Kidney Center is the free-standing hemodialysis facility located at Barnes. The service offers home hemodialysis, CAPD, CCPD and in-center dialysis. It is a fully accredited center that has been in operation for about 27 years. In addition to this 26-station unit, there is a six-bed acute inpatient dialysis facility. In 1993, the Chromalloy Kidney Center saw 182 patients three times a week.

AT A GLANCE

Beds: 1,205
Occupancy Rate: 65%
Average Patient Count: 612
Average Patient Stay: 6.9 days
Annual Admissions: 32,623
Births: 2,184
Outpatient Clinic Visits:
    60,691
Emergency Room/Trauma
    Center Visits: 60,547

HOSPITAL PERSONNEL
Physicians: 1,317
    Board Certified: 75%
Residents: 735
Registered Nurses: 1,553
    BS Degree: 667

ROOM CHARGES (PER DIEM)
Private: $405
Semiprivate: $350
ICU: $1,200

ADDRESS
One Barnes Hospital Plaza
St. Louis, MO 63110

TELEPHONE
(314) 362-5000

In the urology department, Barnes is particularly noted for work in bladder and prostate cancers, kidney stones, and testicular impotency.

A full range of specialists and services treat patients with cancer, including bone cancer, breast cancer, Hodgkin's disease, cancer of the larynx, leukemia, liver cancer, lung cancer, skull base tumors, and testicular cancer. An Outpatient Transfusion Center and the Pheresis Center allow cancer patients to receive blood transfusions as outpatients and thus remain in their homes.

Patients from hundreds of miles away are referred to Barnes's high-risk pregnancy program, which helps women who have delayed pregnancy until later in life; those with pre-existing medical complications, such as diabetes, heart or kidney disease, and hypertension; and those expecting multiple births.

The Health Education and Screening Center and the Community Outreach Program focus on educating the public; their offerings include a television series, printed materials, a speaker's bureau, community forums, and doctors' seminars, all sponsored by Barnes Hospital.

Barnes Home Health helps assure continuity of care after patients leave the hospital, and, in some cases, can even provide an alternative to hospitalization or shorten the stay in the hospital.

In April 1984, Barnes acquired Sutter Clinic in downtown St. Louis, which has evolved into Barnes Care Corporate Health Services and now offers a variety of services, including breast cancer screenings, disability evaluations, and executive physicals, at four locations.

Barnes has a Mammography Screening Center, which was designed specifically with women in mind—serene surroundings and efficient staff, as well as convenient hours for working women, including Saturdays. In addition, Barnes debuted a new Mammography Van in 1992, which saw more than 8,170 women in 1993 at numerous corporations, supermarkets and other public locations, making it one of the largest such programs in the country.

Other special programs and centers include the Alzheimer's Disease Center, the Sleep Center, the Stroke Management and Rehabilitation Therapy Program, the Irene Walter Johnson Rehabilitation Institute, and the Electroconvulsive Therapy Service.

MEDICAL SPECIALTIES

Allergy and Immunology, Anesthesiology, Applied Physiology, Cardiology, Cardiothoracic Surgery, Dentistry, Dermatology, Endocrinology, Gastroenterology, General Surgery, Hematology and Oncology, Infectious Diseases, Neurology, Neurosurgery, Obstetrics/Gynecology, Oncology, Ophthalmology, Orthopedic Surgery, Otolaryngology, Pathology, Pediatric Surgery, Plastic Surgery, Psychiatry, Radiology, Renal Medicine, Rheumatology, Surgical Pathology, Transplantation and Urologic Surgery.

WELL-KNOWN SPECIALISTS

- Dr. William Catalona *Urologic surgery; one of the pioneers in the development of the PSA blood test for prostate cancer*
- Dr. Ralph Clayman *Urologic surgery; authority on minimally invasive surgery techniques; performed the world's first laparoscopic nephrectomy*
- Dr. Joel Cooper *Lung transplant and cardiothoracic surgery; performed the world's first successful single and double lung transplants*
- Dr. James Cox *Surgery for heart arrhythmias, including Wolff-Parkinson-White syndrome*
- Dr. John Fredrickson *Barnes/Washington University chief of otolaryngology; authority on innovative techniques for treatment of head and neck cancer, and of apnea/snoring*
- Dr. Henry J. Kaplan *Ophthalmology; authority on submacular surgery for macular degeneration*
- Dr. Susan Mackinnon *Plastic and reconstructive surgery; recently (1993) performed the first nerve transplant in the United States*
- Dr. Jay Pepose *Ophthalmology; cornea specialist with expertise in using Automated Lamellar Keratoplasty (ALK) for the treatment of severe nearsightedness and moderate farsightedness*
- Dr. James Schreiber *Obstetrics; chairman of the obstetrics/gynecology department; member of a team involved in a multicenter study of the effectiveness of various treatments for miscarriage*
- Dr. Nathaniel Soper *General surgery; associate professor of surgery and director of a new minimally invasive surgery center at Washington Medical School*
- Dr. Paul Weeks *Plastic and reconstructive surgery; experise in reattaching hands and fingers*
- Dr. Samuel Wells *General surgery; chairman of the department of general surgery; expertise in endocrine surgery*

PATIENT SATISFACTION

Patients are randomly surveyed following discharge from the hospital. In the survey, patients are asked to evaluate numerous areas and asked whether or not they would recommend Barnes to their family or friends.

In the 1993 survey, the highest scores were related to satisfaction with the care team—the nurses and physicians. Within the nursing section, care and concern on the part of the nurses rated the highest, with skill level ranking second-highest. With physicians, care, concern and skill were rated equally high.

As to the final question of whether a former patient would recommend the hospital to family or friends, should hospital care be needed, Barnes scored 88%.

RESEARCH

In 1993, Washington University received more than $126 million in medical research grants from the National Institutes of Health, making it one of the top recipients in the country. Also in 1993, 145 foundation grants and corporate giving of $308,000 were received. Among the current research efforts are those described below.

Drs. Paul Lacy and David Scharp are conducting research that may one day eliminate the daily insulin injections for persons with diabetes. The two have successfully transplanted islets of Langerhans, the insulin-producing cells of the pancreas, into patients. Ultimately, this treatment may prevent the life-threatening complications of diabetes, such as heart and kidney failure.

The Center for the Study of Nervous System Injury, headed by Dr. Dennis Choi, is developing strategies to protect the brain and spinal cord from injury due to disease or trauma, as well as working with therapies to promote recovery.

Dr. Eric Whitman, a Barnes cancer specialist, developed a realtime computer system that is used with a specialized procedure, called Isolate Limb Perfusion, to isolate blood flow in certain parts of the body. This technique offers hope to some patients diagnosed with melanoma.

Dr. John DiPersio, Barnes' director of bone marrow transplantation and stem cell biology programs, is well-known for his stem cell research for the treatment of cancer. He is currently researching gene therapy in regard to stem cell transplantation.

Dr. William Powderly, a Barnes infectious disease specialist, is conducting the AIDS Clinical Trials program, which is attempting to determine the effectiveness of various treatments for AIDS patients.

ADMISSIONS POLICY

Upon the request of an attending physician or chief resident with admitting privileges, Barnes will admit elective, private patients that fulfill the appropriate financial criteria. Elective, indigent patients will be admitted within the limits of the charity teaching budget. Patients with life-threatening emergency conditions will be admitted regardless of financial status.

Elective services require full payment prior to services being rendered. Nonelective services require full payment, unless the patient qualifies for charity assistance according to federal poverty guidelines. All self-pay admissions are evaluated for Medicaid application or other federal assistance. Barnes offers bank loans and monthly payment plans to assist payment.

In 1992, Barnes provided $29.4 million worth of charity care, not including bad debt or uncollected bills. In 1993, the figure is estimated at $28.4 million.

PATIENT/FAMILY ACCOMMODATIONS

For relatives of severely ill patients who have traveled a long distance, Barnes offers two facilities. The Queeny Tower, which is on-site, has 39 rooms at $49 per night for a single and $11 for each additional person. The Barnes Lodge is close by. Its room charges are on a sliding scale of up to $20, based on income.

JEWISH HOSPITAL

OF ST. LOUIS

Jewish Hospital of St. Louis is nationally recognized for its long history of quality medical care and research excellence. Long known for its dedication to giving the best patient care possible, Jewish Hospital also focuses on the hospital's clinical strengths, recognition of the contributions of its employees, the excellence of its physician staff, and service to its community. Of the 177 Missouri physicians listed in the second edition of *The Best Doctors in America,* 67 are on staff at Jewish Hospital. From the accolades it has received, one must conclude that Jewish Hospital is carrying out its credo very well.

Jewish Hospital of St. Louis is a 433-bed, acute care teaching hospital affiliated with Washington University School of Medicine. Founded in 1902 with 30 beds by the Jewish community, out of commitment to quality patient care for all people, the hospital quickly grew to a 100-bed facility by 1905. Also in 1902, the Jewish Hospital School of Nursing was founded. The hospital moved to its present location in 1922 and began its now nationally recognized research program at the same time. By 1954, the hospital had expanded to 500 beds, and, in 1963, it began its affiliation with Washington University School of Medicine. Today, Jewish Hospital offers a full range of services and an array of medical and surgical specialties, and its research program ranks among the national leaders for private institutions in

ST. LOUIS, MISSOURI

JEWISH HOSPITAL OF ST. LOUIS IS NATIONALLY RECOGNIZED FOR ITS LONG HISTORY OF QUALITY MEDICAL CARE AND RESEARCH EXCELLENCE.

funding from the NIH. In 1992, Jewish Hospital and Barnes Hospital became affiliated as Barnes-Jewish Inc. Jewish Hospital is a founding member of the BJC Health System, a regional health care system in Missouri and southern Illinois, consisting of Barnes, Jewish, and Christian Hospitals.

In 1993, Jewish Hospital was cited by the Anti-Defamation League for its leadership in helping immigrants from eastern Europe and Russia. The hospital's New American Program is designed to meet the healthcare needs of Jewish refugees and other new arrivals from Russia and other countries of the former Soviet Union by informing patients of the health services available. In 1993, Jewish Hospital treated approximately 530 New American patients each month.

In most hospitals, nurses are hourly employees. Because of Jewish Hospital's commitment to the profession of nursing, nurses are salaried employees, as are all other hospital professionals.

Jewish Hospital is one of a handful of hospitals across the country designing a new way to care for patients through a technique called patient-focused care. The goal of patient-focused care is to provide excellent care in an environment that is centered on patient satisfaction. Patient-focused care principles call for streamlining documentation, moving services closer to patients, redesigning caregiver responsibilities and qualifications, and simplifying unit management.

SPECIAL FACILITIES AND PROGRAMS

Jewish Hospital of St. Louis is noted for excellence in cardiology and cardiovascular surgery, rehabilitation, high-risk obstetrics care, radiation and medical oncology, bone health and geriatrics. The hospital also brings its expertise to the community through a number of specialized, off-site centers that include such services as behavioral medicine, dialysis services, OB/ultrasound, physical therapy and sports medicine, diagnostic imaging, dentistry, and cardiac rehabilitation and diagnostics.

Cardiology services at Jewish Hospital offer patients the most up-to-date diagnostic services and facilities, including state-of-the-art cardiac catheterization and electrophysiology laboratory facilities. Also, research topics in the department include molecular and vascular biology, atherosclerosis and cholesterol metabolism. Jewish Hospital also offers echocardiography, the practice of bouncing sound waves off the heart to form an image that enables physicians to differentiate healthy from unhealthy tissue. The department is currently involved in research that combines physics with cardiology to develop new diagnostic and treatment modalities.

Jewish Hospital's Division of Cardiothoracic Surgery at Washington University has earned an international reputation for its investigations into new and better ways to treat heart, lung and blood vessel diseases. The division has developed a technique to treat the aorta called the switch procedure. The switch procedure involves replacing the diseased aortic valve with the patient's own pulmonary valve, which is then replaced with another human valve. Other procedures used by the division include intraoperative echocardiograms, which enable surgeons to immediately and accurately assess the extent of prior heart damage and whether a particular procedure has been effective. The division also conducts several research studies, among them, studying the use of hypothermia to prevent brain damage and paralysis resulting from the surgical removal of aortic aneurysms.

Through its colorectal cancer services, Jewish Hospital is one of a handful of hospitals nationwide with the expertise needed to minimize the physical pain and emotional stress caused by colorectal conditions. A team of physicians and healthcare professionals from several specialties combines its skills to fight many ailments that can affect the colorectal system. Jewish Hospital's Anal Physiology Lab serves as a Midwest center for those suffering from pelvic floor abnormalities. Jewish Hospital has been able to reduce the need for surgical correction of inflammatory bowel conditions, such as Crohn's disease or ulcerative colitis, by using total parenteral nutrition (TPN). TPN eliminates the need for surgery to treat the ulcerated sores by delivering nutrition directly into the bloodstream. Finally, Jewish Hospital surgeons were the first in the St. Louis metropolitan area to use a minimally-invasive surgical technique called laparoscopy to perform colorectal surgery.

The Jewish Hospital Department of Radiation Oncology uses leading-edge technology and specialized equipment to offer cancer patients less invasive treatment options. For instance, using 3-D imaging and a multileaf collimator, physicians can deliver larger, more effective radiation doses to the tumor while protecting surrounding tissue. In conjunction with the Mallinckrodt Institute of Radiology and the Washington University School of Medicine's Department of Neurosurgery, Jewish Hospital is one of the few facilities in the nation doing work in 3-D radiation.

In order to help cancer patients and their families deal with the psychological and emotional effects of cancer, the Jewish Hospital Auxiliary opened the Cancer Information and Resource Center for Life

AT A GLANCE

Beds: 433
Occupancy Rate: 69%
Average Patient Count: 326
Average Patient Stay: 6.3 days
Annual Admissions: 15,274
Outpatient Clinic Visits:
    90,683
Emergency Room Visits:
    27,899

HOSPITAL PERSONNEL
Physicians: 1,027
    Board Certified: 77%
Residents: 168
Registered Nurses: 616
    BS Degree: 124

ROOM CHARGES (PER DIEM)
Private: $405
Semiprivate: $370
ICU: $1,030

ADDRESS
216 S. Kings Highway
St. Louis, MO 63110

TELEPHONE
(314) 454-7000

and Education (CIRCLE). CIRCLE offers personalized information, support groups and referrals for cancer patients.

Jewish Hospital is an international leader in the study and treatment of bone disease. The Bone Health Program is directed by Louis Avioli and has been cited in national publications as one of the two centers in the United States for exceptional care of osteoporosis. The Bone Health Program offers programs for the prevention, diagnosis and treatment of bone diseases, including a procedure for measuring bone mass, and is staffed by nurses and dieticians who measure calcium use. In addition, the program is involved in a one of a kind study that involves a computer program that enables individuals to answer a series of simple questions to determine whether they may be at risk for osteoporosis.

Jewish Hospital offers expectant mothers a unique service through its High-Risk Obstetrics Team. The high-risk team is made up of the patient's private obstetrician/gynecologist, the Jewish Hospital high-risk pregnancy team, neonatologists from St. Louis Children's Hospital and nurses at both hospitals. The team also provides a genetic counselor to discuss a patient's medical history and chromosomal testing. A hotline, called GENIS, is also available for patients to receive answers about medical and environmental pregnancy risks. The hospital established the city's first successful in vitro fertilization program and offers unique diagnostic procedures, such as chromosomal testing.

To help deal with risks multiple births carry for both mother and babies, Jewish Hospital opened the region's first Center for Multiple Births. The center, affiliated with Washington University School of Medicine, focuses on the special medical and emotional needs of women expecting more than one child. The center's services include obstetrical care, dietary services, physical therapy and social services. Women in the program have the option to participate in long-term studies on multiple births.

The Jewish Hospital Home Care (JHHC) was founded in 1953 and is one of the oldest hospital-based agencies in the nation. It currently ranks as the fourth largest hospital-based agency in St. Louis and fourth largest in Missouri. The agency services about 460 patients a month and averages about 220 visits per day. Currently, there are 24 nurses, one social worker, 16 home health aides, 24 therapists, 10 clerical and support staff members, three intake coordinators, one dietician, four nurse claim interviewers, and five managers employed by the Jewish agency, in addition to 94 volunteers.

Jewish Hospital has long been considered a pioneer in rehabilitative medicine. The 42-bed unit accredited by the Commission on Accreditation of Rehabilitation Facilities (CARF), provides comprehensive rehabilitation services using an interdisciplinary team approach. Physical, occupational and recreation therapists, as well as social workers and nurses, support physicians and family members in assisting patients in their rehabilitative activities and goals. The department offers support groups for patients and their families; an independent-living apartment that helps prepare patients to leave the hospital; an outpatient and sports medicine center in west St. Louis County; more than two decades of service to St. Louis' professional sports teams; a specialized program dedicated to the distinctive needs of performing artists; and interdisciplinary clinics, such as amputee and wheelchair, to meet patients' needs.

Jewish Hospital is continuously upgrading technology to improve the health of the people and communities it serves. Following is a short list of the state-of-the-art equipment which contribute to excellent clinical care at Jewish Hospital: multileaf collimator, portal imaging device, laminar flow surgical suites, thermal radioscope, laparoscopic surgery, CT scanner, diagnostic radioscope, MRI, SPECT, ultrasound, a state-of-the-art electrophysiology laboratory, and two state-of-the-art cardiac catheterization laboratories.

MEDICAL SPECIALTIES

Anesthesiology, Bone and Mineral Diseases, Cardiology, Cardiothoracic Surgery, Dentistry, Dermatology, Emergency Medicine, Gastroenterology, Hematology, Infectious Diseases, Medical Oncology, Neurology, Neurosurgery, Obstetrics/Gynecology, Ophthalmology, Orthopedic Surgery, Otolaryngology, Pathology and Laboratory Medicine, Pediatrics, Plastic Surgery, Psychiatry, Radiation Oncology, Rehabilitation Medicine, Surgery and Urology.

WELL-KNOWN SPECIALISTS

- Dr. Louis V. Avioli   *Bone and mineral diseases; osteoporosis and hormone therapy*
- Dr. James P. Crane   *Obstetrics*
- Dr. Keith Hruska   *Orthopedic surgery; expert in kidney stone treatment, especially for high-risk and repeat patients*
- Dr. Saulo Klahr   *Internal medicine; renal disease*
- Dr. Ira Kodner   *Colorectal surgery; colorectal cancer*
- Dr. Nicholas Kouchoukos   *Cardiothoracic surgery; leading researcher of techniques to treat diseases of the aorta*
- Dr. Stephen S. Lefrak   *Respiratory and critical care; biomedical ethics*
- Dr. Karl Merlile   *Orthopedic surgery; orthopedic oncology*
- Dr. Michael Nelson   *Obstetrics; high-risk pregnancy*
- Dr. Gordon Philpott   *Surgical oncology; breast cancer*
- Dr. Gary Rattain   *Medical oncology; chairman of the Jewish Hospital Cancer Committee*
- Dr. Robert M. Senior   *Respiratory and critical care; specialist in pulmonary disease*
- Dr. Burton Shatz   *Gastroenterology; colorectal cancer and other gastrointestinal cancers/diseases*
- Dr. Ronald Strickler   *Obstetrics/gynecology; high-risk pregnancy; in vitro fertilization*
- Dr. Stephen L. Teitelbaum   *Pathology; expert in bone development, osteoporosis, and hormone therapy*

- Dr. Todd Wasserman   *Radiation oncology; expert in three-dimensional radiation therapy*
- Dr. Samuel A. Wickline   *Cardiology; expert in ultrasonic tissue characterization*

PATIENT SATISFACTION

Patient satisfaction is surveyed independently by NCG Research. Patients are randomly surveyed following discharge from the hospital. In the survey, patients are asked to evaluate numerous areas and asked whether or not they would recommend Jewish Hospital to family and friends.

Survey results indicate that Jewish Hospital is an organization performing at a very high patient satisfaction level. In nearly all areas, scores were above median for the NCG database. In several areas, Jewish Hospital is considered a benchmark hospital in the NCG database. Results also indicated that Jewish Hospital staff excelled in the prompt delivery of quality service.

In particular, the overall or global satisfaction rating by outpatients and inpatients at Jewish Hospital was high—ranging from 88% to 96% rating overall satisfaction with services and care received in various service areas as good or excellent. Inpatient services and outpatient surgery were rated at 96%.

RESEARCH

Jewish Hospital is one of the few hospitals in the United States that maintains a major independent research program. Since the hospital's inception, research that will enhance the delivery of medicine has been one of its missions. Since 1988, the hospital has been in the top dozen or so of hospitals that receive funding from the National Institutes of Health. Current external grant awards from all sources will exceed $12 million in 1994. The hospital, in its support of research over the years, has established endowed chairs for ten of its senior investigators.

In 1993, Jewish Hospital received funding for 80 basic and clinical studies—an increase of 17 grants from 1992. Jewish Hospital researchers were awarded grants for 44% of their proposals—well above the national average of 25%. The hospital received more grant funding than any hospital in Missouri. Only the University of Missouri, Washington University and St. Louis University exceeded Jewish Hospital's research grants.

The hospital has four major research programs. First is the study of bone, including bone resorption, changes in bone due to biological aging, and the prevention and treatment of osteoporosis. Key investigators in this area are Dr. Louis Avioli, one of the country's pioneers in the study of osteoporosis and Dr. Stephen Teitelbaum, a leading bone pathologist. Another program under the direction of Dr. Robert Senior is studying processes or mechanisms that attack tissues in the lung, such as emphysema and pulmonary fibrosis.

Two other programs under the direction of world class investigators at the hospital are studies focused on the pathophysiology of renal disease and uremia, under Dr. Saulo Klahr, the hospital's Physician-in-Chief, and the study of platelet-derived growth factors and its mechanism of action in initiating both normal and abnormal cell growth. Work on the latter is being conducted by Dr. Thomas Dueul, Chief of Hematology and a past nominee for the Nobel Prize in medicine.

Other evidence of the productivity of the research program include the large number of publications produced each year and the recognition received by its faculty. Over 600 articles by hospital researchers are published each year in scientific journals.

ADMISSIONS POLICY

Admission to Jewish Hospital requires an order from a physician. Prospective patients may contact "Physician Choice"—a physician referral service that can be reached at (314) 454-8180 to obtain pertinent information about staff physicians' specialties, office hours, credentials, office location, etc. Patients are admitted if their physician deems an admission as the appropriate level of service.

Patients are required to be able to meet their financial obligations to the hospital. Financial counselors are available to work with patients that are under-insured or uninsured, if significant financial hardship exists. Charity budgets are established each year to treat patients that fall within government poverty guidelines. In 1993, $15 million worth of charity care was provided.

PATIENT/FAMILY ACCOMMODATIONS

Jewish Hospital has established relationships with hotels in the area. The Patient Relations Department works with patients and families to meet their needs.

UNIVERSITY

HOSPITAL

UNIVERSITY OF NEBRASKA
MEDICAL CENTER

OMAHA, NEBRASKA

Located in the heart of the farm belt, University Hospital at the University of Nebraska Medical Center (UNMC) encompasses many of the same medically advanced features as the best hospitals in the largest urban centers in the country. For instance, UNMC is home to the second most active liver transplant program in the country. It has two of the nation's most active and successful bone marrow transplant programs—one for children and one for adults. University Hospital is a Level I trauma center supported by aeromedical transport. It is also a tertiary care facility receiving patients referred from all 50 states and several foreign countries.

University Hospital is the teaching hospital of the University of Nebraska Medical Center's College of Medicine. The medical school was rated 14th among the top comprehensive medical schools out of 66 schools in the 1994 *U.S. News and World Report* annual survey. Many faculty of the College of Medicine and the other UNMC professional schools have clinical appointments to the hospital staff. In all, the colleges of medicine, dentistry, nursing, and pharmacy, and the School of Allied Health Professions, support more than 50 clinical and support services at University Hospital. University Medical Associates operates the Outpatient Care Center located on the UNMC campus adjacent to University Hospital. Here outpatients have access to UNMC faculty physicians

LOCATED IN THE HEART
OF THE FARM BELT,
UNIVERSITY HOSPITAL AT
THE UNIVERSITY OF
NEBRASKA MEDICAL CENTER
(UNMC) ENCOMPASSES
MANY OF THE SAME
MEDICALLY ADVANCED
FEATURES AS THE BEST
HOSPITALS IN THE LARGEST
URBAN CENTERS IN
THE COUNTRY.

and residents. The University Geriatric Center, a comprehensive assessment, treatment, and rehabilitation center for seniors is affiliated with University Hospital. The hospital also operates a 40-bed off-campus inpatient unit in Omaha—University Hospital at Lutheran.

From humble origins as a legislated indigent care facility in 1917, University Hospital has grown into a medical center occupying more than 500,000 square feet. Perhaps the most significant change in its history came in the early 1960s, when University Hospital shifted from a strictly charity care mission to a goal of self-support, while continuing to serve a medically underserved population. In 1966, approximately 20% of revenues were coming from private patients and 80% from legislative appropriations. By 1976, however, 85% of the costs were covered by revenues from patient charges. Today, University Hospital is essentially self-supporting. The move to self-support spurred the growth of University Hospital into the first-rate medical facility it is today.

In addition to transplantation, University Hospital is also nationally recognized for its expertise in cancer treatment, geriatrics, high-risk obstetrics, neonatology, trauma, cardiology, gastrointestinal diseases, oral surgery and urology. It also serves as a regional referral center for the treatment of AIDS and hemophilia. A Mobile Nursing Center serves rural and urban underserved areas, providing health care services and education to diabetics and others with chronic illness or health concerns. This is a joint venture involving UNMC's College of Nursing and the Cornbelt Federation of Cosmopolitan Internal, Inc. The project received a five-year, $887,000 grant from the U.S. Department of Health and Human Services to continue operation of the center that began in spring of 1993.

SPECIAL FACILITIES AND PROGRAMS

The liver transplant program at University Hospital is one of the three most active in the country and the bone marrow transplant one of the five most active. In 1993 alone, UNMC performed 131 liver transplants and 186 bone marrow transplants. In existence for nine years, the liver transplant program has

AT A GLANCE

Beds: 422
Occupancy Rate: 69%
Average Patient Count: 244
Average Patient Stay: 8.3 days
Annual Admissions: 11,173
Outpatient Clinic Visits:
    200,000
Emergency Room/Trauma
    Center Visits: 22,515

HOSPITAL PERSONNEL
Physicians (Attending): 260
    Board Certified: 220
Physicians (Consulting): 195
    Board Certified: 152
Residents: 380
Registered Nurses: 652
    BS Degree: 368

ROOM CHARGES (PER DIEM)
Private: $325
Semiprivate: $280
ICU: $860

ADDRESS
600 South 42nd Street
Omaha, NE 68198

TELEPHONE
(402) 559-4000

treated 526 adults and 238 children. At the 1993 reunion picnic, former patients came from 28 states.

In February 1989, the University of Nebraska Medical Center gained approval to perform pancreas transplants as a joint program with Clarkson Hospital. On April 5, 1989, the first combined pancreas-kidney transplant was performed in the state of Nebraska. Through 1992, a total of 85 combined pancreas-kidney transplants were performed in the program, with 98% patient survival. Approximately half of the transplant recipients were not yet on dialysis prior to transplantation, as the combined pancreas-kidney transplant can be safely performed before diabetic patients need dialysis. It is anticipated that UNMC will continue its current trend of performing 2–3 pancreas-kidney transplants per month.

UNMC places a special emphasis on the treatment of lymphomas and leukemias—malignancies that often respond well to treatment with bone marrow transplantation. To that end, UNMC has built one of the nation's most active bone marrow transplant (BMT) programs, with both adult and pediatric transplant teams performing over 800 transplants since 1983. In fact, almost an entire floor of the hospital is devoted to these patients. The survival rate of 88% is well above the national average. University physicians were recently first in the region, and among very few in the nation, to perform a bone marrow transplant on an outpatient basis. This program is being piloted for breast cancer patients.

The center has the state's only gynecological oncologists, as well as the region's only cytogenetics laboratory that diagnoses and individualizes treatment plans. Because the UNMC's Eppley Institute for Research in Cancer and Allied Diseases is designated as one of 15 National Institutes of Health cancer research laboratories, patients are offered experimental drug and radiation therapies.

The Clinical Care Center of UNMC has been named one of the top 25 in the country for the past three years by *Coping*, a magazine for patients with cancer. Because of the range of treatments available, the center attracts many young people, with an average age of 35. The center pioneered a radical procedure for young bone cancer patients that removes the tumor but saves the vital elements of the leg.

All the major advances in cardiology are available at UNMC. Cutting-edge developments in ultrasound technology are giving UNMC cardiologists advantages in "seeing" how a patient's heart is functioning. One procedure, called the transesophageal echocardiogram, provides unprecedented full-color anatomic detail of the heart. UNMC is one of only a few sites in the country to clinically test intravascular ultrasound, which provides clear images of the inside walls of blood vessels, making it much easier to assess the extent of plaque and cholesterol buildup. UNMC has also been a pioneer in a new procedure called radiofrequency ablation to cure tachycardia, or abnormal rapid heart beat. A full range of open heart surgical procedures, including atherectomy are available as are noninterventional and preventative treatments. The Cardiac Risk Assessment

Clinic tests patients before beginning cardiac rehabilitation and specific programs are designed for individuals as a result of these tests.

The University Geriatric Center is well-known for elder care and research, and claims the state's first geriatrician. Offering comprehensive assessment, treatment and rehabilitation for older adults, the center includes a 14-bed psychiatric unit to help with mental disorders and problematic adjustments to late life.

At UNMC's Perinatal Center, a comprehensive health care team provides care to expectant mothers facing both normal and difficult pregnancies. Services at the Perinatal Center range from sophisticated fetal testing prior to birth to well baby care after birth, and from childbirth education to the latest technology supporting the newborn with special needs. The 14-bed neonatal intensive care unit, led by board-certified specialists in neonatology and a specially trained nursing staff, offers the highest level of patient care for newborns. The unit has the state's only ECMO program, a sophisticated therapy that provides a heart-lung bypass for infants in severe respiratory or cardiac failure. As a partner in the SkyMed helicopter and fixed wing transport system, UNMC also has the option of quickly transporting high-risk pregnant women and critically ill or injured infants to the Perinatal Center. The University Center for Breathing Disorders provides comprehensive follow-up care for infants currently monitored at home for various medical problems and provides on-going premature development follow-up programs.

A full range of other medical services and specialties are provided, using the most modern equipment available. For example, in addition to treating disease or abnormalities of the urinary tract, bladder and kidneys, the Urology Department treats problems of male infertility. A broad range of genetic services, including amniocentesis, genetic counseling and a semen bank are also available. The Department of Oral and Maxillofacial Surgery provides nationally-recognized surgical care for adult and pediatric patients with abnormalities of the facial area and the oral cavity, such as facial lacerations, bone reconstruction, and tooth extractions.

UNMC has established a women's health center—the Leland J. and Dorothy H. Olson Center for Women's Health—to focus on women's health issues and new frontiers of science, medicine, education and nursing practice related to health care for women. A breast cancer resource center was scheduled to open in October 1994.

Other areas of excellence which have received regional and national attention are orthopedics/rotationplasty, reproductive medicine, AIDS research, cystic fibrosis and cancer research. University Medical Associates provides outpatient clinical services in virtually all UNMC departments.

MEDICAL SPECIALTIES

Allergy/Immunology, Arthritis/Rheumatology, Cardiology, Dermatology, Diabetes/Endocrinology, Gastroenterology, Gastrointestinal Surgery, Geriatrics,

Immunology, Infectious Disease, Nephrology, Neurology, Neurosurgery, Obstetrics/Gynecology, Oncology/Hematology, Oral and Maxillofacial Surgery, Orthopedics, Pediatric Surgery, Pediatrics, Plastic Surgery, Psychiatry, Pulmonary Medicine, Radiology, Reproductive Endocrinology/Infertility, Surgical Oncology, Thoracic Surgery, Transplantation, Urology, and Vascular Surgery.

WELL-KNOWN SPECIALISTS

- Dr. James Armitage   *Oncology/hematology; bone marrow transplantation; lymphomas*
- Dr. Carl Camras   *Ophthalmology; glaucoma*
- Dr. Peter Coccia   *Pediatric hematology/oncology*
- Dr. John Colombo   *Pediatric pulmonology*
- Dr. Glenn Dalrymple   *Nuclear medicine*
- Dr. Mark Fleisher   *Psychiatry; mental health/mental retardation*
- Dr. John Foley   *Oncology/hematology; breast cancer*
- Dr. David Folks   *Geriatric psychiatry*
- Dr. Jud Gurney   *Radiology*
- Dr. William Haire   *Oncology/hematology; thrombosis; bleeding disorders*
- Dr. John Kugler   *Pediatric cardiology*
- Dr. James Neff   *Orthopedic and tumor surgery*
- Dr. Maria Olivari   *Cardiovascular disease; transplantation*
- Dr. Jane Potter   *Geriatrics*
- Dr. Stephen Rennard   *Pulmonary and critical care*
- Dr. Layton Rikkers   *Gastroenterologic surgery*
- Dr. Byers Shaw, Jr.   *Transplantation*
- Dr. John Smith   *General vascular surgery*
- Dr. Michael Sorrell   *Gastroenterology*
- Dr. Robert Stratta   *Transplantation*
- Dr. Jon Vanderhoof   *Gastroenterology*
- Dr. Arthur Weaver   *Rheumatology*
- Dr. Anthony Yonkers   *Otolaryngology; head and neck surgery*

PATIENT SATISFACTION

UNMC patients surveyed between the second quarter of 1993 and the first quarter of 1994 indicated 91% overall satisfaction with their care by saying they would recommend the hospital to relatives and friends.

RESEARCH

During 1993, research grants and contracts totalling more than $20 million were awarded to UNMC researchers. More than 75% of this money came from federal and industrial sources. Two-thirds of this external research funding is for cancer research.

The National Cancer Institute (NCI) is sponsoring clinical research that studies the role of radioactively tagged antibodies in the treatment of cancer. Clinicians and researchers are investigating a new cancer treatment—antisense therapy—to combat myeloid leukemia. Dr. Julie M. Vose has led research on the drug PIXY321, which enables people who have undergone an autologous bone marrow transplant to revitalize their blood faster and leave the hospital sooner.

A two-year study funded by the National Institutes of Health is now under way to test BHAP, a new drug compound developed to fight HIV. The drug attacks the HIV virus and allows other antiviral drugs to work more effectively. It is also less toxic and far more potent than other current drugs. Researchers at UNMC have also blocked the AIDS virus from infiltrating the nuclei of some cells by scrambling the signal the virus uses to gain entrance to the cell's nucleus.

UNMC served as one of only three medical centers in the U.S. to test the effectiveness of granulocyte-macrophage colony stimulating factor (GM-CSF) therapy, a procedure intended to stimulate the production of white blood cells and fight life-threatening infections after transplantation. The research results have been favorable and now GM-CSF therapy has become the standard practice at transplant centers across America. At UNMC, it has reduced hospital stays from 40 to less than 30 days.

A UNMC researcher was one of eight scientists involved in a study that may have uncovered a method to diagnose pancreatic cancer earlier. Other scientists were from Creighton University in Omaha, and from the University of Linkoping, Sweden, and the University of Uppsala, Sweden. They were studying a hormone called islet amyloid polypeptide (IAPP) believed to produce insulin resistance, when they saw a link between people who had a pancreatic tumor and diabetes.

Infertility researcher Dr. Christopher DeJonge is one of few investigators in the world studying pre-fertilization events required for successful fertilization. His laboratory features the only sperm micromanipulation technology in Nebraska.

Two UNMC researchers were among nine geneticists to identify a family of genes involved in Marfan syndrome and related connective tissue disorders. A UNMC scientist was the principal investigator of a study which involved the development of the first laboratory test using a person's skin culture to detect Marfan syndrome.

University of Nebraska Hospital is one of 11 hospitals in the country to perform clinical studies with monoclonal antibodies, an experimental cancer treatment.

ADMISSIONS POLICY

A patient can be admitted only by a UNMC physician or through the emergency room. Patients can also be referred to a UNMC physician by their own primary or specialty doctor.

Nebraska residents are required to have health insurance or a 60% deposit for the cost of the procedure. Non-residents must have health insurance or an

80% deposit. There is also a tier-system where the patient can arrange payment. No financial requirements are necessary if the patient is admitted on an emergency basis. The phone number for admissions information is (402) 559-4222.

PATIENT/FAMILY ACCOMMODATIONS

University House, a reasonably priced on-campus hotel for family members and long-term patients, is affiliated with University Hospital.

HOSPITAL FOR

JOINT DISEASES

NEW YORK, NEW YORK

As the largest specialty hospital in the United States, the Hospital for Joint Diseases Orthopedic Institute diagnoses and treats patients with neuromusculoskeletal disorders. The hospital has built a worldwide reputation for its innovative clinical approaches to orthopedic, neurologic, and rheumatic disorders. The Hospital for Joint Diseases treats more than 10,000 patients per year on an inpatient basis and more than 16,000 people annually use its ambulatory care services. In addition, the hospital provides about 100,000 occupational and physical therapy treatments yearly. Nearly 20% of the hospital's patient population comes from outside the immediate hospital community and from as far away as Europe, Latin and Central America, Asia and the Middle East for diagnosis and treatment by nearly 300 specialists.

Since its founding in 1905, the hospital has focused its attention on surgical innovation, medical research, and new advances in patient care. At the turn of the century, orthopedic surgery was in its infancy and doctors could offer very little hope for patients with curvature of the spine, bone cancer, arthritis, and many other orthopedic problems. Today, the Hospital for Joint Diseases Orthopedic Institute can help many of these patients.

THE HOSPITAL HAS BUILT A WORLDWIDE REPUTATION FOR ITS INNOVATIVE CLINICAL APPROACHES TO ORTHOPEDIC, NEUROLOGIC, AND RHEUMATIC DISORDERS.

SPECIAL FACILITIES AND PROGRAMS

Among the hospital's many areas of expertise and specialization are pediatric and general orthopaedic surgery, joint replacement for the treatment of arthritis, foot and hand surgery, back surgery, radiologic scanning techniques, bone replacement, bioengineering, treatment of rheumatoid and non-rheumatoid arthritis, sports medicine, lupus, seizure disorders, movement disorders, and neurosurgery.

Innovative procedures and patient care programs also focus attention on prevention and treatments of occupational injuries, rehabilitative procedures for lower back problems, neuromuscular and developmental disorders, and the treatment of chronic pain associated with musculoskeletal diseases.

The Center for Orthopaedic Oncology offers comprehensive evaluation and management of patients with both benign and malignant disorders of the musculoskeletal system. This division is currently performing limb salvage surgery, including state-of-the-art bone transplantation and custom modular implants, which can greatly help patients with cancer of the musculoskeletal system.

The hospital's Pediatric Orthopaedic Surgery Service is one of the largest in the world, treating between 25 and 50 children at any given time. Children are referred here from as far away as Europe, Latin America, Asia, and Russia.

The Comprehensive Arthritis Service utilizes the combined skills of the hospital's medical and surgical services, as well as allied health professionals, to provide fully coordinated care for both inpatients and outpatients with arthritis.

Other specialized centers help athletes and dancers. The Center for Sports Medicine provides conditioning programs, physical therapy, surgery, and other treatments needed to solve special orthopedic problems. The Center has one of the most active services in arthoscopic surgery.

The Orthopaedic-Arthritis Pain Center was the first nationally accredited inpatient pain center in the New York metropolitan area. Approximately 50% of its patients have resumed a full range of life activities.

The Center for Neuromuscular and Developmental Disorders treats people with cerebral palsy, muscular dystrophy, polio, scoliosis, spina bifida, and a wide variety of other disorders. Most of its patients are children. Other programs for children include the Preschool Program and the center's Communication Laboratory, which has the country's most sophisticated instrumentation for training children with impairments.

The Samuel's Orthopaedic Immediate Care Center, the only urgent care facility for orthopaedic maladies in New York, provides emergency orthopaedic intervention to over 800 people each month.

The Neurosciences program offers comprehensive inpatient, outpatient and surgical services to patients with movement and seizure disorders and has been described as a leading national center for these specialties.

The hospital also recognizes its obligations as a teaching institution. Programs in many disciplines attract physicians, residents and fellows from around the world.

The Hospital for Joint Diseases is a tertiary care facility. To that end, the hospital maintains a 26-bed inpatient rehabilitation center for patients with hip replacements, hip fractures, spinal cord injuries and disorders, fractures and amputations of the lower extremities, arthritis, hemiplegia, paraplegia, multiple sclerosis, Guillain-Barré syndrome and cerebrovascular accidents. An additional 20 inpatient rehabilitation beds for traumatic brain injury patients have been installed. The hospital also maintains outpatient rehabilitation facilities for patients needing physical and occupational therapy.

MEDICAL SPECIALTIES

The Hospital for Joint Diseases maintains broad specialty services in orthopaedics, rheumatology and neurosciences. The following represent those subspecialties in which the Hospital excels.

Arthritis Program; CAMP (Comprehensive Arthritis Management Program); Children's Orthopaedic and Arthritis Institute; Comprehensive Epilepsy Center; Comprehensive Rehabilitation Program; Foot Service; Functional and Stereotactic Neurosurgery Program; Geriatric Falls Program; Geriatric Hip Fracture Program; Hand Service; Harkness Center for Dance Injuries; Headache Program; Ilizarov Program; Joint Replacement Service; Lupus Program; Lyme Disease Center; Metabolic Bone Diseases Center; Movement Disorders Program; Multiple Sclerosis Program; Neurophysiology Center; OIOC (Occupational and Industrial Orthopaedic Center); Orthopaedic Immediate Care Center; Orthopaedic Oncology Service; Orthopaedic and Sports Therapy Center; Pain Center; Shoulder/Elbow Service; Spine Center; TMJ (Temporomandibular Joint) Program; and Traumatic Brain Injury Program.

AT A GLANCE

Beds: 220
Occupancy Rate: 76%
Average Patient Count: 168
Average Patient Stay: 8 days
Annual Admissions: 10,000
Ambulatory Care: 16,000
Outpatient Clinic Visits:
44,254
Emergency Room/Trauma
Center Visits: 4,718

HOSPITAL PERSONNEL
Physicians: 300
Board Certified: 285
Residents: 28
Registered Nurses: 230
BS Degree: 126

ROOM CHARGES (PER DIEM)
Private: $1,175
Semiprivate: $930
ICU: $1,900

ADDRESS
301 East 17th Street
New York, NY 10003

TELEPHONE
(212) 598-6000

WELL-KNOWN SPECIALISTS

- Dr. Steven Abramson   *Inflammatory rheumatology; chairman of Rheumatology*
- Dr. Aleksander Beric   *Neurophysiology*
- Dr. Jill Buyon   *Director of Systemic Lupus Erythematosus Service*
- Dr. Orrin Devinsky   *Seizure disorders (epilepsy); chairman of Neurology*
- Dr. Michael Dogali   *Stereotactic neurosurgery*
- Dr. Victor Frankel   *Ilizarov surgery; hip replacements; chair emeritus of Orthopaedic Surgery*
- Dr. Alfred Grant   *Chief of Neuromuscular and Developmental Disorders*
- Dr. Kathleen Haines   *Pediatric rheumatology, allergy, and immunology*
- Dr. Brian Hainline   *Sports neurology*
- Dr. Joseph Herbert   *Multiple sclerosis*
- Dr. Stephen Honig   *Rheumatology; specialist in chronic pain, metabolic bone disorders*
- Dr. William Jaffe   *Hip and knee replacements; chief of Adult Orthopaedics*
- Dr. Melvin Jahss   *Chief of Orthopaedic Foot Surgery*
- Dr. Kenneth Koval   *Chief of Orthopaedic Fracture Service*
- Dr. Wallace Lehman   *Chief of Pediatric Orthopaedic Surgery*
- Dr. Daniel Luciano   *Neurology (epilepsy)*
- Dr. David Menche   *Associate chief of Sports Medicine*
- Dr. Michael Neuwirth   *Chief of Spine Service*
- Dr. Mark Pitman   *Chief of Sports Medicine*
- Dr. David Present   *Chief of Orthopaedic Oncology*
- Dr. Gary Solomon   *Rheumatology*
- Dr. Stanley Wallach   *Endocrinology; specialist in osteoporosis, Paget's disease*
- Dr. Joseph Zuckerman   *Shoulder and elbow disorders; hip and knee replacements; Surgeon-in-Chief; chairman of Orthopaedic Surgery*

PATIENT SATISFACTION

In early 1994, the hospital instituted a patient satisfaction survey to be conducted by an outside management group. The results of the survey should be available sometime in 1995.

RESEARCH

The Hospital for Joint Diseases spends over $6.1 million annually on research in rheumatology, orthopedic surgery and bioengineering. About $3 million of this comes from the National Institutes of Health.

ADMISSIONS POLICY

Patients are referred by physician or clinic for scheduled admissions. If a patient does not have a physician, the Physician Referral Service will direct him/her to an appropriate doctor. Patients with urgent or emergency orthopaedic trauma may be admitted directly from the Orthopaedic Immediate Care Center, regardless of whether they are physician-referred.

If a patient lacks insurance coverage, an immediate referral is made to the hospital Medicaid specialist for assistance in determining Medicaid eligibility and applications. If Medicaid cannot be obtained, arrangements are made to pay the bill in installments.

Free care at the Hospital for Joint Diseases varies dramatically from year to year. Where at all possible, no patient is denied medical care or referral because of his/her inability to pay. As a tertiary care facility, this includes patients from the entire United States and throughout the world.

HOSPITAL FOR

SPECIAL SURGERY

NEW YORK, NEW YORK

Established in 1863, the Hospital for Special Surgery (HSS) is the oldest orthopedic hospital in the United States. It is a leader in the fields of orthopedics and rheumatology, providing ambulatory care for patients with the entire range of musculoskeletal injuries and diseases.

Strangely enough, this hospital was first brought to our attention by an orthopedist who lives hundreds of miles away from New York. Like many people, we thought the Hospital for Special Surgery (HSS) was simply part of New York Hospital. In fact, while HSS does provide orthopedic and rheumatic service for that institution, relatively few patients are referred from New York Hospital. More than 40% of the 5,000 patients who come there each year are from outside New York and many are from overseas.

What they come for is indeed special surgery. For example, over 1,000 total joint replacements of the hip and knee are performed there annually. This operation, which HSS pioneered over the past 20 years, is performed on patients suffering from advanced osteoarthritis, rheumatoid arthritis and other diseases that have caused such severe deterioration of the joints that no therapy or drug can relieve the pain or restore mobility. In addition, HSS treats bone cancer (the hospital's doctors staff Memorial Sloan Kettering's Bone Tumor Service), spinal disc problems, scoliosis and sports injuries.

ESTABLISHED IN 1863, THE HOSPITAL FOR SPECIAL SURGERY (HSS) IS THE OLDEST ORTHOPEDIC HOSPITAL IN THE UNITED STATES.

Improved surgical procedures in certain areas of orthopedics have reduced the average stay of a patient in the Hospital for Special Surgery to a full week less than the statewide norm. New hip and knee prosthetic replacements designed at HSS and improved surgical and rehabilitation procedures have accounted for reducing the average stay there to about seven days.

The Hospital for Special Surgery is affiliated with Cornell University Medical College and is the site of the college's residency program in orthopedic surgery, an educational opportunity for which more than 300 graduates of medical schools apply each year. Only eight are admitted to the four year HSS program. HSS medical staff hold faculty appointments at the Cornell Medical College.

SPECIAL FACILITIES AND PROGRAMS

Arthroscopic surgery and chemonucleolysis are two procedures for which the hospital is well known. Arthroscopic surgery is surgery that can be accomplished through a large cannulated needle, called an arthroscope, usually on an outpatient basis. Chemonucleolysis is an alternative to back surgery—pressured spinal nerve roots and accompanying pain may be relieved by injecting a herniated disc with an enzyme called chymopapain, rather than operating through the back.

The hospital has also been a leader in implementing a program of autologous blood donations. In this process, blood is drawn on two occasions from the prospective patient two weeks before surgery and banked for use as needed during his or her surgery. This process reduces the risk of contracting AIDS, viral infections and allergic reactions. The hospital is also in the process of expanding a cell saver program, whereby blood aspirated from the wound during surgery is collected, purified and returned to the patient while the operation is still in progress.

Recognizing that there is a need to educate the community about the prevention of orthopedic, rheumatological and musculoskeletal disorders, the

AT A GLANCE

Beds: 160
Occupancy Rate: 73%
Average Patient Count: 117
Average Patient Stay: 7 days
Annual Admissions: 6,089
Outpatient Clinic Visits:
    17,464

HOSPITAL PERSONNEL
Physicians: 171
    Board Certified: 169
Residents: 32
Fellows: 26

ROOM CHARGES (PER DIEM)
Private: $1,275
Semiprivate: $800

ADDRESS
535 East 70th Street
New York, NY 10021

TELEPHONE
(212) 606-1000

hospital has taken a leadership role in promoting and offering community education programs. The Osteoporosis Prevention Program is the most recent effort of HSS to provide public education to the community concerning orthopedic problems. Osteoporosis, a progressive disease affecting 15 million Americans a year, robs bones of minerals, rendering them brittle and more susceptible to fracture. The HSS program was designed to educate men and women on the seriousness of the disease, screen high risk individuals, and offer prevention recommendations. Many other community health education programs offer classes, lectures, seminars, health fairs, tours, and screening clinics on arthritis, back problems, stress management, nutrition and scoliosis.

The Sports Medicine Performance and Research Center is a total care facility providing modern therapeutic techniques, technology and patient education aimed at sports injury avoidance. The Center also evaluates dancers' injuries, offering recommendations on how to avoid potential injury. It is one of the few organizations that offers this vital service free of charge.

The Back Treatment and Learning Center is a recently established outpatient program of the hospital which offers a structured, personalized program of physical therapy emphasizing proper body mechanics, posture, exercise, weight control and stress management.

MEDICAL SPECIALTIES

All orthopedic and rheumatic disease conditions, including: Arthritis, Back pain, Cerebral Palsy, Joint Replacement Surgery, Lupus, Osteoporosis, Scoliosis, Sports Medicine, and Surgery.

WELL-KNOWN SPECIALISTS

- Dr. Charles L. Christian   *General rheumatology and vasculitis; physician-in-chief*
- Dr. Jonathan T. Deland   *Foot and ankle surgery*
- Dr. David L. Helfet   *Orthopaedic surgery; trauma*
- Dr. Richard S. Laskin   *Orthopedic and reconstructive surgery*
- Dr. Eduardo A. Salvati   *Orthopedic surgery; hip surgery*
- Dr. Thomas P. Sculco   *Orthopedic surgery; reconstructive surgery*
- Dr. Francesca M. Thompson   *Orthopedic surgery; foot and ankle surgery*
- Dr. Russell F. Warren   *Orthopedic surgery, sports medicine; surgeon-in-chief*
- Dr. Andrew J. Weiland   *Hand surgery; reconstructive and microsurgery*

PATIENT SATISFACTION

The hospital has been redesigning its survey for the past year. Results are expected in 1995.

RESEARCH

Basic and applied research is conducted at HSS on musculoskeletal disorders.

The National Institutes of Health (NIH) recently granted a five-year, $3 million award to HSS as a specialized research center for the study of systemic lupus erythematosus, one of only two sites in the country.

In 1993, NIH renewed a five-year, $5 million grant to HSS as a multipurpose arthritis center, one of only 13 nationwide.

Other projects include work on free radicals which cause tissue destruction, analysis of what happens to the metals and plastics of artificial joints once transplanted into humans, the development of therapies to treat osteoporosis, and the custom design and fabrication of joint prostheses for surgical arthritis patients.

ADMISSIONS POLICY

A person can become a patient by calling to schedule an appointment with an HSS physician or with one of the 25 specialty clinics in the Ambulatory Care Center. Admission is also available through a New York Hospital emergency room referral. A patient is assured the right to treatment regardless of source of payment or fiscal capacity.

For admissions information, telephone: (212) 606-1241.

MEMORIAL

SLOAN-KETTERING

CANCER CENTER

By all accounts, Memorial Sloan-Kettering (MSK) is one of the most famous cancer treatment and research centers in the world. By any standard, it is also one of the best. Located on Manhattan's Upper East Side and consisting of Memorial Hospital (MH) and the Sloan-Kettering Institute (SKI), it attracts patients from around the world. Almost 60% of Memorial's patients come from beyond New York City; more than 1,000 a year are from other countries. Add to this the fact that nearly half of all patients there are self-referred, and one can sense just how widespread Memorial's reputation is, and why its occupancy rate consistently remains above 80%.

Virtually every form of cancer is treated there; indeed, many types were first identified at Memorial, as well as many of the standard surgical, chemical, and radiation therapies. Founded in 1884 as the New York Cancer Hospital, Memorial was the first American institution devoted exclusively to the care of cancer patients. During the first part of this century, Memorial physicians made important contributions in the use of radiation; in 1926, they developed the first implantable radiation source for use in the treatment of cancer. In 1946, MH physicians began pioneering work in chemotherapy, demonstrating that certain agents developed for chemical warfare were effective against several cancers. Memorial physicians have also led the way in the development of many of the cancer surgical techniques in use to-day. In basic research, scientists at SKI have played a critical role in uncovering the nature of cancer, including the first identification of a genetic basis for cancer susceptibility.

With over 200,000 patient visits or admissions annually, Memorial is one of the largest cancer centers in the United States. In addition, more than 12,000 surgical procedures and over 149,000 radiation treatments are performed each year. One might think that this is simply a large, impersonal academic medical center where patient care is subordinated to research. But in fact, treatment here is personal, intense, and of the highest quality.

In recent years Memorial has made major strides in developing new procedures to treat many forms of cancer, at every stage and for every age group. Substantial progress has been made in the treatment of lymphomas, adult leukemia, breast cancer, testicular cancer, thyroid cancer, prostate cancer—indeed, in almost all types of cancers.

SPECIAL FACILITIES AND PROGRAMS

MSK's new Department of Human Genetics, created in 1992, provides an integrated program of clinical care and research in genetic factors involved in cancer, with an aim of developing better approaches to prevention, risk analysis, detection, and treatment. Researchers are developing methods that can help prevent cancer, particularly in people who, because of a family history or other factors, are at higher than average risk of the disease. People who come to MSK concerned about their risk for cancer will be evaluated through genetic counseling and their risk level defined as precisely as possible, and those found to be at high risk will be advised on how to reduce the chances of developing cancer. They may be invited to participate in a program for men at high risk of prostate cancer, the Colon Cancer Prevention Program, or a breast-cancer prevention program, or advised to visit the Head and Neck Cancer Prevention and Control Clinic.

AT A GLANCE

Beds: 565
Occupancy Rate: 83%
Average Patient Count: 515
Average Patient Stay: 8.3 days
Annual Admissions: 20,659
Outpatient Clinic Visits:
    182,633

HOSPITAL PERSONNEL
Physicians: 423
    Board Certified: 410
Residents: 114
Registered Nurses: 925
    BS Degree: 473

ROOM CHARGES (PER DIEM)
Private: $1,130
Semiprivate: $965

ADDRESS
1275 York Avenue
New York, NY 10021

TELEPHONE
(212) 639-2000

Today, as center investigators continue to refine the techniques of surgery, radiation therapy, and chemotherapy, combinations of these three forms of therapy are increasingly improving survival rates. A prototype of this new combined approach is the treatment of breast cancer. In the past, the standard therapy for breast cancer was radical or modified mastectomy. Today MSK surgeons are able to offer many women with early-stage breast cancer a more conservative form of treatment—lumpectomy. Recent studies suggest that this multidisciplinary approach to the treatment of breast cancer is as effective as mastectomy. After five years, the majority of patients are free of the disease.

In 1992, MSK opened a new outpatient facility, Memorial Sloan-Kettering-64th Street. Under its roof are the Evelyn H. Lauder Breast Center, which meets medical and nonmedical needs of breast-cancer patients, and the Iris Cantor Diagnostic Center, which delivers sophisticated diagnostic imaging services for all cancers.

The Prostate Diagnostic Center at Memorial Sloan-Kettering-65th Street was launched in 1993. Located near MSK's main campus, this off-site facility is a place where men who may be at increased risk for prostate cancer can be evaluated and treated.

Refinements of therapy by Memorial physicians have made possible the preservation of body function in the treatment of a number of other cancers, including colon and rectal cancers, testicular cancer, cancer of the larynx, and soft-tissue sarcomas. For the patient, this may mean preventing a colostomy, retaining normal sexual function, saving the voice, or avoiding amputation.

Some of the most dramatic results have been achieved with childhood cancers. Between 70 and 75% of all children over the age of two with leukemia, for example, will be cured by chemotherapy alone, with an additional 10% cured by other measures, such as bone marrow transplants (compared to only 15 to 20% in 1960). The majority of children with cancer of the bone and Hodgkin's and non-Hodgkin's lymphoma, and an increasing proportion of children with neuroblastoma and certain brain tumors, can also be cured. These dramatic improvements are largely a result of the development of intensive combination therapies, recognition and treatment of sites potentially harboring leukemia that cannot be treated by conventional systemic therapy, the expertise with which doctors at Memorial deliver chemotherapy, and the development of extraordinary support systems for the treatment and prevention of the complications of cancer therapy. About 1,600 children are in active treatment at Memorial Sloan-Kettering at any given time, with nearly 1,400 admissions to the center each year. There are 15,000 outpatient visits each year, which translates into 57 to 60 visits a day in the Pediatric Day Hospital.

Memorial established one of the world's first bone marrow transplantation programs. This program has pioneered in the development of more effective, less toxic preparatory regimens for eradicating leukemia prior to transplant; developed effective treatments for the most common and lethal viral infections complicating transplants; and created successful techniques for transplanting bone marrow between unmatched donors and recipients. These new techniques have far-reaching potential for patients with leukemias and other disorders, certain solid tumors, immune deficiencies, and congenital defects. The center's Bone Marrow Transplantation Service is the region's largest and one of the nation's largest. As a founding member and major participant in the National Marrow Donor Program and its registry of typed volunteer marrow donors, MSK has been able to ensure that a bone marrow "match" for many patients can be found quickly and easily.

Another special feature at Memorial is the Pain Service. When it started in 1982, it was the first of its kind in the country, and has since become a model for other hospitals that must treat patients with the often acute, chronic, and intractable pain associated with cancer.

As impressive as all these services are, the most extraordinary aspect of Memorial, and the key to understanding its preeminent role in cancer care, is the availability of nearly 500 "clinical investigative protocols" that go beyond those regarded as standard. They are recommended when Memorial physicians have reason to believe they will help, and are initiated only with the patient's full understanding and consent.

There is also a full range of services to help patients deal with other cancer-related problems. One of the most important of these is the Psychiatry Service, the first and one of only a few in the country dedicated to cancer patients, offering consultation and treatment of distress, and conducting support programs for patients and their families. Continued communication, counseling, and support is available for cancer survivors. After a patient's treatment ends, the Post-Treatment Resource Program, created in 1988, provides education, counseling, and practical assistance to help ease the transition back to daily life.

Because of its reputation in the nursing community, Memorial is able to recruit highly dedicated, experienced professionals. Nurses excel in providing patient care, teaching patients and their families about cancer, and identifying areas of research that directly affect their practices. Memorial stresses a multidisciplinary approach to patient care, with an emphasis on the coordinating role of nurses.

Memorial also employs several full-time patient representatives to answer questions about hospital policies and procedures, explain patients' rights, and act as advocates for patients or families who need such assistance. In addition, a specially trained social worker is assigned to each clinical service to help patients and families with practical as well as psychosocial problems associated with cancer. The Division of Social Work runs support groups for patients and their families and also coordinates the Patient-to-Patient Volunteer program, now in its twelfth year. The Hospital Chaplaincy provides specially trained chaplains who provide religious services to patients and family members at MSK and other local medical facilities.

MEDICAL SPECIALTIES

Anesthesiology, Bone Marrow Transplantation, Brachytherapy, Breast/Gyneco-logical Oncology, Cardiology, Clinical Chemistry, Clinical Immunology, Clinical Genetics, Critical Care Medicine, Cytogenetics, Dental Service, Dermatology, Developmental Chemotherapy, Endocrinology, Epidemiology and Biostatistics, Gastroenterology and Nutrition, Gastrointestinal Oncology, General Medical Oncology, Genitourinary Oncology, Hematology, Human Genetics, Infectious Disease, Leukemia, Lymphoma, Medical Physics, Medicine, Neurology, Neuro-pathology, Neuroradiology, Nuclear Medicine, Pain Service, Pathology, Pediat-rics, Psychiatry Service, Pulmonary Medicine, Radiation Oncology, Radiology, Radiopharmaceutical Chemistry, Rehabilitation, Renal Medicine, Surgery (which offers specialized services for breast cancer, colorectal cancer, gastric and mixed tumors, gynecological cancers, head and neck cancers, neurosurgery, ophthalmology, orthopedics, pediatrics, plastic and reconstructive surgery, tho-racic surgery, and urological cancers), and Thoracic Oncology.

WELL-KNOWN SPECIALISTS

- Dr. Donald Armstrong   *AIDS; chief of Infectious Disease Service*
- Dr. Joseph R. Bertino   *Medical oncology*
- Dr. George J. Bosl   *Head and neck cancer; testicular oncology; head of the Division of Solid Tumor Oncology*
- Dr. Murray F. Brennan   *Surgical oncology; chairman of the Department of Surgery*
- Dr. Ronald A. Castellino   *Chairman of the Department of Surgery*
- Dr. Alfred M. Cohen   *Chief of the Colorectal Service*
- Dr. Thomas J. Fahey, Jr.   *Physician-in-chief; director of Clinical Programs clinical*
- Dr. William R. Fair   *Prostatic cancer; chief of the Urology Service*
- Dr. Kathleen M. Foley   *Chief of Pain Service*
- Dr. Zvi Fuks   *Radiation oncology; chairman of the Department of Radiation Oncology*
- Dr. David W. Golde   *Leukemia; head of the Division of Hematological Oncology*
- Dr. John H. Healey   *Chief of the Orthopedic Service*
- Dr. Jimmie C. Holland   *Psychiatric oncology; chief of the Psychiatry Service*
- Dr. Alan N. Houghton   *Melanoma; chief of Clinical Immunology*
- Dr. John Mendelsohn   *Medical oncology; chairman of the Department of Medicine*
- Dr. Patricia L. Myskowski   *Skin cancer*
- Dr. Larry Norton   *Chief of the Breast/Gynecological Oncology Service*
- Dr. Richard J. O'Reilly   *Chairman of Pediatrics; head of the Bone Marrow Transplant Service*
- Dr. Jerome Posner   *Tumors of the nervous system; chairman of the Department of Neurology*
- Dr. Jatin P. Shah   *Chief of the Head and Neck Service*

- Dr. Joseph V. Simone   *Pediatric oncology; physician-in-chief, Memorial Hospital*
- Dr. Juan Rosai   *Chairman of the Department of Pathology*
- Dr. Sidney J. Winawer   *Chief of the Gastroenterology and Nutrition Service*

PATIENT SATISFACTION

Results of patient satisfaction surveys at Memorial Sloan-Kettering reveal that patients treated at the hospital hold it in unusually high regard. The percentage of patients rating their care at Sloan-Kettering as good or better in a 1993 survey was 96%, with 56% giving it an excellent rating. Ninety-seven percent said they would recommend the hospital to friends and relatives. More then 98% rated the physician and nursing care received as satisfactory or better.

RESEARCH

Memorial Sloan-Kettering receives about $55 million a year in research grants, making it one of the most heavily funded specialty institutions in the world. About 116 scientists work in research full-time as members of the Sloan-Kettering Institute; in addition, virtually all 423 physicians on staff at Memorial Hospital are also engaged in various kinds of clinical and laboratory research. Thus, one of the great assets of this cancer center is the interaction between its laboratories and clinical areas, which provides opportunities for the application of research findings. For example, clinical trials are underway with immunotherapy agents, such as interferons and interleukins. They are now being studied individually and in combination with other agents to determine their maximum therapeutic potential.

A growth factor that enhances the development and activity of blood cells, identified by MSK scientists, is being used with dramatic success to ameliorate suppression of the immune system that can be caused by chemotherapy. This substance—granulocyte-colony stimulating factor (G-CSF)—is finding broad application in cancer treatment.

Cytodifferentiation agents, which represent an entirely new approach to cancer treatment, are also being pioneered by MSK investigators. Rather than destroy cancer cells, these agents cause cells to lose their malignant properties and behave more normally. Ongoing clinical trials are showing that hexamethylene bisacetamide (HMBA) and all-trans-retinoic acid may induce remission in some patients with certain types of leukemia.

Immunological treatments, using the body's own immune system to fight tumors, represent another exciting new approach to cancer. Some of these treatments make use of monoclonal antibodies, which are genetically engineered versions of normal antibodies that fight infection. Clinical trials of monoclonal antibodies for diagnosis and treatment of cancer are now underway at the center. Another immunological approach under study involves the use of cancer vaccines, which would be given to patients who already had cancer in hopes of stimulating their immune systems to reject the tumor or prevent a recurrence.

Memorial researchers are also exploring gene therapy, an avenue that may launch an entirely new era in medicine. These techniques—in which genes are introduced into cells—may be useful both as new treatments and as adjuncts to today's cancer therapies.

ADMISSIONS POLICY

Anyone who suspects he or she has cancer, or has been diagnosed as having cancer, may contact Memorial Sloan-Kettering, either through his or her physician or by contacting the hospital's Patient Referral Service (1-800-525-2225).

According to the hospital, there is no financial requirement for American citizens (foreign nationals are generally required to pay a deposit). About $30 million a year is allocated for free care.

MOUNT SINAI

MEDICAL CENTER

Mount Sinai Medical Center encompasses one of the nation's oldest and largest voluntary hospitals and one of the country's outstanding medical schools. As with all central city hospitals that have existed for many decades, Mount Sinai faced a crisis in the 1980s in terms of the suitability of its aging plant. Responding to this crisis, Mount Sinai completed one of the largest reconstruction and renovation programs ever undertaken by an academic medical center. Three patient care pavilions were renovated and 11 outmoded buildings were demolished and replaced with the Guggenheim Pavilion, a unique one-million square foot building designed by the internationally-renowned architect, I. M. Pei. As a result, Mount Sinai now has some of the nation's most modern hospital facilities.

Mount Sinai Hospital is a tertiary care hospital located on Manhattan's Upper East Side. It is a regional center for brain injury rehabilitation, hemophilia, AIDS, high risk pregnancy care, neonatal special care services, and pediatric respiratory disease. It is also home to the nation's first hospital division of environmental and occupational medicine and the world's only center for the diagnosis and care of Jewish genetic diseases. Mount Sinai also has well-known services for the care of juvenile diabetes, inflammatory bowel disease, and other autoimmune diseases. The medical center is recognized for cancer

NEW YORK, NEW YORK

MOUNT SINAI MEDICAL CENTER ENCOMPASSES ONE OF THE NATION'S OLDEST AND LARGEST VOLUNTARY HOSPITALS AND ONE OF THE COUNTRY'S OUTSTANDING MEDICAL SCHOOLS.

care, cardiology and neurosurgery, as well as its care of large patient populations with Parkinson's disease, myasthenia gravis, Lou Gehrig's disease, and sarcoidosis.

Since Mount Sinai's establishment in the nineteenth century, its physicians have gained international recognition for some of the most important medical advances of the past century, including the development of the first safe method of blood transfusion and the first portable machine for kidney dialysis. Many illnesses bear the names of the Mount Sinai physicians who identified them, including Crohn's, Buerger's, and Tay-Sachs diseases; the Schick test for diphtheria; and the Master cardiac stress test.

Established in 1852 as the Jews' Hospital in New York, Mount Sinai was initially housed in a four-story building with 45-beds on West 28th Street. Its name was changed shortly thereafter to make it clear that the hospital served patients without distinction to race or religion. The hospital was relocated to its present site in 1904. It has grown into a huge medical complex with 34 operating rooms, serving almost 400,000 people each year.

The Mount Sinai School of Medicine of the City University of New York was established in 1963 and admitted its first students in 1968. Today, the School has an enrollment of nearly 700 M.D. and Ph.D. students taught by a full- and part-time faculty of more than 3,600. The School was the first in the nation to establish a Department of Geriatrics and Adult Development in 1982, and is home to the Derald H. Ruttenberg Cancer Center and the Morchand Center, one of the nation's first centers for clinical competence aimed at improving doctor/patient relationships. As an active center for research of international significance, Mount Sinai School of Medicine is engaged in hundreds of ongoing projects in fields ranging from microbiology and genetic engineering to the prevention and treatment of cancer and cardiovascular disease. Mount Sinai School of Medicine is a national center for research in Alzheimer's disease, schizophrenia, alcoholism, and environmental and occupational hazards and disease.

Mount Sinai is well known for its long history of extraordinary commitment to excellence in patient care, medical education and scientific research. Recognizing that ongoing evaluation of patient care processes are essential to maintaining excellence, Mount Sinai, in 1993, began The Design for Excellence initiative. This quality-enhancement effort melds clinical expertise and high standards with management methods to assure the effectiveness of all patient care services, particularly those areas requiring the coordination of activities in several disciplines.

SPECIAL FACILITIES AND PROGRAMS

In 1967, Mount Sinai established one of the first kidney transplant programs in New York State. Today, it has a full-range adult and pediatric transplant program that includes heart, lung, heart/lung, bone marrow and kidney transplants, as well as one of the nation's largest liver transplant services. The program will soon be performing pancreas transplants as well. In 1993, Mount Sinai performed 31 heart transplants, eight of which were pediatric cases; three lung transplants; two heart/lung transplants; 47 kidney transplants; and 174 liver transplants, 21 of which were pediatric cases, and which included the first living-related donor liver transplant in New York State.

Mount Sinai also has an extensive bone marrow transplantation program that includes use of the procedure in the treatment of advanced breast cancer. In 1993, the program performed 64 autologous, stem cell and allogenic bone marrow transplant procedures.

The revolutionary design of the Guggenheim Pavilion includes numerous features that increase the efficiency of patient-care services, while providing every patient room in its three 11-story towers with a view of either the outdoors, or one of two landscaped atriums that have been carved from the building's core. The Pavilion houses both private and semiprivate rooms, as well as medical, surgical, cardiac and cardiothoracic intensive care units, a surgical suite housing 22 of Mount Sinai's operating rooms, diagnostic facilities for nuclear and rehabilitation medicine and Mount Sinai's Emergency Room and Walk-In Clinic.

Mount Sinai's campus also includes special facilities for comprehensive cancer and cardiovascular care, AIDS, skull base and laparoscopic surgery, high-risk pregnancy and neonatal special care, geriatrics, pain management, and pediatrics.

In 1993, 55 patients were treated in Mount Sinai's chronic outpatient dialysis program and 70 patients participated in an outpatient (home) peritoneal dialysis program. A total of 13,051 treatments were performed at Mount Sinai's dialysis facility, which is currently equipped with 12 treatment stations, but scheduled to add 24 new outpatient and 6 new inpatient stations later in 1994.

Mount Sinai has a 50-bed inpatient rehabilitation unit that offers special services, such as Functional Electronic Stimulation and a Model System of Care, for spinal cord injury and traumatic brain injury. Mount Sinai's Rehabilitation Medicine program also includes two satellite outpatient sports and physical therapy facilities.

AT A GLANCE

Beds: 1,167
Occupancy Rate: 89%
Average Patient Count: 967
Average Patient Stay: 8.2 days
Annual Admissions: 43,625
Births: 5,426
Outpatient Clinic Visits:
    290,696
Emergency Room/Trauma
    Center Visits: 62,649

HOSPITAL PERSONNEL
Physicians: 1,643
    Board Certified/Eligible:
    1,348
Residents: 656
Registered Nurses: 1,608
    BS Degree or Higher:
    1,175

ROOM CHARGES (PER DIEM)
Private: $1,375
Semiprivate: $1,200
ICU: $2,580

ADDRESS
One Gustave Levy Place
New York, NY 10029

TELEPHONE
(212) 241-6500

Mount Sinai is a New York State-designated AIDS Center; a New York State-designated regional center for neonatal special-care services; a National Institute of Aging-designated Alzheimer's disease research center; a U. S. Department of Health and Human Services-designated regional center for the care of children with respiratory diseases; a U. S. Department of Health and Human Services-designated regional hemophilia center; a regional traumatic brain injury rehabilitation and prevention center; and a National Institute of Alcoholism and Alcohol Abuse research treatment center.

The hospital is home to the nation's first hospital division of environmental and occupational medicine, as well as the nation's only medical school department of geriatrics and adult development. Mount Sinai's obstetrics, gynecology and reproductive medicine services include special programs for the care of high-risk infants, and the treatment of menopause and osteoporosis, as well as an Assisted Reproductive Technologies Program for the treatment of infertility that includes the first ovum donation program in New York City. The Mount Sinai Children's Heart Center performs pediatric heart transplants and other complex life-saving cardiac surgery on infants and children.

MEDICAL SPECIALTIES

Adolescent Medicine, AIDS, Allergy, Alzheimer's Disease, Anesthesiology, Assisted Reproductive Technologies, Autoimmune Diseases, Breast Diseases, Cancer and Neoplastic Diseases, Cardiac Catheterization, Cardiology (Adult and Pediatric), Cardiothoracic Surgery, Cardiovascular Surgery, Community Medicine, Dentistry, Dermatology, Diabetes, Endocrinology, Environmental Medicine, Gastroenterology, General Medicine, Genetics, Geriatrics, Hematology/Oncology, Hemophilia, Infectious Diseases, Infertility, Internal Medicine, Jewish Genetic Diseases, Kidney Transplantation, Liver Diseases, Neonatology, Nephrology, Neurology, Neurosurgery, Nuclear Medicine, Obstetrics/Gynecology, Occupational Medicine, Oncology, Ophthalmalogy, Orthopedics, Otolaryngology, Pathology, Pediatrics, Plastic Surgery, Preventive Medicine, Psychiatry, Pulmonary Diseases, Radiology, Rehabilitation, Rheumatology, Sports Medicine, Surgery, Thoracic Surgery, Thrombosis, Transplantation, and Urology.

WELL-KNOWN SPECIALISTS

- Dr. Arthur H. Aufses, Jr. *Chairman of the General Surgery Department*
- Dr. Richard L. Berkowitz *Maternal/fetal Medicine; chairman of Obstetrics, Gynecology, and Reproductive Sciences*
- Dr. Lewis Burrows *Surgery; kidney transplants*
- Dr. Robert N. Butler *Psychiatry; founder and chairman of the Geriatrics Department*
- Dr. Carmel Cohen *Gynecology; cervical cancer*
- Dr. Kenneth Davis *Psychiatry; director of the Alzheimer's Disease Research Center*

- Dr. Valentin Fuster *Director of the Mt. Sinai Cardio-Vascular Institute*
- Dr. Fredda Ginsberg-Fellner *Pediatric endocrinology; juvenile diabetes*
- Dr. Richard Golinko *Pediatric cardiology*
- Dr. Randall Griepp *Chief of Cardiothoracic Surgery*
- Dr. Kurt Hirschhor *Medical genetics; chairman of Pediatrics*
- Dr. James F. Holland *Chairman of Oncology*

PATIENT SATISFACTION

Mount Sinai has been conducting systematic patient surveys since the late 1950s. The feedback provided by these surveys is incorporated into Mount Sinai's ongoing efforts to enhance its programs and services.

Mount Sinai currently conducts quarterly confidential telephone surveys of a large proportionate sample of patients. The results of these surveys are reviewed by an interdepartmental, multidisciplinary standing committee composed of department heads, supervisors and senior management. Mount Sinai also conducts special surveys to obtain information on specific programs and services.

Results of patient surveys are overwhelmingly positive, with patients consistently expressing high levels of satisfaction with Mount Sinai, its programs, and its services.

RESEARCH

Mount Sinai has been a leader in medical research since its earliest days, and is an active center for wide-ranging scientific investigation of international significance. Total funding in 1993 was just short of $120 million.

In recent years, Mount Sinai researchers have explained the mechanism by which asbestos causes cancer; created the first genetically engineered influenza vaccine; performed the first blood transfusion in an unborn fetus; isolated and cloned the protein that triggers blood coagulation; identified the gene for Marfan syndrome; and identified a marker for preterm birth.

Mount Sinai is engaged in hundreds of ongoing clinical and basic science research projects in fields ranging from microbiology and genetic engineering to the prevention and treatment of cancer and cardiovascular disease. Focal points of interdisciplinary research activities include the Derald H. Ruttenberg Cancer Center, The Mount Sinai Cardiovascular Institute, the Dr. Arthur M. Fishberg Research Center in Neurobiology and the Brookdale Center for Molecular Biology.

Reaffirming its commitment to scientific investigation, Mount Sinai recently began construction of a $200 million biomedical research and clinical facility. The 18-story building will house New York's most modern research laboratories and support facilities for work on cancer, cardiobiology, neurosciences, immunology, and genetics. Construction of the research building continues Mt. Sinai's reconstruction and renovation program.

ADMISSIONS POLICY

Patients can be admitted to Mount Sinai in several ways. Referrals can be made by individual physicians, Mount Sinai's more than 100 specialty clinics, or the allied and affiliated institutions and physician groups that comprise the Mount Sinai Health System Network. Patients also can be admitted directly through the Adult or Pediatric Emergency Room. In addition, there is an active Ambulatory Surgery Program.

Prospective patients wishing to see Mount Sinai physicians can either call their offices directly, or call 800-MD-SINAI (800-637-4624) to reach a registered nurse at a computerized referral service that can direct them to more than 600 specialists throughout the New York metropolitan area. Mount Sinai's Faculty Practice Associates maintains a separate facility on the medical center campus, with private offices for physicians in a broad range of specialties who are available to prospective patients.

In addition to direct payment from patients, Mount Sinai accepts reimbursement from private health insurance, certain managed care plans, Blue Cross/Blue Shield, Medicare and Medicaid. The hospital also will consider alternative arrangements in instances in which reimbursement cannot be provided. In 1993, Mount Sinai provided $42 million worth of free or subsidized care.

PATIENT/FAMILY ACCOMMODATIONS

Mount Sinai has arrangements for reduced rates at a number of local hotels. Current information on these arrangements is contained in the hospital's *Guide to Transportation and Lodging*, available from the Admitting Department.

NEW YORK

HOSPITAL-CORNELL

MEDICAL CENTER

In New York City, there are 66 acute-care hospitals, ranging from huge academic medical centers with more than 1,000 beds, to specialty hospitals that provide care only for certain problems, to small community hospitals. These 66 hospitals include several that are listed in this book. According to the *U.S. News & World Report* annual survey, eight of these hospitals stand out from the rest. Among these elite hospitals, New York Hospital (NYH) ranked among the top five in more medical specialty categories than any other New York City hospital.

Chartered by King George III in 1771, New York Hospital was the first hospital in New York City and is the second oldest in the United States. The Medical Center grew out of an affiliation with Cornell University's Medical College, which began in 1912. Housed today on the City's upper east side, the New York Hospital-Cornell Medical Center consists of The New York Hospital, the Cornell University Medical College, and the Graduate School of Medical Sciences.

Since its inception, the medical center has built a reputation as a referral and research center of national renown. New York Hospital has been a pioneer in treating mental disorders, dating back to 1821 with the opening of the Bloomingdale's Asylum. New York Hospital was listed by *McCall's* magazine in June 1994 as one of the top 10 hospitals for women

NEW YORK, NEW YORK

SINCE ITS INCEPTION, THE MEDICAL CENTER HAS BUILT A REPUTATION AS A REFERRAL AND RESEARCH CENTER OF NATIONAL RENOWN.

in the country. It is a New York State-designated regional trauma center, a State-designated regional burn center, and Level III regional center for neonatal special care, as well as a New York State AIDS center. New York Hospital also had the most number of doctors listed in *New York Magazine's* 1991 survey on the best doctors in New York.

The recently-launched New York Hospital Modernization Project includes the construction of a new hospital building over the FDR Drive and the renovation of the existing facility's infrastructure. The new 12-story, 850,000 square foot building, which is expected to open in January of 1998, will have a capacity of 776 beds, and will house the emergency room, inpatient operating rooms, obstetric services, the neonatal and burn units, and general pediatric, medical/surgical, and psychiatric beds. At the completion of the entire project, all of the patient care areas will be equipped with totally modern facilities, in keeping with up-to-date medical practices.

SPECIAL FACILITIES AND PROGRAMS

New York-Cornell cardiothoracic surgeons offer surgical treatment of congenital and acquired defects of heart and major blood vessels, esophagus, and diaphragm. This includes pediatric and congenital heart surgery, coronary-artery bypass, valve repair and replacement, heart and pericardium (surrounding sac) repair, and implantation of automatic defibrillator. A wide array of cardiac services are also available.

The Coronary Risk Reduction Program is a rehabilitative and preventive program designed specifically for individuals who have had a heart attack or coronary bypass surgery, as well as for persons at a high risk for coronary heart disease. The Program focuses on the modification of risk factors, such as diet, exercise and stress, which may significantly reduce the chance of a second heart attack. The Echocardiography Laboratory offers evaluation of cardiac structure and function by imaging echocardiography and the full range of conventional and color flow Doppler techniques. Innovative services include transesophageal intraoperative echocardiography performed on both outpatients and inpatients. The Cardiac Catheterization Laboratory provides high quality diagnostic cardiac angiography, complemented by state-of-the-art interventional cardiology encompassing coronary balloon angioplasty, atherectomy, excimer laser angioplasty, and valvuloplasty on a 24-hour basis. Interface with the Department of Pediatrics extends interventional and therapeutic procedures to infants and children. The Nuclear Cardiology Service, a joint operation of the Division of Cardiology and the Division of Nuclear Medicine, provides several modalities for quantifying right and left ventricular function and myocardial perfusion. These procedures are useful in the diagnosis of coronary artery disease, and in prognostication and management decision-making for patients with coronary, valvular, congenital and cariomyopathic conditions.

The Rogosin Kidney Center (RKC) of The Rogosin Institute (RI) specializes in research and treatment of kidney disease. RI is an independent, not-for-profit institution affiliated with The New York Hospital and Cornell University Medical College. RI members have appointments in both the hospital and college. The Rogosin Kidney Center pioneered dialysis treatments in NYC and currently provides over 75,000 dialyses per year. All forms of dialysis are offered. RKC is one of the largest and most successful dialysis centers; it has half the morbidity and mortality rates of other chronic dialysis centers in the country. The Kidney Center performed the first kidney transplant in the metropolitan area. As a result of RKC's research and care, the center maintains a transplant program with success rates second to none for related and cadaver transplants. RI's Immunogenetics and Transplantation Center does the tissue typing and monitoring for transplantation at the NYH and, in addition, the tissue typing for heart, liver and kidney transplants for two other major medical centers in NYC. In 1993, sixty-nine transplants were done at NYH, placing the Center first among the seven transplant centers located within New York City.

The New York-Cornell Regional Burn Center is the largest specialized facility in the U.S., and treats more than 1,000 inpatients and 3,000 outpatients, both adults and children, per year.

Obstetric and gynecologic services are provided at the Lying-In Hospital located in the NYH-CMC facilities. It is one of the best hospitals for women in the country. The hospital's Center for Reproductive Medicine and Infertility has one of the highest in vitro fertilization success rates in the country. It offers the latest treatments for infertility, including intra-cytoplasmic sperm injection (ICSI), a new procedure for male infertility. It also provides treatment for endocrine disorders and disorders associated with menopause.

The Division of Hematology/Oncology at New York-Cornell initiated a bone marrow transplantation program in March, 1994. The specialized therapy offered by this program involves the removal of

AT A GLANCE

Beds: 1,310
Occupancy Rate: 88.3%
Average Patient Count: 1,157
Average Patient Stay: 8.2 days
Annual Admissions: 39,515
Births: 4,068
Outpatient Clinic Visits:
    238,133
Emergency Room/Trauma
    Center Visits: 40,729

HOSPITAL PERSONNEL
Physicians: 1,552
    Board Certified: 1,263
Residents: 541
Registered Nurses: 1,287
    BS Degree: 850

ROOM CHARGES (PER DIEM)
Private: $1,231–$1,682
Semiprivate: $968
ICU: $2,051–$2,516

ADDRESS
525 East 68th Street
New York, NY 10021

TELEPHONE
(212) 746-5000

bone marrow cells or other specialized cells from the blood of a patient with cancer or a hematologic malignancy. These cells are processed, frozen, and stored for future use. Patients are treated for their malignancy with high doses of chemotherapy and/or radiotherapy. Their own stems cells are then thawed and reinfused to minimize the toxicity of the treatments. In this manner, patients can receive much higher doses of chemotherapy than previously tolerated.

The Department of Rehabilitation Medicine has three physicians specializing in Physical Medicine and Rehabilitation, 13 residents in training, and 75 occupational and physical therapists providing inpatient and outpatient rehabilitation services to adults and children. The Department has (in connection with the Hospital for Special Surgery) a Hand Rehabilitation Program. Other specialists and services include treatment for the back and neck, as well as sports injuries, pool therapy, treatment for neurological dysfunctions, and cognitive rehabilitation services.

Diagnostic and surgical urology services are provided for pediatric and adult patients. Disorders of adrenal glands, kidney, ureter, bladder, prostate, urethra, and testes are treated, as well as incontinence, male sexual problems, and infections. Lithotripsy (nonsurgical removal of kidney stones), laser lithotripsy and laparoscopy are also available.

The Department of Neurosurgery diagnoses and treats pediatric and adult disorders of the brain, spinal cord, and peripheral nerves; tumors of the nervous system, vascular disorders that cause stroke and brain hemorrhage; and ruptured disc and spinal stenosis.

The Center for Special Studies, the designated AIDS Care Center for treatment and counseling, is a NIH-funded AIDS Clinical Trials Unit. It houses the largest contiguous space for care and research of AIDS and HIV-related diseases in New York City.

New York Hospital-Cornell Medical Center also operates the largest inpatient geriatric psychiatric service in the country. The Neuromuscular Disease Center provides comprehensive diagnosis and treatment of patients with disorders of the motor and sensory nerves. The Neurobehavior Evaluation Program evaluates patients with unexplained changes in thought, language, memory, mood, personality, perception, or behavior. Other specialty centers include care for multiple sclerosis, ALS, Alzheimer's disease, pediatric asthma and allergy, pain management, cystic fibrosis, and breast problems.

MEDICAL SPECIALTIES

Anesthesiology, Allergy, Burn and Trauma Surgery, Cardiology, Cardiothoracic Surgery, Dental and Oral Surgery, Dermatology, Digestive Diseases, Emergency Medicine, Endocrinology, General Internal Medicine, General Surgery, Gerontology, Hematology/Oncology, Infectious Disease, Molecular Medicine, Nephrology, Neurology, Neurosurgery, Nutrition, Obstetrics/Gynecology, Ophthalmology, Orthopedics, Otorhinolaryngology, Pathology, Pediatrics, Pharmacology, Plastic

Surgery, Psychiatry, Pulmonary Medicine, Radiology, Rehabilitation Medicine, Rheumatic Diseases, Urology, and Vascular Surgery.

WELL-KNOWN SPECIALISTS

- Dr. Jack D. Barchas   *Psychiatry*
- Dr. Kenneth Berns   *Microbiology*
- Dr. Esther Breslow   *Biochemistry*
- Dr. D. Jackson Colemen   *Ophthalmology*
- Dr. John M. Daly   *Surgery*
- Dr. Michael Deck   *Radiology*
- Dr. Daniel M. Knowles   *Pathology*
- Dr. Donald A. Fischman   *Cell biology and anatomy*
- Dr. Lorraine J. Gudas   *Pharmacology*
- Dr. George W. Hambrick, Jr.   *Dermatology*
- Dr. O. Wayne Isom   *Cardiothoracic surgery*
- Dr. William J. Ledger   *Obstetrics and gynecology*
- Dr. Robert Millman   *Public health*
- Dr. Ralph Nachman   *General medicine*
- Dr. Maria I. New   *Pediatrics*
- Dr. Fred Plum   *Neurology*
- Dr. John J. Savarese   *Anesthesiology*
- Dr. W. Shain Schley   *Otorhinolaryngology*
- Dr. E. Darracott Vaughan   *Urology*
- Dr. Erich E. Windhager   *Physiology and biophysics*

PATIENT SATISFACTION

The latest statistics available for 1994 show overall patient satisfaction with New York Hospital-Cornell Medical Center to be 96%.

RESEARCH

Research funding for 1993 at NYH-CMC was $55 million, 75% of which comes from federal grants, including NIH grants.

Cornell Medical Center houses a number of well-known research institutes. The Institute of Human Neurosciences conducts research on the major degenerative and organic disorders of the brain. The Institute for Prevention Research focuses on the major public health problems of our times—AIDS, substance abuse, cancer, cardiovascular disease, and teenage pregnancy. The complex also houses the Cystic Fibrosis Gene Therapy Research Center and the Margaret M. Dyson Vision Research Unit among other facilities.

Medical and scientific advances accomplished at NYH-CMC are numerous. Some of the most significant recent research accomplishments are described below.

The first successful clinical use of IVF micromanipulation to help sperm penetrate and fertilize an egg occurred there in 1988 under the direction of Dr. Jacques Cohen. Drs. Ralph Nachman and Katherine Hajjar identified a little-known blood cholesterol (lipoprotein a) as an independent risk factor for heart attacks. The first U.S. use of an innovative no-scalpel vasectomy technique to reduce patient bleeding, discomfort and recovery time was done at CMC in 1989. The same year, Dr. Jacques Cohen became the first to use "assisted hatching" to aid human embryos in implanting on the uterine wall. The 1990s have brought the discovery of the mechanism by which herpes enters cells; the first demonstration of how glutathione, a vital amino acid, suppresses the HIV virus in human cell cultures, resulting in several new AIDS drugs; significant research on the role of nitric acid in human metabolism; the first successful use of thorascopy in New York City; and the first demonstration that renin, the blood pressure and kidney hormone, is a key predictor of heart attacks.

ADMISSIONS POLICY

Patients can be admitted via the emergency room, private physicians, or the clinic services at New York Hospital-Cornell Medical Center.

Patients who do not have insurance or those whose insurance plans do not accept full responsibility for hospital services provided will be asked to pay a deposit toward the estimated cost of their stay at the hospital. The Admitting Office and Patients Accounts staff is available for patient assistance. Free care provided by NYH-CMC amounted to more than $27 million in 1993.

Special number for Admissions Information: (212) 746-4250.

PRESBYTERIAN

HOSPITAL

Many health care professionals consider Presbyterian to be New York's foremost hospital. And for good reasons—Presbyterian led all New York hospitals by far in the number of doctors listed in the 1994-1995 edition of *The Best Doctors in America*—117, in all. It was also New York's only full-service hospital listed among the best of the best in last year's *U.S. News* annual survey. In a city of top-notch hospitals, this says volumes about the excellence of this medical institution. Given the kind of medical services offered, it also should come as no surprise. Presbyterian has, for example, one of the nation's most active transplantation programs, is a federally designated Comprehensive Cancer Center, and is the site of the largest stroke patient caseload in the world. Presbyterian draws patients from throughout the New York metropolitan area and beyond, including a number of patients from abroad. For instance, a number of Bosnian children who suffer from a variety of eye diseases have recently been treated at Presbyterian.

The Columbia-Presbyterian Medical Center, which opened in 1928, consists of Presbyterian Hospital and the Columbia University Health Sciences Division. The alliance of these two institutions created the first academic medical center, where leading centers for patient care, biomedical research, and health sciences education combined their expertise at a single location to accomplish common goals

COLUMBIA-PRESBYTERIAN
MEDICAL CENTER

NEW YORK, NEW YORK

MANY HEALTH CARE
PROFESSIONALS CONSIDER
PRESBYTERIAN TO BE NEW
YORK'S FOREMOST HOSPITAL.

of providing the highest quality health care; advancing knowledge about the cause of illness, preventing and treating disease and disability; and training health care practitioners.

Today, Presbyterian is one of the largest private hospitals in the nation, handling more than 800,000 patient visits each year. Virtually every medical specialty is represented among the Hospital's clinical services. Presbyterian comprises the Milstein Hospital Building, Babies & Children's Hospital of New York, Edward S. Harkness Eye Institute, Neurological Institute of New York, New York Orthopaedic Hospital, Sloane Hospital for Women, Squier Urological Clinic, Vanderbilt Clinic, and the Allen Pavilion, a community hospital located at the northern tip of Manhattan.

Columbia's Health Sciences Division includes the College of Physicians & Surgeons (P&S), the Schools of Nursing, Public Health, and Dental & Oral Surgery, and allied health programs, plus more than a dozen specialized centers and institutes. Also located on campus is the New York State Psychiatric Institute, which is closely affiliated with both Columbia and Presbyterian.

Particularly noteworthy are a large number of clinical "firsts" accomplished at Columbia-Presbyterian over the years. The medical center is credited with the invention of the oxygen tent, which was used in the early treatment of patients with severe ear and lung disease. It was the site of the first clinical use of penicillin in this country. Columbia-Presbyterian scientists discovered bacitracin, a powerful antibiotic. The first amniocentesis procedure in the United States was also performed at Columbia-Presbyterian. More recently, the first successful pediatric heart transplant was completed at the Hospital; and it was also the location for the birth of the first test tube baby in New York City.

To adjust to the current healthcare environment, Columbia-Presbyterian, which is primarily a tertiary-care facility, has begun a concerted effort to expand its primary care reach. The Ambulatory Care Network, Presbyterian's expanding network of community health centers, is a critical component of the hospital's drive to become a comprehensive healthcare provider. Beyond ambulatory care, it is building a healthcare network that will consist of strategically located primary care providers; an organized group of medical/surgical subspecialists providing secondary and tertiary care in a capitated system; a network of low-cost, community-based inpatient facilities providing primary and secondary hospital care; access to long-term care facilities; and a home-care delivery system. This program is in its second year of implementation.

SPECIAL FACILITIES AND PROGRAMS

Presbyterian Hospital transplantation programs include heart, heart-lung, lung, kidney, and bone marrow transplantation. In 1993, Presbyterian Hospital performed 58 heart transplants, including eight pediatric cases. Since 1977, the hospital has performed nearly 700 transplants, including 96 on children. The one-year survival rate for heart transplant patients is 80%. Presbyterian Hospital began lung transplantation in 1989. In 1993, the hospital performed two heart-lung transplantations; 25 lung transplantations; and seven double-lung transplantations. The hospital also performed 52 kidney transplantations in 1993.

Cardiology is one department with a long and distinguished history, which includes a Nobel Prize for medicine and credit for developing many of the techniques for treating heart disease. The Arrhythmia Control Center is regarded as one of the most sophisticated programs of its kind. Other services include open heart surgery and pacemaker evaluation and insertion. The Heart Failure Center was opened in 1993 to treat the underlying causes of heart failure, a leading cause of death and disability affecting some 400,000 people in the New York metropolitan area alone. The process begins with a variety of diagnostic machinery—ultrasound, positron emission tomography, magnetic resonance imaging, and computerized exercise tests—that yield a precise picture of the damage to the heart and how it is affecting the patient. Using this data, the Center's cardiologists prescribe a regimen of drugs and exercise designed to ease the workload of the heart while healing the damage. In some instances, patients are found to have previously undiagnosed conditions that are amenable to surgical intervention, such as coronary bypass or valve surgery. Also at the Center, Dr. Eric Rose and his colleagues are testing the partially implantable left ventricular assist device as a promising alternative to heart transplantation.

The new Sol Goldman Children's Heart Center at Babies and Children's Hospital consolidates all the diagnostic and treatment facilities of the pediatric cardiology and pediatric cardiac surgery services in a colorful setting designed with children in mind. Previously, the services, regarded by many as the finest in the world, had been scattered throughout the Medical Center.

The full spectrum of pediatric services is available at Babies and Children's Hospital. The High-Risk Pregnancy Program and the Perinatal Center serve as important referral centers for the tri-state area of Connecticut, New Jersey and New York. The

AT A GLANCE

Beds: 1,537
Occupancy Rate: 84%
Average Patient Count: 1,288
Average Patient Stay: 8.9 days
Annual Admissions: 54,011
Births: 5,685
Outpatient Clinic Visits: 431,891
Emergency Room/Trauma Center Visits: 110,085

HOSPITAL PERSONNEL
Physicians: 1,590
  Board Certified: 85%
Residents: 737
Registered Nurses: 1,640
  BS Degree: 823

ROOM CHARGES (PER DIEM)
Private: $1,400–$1,600
Semiprivate: $1,225
ICU: $1,625–$4,300

ADDRESS
New York, NY 10032-3784

TELEPHONE
(212) 305-2500

neonatal intensive care unit has an outstanding reputation. Approximately 95% of two-to-three-pound babies treated here survive. In pediatrics, the entire gamut of major childhood diseases are treated—asthma, cystic fibrosis, and juvenile diabetes, to name a few. There are also special programs for children with arthritis, cancer, liver diseases, and sickle-cell anemia, among many others.

Neurology has been one of the most important specialties of Presbyterian for over 80 years. Renowned for its work in child neurology, epilepsy, neuromuscular disease and strokes, the medical center is today the world headquarters for the Parkinson's Disease Foundation. Microsurgery performed here includes conventional microsurgery for victims of stroke and other neurological disorders. Since 1989, the Department of Neurological Surgery has performed more than 200 stereotactic radiosurgery procedures. The technique is used to treat a variety of brain tumors, as well as arteriovenous malformations—dangerous tangles of blood vessels that can break and lead to strokes or seizures.

The diagnosis of and treatment of cancer is another area in which Columbia-Presbyterian has achieved special status. As a federally designated Comprehensive Cancer Center, the medical center is equipped to provide the latest treatments for almost every form of cancer, from Hodgkin's disease to melanoma. The Radiation Oncology Department offers access to the most up-to-date forms of radiation therapy, in conjunction with a full range of medical and surgical options. Each year, over 2,000 cancer patients come to Presbyterian, making it one of the largest cancer centers in the region. The medical center is using cutting edge treatments, such as gene-therapy and autologous bone marrow transplantation, in its fight against cancer.

Obstetrics/gynecology has a long and distinguished history at Columbia-Presbyterian. Programs for women range from in vitro fertilization to a menopause clinic. There is also a Center for Women's Health in midtown Manhattan at the doctors' offices in the Columbia-Presbyterian/Eastside facility.

Presbyterian Hospital is renowned for many other special treatment centers and specialties. The following lists some of the most important ones; many are multidisciplinary and involve basic and clinical research. Special centers include the Pain Center, the Arthritis Diagnostic and Treatment Center, the AIDS Center, the Movement Disorders Center, the Genetic Counseling Center, the Memory Disorders Center, The Multiple Sclerosis Clinical Care Center, Diagnostic Center, the Center for Spinal Disorders, the Center for Sports Medicine, the International Shoulder Center, the Pediatric Epilepsy Monitoring Center and the Interventional Neuroradiology Center. Among the specialty diagnostic and treatment expertise available at the medical center are care services in psoriasis, lipid disorders, Lou Gehrig's disease, botulinum toxin therapy for spasmodic dysphonia, and KTP and YAG laser treatment for otolaryngologic vascular lesions. Facilities unique to the New York metropolitan area include the Specialized Center for Research in Atherosclerosis, the Pediatric Lipid Center and the ECMO unit for oxygen-deprived infants and children.

A special mention should be made of the Columbia-Presbyterian nursing program, which is among the nation's best. About half of the nurses are educated at the bachelor's level or beyond. In the ambulatory care, critical care and emergency services departments, prior experience is a must. Critical-care nurses receive extensive training at Columbia-Presbyterian, including specially supervised work in areas such as cardiology, general surgery, neonatology, neurology and neurosurgery.

MEDICAL SPECIALTIES

Allergy, Anesthesiology, Cardiology (Adult and Pediatric), Dentistry, Dermatology, Endocrinology, Gastroenterology, Geriatrics, Hematology, Immunology, Infectious Diseases, Medical Genetics, Nephrology, Neurological Surgery, Neurology, Obstetrics/Gynecology, Oncology, Ophthalmology, Organ Transplantation, Orthopedic Surgery, Otolaryngology, Pathology, Pediatrics, Plastic and Reconstructive Surgery, Psychiatry, Radiation Oncology, Radiology, Rehabilitation Medicine, Rheumatology, Surgery, Urology and Vascular Surgery.

WELL-KNOWN SPECIALISTS

- Dr. Philip O. Alderson *Radiology*
- Dr. Peter Altman *Pediatric surgery*
- Dr. Karen H. Antman *Medical oncology*
- Dr. Myles M. Behrens *Ophthalmology*
- Dr. John Brust *Neurology*
- Dr. Harold M. Dick *Orthopedic surgery*
- Dr. Stanley Fahn *Neurology*
- Dr. Mieczyslaw Finster *Anesthesiology*
- Dr. Anne A. Gershon *Pediatrics*
- Dr. Alexander Glassman *Psychiatry*
- Dr. Paul Lo Gerfo *Surgery*
- Dr. Richard P. Mayeux *Neurology*
- Dr. Robert B. Mellins *Pediatrics*
- Dr. Jay P. Mohr *Director of the Stroke Center*
- Dr. Audrey Penn *Neurology*
- Dr. Donald O. Quest *Neurological surgery*
- Dr. Stephen L. Trokel *Ophthalmology*

PATIENT SATISFACTION

Presbyterian Hospital is now conducting an ongoing Patient Satisfaction Survey. Survey data collected in March/April, 1994 show the following results. Well over 90% of all patients were satisfied with the services they received. Some 98% of inpatients surveyed expressed satisfaction with the services. For ambulatory patients, the rate of those satisfied with their care was 93%.

The Best Hospitals in America

RESEARCH

The College of Physicians and Surgeons, the research and education arm of Columbia-Presbyterian Medical Center, is the sixth largest medical school recipient of National Institutes of Health (NIH) funding. Total annual FY 1993 dollar amount of peer review research funds granted to P&S by NIH was $140,903,608.

The largest clinical activity at Columbia-Presbyterian is in cancer care. Clinical research in progress includes: Taxol therapy for breast cancer and Suramin therapy for prostate cancer; gene therapy to increase tolerance to high doses of chemotherapy; tumor markers; colon cancer causation, prevention and treatment; and bone marrow transplant program.

Columbia-Presbyterian is also very active in research and treatment of cardiovascular disease. In adult cardiology there are two nationally famous research programs, one for arrhythmia, the other for atherosclerosis; the latter is one of only eight special research centers in the country funded by the NIH. Because of its expertise in heart disease, the medical center was also selected as a site for a national study of TPA (tissue plasminogen activator), a clot-dissolving drug. It is also a major center for treatment and research in heart failure.

Sleep disorders, male infertility, and psoriasis are some of the other adult subjects under study.

Recent discoveries by Columbia-Presbyterian physicians include the gene for Wilson's disease, a rare condition affecting copper metabolism; the oncogene for diffuse large cell lymphoma, the most lethal cancer of the immune system; the mammalian gene for normal learning and memory; an artificial enzyme that could prevent cocaine's addictive action in the brain; and identification of a major HIV protein that helps explain how HIV multiplies and suppresses immunity.

Other research activities include HIV studies to treat HIV-infected children, as part of the NIH program of the pediatric AIDS clinical trials group. There are also studies on the effect of pregnancy on HIV-infected women; determinants of perinatal transmission; the natural history of children born to HIV-infected mothers; and resistant pneumococcal carriage in HIV-infected children.

The hospital is very active in pediatric cardiology research. Studies include the evaluation of long-term, continuous prostacyclin treatment of primary pulmonary hypertension; the evaluation of nitric oxide as pulmonary vasodilator and palliative balloon atrial septostomy in treatment of severe pulmonary hypertension; noninvasive diagnosis of rejection in infants and young children following heart transplantation; and a multicenter trial of respiratory syncytial virus.

The hospital is a leader in cystic fibrosis treatment and research. It is a national referral center to study potential antibiotic combinations, antibiotics under development, and resistance mechanisms from multiresistant organisms isolated from patients with cystic fibrosis.

In pediatric neurology, a Presbyterian physician, Dr. Darryle DeVivo, received the coveted Neurological Sciences Academic Development Award, given to only five institutions in the United States. The Award permits pediatric neurology residents to obtain five additional years of NIH-supported research, integrated with their clinical training.

Columbia-Presbyterian's Comprehensive Sickle Cell Center is one of ten in the nation sponsored by the NIH. Research includes studies in the genetics of sickle cell diseases; development of "genetic engineering" techniques for patients with hemoglobinopathies; studies of the area of formation of hemoglobin crystal, and the area of microcirculation; and study of stroke in sickle cell disease.

Perinatal research includes the study of the cardiorespiratory responses of critically ill neonates; study of adjustments made postnatally by the infant with congenital diaphragmatic hernia and the perioperative responses of infants with transposition of the great vessels; and the study of parenchymal brain lesions in very low birth weight premature infants, which are strongly correlated with poor neurologic outcome, in particular cerebral palsy.

ADMISSIONS POLICY

Admission can be arranged through the patient's own physician. To find a Presbyterian Hospital physician, patients should call (212) 305-5156. The referral number for doctors to call is (212) 305-5222, or (800) 227-CPMC for doctors who are out-of-state. Pediatricians should call (800) 245-KIDS.

Although officially there is a financial requirement for admission for elective procedures, the hospital rarely turns away anyone needing care; each year, it provides millions of dollars in care for the indigent.

ROSWELL PARK

CANCER INSTITUTE

BUFFALO, NEW YORK

Founded in 1898, Roswell Park Cancer Institute (RPCI) is one of the oldest and largest comprehensive cancer centers in the world. As a National Cancer Institute-designated Comprehensive Cancer Center, Roswell Park provides patients with a full-range of oncology diagnostic and treatment services, including access to therapies not available elsewhere in the region. Specialized treatments and services include bone marrow transplantation, high dose chemotherapy or radiation therapy, photodynamic therapy, a pediatric follow-up clinic for adolescents and young adults treated for childhood cancer, a Regional Center for Maxillofacial Prosthetics (one of 12 in the country), and new therapeutic regimens based on the most recent advances in biomedical pharmacology, immunology and biological response modifiers. About 13 percent of Roswell Park's patients come from outside its prime service area.

From its origin, Roswell Park has built a reputation as a major innovator in cancer care. For instance, in 1904, Dr. G. H. A. Clowes initiated the first cancer chemotherapy program in the United States. In 1934, Dr. William H. Wehr became one of the first physicians in the nation to use radium in the treatment of cancer. In the early 1950s, Dr. Vahram Bakamjian developed the deltopectoral, or Bakamjian flap to reconstruct head and neck areas

FOUNDED IN 1898, ROSWELL PARK CANCER INSTITUTE (RPCI) IS ONE OF THE OLDEST AND LARGEST COMPREHENSIVE CANCER CENTERS IN THE WORLD.

following disfiguring cancer surgery. Today, the Bakamjian flap is used worldwide and is still considered the state-of-the-art in reconstructive surgery. In 1993, the James T. Grace, Jr. Cancer Drug Center opened at Roswell Park, becoming the only academic center in the U.S. which has the capability of taking drug development from its conceptual stage in the chemistry laboratory through testing of the compound in clinical trials. Advancements in the art of cancer diagnosis and treatment continue at Roswell Park today. For example, Dr. Michael Caliguri is using a novel technique—the polymerase chain reaction—to monitor the successful engraftments of donor marrow cells to detect as little as one tumor cell in the midst of one million donor cells.

Roswell Park is currently in the midst of a $241 million modernization program begun in 1992. When completed in 1997, it will have a new 151-bed hospital, diagnostic and treatment center, outpatient clinics, and medical research laboratory, as well as totally renovated education, research and support buildings.

The Roswell Park Division of the Graduate School of S.U.N.Y. Buffalo enrolls nearly 300 pre- and post-doctoral students annually. The Institute is involved in the training of 125 residents and clinical fellows each year. Many of these trainees come from abroad. RPCI sponsors educational programs for the general public, workshops and seminars for allied health professionals, and continuing medical education for physicians and nurses in New York, Ohio and Pennsylvania. RPCI also conducts a nationally recognized program which provides scientific training for top-ranked minority high school and college students.

While the range of Roswell Park physicians' expertise and the research that is conducted is impressive for its breadth and depth, Roswell Park's results are even more impressive. For instance, RPCI performs the fewest cancer-related amputations in the nation, and it has some of the best success rates nationwide in treating colorectal cancer, malignant melanoma and uterine cancer.

AT A GLANCE

Beds: 124
Occupancy Rate: 82%
Average Patient Count: 102
Average Patient Stay: 7.6 days
Annual Admissions: 4,900
Outpatient Clinic Visits:
    95,000

HOSPITAL PERSONNEL
Physicians: 96
    Board Certified: 86
Residents: 49
Registered Nurses: 392
    BS Degree: 102

ROOM CHARGES (PER DIEM)
Private: $528
Semiprivate: $528
ICU: $1,550

ADDRESS
Elm & Carlton Streets
Buffalo, NY 14263-0001

TELEPHONE
(716) 845-2300

SPECIAL FACILITIES AND PROGRAMS

Roswell Park has been performing both autologous and allogenic bone marrow transplants since 1991. As one of only 72 National Marrow Donor Program-accredited transplant centers, Roswell Park gains access to more than 885,000 potential donors listed in the National Registry, which allows the Institute to conduct preliminary and formula searches for compatible, unrelated donors for its patients. In addition, as an accredited Collection Center, Roswell Park serves as a regional referral center for harvesting the bone marrow of regional registrants. The Bone Marrow Transplant Unit at Roswell Park occupies dedicated space of approximately 18,000 square feet over two floors, built to minimize the possibility of infection. Six beds are dedicated for allogenic transplants and 25 for autologous transplants and high-dose chemotherapy. Since its founding, the unit has performed 97 transplants and is building toward an annual capability of 120 to 150 procedures. The unit director, Dr. Geoffrey Herzig, pioneered the chemotherapeutic doses necessary for true ablation of bone marrow prior to transplantation. Dr. Herzig is internationally known for reporting the best long-term survival rates for leukemia patients undergoing transplants.

Roswell Park is one of the few facilities to offer the use of photopheresis to treat T-cell lymphoma. This safe, effective procedure now has the seal of approval from the FDA as the standard form of therapy for treating the advanced form of this extremely debilitating and potentially fatal malignancy of the white blood cells.

The RPCI Department of Radiation Medicine is a leader in western New York in the use of high-dose brachytherapy, a new, more efficient method of delivering radiation directly to tumors. In brachytherapy, which lasts from three to ten minutes, a powerful radioactive pellet—the size of a grain of rice—is attached to a thin, flexible catheter and placed directly on or near the tumor. A very high dose of radiation is then delivered, and remains essentially confined to the tumor area, sparing the surrounding healthy tissue.

The Department of Radiation Therapy is equipped with the Clinac 2100C Radiotherapy Linear Accelerator, the first of its kind installed in the Buffalo area. This permits more pinpointed doses of radiation to be delivered to the site of the malignancy.

Roswell Park is one of the leading centers in the use of the highly sophisticated, highly sensitive diagnostic tool known as flow cytometry. Use of flow cytometry allows scientists to diagnose and monitor the progress of cancer by determining minute differences between malignant and normal cells.

Photodynamic therapy (PDT) is a new cancer treatment that was pioneered at Roswell Park by Dr. Thomas Dougherty in the 1970s. Today, the procedure, which combines lasers, a fluorescent dye (Photofrin), and fiberoptics, is being used on thousands of cancer patients for whom surgery is not possible or who cannot tolerate additional chemotherapy and radiation. Researchers say that this investigational therapy, with its limited side effects, shows tremendous promise as a way to detect, treat, and in some cases, cure certain cancers. Currently,

Roswell Park is involved in national multicenter studies of PDT to determine its effectiveness against lung and early-stage bladder tumors. A recently-awarded $5 million grant from the National Cancer Institute will permit the testing of PDT against certain skin cancers. These studies represent the final stage before the FDA lifts the therapy's investigational status and approves it for widespread use in the United States.

Roswell Park is the headquarters of the Regional Center for Maxillofacial Prosthetics, one of only a dozen such centers in the United States. Protheses, artificial devices to replace missing parts of the body, are custom designed to help rehabilitate cancer and trauma patients with head and neck defects or injuries. Roswell Park is pioneering a new method of attaching prostheses using titanium implants and magnets.

Roswell Park has a comprehensive Pain Management Program which develops and applies new and evolving techniques for managing pain in cancer patients. A multidisciplinary team of professionals combines the appropriate medical, surgical, pharmacological, psychosocial and behavioral skills to construct an individualized program designed to control and alleviate pain.

The Department of Dermatology operates a clinic devoted exclusively to a certain group of skin tumors. The Pigmented Tumor Clinic diagnoses, treats and monitors benign tumors, such as moles, as well as potentially life-threatening skin cancers such as melanoma. Roswell Park currently boasts the nation's highest survival rates for malignant melanoma—85% at five years. The Clinic was designed to determine risk factors, including genetic predisposition, to certain pigmented tumors and to establish standardized treatment guidelines.

Among the 37 specialized cancer treatment facilities are the AIDS-related Neoplasia Clinic, the Ambulatory Surgical Center, the Brain Tumor Treatment Center, Cancer Control and Epidemiology, the Cancer Screening Clinic (free), the Clinical Neuroelectrophysiology Unit, the Cytogenetics Lab, the Diethylstilbestrol (DES) Screening Clinic, the Gilda Radner Familial Ovarian Cancer Registry, the Molecular Diagnostics Laboratory, the Outpatient Chemotherapy Clinic, and the Prostate Cancer Screening Clinic.

MEDICAL SPECIALTIES

Anesthesiology and Pain Management, Bone Marrow Transplantation, Dentistry and Maxillofacial Prosthetics, Dermatology, Diagnostic Imaging, Gynecologic Oncology, Hematologic Oncology, Investigational Therapeutics, Laboratory Medicine, Neurology, Neurosurgery, Pathology, Pediatrics/Adolescent Treatment, Psychology Services, Radiation Medicine, Solid Tumor Oncology, Surgical Oncology, and Urologic Oncology.

WELL-KNOWN SPECIALISTS

- Dr. Clara Bloomfield   *Hematologic malignancies; chairman of the Department of Medicine*

- Dr. Harold O. Douglass, Jr. *Surgical oncology; upper gastrointestinal and endoscopy*
- Dr. Daniel Greem *Pediatrics; creator of a Pediatric Long-Term Follow-up Clinic*
- Dr. Geoffrey Herzig *Chief of the Divisions of Bone Marrow Transplantation and Hematologic Oncology*
- Dr. Robert Huben *Renal cell, prostate, bladder, and testicular carcinoma; chairman of Urologic Oncology*
- Dr. Constantine Karakousis *Surgical oncology; specialist in soft tissue melanoma and bone service*
- Dr. Enrico Mihich *Chairman of the Department of Experimental Therapeutics*
- Dr. Hector Nava *Surgical oncology; upper gastrointestinal and endoscopy service; photodynamic tumor destruction*
- Dr. Nicholas Petrelli *Lower gastrointestinal service; chairman of Surgical Oncology*
- Dr. M. Steven Piver *Chairman of Gynecologic Oncology; director of the Gilda Radner Familial Ovarian Cancer Registry*
- Dr. Derek Raghaven *Chief of the Divisions of Solid Tumor Oncology and Investigational Therapeutics*
- Dr. Norman Schaaf *Chairman of Dentistry and Maxillofacial Prosthetics*
- Dr. Donald Shedd *Head and neck surgery and oncology; rehabilitation of speech and swallowing; salivary gland tumors; reconstruction of head and neck defects; endoscopy of head and neck*
- Dr. Thomas B. Tomasi *President and CEO of RCPI*

PATIENT SATISFACTION

The Roswell Park Patient Satisfaction Survey is distributed, by mail, to all Roswell Park inpatients who are discharged to home. Questionnaires are mailed to the patient's home within two business days of discharge, and include a postage paid reply envelope to facilitate return. The most recent report on the survey was issued in March 1994 and covers the period from 10/93 to 1/94.

Overall, patients gave Roswell Park very high marks, citing as strengths the competence of the medical and nursing faculties, Roswell's expertise in cancer care and treatment, and the caring and compassionate atmosphere they encountered at Roswell Park. Patients frequently commented that they would not consider seeking cancer treatment anywhere but Roswell Park.

The most recent findings follow. Over 99% of all respondents said that they were extremely or very satisfied with the medical care provided to them by Roswell Park physicians. Over 94% stated that they were either extremely or very satisfied with the nursing care they received at Roswell Park. Over 95% of respondents indicated that they were either extremely or very satisfied with their stay at Roswell Park. Over 97% of respondents indicated that they were either extremely or very likely to recommend Roswell Park to others.

RESEARCH

For the fiscal year ending March 31, 1993, grant and contract revenue was $25.2 million. Among the significant current research activities are the following.

Roswell Park's Colorectal Service is collaborating with the Department of Social and Preventive Medicine at the State University of New York at Buffalo in a large-scale Polyp Prevention Trial, sponsored by the National Cancer Institute. The trial is studying the effect of dietary fat and fiber on polyp formation.

In 1980, Dr. Maire Hakala, a scientist in Roswell Park's Grace Cancer Drug Center, pioneered the development of the drug combination 5-FU and leucovorin. Today, clinical trials with this chemotherapy indicate a significant improvement in the response rate of patients with colorectal carcinomas—from 15% to 45%. Dr. Nicholas J. Petrelli, chief of the Department of Surgical Oncology, is conducting several clinical trials with this important drug combination.

One study in bone marrow transplantation is underway to assess the effectiveness of growth factors (drugs which hasten the return of infection-fighting white blood cells) and their impact on stimulating patient recovery and reducing the risks of infection—a major drawback of BMT. Another study will determine the role of autologous BMT in treating women with advanced breast cancer. A third study offers the hope of cure to leukemia patients who may one day face the possibility of relapse.

A five-year ACS study on prostate cancer detection conducted by the Society's National Prostate Cancer Detection Project evaluated the current standard test for prostate cancer detection, digital rectal examination, as well as two new diagnostic tests, transrectal ultrasound and the prostate-specific antigen (PSA) blood test, which was pioneered by Roswell Park researchers.

In one recent study, Dr. Clement Ip, an RPCI research scientist, compared garlic crops grown in selenium-enriched soil to those grown in normal soil. The two types of garlic were milled into powders and fed to experimental rats which had been treated with a carcinogen to induce breast tumors. The selenium-enriched garlic was far superior to regular garlic in suppressing breast cancer. Ip has also been investigating the anticancer properties of conjugated linoleic acid (CLA), a naturally-occurring fatty acid found primarily in dairy products and meat. CLA is unique because its effectiveness in the animal model is expressed at concentrations close to human consumption levels, and, unlike most fatty acids, CLA prevents rather than stimulates cancer development.

Roswell Park is one of only a handful of research facilities in the country conducting clinical trials to assess the effectiveness of Taxol and carboplatin in patients with advanced cancer. Dr. Patrick Creaven, Senior Investigator, and Dr. Derek Raghaven, chief of the Division of Solid Tumor Oncology and Investigational Therapeutics, both internationally recognized for their roles in the early development of platinum compounds, will head these important studies.

The researchers hope to determine optimal drug dosages (beginning with a low dose with gradual increases as safely tolerated by patients). They will also evaluate side effects, and identify—and later target—those cancers that respond best to the Taxol-carboplatin regimen. The study, which is already in progress, will continue for approximately six to nine months.

ADMISSIONS POLICY

Patients with cancer or suspected cancer can be referred by their physicians to a Roswell Park Clinic. A Roswell Park staff physician is the only one who can schedule an inpatient admission. Patients also can self-refer by calling the Patient Referral Office at 1-800-ROSWELL.

U.S. citizens are admitted regardless of ability to pay. Patients from other countries are asked to make payment prior to admission based on estimated costs. U.S. citizens with no insurance are encouraged to apply for Medicaid or sign a payment agreement.

Special phone number for admissions information (716) 845-3127.

STRONG MEMORIAL

HOSPITAL

Strong Memorial Hospital is named for Henry Alva and Helen Griffin Strong, whose daughters donated $1 million in 1921 toward the construction of the hospital that would honor their parents. Henry Alva Strong was an early investor and business associate of George Eastman, founder of the Eastman Kodak Company. Eastman himself was instrumental in helping to create the School of Medicine and Dentistry when, in 1920, he gave $5 million to the University of Rochester to help start the new medical school.

Strong Memorial is the primary teaching hospital for the University of Rochester Schools of Medicine, of Dentistry, and of Nursing. One of the most respected hospitals in the Northeast, Strong is particularly well regarded by its former patients, as demonstrated in a 1993 patients' survey conducted by the hospital, where over 95% of all respondents would return to Strong if they required hospitalization in the future.

Strong Memorial is the regional referral center for upstate New York Finger Lakes Region's 1.5 million residents. The hospital provides care for approximately 29,000 inpatient stays and 475,000 outpatient visits each year. Recently designated by New York State as a regional trauma center, Strong Memorial's Emergency Department is the busiest in the region, treating patient ailments ranging from cuts and bruises to severe burns and serious multi-organ trauma and head injury.

UNIVERSITY OF ROCHESTER

ROCHESTER, NEW YORK

ONE OF THE MOST RESPECTED HOSPITALS IN THE NORTHEAST, STRONG IS PARTICULARLY WELL REGARDED BY ITS FORMER PATIENTS, AS DEMONSTRATED IN A 1993 PATIENTS' SURVEY CONDUCTED BY THE HOSPITAL, WHERE OVER 95% OF ALL RESPONDENTS WOULD RETURN TO STRONG IF THEY REQUIRED HOSPITALIZATION IN THE FUTURE.

The University of Rochester Schools of Medicine and of Dentistry offer programs leading to the M.D. degree and to the M.S. and Ph.D. degrees in basic biomedical science. The School of Nursing became an independent school of the university in 1972, after almost 50 years as a department within the medical school. The school offers programs of study leading to the B.S., M.S., and Ph.D. degrees in nursing, as well as a post-doctoral clinical scholars program. Strong's nursing staff is particularly well educated, with 100% having at least a bachelor's degree.

The Office of Continuing Professional Education is a clearinghouse of information for more than 4,000 physicians in upstate New York. It provides a catalog of regularly scheduled education programs available at the medical center and its affiliated hospitals.

The hospital's departments and divisions offer a variety of fellowships for highly specialized and advanced training in pediatric cancer, hand and spine surgery, cardiology, obstetrics and gynecology, hematology, and many others. At any given time, approximately 570 physicians are pursuing residency and fellowship programs at Strong Memorial, including a newly approved program in emergency medicine.

SPECIAL FACILITIES AND PROGRAMS

The Department of Pediatrics, known as the Strong Children's Medical Center, provides specialized services for critically and chronically injured or ill children from the region, including a state-of-the-art children's intensive care unit and a neonatal intensive care unit for the region's premature and seriously ill newborns. Babies as small as one pound have been successfully cared for in this unit, which did pioneering work in the development of a surfactant drug therapy to help premature babies breathe properly.

Strong's specialized Pediatrics Services also include the region's Birth Defects Center, pediatric cardiology, a cystic fibrosis program, pediatric gastrointestinal nutrition, genetics, infectious diseases, pediatric neurology, sudden infant death syndrome, and the Rochester Adolescent Maternity Program. The Adolescent Medicine Unit offers a variety of services geared to teenagers and has a special interest in treating eating disorders, such as anorexia nervosa and bulimia. Each pediatric unit contains a playroom, and a special classroom on the pediatric floor allows patients away from school for extended lengths of time to keep up with their education.

Strong provides special care to severely burned patients in a nine-bed unit equipped with a hydrotherapy tub room and an operating room. The Burn Unit coordinates the services of medical, nursing, surgical, physical and occupational therapy, and psychiatric staff.

Strong's department of psychiatry is well known. The hospital houses the department's outpatient clinics, treatment areas, research laboratories, faculty and staff offices, and inpatient care units. Services are designed to respond to every kind of mental healthcare need and to function in close association with the other medical center departments nearby. Its newest capability is an inpatient Child and Adolescent Psychiatry Unit, the only one in the region. Outpatient services include the Alzheimer's Disease and Memory Disorders Clinic, the Child and Adolescent Psychiatry Clinic, the Family and Marriage Clinic, the Methadone Maintenance Treatment Program, the Stress Clinic, and the Tourette Syndrome Clinic. The department also runs the Pain Treatment Center, the area's only comprehensive pain facility, which treats chronic pain from a multidisciplinary approach. The Alcoholism and Alcohol Abuse Program is certified as an outpatient clinic by the New York State Division of Alcoholism.

Two adult intensive care units, comprised of 44 beds, provide facilities for cardiac care and respiratory patients, as well as others requiring complex and closely monitored medical and surgical care. In 1993, Strong was designated the Finger Lakes Regional Trauma Center. In 1994, it received approval to inaugurate an Emergency Medicine Residency Training Program. The 20-bed Rehabilitation Unit and its specialized occupational therapy (OT) and physical therapy (PT) services are another regional resource. Patient rooms there are larger, three are equipped with hoists to move paralyzed patients, and corridors and rooms alike are designed to allow for wheelchairs and other large equipment used in rehabilitation. Strong and the University of Rochester Medical Center have been designated by the U.S. Department of Education as one of fewer than 20 Spinal Cord Injury Centers in the country.

Strong's Ambulatory Surgical Center has accommodations for 24 patients. A wide variety of medical and surgical procedures are performed there, including blood transfusions, chemotherapy, pacemaker battery replacements, and X-ray studies.

The Strong Heart Program at the University of Rochester Medical Center is a unique preventive service that utilizes the skills of a heart specialist, behavioral psychologist, nurse practitioner, and nutritionist to identify people at risk for cardiovascular disease. This program seeks to help high-risk individuals

AT A GLANCE

Beds: 722
Occupancy Rate: 93%
Average Patient Count: 670
Average Patient Stay: 7 days
Annual Admissions: 29,000
Births: 4,000
Outpatient Clinic Visits:
    475,000
Emergency Room/Trauma
    Center Visits: 58,000

HOSPITAL PERSONNEL
Physicians: 1,252
Dentists: 59
Residents: 573
Registered Nurses: 1043
    BS Degree or Higher:
    100%

ROOM CHARGES (PER DIEM)
Private: $725
Semiprivate: $685
ICU: $1,680

ADDRESS
601 Elmwood Avenue
Rochester, NY 14642

TELEPHONE
(716) 275-2644

cope with stress, quit smoking, and develop exercise and nutrition programs. After a physical examination and laboratory test, the patient's heart attack risk profile is assessed. The Cardiac Rehabilitation Program works with people who have undergone heart surgery or have heart disease in an effort to improve their heart function and fitness level. It utilizes state-of-the-art monitoring techniques and the latest knowledge in exercise and patient education and encourages participation by the patient's family.

Strong was the first hospital in upstate New York to begin using a lithotriptor to treat patients suffering from kidney stones. Operated under the auspices of the Department of Urology, the lithotriptor is part of Strong's Kidney Stone Treatment Center. Also under the auspices of the Department of Urology is Strong's Sperm Bank and Andrology Program, which provides a variety of services, including artificial insemination and sperm testing and analysis.

The University of Rochester Cancer Center's headquarters are located at Strong Memorial Hospital. The Cancer Center includes special departments in gynecologic oncology, medical oncology, nursing oncology, pediatric hematology/oncology, psychosocial oncology, and radiation oncology.

A new Department of Environmental Medicine offers a unique combination of research and clinical care for environmental and occupational illnesses.

The hospital is the region's center for kidney, pancreas, and liver transplantation. An exciting new treatment for epilepsy, in which neurologists "map" the brain and neurosurgeons "rewire" misfunctioning circuits, was recently introduced by Strong Memorial Hospital.

In the 1980s, the hospital began upstate New York's first in vitro fertilization program, offering infertile married couples a new technology and new hope for helping them to conceive a child. A few years later, upstate New York's first sperm bank was started at Strong Memorial, providing a full range of male infertility services and facilitating the donation and frozen storage of sperm. A new birth center was opened in 1987.

In 1989, the hospital opened the Samuel E. Durand Bone Marrow Transplantation Unit, the only one in upstate New York dedicated exclusively to bone marrow transplantation as a cure for leukemia and other blood-related cancers and diseases. This specialized unit enables transplantation specialists to perform both autologous (using the patient's own bone marrow) and allogeneic (using donated marrow) procedures. The unit features a highly sophisticated air filtration and ventilation system that minimizes the chances for patients to become infected as they undergo the 50-day procedure.

Strong Memorial also has a number of innovative and interesting programs that rely less on technology and more on new ways to manage patient care.

Following the new direction for providing treatment to psychiatric patients on an outpatient rather than an inpatient basis, the hospital opened Strong Ties at a centrally located off-site facility to provide day treatment and services to functional emotionally and mentally ill patients, offering them support, counseling and treatment. The new building offers a variety of facilities for group activities and for enhancing independent living skills. Back at the hospital, inpatient psychiatry units have been renovated and reorganized to improve the continuum of psychiatric care for patients; a new unit devoted to children and adolescents opened in the Spring of 1993 and serves the entire region.

Strong Memorial's Work Re-entry Program helps people injured on the job to get back to work. Physicians, psychologists, and therapists use sophisticated tools to assess an injured worker's physical capabilities, and then to design a program that strengthens physical skills and dexterity, as well as enables injured workers to relearn job skills and, if necessary, manage chronic pain.

Also in 1989, the hospital's Daisy Marquis Jones Rehabilitation Center was opened—a newly designed and enlarged facility within the hospital for physical and occupational therapy for patients who have had strokes, spinal cord injuries, and related illnesses and conditions. For many years, the hospital has been a federally designated spinal cord injury rehabilitation center, recognizing the hospital's expertise in orthopedics, surgery, neurology and rehabilitation medicine.

Medical services at Strong cover a wide spectrum of specialties. The best known are Emergency Care, Oncology, Orthopedics, Pediatrics, Psychiatry, and Neurology.

Other special programs include diabetes self-management, the Strong Heart and Cardiac Rehabilitation programs, the dialysis unit, medical and surgical intensive care units, long-term care, a burn unit, and in vitro fertilization. Specialties within the Department of Orthopedics include the Regional Spinal Cord Injury Center, sports medicine, joint replacement and hand surgery, and a comprehensive musculoskeletal program.

MEDICAL SPECIALTIES

Allergy and Immunology, Cardiology, Cardiovascular Surgery, Dentistry, Dermatology, Emergency Medicine, Endocrinology and Metabolism, Infectious Diseases, Nephrology, Neonatology, Neurology, Neurosurgery, Obstetrics/Gynecology, Oncology/Hematology, Orthopedics, Pediatrics, Psychiatry, Psychology, Radiation Oncology, Radiology, Surgery, Thoracic Surgery, and Urology.

WELL-KNOWN SPECIALISTS

- Dr. Marvin S. Amstey   *Obstetrics and gynecology; infectious disease*
- Dr. John M. Bennett   *Medical oncology/hematology; breast cancer; leukemia; lymphomas*
- Dr. John G. Brooks   *Pediatrics; pediatric pulmonology*
- Dr. Edward B. Clark   *Pediatrics; pediatric cardiology*
- Dr. Richard H. Feins   *Thoracic surgery*
- Dr. Charles Francis   *Medical oncology/hematology; disorders of bleeding; thrombosis*
- Dr. J. Timothy Greenamyre   *Adult neurology; movement disorders*

- Dr. Robert C. Griggs   *Adult neurology; neuromuscular diseases*
- Dr. Caroline Breese Hall   *Pediatrics; pediatric infectious disease*
- Dr. Robert J. Joynt   *Adult neurology; degenerative diseases*
- Dr. F. Marc LaForce   *Infectious disease; hospital-acquired infections*
- Dr. Stephen I. Rosenfeld   *Allergy and immunology; general allergy and immunology*
- Dr. Philip Rubin   *Radiation oncology*
- Dr. Seymour I. Schwartz   *General surgery; gastroenterologic surgery*
- Dr. James R. Woods   *Obstetrics/gynecology; addiction medicine; addiction during pregnancy; maternal and fetal medicine*

PATIENT SATISFACTION

Patient satisfaction is a high priority at Strong Memorial Hospital. All inpatients and ambulatory surgery patients receive surveys so that they may rate the care and services provided and make any specific comments about their hospital experience.

In 1993, the overall quality of care at Strong Memorial Hospital was rated as excellent or good by 92% of the inpatient survey respondents and 95% indicated they would recommend or return to Strong; 99% of the Ambulatory Surgery patients returning the form rated the care as excellent or good and said they would return.

RESEARCH

Strong Memorial Hospital is one of a handful of federally-designated and funded AIDS research and treatment centers. Infectious disease researchers are conducting clinical trials of new medicines that combat the AIDS virus and are contributing to the national effort to treat and eventually cure the disease. In addition, research into an effective AIDS vaccine is also conducted at Strong Memorial, one of the original five federally-designated AIDS Vaccine Evaluation Units in the nation.

The hospital's Clinical Research Center is a unit where patients and study subjects can stay for several days or weeks as physicians conduct research into a variety of illnesses and therapies; of particular note is the research involving neuromuscular diseases such as muscular dystrophy.

Beginning in 1987, Strong Memorial neurologists coordinated and directed an 800-patient nationwide clinical trial on the effectiveness of a new drug, deprenyl, in delaying and slowing the progression of Parkinson's disease. The Associated Press included as one of its top ten medical stories of 1989 the very positive results of that study. The Parkinson's Study Group continues to conduct clinical trials on other promising drugs for the treatment of Parkinson's disease.

In fiscal year 1993, the University of Rochester's School of Medicine and Dentistry received more than $87 million in sponsored research grants, putting it in 22nd place among the nation's 126 medical schools. Most of the clinical work takes place in Strong Memorial Hospital, enabling Rochester patients to receive the latest and newest therapies.

ADMISSIONS POLICY

Admission is via referral from physicians with admitting privileges, from their offices, the emergency department, outpatient clinics, or transfer from another facility. Patients without an attending physician are assigned one. Referring physicians without admitting privileges may contact Strong Referral for the name of a physician with privileges.

The hospital expects admission accounts to be secured with verified third-party benefits, prepayment, or payment arrangements. Financial counseling is provided for those who need it. Financial counselors may recommend charity allowances. A charity care policy is in place for patients who want to pay but are unable, due to verified low income or resources, or severe financial hardship due to illness. A sliding fee scale is also available.

PATIENT/FAMILY ACCOMMODATIONS

For outpatients receiving care at the hospital, the Goler Motel Unit is available. The rates are: single, $45; double, $49. Weekly and monthly rates are also available.

TISCH

HOSPITAL / RUSK

INSTITUTE

NEW YORK UNIVERSITY
MEDICAL CENTER

NEW YORK, NEW YORK

In a city well-known for self-promotion and self-congratulations, it is surprising to find that the hospitals in New York, even those with world-class reputations, keep low profiles. Consequently, the availability of specialized, hard-to-find medical services is made known through an informal network of physicians and hospital professionals. This may help explain why the hospitals of New York University (NYU) Medical Center, virtually unknown outside New York City, except among doctors, consistently run occupancy rates in excess of 85%.

NYU Medical Center is a major academic medical enterprise consisting of the NYU School of Medicine; Bellevue Hospital, one of the nation's most respected municipal hospitals; Tisch Hospital, a major referral center staffed by the faculty of the NYU School of Medicine; Rusk Institute, the world's largest university-affiliated center for treating and training disabled adults and children; the Arnold and Marie Schwartz Health Care Center; and the research laboratories at the NYU Medical Center campus and at Sterling Forest in Rockland County.

TISCH HOSPITAL IS THE FLAGSHIP HOSPITAL OF NYU MEDICAL CENTER. BECAUSE THE FACULTY OF THE NYU SCHOOL OF MEDICINE SERVES AS THE MEDICAL STAFF OF TISCH HOSPITAL, IT IS NOT SURPRISING THAT PEOPLE ARE DRAWN THERE FROM ALL POINTS OF THE NATION AND OVERSEAS.

Tisch Hospital is the flagship hospital of NYU Medical Center. Because the faculty of the NYU School of Medicine serves as the medical staff of Tisch Hospital, it is not surprising that people are drawn there from all points of the nation and overseas.

In fact, 15% of the patient population comes to NYU from outside New York State.

Patients come to Tisch Hospital for treatment of almost every kind of illness. The hospital has achieved national recognition in numerous specialties, including dermatology, geriatric medicine, neurosurgery (volumetric stereotactic procedures), pediatric neurosurgery, otolaryngology (one of the few hospitals performing multichannel cochlear implants), rheumatology, and urology (treatment for, and research on, prostate disorders, including cancer). Tisch Hospital is also internationally recognized as a regional center for the study and treatment of heart disease; more than 1,400 open heart procedures are performed there each year. In addition, more than 2,500 infants are born there annually, many of them the result of high-risk pregnancies.

What patients find at Tisch Hospital, in addition to a group of highly regarded physicians, is a modern facility equipped with the latest technological advances, including four state-of-the-art magnetic resonance imaging (MRI) machines. They also find a nursing staff that is among the most carefully selected and trained in the country. More than 80% of its nurses hold a minimum of a bachelor's degree.

Evidence of the caliber of Tisch Hospital is its consistently high scores in accreditation surveys. In fact, in the most recent triennial accreditation survey, Tisch Hospital received a summary grid score of 92 (out of a top score of 100). Also, in the latest annual report of the performance of New York State hospitals offering cardiac bypass surgery, Tisch Hospital was again cited for the lowest state-wide risk adjusted mortality rate (1.38%).

The Howard A. Rusk Institute of Rehabilitation Medicine is the world's first university-affiliated facility devoted entirely to rehabilitation medicine. Established in 1948 by Dr. Rusk (considered the father of rehabilitation medicine), its patients are referred from all over the world. Rusk Institute treats neurological, orthopedic and a wide variety of physical disabilities in children and adults on both an inpatient and outpatient basis. Treatment programs range from stroke, spinal cord, cardiac and pulmonary rehabilitation to pain management.

AT A GLANCE

TISCH HOSPITAL

Beds: 726
Occupancy Rate: 87%
Average Patient Count: 623
Average Patient Stay: 8.7 days
Annual Admissions: 26,029
Births: 2,258
Outpatient Clinic Visits:
    36,683
Emergency Department
    Visits: 19,216

RUSK INSTITUTE

Beds: 152
Occupancy Rate: 92%
Average Patient Count: 140
Average Patient Stay: 35.3
    days
Annual Admissions: 1,447
Outpatient Clinic Visits:
    45,462

TISCH HOSPITAL/RUSK INSTITUTE

HOSPITAL PERSONNEL
Physicans: 1,227
    Board Certified: 1,106
Residents: 975
Registered Nurses: 1226
    BS Degree: 80%

ROOM CHARGES (PER DIEM)
Private: $927
Semiprivate: $735
ICU: $1,943

ADDRESS
560 First Avenue
New York, NY 10016

TELEPHONE
(212) 263-7300

SPECIAL FACILITIES AND PROGRAMS

Some of the best known services at Tisch Hospital are available on an outpatient basis. The Day Surgery Unit, for example, the first ambulatory surgical unit on the East Coast, offers elective surgery for more than 200 procedures without requiring an overnight hospital stay. Approximately 8,500 patients were treated there in 1993.

The Institute of Reconstructive Plastic Surgery treats a wide variety of problems including aesthetic (cosmetic) surgery, birth defects, severe deformities due to cancer-related removal of large areas of tissue and bone (breast reconstruction, for example) and post-traumatic problems of automobile injuries and burns. The Variety Center for Craniofacial Rehabilitation, located in this institute, treats severe congenital facial deformities such as cleft palate and other disorders. Specialists at the institute also excel in microsurgery and reconstructive surgery of the hand.

NYU Medical Center's work in dermatology has a long history and is internationally recognized for major advances in the research and treatment of skin cancer and numerous other skin disorders. The Harris Skin and Cancer Pavilion, staffed by the medical center's Department of Dermatology, focuses on the diagnosis and treatment of disorders of the skin, hair and nails. Among the specialized units are those dealing with skin cancer, melanoma and pigmented lesions, blistering diseases, dermatologic and laser surgery, psoriasis, hair and nail disorders, and photosensitive dermatosis. The recently inaugurated Center for Skin Health and Appearance focuses on cosmetic dermatologic problems.

The care and treatment of cancer patients is one of the most important services at Tisch Hospital—over 2,500 new cancer patients are admitted every year. Funded, in part, by the National Cancer Institute, the Kaplan Comprehensive Cancer Center offers the latest clinical services in chemotherapy, hormonal therapy, radiation therapy, and surgery. Among their particularly renowned specialties, NYU physicians excel in treating breast cancer, cancers affecting children, and lung, ovarian, and skin cancer. Melanoma is the focus of an internationally cited NYU program that has treated the largest number of patients in the world, while developing new surgical and medical procedures to combat the disease.

In addition, the Stephen D. Hassenfeld Children's Center for Cancer and Blood Disorders offers an innovative and comprehensive outpatient program. Staff at the center continually evaluate promising new treatment methods, while at the same time working toward improving the children's response to treatment by helping them and members of their families to deal with the emotional and social impact of their medical condition.

Tisch Hospital's Cooperative Care Unit (known as Co-Op Care) was created in 1979 to provide cost-effective health care in a more compassionate environment in which relatives or friends play an active role in the patient's care. Criteria for admission and continued stay in Co-Op Care are identical to those of a traditional acute-care hospital, except that a patient must not require constant nursing observation and must be able to move independently or with the aid of crutches, a walker, or a wheelchair. Patients are admitted to the unit directly by their physician from the outside (as for chemotherapy or an invasive diagnostic procedure such as coronary angioplasty), or they are transferred from other wings of Tisch Hospital.

Central to the Co-Op Care approach is the care partner, usually a relative or close friend, who lives with the patient between four and 24-hours-a-day. The partner pays nothing for room and board. The care partner is trained by the hospital staff to supplement many of the services traditionally handled by nurses. Visiting is unrestricted; patients can wear street clothes and are themselves partly responsible for administering the medications prescribed by their physician. And, unlike the typical hospital logistics, visits with physicians are by appointment, not merely at their discretion.

Co-Op Care has been remarkably cost effective—the average patient bill in this unit is one-third less than for a stay of comparable length in the traditional hospital environment. Furthermore, the cooperative care approach has been shown to foster better patient adherence with the prescribed medical regimen, as well as a highly positive attitude among patients and their loved ones. The NYU Medical Center program serves as a model for similar programs being considered at other health-care institutions.

Treatment at the Rusk Institute is based on the team approach, involving specialists in psychiatry, physical therapy, psychology, occupational therapy, social services, speech pathology, and vocational rehabilitation, all working in conjunction with medical specialists in other divisions of the medical center. The total-care approach takes into consideration the psychological aspects of rehabilitation and the patient's vocational requirements. Rusk has pioneered in the development of support services, including a breast cancer support group that has become the model for other such groups, and the Cancer Rehabilitation Service, which provides continuity of care and support for cancer patients and their families during all phases of treatment. This service is available both to cancer patients of the medical center and by referral.

MEDICAL SPECIALTIES

Allergy/Immunology, Anesthesiology, Cardiology, Dermatology, Dentistry, Diagnostic Radiology, Emergency Medicine, Endocrinology, Family Practice, Gastroenterology, Hematology, Infectious Diseases, Internal Medicine, Nephrology, Neuro/Vascular Interventional Radiology (includes Endovascular Grafting and Selective Chemoembolization), Neurological Surgery and Pediatric Neurosurgery, Obstetrics and Gynecology (including complete Perimenopausal and Menopausal Evaluations, Infertility Evaluation and Oocyte Donation, In Vitro Fertilization), Oncology, Ophthalmalogy, Orthopedic Surgery, Otolaryngology (includes Otology and Plastic and Reconstructive Surgery), Pathology, Pediatrics,

Physical Medicine and Rehabilitation, Plastic Surgery (includes Craniofacial Surgery, Hand Surgery, and Microsurgery), Preventive Medicine, Psychiatry, Pulmonary Disease, Rheumatology, Sports Medicine, Surgery, Thoracic Surgery, Urology and Vascular Surgery.

WELL-KNOWN SPECIALISTS

- Dr. Vallo Benjamin   *Neurosurgery; spinal surgery*
- Dr. Alex Berenstein   *Embolization; inventor of a nonsurgical procedure to treat certain vascular disorders*
- Dr. Noel Cohen   *Otolaryngology; multichannel cochlear implants*
- Dr. Fred J. Epstein   *Pediatric neurosurgery; pioneer in developing a procedure for removing tumors from the spinal cord and brain stem of infants and children*
- Dr. Alvin Friedman-Kein   *Dermatology and microbiology; AIDS treatment*
- Dr. Marc Galanter   *Psychiatry; alcoholism and drug abuse*
- Dr. Stuart Garay   *Clinical medicine; pulmonary medicine*
- Dr. Roy Geronemus   *Dermatology; surgical dermatology*
- Dr. Ronald Hoffman   *Otology and neuro-otology; director of the Balance Center*
- Dr. Glenn Jelks   *Ophthalmology; plastic surgery; oculoplastic and orbital surgery*
- Dr. Patrick Kelly   *Neuro-oncology; deep-seated brain tumors; world pioneer in the development of computer-assisted volumetric stereotactic resection*
- Dr. Alfred Kopf   *Dermatology; specialist in melanoma and other types of skin cancer*
- Dr. Jeffrey Minkoff   *Orthopedic surgery; sports medicine*
- Dr. Lila Nachtigall   *Menopause; prominent researcher in estrogen replacement therapy*
- Dr. Barry Reisberg   *Psychiatry; specialist in Alzheimer's disease*
- Dr. Cecilia Schmidt-Sarosi   *Obstetrics/gynecology; director of Clinical Reproductive Endocrinology and the In Vitro Fertilization Program*

PATIENT SATISFACTION

NYU Medical Center receives very high marks from former patients. In the latest inpatient survey, taken during the second quarter of 1994, 93% of respondents found their care to be good to excellent, while 96% said they would recommend the hospital to friends and relatives.

RESEARCH

NYU Medical Center receives approximately $90 million in research funding annually—$65 million from federal sources. Much of the important research supplements the Medical Center's best-known clinical services in cardiology, cardiovascular surgery, neurosurgery, reconstructive plastic surgery (especially microsurgery), rehabilitation medicine, and rheumatology.

The newly constructed Skirball Institute of Biomolecular Medicine is the latest manifestation of this research commitment. The interdisciplinary facility will initially emphasize collaborative research in three broad areas: developmental genetics, neurobiology, and molecular pathogenesis (human defense mechanisms), areas in which innovative research has been ongoing.

NYU Medical Center's federally-funded Kaplan Comprehensive Cancer Center is the site of basic and clinical research in every key area of oncology. Cancer research accounts for over 40% of the total research budget; in addition to a melanoma program, research is ongoing in the therapy of breast and ovarian cancers. Nationwide clinical trials are exploring drug and radiation therapies, with special trials for the treatment of brain and gastrointestinal tumors.

NYU Medical Center is one of 13 federally-designated Centers for AIDS Research, with one of the nation's largest programs of clinical trials evaluating drugs to treat both HIV and infections and cancers contracted by people with AIDS. More than 40 physicians and scientists are involved in AIDS-related basic and clinical research.

The Department of Pharmacology conducts internationally recognized research on signal transduction, the mechanisms by which chemical messages are sent from the cell membrane to the nucleus. This is expected to reveal key insights into such vital functions as cell division and glucose metabolism, and lead to new therapies for cancer and diabetes.

Research on prostate cancer and benign prostatic hypertrophy (BPH) includes the largest worldwide study comparing two drugs for the treatment of BPH. NYU Medical Center will be the first test site in the United States for transurethral needle ablation, a nonsurgical procedure for BPH.

The Nelson Institute of Environmental Medicine has developed biomarkers to detect human exposure to possible harmful chemicals. A large study (funded by a $406,000 grant from the Charles A. Dana Foundation) examines the prevention, early diagnosis, and treatment of environmentally-related diseases. Other studies focus on chemical and radiation carcinogens, radon exposure, toxicology epidemiological-biostatistical investigations in AIDS, breast cancer, colon cancer, and melanoma.

Other major research programs include those in Alzheimer's disease, depression in older people, hypertension, Parkinson's disease, physiology and biophysics, sexually transmitted diseases, stroke and vaccine development.

ADMISSIONS POLICY

Patients are admitted to Tisch Hospital by a physician on staff or through the Emergency Room, where a physician is assigned as needed. To set up an appointment with an NYU physician in any one of its specialty areas, call the Physician Referral number: (212) 263-5000.

Tisch Hospital accepts self-paying patients, as well as those covered by Medicare, Medicaid, and other third-party payers. Emergency patients are treated immediately in the emergency room, regardless of payment status. Approximately $12 million in free care is provided per annum.

For Tisch Hospital admissions information, call: (212) 263-5006.

PATIENT/FAMILY ACCOMMODATIONS

Greenburg Hall Family Housing, located directly across the street from the Hospital, consists of seven apartments reserved for patient families. The rate is $95 per night for the apartments.

DUKE UNIVERSITY

MEDICAL CENTER

Education is an integral aspect of most of the hospitals we have included in this book, because increasing specialization in medicine has brought a corresponding need for postgraduate training for physicians. In the past few decades, Duke University has become a formidable training ground for specialists.

Each year, about 800 M.D.'s and Ph.D.'s receive advanced training in the clinical and basic sciences. Another 150 trainees are in paramedical programs. In addition, about 50 nurses are in a new specialized master's curriculum that prepares them for advanced clinical practice and administration.

Medical training is similarly impressive—the Duke University School of Medicine is one of the finest in the country. Admission is highly selective. In 1993, for example, there were 5,922 applicants for 100 openings.

In addition to being on the staff of the hospital, Duke's physicians hold appointments at the medical school and usually do research in their fields. Consequently, patients benefit from Duke's educational facilities and from its extensive corresponding research. More than 100 medical center doctors are listed in *The Best Doctors in America*.

Duke University Hospital is the major private tertiary care center in the Southeast. In some clinical

**DURHAM,
NORTH CAROLINA**

DUKE UNIVERSITY HOSPITAL IS THE MAJOR PRIVATE TERTIARY CARE CENTER IN THE SOUTHEAST. IN SOME CLINICAL SUBSPECIALTIES, SUCH AS BONE MARROW TRANSPLANTATION AND OPEN HEART SURGERY, PATIENTS ARE REFERRED FROM ALL OVER THE WORLD.

subspecialities, such as bone marrow transplantation and open heart surgery, patients are referred from all over the world. The range of services available at Duke covers just about every medical specialty and subspecialty.

SPECIAL FACILITIES AND PROGRAMS

One of the major areas of concern at Duke is children's health and related pediatric problems. The Children's Medical and Surgical Center was designed as a compact, child-oriented unit within Duke University Hospital with quick access to the specialists and facilities of the entire medical center. Duke is a major center for the treatment of children with severe combined immunodeficiency disease (SCIDS) and is a major referral center for children with cardiac disease. It has one of the most modern facilities available anywhere for pediatric cardiac catheterization, as well as a first-rate neonatal intensive care unit for treating premature infants. The pediatric metabolism lab is the only one in the country devoted entirely to the analysis of clinical samples, and its high-tech equipment can diagnose rare metabolic diseases and Reye's syndrome. The Child Guidance Clinic is the home of the Durham Community Guidance Clinic for Children and Youth, a service of the Department of Psychiatry.

In other areas of psychiatry, Duke is a major referral center for patients with eating disorders, particularly anorexia nervosa. Duke also offers an interdisciplinary approach to the treatment of chronic pain. The Duke Diet and Fitness Center is part of the Department of Community and Family Medicine and is one of the best-known facilities in North Carolina. The program concentrates on self-education, so participants can develop a weight control and exercise program that can be maintained after they leave. The program focuses on four areas: medical, behavioral, dietary and nutritional, and fitness. Participants are asked to spend at least four weeks in Durham, although six to eight are recommended.

Duke has had a kidney transplant program for nearly twenty years, and heart and liver programs were initiated in 1984. In 1993, Duke surgeons transplanted 19 hearts, 21 livers, 54 kidneys, 15 lungs, and 13 kidneys and pancreases in combination. Duke is a regional referral center for microsurgery and replantation of severed limbs. Its plastic surgeons specialize in breast reconstruction, treatment of cleft palate, and the specialized treatment of patients in the Burn Unit.

The Duke Comprehensive Cancer Center houses inpatient and outpatient programs in oncology and treats more than 6,000 patients a year. Autologous bone marrow transplants are used to treat recalcitrant cases of breast cancer, leukemia, lymphoma, and melanoma. Other innovative techniques include hyperthermia to enhance the effectiveness of chemotherapy. Extensive radiation therapies are also available. Duke opened the nation's first outpatient bone marrow transplant clinic for the treatment of breast cancer.

Duke specialists use a number of procedures, including in vitro fertilization, to treat couples with infertility problems. The Obstetrics/Gynecology Department offers clinics for patients with pelvic pain, premenstrual syndrome, sexual dysfunction, and sexually transmitted diseases. A lab for prenatal diagnosis of disease includes facilities for chorionic villi sampling. Duke is a major regional referral center for high-risk obstetric patients.

The Duke University Eye Center is a clinical and research unit, the only one of its scope between Baltimore and Miami. A faculty member originated the technique of vitrectomy, in which the clouded vitreous humor of the eye is removed and replaced with clear fluid. Other specialists here use innovative procedures to treat a variety of unusual eye diseases. For instance, the retinal tack, a Duke invention, has been used in several patients to smooth out badly folded and torn retinas. Duke is one of the few places in the country to perform epikeratophakia, which involves suturing a lens onto an eye.

The large Neurosciences Division includes an extensive study of Alzheimer's disease and certain inherited neurological disorders, such as Huntington's disease and muscular dystrophy. A special program offers a comprehensive approach to people who have or are at risk of developing heart disease. Several physicians specialize in the treatment of rheumatoid diseases, especially the myriad types of arthritis. The Hypertension Center treats and educates patients afflicted with the "silent killer," high blood pressure.

The Center for the Study of Aging and Human Development, the first and longest continuously funded such center in the country, studies what happens biologically, psychologically, economically, and socially as people grow older. The center has conducted many long-term studies, including the first longitudinal study in normal aging. The Geriatric Evaluation and Treatment Clinic provides initial assessment and continuing care, refers patients to specialty clinics when necessary, and works with family members.

As would be expected in an institution of this size and breadth, Duke has extensive facilities for diagnostic and therapeutic radiology. The Emergency Room has a Level I trauma rating and two Life

AT A GLANCE

Beds: 1,125
Occupancy Rate: 80%
Average Patient Count: 804
Average Patient Stay: 8.1 days
Annual Admissions: 36,000
Births: 2,000
Outpatient Clinic Visits:
   548,676
Emergency Room/Trauma
   Center Visits: 43,116

HOSPITAL PERSONNEL
Physicians: 1,274
Residents/Fellows: 855
Registered Nurses: 1,624
   BS Degree: 50%+

ROOM CHARGES (PER DIEM)
Private: $470
ICUs: $1,000–$2,035

ADDRESS
Durham, NC 27710

TELEPHONE
(919) 684-8111

Flight helicopter ambulances to transport trauma victims and acutely ill patients within a radius of 150 miles.

Eight compression chambers provide hyperbaric oxygen therapy for a number of conditions, such as acute cyanide and carbon monoxide poisoning, gas gangrene, and certain soft-tissue infections. Duke is part of the national Divers Alert Network, providing immediate care, transportation, and compression chamber treatment for diving accident victims in the southeastern United States.

Other major specialty clinics are devoted to diabetes, epilepsy, prosthetics and orthotics, pulmonary rehabilitation, sickle cell anemia, stroke, and swallowing disorders.

Medical personnel from Duke serve the 484-bed Veterans Administration Medical Center; Lenox Baker Children's Hospital, a 40-bed rehabilitation center for children; and Duke personnel staff outreach programs that cover the state.

The range and diversity of services at Duke is even more impressive when one considers that at the time of its founding, North Carolina ranked forty-fourth in the nation in personal income, and medicine in the state was practically a cottage industry. The original 400-bed hospital opened in 1930, funded by James Buchanan Duke, a Durham native who had become a major U.S. industrialist. In his will he designated $4 million to be used to erect a medical school, hospital, and nurses' residence at Duke University.

Today almost 80% of Duke's patients come from North Carolina; the rest come from other states and from around the world.

MEDICAL SPECIALTIES

Allergy, Anesthesiology, Audiology, the Burn Unit, Cardiology, Dermatology, Endocrinology, Family Planning, Gastroenterology and Hepatology, Genetics, Geriatric Psychiatry, Gynecology, Hematology, Hyperbaric Medicine, Infectious Diseases, Infertility, Internal Medicine, Maternal Fetal Medicine, Medical Speech Pathology, Metabolism, Nephrology, Neurosurgery, Nuclear Medicine, Obstetrics, Occupational Therapy, Oncology, Ophthalmology, Oral Surgery, Orthodontics, Orthopedics, Otolaryngology, the Pain Clinic, Pathology, Pediatrics, Pediatric Surgery, Physical Therapy, Plastic and Maxillofacial Surgery, Proctology, Psychiatry, Psychoanalysis, Psychology, Pulmonary Disease, Radiology, Rehabilitation Medicine, Radiology, Rehabilitation Medicine, Rheumatic and Genetic Disease, Speech and Hearing, Surgery, Thoracic Surgery, Trauma Surgery, and Urology.

WELL-KNOWN SPECIALISTS

- Dr. Brenda Armstrong   *Pediatric cardiology*
- Dr. R. Randal Bollinger   *Liver and kidney transplantation*
- Dr. Rebecca Buckley   *Pediatric immunology; specialist in severe combined immunodeficiency syndrome*
- Dr. Bernard Carroll   *Psychiatry*

- Dr. R. Edward Coleman   *Diagnostic radiology*
- Dr. John Falletta   *Pediatric oncology*
- Dr. Henry Friedman   *Pediatric oncology; specialist in pediatric brain tumors*
- Dr. Joseph C. Greenfield, Jr.   *Cardiology*
- Dr. Charles Hammond   *Infertility*
- Dr. Arthur Haney   *Infertility*
- Dr. Samuel Katz   *Pediatric infectious diseases and immunizations*
- Dr. Robert Machemer   *Ophthalmology; specialist in vitrectomy*
- Dr. Blaine Nashold   *Neurosurgery; specialist in pain*
- Dr. William Peters   *Oncology; specialist in autologous bone marrow transplantation*
- Dr. Sheldon Pinnell   *Dermatology*
- Dr. Edward Pritchett   *Cardiology*
- Dr. Leonard Prosnitz   *Radiation oncology*
- Dr. Charles Roe   *Pediatric genetics and metabolism*
- Dr. Allen Roses   *Neurology; head of the Alzheimer's disease program*
- Dr. David C. Sabiston, Jr.   *Cardiothoracic surgery*
- Dr. Donald Serafin   *Plastic surgery and microsurgery*
- Dr. James Urbaniak   *Orthopedic surgery and microsurgery*
- Dr. Redford Williams   *Behavioral medicine*

PATIENT SATISFACTION

In a mid-1994 survey of Duke patients, 97.4% of the respondents were satisfied with their care (59.1% of them were extremely satisfied), and 98.2% said they would return if they needed hospital care in the future.

RESEARCH

For 1993, Duke and its researchers received $107 million in grants from the National Institutes of Health, covering a total of 414 individual projects. This ranked Duke seventh among U.S. research universities. The two major thrusts in research at Duke are molecular genetics and the neurosciences.

Duke is home to one of 52 Howard Hughes Medical Institutes, where groundbreaking research is being conducted in the areas of adrenergic receptors, the molecular mechanisms of insulin, and regulation of gene expression. The University is also a designated Center for AIDS Research.

The Duke Heart Center is currently conducting two projects for the U.S. Agency for Health Care Policy and Research—one is a massive five-year effort to define appropriate indications for the use of cardiac catheterization, angioplasty, and bypass surgery; the other, a three-year effort to establish national guidelines for the care of patients with unstable angina.

The Duke Center for the Study of Aging is conducting one of the nation's largest studies of the elderly. The Joseph and Kathleen Bryan Alzheimer's

Disease Research Center has been a leader in applying molecular genetic strategies to Alzheimer's research.

Because of its long history of research in immunology and rheumatology, Duke was one of three institutions named by the NIH as a specialized center for arthritis research.

The Duke Comprehensive Cancer Center was established in 1972 as one of the first federally-designated centers offering a multidisciplinary approach to the disease. The Center has established a reputation for excellence in studies of the immune responses to tumors, such as those in the brain, breast, kidney and colon. The Center is also known for research in bone marrow transplantation, hyperthermia, and pediatric brain tumors.

ADMISSIONS POLICY

There are three ways to enter Duke University Hospital: preadmission (patients referred to Duke by their personal physicians are scheduled for hospitalization by their Duke physicians), through the emergency/trauma center, or after examination in one of Duke's clinics.

There is no financial requirement for patients entering through the emergency room. Nonemergency patients must have some kind of insurance. If insurance does not cover the estimated bill, a deposit is required. If a deposit is not possible, the patient may receive a waiver from a physician or hospital administrator. A waiver may also be granted if the service would be a significant teaching case. Duke provides more than $12 million annually in charity discounts and uncollectible debts.

UNIVERSITY OF NORTH

CAROLINA HOSPITALS

University of North Carolina Hospitals (UNCH), which comprises North Carolina Memorial Hospital, North Carolina Neuropsychiatric Hospital, North Carolina Children's Hospital and North Carolina Women's Hospital, opened in 1952 as the state's primary referral hospital. It is the academic medical center for the University of North Carolina at Chapel Hill (UNC-CH) School of Medicine. It is also a research center and a primary care hospital for the people of North Carolina.

UNCH has 665 beds, 1,285 licensed nurses, and 750 attending physicians, who are also on the faculty at the UNC-CH School of Medicine. Each year, UNCH admits more than 24,500 patients and provides outpatient care to more than 529,000 patients through emergency, clinic, and ancillary service areas. These patients come to Chapel Hill from all 100 North Carolina counties, neighboring states, and from throughout the country and around the world. Many outpatients are seen in the new Ambulatory Care Center, which opened in 1993 and can accommodate up to 250,000 patient visits a year. In addition, UNCH is designated as a Level I trauma center.

A pioneer in many medical developments, UNCH opened the nation's first intensive care unit in 1953. Since then, the hospitals have expanded intensive care services to include 10 specialized intensive care units. One of these is the North Carolina

CHAPEL HILL,
NORTH CAROLINA

UNCH IS A HEALTH SCIENCE
COMPLEX THAT IS ONE OF
THE MOST COMPREHENSIVE
IN THE COUNTRY.

Jaycee Burn Center, which offers one of the Southeast's leading programs in burn treatment, research, and education.

UNCH is continuing to look toward the future and its role in meeting the health care needs of the state. In 1993, the medical center introduced a new service, UNC HealthLink, a telephone service that gives consumers easy access to appointments and care. As part of a major facility replacement program, UNCH began construction of a new neuropsychiatric hospital, which was to include an enlarged emergency department, and was scheduled for completion in late 1994. There are also plans for a new North Carolina Children's Hospital, a new North Carolina Women's Hospital, and a Support Services facility.

UNCH is a health science complex that is one of the most comprehensive in the country. This complex includes five professional schools—dentistry, medicine, nursing, pharmacy, and public health—with a combined enrollment of 3,000 students, a number of prestigious centers and institutes, and the largest health sciences library in the South.

The medical center is recognized nationally for expertise and innovation in caring for people with a variety of medical problems, including arthritis, autism, burns, cancer, coagulation disorders, cystic fibrosis, genetic disorders, growth disorders, infertility, and neuromuscular diseases. It is a major center for the care of high-risk mothers and infants. In all, there are over 160 outpatient clinics at North Carolina Memorial offering services ranging from general medical care to treatment for highly specialized problems.

SPECIAL FACILITIES AND PROGRAMS

The UNC medical center is nationally recognized for the specialized care it offers patients with a variety of health problems. It has centers for research in cancer, hemostasis and thrombosis, cystic fibrosis, environmental health, arthritis, sexually transmitted diseases, digestive diseases, health promotion and disease prevention, and geriatrics. Other areas of note are trauma care, neurosurgery, heart disease, autism, growth disorders, hemophilia, infertility, nephrology, and alcohol-related problems. The UNC Lineberger Comprehensive Cancer Center is one of only 27 programs designated a comprehensive cancer center by the National Cancer Institute. The UNC AIDS Clinical Trials Unit is one of 36 centers designated by the National Institutes of Health to improve diagnosis and investigate new treatments for people who are infected with the human immunodeficiency virus (HIV).

In addition, the transplantation program at UNCH is recognized as the most comprehensive in the state and among the best in the country. The staff regularly performs heart, lung, heart/lung, kidney, liver, pancreas and bone marrow transplants. About 130 transplant procedures are performed each year.

The Radiation Oncology Center serves cancer inpatients and outpatients and provides those patients with access to advanced technology. The center also houses research facilities and a motel unit.

The North Carolina Jaycee Burn Center is one of the most comprehensive burn facilities in the country. Patients receive acute and intermediate care, physical therapy and rehabilitation, and reconstructive surgery. The burn center staff also provides emotional support and psychiatric counseling for burn patients and their families.

The hospital offers a full range of gynecological and obstetrical services, including in vitro fertilization. The staff uses many different medical and surgical techniques to give infertile couples new hope for achieving pregnancy.

The elderly and disabled are helped through Lifeline, a service providing quick access to medical assistance when needed. Subscribers wear a small button on a chain around their necks. Pressing the button transmits a signal to the Emergency Room at North Carolina Memorial, where staff can make sure that appropriate medical care is provided.

To save costs and provide improved services to patients, UNCH offers Day-Op, an ambulatory surgical program where patients arrive in the morning and are usually discharged in time to spend the evening with their families. Under an innovative Outpatient Admissions Program, patients are allowed to stay in the hospital for up to 23 hours as an outpatient. The program is designed for patients who may not be well enough to go home after a minor surgical or diagnostic procedure, but are not sick enough to be admitted as an inpatient.

MEDICAL SPECIALTIES

Anesthesiology, Cancer, Cardiology, Critical Care Medicine, Dentistry, Dermatology, Digestive Diseases and Nutrition, Emergency Medicine, Endocrinology and Metabolism, Epidemiology, Family Medicine, Hematology, Infection Control, Infectious Diseases, Medical Genetics, Nephrology, Neurology, Obstetrics/Gynecology, Oncology, Ophthalmology, Pathology, Pediatrics, Psychiatry, Radiation Oncology, Radiology, and Surgery.

AT A GLANCE

Beds: 665
Occupancy Rate: 76%
Average Patient Count: 488
Average Patient Stay: 6.1 days
Annual Admissions: 24,526
Births: 2,160
Outpatient Clinic Visits:
    493,000
Emergency Room/Trauma
    Center Visits: 37,000

HOSPITAL PERSONNEL
Physicians: 750
Residents: 471
Registered Nurses: 1,188
    BS Degree: 51%

ROOM CHARGES (PER DIEM)
Private: $475
Semiprivate: $450–$460
ICU: $1,625

ADDRESS
101 Manning Drive
Chapel Hill, NC 27514

TELEPHONE
(919) 966-4131

WELL-KNOWN SPECIALISTS

- Dr. Richard C. Boucher   *Pulmonology; specialist in cystic fibrosis*
- Dr. Ronald J. Falk   *Nephrology; specialist in chronic renal disease*
- Dr. Paul A. Godley   *Oncology; specialist in prostate cancer*
- Dr. Jaroslav F. Hulka   *Obstetrics and gynecology; specialist in reproductive endocrinology*
- Dr. Edison Liu   *Oncology; specialist in breast cancer*
- Dr. H. D. Peterson   *Surgery; specialist in burn care*
- Dr. Harold R. Roberts   *Hematology; specialist in thrombosis and hemostasis*
- Dr. Charles Van der Horst   *Specialist in acquired immunodeficiency syndrome*
- Dr. John B. Winfield   *Specialist in rheumatology/immunology*
- Dr. Steven H. Zeisel   *Specialist in nutrition*

PATIENT SATISFACTION

UNCH has conducted patient satisfaction surveys since 1985, using in-house computer-assisted telephone surveying. The surveys are conducted by trained volunteers seven to 10 days after patient discharge. UNCH completes 500 surveys per quarter, or 2,000 surveys per year. This is approximately 10% of the hospital's total discharges. Surveying of outpatients will begin in 1995.

Patient ratings are high. Ninety-four percent of surveyed patients report being satisfied or very satisfied with their overall experience at UNCH. Ninety-five percent say they were satisfied or very satisfied with the courtesy and friendliness of their nurses. Ninety-eight percent were satisfied with the courtesy and friendliness of the doctors at UNCH. Ninety-five percent of the patients surveyed say that they would recommend UNCH to others.

RESEARCH

The Verne S. Caviness General Clinical Research Center, which is part of UNCH, receives about $3,025,000 each year in grant and foundation money.

At the Lineberger Cancer Research Center, scientists investigate AIDS, chemical carcinogenesis, immunology, cancer cell biology, drug development, recombinant DNA, and viruses. Researchers have found what appears to be an important clue to the mystery of why one or more kinds of cancer spread throughout the body. They have discovered that molecules believed to be part of a key signaling mechanism among cells are significantly more common in patients with some forms of cancer, including colon and breast cancer, than in people without the disease.

A first-of-its-kind study of treatment for progressive brain disease in AIDS patients was commissioned in January of 1994. UNC is participating in this study with Columbia, Johns Hopkins and Yale Universities, the University of California at San Francisco, Washington University at St. Louis, the Universities of Miami and Minnesota, UCLA and Mt. Sinai Medical Centers, and Massachusetts General Hospital.

The Arthritis Research Center coordinates research into the cause and treatment of this crippling disease. The center also sponsors research seminars to educate physicians on the latest advances in arthritis care. In late 1985, the center—one of two federally funded arthritis centers in the Southeast and 12 across the U.S.—was awarded a $1.6 million grant from the National Institute of Arthritis and Musculoskeletal and Skin Diseases.

The Center for Thrombosis and Hemostasis studies blood and clotting disorders. The Comprehensive Hemophilia Diagnosis and Treatment Center, a part of the research center, follows 400 hemophiliacs throughout the Southeast to evaluate their treatment and progress.

The Cystic Fibrosis Research Center studies the cause of this fatal lung disease and digestive system disorder and was one of the first three such centers in the United States.

ADMISSIONS POLICY

Patients must be referred to a physician on staff at UNCH. They cannot admit themselves.

Patients must also have a guarantor financial statement. If patients have no insurance, UNCH will see if they qualify for financial assistance from Medicaid, Children's Special Health Services, the Sickle Cell Program, Cancer Program, or Vocational Rehabilitation. UNCH reserves the right to deny care for elective admissions, but does not deny care in cases of medical emergency, regardless of ability to pay. Last fiscal year over $33 million in indigent care was provided.

Phone number for admissions information: (919) 966-2051, from 7 a.m. to midnight.

PATIENT/FAMILY ACCOMMODATIONS

Hotel rooms are available for $6.00 per night.

CLEVELAND CLINIC

FOUNDATION

In medical circles around the country, the Cleveland Clinic is regarded as one of the finest institutions in the world. Hyperbole comes easily, because almost everything about the Cleveland Clinic is out of the ordinary. The clinic's list of medical breakthroughs reads like a history of modern medicine. Cleveland Clinic founder George W. Crile, Sr. performed the first laryngectomy and the first human-to-human blood transfusion. His son, George, pioneered the use of the simple mastectomy and other therapies for breast cancer that were less disfiguring than the then-standard radical mastectomy.

The clinic has also been a pioneer in kidney transplantation, primarily through the efforts of Dr. Willem Kolff, who created the artificial kidney (also known as dialysis) using an old Maytag washing machine. In 1951, another clinic doctor, George Phalen, identified carpal tunnel syndrome (the repetitive stress injury that today afflicts many people who use keyboards) and developed a test for diagnosing it and enabling treatment. And in 1967, clinic heart surgeon Rene Favaloro performed the first successful coronary bypass operation.

The clinic was founded just after World War I by four Cleveland physicians—Drs. George W. Crile, Frank Bunts, William Lower, and John Phillips—who had discovered the advantages of the then-revolutionary group practice concept in their work

IN MEDICAL CIRCLES AROUND THE COUNTRY, THE CLEVELAND CLINIC IS REGARDED AS ONE OF THE FINEST INSTITUTIONS IN THE WORLD.

near the battlefields of France. On February 26, 1921, a new four-story clinic building was officially opened.

Since then, the Cleveland Clinic has evolved as a multifaceted organization which consists of four major divisions: the clinic, the hospital, the educational division and the research division. All four divisions are included in the private, not-for-profit practice of medicine that distinguishes the Cleveland Clinic from many other institutions. As a consequence, in 1979, Congress recognized the Cleveland Clinic Foundation (the official name of the institution) as a center of medical excellence—a National Health Resource. The foundation's Division of Education was incorporated as a postgraduate medical school in 1935 and was one of the first institutions to promote continuing medical education. Today, it is recognized as the largest post-graduate medical facility in the United States that is not connected with a medical school or university.

Located on a 100-acre campus on Cleveland's east side, the Cleveland Clinic Foundation is the second largest medical group practice in the world. The facility consists of 30 buildings on 125 acres, including a 12-story outpatient clinic. Similar to the Mayo Clinic, Cleveland Clinic doctors band together and pool services. Each staff physician is a specialist in one or more areas of medicine. None has an outside practice and none sees patients at any other hospital. Fifty-six Cleveland Clinic physicians were listed in the latest edition of *The Best Doctors in America* and many others are known to excel in their specialties.

In 1992, the clinic signed a formal affiliation agreement with Kaiser Permanente, the nation's largest health maintenance organization. The agreement paved the way for Kaiser's 200,000 members in Northeast Ohio to be referred to the Cleveland Clinic for high-quality specialty care.

SPECIAL FACILITIES AND PROGRAMS

Since 1963, when the Cleveland Clinic performed the first transplant in Ohio and became a recognized

AT A GLANCE

Beds: 880
Occupancy Rate: 69%
Average Patient Count: 604
Average Patient Stay: 7.4 days
Annual Admissions: 29,857
Outpatient Clinic Visits:
    760,674
Emergency Department
    Visits: 15,987

HOSPITAL PERSONNEL
Physicians: 503
    Board Certified: 472
Residents: 883
Registered Nurses: 2,038
    BS Degree or Higher: 795

ROOM CHARGES (PER DIEM)
Private: $705
Semiprivate: $650
ICU: $1,700

ADDRESS
9500 Euclid Avenue
Cleveland, OH 44195

TELEPHONE
(216) 444-2200

pioneer in the field of organ transplantation, it has expanded the staff, resources, and technical support necessary to stay in the forefront of transplant technology. In addition to the more than 1,700 kidney transplant operations performed at the clinic since 1963, bone, bone marrow, cornea, heart, heart/lung, liver, lung, and pancreas transplantation programs have been established with success rates commensurate with other leading health care institutions. The clinic offers one of the most successful and comprehensive programs available for multiorgan transplants. In 1993 alone, 233 organ transplant procedures and 169 bone marrow transplants were completed—numbers well above the average.

The Cleveland Clinic Heart Center staff represents one of the largest cardiac specialty groups in the world and provides patients with access to the full breadth and depth of cardiac care. Heart Center volume speaks for itself: in 1992, 3,424 open heart surgeries, 1,048 valve surgeries, 4,802 diagnostic catheterization procedures, 1,982 interventional catheterization procedures, 13,558 echocardiograms and dopplers, 368 permanent pacemaker insertions, 133 cardiac defibrillator implants, 639 electrophysiology studies, 8,425 stress tests, and 93,247 electrocardiograms were performed. The clinic was one of only a handful of medical centers to perfect cardiomyoplasty, a pioneering surgical technique that can eliminate the need for a heart transplant or an artificial heart in patients suffering from heart failure.

The foundation has created one of the foremost epilepsy diagnostic, treatment, and research programs in the country. A testing site for new drugs, the foundation is working to increase the percentage of patients who respond to medical treatment. Some difficult cases require surgery, for which the foundation helped develop sophisticated testing techniques that allow surgeons to pinpoint, and remove, the source of seizures in the brain. Although difficult cases make up only 2% of the epileptic population, 20% of these surgeries are performed at the Cleveland Clinic.

The clinic is one of four U.S. medical centers that cooperated on the design and testing of innovative cementless replacement joints. These prostheses are expected to last longer than earlier cemented models and feature a porous metal coating that allows bones to grow into it, locking the implant into place. In 1992, the clinic performed its first successful knee transplant, a procedure that is done in fewer than 10 medical centers in the country. It also established an Institute for Physical Medicine and Rehabilitation to help patients recover from strokes, brain tumors, multiple sclerosis, amputations, and other disabling conditions.

The clinic's pioneering work in tissue spectroscopy, in which tissues are exposed to weak laser light from an optical fiber probe, has translated into a 92% success rate at detecting colon cancer. The procedure, which does not require removing tissue samples from the body, is more comfortable for the patient and far less risky, and may eventually replace all other early detection systems. The clinic has also pioneered less-than-radical surgery for breast and thyroid cancer and a surgical stapling technique which helps preserve normal bowel function in nine out of ten rectal cancer patients.

Like the Mayo Clinic, the Cleveland Clinic has recently expanded its operations to bring its quality care to patients in the sunbelt. In 1988, it opened a satellite clinic in Fort Lauderdale, Florida, offering patients a full range of medical and surgical specialties. Its 72-member staff handled close to 100,000 patient visits in 1992, more than twice as many as the year before.

MEDICAL SPECIALTIES

Adolescent Medicine, Allergy and Immunology, Anesthesiology, Broncho-esophagology, Cardiovascular Diseases, Critical Care medicine, Dermatology, Dermatopathology, Diabetes, Endocrinology, Gastroenterology, General Medicine, Geriatrics, Gynecology, Hematology/Oncology, Immunopathology, Infectious Diseases, Internal Medicine, Laryngology, Nephrology, Neurology, Neuropathology, Nuclear Medicine, Occupational Medicine, Oncology, Ophthalmology, Otology, Otorhinolaryngology, Pathology, Pediatrics, Pharmacology, Psychiatry, Pulmonary Diseases, Radiology, Rheumatology, Rhinology, and Surgery.

WELL-KNOWN SPECIALISTS

- Dr. Brian Bolwell   *Medical oncology/hematology*
- Dr. David Bronson   *Internal medicine*
- Dr. William Carey   *Gastroenterology*
- Dr. Vincent Dennis   *Nephrology*
- Dr. Charles Fisher   *Pulmonary and critical care medicine*
- Dr. Kathleen Franco   *Psychiatry*
- Dr. Robert Graor   *Cardiovascular disease*
- Dr. William Hart   *Anatomic pathology*
- Dr. Michael Henderson   *General surgery*
- Dr. Gary Hoffman   *Rheumatic disease*
- Dr. Bret Lashner   *Gastroenterology*
- Dr. David Longworth   *Infectious disease*
- Dr. Roger Macklis   *Radiation oncology*
- Dr. Michael McKee   *Psychology*
- Dr. Roger Mee   *Thoracic surgery*
- Dr. Vinod Sahgal   *Rehabilitation medicine*
- Dr. Marshall Strome   *Otolaryngology*
- Dr. George Tesar   *Psychiatry*

PATIENT SATISFACTION

The Cleveland Clinic has traditionally enjoyed high esteem among its former patients. The latest survey results show that this remains true today. The satisfaction level with the overall Cleveland Clinic experience was graded at 97%.

Physicians register 98% satisfactory ratings, while 98% of patients also expressed satisfaction with the medical care they received.

RESEARCH

Conducting leading-edge research to unravel the mysteries of disease has been a cornerstone of the clinic since its founding. The Cleveland Clinic received $47 million in grants and other revenue in 1993 to support its research efforts. These funds support 118 research scientists and 125 research fellows, as well as 352 technical and support personnel.

The foundation has been a pioneer in the development of kidney dialysis and the artificial heart, and in the identification of the hormones that affect blood pressure and hypertension and their links to the hardening of the arteries. Innovations at the foundation have included the first artificial kidney, built in the late 1940s and housed in an old Maytag washing machine, and the first heart bypass operation, performed in 1967.

Current projects include research into the causes of cancer, and the control and prevention of ALS and other neurosensory disorders. Special research related to the hospital's best-known specialties includes the development of blood purification techniques to help liver transplant patients, laser catheterization to unclog narrowed arteries, and the testing of t-PA, a powerful, genetically engineered drug to dissolve blood clots.

In 1992, the clinic's Research Institute received a four-year grant from the National Institutes of Health, totalling nearly $1 million, to study the genetic expression of the human parainfluenza virus, which can be deadly to children under two years old.

There is even a clinic devoted specifically to fainting, which is a daily threat to patients with extremely low blood pressure. The Syncope Clinic includes a neurologist, otolaryngologist, cardiologist, and an electrophysiologist to investigate ways of preventing cardiac arrhythmias and nervous system disorders in these patients.

ADMISSIONS POLICY

Any patient who is referred to a Cleveland Clinic Hospital staff physician may be admitted. Admission approval is based upon the staff physician's assessment of the patient's medical needs.

There are no specific financial guidelines for admission. Each case is reviewed on an individual basis. In cases where financial liabilities are identified prior to admission, financial counselors will work with the patient and the patient's family to identify payment alternatives. No patient who is in need of care will be denied care because of inability to pay. Charity care provided in 1993 totalled $35.1 million.

PATIENT/FAMILY ACCOMMODATIONS

The Cleveland Clinic Guesthouse, a 197-room, limited service lodging facility, is available for short- and long-term stays. The standard room rate is $63, a kitchenette is $77, and an apartment is $140. Weekly and monthly rates are also available. For reservations, call (800) 833-0303. In addition, a 400-room hotel, located near the Cleveland Clinic facility, offers reduced rates for patients and their families.

OHIO STATE

UNIVERSITY

MEDICAL CENTER

COLUMBUS, OHIO

Recognizing its "high level of commitment to the pursuit of excellence in patient care," the Joint Commission on Accreditation of Healthcare Organizations gave its highest ranking, accreditation with commendation, to the Ohio State University Medical Center (OSUMC). OSUMC is also regularly recognized as one of the best in various other studies and surveys. Its patients also give the hospital high marks, with 98% in a recent survey praising the facility's responsiveness to their needs—far better than the national average.

OSUMC boasts a broad list of nationally recognized programs that speak strongly for its reputation among health care professionals. Ohio State University Hospitals is the nation's ninth most active organ transplant center, with almost 300 solid organ transplants being performed in a typical year. It is also one of six perinatal referral centers in Ohio for high-risk obstetrical care and the only Level III facility in central Ohio. It is a participant in the Medicare Coronary Artery Bypass Graft Demonstration Project and is one of a limited number of medical centers throughout the country using the excimer "cool" laser to treat patients with clogged heart arteries.

Specialties that have brought particular recognition to the hospitals include endocrinology, obstetrics/gynecology, cardiology, transplant surgery, neurology, otolaryngology, orthopedics, rehabilitation, and psychiatry. The OSUMC-affiliated School

OSUMC BOASTS A BROAD LIST OF NATIONALLY RECOGNIZED PROGRAMS THAT SPEAK STRONGLY FOR ITS REPUTATION AMONG HEALTH CARE PROFESSIONALS.

of Medicine is also nationally recognized as among the best overall—second only to Oregon Health Sciences University—in the training of primary care physicians, as rated by *U.S. News & World Report*.

As a referral center for the more than 2.5 million residents of central and southern Ohio, as well as for patients throughout the country, OSUMC is recognized as one of the nation's leading medical centers. Associated with the nation's fourth largest college of medicine, the Center trains more than 1,400 medical students and residents annually. Patient care facilities at OSUMC consist of the Arthur G. James Cancer Hospital and Research Institute, in addition to University Hospitals.

University Hospitals also has numerous community programs and facilities for ease of patient care and access. With seven locations throughout Columbus, MedOHIO Physician Care Centers offer continuing primary care with convenient hours that facilitate prompt treatment when other medical alternatives are not available. Additionally, they provide an extensive occupational medical program and medical care in urgent situations, as well as continuing care on a general basis. The Healthcare Consortium of Ohio, founded by OSUMC, allows area hospitals to work together to better meet the needs of their communities. OSUMC also sponsors numerous educational seminars, support groups, wellness screening, and The Health Team, a partnership with the University Medical Center and a local television station, WCMH-4, that features health information and free monthly events.

SPECIAL FACILITIES AND PROGRAMS

Research efforts at OSUMC have established its Cardiovascular Services as one of the premier heart programs in the nation. Recently, OSUMC was selected as one of the first four hospitals in the nation to be a Medicare Participating Heart Bypass Center. University Hospitals was also the first hospital in its area to have a Heart Rhythm Lab for diagnosing abnormal heart rates so proper treatment could be prescribed. OSUMC performed the first heart transplant in central Ohio, and was among the first in the

AT A GLANCE

Beds: 706
Occupancy Rate: 74%
Average Patient Count: 524
Average Patient Stay: 6.7 days
Annual Admissions: 28,504
Births: 3,693
Outpatient Clinic Visits:
    231,860
Emergency Room/Trauma
    Center Visits: 44,518

HOSPITAL PERSONNEL
Physicians: 477
    Board Certified: 405
Residents: 466
Registered Nurses: 1,219
    BS Degree: 670

ROOM CHARGES (PER DIEM)
University Hospitals
Private: $285
Semiprivate: $260
ICU: $1,050
James Hospital
Private: $450
ICU: $1,100

ADDRESS
410 West 10th Avenue
Columbus, OH 43210-1228

TELEPHONE
(614) 293-8000

nation to perform cardiac catheterization. Among the more routine services available are coronary bypass surgery, outpatient catheterization, and laser treatment for clearing clogged arteries. For all of these procedures, and for general coronary care, the University Medical Center is the first choice of heart patients in central Ohio and beyond.

From obstetrics and gynecologic services to preventive care, OSUMC provides a full range of services to meet a woman's medical needs at every stage of her life. Special services include gynecologic oncology, maternal-fetal medicine, and reproductive endocrinology and infertility. The Division of Gynecologic Oncology provides the most advanced methods of cancer diagnosis and treatment for women throughout Ohio and the Midwest. The Division of Maternal-Fetal Medicine treats high-risk patients from a 33-county area in Ohio. The University Medical Center pioneered the use of in vitro fertilization in Ohio, and today remains at the forefront of new diagnostic and treatment options for couples experiencing infertility problems.

The Organ Transplantation Program is one of the most technologically advanced in the United States and is the only solid organ transplant program in central Ohio. Currently, an organ transplant is performed every 24 hours. Nationally, OSUMC is among the top five in kidney transplants performed, and is one of the leading centers in the world for combined kidney-pancreas transplants, based on volume and success rates. Through 1993, University Hospitals had performed more than 2,700 transplants, including 2,199 kidneys, 200 pancreases, 182 livers, and 121 hearts. In 1993 alone, 136 kidney and 53 kidney-pancreas transplant procedures were performed.

The rehabilitation program at Ohio State is nationally recognized as a leader in this area, noted for expertise in electrodiagnosis, which includes electromyography and nerve condition studies. The program treats people who have experienced debilitating injuries and illnesses, such as head and spinal cord injuries, strokes, burns, chronic pain, and neuromuscular conditions. At Dodd Hall, a CARF (Commission on Accreditation of Rehabilitation Facilities) accredited facility, the staff's goal is to help patients regain their maximum level of functioning and go on to lead independent and productive lives. OSUMC's unique community re-entry program simulates the home, work, school, and community environments and allows patients to "practice" independent living skills in a controlled setting. From acute rehabilitation care to outpatient visits at the Stoneridge Medical Center in Dublin, patients work with a team of rehabilitation professionals—physicians, nurses, physical and occupational and speech therapists, psychologists, and social workers—to ease the way along the challenging road of rehabilitation.

The Neurosciences staff treats patients with a wide range of neurological disorders, including chronic headaches, Alzheimer's disease, multiple sclerosis, epilepsy, Parkinson's disease, and many others. Patient care is supported with strong emphasis on research, treatment, and prevention of strokes, muscular dystrophy, and other degenerative diseases. The psychiatry program assists adults, adolescents, and children with varying degrees of mental illness. OSUMC established the first inpatient child psychiatry unit in central Ohio, attending to the needs of children ages 12 and younger.

The most advanced diagnostic procedures for the entire spectrum of otolaryngologic (head and neck) conditions are provided by the Department of Otolaryngology. The department is a recognized national leader in a number of specialized areas, including head and neck oncology and facial plastic and reconstructive surgery. Subspecialties include hearing problems, head and neck tumors, cranial base surgery, neurotology, balance disorders, multidisciplinary voice disorders, endoscopic sinus surgery, and facial paralysis.

The Emergency Department at the Ohio State University Hospitals provides comprehensive emergency services, including round-the-clock Level I trauma care. Staffed by board-certified staff and emergency medicine specialty residents, the department offers expert care for both urgent and emergency conditions. The emergency staff is backed up by in-house specialists in all of the disciplines required for comprehensive emergency care. Specialized facilities located in the Emergency Department include resuscitation suites, CAT scanner, and a hyperbaric medicine chamber. The SKYMED helicopter service provides advanced emergency care and rapid transport to the facility.

As the first fully dedicated cancer hospital in the Midwest, the 128-bed Arthur G. James Cancer Hospital is one of a very few independent cancer hospitals in the nation to be linked with a major academic and medical research center. Opened in 1990, the hospital is a National Cancer Institute Comprehensive Cancer Center. The center has deep roots at Ohio State, which has developed a reputation over the years for innovative cancer research and patient care. The title "Comprehensive Cancer Center" refers to the organization which facilitates interactive and interdisciplinary research teams encompassing more than 200 faculty members from 11 different colleges.

Each year, the James Hospital treats as many as 4,800 inpatients and nearly 75,000 outpatients from Ohio and around the world. It offers a full spectrum of cancer diagnosis and care services, including bone marrow transplantation, breast care, and treatment for cancer pain, as well as the full range of specific anatomy and cancer-specific services. It is also an official center for the testing of new anti-cancer drugs.

The Male Cancer Early Detection Clinic opened in 1991 to provide comprehensive detection and treatment options for prostate, bladder, and testicular cancers. Periodic screenings for prostate cancer are held at no charge. The Cancer Pain Control Clinic also opened in 1991 to offer a multidisciplinary approach to relieving cancer pain. Treatments involve representatives from pharmacology, occupational and physical therapy, acute pain service, social work, and pastoral care.

The American Cancer Society Babe Zaharias Women's Cancer Center specializes in the prevention, diagnosis, and screening of cancers affecting women, including breast, ovarian, and cervical cancers. The center currently focuses on breast cancer. When a woman is diagnosed with breast cancer at the center, she is counseled by an interdisciplinary team of specialists, generally the same day. More than 200 patients per month are seen by the center.

The James Hospital is one of only a handful of U.S. hospitals to provide radiation treatments in the operating room. Known as Intraoperative Radiation Therapy, it allows the physician to deliver high-dose radiation directly to a tumor exposed during surgery. At the same time, it spares healthy overlying tissue from exposure to the radiation beam.

MEDICAL SPECIALTIES

Anesthesiology, Cardiology, Dentistry, Emergency Medicine, Family Medicine, Internal Medicine, Neurology, Obstetrics/Gynecology, Oncology, Ophthalmology, Otolaryngology, Pathology, Pediatrics, Physical Medicine, Preventive Medicine, Psychiatry, Radiology, and Surgery.

WELL-KNOWN SPECIALISTS

- Dr. Larry Copeland   *Obstetrics/gynecology; director, Division of Gynecologic Oncology*
- Dr. Paul Dorinsky   *Pulmonary specialist*
- Dr. Christopher E. Ellison   *General surgery*
- Dr. William B. Farrar   *Surgical oncology*
- Dr. Ronald M. Ferguson   *Surgery; chairperson, Department of Surgery*
- Dr. Steven G. Gabbe   *Chairperson; Department of Obstetrics and Gynecology*
- Dr. Lee Hebert   *Director, Division of Nephrology*
- Dr. Jay D. Iams   *Director, Division of Maternal-Fetal Medicine*
- Dr. Ernest W. Johnson   *Physical medicine*
- Dr. Moon H. Kim   *Endocrinology; director, Division of Reproductive Endocrinology*
- Dr. John T. Kissel   *Neurology*
- Dr. Calvin Kunin   *Preventive medicine*
- Dr. Richard Lembach   *Ophthalmology*
- Dr. Richard P. Lewis   *Cardiology*
- Dr. Carl V. Lier   *Cardiology; director, Division of Cardiology*
- Dr. Earnest Mazzaferri   *Internal medicine; chairperson, Department of Internal Medicine*
- Dr. Jerry R. Mendell   *Neurology; director, Division of Neurology*
- Dr. Subir K. Nag   *Otolaryngology; chief of Brachytherapy*
- Dr. Henry A. Nasrallah   *Psychiatry; chairperson, Department of Psychiatry*
- Dr. Richard W. O'Shaughnessy   *Obstetrics; director, Fetal Therapy Program*
- Dr. E. Mitchel Opremcak   *Ophthalmology*
- Dr. George W. Paulson   *Neurology*
- Dr. William Pease   *Physical medicine*
- Dr. Robert Ruberg   *Plastic surgery; director, Division of Plastic Surgery*

- Dr. David E. Schuller   *Clinical oncology; director, Comprehensive Cancer Center*
- Dr. Michael J. Sullivan   *Plastic surgery; specialist in facial plastic surgery*
- Dr. Elizabeth Weller   *Psychology; director, Division of Child and Adolescent Psychiatry*
- Dr. Duane Bradley Welling   *Otolaryngology; director of Otology and Neurotology*

PATIENT SATISFACTION

University Hospitals' inpatient satisfaction rating for the quarters of 1993 ranged from 8.47 to 8.79 on a scale of 1 to 10, with 10 being extremely satisfied. Ambulatory surgery satisfaction was rated between 8.74 and 8.90 for the same period.

Patients at the Arthur G. James Cancer Hospital report themselves well pleased with their treatment. The most recent surveys noted overall satisfaction between 8.97 and 9.32 on a scale of 10. Satisfaction with nurses and physicians averages about 9.0.

RESEARCH

Total grant support in 1993 was $49.5 million. About $28 million was supplied by the National Institutes of Health. Major areas of activity include neurosciences, cancer, immunology, experimental drugs, molecular biology, and environmental toxicology.

Among the well-known accomplishments of the Ohio State research program is a widely published and recognized work in psychoneuroimmunology which has established a link between stress and deterioration of the body's immune system.

In OSU's renowned heart failure research program, the largest of its kind in the nation, researchers are known for their discovery of the beneficial effects of a number of heart failure drugs, such as dubotamine, used for acute or severe heart failure.

OSU is also participating in a multicenter clinical trial for the evaluation of new drugs to fight the HIV virus.

At the Comprehensive Cancer Center, the understanding of cancer causes and treatments grows through research that takes many forms. It ranges from basic research in cell biology and tumor viruses to development of new surgical techniques and clinical drug trials. A few examples will suffice. The Brain Tumor Research Center is striving to improve the detection and treatment of brain tumors. A new technology with long-range promise for the treatment of brain tumors is Boron Neutron Capture Therapy, an example of physicians at the James Hospital working with basic Cancer Center scientists to combat the disease. Clinical scientists from the Head and Neck Oncology Program are working in tandem with other researchers to study new treatment strategies for patients with advanced head and neck cancers. In 1991, the Gynecological Oncology Program became the first in America to gain approval from the National Cancer

Institute to use the drug Taxol in a special protocol for advanced ovarian cancer patients for whom other treatments had failed. A procedure that could markedly improve the surgical treatment of certain cancers is being developed by Ohio State researchers. The procedure is known as Radioimmuno-Guided Surgery (RIGS). It relies on a radioactive antibody that is targeted to a patient's cancer and on an electronic probe, which acts as a gamma detector, that is used during surgery to locate unseen cancer cells.

ADMISSIONS POLICY

Orders for admission are accepted only from credentialed OSUMC attending faculty and courtesy staff.

Customary demonstration of adequate third party coverage and/or ability to pay is required. If a patient lacks insurance, Patient Financial Services will work with the patient to obtain coverage in elective situations. Emergent/urgent care is not denied to anyone, regardless of ability to pay. OSUMC absorbed about $30 million in charity care and bad debt in fiscal year 1993.

PATIENT/FAMILY ACCOMMODATIONS

University Ramada Inn offers a special rate for patients and/or families of $34 plus tax per night for 1–4 people.

UNIVERSITY HOSPITALS

OF CLEVELAND

University Hospitals of Cleveland (UHC) is a 947-bed academic medical center serving its community and the nation through patient care, research, and teaching. Its main campus includes Alfred and Norma Lerner Tower; Samuel Mather Pavilion and Lakeside Hospital for adult medical/surgical care; University MacDonald Womens Hospital; Rainbow Babies and Childrens Hospital; University Psychiatric Center (Hanna Pavilion); and Bolwell Health Center.

UHC is affiliated with, but separate from, the adjacent Case Western Reserve University of Medicine. The hospitals' attending physicians are all faculty members at the medical school.

The origin of UHC was the establishment in 1863 of the "Home for the Friendless." Lakeside Hospital, dedicated in 1931, was the original hospital of the Medical Center. In 1967, the original Lakeside Hospital was expanded. Rainbow Babies and Childrens Hospital dates back to the founding of Rainbow Cottage in 1887 and Childrens Hospital in 1902. In 1972, Rainbow Hospital joined Babies and Childrens Hospital.

In February 1994, University Hospitals opened two new world-class facilities on its campus: the Alfred and Norma Lerner Tower and Samuel Mather Pavilion. This biggest-ever expansion allows University Hospitals to offer its patients a new dimension

CLEVELAND, OHIO

IN 1994, FOR THE FOURTH YEAR IN A ROW, *U.S. NEWS & WORLD REPORT* NAMED RAINBOW BABIES AND CHILDRENS HOSPITAL ONE OF THE TOP SIX PEDIATRIC HOSPITALS IN THE COUNTRY.

in clinical excellence for a referral, diagnostic, and treatment center. The Lerner Tower's 210 private patient rooms, located on seven floors, replaced beds in Lakeside Hospital and Hanna House. Most of the tower's floors are dedicated to a single patient population, such as organ transplantation or cancer. The adjoining Mather Pavilion incorporates four stories of patient care facilities, including ambulatory services, diagnostic centers, surgical suites, intensive care units, and laboratories.

SPECIAL FACILITIES AND PROGRAMS

In 1994, for the fourth year in a row, *U.S. News & World Report* named Rainbow Babies and Childrens Hospital one of the top six pediatric hospitals in the country. Rainbow is a 244-bed comprehensive pediatric medical and surgical facility dedicated to excellence in family-centered care. With more than 30 major divisions, it is a principal referral center for Ohio and nearby states, and is nationally recognized for excellence in many pediatric subspecialties and pediatric intensive care. Each year, more than 86,000 infants, children, and adolescents are served by the hospital, with approximately 10,000 admitted for inpatient care. The Rainbow Pediatric Trauma Center is the only Level I pediatric trauma center in northeast Ohio, as designated by the American College of Surgeons.

With 106 beds and 52 bassinets, University MacDonald Womens Hospital is the largest and most comprehensive hospital for women in Ohio. Along with comprehensive maternity services, University MacDonald offers a full spectrum of women's surgical services: infertility services; breast health services through the MacDonald Breast Center and the MacDonald Mobile Mammography Van; gynecologic oncology services in conjunction with University Hospitals' Ireland Cancer Center; and an array of experts who are leaders in the diagnosis, treatment, and research of menopause, incontinence, menstrual disorders, and infertility. University MacDonald is licensed by the state of Ohio as a Level III facility, the highest classification available to any hospital offering maternity services. The expertise of Rainbow's 38-bed Neonatal Intensive Care Unit is just seconds away, providing exceptional care for high-risk pregnancies and at-risk newborns.

University Hospitals has two cardiac catheterization labs. One lab is for digital bi-plane catheterization, which takes two views of the arteries of the heart at once, improving diagnostic capabilities and providing a better view during interventional processes.

The Neuroscience Intensive Care Unit makes available rapid diagnostic tools and advanced treatment procedures, making permanent brain damage preventable in stroke victims.

The University Ireland Cancer Center was established in 1985 to coordinate all inpatient and outpatient oncology activities. The center is one of only two National Cancer Institute-designated clinical cancer centers in the state of Ohio. Since its inception, the center has developed several major clinical programs. It has been a leader in the development of autologous bone marrow transplantation for the treatment of both hematopoietic malignancies and solid tumors. Other procedures developed include a method of treating marrow ex vivo and a technique for collecting stem cells from peripheral blood. A major commitment has also been made to the development of basic and clinical research programs in colon cancer. A comprehensive Breast Cancer Center has been established as well.

The center's Department of Radiation Oncology offers the most up-to-date technology, including three linear accelerators, a Sieman Stabilitan Superficial and Orthovoltage unit, and a simulator. A Positron Emission Tomography unit and support cyclotron are also available.

In 1990, the University Ireland Cancer Center opened a 27,000 square foot outpatient facility with specially designed exam, consultation, and therapy areas for adults and children. This facility also includes on-site laboratory and pharmacy services.

The University Musculoskeletal Institute combines the talents of internationally recognized specialists in orthopedics, rheumatology, neurological surgery, neurology, and radiology to treat problems of simple movement. The Institute provides patients with expert diagnosis, follow-up treatment, and rehabilitation. Areas of treatment include arthritis, joint replacement, disease or traumatic injury to the spinal cord, pain reduction, pediatric orthopedics, oncology, sports medicine, osteoporosis, and rehabilitation.

Nearly 500,000 strokes occur in America each year; 145,000 are fatal. The University Cerebrovascular Center consists of physicians, scientists, and nurses, all working toward a better understanding of the blood vessels that supply the brain. Specialists in neurological surgery, neuroradiology, emergency medicine, neurology, nursing, and physical and occupational therapy provide patient care.

The Alzheimer Center of University Hospitals has the nation's largest staff of experts in an academic medical institution dedicated to discovering and using state-of-the-art solutions to the problems

AT A GLANCE

Beds: 939
Occupancy Rate: 80%
Average Patient Count: 567
Average Patient Stay: 5.9 days
Births: 4,151
Annual Admissions: 35,171
Outpatient Clinic Visits:
   85,586
Emergency Room/Trauma
   Center Visits: 65,634

HOSPITAL PERSONNEL
Physicians: 1,372
   Board Certified: 890
Residents: 664
Registered Nurses: 1,831
   BS Degree or Higher:
   1,337

ROOM CHARGES (PER DIEM)
Private: $540–$875
Semiprivate: $453–$782
ICU: $1,745–$1,812

ADDRESS
11100 Euclid Avenue
Cleveland, OH 44106

TELEPHONE
(216) 844-1000

raised by Alzheimer's disease. Housed in the Joseph M. Foley Elder Health Center, the Alzheimer Center integrates specialists to provide for the patient's entire physical and mental well-being.

The University Psychiatric Center is an 80-bed hospital housed in the Howard M. Hanna Pavilion. The center provides specialized services to meet the needs of schizophrenia patients, mood and personality disorder patients, older adults with mental health problems, and patients with other psychiatric illnesses. A biopsychosocial assessment and treatment process is the hallmark of patient care, as provided by a team of psychiatrists, psychologists, nurses, and social workers.

Complicated major surgery, as well as ambulatory surgery, is performed in Lakeside Hospital, which consists of 280 medical and surgical beds, including the cardiac monitoring unit, surgical intensive care unit, and medical intensive care unit. Twenty-eight operating rooms provide ample surgical space. Through the work of the late Dr. Claude Beck, UHC was a world pioneer in heart surgery from the 1920s on and remains, today, a respected center for heart surgery.

University Hospitals also provides an impressive array of special services. The staff performs 70 to 80 kidney transplants annually, 15 to 20 kidney and pancreas transplants, and 15 to 20 liver transplants. Eighty-five bone marrow transplants are done annually. Hemodialysis treatments number 10,000 per year.

MEDICAL SPECIALTIES

Airway Diseases, Anesthesiology, Cardiology, Clinical Pharmacology, Critical Care, Dermatology, Endocrinology and Hypertension, Family Medicine, Gastroenterology, Geographic Medicine, Hematology and Oncology, Infectious Diseases, Internal Medicine, Nephrology, Neurological Surgery, Neurology, Obstetrics/Gynecology, Ophthalmology, Orthopaedics, Otolaryngology, Pathology, Pediatrics, Plastic Surgery, Psychiatry, Pulmonary and Critical Care Medicine, Rheumatic Diseases, Radiology, Surgery, Urology.

WELL-KNOWN SPECIALISTS

- Dr. Baka Arafah   *Endocrinology*
- Dr. John Carey   *Infectious diseases (AIDS)*
- Dr. Suzanne Cassidy   *Pediatric genetics*
- Dr. D. L. Dudgeon   *Pediatric surgery*
- Dr. Alex Gelha   *Cardiothoracic surgery*
- Dr. Maureen Hack   *Neonatology*
- Dr. Jerome Kowal   *Geriatrics*
- Dr. Jennifer Kriegler   *Neurology; specialist in chronic pain*
- Dr. Hillard Lazarus   *Oncology*
- Dr. E. Regis McFadden   *Pulmonary medicine*
- Dr. Roland Moskowitz   *Rheumatology*
- Dr. Warren Selman   *Microvascular surgery*

- Dr. Wulf Utian   *Reproductive endocrinology; menopause*
- Dr. George Van Harr   *Pediatric cardiology*
- Dr. Albert Waldo   *Cardiology*

PATIENT SATISFACTION

Since 1987, 94% of patients surveyed have rated the quality of care at University Hospitals as "very good" or "excellent"; 97% said they would return if they needed hospital care in the future; and 97% also said they would recommend University Hospitals to others. Physician care was rated as "very good" or "excellent" in 92% of the cases; nursing care in 91%.

RESEARCH

Total National Institutes of Health funding is $65,145,000. In addition, 1993 foundation gifts totaled $2,508,092. The Department of Medicine at University Hospitals of Cleveland ranks 15th in the U.S. in research funding by the NIH. Pediatrics is in the top 11.

The University Ireland Cancer Center is one of only two National Cancer Institute designated sites in Ohio, providing patients with access to the most current clinical research trials.

In the area of basic research, the University Ireland Cancer Center joins its academic counterpart, Case Western Reserve University, to form a comprehensive biomedical research program that is supported by more than $17 million annually. Research areas include radiation biochemistry, environmental carcinogenesis; tumor metabolism; molecular biology; molecular virology; and hematopoietic and immune cell biology.

The University Ireland Cancer Center Bone Marrow Transplant Program was the first center both nationally and internationally to study the use of a new highly potent anti-nausea medication to prevent vomiting during bone marrow transplants.

The University Ireland Cancer Center was among the first group of transplant centers to be designated by the Eastern Cooperative Oncology Group, a national multi-institution organization that coordinates clinical trials. Other members of this elite group include Johns Hopkins, the Mayo Clinic and the University of Pennsylvania. The cancer center also participates in the Childrens Cooperative Study Group.

The Rainbow Cystic Fibrosis Center, the largest research and care center in the U.S., has been recognized for creating the first successful approach to managing this number-one ranked genetic killer of children.

Neonatologists and respiratory therapists at Rainbow pioneered "jet ventilation therapy," an innovation that more effectively supports infants with underdeveloped lungs.

Rainbow's Center of Pediatric Pharmacology is one of a handful of programs throughout the world where development and testing of new medications for children takes place.

Rainbow has taken a leading role in identifying biofeedback, music therapy, and other relaxation techniques to help children cope with pain, cancer, and frequent or extended hospital stays.

University Hospitals was a co-developer of the first new drug in 20 years for the treatment of schizophrenia—clozapine, which was approved by the FDA in 1989.

ADMISSIONS POLICY

Arrangements for all admissions to University Hospitals, other than obstetric and gynecologic, are made in advance between the physician and the Humphrey Building Admitting Reservations Office. Obstetric and gynecologic patients are admitted to MacDonald House and arrangements are made through the Admitting Office located there.

If patients do not have a doctor on staff, they will be admitted under the staff service of that specialty. They will then be assigned to the attending physicians on call. If a patient lacks insurance, he/she will be contacted by a Financial Counselor to review what is available and what they are qualified for.

OREGON HEALTH

SCIENCES UNIVERSITY

HOSPITAL

Of the more than 100 academic health centers in the United States, Oregon Health Sciences University (OHSU) is one of the few that is independent of a larger university campus and administration. As part of the Oregon State System of Higher Education, OHSU is the only institution of medical education in the state. It is home to Schools of Medicine, Dentistry and Nursing. Its patient care units consist of University Hospital, the University medical and dental clinics, the Child Development and Rehabilitation Center, and Doernbecher Children's Hospital. Research is conducted at the Biomedical Information Communication Center, the Center for Research on Occupational and Environmental Toxicology, and the Vollum Institute for Advanced Biomedical Research.

OHSU's two hospitals and their clinics serve as primary clinical teaching facilities for the OHSU School of Medicine and provide tertiary care for the people of Oregon. Patients from every county in Oregon were treated at OHSU last year; other patients came from as far away as Alaska and New York. About 7% of all patients treated come from outside Oregon. University Hospital, the focal point of patient care at OHSU, represents the 1973 joining together of Medical School Hospital, Multnomah County Hospital, Doernbecher Children's Hospital and University Clinics. It provides services ranging

PORTLAND, OREGON

FOR GENERATIONS, OHSU HAS BEEN AT THE VANGUARD OF BIOMEDICAL ADVANCES, EARNING A NATIONAL REPUTATION FOR ITSELF AND ITS COMMITMENT TO SERVICE.

from primary medical care to highly sophisticated care for patients with complicated illnesses. For generations, OHSU has been at the vanguard of biomedical advances, earning a national reputation for itself and its commitment to service. In July 1989, University admitted its one millionth patient.

University Hospital boasts many firsts, particularly in the area of coronary care. In 1957, Oregon's first open heart surgery was performed there and in 1985 the state's first heart transplant program was begun. In 1960, for the first time, a malfunctioning heart valve was replaced at the hospital with an artificial valve developed by an OHSU faculty member and his engineer associate. Surgeons at the Doernbecher Children's Hospital performed Oregon's first pediatric open heart surgery in 1958 and the state's first pediatric heart transplant in 1987. University Hospital physicians have made major advances in the techniques of coronary arteriography, developing the standard method now used worldwide. A catheter designed by an OHSU faculty physician has proven to be an effective therapy for treatment of hardening of the arteries. The method has been adapted to the coronary system and often replaces surgical treatment.

The OHSU School of Medicine was ranked No. 1 among comprehensive medical schools in the *U.S. News & World Report* national survey of medical schools. Comprehensive medical schools are those "more oriented toward training primary care doctors."

SPECIAL FACILITIES AND PROGRAMS

The Neurology Department is one of the fastest developing academic departments on the West Coast. Faculty specialists collaborate with other OHSU specialists, such as neuropsychologists, in multidisciplinary clinical programs. Many of these programs are unique in the Northwest, including clinics for movement disorders, such as Parkinson's disease; stroke; dizziness; epilepsy; Alzheimer's disease and related disorders; and multiple sclerosis/neuroimmunology (which also offers plasmapheresis for disorders such as Guillain-Barré syndrome). The Northwest's only neurogerontology program has recently been developed; and, in collaboration with the new Center for Research on Occupational and Environmental Toxicology, a program in neurotoxicology is under development. Other services include clinical neurophysiology (electroencephalography, electromyography, evoked potentials).

Home of the High Risk Cancer Family Clinic, University Hospital specializes in examining and screening families who have a history of breast, colon, or endometrial cancers, or malignant melanomas. Based on the results of this screening, an individualized check-up routine is established, risks are identified, and prevention advice is given.

Other faculty are exploring cancer treatments through the study of living cells. Effects of anti-cancer drugs, hormones, growth factors, and interferons are studied using cancer cell cultures; and the OHSU Osgood Leukemia Laboratory studies live bone marrow cells to examine their behavior and pinpoint better treatment. Other investigators are studying oncogenes, hormone receptors, and drug resistance to improve cancer therapy.

The Hormone Receptor Laboratory provides specialized expertise in hormone receptor analysis. Evaluation of steroid receptor profiles is of considerable significance in selecting the appropriate therapy for breast cancer patients.

OHSU faculty have pioneered remarkable techniques in the treatment of brain tumors by overcoming the protective mechanism called the blood-brain barrier, which prevents anti-cancer drugs from reaching the brain.

The Ophthalmology Department of OHSU is the fastest growing academic eye program in America. The majority of its faculty have national and international reputations in their subspecialties. In 1948, funded by a grant from the Oregon State Elks Association, members of the Department of Ophthalmology developed the first ocular microscope that greatly improved the safety of eye surgery.

The National Registry of Drug Induced Ocular Side Effects is located at OHSU. This registry is used by the Food and Drug Administration, drug companies and physicians from 30 countries, and offers the world's only data center for the collection and dissemination of information on drugs, chemicals and environmental factors that affect the visual system.

A new $23 million Casey Eye Institute is currently under construction. It will be the only academic eye research and treatment center west of St. Louis and north of San Francisco.

University Hospital has the largest and most active kidney center in the five-state Northwestern region. It has performed nearly 1,500 transplants since conducting its first and the world's 18th in 1959. This program features the Portable Home Kidney Dialysis Service, the nation's first center to offer at-home kidney dialysis. Faculty have developed improved techniques for removal of kidney stones, using ultrasound and shockwaves, instead of the conventional kidney stone surgery.

AT A GLANCE

Beds: 347
Occupancy Rate: 79%
Average Patient Count: 273
Average Patient Stay: 5.7 days
Annual Admissions: 16,917
Births: 2,600
Outpatient Clinic Visits: 294,907
Emergency Room/Trauma Center Visits: 24,750

HOSPITAL PERSONNEL
Physicians: 499
  Board Certified: 433
Residents: 284
Registered Nurses: 937
  BS Degree: 600

ROOM CHARGES (PER DIEM)
Private: $430–$720
Semiprivate: $430–$720
ICU: $886–$2,116

ADDRESS
3181 SW Sam Jackson Park Road
Portland, OR 97201-3098

TELEPHONE
(503) 494-8311

The Reproductive Biology Program, involving University Hospital, the School of Medicine, and the Oregon Regional Primate Research Center, is one of the strongest in the country. Fifty-two babies have been born to previously infertile couples in the last year with the help of the OHSU In Vitro Fertilization and GIFT Services. The reproductive program is the first in the Northwest to offer the option of in vitro fertilization.

The Department of Psychiatry is unique in academic centers for its work with patients from many cultures. Its programs combine treatment, research, and training. The Indochinese Clinic treats Cambodian, Laotian, Hmong, Vietnamese, and Mein refugees. It also provides training for paraprofessionals who care for these Southeast Asians in community clinics and conducts research among the Vietnamese group.

Another program focuses on three Native American Indian tribes, the Hopi, the Blackfeet, and the Warm Springs. Research is underway to better understand unique patterns of depression and methods of treatment for Native Americans.

University Hospital is the state's major organ transplant center, performing 17 liver, 124 kidney, 25 heart, 164 cornea, and three pancreas transplants last year. In Oregon, kidney, heart, liver, and pancreas transplants are offered only at OHSU.

University Hospital was named one of two Level I trauma centers in 1988 by the Oregon State Health Division. Serving the Portland metropolitan area, Level I hospitals manage the most severely injured patients, provide trauma-related medical education, and conduct research in trauma care. University Hospital has an Adult Trauma Transport Program which provides inter-hospital transport of critically ill patients from throughout the region.

As a leader in emergency care and training, University Hospital has been designated the Medical Resource Hospital to serve the Portland metropolitan area. As the resource hospital, University Hospital is staffed 24 hours-a-day with pediatric, surgical, orthopedic, psychiatric and other medical specialists to provide medical advice to ambulance/rescue personnel.

The Oregon Poison Center provides 24-hour emergency telephone assistance and first-aid instructions. The center's physicians answer inquiries about drugs, toxic substances, and poisonings. Staff members have access to computerized listings of 400,000 drugs, poisons, and toxic chemicals and their effects and antidotes.

University Hospital is also well-known for its programs in neurology, surgery, internal medicine, high-risk pregnancy, genetics, family medicine, otolaryngology, and psychiatric crisis intervention.

Other hospital services include specialized immunology and allergy laboratory testing, hormone receptor assays for breast and prostate cancer patients, noninvasive vascular and urodynamics laboratories, radiography, and the most modern diagnostic procedures for evaluating cardiac, gastrointestinal, and pulmonary problems.

Doernbecher Children's Hospital, Oregon's only public hospital for children, will celebrate its 70th birthday in 1996. Doernbecher offers the most comprehensive range of pediatric services in the state. Children come here for many reasons. Some are healthy and visit the Well Baby Clinic—others come with life-threatening illnesses or injuries. As the regional center for the treatment of the most complex heart surgery cases in children, Doernbecher and its OHSU affiliate, the Child Development and Rehabilitation Center (CDRC), provide the latest technology and specialists to diagnose and treat the majority of the 400 babies born in Oregon each year with congenital heart defects.

Doernbecher's unique neonatal and pediatric emergency transport systems, the first such systems in Oregon, are able to send a "transportable hospital" of highly trained specialists with state-of-the-art equipment directly to critically ill newborns and older children throughout the region. Last year, nearly 500 critically ill and injured children were transported.

The Neonatal Intensive Care Unit and Pediatric Intensive Care Unit specialize in the care of children with serious and life-threatening illnesses. Together, they care for more than 1,100 premature infants and critically ill children annually.

Infants at risk for breathing problems, including sudden infant death syndrome (SIDS) or "crib death," are evaluated and monitored through the Infant Monitoring Project. Parents learn to use equipment and techniques that alert them to changes in their child's respiration or heart rates.

OHSU is home to the Elks Children's Eye Clinic, an internationally known facility that has served as a model for other university-based eye clinics for children. More than 35,000 young patients have made in excess of 125,000 visits to the clinic; for many, these services otherwise would not have been available. Premature children can be especially at risk for blindness, and ophthalmologists there are leading a national study to prevent sight loss in these tiny infants.

Doernbecher diagnoses and cares for most (about 90%) of Oregon's young cancer victims. It is Oregon's first and only health center participating in the Children's Cancer Study Group, a consortium of specialists around the country who are researching and treating cancer in children. Nearly a third of the children at Doernbecher suffer from cancer, and about half of these have leukemia.

With 7,600 active patients (38,200 annual visits), CDRC provides diagnosis, treatment, and rehabilitation for handicapped people and their families throughout the state.

In addition to its clinics at OHSU, CDRC operates clinical facilities in Eugene and Medford. Staff members travel to Bend, Coos Bay, Corvallis, Pendleton, and Roseburg to see patients and offer specialized training to community health care practitioners. CDRC is widely recognized for its work in genetics and operates four genetics clinics: the Diagnostic and Counseling Clinic, the Chromosome and Dysmorphology Clinic, the Metabolic Clinic, and the Prenatal Counseling and Diagnostic Clinic.

Other Doernbecher pediatric specialties include: endocrinology, gastroenterology, immunology, neurology, psychiatry, pulmonary medicine, and renal medicine.

MEDICAL SPECIALTIES

Allergy/Immunology, Audiology, Cancer Care, Cardiology, Cardiothoracic Surgery, Critical/Intensive Care Medicine, Dentistry, Dermatology, Diabetes, Endocrinology, Family Medicine, Gastroenterology, General Medicine, Hematology/Medical Oncology, Immunology, Internal Medicine, Neurology, Obstetrics/Gynecology, Occupational Disease, Oncology, Ophthalmology, Orthopedics, Otolaryngology, Pediatrics, Plastic Surgery, Psychology, Pulmonary Medicine, Radiation Oncology, Renal Medicine, Reproductive Biology, Surgery, Transplantation Medicine, Trauma Care/Emergency Medicine, Urology, and Vascular Medicine.

WELL-KNOWN SPECIALISTS

- Dr. Grover Bagby *Hematology/oncology*
- Dr. Joseph Bloom *Psychiatry; specialist in forensic psychiatry*
- Dr. Sonia Buist *Pulmonary/critical care medicine; specialist in asthma treatment*
- Dr. William Conner *Endocrinology, metabolism, and clinical nutrition*
- Dr. Linn Goldberg *Director of Human Performance Lab; expert in adolescent use of anabolic steroids*
- Dr. Frederick Keller *Interventional radiology; specialist in non-invasive therapies*
- Dr. Peter Kohler *Endocrinology*
- Dr. Alfred Lewy *Psychiatry; specialist in seasonal affective disorder*
- Dr. Robb Moses *Medical genetics; specialist in Fanconi's syndrome research*
- Dr. Edward Neuwelt *Neurology; specialist in treating brain tumors*
- Dr. Susan Tolle *General and oral pathology; ethicist known for end-of-life issues*
- Dr. Donald Trunkey *Surgery; specialist in trauma treatment*

PATIENT SATISFACTION

OHSU uses a nationally-recognized survey system, Press Ganey Associates, to track inpatient and outpatient satisfaction. Quarterly reports, with departmental detail scores and comments, are distributed to all departments. The Quality Management Department works with individual departments to help them understand how the information can be integrated into departmental quality assessment and improvement activity. An executive summary that highlights areas of greatest potential for improvement is presented to medical staff and administrative leaders at the Quality Council (the multidisciplinary forum responsible for overseeing hospital-wide quality improvement activities).

Eighty-six percent of respondents to a second quarter 1994 inpatient survey said that they found the overall quality of the care received at OHSU Hospital "good" to "very good". Eighty-eight percent said they were likely to recommend the hospital to friends and family. Physician care received "good" to "very good" ratings in 90% of the responses; nursing care received the same ratings from 92% of respondents.

RESEARCH

Research and training grants to OHSU exceed $50 million per year. Eighty-three percent of these funds are obtained from out-of-state sources.

Examples of OHSU scientists' contributions to medicine include the use of catheters to clear clogged arteries, the creation of a way to cross the blood-brain barrier to treat brain tumors with chemotherapy, and cryotherapy for preventing blindness in premature infants. One new research group developed methods to detect, at an early treatable stage, the adverse effects of occupational chemicals on the nervous system. Advances in neuroscience include the cloning of neurotransmitter molecules and their receptors on nerve cell membranes, providing important insights into the biological basis of drug addiction, Parkinson's disease, schizophrenia, and many other neurological disorders.

The university is the center of a research consortium that combines the efforts of scientists from many institutions, including the Veterans Affairs Medical Center, the Shriners Hospital for Crippled Children, the Oregon Graduate Institute for Science and Technology, Kaiser Permanente's Center for Health Research, the Earl A. Chiles Research Center at Providence Medical Center, and the Neurological Sciences Institute of Good Samaritan Hospital.

Since the opening of the Vollum Institute for Advanced Biomedical Research in 1987 and the Center for Research on Occupational and Environmental Toxicology (CROET), significant new sums of money have been received for neuroscience research. CROET's research, along with that of Oregon State University, gives Oregon one of the country's strongest research programs in toxicology.

From the engineering of proteins to the cloning of genes governing cell growth and proliferation, biochemists and molecular biologists are probing the fundamental molecular events that underlie health and disease. Investigations include the biosynthesis of connective tissue for wound healing; the cloning of cell membrane receptors; delineating the role of growth factor receptors in normal and malignant cell growth; designing new hemoglobin molecules to serve as blood transfusion substitutes; and probing the actions of viruses and parasites in causing disease.

The scientists at the Vollum Institute for Advanced Biomedical Research are devoted to studying the brain and its neurons at the molecular level. Research teams have focused on the synapse, the site at which an impulse shoots from one nerve cell to another. Chemical messenger molecules called neurotransmitters are released at the synapse. A fundamental understanding of neurotransmitters may reveal how the brain works and how it is affected by such conditions as schizophrenia, depression, and drug addiction. It is critical to understanding such diseases as Alzheimer's, Parkinson's, and Huntington's.

Vollum researchers are tracking neurotransmitters from gene to synapse and beyond—how they are produced, modified, and released by the firing neuron, and how they are able to initiate an impulse in the receiving neuron.

Routinely used are the latest and most sophisticated equipment and methods, including recombinant DNA and gene transfer techniques; isolating, sequencing and mapping of genes and proteins; and use of monoclonal antibodies to determine with great accuracy if particular molecules are present within a cell. Institute scientists collaborate with basic researchers in the School of Medicine, such as the departments of biochemistry, microbiology and immunology, medical genetics, cell biology and anatomy, physiology, neurology, and diagnostic radiology.

ADMISSIONS POLICY

A potential patient must be accepted by a physician on staff. This may include a referral from an outside physician, but an OHSU physician must be attending.

If the patient has no third party coverage, other arrangements are made. If the service is elective, the patient is financially screened and will be responsible for full or partial payment. The patient is also screened for Medicaid eligibility and possible teaching allowance. Each year, OHSU provides more than $34 million in free care.

The special number for admissions information is (503) 494-8136.

GEISINGER MEDICAL

CENTER

When it comes to rural health care, the Geisinger health care system is among the elite. The Geisinger system of group practice and managed care has been cited by various authorities, including Hillary Rodham Clinton, as a national model for health care reform. Geisinger serves more than 2.1 million people from Pennsylvania's northeastern corner to its midpoint—and thousands of others through widely distributed outreach programs. Crucial to the Geisinger concept of managed care is Geisinger Health Plan (GHP), which has approximately 145,000 members. Founded in 1972 as one of the first rural health maintenance organizations (HMOs) in the United States, GHP is now the nation's largest rural HMO. The Geisinger Clinic's approximately 500 salaried physicians offer GHP services at 48 primary care locations and 13 community hospitals in 25 Pennsylvania counties. Through the Geisinger Clinic, GHP also has agreements with 433 private practice doctors in central and northeast Pennsylvania to deliver services complementing those that Geisinger specialists offer.

Founded in 1915 as the George F. Geisinger Memorial Hospital, the hospital was designed as a regional care facility that would offer specialized services to people in rural areas. Dr. Harold Foss was Geisinger's first chief of staff, and he served in that capacity from 1915 until 1958. Trained at the Mayo Clinic, Foss advocated the group practice of medicine

DANVILLE, PENNSYLVANIA

WHEN IT COMES TO RURAL HEALTH CARE, THE GEISINGER HEALTH CARE SYSTEM IS AMONG THE ELITE.

and hired specialty-trained physicians who formed the full-time, salaried, closed staff of the hospital. The original 70-bed hospital has grown to be one of the nation's most modern rural medical centers and now has 577 beds.

Geisinger has two hospitals. The Geisinger Medical Center in Danville delivers specialized care, including emergency medicine, cardiovascular surgery and neonatal intensive care, among 75 specialties and subspecialties. Geisinger Medical Center has two helicopters and provides trauma care 24 hours-a-day. It has been designated as one of five tertiary care centers in the state of Pennsylvania. The medical center is also home to the Janet Weis Children's Hospital. Its other specialized care centers focus on kidney, neurosciences, trauma, heart, cancer, and infertility treatment. The Geisinger Wyoming Valley Medical Center serves the eastern portion of the Geisinger health care network with comprehensive maternity programs and pediatric services, five medical/surgical units, the Frank M. and Dorothea Henry Cancer Center, and a complete emergency department.

Though it is not affiliated with a medical school, Geisinger supports numerous educational programs. Since its founding, it has trained more than 2,400 interns, residents, and fellows; graduated more than 3,200 registered nurses; and developed training programs in nine allied health professions. The training programs include cardiovascular technology, dietetic internship, histotechnology, medical technology, nurse anesthesia, nursing (a diploma program), radiation therapy technology, radiographic technology, and pastoral care.

SPECIAL FACILITIES AND PROGRAMS

Geisinger offers a complete array of cardiac diagnostic and treatment services through its Heart Center. The medical center's comprehensive diagnostic services include cardiac catheterization, electrocardiogram, echocardiography, electrophysiology, esophageal echocardiography, non-stress Persantine/Thallium testing, and stress testing. Once diagnosed, heart patients receive treatment ranging from the most basic advice to advanced cardiovascular surgery.

Geisinger Medical Center's complete program of treatment alternatives include Acute Intervention in Myocardial Infarction (AIMI), an aggressive, comprehensive program to treat heart attack patients within six hours of the onset of symptoms. The Heart Center's team of specialists uses treatments and procedures such as clot dissolving drugs, catheterization, and balloon angioplasty to prevent death and stop heart damage. With the same procedure as cardiac catheterization, physicians inject blood thinners and clot dissolving drugs directly into the hearts of patients experiencing a coronary heart attack. Balloon angioplasty is used to expand clogged blood vessels.

Geisinger Clinic physicians, in collaboration with national clinical drug trials, can also offer patients the latest therapies for heart disease. Drugs, pacemakers and cardiac defibrillators are used to regulate irregular heart beats.

Geisinger's heart surgery specialists repair holes in the heart and treat valve problems. They also perform artery bypass grafting and other open heart repair procedures. The cardiac intensive care and cardiovascular special care units provide two levels of care for critically ill cardiac patients.

For postoperative patients and heart attack sufferers, as well as to ward off heart attack in high-risk individuals, the cardiac rehabilitation program makes exercise specialists available to design and monitor personalized exercise programs.

Among Geisinger Clinic's pediatric subspecialists are cardiologists and cardiovascular surgeons who treat congenital heart disease and monitor children whose family history points to the possibility of adult heart disease. Geisinger Medical Clinic staffs the most comprehensive pediatric cardiology department in the region. The Geisinger Clinic also offers pediatric cardiology outreach clinics in several communities in Pennsylvania, bringing specialized care to rural areas in particular.

Geisinger Medical Center is the home of the Kiwanis Children's Heart Program, the fund-raising initiative of more than 250 Kiwanis Clubs in Pennsylvania. The Kiwanis Foundation has invested more than $250,000 in the children's heart program at Geisinger. Begun in 1984, the program has created an endowment to support Geisinger's pediatric cardiology services.

Physicians in the Department of Cardiology in Danville now offer transluminal extraction catheter (TEC) atherectomy, a procedure recently approved by the FDA, to treat coronary stenosis.

When performing TEC, the interventional cardiologist threads a blade-equipped catheter into the occluded artery. As it bores through the plaque, the device sucks off the shavings through a central lumen. This differs from the directional coronary atherectomy, which collects the plaque in a nosecone section of the catheter. Like DCA, the goal of TEC is to remove atherosclerotic plaque and decrease trauma to the vessel, which can cause acute complications.

Ideal candidates for TEC include patients with saphenous venous graft lesions or thrombosis in large, straight, noncalcified native coronary vessels.

AT A GLANCE

Beds: 577
Occupancy Rate: 72%
Average Patient Count: 415
Average Patient Stay: 7.6 days
Annual Admissions: 19,893
Births: 1,317
Outpatient Clinic Visits:
    505,740
Emergency Room/Trauma
    Center Visits: 33,307

HOSPITAL PERSONNEL
Physicians: 520
    Board Certified: 251
Residents: 214
Registered Nurses: 652

ROOM CHARGES (PER DIEM)
Private: $473–$599
Semiprivate: $410–$468
ICU: $1,701

ADDRESS
100 North Academy Avenue
Danville, PA 17822

TELEPHONE
(717) 271-6211

Currently, many of these patients require bypass surgery because conventional angioplasty is associated with a high risk of complications. The success and complication rates parallel those for DCA and angioplasty in low-risk lesions. Typically, angioplasty immediately follows TEC to smooth out remaining atheroma and to improve luminal diameter.

At the cancer center of Geisinger Medical Center, highly-skilled health care professionals work with the most advanced technology to evaluate, diagnose, and treat patients with cancer. The physician staff of Geisinger Medical Center's cancer center includes cancer specialists trained at major cancer treatment centers across the United States and Canada. These physicians work together with other well-trained health care professionals equally dedicated to treating patients with cancer, such as nurses, nutritionists, psychologists, social workers, technicians, technologists, therapists, and chaplains.

The cancer center receives funding from the Community Clinical Oncology Program sponsored by the National Cancer Institute (NCI). Recognized by the NCI as a model cancer program, Geisinger's cancer center received the second highest priority score for funding in the nation.

The most modern diagnostic tools, including endoscopy radiology and laboratory medicine, as well as all of the surgical specialties, are available at the cancer center. Center physicians use the latest techniques in chemotherapy, radiation therapy, surgery, and symptom-dissected care in the treatment of cancer.

Pediatric oncology offers a multidisciplinary approach to treating childhood cancer. Although the treatment plan is coordinated by a pediatric oncologist, the care is provided by a heath care team consisting of the oncologist, a pediatric psychologist, a pediatric nurse specialist, a pediatric social worker, a child life activities specialist, and a teacher. The team maintains active involvement with radiation oncology and all pediatric surgical services, including cardiovascular and thoracic surgery, dentistry, neurosurgery, ophthalmologic surgery, orthopaedic surgery, otolaryngologic surgery, and urologic surgery. The departments of laboratory medicine, pathology, and radiology designate staff and equipment to deal with the particular needs of this singular group.

The fertility center combines routine care, support groups, and assisted reproductive techniques to help infertile couples conceive a child. The services offered by Geisinger's fertility center include routine workups for infertility, appropriate medical and surgical intervention to correct anatomic or physiologic problems identified in either partner, and application of assisted reproductive procedures such as in vitro fertilization (IVF), gamete intrafallopian transfer (GIFT), tubal embryo transfer (TET), and zygote intrafallopian transfer (ZIFT).

Comprehensive treatment options are available for both partners. Urology treatment includes medical options, such as hormonal treatments to boost sperm count, and surgical interventions such as vasectomy reversal, varicocelectomy, and treatment of ductal obstructions. In addition to medically managing ovulation disorders, the center offers advanced operative laparoscopy and hysteroscopy, conventional laparotomy, and microsurgery. The staff can evaluate and treat premenstrual syndrome, premature ovarian failure and menopause. The entire gamut of advanced reproductive technology is available for the 10% to 15% of couples for whom less aggressive therapy fails.

The andrology and embryology laboratory, an integral component of the fertility program, was certified by the College of American Pathologists in 1993, the first year that accreditation had been offered. The laboratory offers a full range of services, from semen analysis evaluation of sperm viability to cryopreservation of embryos and sperm.

Geisinger Fertility Center statistics for the 1993 calendar year exceeded national standards. The GIFT program documented a clinical pregnancy rate of 40% per retrieval; the combined rate for ongoing pregnancies and delivery was 32%. These rates are above the national rates of 34% and 27% respectively. The IVF program evidenced a clinical pregnancy rate of 26% per retrieval; the combined rate of ongoing pregnancies and deliveries is 20%. The national rates are 19% and 15% respectively. Eleven transfers of previously frozen embryos have yielded two pregnancies and one birth to date.

Geisinger gastroenterologists have offered endoscopic papillotomy and sphincterotomy for more than a decade. In that time, the diagnostic and therapeutic modalities for treatment of hepatobiliary and pancreatic disease has expanded to include the following services: preoperative evaluation of the bile ducts, endoscopic sphincterotomy, stenting or sphincterotomy, sphincterotomy and stone extraction, dilation of benign strictures of the biliary tree, endoscopic or percutaneous stent placement for malignant obstruction of the bile duct, and mechanical lithotripsy of common bile duct stones.

Endoscopic retrograde cholangio-pancreatography (ERCP) represents an efficacious procedure for diagnosing pancreatic carcinoma, chronic pancreatitis, and sclerosing cholangitis, especially when noninvasive radiographic studies are inconclusive. ERCP has been shown to be particularly helpful in evaluating recurrent pancreatitis in children.

Geisinger offers a pediatric inflammatory bowel disease (IBD) clinic in Danville on the first and third Tuesdays of the month. The IBD clinic represents the first organized pediatric program of its kind in central and north central Pennsylvania.

Children suffering from inflammatory bowel disease deal with specific physical problems that carry significant social stigmas. A multidisciplinary approach assures that both the physical and emotional manifestations of IBD are addressed. The team staffing the IBD clinic includes physicians who are board-certified in pediatrics and gastroenterology, and a nutritionist and a psychologist, both of whom specialize in treating pediatric patients. Nutritional support for children with IBD is important. While the nutritional demands imposed by the disease require a hypercaloric diet, pediatric patients are often reluctant to eat because of the discomfort. Yet, there must be meticulous management of nutritional and pharmacologic therapy to reduce the risk of complications, such as growth retardation and delayed onset of puberty.

A high-risk obesity clinic at the medical center in Danville offers treatment and follow-up care for severely obese patients (50% or more overweight) with co-morbidities, including, but not necessarily limited to, hypertension, cardio-pulmonary disease, destructive joint disease, diabetes mellitus, and gallbladder disease. Patients should be highly motivated individuals who have failed other attempts at weight reduction. The treatment team, which includes a physician, psychologist, dietitian, and exercise physiologist, plans a treatment course tailored to the patient. Eligible patients may be offered closely supervised, very low calorie diets. Patients remain in the program as long as support is necessary. The Geisinger physician sends regular progress reports to the patient's primary physician.

Patients suffering from malnutrition may be referred to the nutrition clinic directed by nutrition physicians at the medical center in Danville. Typical consultations are for malnutrition in patients with surgeries, trauma, gastrointestinal diseases, or eating disorders. Treatment modalities include total parenteral nutrition (TPN), peripheral parenteral nutrition, tube-feeding, and oral supplementation. Nutrition clinic team members include physicians, dietitians, nurses, pharmacists, and social workers. Extensive experience with home TPN and tube feeding helps implement the primary care physician's treatment plan for these difficult patients. To provide optimal care, the team works closely with the patient's primary physician and the home care vendor.

The standard of care for treating acute pain requires a dedicated team trained to manage this difficult condition. Geisinger's pain management team in Danville includes a nurse coordinator, an anesthesiologist, and a resident. The anesthesiologist develops a treatment plan in concert with the patient's primary service physician. The nurse coordinator attends daily rounds, tracks patient's progress, attends to mechanical problems, and provides care continuity. Attending staff coverage is available 24 hours-a-day.

The population for the acute pain service includes postsurgical patients, some patients on the medical and trauma services, and patients whose conditions require complex drug management, such as drug addicts and pediatric patients.

Pain management techniques offered by the acute pain management service include intravenous patient-controlled analgesia and patient-controlled epidural analgesia (PCEA). The insertion and drug management of PCEA remains the purview of the anesthesiologist. The emphasis of patient-controlled analgesia allows the patient to be comfortable and hastens recovery.

The Department of Psychiatry and Behavioral Medicine in Danville has initiated an outpatient assessment program to improve access for patients requiring urgent or routine care. The assessment team, which includes a master's level clinician, a psychotherapist or psychiatric clinical nurse specialist, and a psychiatrist, determines the appropriate course of care for the patient. This can include follow-up evaluation by a psychiatrist or psychotherapist, admission to the hospital, or referral to an outside agency, when appropriate.

The outpatient assessment program negates the need for a patient to make a return appointment to begin treatment. After the initial examination, the team convenes to determine whether the patient requires drug therapy, a psycho-supportive behavioral approach, or a combination of the two. The patient, who is invited to stay at the medical center while the team meets, receives a follow-up appointment the same day. Patients seen through this clinic will not have to make a return trip to receive medication or begin psychiatric consultation. When the condition warrants the decision, a patient may be admitted to the hospital on the same day as the initial evaluation.

Primary care physicians are urged to call the assessment team members to evaluate patients who are not responding to standard therapy. After the consultation, the patient is referred back to his or her primary care physician for ongoing treatment. Patients whose conditions are medically complicated are likely referrals to the outpatient assessment program, as are individuals suffering from depression or anxiety disorders. Doctors should call the department's emergency service for patients who are suicidal, psychotic, violent, or require hospitalization.

The Geisinger program for alcohol and chemical detoxification and rehabilitation is system-wide. It includes the 77-bed Marworth inpatient treatment center in Waverly, Pennsylvania, which addresses the physical, social, psychological, and family issues of dependency and recovery and coordinates outpatient chemical dependency services wherever Geisinger provides health care.

Geisinger Medical Center averages between 40 and 45 kidney transplants per year. The program began in 1981 as part of a Geisinger commitment to the Pennsylvania Department of Health to create a rural kidney transplant program. For many years, Geisinger's was the only rural kidney transplant center in the United States. Included in the transplant totals above are adult transplants and four or five pediatric transplants per year. Working with the team of two transplant surgeons is a four-person operating room team, plus four adult nephrologists and two pediatric nephrologists. Geisinger's transplant program serves 10 kidney dialysis programs at hospitals over an area with a 150-mile radius, covering 31 counties or 40% of the state of Pennsylvania. Geisinger Medical Center, which in the late 1960s had one of the earliest kidney dialysis programs in the United States, has 130 patients on dialysis, including 30 on continuous ambulatory peritoneal dialysis.

Geisinger Medical Center is accredited as a Level I Regional Resource Trauma Center, based on its provision of comprehensive trauma care 24 hours-a-day and its outreach educational and research programs in trauma care. The trauma center includes a two-helicopter Life Flight rapid response retrieval program, which from July 1992 through June 1993 provided emergency medical transportation to 1,236 critically ill and injured adults, children, and newborns and served more than 100 hospitals in five states and the District of Columbia.

The helicopters average 3.3 flights per day and are available around the clock. Since the program began in 1981, these "flying emergency room" helicopters staffed by doctors, nurses, and paramedics have transported more than 12,000 patients from other hospitals and from accident scenes.

Other centers at Geisinger include a hyperbaric medicine program, an eye bank, and a neurosciences center.

For patients who do not require full hospitalization, Geisinger provides HotelCare, allowing patients to receive quality nursing care at a reduced cost. The HotelCare room is designed so that friends and loved ones can remain close. There is an exam room on site and special diets are available.

MEDICAL SPECIALTIES

Allergy, Cardiovascular Medicine, Cardiovascular and Thoracic Surgery, Critical Care Medicine, Dental Medicine and Surgery, Dermatology, Emergency Medicine, Endocrinology, Family Practice, Gastroenterology and Nutrition, General Internal Medicine, General Surgery, Hematology/Oncology, Hyperbaric Medicine, Infectious Diseases, Neonatology, Nephrology, Neurology, Neurosurgery, Obstetrics/Gynecology, Ophthalmology, Orthopedics, Otolaryngology, Pediatrics, Physical Medicine and Rehabilitation, Plastic Surgery, Psychiatry and Behavioral Medicine, Radiology, Rheumatology, Thoracic Medicine, Transplant Surgery, Urology, and Vascular Surgery.

WELL-KNOWN SPECIALISTS

- Dr. Frank Bartone   *Urology*
- Dr. J. Mostyn Davis   *Family medicine*
- Dr. John Deitrick   *Surgery*
- Dr. Stuart Heydt   *President and C.E.O. of Geisinger*
- Dr. William Jeffreys   *Neurology*
- Dr. Thomas Kennedy   *Otolaryngology and head and neck surgery*
- Dr. Charles Laubach   *Cardiology*
- Dr. Howard Morgan   *Cardiology*
- Dr. Michael Ryan   *Pediatric osteopathics*
- Dr. Diane Schuller   *Allergy and immunology*
- Dr. Donald Vrabec   *Otolaryngology and head and neck surgery*
- Dr. John West   *Organ transplantation*

PATIENT SATISFACTION

In the most recent survey, 95% of discharged patients responding said they would return to Geisinger for care. Ninety-three percent would recommend it to others. Overall quality of care was rated as excellent or good by 97%, with 70% giving an excellent rating. Other areas with high satisfaction scores were medical outcome, physician care, and nursing care.

RESEARCH

In May 1987, Geisinger opened its Sigfried and Janet Weis Center for Research. This 63,360-square-foot center for basic research is located adjacent to Geisinger Medical Center in Danville. Geisinger also serves as the regional hub for physician graduate medical education and allied health schools that include laboratory technology and pastoral care.

An annual budget of about $10 million supports Geisinger's research program, which included 408 active projects during the fiscal year ending June 30, 1993. The basic research program focuses on the mechanisms of cardiovascular disease, as studied at the cellular and molecular levels. The research is carried out in 10 independent laboratories, all of which are funded by the National Institutes of Health.

Geisinger Clinic's recent dedication of the Sigfried and Janet Weis Center for Research completed the final component of the most comprehensive cardiac program in the region. A national-caliber team of research scientists is headed by Howard Morgan, M.D., a former president of the American Heart Association. Geisinger Clinic scientists are studying heart disease at the cellular and molecular levels, looking into such mysteries as the causes of heart enlargement, the death of heart muscle following a heart attack, the relationship of hormones to heart disease, the cellular impact on blood pressure regulation, and the relationship between heart muscle and an increased work demand.

ADMISSIONS POLICY

The Medical Center has always operated under the closed medical staff concept. Patients are admitted to the Medical Center only by physicians employed by a group practice corporate entity related to the Medical Center.

Patients are counseled by a member of the Business Services' financial counseling staff and arrangements are made for payment and/or referral to government agencies such as Medical Assistance. In 1992-1993, the Medical Center incurred $10.3 million in uncompensated care costs.

Special phone number for admissions information: (717) 271-6206.

PATIENT/FAMILY ACCOMMODATIONS

Patients in the HotelCare program stay at the Pine Barn Inn, a privately operated hotel on the grounds of Geisinger Medical Center.

HOSPITAL OF THE

UNIVERSITY OF

PENNSYLVANIA

**PHILADELPHIA,
PENNSYLVANIA**

Anyone in the medical community will tell you that the Hospital of the University of Pennsylvania is rated at the top in just about every category that matters in modern medicine. Over 20% of the physicians there, for example, are listed in the second edition of *The Best Doctors in America*, the most comprehensive survey of outstanding doctors in the U.S. Research grants in 1993 totaled almost $150 million, making Pennsylvania one of the most important medical centers in the world.

HUP provides a comprehensive range of inpatient and outpatient services, including highly specialized tertiary and quaternary levels of care. As a regional referral center and teaching institution, HUP provides sophisticated diagnostic and therapeutic radiology and clinical laboratory services. HUP is designated as a Level I Regional Resource Trauma Center by the Pennsylvania Trauma System Foundation and is capable of transporting patients in need of immediate care via HUP's PennSTAR program air ambulance. PennSTAR provides inter-hospital air medical transportation for patients requiring the technology of care available only at a tertiary/quaternary care facility. The hospital's Emergency Department is one of the busiest in the city. Adjacent to the emergency room is a walk-in clinic, where patients with non-urgent medical problems are treated on a first-come, first-served basis. HUP is the only Delaware

Valley hospital that performs transplants of all major organs—its kidney transplant program celebrates its 28th anniversary in 1994. HUP is also an international referral center for complicated heart problems. In addition, HUP houses one of only 28 cancer centers in the United States to be designated a Comprehensive Cancer Center by the National Cancer Institute.

Anticipating changes in the health care environment, as well as the needs of the University Medical Center, the University established the University of Pennsylvania Health System in July of 1993. The components of the system are: the Medical Center (comprising the School of Medicine and HUP), a new integrated provider network (including the Clinical Care Associates of the University of Pennsylvania, which provides primary care services to the community), a managed care entity, and a management services organization to meet the challenge of a capitated environment. The network will expand the availability of Penn-trained doctors at the primary care level.

SPECIAL FACILITIES AND PROGRAMS

HUP is home to 72 specialized centers, institutes and programs. Among the more noteworthy is the hospital's Cancer Center, which conducts cancer research and provides advanced multi-method treatment programs for breast cancer, lung cancer, head and neck cancer, leukemia, lymphoma, pigmented lesions and melanoma, gynecological cancers, and urologic cancers. There is also a bone marrow transplantation program.

The Breast Cancer Program has earned an international reputation for treating early breast cancer with lumpectomy and radiotherapy as an alternative to mastectomy. In conjunction with the Breast Cancer Program, the Radiation Therapy Department of HUP, one of the most active in the country in both treatment of patients and training of radiation therapists, has a national reputation in research in and treatment of breast cancer following lumpectomy.

The world-renowned Pigmented Lesion Clinic and Melanoma Program is one of the foremost

AT A GLANCE

Beds: 725
Occupancy Rate: 81%
Average Patient Count: 585
Average Patient Stay: 7.6 days
Annual Admissions: 30,073
Births: 2,707
Outpatient Clinic Visits: 470,901
Emergency Room/Trauma Center Visits: 53,747

HOSPITAL PERSONNEL
Physicians: 610
  Board Certified: 98%
Residents: 1,031
Registered Nurses: 1,056
  BS Degree or Higher: 731

ROOM CHARGES (PER DIEM)
Private: $1,020
Semiprivate: $939
ICU: $1,759

ADDRESS
3400 Spruce Street
Philadelphia, PA 19104

TELEPHONE
(215) 662-4000

patient care and research efforts in the evaluation and treatment of moles. The clinic, in the Department of Dermatology, is the largest facility in the United States for the diagnosis and treatment of melanoma. The hospital is the only major medical center between New York and Washington, DC using Mohs surgery for the removal of cutaneous malignant tumor tissue. It is also one of the few centers in the United States using phototherapy to treat psoriasis and other light-related diseases.

In vitro fertilization and endoscopic surgery were also pioneered at HUP, and the hospital is one of six in the United States to be designated by the National Institutes of Health to conduct infertility research and treatment. The Division of Human Reproduction was among the first to attempt to treat tubal disease with microsurgery. High-risk obstetrics involving patients threatened by diabetes mellitus, Rh factor, and premature birth is another major area of concentration.

HUP continues to be a leader in imaging technology. Its radiologists have contributed to the development of MRI (magnetic resonance imaging), PET (positron emission tomography), MRS (magnetic resonance spectroscopy) and CT (computerized tomography).

The Scheie Eye Institute, founded by Dr. Harold G. Scheie, and known throughout the world for its contribution to vision research and treatment, is also a part of the University of Pennsylvania Medical Center.

HUP receives patients from all over the world to be treated for complicated heart problems. For instance, HUP doctors developed the "Pennsylvania Peel," a surgical technique used the world over to cure life-threatening arrhythmias. Comprehensive cardiac services range from evaluation to heart transplantation.

One of the best facilities for hip replacement and revision, HUP is also renowned for ambitious multidisciplinary efforts in its metabolic bone disease unit. Capacitive coupling, using electrical impulses to stimulate bone growth to nonunion fractures, was developed in the Department of Orthopaedic Surgery. Joint transplantation, available in only three other centers in North America, is being developed at the Joint Reconstruction Center.

The Department of Psychiatry provides comprehensive consultation, evaluation, and management of all psychiatric disorders, including acute psychoses. A number of specialty programs, including Affective Disorders, Brain and Behavior Research, Geropsychiatry, and Pain Management, provide advanced diagnostic evaluation and acute care, both inpatient and outpatient. Cognitive therapy, a technique for relieving negative emotions, was developed here.

Programs in Dental Medicine include an interdisciplinary group of dentists and physicians specializing in the diagnosis and treatment of facial pain and temporomandibular joint disease; a section on cosmetic and functional deformities of the teeth, mouth, and jaws; and the use of maxillofacial prosthetics to replace facial structures lost to disease, surgery, or accident.

The Otorhinolaryngology Department has pioneered developments for successful cochlear implants. The Smell and Taste Center's 12-stage air-dilution human olfactometer—the only one in the world—provides computer-based measurement of nasal airflow and taste functions, allowing researchers to study the smell and taste functions.

The Institute for Environmental Medicine serves as a regional focus for hyperbaric therapy. Besides research, these facilities are used for the emergency treatment of patients requiring exposure to increased oxygen pressures, as in the treatment of air embolism, the bends, carbon monoxide poisoning, or gas gangrene. They are also used for elective treatment of specific chronic defects of healing, such as in osteoradionecrosis and osteomyelitis.

HUP offers the only program in the Delaware Valley that performs transplants of all major organs—kidney, heart, liver, lung, and pancreas. It also performs autologous bone marrow transplants for hematologic malignancies and some solid tumors. Kidney dialysis is provided on an inpatient and outpatient basis.

MEDICAL SPECIALTIES

Allergy and Immunology, Anesthesiology, Cardiology, Dental Medicine, Dermatology, Diabetes, Emergency Medicine, Endocrinology, Gastrointestinal Medicine, General Internal Medicine, Hematology/Oncology, Infectious Diseases, Neurology, Obstetrics/Gynecology, Ophthalmology, Orthopaedic Surgery, Otorhinolaryngology, Pathology and Laboratory Medicine, Pediatrics, Psychiatry, Pulmonary and Critical Care Medicine, Radiation Oncology, Radiology, Rehabilitation Medicine, Renal Electrolyte, Rheumatology, and Surgery.

WELL-KNOWN SPECIALISTS

- Dr. Abass Alavi   *Nuclear medicine; specialist in treatment of the brain*
- Dr. Leon Axel   *Cardiovascular radiology; specialist in MRI*
- Dr. Clyde F. Barker   *Surgery; specialist in transplantation*
- Dr. Stuart L. Fine   *Ophthalmology; specialist in medical retinal diseases*
- Dr. Barbara Fowble   *Radiation oncology; specialist in breast cancer*
- Dr. Thomas A. Gennarelli   *Neurosurgery; specialist in trauma*
- Dr. Alan M. Gewirtz   *Medical oncology/hematology; specialist in bleeding disorders, thrombosis*
- Dr. Cynthia Guzzo   *Dermatology; specialist in psoriasis*
- Dr. Daniel G. Haller   *Medical oncology/hematology; specialist in gastrointestinal oncology*
- Dr. Mark A. Kelley   *Medicine; specialist in pulmonary and critical care*
- Dr. David W. Kennedy   *Otolaryngology; specialist in sinus and nasal surgery*
- Dr. Paul A. Lotke   *Orthopaedic surgery*
- Dr. David E. Pleasure   *Neurology*
- Dr. Ernest F. Rosato   *General surgery; specialist in gastroenterology*
- Dr. Donald H. Silberberg   *Neurology; specialist in infectious and demyelinating diseases*

- Dr. Peter J. Snyder   *Endocrinology and metabolism; specialist in neuroendocrinology*
- Dr. Richard W. Tureck   *Obstetrics/gynecology; specialist in reproductive endocrinology*
- Dr. Keith N. Van Arsdalen   *Urology; specialist in endo-urology*
- Dr. Richard Whittington   *Radiation oncology; specialist in gastrointestinal cancer*
- Dr. James M. Wilson   *Director, Institute of Human Gene Therapy*
- Dr. Burton Zweiman   *Medicine; specialist in allergy/immunology*

PATIENT SATISFACTION

HUP conducts regular patient satisfaction surveys through an outside research agency. Data is collected by sending a questionnaire to 50% of patients within five to seven days after discharge. In the most recent survey, respondents rated HUP "very good" or "good" on 85% of the items listed. Professional services provided by physicians and nurses; social service personnel; and physical, respiratory and occupational therapists received the highest ratings.

RESEARCH

In 1993, the School of Medicine ranked fifth nationally in NIH (National Institutes of Health) funding to medical schools, receiving more NIH funding than all other Philadelphia-based medical schools combined. Penn received 1,273 sponsored research awards, totaling $149 million. NIH support for the year totaled $117.6 million.

The School of Medicine has active research programs in every area of modern biomedical research, with major emphasis in molecular genetics, cancer, biomedical imaging, diabetes, immunology, infertility, reproductive genetics, neurogenetics, and behavioral disorders.

Through the Institute for Human Gene Therapy, a current major focus at HUP is gene therapy, which promises to be the key to stopping many deadly diseases, including cystic fibrosis, AIDS and cancer. In addition, recent discoveries at HUP allow a transplant process in animal models that has the potential to prevent the development of diabetes in humans.

ADMISSIONS POLICY

All patients at HUP must be admitted by a staff physician. Self-referring patients and physicians should call (800) 789-7366 or 662-7366 in Philadelphia.

Although HUP does not have a specific number of beds for, or a specific dollar amount of, indigent care, the hospital has an open-door policy, so that no one in need of medical attention is turned away because of money. In fiscal year 1993, the total value of charity care was over $72.6 million.

MILTON S. HERSHEY

MEDICAL CENTER

Heart disease continues to be the leading cause of death in the United States, claiming approximately one million lives each year. However, diagnostic and therapeutic procedures to prevent death from cardiac disease have greatly improved. The concept of replacing the function of the human heart with a mechanical substitute is far from new, but few hospitals in the country have been as involved with artificial organs as University Hospital at the Milton S. Hershey Medical Center.

In medical circles, perhaps the best-known artificial organ is the "Penn State Heart" designed and developed by Dr. William S. Pierce and members of a research team of the Pennsylvania State University Colleges of Medicine and Engineering. A prototype of the Penn State Heart was first used in December of 1976, and since then has been implanted in more than 250 patients. The present version of the Penn State Heart made its debut in October of 1985, sustaining a patient's life for 11 days. Since then, the longest a patient's life has been sustained with the heart is 390 days. The air-powered artificial heart was designed specifically as a "bridging device" until a human donor heart becomes available. Refinements in the Penn State Heart make it significantly different from artificial hearts designed elsewhere, and it has been used in more than 15 other health care institutions in the U.S. and abroad.

PENNSYLVANIA STATE
UNIVERSITY

HERSHEY, PENNSYLVANIA

THE CONCEPT OF
REPLACING THE FUNCTION
OF THE HUMAN HEART WITH
A MECHANICAL SUBSTITUTE
IS FAR FROM NEW, BUT FEW
HOSPITALS IN THE COUNTRY
HAVE BEEN AS INVOLVED
WITH ARTIFICIAL ORGANS
AS UNIVERSITY HOSPITAL AT
THE MILTON S. HERSHEY
MEDICAL CENTER.

Research is only one part of the work performed at the Milton S. Hershey Medical Center. It also serves as a full-service tertiary care institution, the only one between Pittsburgh and Philadelphia. Hershey is a referral center for patients sent by their physicians in communities throughout Pennsylvania, and also provides primary care for residents of the surrounding area. It is also an accredited regional Resource Trauma Center, with additional qualifications in pediatric trauma.

In 1963, the M. S. Hershey Foundation offered $50 million to Pennsylvania State University to establish a medical school in Hershey. With this grant and $21.3 million from the U.S. Public Health Service, the University built a medical school, teaching hospital, and research center. Ground was broken in 1966, and Penn State's Milton S. Hershey Medical Center opened its doors to its first students in 1967 and accepted the first patients at University Hospital in 1970. The medical center is comprised of Penn State's College of Medicine, University Hospital, and Penn State University Children's Hospital. The medical center has about 5,500 employees and enrolls more than 500 students annually. The newly expanded University Physicians Center is connected to the hospitals and consists of a multispecialty group practice of University Hospitals' physicians. A number of satellite practice sites in central Pennsylvania have been established, and others are planned.

To accommodate continued growth in the number of patients who seek care at University Hospitals and to prepare for new academic programs, the medical center is completing a $214 million expansion. Recent construction includes a seven-story hospital addition and main entrance; a seven-story Biomedical Research Building; expansion of both the University Physicians Center and Center for Emergency Medical Services; and several smaller projects.

SPECIAL FACILITIES AND PROGRAMS

The 467-bed University Hospitals are responsible for providing high-quality medical care while serving as settings for educational and research programs. The University Hospitals have a number of specialized centers, including the Penn State Cardiovascular Center and Center for Primary Care, as well as others for sports medicine, newborn intensive and surgical care, hemophilia, sleep disorders, muscular dystrophy, and emergency medical services. The hospitals also have comprehensive programs in high-risk obstetrics, infertility, oncology, diabetes, multiple sclerosis, genetics, and spinal cord injuries.

The Neonatal Intensive Care Unit serves as the regional center for central Pennsylvania in the treatment of critically ill newborns whose problems range from premature and respiratory distress to congenital heart defects requiring open heart surgery. University Hospital is one of four to participate in the Neonatal Surgery Program of the Pennsylvania Department of Health, established to treat infants with congenital malformations of the intestinal, respiratory and urinary tracts. The Neonatal Unit has 26 beds, and more than 700 infants are referred annually from more than 50 hospitals in 20 counties. The hospital also owns and operates its own mobile neonatal intensive care unit to transport neonatal infants.

The Pediatric and Adult Heart Surgery program has been designated as one of four official centers in the Commonwealth of Pennsylvania for state-sponsored programs in child cardiac care. Patients of all ages with either congenital or acquired diseases are managed in the program, and more than 500 operations are performed annually.

The Child Psychiatry Unit provides comprehensive diagnostic assessment and intensive treatment for children ages 3 to 13 who suffer from a variety of behavior and conduct disorders, including anorexia nervosa, child abuse, depression and suicide, childhood psychosis, autism, learning disorders, and hyperactivity. This unit, in addition to promoting a homelike atmosphere, includes several innovative design features, such as a closed nursing observation area for viewing children with special medical problems and audiovisual therapy—taping children and their parents together—for the purpose of assessing and monitoring treatment.

Adult Cancer is treated by faculty from many departments. Scientific programs have been established in the divisions of oncology, gynecologic oncology, hematology, endocrinology, otorhinolaryngology, and plastic and reconstructive surgery. Established protocols and investigational methods are used to treat more than 1,000 new patients each year with the primary diagnosis of cancer.

The University Hospital also serves as the center for the Central Pennsylvania Oncology Group, an outreach program that includes 91 physicians and nurses affiliated with 32 community hospitals.

The Department of Gynecology and Obstetrics offers a wide range of outpatient and inpatient diagnostic and treatment regimens, including evaluation for problems relating to endocrinology—infertility, premenstrual syndrome and menopause. For women who have gynecological cancer, the department provides complete services, including evaluation and all forms of treatment. In addition, the

AT A GLANCE

Beds: 504
Occupancy Rate: 80.9%
Average Patient Count: 408
Average Patient Stay: 8.2 days
Annual Admissions: 17,587
Physician Office Visits:
    242,302
Emergency Room/Trauma
    Center Visits: 28,825

HOSPITAL PERSONNEL
Physicians: 312
    Board Certified: 270
Residents: 378
Registered Nurses: 1,029
    BS Degree: 49%

ROOM CHARGES (PER DIEM)
Private: $460–$605
ICU: $1,550

ADDRESS
P.O. Box 850
Hershey, PA 17033

TELEPHONE
(717) 534-8521

staff's clinical expertise includes family-centered care for normal and high-risk pregnancies, family planning, general gynecology, and gynecologic urology.

University Hospital is the designated site of the Capital Area Poison Center, which serves residents throughout south central Pennsylvania. As a service of the University Hospital, the poison center maintains a comprehensive collection of information on product formulation and treatment of poisons. As an affiliate of the American Association of Poison Control Centers, the center functions as an information and referral network for seven area hospitals. In 1993, the poison center responded to more than 31,000 calls.

The Short Stay Unit offers treatment on an outpatient basis, which is usually more convenient and less costly for the patient. The Pain Management Clinic is part of this unit. A program of the department of anesthesiology, the clinic combines various specialties in the diagnosis and treatment of people with persistent pain problems. The two main techniques used by physicians within the pain clinic are TENS (transcutaneous electrical nerve stimulus) and biofeedback. TENS produces relief from pain and also prompts the release of endorphins, a naturally occurring bodily substance that inhibits the transmission of pain by the nerves. Biofeedback teaches patients how to knowingly control parts of the body not normally under conscious control. While this technique helps in the management of pain, it can even alter the patient's perception of pain.

Within the psychiatric department, the Sleep Disorders Clinic and Laboratory is one of the most advanced clinics of its kind in the world. It has achieved breakthroughs in the diagnosis and treatment of insomnia, narcolepsy, and night terrors, as well as sleep apnea, a condition in which oxygen in the blood of a sleeping person drops to dangerously low levels.

Senior citizens receive complete psychiatric and medical examinations, as well as neuropsychological testing, in the comprehensive psychogeriatric outpatient program that is part of the psychiatric department. University Hospital is designing an inpatient geriatric psychiatry unit and developing a partial hospitalization program for geriatric patients.

In 1982, Pennsylvania State University assumed control of the Elizabethtown Hospital and Rehabilitation Center, a 50-bed hospital providing rehabilitation services for severe and complicated disabilities. Elizabethtown offers comprehensive programs in spina bifida, brain surgery, pediatric orthopaedics, neurodevelopmental disability, and spinal cord injury. The orthopedic service provides a variety of family-oriented services to correct or prevent deformities in children. The neurodevelopmental service treats learning and developmental problems, such as cerebral palsy and traumatic head injury. Adolescent and adult patients with spinal cord injuries and deterioration receive rehabilitation services. Plans have been made to relocate the hospital to the Hershey Medical Center campus. In 1993, the University Hospital Rehabilitation Center (UHRC) received a three-year reaccreditation from the Commission on Accreditation of Rehabilitation Facilities (CARF). UHRC successfully met the high standards of performance in Comprehensive Inpatient Rehabilitation: Hospitals; Spinal Cord

Injury Program; and Brain Injury Program: Medical Inpatient—Adult/Pediatric. No other institution in south central Pennsylvania has achieved such accreditation.

The Department of Anesthesia's Simulation Development and Cognitive Science Laboratory was honored by the American Society of Anesthesia's Anesthesia Patient Safety Foundation.

The Department of Family and Community Medicine has received a Robert Wood Johnson planning grant to fund its Generalist Physician Initiative. The project's goal is to increase the percentage of College of Medicine graduates who choose a career path in general internal medicine, family and community medicine, or general pediatrics to 50% by 1988. These graduates will help to alleviate the shortage of primary care providers in rural, small-town, and medically underserved areas.

University Hospital has increased its transplantation programs, performing about 150 procedures per year. Heart, kidney, pancreas (including combined pancreas/kidney), liver, and cornea transplants are offered. Efforts to establish an autologous bone marrow transplant program are underway and the program is expected to begin operation in 1995.

MEDICAL SPECIALTIES

Anesthesiology, Cardiology, Cardiothoracic Surgery, Dermatology, Emergency Medicine, Endocrinology, Family and Community Medicine, Gastroenterology, Hematology, Infectious Diseases, Internal Medicine, Neonatology, Nephrology, Neurology, Neurosurgery, Obstetrics/Gynecology, Oncology, Ophthalmology, Orthopedics, Pediatric Neurosurgery, Pediatric Surgery, Pediatrics, Pulmonary/Critical Care Medicine, Psychiatry, Radiology, Reproductive Endocrinology and Fertility, Rheumatology, Surgery, and Urology.

WELL-KNOWN SPECIALISTS

- Dr. George W. Blankenship, Jr. *Ophthalmology; specialist in retinal diseases and vitreo-retinal surgery*
- Dr. Cheston M. Berlin, Jr. *Chair of American Academy of Pediatrics' Committee on Drugs; chief of general pediatrics*
- Dr. M. Elaine Eyster *Hematology; specialist in AIDS/hemophilia research*
- Dr. Anthony Kales *Psychiatry; director of the Sleep Research and Treatment Center*
- Dr. Gordon L. Kauffman *Gastroenterologic surgery; chief of surgery*
- Dr. Kenneth L. Koch *Gastroenterology; specialist in motion sickness research*
- Dr. Thomas M. Krummel *Pediatric surgery; specialist in wound healing research*
- Dr. Rodrigue Mortel *Specialist in endometrial cancer*
- Dr. William S. Pierce *Cardiothoracic surgery; pioneer in developing the Penn State Heart*

- Dr. Herbert Y. Reynolds *General pulmonary and critical care; specialist in asthma*
- Dr. Michael T. Snider *Respiratory and intensive care; specialist in artificial lung research*
- Dr. Brian L. Thiele *Surgery; specialist in vascular surgery*
- Dr. Steven J. Wassner *Pediatrics; specialist in pediatric nephrology*
- Dr. Mark D. Widome *Pediatrics; chair of American Academy of Pediatrics' Council on Child and Adolescent Health*
- Dr. Clifford W. Zwillich *Pulmonary critical care; specialist in pulmonary disease and critical care*

PATIENT SATISFACTION

The latest patient survey results show high satisfaction ratings for Hershey Medical Center. Ninety-four percent of outpatient respondents considered themselves "very" or "somewhat" satisfied with their visit. Ninety-seven percent of the outpatients would recommend the services to a friend or a family member.

On inpatient service, Hershey has consistently rated between 3.7 and 3.9 on a 4.0 scale (4.0 = very satisfied) in overall patient satisfaction over the past two years. Ratings on "likelihood to choose University Hospital again" have ranged between 3.65 and 3.75. On "likelihood to recommend," the ratings have been between 3.7 and 3.8. All of these are higher than the average of other Mid-Atlantic hospitals.

RESEARCH

As part of Penn State, Hershey conducts basic and clinical research in many different fields of medicine. Cancer research at Hershey is internationally acclaimed; awards in this area alone approached $7 million. In all, standard contract dollars in research at the medical center totalled over $36 million in 1992-93.

Currently, a $5.4 million, three-year National Institutes of Health contract is enabling Gerson Rosenberg, Ph.D., and William Pierce, M.D., to continue work on developing a permanently implantable electric heart. They are known worldwide for their air-driven Penn State Heart and ventricular assist device, which is routinely used in patients awaiting heart transplantation.

Research on Prader-Willi syndrome by Maria Mascari, Ph.D., and Peter Rogan, Ph.D., has resulted in a new test for the disease and has linked it to a genetic defect.

A study by Thomas Lloyd, Ph.D., showing that extra calcium increases bone density in adolescent girls, may help prevent later osteoporosis.

Motion sickness studies for NASA have been done in the gastroenterology lab by Dr. Kenneth Koch. Koch is known nationally as an authority on treating motion sickness.

AIDS research by Dr. M. Elaine Eyster has been recognized nationally for its advancement in treatment of HIV-positive hemophiliacs.

Dr. Ernest Manders' work with soft tissue expansion has changed the lives of patients in need of reconstructive surgery, from facial reconstruction to treatment for baldness.

ADMISSIONS POLICY

Most patients are admitted to Hershey via doctor referral. However, patients are also admitted through the clinics. Some of these clinics see patients on a walk-in basis without an appointment.

Urgent and emergency patients are admitted regardless of their financial condition. Elective admissions not fully covered by insurance would be requested to pay any difference in fees. About $1.3 million in indigent care was provided in 1993.

PRESBYTERIAN

UNIVERSITY

HOSPITAL

To the people who live and work in Pittsburgh, ready access to a number of first-rate hospitals is an important reason why their city has come to be regarded as one of the most desirable places to live in the nation. Unlike Boston, Houston, or New York, Pittsburgh is not a city most people think of as a leading medical enclave, but doctors and those in hospital administration know that in recent years Presbyterian University Hospital, the principal teaching institution of the University of Pittsburgh School of Medicine, has emerged as one of America's outstanding medical facilities.

Although researcher Jonas Salk developed his polio vaccine here in the 1950s, Presbyterian was basically a highly regarded teaching hospital and a well-known regional tertiary care center. However, in 1980, a surgeon named Thomas Starzl arrived at Presby, as it is called, and almost single-handedly transformed the hospital into one of the world's foremost organ transplantation centers. A man of enormous energy and imagination, Starzl was the key figure in designing the techniques used in liver transplantation. He was also instrumental in developing the drug which suppresses the body's natural tendency to reject a new organ. The impact of his work can perhaps be best appreciated by quoting a dean of the UCLA medical school where Starzl had originally planned to bring his program: "The loss of

The Best Hospitals in America

Tom Starzl was the greatest recruiting loss to UCLA in thirty years."

Although transplantation was the key to putting Presby on the national map, it is hardly the only specialty that ranks among the best in the country. A July 1993 survey in *U.S. News & World Report* ranked the University of Pittsburgh Medical Center among the best in the following specialties: AIDS, cancer, cardiology, endocrinology, geriatrics, neurology, orthopedics, otolaryngology, and rheumatology. Other surveys have cited gastroenterology and psychiatry at UPMC for recognition as well. In addition, physicians practicing at Presby are frequently cited in magazines and newspapers as leading practitioners in their fields. More than 100 UPMC specialists were listed in the most recent edition of *The Best Doctors in America*.

The University of Pittsburgh Medical Center (UPMC), with 1,221 beds, is a regional and national medical resource. It includes Presbyterian University Hospital, Montefiore University Hospital, Western Psychiatric Institute and Clinic, the Pittsburgh Cancer Institute, Falk Clinic, the Eye & Ear Institute, and the schools of the health sciences. These schools include medicine, nursing, health and rehabilitation sciences, dental medicine, pharmacy, and the Graduate School of Public Health.

In 1993, UPMC had approximately 32,000 medical/surgical admissions. Of these, 48% came from outside of Allegheny County, where UPMC is located. About 15% came from out of state.

SPECIAL FACILITIES AND PROGRAMS

The UPMC organ transplant program is the world's largest and busiest. On the average, one transplant is performed every 12 hours. The medical center performs the most liver and lung transplants, and implants more artificial hearts than any other institution in the United States. It is one of the only centers that transplant both whole pancreases and pancreatic islet cells. Its surgeons have the most extensive experience in the world in transplantation of intestinal and multivisceral grafts. UPMC performed more than 1,200

AT A GLANCE

Beds: 1,221
Occupancy Rate: 84%
Average Patient Count: 939
Average Patient Stay: 10.4 days
Annual Admissions: 32,807
Outpatient Clinic Visits: 371,500
Emergency Room/Trauma Center Visits: 56,295

HOSPITAL PERSONNEL
Physicians: 1,295
  Board Certified: 935
Residents: 564
Registered Nurses: 1,910
  BS Degree: 681

ROOM CHARGES (PER DIEM)
Private: $585–$655
Semiprivate: $525
ICU: $2,530

ADDRESS
200 Lothrop Street
Pittsburgh, PA 15213

TELEPHONE
(412) 647-8762

transplantation procedures in 1993. Of these, about 750 involved liver procedures, either liver-only transplants or transplants of livers and other organs. Cardiothoracic transplants numbered 136, kidney transplants 202, and 86 cellular transplants.

The Pittsburgh Cancer Institute (PCI) is designated by the National Cancer Institute as a Comprehensive Cancer Center. Created in 1984, the Institute is noted for cancer diagnosis, treatment, research, and education in an environment that fosters collaboration among scientists and clinicians across a broad spectrum of expertise. PCI is one the country's foremost centers in investigating treatment strategies using biological response modifiers, gene therapy, and unique and promising cancer vaccines. An important figure in cancer research is Dr. Bernard Fisher, a leader in developing clinical trials for treating breast and colorectal cancers.

The PCI Outpatient Clinic is a large, comprehensive walk-in clinic which sees 1,200 patients each month. In this setting, patients can receive chemotherapy or diagnostic and follow-up care. Patients are seen by a team that includes physicians, oncology nurses, pharmacists, psychologists, social workers, dieticians, dentists, financial counselors and others. The clinic facilities include specialized treatment rooms, an in-house pharmacy, and a patient/family kitchen. The clinic is near a PCI educational room that provides literature and videocassettes on cancer management and support. In addition, the clinic is next to a UPMC salon for those patients with hair-care needs.

The PCI Comprehensive Breast Care Center provides services including breast imaging, diagnostic services, health education, multidisciplinary treatment planning and psychological support services. Breast imaging services include screening and diagnostic mammograms. If a diagnostic or screening mammogram detects an abnormality, further tests (ultrasound-guided needle aspirations and needle biopsy or stereotactic needle biopsy) may be performed, most during the same day of the initial visit. Other diagnostic testing includes sonograms, ductograms, and pneumocystograms. A preliminary diagnosis is generally available the same day.

Led by Dr. Peter Jannetta, who developed a procedure called microvascular decompression to treat severe facial pain, cranial nerve dysfunction, and hypertension, the Department of Neurological Surgery is distinguished by research and patient care in ten specialized areas. Among them are the Specialized Neurological Surgical Center, which was the first in the country to use the gamma knife clinically to treat previously inoperable lesions in the brain without the need for surgical incision, and the Center for Cranial Base Surgery, which also was the first of its kind in the country.

Since becoming an accredited Level I Trauma Center in 1986, the UPMC Trauma Center has grown significantly—in the past year alone, by 27%. The Center has three dedicated trauma treatment rooms, X-ray, and computerized tomography (CT) scan. In addition, two hospital units are dedicated for trauma patients, with another scheduled to open later this year. Within the Emergency

Department is the Chest Pain Evaluation Center for emergency treatment of patients with chest pain. Because of its resources and size, the Trauma Center never diverts patients. It also benefits from the availability of numerous specialists, including orthopedic trauma surgeons and neurotrauma surgeons.

The Heart Institute diagnoses and treats potentially fatal heart problems. Services include the Chest Pain Evaluation Center, the Heart and Vascular Disease Prevention Center, cardiopulmonary rehabilitation, exercise physiology, treatment of congestive heart failure, cardiac catheterization, electrophysiology, and nuclear cardiology. The High Risk Heart Surgery Program is for patients who may be at risk for open heart surgery or who have been turned down for surgery elsewhere.

The Arthritis Center offers research-based care for patients with rheumatoid and osteoarthritis, as well as connective tissue diseases such as scleroderma. The Benedum Geriatric Center has outpatient services for the frail elderly who are at risk for institutionalization. Physicians from the center provide medical services to Canterbury Place, a skilled nursing and residential care facility affiliated with UPMC. Other specialized clinics include the Microvascular/Cranial Nerve Center, the Cerebrovascular Surgery Center, the Comprehensive Spine Center, the Toxicology Treatment Program, the Musculoskeletal Institute, and the Center for Sports Medicine.

MEDICAL SPECIALTIES

AIDS, Anesthesiology, Cancer, Cardiology, Cardiothoracic Surgery, Dental Medicine, Dermatology, Emergency and Trauma, Endocrinology, Environmental/Occupational Health and Toxicology, Epilepsy, Gastroenterology, Genetics, Geriatrics, Hematology/Oncology, Hypertension and Clinical Pharmacology, Immunopathology, Infectious Diseases, Medicine, Molecular Diagnostics, Neurology, Neurosurgery, Nuclear Medicine, Ophthalmology, Orthopaedic Surgery, Otolaryngology, Pathology, Plastic Surgery, Psychiatry, Pulmonary Medicine, Radiology, Rehabilitation Medicine, Renal-Electrolyte Medicine, Rheumatology, Sports Medicine, Surgery, Transplantation, Urology and Urological Surgery, and Vascular Surgery.

WELL-KNOWN SPECIALISTS

- Dr. Edward D. Ball   *Hematology/oncology; specialist in bone marrow transplantation*
- Dr. John Barranger   *Human genetics; specialist in treatment of Gaucher's disease*
- Dr. Robert J. Corry   *Transplant surgery; specialist in pancreatic transplantation*
- Dr. Bartley Griffith   *Cardiothoracic surgery; specialist in heart and lung transplantation*
- Dr. Thomas Hakala   *Urology; specialist in renal transplantation and urologic cancer*

- Dr. Robert Hardestry   *Cardiothoracic surgery; specialist in heart and lung transplantation*
- Dr. L. Dade Lunsford   *Neurosurgery; specialist in treatment of brain lesions*
- Dr. Thomas A. Medsger, Jr.   *Rheumatology; specialist in connective tissue diseases*
- Dr. Jorge Railela   *Transplant medicine; specialist in liver disease*
- Dr. Donald L. Trump   *Medical oncology/hematology/pharmacology; specialist in genito-urinary cancer*
- Dr. Savio L-Y Wo   *Orthopaedic surgery; specialist in biomechanics*

PATIENT SATISFACTION

Approximately 60% of all inpatients (with the exception of intensive care units) are surveyed upon discharge. In addition, all patients in the following areas are surveyed: Emergency Department, Same Day Surgery, Intensive Care Units, and Ambulatory Care. On a five point scale from excellent to poor, the majority of areas within UPMC receive a 4, or "very good" rating.

RESEARCH

The University of Pittsburgh Medical Center is involved in 1,299 research projects totaling more than $599 million.

Through research at the McGowan Center for Artificial Heart and Lung Research, patients with end-stage heart disease are implanted with temporary heart assist devices as a bridge to heart transplantation. The UPMC is the only center in the country with FDA approval to discharge patients implanted with the Novacor device while they await transplantation.

Use of the immunosuppressant cyclosporine was key to the UPMC's early achievements in transplantation. Beginning in 1982, the UPMC conducted the original exclusive trials on the drug, which enabled successful transplantation to occur on a larger scale.

While researchers continue to study other potential immunosuppressants, they are also investigating new applications for the drugs currently available. Cardiothoracic transplant surgeons are studying the use of aerosolized cyclosporine to control rejection in lung transplant patients.

Pioneering work at Pittsburgh altered the standard treatment for breast cancer, improving survival rates while replacing radical surgery (mastectomy) with less extensive procedures (lumpectomy and segmental mastectomy). In 1992, the National Surgical Adjuvant Breast and Bowel Project began the first large-scale breast cancer prevention trial. Sixteen thousand healthy women at increased risk for breast cancer will be randomized to receive at least five years of tamoxifen or placebo. In addition to evaluating the effects of tamoxifen on reducing the incidence of breast cancers, cardiovascular events and bone marrow fractures will also be monitored.

The PCI has a core grant from National Cancer Institute (NCI), making it one of only 27 NCI-designated comprehensive cancer centers in the country. The grant provides support for translating clinical and basic sciences research into innovative cancer prevention, diagnosis, and treatment methods. PCI has more than 100 active clinical protocols for various cancers.

Other significant federal grants awarded to UPMC researchers include the Prostate Cancer Prevention Trial for men at increased risk of this disease; the Prostate, Lung, Colorectal, and Ovarian Cancer Screening Trial, designed to determine whether certain cancer screening tests save lives; grants for Specialized Programs of Research Excellence in lung cancer and gastrointestinal cancer; and the Women's Health Initiative, a 15-year commitment to advancing research on chronic diseases (including breast cancer) that affect women.

Other areas of major research include AIDS, Genetics, Geriatrics, Trauma and Critical Care Medicine, Pain Evaluation and Treatment, Ophthalmology, and Otolaryngology.

ADMISSIONS POLICY

UPMC patients are admitted either through physician's referrals, preferred provider organizations, the Emergency Department, or through Falk Clinic, the UPMC's outpatient facility. Patients without a physician will have one from the hospital staff assigned to them.

A patient without insurance or full means to pay completes a medical assistance application and/or a free care application. If the patient does not qualify for free care or medical assistance, he will be considered a self-pay patient and payment terms are set up if necessary. About $28 million worth of indigent care was provided in 1993.

PATIENT/FAMILY ACCOMMODATIONS

Families of patients who have long hospital stays can take advantage of low cost housing at Family House or Family House Inn. Rates at Family House are $15/night/single and $20/night/double. Rates at Family House Inn are $25/night.

There are three other hotels close to the UPMC with 127 private rooms, most with private baths and with common living areas and kitchens.

THOMAS JEFFERSON

UNIVERSITY

HOSPITAL

PHILADELPHIA, PENNSYLVANIA

Thomas Jefferson University is a major academic health center that includes the largest private medical school in the country, as well as schools for nursing, allied health fields, and graduate studies. Jefferson provides outstanding medical care through its University Hospital and the affiliated Ford Road and Children's Rehabilitation Hospitals. With 19 departments of clinical specialties and more than 1,000 staff physicians, Jefferson was recently placed among the top one percent of hospitals across the country by *U.S. News & World Report* in most of the areas covered by its "Best Hospitals" survey. In addition, almost 60 Thomas Jefferson physicians were listed in the second edition of *The Best Doctors in America*. With historic roots dating back to 1824, Jefferson also has a long and distinguished record in biomedical research. Jefferson researchers were responsible for the development of the first heart-lung machine, which made open heart surgery possible; the invention of the first artificial tendon for reconstructive hand surgery; and the discovery of erythropoietin, an important kidney hormone.

Philadelphia physician George McClellan founded Jefferson Medical College in 1824. In 1877, a 125-bed hospital was opened, one of the first in the nation affiliated with a medical school. From these beginnings, a 13-acre center-city campus has grown, housing the hospital, educational facilities, and research

WITH 19 DEPARTMENTS OF CLINICAL SPECIALTIES AND MORE THAN 1,000 STAFF PHYSICIANS, JEFFERSON WAS RECENTLY PLACED AMONG THE TOP ONE PERCENT OF HOSPITALS ACROSS THE COUNTRY BY *U.S. NEWS & WORLD REPORT* IN MOST OF THE AREAS COVERED BY ITS "BEST HOSPITALS" SURVEY.

The Best Hospitals in America

laboratories. The Thomas Jefferson University Hospital is the largest and most visible part of this complex. Housed in the Gibbon Building, which was opened in 1978, the hospital is an advanced facility. Each patient floor functions as a mini-hospital with its own pharmacy, admissions office, and disease identification and treatment facilities. Other floors house doctors' offices where outpatients are treated. Thomas Jefferson University Hospital is the second largest in the city of Philadelphia.

Jefferson's outstanding research accomplishments have supported academic training at Thomas Jefferson University almost from the beginning. Nineteen Jefferson teachers and graduates have been physicians to U.S. presidents, including Thomas Jefferson. Dr. Samuel D. Gross, immortalized in Thomas Eakin's famous painting, was the nineteenth-century dean of American surgery. Dr. Carlos Finlay, an alumnus, discovered the carrier of yellow fever, and Dr. Chevalier Jackson made bronchoscopy a new specialty. Alumnus Dr. J. Marion Sims founded the specialty of gynecology, and alumnus Dr. Jonathan Letterman, Medical Director of the Army of the Potomac, set up the first MASH-type field operations. Dr. Victor Heiser, also a graduate, organized the forerunner of the U.S. Public Health Service. In modern times, open heart surgery, artificial hearts, and heart vessel bypasses became possible when Dr. John H. Gibbon, Jr., a Jefferson alumnus and professor, successfully used his heart-lung machine in 1953. More recently, Dr. Allan J. Erslev discovered the hormone that controls red blood cell production; Dr. James Hunter invented the first artificial tendon for reconstructive hand surgery; Dr. Jewell Osterholm used microsurgical grafting to reduce the effects of stroke; Drs. Laird Jackson and Ronald Wapner began work in 1983 on chorionic villus sampling for the detection of congenital defects early in gestation; and Dr. Louis D. Lowry and Philip A. Katz, Ph.D., invented an artificial larynx to restore natural speech. In 1984, the University's surgeons successfully performed the Delaware Valley's first liver transplant. The same year, Dr. Robert C. Gallo, a Jefferson graduate,

AT A GLANCE

Beds: 717
Occupancy Rate: 78.9%
Average Patient Count: 505
Average Patient Stay: 7.8 days
Annual Admissions: 25,411
Births: 2,602
Outpatient Clinic Visits:
　304,916
Emergency Room/Trauma
　Center Visits: 42,800

HOSPITAL PERSONNEL
Physicians: 934
　Board Certified: 89%
Residents: 645
Registered Nurses: 996
　BS Degree: 548

ROOM CHARGES (PER DIEM)
Private: $1,140
Semiprivate: $1,140
ICU: $2,350

ADDRESS
111 South 11th Street
Philadelphia, PA 19107-5098

TELEPHONE
(215) 955-6460

was a codiscoverer of the HIV virus and proved that it is responsible for Acquired Immune Deficiency Syndrome (AIDS).

Over the past decade, Thomas Jefferson University has committed itself to assembling a top research faculty to complement the University's excellence in medical education and patient care. In 1986, the University created the Jefferson Institute of Molecular Medicine, an interdisciplinary research and teaching entity that unites researchers investigating a variety of diseases at the molecular level. Under the leadership of Dr. Darwin J. Prockop, the Institute is dedicated to understanding the genetic basis of human diseases and to developing better techniques to diagnose and treat them. The Jefferson Cancer Institute, established in 1991 and led by renowned cancer geneticist, Dr. Carlo M. Croce, brings together top researchers working on the molecular and genetic mechanisms of cancer and related diseases.

SPECIAL FACILITIES AND PROGRAMS

As the largest single radiation facility for cancer treatment in the Delaware Valley, the Bodine Center for Cancer Treatment cares for 140 cancer patients daily and gives 40,000 radiation therapy treatments yearly. Established in 1987, the Bodine Center provides cutting-edge technology and state-of-the-art equipment, including laser-guided treatment beams and computer-designed planning and treatment. These features, combined with highly trained staff, have made the Bodine Center for Cancer Treatment one of the leading facilities in the nation.

One of the most respected mammography programs in the country provides diagnostic X-rays and their interpretation to more than 20,000 women and their physicians each year at Jefferson. The Breast Imaging Center at Jefferson has served as a model for quality-assurance programs in mammography and is a leader in the area of promoting screening and early detection of cancerous breast lesions. Jefferson radiologists have helped originate many improvements in mammography, including such recent innovations as needle-hookwire prebiopsy localization studies and mammographic film-processing quality control.

Thomas Jefferson University Hospital has joined with Chestnut Hill, Methodist, Grand View, Lower Bucks, and Wills Eye Hospitals, and with the Alfred I. duPont Institute for Children, in forming the Jefferson Cancer Network. The network was established to give patients at member hospitals access to the latest developments in cancer research, technology, and treatment. Cancer specialists at Jefferson and each member hospital work together to provide patients a broader range of treatment options, often delivered in their own hospital by their own doctors. One emphasis of the network is to speed the application of basic cancer discoveries into clinical settings around the Delaware Valley through the use of collaborative clinical trials. The staff at Jefferson Clinical Trials Support Service works closely with clinicians and cancer researchers to centralize data management and to support the efforts of individual clinical researchers in designing and developing new research protocols. The Clinical Trials Support Service acts as the resource office for clinical trials information.

The Colorectal Cancer Center is a multidisciplinary center for the study, prevention, and treatment of rectal cancer, offering expert primary prevention (lifestyle modification counseling) and secondary prevention (early detection through flexible sigmoidoscopy and colonoscopy). A program utilizing high-dose preoperative radiation and special sphincter-preservation surgical techniques has been in place since 1976, and the results promise to provide substantial new hope for patients with rectal cancer. A highly refined treatment selection process utilizes the expertise of surgeons, oncologists, surgical pathologists, radiation therapists, geneticists, nurses, and ultrasound specialists, among others. A weekly conference reviews the management of new patients as well as those already under treatment or follow-up observation. The center provides consultative services for oncology specialists nationwide.

At the Urologic Cancer Center, two full-time oncologists participate in a multidisciplinary approach to treating urologic cancer. The group, which also includes neoplastic disease specialists, radiation oncologists, and radiology specialists, uses the latest treatment modalities. The specialists make extensive use of contemporary techniques for diagnosing and evaluating urologic malignancies. Physicians at the Urologic Cancer Center can evaluate patients in one visit and recommend or plan a treatment regimen. Referring physicians can receive second opinions or treatment plans for their patients.

Jefferson's divisions of cardiology and cardiothoracic surgery provide state-of-the-art evaluation and treatment for patients with cardiac disease. Patients may be managed by an array of modalities such as medication, dietary adjustments, exercise, angioplasty, ablation, or surgery, to name but a few of the treatment options.

Cardiovascular disease prevention applies both to patients who have heart disease and to those hoping to avoid it. Jefferson's staff evaluates the unique needs of each patient to develop an individualized approach of risk reduction. Some of the most exciting developments in cardiology are preventive, and Jefferson physicians are applying them to help their patients. Heart disease can actually be reversed with lifestyle changes and through medical therapy with such agents as cholesterol-lowering drugs. Jefferson cardiologists have specific expertise in providing risk-factor reduction for patients who have heart disease as well as for patients at risk of developing heart disease.

The Cardiac Rehabilitation Program is one of the oldest such services in Philadelphia. Instituted 15 years ago, the program provides full care to the cardiac-disabled, including physical and occupational therapies, psychological counseling, and vocational redirection. Patients may either begin treatment early in their hospital course, following their acute cardiac illness, or in the period after their cardiac surgery. Also, the program may begin in the hospital and continue as an outpatient program, as the need requires. A skilled rehabilitation physician identifies the appropriate prescription for the initial phases of rehabilitation.

Close cooperation with the primary physician or cardiologist assures optimal care, especially when changes in medical status occur. The facility has full equipment to allow proper monitoring of response to activity, including telemetry.

Jefferson's extensive and longstanding kidney transplant program is staffed by experienced nephrologists and surgeons from the hospital's Division of Transplant Surgery. These specialists work in close coordination to provide the best team-care possible and to match the right recipient with an available donor organ. Assiduous long-term follow-up care also contributes to the program's high success rate. Jefferson's transplant program performed 73 renal transplants in fiscal year 1993.

The Kidney Dialysis Program at Jefferson consists of acute, intermediate, and self-dialysis. Acute care at the six-station acute unit is provided by registered nurses trained to treat patients with acute and chronic renal failure, as well as pre- and post-operative transplant patients. Other procedures provided include CAVH, CAVHD, hemoperfusion, and hemodialysis. More than 2,500 treatments were provided in 1993. The intermediate dialysis unit is a 20-station outpatient center that performed over 14,000 procedures last year. The Self-Dialysis Program is a home dialysis program staffed by specially trained registered nurses. In-center, staff-assisted hemodialysis services are also provided at Jefferson's Ford Road Campus.

Jefferson is the home of a well-respected liver disease treatment program. The Division of Gastroenterology and Hepatology is a referral center for diagnosing patients with acute or advanced chronic liver disease. The program takes advantage of detailed nutritional testing and other diagnostics, as well as leading-edge nutritional and medical therapies, including the use of interferon for treating chronic viral hepatitis. Program staff can refer end-stage patients for transplantation at Jefferson and serve as important components of the screening, testing, and long-term follow-up aspects of the transplant program. Designated the first Liver Transplant Center in the Delaware Valley in 1984, the Jefferson center offers an experienced team of surgeons, anesthesiologists, nurses, and hepatologists. Livers for the transplant operations performed at Jefferson are obtained through the Delaware Valley Transplant Program.

Gastroenterologists of the Liver Disease Prevention Center collaborate with surgeons, radiologists, and nuclear medicine and oncology experts in this center's efforts at combating hepatitis B and other liver disease and in detecting liver cancer at an early stage. The center runs a hepatitis-B vaccine clinic and serves as an important resource for hundreds of thousands of Asian-Americans in the region and other groups at risk for the disease.

Located on the Thomas Jefferson University Hospital Ford Road Campus, the Osteoporosis Center offers prevention, diagnosis, and treatment for osteoporosis and related problems and provides multidisciplinary care coordinated with the referring physician. Specialists in orthopaedic surgery, rheumatology, and endocrinologic and metabolic diseases evaluate and manage patients with, or at risk of, such conditions. Dual-energy X-ray absorptiometery

(DEXA), quantitative computerized tomography (CT), and single- and dual-photon densitometry assist in diagnosis. Treatments may include dietary consultation and medical and physical therapy.

The Pain Center cares for patients with chronic, intractable pain due to reflex sympathetic dystrophy, musculoskeletal disorders, or neuropathies (including post-herpetic neuralgia). The center's staff also assists in optimizing pain medication for cancer patients. The primary objective is to improve patient functionality rather than "cure" the pain. To that end, the center offers a variety of treatment options that are of a somatic (nerve blocks and physical therapy) and psychosomatic (biofeedback, hypnosis, and group therapy) nature. The multidisciplinary pain management team includes anesthesiologists, psychiatrists, psychologists, neurologists, physiatrists, surgeons, orthopedists, neurosurgeons, and others as needed.

The Comprehensive Rehabilitation Center at Thomas Jefferson University Hospital consists of 32 beds for those in need of intensive inpatient rehabilitation services. The center provides high-quality patient care focused on maximizing independence and facilitating appropriate discharge. Skilled consultants are available who can provide monitoring and treatment during the period of physical restoration. The center is staffed by nurses specially trained in the rehabilitation process who can also provide traditional nursing intervention.

Jefferson's Surgical Center provides a modern and attractive facility to serve the increasing number of patients undergoing surgery on an outpatient basis. The center accommodates a full range of surgical specialties in its four operating rooms. Patients and surgeons benefit from the personalized approach of the center's staff and the medical backup of Jefferson's full medical center. The center supplies a fourth option to Jefferson's Surgical Program, which also includes the Short Procedure Unit for medical and more complex outpatient procedures, Surgery Day of Admissions for elective surgery requiring only a postoperative stay, and inpatient surgery for major surgical care requiring prior inpatient workup.

Jefferson is an officially designated Level I Regional Trauma Center. It is one of only 14 hospitals in the U.S. that are both an official Regional Trauma Center and a Regional Spinal Cord Injury Center (RSCIC). Patients with the most serious multisystem traumas are brought to Jefferson by the emergency medical squads and by physician-initiated transfer from other hospitals. As a Level I Center, Jefferson also conducts research and continuing education programs for health professionals in trauma care. In affiliation with the Magee Rehabilitation Hospital, Jefferson is designated one of the nation's 13 regional Model Demonstration and Research Spinal Cord Injury Systems. The center, which has treated more than 1,500 patients, provides for the multidisciplinary coordination of emergency and acute medical/surgical care, rehabilitation beginning at the onset of acute care, vocational evaluation and training, and lifetime follow-up care of persons with spinal cord injuries. With over 70% of persons with spinal cord injury admitted within three days of injury, Jefferson's RSCIC has demonstrated a mortality rate of 4% (as compared to the 20% national average) and significantly reduces the severe secondary complications of traumatic spinal cord injury.

Other adult treatment centers at Thomas Jefferson University Hospital include the Arthritis Center, the AIDS Clinical Trial Group, the Tay-Sachs Prevention Program, Alcohol and Substance Abuse Programs, the Cerebrovascular Disease Center, the Endocrinology/Diabetes Center, the Environmental Medicine and Toxicology Clinic, and the Hearing Center.

The Jefferson Center for Women's Medical Specialties offers a full range of obstetric and gynecologic services provided by skilled, sensitive physicians concerned about the unique health care needs of women. The center is staffed by specialists and subspecialists who are full-time clinical faculty members of Thomas Jefferson University's department of obstetrics and gynecology. Services include well-woman care and general gynecology, normal and high-risk maternity care, obstetric ultrasound, genetic screening, infertility treatment, gynecologic cancer care, gynecologic ultrasound, and gynecologic urology.

A full range of pediatric services is also provided. Children's Rehabilitation Hospital meets the very special needs of children (birth to age 18) who have chronic medical problems stemming from prematurity, pediatric head and spinal cord injury, pediatric asthma, pediatric diabetes, birth defects such as cerebral palsy, and other medical conditions. Coordinated care involves pediatricians; physicians specializing in physical and rehabilitation medicine; pediatric nurses; dietitians; physical, occupational and speech therapists; social workers; psychologists; and the referring physician. Programs for premature babies and for children are offered in modern facilities and in a friendly neighborhood atmosphere that invites family participation. Medical care offers the expertise of Jefferson pediatricians and access to Jefferson resources. The Children's Center for Seizure Disorders offers multidisciplinary care from specialists in psychiatry, child development, rehabilitative medicine, nutrition, and pharmacology for the evaluation and treatment of pediatric seizure disorders. The Children's Center for Cerebral Palsy and Neuromuscular Disorders aids in the evaluation and treatment of neuromuscular disorders, including cerebral palsy in pediatric, adolescent, and adult patients. The services are interdisciplinary, employing specialists in neurology, orthopaedics, and neurosurgery. Assessment studies may include electrophysiologic tests, neuroradiologic imaging, tests for neurodegenerative diseases and inborn errors of metabolism, examination of nerve and muscle, and evaluation of growth and development. Available therapies include orthopaedic surgery; neurosurgical procedures, such as selective dorsal rhizotomy and spinal-cord stimulator implants; and physical, occupational, or speech therapies.

Jefferson is one of only two hospitals in the Delaware Valley, and one of approximately 60 nationwide, to perform extracorporeal membrane oxygenation (ECMO). The procedure, which oxygenates a baby's blood outside the body, gives lungs that were severely damaged at birth a chance to heal. ECMO can save the life of a newborn suffering from meconium aspiration or other critical neonatal pulmonary problems. Experienced neonatologists, pediatric surgeons, ultrasonographers, respiratory therapists and nurses contribute their expertise in carrying out the cardiopulmonary bypass. An essential extension of its sophisticated neonatologic services, Jefferson's Special Babies Program affords clinical follow-up on an outpatient basis for babies that were severely premature or who required intensive monitoring or ECMO support neonatally.

MEDICAL SPECIALTIES

Allergy and Immunology, Anesthesiology, Cardiology, Clinical Pharmacology, Dermatology, Endocrinology, Gastroenterology, Gynecologic Oncology, Medical Oncology/Hematology, Neonatology, Nephrology, Neurology, Neurosurgery, Obstetrics/Gynecology, Ophthalmology, Orthopedics, Otolaryngology, Pediatrics, Physical Medicine and Rehabilitation, Plastic Surgery, Primary Care/Family Medicine, Psychiatry, Pulmonary and Critical Care Medicine, Radiology, Rheumatology, Surgery, Surgical Oncology, Trauma Medicine, Urology, and Vascular Surgery.

WELL-KNOWN SPECIALISTS

- Dr. Salman Akhtar   *Psychiatry; specialist in psychoanalysis*
- Dr. Demetrius H. Bagley   *Urology; specialist in endocrinology*
- Dr. David Berd   *Neoplastic diseases; specialist in immunotherapy, cancer, and biotherapy*
- Dr. Joseph Calhoun   *Ophthalmology; specialist in pediatric ophthalmology*
- Dr. Elisabeth Cohen   *Ophthalmology; specialist in corneal diseases and transplantations*
- Dr. Jerome Cotler   *Orthopedic surgery; specialist in spinal surgery*
- Dr. O. Richard Dypp   *Obstetrics/gynecology*
- Dr. Sheldon Goldberg   *Cardiovascular disease*
- Dr. Franz Goldstein   *Gastroenterology*
- Dr. Leonard Graziani   *Pediatric neurology*
- Dr. William Holloway   *Infectious diseases*
- Dr. Robert Knobler   *Neurology*
- Dr. Stephen Lawless   *Pediatrics; specialist in pediatric critical care*
- Dr. Stephen McGeady   *Allergy and immunology*
- Dr. James Reilly   *Otolaryngology; specialist in pediatric otolaryngology*
- Dr. Lawrence Schneider   *Hand surgery*
- Dr. Gordon F. Schwartz   *Surgical oncology; specialist in breast cancer*
- Dr. Brendan Teehan   *Nephrology*
- Dr. Ronald Wapner   *Obstetrics/gynecology*

PATIENT SATISFACTION

Inpatient satisfaction surveys are conducted continuously and scores are monitored quarterly. Patient satisfaction surveys are also in place for many outpatient areas (e.g., emergency department, outpatient surgery) and office practices (e.g., department of medicine, obstetrics and gynecology). Results are provided to senior officers, managers and administrators to help them improve operations, and action plans are developed by the services marketing department to address patient satisfaction issues.

Over the past two years an average of 92% of patients surveyed expressed satisfaction with Thomas Jefferson. Ninety-six percent would return and 96% would recommend the hospital to family and friends.

RESEARCH

Total research revenue at Thomas Jefferson University in 1993 was $60 million. Jefferson's efforts are focused in hematological, cardiovascular, and pulmonary disease; neurosciences and rehabilitation medicine; skin, bone, and extracellular biology; alcohol, liver, and metabolic diseases; cancer; genetics, developmental biology, and birth defects; and immunology and health services.

Research in cardiovascular disease has long been a commitment at Thomas Jefferson University, exemplified by the pioneering work of John H. Gibbon, Jr., M.D., who in 1953 performed the first successful open heart surgery using the heart-lung machine. Today Jefferson maintains an international reputation as a center of excellence in cardiopulmonary research. Scientists exploring cardiac diseases across the broad spectrum of research areas are based in two departments: the department of medicine, which includes the Cardeza Foundation in Hematologic Research—one of the largest blood research institutions in the country—and the divisions of cardiology, pulmonary diseases, and critical care and clinical pharmacology; and the department of physiology, which has a major concentration of federally-funded studies in cardiovascular and pulmonary physiology. Other centers include researchers in surgery, radiology, and biochemistry and molecular medicine. The college has been on the forefront in the development of new techniques for the treatment of patients with heart attacks and the development of new technologies designed to improve the recovery of patients with life-threatening strokes. More recently, research has expanded to include molecular studies on the role endothelial cells play in regulating not only blood coagulation, but blood pressure and blood vessel smooth muscle growth. The university holds several patents in the area of vascular graft technology and technologies for reducing vascular wall growth following angioplasty. About 60% of the support for hematological, cardiovascular and pulmonary disease research comes primarily from the National Institutes of Health.

In neurosciences and rehabilitation medicine, investigators in both the basic and clinical sciences are actively involved in diverse research on the structure, function and molecular basis for nervous activity. Lance L. Simpson, Ph.D., Director of the Division of Environmental Medicine and Toxicology, is a recipient of the Javits Neuroscience Investigator Award, presented by Congress in conjunction with the National Institutes of Health. Dr. Simpson is leading a multidisciplinary investigation on toxins, particularly those that are synthesized by bacteria. Recently, Jefferson established a Center for Neurovirology under the direction of Dr. Hilary Koprowski, a world-renowned investigator in the development of vaccines against neuroviruses. The Center is directing its research activities in the areas of rabies, multiple sclerosis, and depressive disorders of possible viral nature. The Center has recently been named a World Health Organization Collaborating Center for Neurovirology. Faculty in Jefferson's departments of surgery, orthopedic surgery, and rehabilitative medicine are involved in numerous studies on the treatment of spinal cord injury and stroke. Jefferson holds several patented technologies in the areas of stroke treatment.

The Director of the Jefferson Institute of Molecular Medicine, Dr. Darwin J. Prockop, is an internationally recognized authority on collagen whose research involves the nature of mutations that produce diseases of connective tissue. In his studies, he is establishing the pathways by which collagen is synthesized and is looking at how cells manipulate and regulate the process. Dr. Prockop has a particular interest in the gene defects that produce osteogenesis imperfecta, or brittle bone diseases, and more common diseases such as osteoporosis, osteoarthritis, and blood vessel disease.

Other research interests revolve around biochemistry and molecular biology of connective tissue in relation to skin diseases. The goal of this research is to elucidate the underlying molecular defects in collagen, elastin, and the basement membrane zone macromolecules in acquired and heritable connective tissue disorders. In particular, the dermatology group is interested in structural and regulator mutations that lead to altered synthesis of the extracellular matrix components in heritable connective tissue diseases primarily affecting the skin.

The Alcohol Research Center is composed of investigators with backgrounds in biochemistry, biophysics, pathology, and pharmacology who are demonstrating the relationship between the structural and functional effects of alcohol on cells and subcellular structures, the adaptations occurring during long-term exposure of the organism to alcohol, and the molecular basis for irreversible cell damage and resulting collagen deposition associated with chronic alcohol ingestion. The center is under the direction of Dr. Emanuel Rubin, internationally known for his multidisciplinary efforts to establish a molecular basis for behavioral tolerance to alcohol. The center is supported by two major grants from the National Institutes of Health.

Established in 1991, the Jefferson Cancer Institute occupies nearly 120,000 square feet of modern research space with access to additional state-of-the-art support services. The Institute has fully equipped structural biology facilities, including nuclear magnetic resonance (NMR) and X-ray crystallography centers for analysis of protein structure and peptide and nucleotide synthesis facilities. All of these facilities are connected to a mini-supercomputer for graphic analysis, modeling and display. The research program focuses on the involvement of cellular proto-oncogenes and cancer suppressor genes in the pathogenesis of human cancer. Much of the research concerns the molecular mechanisms involved in the pathogenesis of human leukemias and lymphomas. Clinical research strengths are developing in human solid tumor research, including prostate cancer, colorectal cancer, and breast and brain tumors. Nearly 200 scientists are involved in the basic molecular biology, biochemistry, cell biology, immunology, and developmental aspects of cancer. Overall, support for cancer-related research has increased nearly fourfold in the last eight years. Over 85% of this research support is from the National Institutes of Health.

Jefferson is recognized both nationally and internationally as a center for basic and clinical research in the areas of genetics, developmental biology, and birth defects. The Jefferson faculty includes three past presidents of the American Teratology Society, one of whom has been further recognized as a Merit Scholar of the National Institutes of Health. The faculty in these programs hold the only two training grants in this specialty awarded by the National Institutes of Health. They represent faculty from biochemistry and molecular biology; medical genetics; pediatrics; obstetrics and gynecology; radiology; urology; and anatomy and developmental biology. There are several interdisciplinary faculty groups, also including faculty in the Jefferson Institute of Molecular Medicine and the Jefferson Cancer Institute. During 1992, these faculty groups received over $8 million in awards for the yearly support of their research. Most of these funds represent peer-reviewed awards from the National Institutes of Health. The utilization of chorionic villus sampling for the early detection of birth defects in women in the first ten weeks of pregnancy was pioneered at Jefferson, and the faculty are active in the utilization of such tissue for the early diagnosis of birth defects and other genetically linked diseases, such as familial colorectal cancer, and other forms of cancer.

The Immunology Program focuses on the identification of the immune mechanisms that may be manipulated in designing effective therapeutic modalities to control tumor cell growth by lymphocytes and by cells of the nonadaptive system of defense. The interests of the faculty are varied and include aspects of basic cellular immunobiology, the functional aspects of lymphocyte biology and their clinical applications. The faculty in the program uses approaches dealing with definition of the mechanisms that modulate lymphocyte functions, both cell-mediated and humoral immunity; the role of cytokines in host-tumor response; and the characterization of molecules involved in recognition of normal or tumor cells. The strength of the program is in the immunobiology of cancer, with emphasis on its functional aspects.

The Center for Research in Medical Education and Health Care is dedicated to the improvement of the medical education process and to the development of a greater understanding of factors that affect both the quality and cost of health care.

ADMISSIONS POLICY

Patients can be admitted by any physician who has staff privileges at Jefferson. Since Jefferson is a tertiary teaching center, referrals can be made directly between physicians, or patients can call the JEFF NOW Physician Referral Service.

Each scheduled admission is certified with regard to financial coverage. This certification takes place prior to admission. If insurance coverage has provisions for deductibles and co-insurance, these amounts are sought prior to admission. If a patient lacks insurance coverage, the hospital will seek statewide medical assistance. If the individual does not qualify for medical assistance, the hospital then has the patient fill out a free care application. Approximately $5 million in free care is provided per year.

Special phone number for admissions information: (215) 955-6483.

PATIENT/FAMILY ACCOMMODATIONS

The hospital has an agreement with Holiday Inn, where rooms are available at $72/night for patients and family, including individual breakfast and local calls. Five apartments are available in Barringer Hall at $50/night, with full accommodations.

WILLS EYE HOSPITAL

Wills Eye Hospital, established in 1832 through a bequest to the city of Philadelphia by James Wills, a Quaker merchant, is a 115-bed non-profit specialty institution whose clinical expertise and sophisticated diagnostic and treatment procedures make it a worldwide referral center. Wills Eye Hospital has been ranked one of the best hospitals in the United States by *U.S. News & World Report* for five consecutive years. Programs maintained by the hospital are organized along the traditional divisions of patient care, education, and research activities.

The first Wills Eye Hospital, containing 70 beds, was located at the southwest corner of 18th and Race Streets in Philadelphia, opposite what is now Logan Circle. As a specialty institution from its inception, Wills played a vital role in establishing ophthalmology as a separate branch of medicine in this country.

By the early 1900s, Wills had outgrown its quarters. In 1932, the hospital relocated to a new building at 16th and Spring Garden Streets. The new hospital expanded the inpatient bed capacity to 120, increased outpatient service areas, and provided additional conference and teaching facilities.

In the 1960s, Wills began to develop subspecialty services, in addition to its General Ophthalmology Services (now the Cataract and Primary Eye Care

The Best Hospitals in America

Service). Dealing with particular diseases or parts of the eye, these services now number nine: Contact Lens, Cornea, Glaucoma, Neuro-Ophthalmology, Oculoplastics, Oncology, Pathology, Pediatric Ophthalmology and Retina.

In 1972, Wills affiliated with Jefferson Medical College of Thomas Jefferson University. As a result, Wills now serves as Jefferson's Department of Ophthalmology. All Jefferson medical students receive their basic eye instruction and training at Wills.

With its continued growth, Wills once again needed larger quarters. The new Wills Eye Hospital, located at 900 Walnut Street, opened in 1980 and is nearly twice as large as the previous building. An ultramodern facility, and winner of several design awards, the new hospital features greatly expanded outpatient services in keeping with the increasing trend toward outpatient care in ophthalmology.

For common eye problems to rare sight-threatening diseases, Wills provides general eye care and nine subspecialty services, attracting patients from the Delaware Valley area, across the country, and around the world.

During its 162-year history, the hospital's staff has pioneered in the development of innovative techniques in ophthalmology. The first implantation of an artificial intraocular lens to replace the cataract patient's own clouded lens was performed in the United States in 1952 by Drs. Warren Reese and Turgut Hamdi of the hospital staff. Other revolutionary cataract surgery procedures were developed by former Wills resident Charles Kelma, M.D. A vitrectomy machine, now widely used for eye microsurgery, was invented in 1972 by Wills physician Jay L. Federman, M.D.

The sophistication of care delivered at Wills can be evidenced by the following descriptions of the activities performed by its specialty services.

SPECIAL FACILITIES AND PROGRAMS

The Cataract and Primary Eye Care (CPEC) Service provides treatment to patients with needs ranging from routine eye examinations to cataract surgery.

AT A GLANCE

Beds: 115
Occupancy Rate: 33%
Average Patient Count: 38
Average Patient Stay: 2 days
Annual Admissions: 3,952
Outpatient Clinic Visits:
     59,936

HOSPITAL PERSONNEL
Physicians: 441
     Board Certified: 432
Residents: 33
Registered Nurses: 138
     BS Degree: 25

ROOM CHARGES (PER DIEM)
Private: $855
Semiprivate: $750

ADDRESS
900 Walnut Street
Philadelphia, PA 19107-5598

TELEPHONE
(215) 928-3000

The Refractive Surgery Unit, which is part of CPEC and the Cornea Service, offers astigmatic and radial keratotomy (RK) surgery to reduce or eliminate astigmatism and nearsightedness. The Unit is also studying the excimer laser to reduce or eliminate astigmatism and nearsightedness and to treat superficial corneal scars and corneal dystrophies, as well as recurrent corneal erosions.

The Contact Lens Service evaluates and fits patients of all ages and medical conditions with the latest in contact lens technology. The Service is participating in a study with 15 other eye care centers in the U.S., Europe and Japan on new disposable contact lenses that are designed to be thrown away after one use.

The Cornea Service, which houses the Lions Eye Bank of the Delaware Valley, treats patients with corneal or external ocular disease and is a leading center for corneal transplants. The corneal topography video computer camera has numerous applications in the treatment of various disorders and diseases of the cornea. Most recently, it has been used in conjunction with the hospital's excimer laser on patients with corneal scarring. It also aids surgeons in performing radial keratotomy.

The Glaucoma Service, the largest in the country, offers patients the availability of glaucoma surgery sooner than ever before with state-of-the-art lasers. The Glaucoma Service Diagnostic Laboratory provides advanced computerized techniques to uncover the earliest signs of glaucoma in suspected patients, as well as charting the progression of the condition in patients who have already been diagnosed.

The Neuro-Ophthalmology Service diagnoses disorders which produce visual symptoms that are not due to eye disease itself. The service was one of 15 centers nationwide that participated in the National Eye Institute's Optic Neuritis Treatment Trial. The next phase of the investigation, the Longitudinal Optic Neuritis Study (LENS), involves following the patients from the original study to determine the long-range outcome from an ocular and neurological standpoint.

The Oculoplastic Service, also the largest service of its kind in the country, provides fascia lata tissue for use in the repair and reconstruction of the eyelids and other delicate structures surrounding the eye. The Fascia Lata Bank is the first in the United States and is utilized by surgeons throughout the country. As part of the Oculoplastic Service, the Cosmetic Surgery Unit offers cosmetic surgery that includes plastic surgery of the upper eyelids, lower eyelids, and eyebrows, as well as chemical peels.

The Oncology Service provides treatment for ocular tumors. Patients are also offered a state-of-the-art orbital implant which allows an artificial eye to move like a healthy eye.

The Pediatric Ophthalmology Service treats the unique ocular problems of children, including strabismus (crossed eyes) and amblyopia (lazy eye). Physicians can also perform cataract surgery on infants as early as a few weeks old. Expeditious removal of cataracts enhances a child's chances for better vision.

A pediatric contact lens service at Wills fits and stocks lenses exclusively for children.

The Retina Service has diversified into units to treat specific conditions such as vascular disease, macular disease, and uveitis, as well as hereditary and degenerative diseases. The Retina Service staff also includes a retinal oncologist who specializes in retinal tumors and cancer.

The Foerderer Center for the Study of Eye Movement Disorders in Children is equipped with state-of-the-art recording instruments and computers, allowing specialists to accurately monitor eye movements and brain wave responses to help in diagnosing and treating the most common visual problems in children.

The Vascular Studies Laboratory is at the forefront in using a number of new techniques to estimate ocular blood flow, a critical factor in assessing carotid disease and other vascular diseases affecting the eye. The color flow Doppler, a diagnostic device designed to monitor blood flow in the heart and legs, was adapted by two former Wills fellows for use in ophthalmology for patients with ocular tumors and vascular disorders.

The Day Surgery Unit offers specialized nursing care and streamlined admitting procedures to provide greater comfort and convenience for same-day surgery patients.

The Center for Sports Vision offers eye care, injury prevention, and treatment for the athlete, both professional and amateur, 24 hours-a-day.

The Low Vision Service offers help to patients whose eyesight cannot be corrected medically, surgically, or with lenses. Special low vision aids enable them to use their remaining vision to the best advantage.

Services also include Visual Physiology, Diagnostic Photography, Pathology, and a 24-hour Emergency Service and Ocular Trauma Center.

Other services at Wills include cosmetic surgery; the Fascia Lata Laboratory, a major distributor of tissue to surgeons at over 100 hospitals; the Foerderer Center for the Study of Eye Movement Disorders in Children; the Glaucoma Service Diagnostic Laboratory; the Lions Eye Bank of Delaware Valley; the Low Vision Center; and the outpatient Refractive Surgery Unit. The Vascular Studies Laboratory performs noninvasive tests to determine the health of large blood vessels supplying blood to eyes and brain. Phototherapeutic keratectomy, using the excimer laser, is available to treat corneal scars, dystrophies and recurrent corneal erosions.

During the 1980s, dramatic advances in ophthalmic technology and tightening of government regulations resulted in a dramatic shift from inpatient to outpatient care being delivered by the hospital. In response to the changing health care environment, and also to meet the needs of an aging population, Wills added several complementary non-ophthalmic services to its list of medical disciplines. The four endeavors are hand surgery, geriatric psychiatry, diabetes treatment, and a neurosurgery program.

MEDICAL SPECIALTIES

General Ophthalmology Service and nine subspecialties: Contact Lenses, Cornea, Glaucoma, Neuro-Ophthalmology, Oculoplastics, Oncology, Pathology, Pediatric Ophthalmology, and Retina.

WELL-KNOWN SPECIALISTS

- Dr. Raymond E. Adams   *Director of the Cataract and Primary Eye Care Service (CPEC)*
- Dr. William E. Benson   *Director of the Retina Service*
- Dr. Thomas M. Bosley   *Neuro-ophthalmology*
- Dr. Joseph H. Calhoun   *Director of the Pediatric Ophthalmology Service*
- Dr. Elisabeth J. Cohen   *Co-director of the Cornea Service*
- Dr. Jay L. Federman   *Co-director of the Retina Service*
- Dr. Joseph C. Flanagan   *Director of the Oculoplastic Service*
- Dr. Peter L. Laibson   *Director of the Cornea Service*
- Dr. Robert D. Reinecke   *Director of the Foerderer Center*
- Dr. Barry W. Rovner   *Medical director, geriatric psychiatry program*
- Dr. Peter J. Savino   *Director of the Neuro-Ophthalmology Service*
- Dr. Jerry A. Shields   *Director of the Oncology Service*
- Dr. George L. Spaeth   *Director of the Glaucoma Service*
- Dr. William Tasman   *Ophthalmologist-in-Chief of Wills; attending surgeon on the Retina Service*

PATIENT SATISFACTION

Each patient admitted to Wills receives a patient handbook containing a questionnaire for their comments and a return envelope. Patients are asked to comment on, among other items, the hospital's admissions procedures, its nursing staff, cleanliness and comfort of their room, and food, as well as their general impression of the Hospital.

Questionnaires are forwarded to the hospital's administration who review them, refer problem areas to the appropriate department, and also ensure that the positive reactions are received.

In the past year, 3,685 patients were admitted to Wills. Of those, 295 returned the questionnaires. Favorable comments totaled 89% of the forms returned.

RESEARCH

In clinical studies, a major aspect of the research is concerned with improving the current diagnostic capabilities for particular eye diseases, such as glaucoma. Studies to improve methods of treatment are always underway, as well. Physicians in the Retina Service are presently participating in two retinopathy of prematurity studies; Glaucoma Service physicians are studying the best treatment approach for open-angle glaucoma; and the Cornea Service is in the third year of a five year investigation into the medical treatment of active and inactive herpetic eye disease.

Scientific research at Wills focuses on inflammatory diseases of the eye, macular degeneration, and ocular oncology. The research laboratories consist of modern state-of-the-art facilities specifically designed to carry out new molecular biology studies.

Significant research achievements of the research division, headed by Larry A. Donoso, M.D., Ph.D., include the identification of specific sites in a retinal protein which is responsible for a severe ocular inflammatory condition; the identification and cloning of an antigen which is present in malignant melanomas of the eye; and, in conjunction with laboratories at Harvard Medical School, the identification of the chromosomal location of a gene involved in a form of hereditary macular degeneration, a condition which can lead to severe visual impairment.

Approximately $3.5 million comes from grants, specific purpose and unrestricted gifts.

ADMISSIONS POLICY

Admissions can be made through a staff physician, an outside referring physician, or the Emergency Room.

The financial requirement for patients is either insurance or cash. If patients lack insurance, and meet medical assistance criteria, that is accepted. Otherwise, if the patient is financially able, payment arrangements will be made through the Billing Office. Last year, about $900,000 in free care was provided.

Special phone number for admissions information: (215) 928-3311.

VANDERBILT

UNIVERSITY

HOSPITAL

VANDERBILT UNIVERSITY
MEDICAL CENTER

NASHVILLE, TENNESSEE

In discussing Vanderbilt University Medical Center (VUMC), we want to emphasize that this is indeed an institution way ahead of other hospitals in its innovative programs and responsiveness to new health care needs. The medical center is a comprehensive health care facility which combines patient care, biomedical research, and the education of health professionals. Through its programs, it has become a major referral center for the Southeast and the entire nation.

The medical center, which consists of Vanderbilt Hospital, the School of Medicine, and the School of Nursing, can trace its roots back to the mid-1800s. The School of Medicine began at the University of Nashville in 1850, some 23 years before Vanderbilt University was established. It became part of Vanderbilt in 1874 and awarded its first Vanderbilt medical degrees to 61 graduates in 1875.

IN DISCUSSING VANDERBILT UNIVERSITY MEDICAL CENTER (VUMC), WE WANT TO EMPHASIZE THAT THIS IS INDEED AN INSTITUTION WAY AHEAD OF OTHER HOSPITALS IN ITS INNOVATIVE PROGRAMS AND RESPONSIVENESS TO NEW HEALTH CARE NEEDS.

Throughout its history, Vanderbilt University Medical Center has made relentless efforts to provide the best and newest in medical care. Over the past 14 years, VUMC has remained in the forefront of patient care.

The present Vanderbilt University Hospital was completed in 1980. The twin-towered structure, which includes Children's Hospital, houses one of the most modern health care facilities in the nation.

The Best Hospitals in America

The Vanderbilt Clinic, adjacent to the hospital, houses outpatient medical and surgical practices, the Henry-Joyce Cancer Clinic and Clinical Research Center, diagnostic clinical laboratories, and various other support services.

Medical Research Building I, a major biomedical research facility at the Medical Center, opened in the spring of 1989. That year also saw the opening of the Kim Dayani Human Performance Center, which provides comprehensive clinical and research programs in health promotion, as well as fitness and rehabilitation facilities for patients, Vanderbilt employees, and the community. In 1993, construction was completed on the Vanderbilt Stallworth Rehabilitation Hospital, the only freestanding facility of its kind in Tennessee, as well as on the Annette and Irwin Eskind Biomedical Library.

Recent construction includes the renovation and expansion of research centers, laboratories, and medical offices in Medical Center North; the addition of four floors to Medical Center East; and a second Medical Research Building, which will house much of the research arm of the Vanderbilt Cancer Center.

Vanderbilt's Cooperative Care Center clearly shows the Hospital's determination to meet patient needs without unnecessarily escalating the cost of medical services, and therefore reflects one of the most sensible contemporary trends in health care. One of only two such centers in the country, the Cooperative Care Center involves family members actively in the care of the patient during hospitalization. A typical patient in this unit is someone with a chronic disease, such as diabetes, who is having an acute episode of his or her illness, such as insulin shock. In the center, the patient is brought through the acute episode and then, along with family members, is educated to avoid a recurrence. Long range preventive steps are planned and implemented. A major side benefit of this kind of care is that treatment at the Center often reduces the cost of a patient's care by at least one third.

Many other services offered at Vanderbilt are unique in the state and, in some instances, in the

AT A GLANCE

Beds: 661
Occupancy Rate: 80%
Average Patient Count: 507
Average Patient Stay: 6.8 days
Annual Admissions: 28,154
Births: 2,018
Outpatient Clinic Visits:
 361,903
Emergency Room/Trauma
 Center Visits: 46,252

HOSPITAL PERSONNEL
Physicians: 914
 Board Certified: 752
Residents: 545
Registered Nurses: 879
 BS Degree: 527

ROOM CHARGES (PER DIEM)
Private: $353
Semiprivate: $352
ICU: $873

ADDRESS
1161 21st Avenue South
Nashville, TN 37232-2390

TELEPHONE
(615) 322-5000

United States. Vanderbilt Children's Hospital, for example, is a prototype for some dozen universities around the country who would like to duplicate this "hospital within a hospital" organization model. Although it occupies two floors within Vanderbilt Hospital, Children's Hospital maintains a separate identity. This organization has enabled Children's Hospital to have the best of both worlds—the support of a comprehensive teaching and research medical center and the skills and expertise of a dedicated pediatric faculty. During 1984, Children's Hospital became the first member of its type to be admitted to the National Association of Children's Hospitals, which previously admitted only freestanding facilities with their own buildings.

Innovative programs at Vanderbilt, such as cooperative care, are reinforced by traditional medical services and backed up by nationally visible biomedical research. Patient care statistics for last year indicate that Vanderbilt's primary business is secondary and tertiary referrals from local and regional physicians. The many clinics and centers at Vanderbilt offer patients a variety of medical specialties. Fifty-nine of VUMC's physicians were named in *The Best Doctors in America*, a comprehensive survey which asked doctors to select the leading practitioners in their fields.

Vanderbilt is committed to the education of nurses who, in addition to their expertise in advanced clinical practice, are articulate patient advocates, are able to speak for nursing at policy-making levels in health care institutions, are prepared to deliver hands-on care to patients, and bring a lively spirit of inquiry and enthusiasm to their professional and personal lives.

SPECIAL FACILITIES AND PROGRAMS

The Vanderbilt Transplant Center is a multidisciplinary alliance of transplant specialists. Its participants are dedicated to the efficient, long-term care of the patient through the application of advances in tissue typing, immunosuppression, and organ and tissue procurement. Each transplant program within the center represents a collaboration of both medical and surgical professionals working clinically and in transplantation science.

The results of this teamwork are seen in VTC's excellent one-year survival rates on organ transplants. Of 30 heart transplant recipients in the most recent year for which data are available, 88% survived for at least one year; 98% of the 67 kidney recipients survived over the same period; the rate for combined kidney/pancreas transplants is 87%; for liver transplants, 86%; and lung transplants, 82%. The Center also performed 96 bone marrow transplants in fiscal year 1993.

The newly formed Vanderbilt Cancer Center incorporates all cancer-related activities at Vanderbilt University Medical Center. Its mission is to foster interdisciplinary patient care and cooperative bench-to-bedside research activities, as well as to connect basic and clinical research with clinical care activities. The Cancer Center is also dedicated to training the next generation of biomedical scientists and physicians. The primary patient care arm of the Vanderbilt Cancer Center, the Henry-Joyce Cancer Clinic and Clinical Research Center, is a major regional referral center for the treatment of both adult and pediatric cancers. Patients are evaluated and treated by a broad array of specialists, including medical and pediatric oncologists, surgeons, psychiatrists, and social services consultants. This team approach provides patients with prompt expert attention, while providing each patient with the best and most comprehensive treatment plan available.

The Arthritis and Joint Replacement Center represents the combined effort of orthopaedic surgeons and rheumatologists to provide comprehensive care for patients with arthritis and related disorders. The Center provides outpatients with easily accessible evaluation and continuing care by housing a satellite laboratory, radiology suite, social services, physical and occupational therapy facilities, and educational services.

Same-day service for diagnosis of breast problems is offered through the Breast Diagnostic Center. Personalized counseling regarding the most appropriate treatment is also provided. A mammography program for the detection of breast cancer is available, as well as immediate evaluation of fine needle aspiration of breast lumps. Self-referred patients are accepted.

A 20-bed facility uniquely designed, equipped, and staffed for burn victims, the Vanderbilt Burn Center is the only Level I burn center in the middle Tennessee area. In addition to patient care, the center emphasizes research and education and improves the quality of care available to burn victims throughout the region.

The purpose of the Chronic Disease Rehabilitation Program is to retard the progression of different forms of chronic disease and to help patients decrease symptoms or complications and attain maximum functional capabilities. It consists of warm-up and individually prescribed cardiovascular exercises, strength training, cool-down and relaxation techniques, dietary counseling, assistance with quitting smoking, and patient education classes. Appropriate candidates for this program are persons with heart (heart attack, bypass surgery, balloon angioplasty, cardiac transplants), pulmonary, or kidney disease, and other chronic diseases for which exercise intervention is deemed appropriate.

Children's Hospital provides a complete range of medical services and treatment for patients ranging in age from newborn to adolescents. With over 150 beds and a staff of nearly 600 doctors and nurses, Children's Hospital treats almost all diseases that affect children. Among the excellent pediatric programs are the following:

The Junior League Children's Lung Cancer Center is a collaborative effort of the Junior League of Nashville, which provided start-up funds for personnel and facility renovations and for Vanderbilt University Medical Center. Dedicated in January 1991, the center focuses on pulmonary research, diagnosis, and treatment of infants, children, and young adults with lung problems. Four physicians and three nurse clinicians also provide consultation services to area physicians and coordinate chronic care via home health nursing agencies. Services within the center include the Cystic Fibrosis Program, the Pediatric Pulmonary Function Laboratory, the Infant Chronic Lung Disease Program and Pediatric Flexible Bronchoscopy.

The Child Development Center (CDC) is a specialized diagnostic clinic of Vanderbilt Children's Hospital. As a referral center serving 40 counties in Middle Tennessee, the CDC provides thorough diagnostic assessment and recommendations to children and young adults with developmental problems, such as mental retardation, autism, cerebral palsy, attention deficit and hyperactivity disorders, and learning disabilities. Through its recommendations, the CDC attempts to link patients with the necessary treatment and social agencies. The Behavioral Pediatrics Clinic, a service of CDC, provides consultation, evaluation, and intervention services for children between birth and 12 years of age who exhibit common behavior problems, including temper tantrums, noncompliance, over-activity, fears, and difficulty with eating, sleeping, or toilet routines. The CDC also has a summer day treatment program for children with attention deficit hyperactivity disorders.

Other special adult centers include the Vanderbilt Institute for Treatment of Addiction, the Sports Medicine Center, the Pain Center, the Parkinson's Disease Center, and the Middle Tennessee Poison Center.

MEDICAL SPECIALTIES

Anesthesiology, Burn Treatment, Cancer, Cardiology, Clinical Pharmacology, Dermatology, Diabetes, Emergency/Trauma Medicine, Endocrinology/Metabolism, Endoscopy, Gastroenterology, Genetics, Hematology, Hypertension, Infectious Diseases, Infertility, Intensive Care, Nephrology, Nutrition, Neonatal Intensive Care, Neurology, Neurosurgery, Obstetrics/Gynecology, Oncology, Ophthalmology, Orthopedic Surgery, Orthopedics and Rehabilitation, Otolaryngology, Pediatric Surgery, Pediatrics, Plastic Surgery, Preventive Medicine, Psychiatry, Radiation Therapy, Radiology, Renal Medicine, Rheumatology, Speech Pathology, Surgery, Thoracic and Cardiac Surgery, Transplantation Surgery, and Urology.

WELL-KNOWN SPECIALISTS

- Dr. Frank H. Boehm   *Obstetrics/gynecology*
- Dr. Preston W. Campbell, III   *Pediatrics*
- Dr. Robert B. Cotton   *Pediatrics; specialist in neonatology*
- Dr. Jayant K. Deshpande   *Pediatrics; director of division of critical care and anesthesiology*
- Dr. Stephen S. Feman   *Ophthalmology*
- Dr. Gerald M. Fenichel   *Neurology*
- Dr. Michael E. Glasscock, III   *Otolaryngology*

- Dr. Thomas P. Graham, Jr.   *Pediatrics; director of the division of Pediatric Cardiology*
- Dr. Neil E. Green   *Orthopedics and rehabilitation*
- Dr. Mark T. Jennings   *Neurology*
- Dr. Peter T. Loosen   *Psychoneuroendocrinology*
- Dr. Richard A. Margolin   *Geriatric psychiatry*
- Dr. Samuel R. Marney, Jr.   *Allergy and immunology*
- Dr. John Hughes Newman   *Pulmonary medicine*
- Dr. Barry Nurcombe   *Child and adolescent psychiatry*
- Dr. David N. Orth   *Endocrinology*
- Dr. C. Leon Partain   *Radiology*
- Dr. William Schaffner   *Preventive medicine*
- Dr. Joseph A. Smith, Jr.   *Urology*
- Dr. Sulramanian Suran   *Experimental neurology*

PATIENT SATISFACTION

During the past three years, Vanderbilt University Hospital has participated in the University Hospital Consortiums's Patient-Centered Care Survey Program to facilitate measurement of inpatient satisfaction. Within this initiative, 12 key areas of patient care are measured: admitting process, physician care, nursing care, resident/intern care, surgical care, pain control, discharge process, billing information, nutrition information, food service, housekeeping, and facility maintenance.

Results of an inpatient survey fielded in the spring of 1994 indicated that 90% of those surveyed would return to Vanderbilt University Hospital and that an unusually high 86% felt they had received excellent care. Compared to other university hospitals, Vanderbilt scored above average in overall satisfaction, as well as within the key areas of physician care, nursing care, the discharge process, and facility maintenance.

RESEARCH

For the fiscal year ending June 30, 1993, a total of 667 grants and contracts, valued at approximately $103.6 million, were awarded across 14 research centers at Vanderbilt Medical Center, including the School of Nursing. The federal government supports over 65% of research. Vanderbilt University Hospital has been designated a General Clinical Research Center by the National Institutes of Health.

In 1993, VUMC positioned itself as a world-class cancer research and treatment center with the establishment of the Vanderbilt Cancer Center, designed to strengthen the links between basic researchers and clinicians. Strategies to move research findings quickly to the patient-care setting include improving communication between basic and clinical scientists, fostering translational research (projects with clinical application), and establishing a number of core laboratories.

VUMC is participating in a nationwide prostate cancer trial, sponsored by the National Cancer Institute, testing the efficacy of the drug finasteride in preventing prostate cancer.

VUMC continues to be involved in the fight against AIDS, on both the research and the clinical fronts. Researchers working on a potential AIDS vaccine have entered the final push toward a large-scale efficacy trial. VUMC researchers are examining whether an immune-boosting vaccine given to pregnant women infected with HIV can protect their unborn babies from the disease.

Other research achievements are in cardiovascular medicine; pharmacology; cancer genetics, namely on the gene known as p53, the most frequently mutated gene in human cancers; a new stenting method that reduces the risks of angioplasty; formation of a Rare Disorders Network, designed to increase the viability of rare disorders; a laser-assisted technique for snoring; and research aiming to counteract the effect of zero gravity on astronauts.

The Elizabeth B. Lamb Center for Pediatric Research was established in the Department of Pediatrics and at Children's Hospital in 1990. It is dedicated to basic research to determine how microbial organisms (viruses, bacteria, fungi, or parasites) cause disease. The center includes laboratories for the study of viral diseases in order to develop strategies to prevent and treat viral infections. The center plays a strong role in teaching medical students, graduate students, fellows and house officers about infectious diseases in children, and in fostering collaboration among specialists in the clinical and basic sciences throughout the medical center. The center also sponsors an annual visiting professorship and a monthly seminar series.

The Arthritis and Lupus Center conducts research to identify the causes of, and improved treatments for, inflammatory rheumatic diseases. The program includes basic immunology research, participation of more than 500 patients in treatment research protocols, and the monitoring of more than 3,000 patients throughout the United States. These studies have led to important advances in the management of rheumatoid arthritis, systemic lupus erythematosus and other rheumatic diseases.

Other research centers include the Center for Biomedical Informatics, the Center for Fertility and Reproductive Research, the Specialized Center of Research in Hypertension, the Specialized Center of Research in Newborn Lung Disease, and the Vanderbilt Voice Center.

ADMISSIONS POLICY

Patients must be admitted to Vanderbilt by a physician with admitting privileges. They may be admitted through the Admitting Office, The Vanderbilt Clinics, and the Emergency Department.

All patients treated at Vanderbilt are expected to make adequate arrangements for payment of their hospital bills. Payment is defined as verified insurance benefits or payment arrangements representing either the patient's portion above coverage limits, or payment in full. Exceptions are made when the admission and/or treatment is an emergency, as determined by the attending physician. After the emergency condition has ended, the patient comes under the standing financial policies. Exceptions to the financial requirement are also made when the needed services can be obtained only at Vanderbilt. Almost $26 million in free annual care was provided in 1993.

Special phone number for admissions information: (615) 322-2225.

BAYLOR UNIVERSITY

MEDICAL CENTER

Founded as the Texas Baptist Sanitarium over 80 years ago, Baylor University Medical Center (BUMC) serves patients from Texas, the southwest, and around the world. It is the second largest church-related hospital in the United States, according to the *AHA Guide to the Health Care Field,* and is the largest private hospital in the state of Texas.

The medical center is the nucleus of a system that includes Baylor Medical Center, Ennis; Baylor Medical Center, Gilmer; Baylor Institute for Rehabilitation (formerly Swiss Avenue Hospital) in Dallas; Baylor Medical Center, Grapevine; and Baylor Medical Center, Waxahachie. These community hospitals provide primary and secondary acute care, as well as long-term and specialized care, and constitute a referral base for Baylor University Medical Center in Dallas.

Research and the application of its findings are the hallmarks of Baylor University Medical Center, a five-hospital complex. In many medical specialties, Baylor physicians are applying state-of-the-art treatments. For example, Baylor researchers are preparing for the first clinical trials of gene therapy for cancer. They hope that by inserting cancer-killing genes into only cancer cells they may be able to eliminate the severe side effects of chemotherapy. In another development, Baylor physicians pioneered the use of a new immunosuppressive drug, FK506, to decrease rejection in liver transplants. Baylor is

FOUNDED AS THE TEXAS BAPTIST SANITARIUM OVER EIGHTY YEARS AGO, BAYLOR UNIVERSITY MEDICAL CENTER (BUMC) SERVES PATIENTS FROM TEXAS, THE SOUTHWEST, AND AROUND THE WORLD.

now one of the few transplant centers approved to use FK506 in small bowel transplants.

TelMed, a tape library of health information, is available by phone (214/820-4000) and has received more than one million calls since its inception in 1980. Community programs in weight loss, stress management, pregnancy and birth, chemical and alcohol addiction, and home health care are also available.

Education is a major concern at the medical center. The A. Webb Roberts Center for Continuing Education in Health Sciences presents educational programs for physicians, nurses, and allied health professionals.

SPECIAL FACILITIES AND PROGRAMS

Baylor's program of liver and kidney transplants is one of the largest in the country, with one of the highest survival rates. Over 372 kidney and 933 liver procedures have been performed since the program started in 1985. Baylor surgeons also perform heart transplants.

Baylor's Sammons Cancer Center conducts active research in genetics, interleukin-2, monoclonal antibodies, immunotoxins, and advanced laser applications. In 1993 alone, the Center did 162 bone marrow transplants.

The Cancer Center practices a multidisciplinary approach to cancer, combining oncology, hematology, surgery, radiation oncology, and many other disciplines. In addition, patients learn to cope with their illness with the help of special support groups. The families of cancer patients also learn about the emotional and physical impact of cancer.

More than 25 subspecialties of cardiology are practiced at the Hunt Heart Center. Physicians there apply advanced procedures for the diagnosis, treatment, and rehabilitation of patients; they also conduct research in heart disease.

The Diagnostic Center for Digestive Diseases, one of only two such centers in the world, deals with chronic illnesses of the digestive tract, such as peptic ulcers, hepatitis, Crohn's disease, and cancer of the

AT A GLANCE

Beds: 1,455
Occupancy Rate: 63%
Average Patient Count: 917
Average Patient Stay: 5.4 days
Annual Admissions: 36,554
Births: 3,714
Outpatient Clinic Visits: 333,279
Emergency Room/Trauma Center Visits: 57,631

HOSPITAL PERSONNEL
Physicians: 650
Residents: 165
Registered Nurses: 1,081

ROOM CHARGES (PER DIEM)
Private: $397
Semiprivate: $394
ICU: $1,100

ADDRESS
3500 Gaston Avenue
Dallas, TX 75246

TELEPHONE
(214) 820-2264

digestive organs. The Center conducts research and provides patient care for both children and adults.

The orthopedic service at BUMC is highly renowned in Dallas and throughout north Texas. Physicians perform surgical reattachment of limbs and special hand surgery, as well as other advanced orthopedic techniques.

Baylor's nationally known Psoriasis Center has been in operation for seven years. A comprehensive ambulatory center for the treatment of psoriasis, the facility offers the latest treatments, including Goeckerman therapy, which utilizes crude coal tar and UV light; PUVA therapy; and Ingram therapy.

At the Blanche Swanzy Lange Special Care Nursery, neonatologists help care for premature and high-risk babies.

Baylor also provides specialized care for the very young and the very old. Designed like a Victorian home, the Pediatric Center for Restorative Care is a medical facility for seriously ill and technology-dependent children. Services include therapy, family education counseling, hospice care for terminally ill children, as well as spiritual and bereavement counseling. The center can accommodate families on a 24-hour basis, both as inpatients and outpatients.

The elderly receive care in four community-based centers that provide primary medical care. These centers also offer specialty care for incontinence, Alzheimer's disease, foot pain, and imbalance.

Laser surgery is an important part of the work at Baylor. While there is no organized program or center, lasers are utilized in clinical practice and in research. The medical center also maintains "centers of excellence" in ambulatory surgery, arthritis, breast cancer, diabetes, drug/alcohol dependency, emergency medicine, medical imaging, physical medicine, psoriasis, and visual function testing.

MEDICAL SPECIALTIES

Cardiology; Digestive Diseases; Gynecology; Intensive Care; Laser Surgery; Liver, Heart, and Kidney Transplants; Neonatology; Neurology; Ophthalmology; Oncology; Orthopedics; Otolaryngology; and Rehabilitation.

WELL-KNOWN SPECIALISTS

- Dr. Fritz E. Barton   *Plastic surgery; specialist in reconstructive surgery*
- Dr. Andrew Chubick   *Rheumatology*
- Dr. John Fordtran   *Gastroenterology*
- Dr. Thomas Gonwa   *Kidney transplants*
- Dr. A. Alan Menter   *Dermatology; specialist in psoriasis*
- Dr. William C. Roberts   *Cardiology*
- Dr. Rand William Spencer   *Ophthalmology; specialist in vitreo-retinal surgery*
- Dr. Harold C. Urschel, Jr.   *Thoracic surgery*

PATIENT SATISFACTION

In a 1994 survey, about 98% of previous inpatients reported that they would recommend Baylor to a friend or family member. More than 90% of outpatients said they would recommend Baylor.

RESEARCH

The Baylor Research Institute is a major component of the Baylor Medical Center Group. With approximately $5.5 million in funding, the Foundation conducts research in more than 130 different and diverse projects. More than 60% of the Institute's work is in clinical research, covering such areas as organ transplants, oncology, photobiology, cardiology, psoriasis, digestive diseases, muscles and sports medicine.

Two Baylor researchers recently developed a technique for imaging breasts using MRI to find tumors as small as three millimeters.

Another ongoing research project is a study of how to spur blood cell growth to help patients recover faster from bone marrow transplants.

ADMISSIONS POLICY

Although physician referral is not required for admission, upon arrival at the hospital, all patients are admitted by a Baylor physician.

BUMC accepts assignment from insured patients. Noninsured patients may be asked for a deposit before admission.

Baylor provides the community with many services. For example, anyone who is new to Dallas and is seeking a physician can call the center's Helpline at 214/820-3312. It's a free physician referral service where callers can choose a doctor from an extensive list of qualified candidates.

M . D .   A N D E R S O N

C A N C E R   C E N T E R

UNIVERSITY OF TEXAS

HOUSTON, TEXAS

In 1941, a hospital was established to serve Texans afflicted with cancer. Today, the University of Texas M.D. Anderson Cancer Center is a comprehensive facility that serves not only Texans, but patients from around the world. M.D. Anderson patients come from all 254 Texas counties, as well as from all 50 states and more than 50 foreign countries. They come for cancer diagnostic and treatment services that are among the most extensive in the world. Patients also come because of Anderson's reputation for quality care. In 1992, M.D. Anderson received accreditation with commendation from the Joint Commission on Accreditation of Healthcare Organizations (JCAHO). Only 3.7% of hospital surveys made by the JCAHO during 1992 resulted in accreditation with commendation. To qualify for this distinction, M.D. Anderson received perfect or near perfect scores in important categories, including nursing care, surgical services, diagnostic radiology and laboratory medicine, infection control, rehabilitation medicine, patient and family education, and medical staff credentialing. In addition, 56 of Anderson's physicians were named in *The Best Doctors in America*.

M.D. ANDERSON PATIENTS COME FROM ALL 254 TEXAS COUNTIES, AS WELL AS FROM ALL 50 STATES AND MORE THAN 50 FOREIGN COUNTRIES. THEY COME FOR CANCER DIAGNOSTIC AND TREATMENT SERVICES THAT ARE AMONG THE MOST EXTENSIVE IN THE WORLD.

M.D. Anderson offers all clinical oncology specialties and many subspecialties that are available in only a few other comprehensive cancer centers. For example, the Division of Pathology includes 30 full-

The Best Hospitals in America

time board-certified pathologists, with two or three experts available in each surgical pathology subspecialty of head and neck, gastrointestinal, and genitourinary cancer. In addition, M.D. Anderson's pathologists offer such unique diagnostic tests as DNA content probes and techniques to measure proliferative factors and cell death rates. M.D. Anderson is internationally known for such specialized cancer services as treatment of deep-seated brain tumors; management of all childhood cancers; bone marrow transplantation for leukemia, lymphoma, multiple myeloma and breast cancer; radical liver, pancreas and pelvic surgery; clinical chemotherapy trials; cyclotron radiation therapy; microvascular surgery; total body irradiation for leukemia; stereotactic surgery for brain tumors; skull base surgery; intraoperative radiotherapy; interventional radiology; management for extremely rare tumors; cancer treatment for pregnant women; and cryotherapy for prostate and liver cancers. Some of the newest clinical innovations include advanced combination biologic therapy and gene therapy for hematologic malignancies like leukemia and such solid tumors as ovarian, breast and lung cancers. M.D. Anderson is also pioneering the new field of chemoprevention, which focuses on administering natural and synthetic compounds that can prevent or delay development of pre-cancerous lesions and second primary tumors in high-risk patients.

Starting with pioneering interferon studies in the mid-1970s, the world's largest clinical test of biologic substances has been conducted at M.D. Anderson. More than 25 natural and synthetic body proteins and other compounds that can stimulate, modify or restore the immune system now are being analyzed, either singly or in combination. The synergistic effects of giving biologics with chemotherapy mean additional treatment options for many patients.

Several examples of combination therapy and innovative supporting methods developed or refined at M.D. Anderson are conservation surgery followed by radiotherapy, so many women with breast cancer can avoid radical mastectomy without

AT A GLANCE

Beds: 518
Occupancy Rate: 76%
Average Patient Count: 396
Average Patient Stay: 7.7 days
Annual Admissions: 18,701
Outpatient Clinic Visits:
    586,979

HOSPITAL PERSONNEL
Physicians: 372
    Board Certified: 349
Residents: 148
Registered Nurses: 918
    BS Degree: 503

ROOM CHARGES (PER DIEM)
Private: $390
Semiprivate: $355
ICU: $1,100

ADDRESS
1515 Holcombe Blvd.
Houston, TX 77030

TELEPHONE
(713) 792-2121

The Best Hospitals in America

403

compromising survival rates; collaboration of surgeons, radiotherapists, and/or medical oncologists to help patients preserve normal bowel functions or retain speaking and eating abilities; limb-salvage treatment in which bone cancer patients take chemotherapy before and after surgery, thereby avoiding amputation of affected arms or legs; application of surgical lasers to remove previously inoperable brain tumors, excise bladder cancers, and extend therapy options for other tumors; and tiny drug-delivery pumps, concealed by clothes, carried in shoulder bags, or worn on belts, which have freed thousands of patients from hospital confinement and allowed them to continue normal activities. Some combination therapies for rare tumors, as well as more common cancers, are available only at M.D. Anderson and perhaps a handful of other centers. More patients are treated on an outpatient basis at M.D. Anderson than at any other cancer center. All of the treatment programs are supported by the largest and most automated hospital-based pharmacy in the United States.

M.D. Anderson's Division of Nursing and Pharmacy provides interdisciplinary services to all clinicians and their patients. Teams of nurses are trained in specific types of cancer-site care and in management of such combined therapies as multiple anti-cancer drugs with radiotherapy and/or biologic therapy. The Division of Pharmacy, which is the largest and most automated hospital-based pharmacy in the world, provides increasing support as the drug component of cancer care becomes more important. Clinical pharmacists prepare in excess of 5,000 intravenous fluid doses per day and more than 4,000 portable chemotherapy pumps a month. During the past year, a pharmacoeconomics program was started to compare costs and outcomes of drug therapy, which averages 30% of cancer patients' expenses, and to ensure that the drug therapy the patients are receiving is cost effective and optimal.

Other supportive specialties include dieticians dedicated to individual types of cancer, patient care coordinators, chaplains, social workers, patient advocates, and translators, as well as volunteers for numerous support services and medical ethicists.

SPECIAL FACILITIES AND PROGRAMS

M.D. Anderson has led the world in developing comprehensive outpatient cancer services that can be delivered in an ambulatory setting. The approximately 2,300 patient visits that are now recorded daily in the more than 50 outpatient clinics range from extensive radiotherapy services to the diagnosis and treatment of extremely rare endocrine tumors. Patients benefit both financially and emotionally in an outpatient environment. Specialized outpatient facilities include the world's largest ambulatory center for chemotherapy, with 68 private rooms where patients can receive anti-cancer drugs and supportive therapy for up to 24 hours without hospital admissions. A nearby satellite ambulatory treatment center opened in 1993 and provides faster, more convenient chemotherapy and other services for patients who do not need to go to the main complex. The Ambulatory Surgery Center provides facilities where about 3,000 patients can undergo such operations as lumpectomies and modified radical mastectomies for breast cancer, excision of head and neck lesions, some urologic procedures and diagnostic laparoscopies without being admitted to the hospital. The nation's largest radiotherapy department offers the widest array of treatment equipment, one of the few intraoperative radiotherapy units, and many other innovative therapy strategies combining chemotherapy, surgery, and biological therapy.

A separate clinic has been established for patients with so-called "mystery" cancers (a condition in which the primary cancer remains unknown) that affect 5–7% of cancer patients; physician specialists who staff this clinic have the world's largest databank on such cancers and have started several clinical trials for subsets of patients with common problems.

M.D. Anderson conducts one of the two largest bone marrow transplantation programs in the country. Since the program started in late 1975, more than 2,500 procedures have been performed. Approximately 275 bone marrow transplants are performed annually. Both autologous and allogeneic transplantation procedures are offered. An autologous bone marrow transplant involves removal of a patient's own bone marrow while he or she is in remission and freezing it until it is returned to the patient after high-dose chemotherapy. Allogeneic bone marrow transplants use bone marrow from tissue-compatible donors, usually a sibling or parent. More recently, transplantation of histologically matched bone marrow from unrelated donors has been made possible through a national program that recruits potential donors for listing in a computerized registry. More autologous bone marrow transplants have been done at M.D. Anderson than anywhere in the world. The institution also has been at the forefront in developing techniques for blood stem cell transplants for patients whose bone marrow cannot be extracted from their pelvic area.

A 20-bed protected environment is provided for patients who are particularly susceptible to life-threatening infections. It is the only such facility in the world. Patients recovering from some types of bone marrow transplants, as well as those taking high-dose chemotherapy for leukemia, lymphoma, multiple myeloma, and such common cancers as cancer of the breast and lung, may spend four to six weeks in one of the isolation rooms, where everything they eat, wear, and use is sterilized.

Funded by a $2.34 million grant from the National Cancer Institute, the Brain Tumor Center is a multidisciplinary clinical and research unit, within the University of Texas M.D. Anderson Cancer Center, devoted to the development of improved treatments for brain tumors. It is one of the largest such centers in North America with respect to clinical and laboratory personnel and research, with major multidisciplinary programs in anti-cancer drug development and the molecular biology and genetics of gliomas. Patient clinics and services within the Brain Tumor Center include the Adult Neuro-Oncology Clinic, the Pediatric Neuro-Oncology Clinic, the Neurosurgery Clinic, the Radiotherapy Clinic, the Neurofibromatosis Clinics, the Neuropsychology Service, the Neuroimaging Services, and the Neuropathology Service.

Other special programs include a cancer rehabilitation and pain management program, including a special hospital wing devoted entirely to pain and symptom control, restorative therapies, and transitional care. Disease site centers for patients with breast, lung, head and neck, gastrointestinal, and other cancers are being set up to allow patients to see all medical team members in one location, thereby greatly reducing the time needed for evaluation, diagnosis, and treatment planning.

As with all excellent cancer centers, technology plays a major role at M.D. Anderson. Highly specialized surgical equipment includes lasers for specific cancer problems and tools for delicate reconstructive procedures. Stereotactic radiosurgery equipment that permits surgery without a knife for otherwise inoperable brain tumors, and intraoperative radiotherapy machines that allow high-dose radiation to be delivered to tissues exposed during surgery, are available at only a few centers, including M.D. Anderson.

Specialized laboratory medicine equipment includes machines in a molecular diagnostic laboratory, a cytogenetics laboratory, and a flow cytometry center, all of which enable clinicians to identify cancer cells earlier and plan precise treatment regimens. After therapy, these methods provide markers for minimal residual disease or relapse. Pathology prognostic tests unavailable elsewhere include DNA content probes and techniques to measure hormone receptors, proliferative factors, and cell death rates.

The latest generation of nuclear imaging machinery provides improved testing and diagnosis for many cancers, especially those earmarked for radioimmunotherapy. Diagnostic imaging machinery includes numerous units for computerized tomography, magnetic resonance imaging, and ultrasound scanning. The range of ultrasound scanning, for instance, includes vascular and intracavitary examinations. M.D. Anderson helped develop the original blood cell separator 15 years ago, and has pioneered using improved models to extend blood component therapy to the majority of patients. This equipment is also critically important for specialized stem cell transplants in patients unable to undergo bone marrow transplants because of a lack of tissue-matching donors.

While some types of cancer can be successfully treated at community hospitals, others require a variety of specialized services not usually found in community health networks. These services, which M.D. Anderson provides, include sophisticated risk assessment for cancer, comprehensive multidisciplinary treatment planning, and full-service cancer prevention programs.

M.D. Anderson's approach to cancer care goes far beyond actual treatments and includes an extensive Patient Education Office, a patient/family library that is a branch of the Houston Public Library, and numerous supportive programs. Patients and their families are encouraged to participate in the Anderson Network, a volunteer group of more than 800 patients and former patients who provide practical and emotional support. The Anderson Network Hospitality Room at M.D. Anderson is open daily for the benefit of patients wanting to stop by for coffee, juice, and a reassuring conversation. Public education has long been a strength of M.D. Anderson, which operates a CancerWISE Community Speakers Bureau and provides regular tours to various groups of students, civic leaders and international visitors. With support from the National Cancer Institute, M.D. Anderson also provides the Cancer Information Service, a toll-free service for residents of Texas and Oklahoma. Since its inception in 1975, M.D. Anderson's Cancer Information Service has helped more than 350,000 callers obtain the latest information about cancer and related topics.

Among the services that M.D. Anderson offers to help colleagues in communities throughout Texas is the Texas Outreach Program, which includes projects focusing on skin cancer prevention, cervical cancer prevention and detection for economically disadvantaged women in the Rio Grande Valley, and a statewide neuroblastoma screening service. A related service is the Radiologic-Pathologic Institute, which is providing long-distance diagnostic support to doctors across the state and beyond.

MEDICAL SPECIALTIES

Anesthesiology and Critical Care, Breast and Gynecologic Medical Oncology, Clinical Immunology and Biological Therapy, Clinical Investigation, Dental Oncology, Diagnostic Radiology, Gastrointestinal Medical Oncology and Digestive Diseases, Genitourinary Medical Oncology, Gynecologic Surgical Oncology, Head and Neck Surgery, Hematology, Laboratory Medicine, Medical Specialties (Cardiology, Dermatology, Endocrinology, General Internal Medicine, Geriatrics, Infectious Diseases, Nephrology, Pulmonary and Critical Care Medicine, Rehabilitation Medicine), Melanoma/Sarcoma Medical Oncology, Neuro-oncology (Psychiatric Oncology, Pain Management and Behavioral Psychology), Neurosurgery, Nuclear Medicine, Pathology, Pediatrics, Radiotherapy, Reconstructive and Plastic Surgery, Surgical Oncology, Thoracic and Head and Neck Medical Oncology, Thoracic and Cardiovascular Surgery, and Urology.

WELL-KNOWN SPECIALISTS

- Dr. Jaffer A. Ajani   *Medical oncology/hematology; specialist in gastrointestinal oncology*
- Dr. Frederick C. Ames   *Surgical oncology; specialist in breast cancer and melanoma*
- Dr. K. Kian Ang   *Radiation oncology; specialist in head and neck cancer*
- Dr. Charles M. Balch   *Surgical oncology; specialist in breast cancer and melanoma*
- Dr. W. Archie Bleyer   *Pediatrics; specialist in pediatric hematology/oncology*
- Dr. Gerald P. Bodey   *Infectious diseases; specialist in cancer and infections*
- Dr. Fernando Cabanillas   *Medical oncology/hematology; specialist in lymphomas*
- Dr. Richard Champlin   *Medical oncology/hematology; specialist in bone marrow transplantation, leukemia, and lymphomas*
- Dr. James D. Cox   *Radiation oncology; specialist in lung cancer*

- Dr. Luis Delclos *Radiation oncology; specialist in brachytherapy and gynecologic cancer*
- Dr. Patricia J. Eifel *Radiation oncology; specialist in gynecologic cancer*
- Dr. W. Keith Hoots *Medical oncology/hematology; specialist in disorders of bleeding, and thrombosis*
- Dr. Hagop Kantarjian *Medical oncology/hematology; specialist in leukemia*
- Dr. E. Edmund Kim *Nuclear medicine; specialist in nuclear medicine and oncology*
- Dr. Bernard Levin *Gastroenterology, medical oncology; specialist in gastrointestinal cancer, and gastrointestinal oncology*
- Dr. Christopher J. Logothetis *Medical oncology/hematology; specialist in genitourinary cancer*
- Dr. John A. Murray *Orthopedic surgery; specialist in tumor surgery*
- Dr. Jack A. Roth *Thoracic surgery; specialist in thoracic surgery, and thoracic oncology surgery*
- Dr. Raymond Sawaya *Neurological surgery; specialist in tumor surgery*
- Dr. Andrew C. von Eschenbach *Urology; specialist in urologic oncology*
- Dr. W. K. Alfred Yung *Neurology; specialist in adult neuro-oncology*

PATIENT SATISFACTION

M.D. Anderson's satisfaction survey process is currently being redesigned. Until February 1994, a card was available in patient care areas which allowed patients free-lance opportunity to comment as well as grade services by category. The card was changed and the category by service sections were eliminated. The current card allows comments only.

A committee to develop a formalized patient satisfaction survey process is in place. The process of selecting a vendor to outsource the formal survey is being finalized.

For the five months ending January 1994, overall patient satisfaction with services based on care and compassion shown was rated at 88%, based on the old free-form survey system.

RESEARCH

Research expenditures for fiscal year 1993 were $127.5 million. External research support received totaled $72.3 million. M.D. Anderson was first in the number of grants awarded by the National Cancer Institute.

Many major advances in cancer research over the past half-century have been made at M.D. Anderson, where interdisciplinary teams of scientists collaborate with clinical colleagues. One of the most important achievements has been better understanding of the genesis of cancer at the molecular level. M.D. Anderson is home to the world's largest program in cancer metastasis, which remains the primary cause of failed therapies; teams of scientists are working to understand why certain cancers spread from primary to distant sites, as well as on novel strategies to prevent metastasis. Researchers are also doing pioneering work in clarifying the role of numerous environmental factors in the inception of cancer.

Some specific basic and clinical research contributions include the first observation of virus-like particles in human cancer tissues, opening the way for worldwide studies on the role of viruses in cancer; the development of a banding technique to identify all 46 chromosomes and methods to detect genetic-associated cancers and to monitor therapy; the design of a cold chamber cryostat that dramatically improved the ability of pathologists to diagnose cancer while patients were in surgery, and also to quickly provide surgical specimen slides to expedite therapy planning; a technique to enclose toxic drugs in microscopic fatty capsules known as liposomes, so higher doses can go directly to tumors; and the discovery of the T-cell receptor that has a critical role in the body's defense against foreign tissues, tumor cells, and some viruses.

Powerful DNA probe tests that can detect recurring leukemia and lymphoma, when the malignant cells comprise 1% or less of all cells, were developed at Anderson.

Trials of potentially far-reaching techniques to activate patients' white blood cells and target treatment to attack only malignant cells, an approach that could revolutionize management of cancer metastasis, are currently underway.

Anderson scientists and physicians are also conducting studies to design individual vaccines which would protect patients from recurrent malignant melanoma, as well as from ovarian and colon cancers.

M.D. Anderson is one of 270 institutions around the country enrolling women in a clinical trial to determine whether the drug tamoxifen can be used to prevent breast cancer in women at high risk for the disease. By the fall of 1993, M.D. Anderson had enrolled more than 220 participants in the trial—the largest number of any participating institution. M.D. Anderson researchers hope to enroll a total of 300 women.

ADMISSIONS POLICY

Admission to M.D. Anderson Cancer Center is based on referral by the patient's physician. Members of the medical staff at M.D. Anderson are employed by the cancer center and do not participate in private practice or have admitting privileges elsewhere.

Patients are required to provide proof of acceptable insurance coverage or make a deposit equal to the estimated cost of their treatment. Texas residents may apply for assistance and each case is handled on an individual basis.

Because M.D. Anderson is a state chartered and supported hospital, it provides cancer care to all citizens of Texas, regardless of ability to pay. Indigent care and government contractual adjustments amounted to $187 million in fiscal year 1993.

Special phone number for admissions information: (713) 792-6161.

PATIENT/FAMILY ACCOMMODATIONS

Accommodations for patients and their families are available at the Jesse H. Jones Rotary House International at special rates of $66–$69 for hotel rooms and $84–$89 for suites.

METHODIST HOSPITAL

Founded in 1919 in downtown Houston, Methodist Hospital today is a 1,527-bed complex located in the world-renowned Texas Medical Center. One of the largest private non-profit hospitals in the nation, it is staffed by more than 6,000 professionals and support personnel. As a complete acute-care facility, Methodist provides comprehensive medical services in all adult specialties. The hospital's 3.3 million square feet of space houses one of the most complete centers for patient care and service in the world. Methodist Hospital's mission of patient care, research, and education is supported by its non-profit status, which means that all revenues in excess of expenses, or "profits," are reinvested in the organization.

Methodist is the primary adult teaching hospital for Baylor College of Medicine, one of the country's leading institutions of medical education and research. All 856 members of the active medical staff hold concurrent faculty appointments at Baylor. Through its affiliation with Baylor College of Medicine, millions of dollars in research programs are translated directly into innovative patient treatments at the hospital. And through community-based activities, this care is also being provided through Methodist's preventive health screenings for the public and through direct patient care programs in Houston's hospital district facilities. Methodist also

THE HOSPITAL'S 3.3 MILLION SQUARE FEET OF SPACE HOUSES ONE OF THE MOST COMPLETE CENTERS FOR PATIENT CARE AND SERVICE IN THE WORLD.

sponsors training programs for nursing, as well as most of the allied heath professions.

Methodist Hospital has long been famous for its innovations in cardiology and cardiovascular surgery, and is the home of famed heart surgeon Dr. Michael E. DeBakey. Working with Baylor College of Medicine, the hospital developed one of the largest transplant centers in the country, the Multi-Organ Transplant Center, and is also known for its use of state-of-the-art technology and innovative diagnostic and surgical treatments for cancer and aneurysms. In addition, the high-quality, high-value patient care has been extended beyond the hospital's walls through the rapidly growing Home Health Care service and the Sid W. Richardson Institute for Preventive Medicine. Lesser known is the fact that Methodist also is one the world's leading facilities in epilepsy research and in treating children with epilepsy.

The hospital is a major surgical center, with more than 70 operating rooms. Methodist orthopedic surgeons are established leaders in bone and joint surgery, and its neurosurgeons have earned worldwide recognition for advances in surgery of the brain and spinal cord. Methodist also is a center for ear, nose, throat, and eye care.

Methodist is also an internationally known referral center serving about 40,000 inpatients and performing nearly one million outpatient surgical procedures annually. A little more than half the patients come from outside the Houston area; in 1993, they came from all 50 states and 88 foreign countries. Through the Methodist Health Care Network, Methodist is affiliated with 39 institutions in Texas, Louisiana, Mexico, Guatemala, Italy, Venezuela, Turkey, and Peru. The hospital's connection to the United Methodist Church incorporates the spiritual component of health and healing into patient care. Methodist's department of Pastoral Services and Education is a resource to help people as they struggle with the difficult issues associated with illness. The hospital's services include everything from primary to tertiary care. Even a brief description of the programs offered at Methodist indicate why so many people are willing to travel long distances to obtain treatment there.

SPECIAL FACILITIES AND PROGRAMS

In conjunction with Baylor College of Medicine, and under the direction of Drs. Michael DeBakey and Antonio Gotto, Jr., Methodist's comprehensive transplant center performs bone marrow, cornea, heart, heart-lung, kidney, and liver transplants. Through the multidisciplinary resources available there, patients receive comprehensive care before the transplant and long-term follow-up care. Methodist's Multi-Organ Transplant Center performed 115 transplants in 1993, including heart, kidney, liver, lung, pancreas, cornea, and bone marrow.

The hospital believes an organized cardiac rehabilitation program is a beneficial method of providing cardiac patients and their families with education, as well as physical and psychological support during their hospitalization. The goal of cardiovascular pulmonary rehabilitation is to restore the cardiac patient to optimal physical, social, emotional, psychological, and vocational status during and after hospitalization. A multidisciplinary team of registered nurses, dieticians, exercise physiologists, physicians, social workers, and chaplains custom designs a program for each patient. Some of the areas of focus are stress management, lifestyle changes, benefits of exercise, the heart-healthy diet, smart shopping and dining out, risk factors of heart diseases, prescription for wellness, self-measurement of pulse and blood pressure, relaxation, and laughter.

The Methodist Hospital Kidney Dialysis Program specializes in the treatment of acute and chronic renal disease. The outpatient chronic renal disease program offers nurse-assisted and self-care hemodialysis, as well as home dialysis. The inpatient acute care program offers hemodialysis and peritoneal dialysis. The programs treat over 500 patients annually.

Methodist is the home of the world's first center devoted to neurosensory disorders, which includes the Blue Bird Circle Clinic for Pediatric Neurology, the only center in the Southwest devoted to pediatric neurology. It offers diagnosis and treatment for epilepsy, as well as for a variety of other neurological disorders in children. The Cullen Eye Institute offers cornea transplants, intraocular lens implants, radial keratotomy, and ultrasound treatment of glaucoma. The Institute for Otorhinolaryngology and Communicative Disorders encompasses ear, nose, and throat care, as well as speech pathology and therapy. The Jerry Lewis Neuromuscular Disease Research Center investigates multiple sclerosis, ALS, and a variety of other disorders.

The hospital has the largest facility for outpatient surgery in the nation; 42 percent of all its surgical procedures in 1993 were performed on an outpatient basis.

The Sid W. Richardson Institute for Preventive Medicine of the Methodist Hospital was established in 1980 to reduce the risk of serious disease by providing individual and group programs of diet and exercise

AT A GLANCE

Beds: 1,527
Occupancy Rate: 67%
Average Patient Count: 743
Average Patient Stay: 7.7 days
Annual Admissions: 31,903
Births: 2,543
Outpatient Clinic Visits:
 891,044
Emergency Room/Trauma
 Center Visits: 17,922

HOSPITAL PERSONNEL
Physicians: 1,625
 Board Certified: 1,347
Residents: 208
Registered Nurses: 1,714

ROOM CHARGES (PER DIEM)
Private: $335
Semiprivate: $300
ICU: $1,065

ADDRESS
6565 Fannin
Houston, TX 77030

TELEPHONE
(713) 790-3311

under constant scientific evaluation. The Institute includes a health and fitness club, nutrition education, cardiac rehabilitation programs, and corporate fitness programs.

The hospital's physicians are pioneering the use of the endoscope in surgery. With small, thin tubes equipped with cameras and surgical tools, doctors can perform complex procedures by making only tiny incisions in the abdomen and chest, thereby minimizing patient trauma and recovery time.

Methodist's state-of-the-art technology and procedures include a lithotriptor for non-surgical treatment of kidney stones; complete imaging capabilities, including an in-house suite for magnetic resonance imaging; advanced anesthesia monitoring equipment; 36 lasers and laser equipment; surgical microscopes for reconstructive microvascular and microneural surgery; a gamma knife; renal monoplane hyperbaric chambers; a computed tomographic machine and MRI-guided stereotactic surgery; stereotactic radiosurgery; a thermography machine; an X-knife; biplane digital angiography; a computerized electromyography and somatosensory machine; and large facilities for diagnostic cardiac procedures.

Methodist is distinguished for many other medical services, including the Institute for Preventive Medicine; Aeromedical Services, a helicopter-based patient transport service; the Chronic Pain Management Center; the Digestive Disease Center; and the Asthma Institute.

MEDICAL SPECIALTIES

Allergy & Immunology, Cardiology, Cardiovascular Surgery, Dermatology, Endocrinology, Gastroenterology, General Surgery, Geriatrics, Gynecology, Hematology, Infectious Diseases, Internal Medicine, Medical Oncology, Nephrology, Neurology, Neurophysiology, Neurosurgery, Obstetrics, Organ Transplantation, Orthopedics, Otorhinolaryngology, Pathology, Pediatrics, Physical Medicine and Rehabilitation, Plastic Surgery, Psychiatry, Pulmonary Diseases, Radiology, Radiotherapy and Urology.

WELL-KNOWN SPECIALISTS

- Dr. Bobby R. Alford *Otolaryngology, otology, neurology*
- Dr. Stanley H. Appel *Neurology; specialist in ALS, Alzheimer's disease, and neuromuscular disorders*
- Dr. David S. Baskin *Neurology, neurosurgery; specialist in the treatment of stroke-caused paralysis and Alzheimer's disease*
- Dr. C. Eugene Carlton, Jr. *Urology, urological diseases, prostate cancer*
- Dr. Michael DeBakey *Surgery; specialist in cardiovascular and transplant surgery*
- Dr. Alan J. Garber *Endocrinology and metabolism; specialist in diabetes*
- Dr. Antonio Gotto, Jr. *Internal medicine, atherosclerosis, lipid metabolism*
- Dr. Donald P. Griffith *Urology, endocrinology*
- Dr. Robert G. Grossman *Neurological surgery, epilepsy surgery*

- Dr. J. Alan Herd   *Internal medicine, cardiology*
- Dr. Jimmy F. Howell   *Surgery; specialist in cardiovascular and thoracic surgery*
- Dr. David Huston   *Internal medicine; specialist in immunology and immunodeficiency*
- Dr. Joseph Jankovic   *Neurology; specialist in movement disorders*
- Dr. Raymond H. Kaufman   *Obstetrics/gynecology; specialist in genital dermatological diseases*
- Dr. Alice R. McPherson   *Ophthalmology; specialist in disorders of the retina*
- Dr. George P. Noon   *Surgery; specialist in cardiovascular, thoracic, and vascular surgery, and heart, kidney, and lung transplantation*
- Dr. Peter Scardino   *Urology; urologic oncology*
- Dr. Melvin Spira   *Plastic and reconstructive surgery*
- Dr. Hugh S. Tullos   *Orthopedic surgery; specialist in hip surgery*
- Dr. Hartwell H. Whisennand   *Surgery; specialist in liver transplants*

PATIENT SATISFACTION

Ninety-five percent of Methodist inpatients and outpatients surveyed by Professional Research Consultants would recommend the Methodist Hospital to others; 97% of inpatients and outpatients said they had either an excellent or good impression of Methodist; and 94% said they were very satisfied with the quality of care they received.

RESEARCH

In 1993, research funding for Baylor College of Medicine amounted to over $163.3 million.

Major research facilities at Methodist include the DeBakey Heart Center, which houses two federally designated Specialized Centers of Research dedicated to the study of heart failure and atherosclerosis; one of three centers in the nation established for the study and treatment of Alzheimer's disease; one of five of the nation's amyotropic lateral sclerosis (ALS) clinics funded by the Muscular Dystrophy Association (MDA); one of two centers in the nation to receive National Institutes of Health (NIH) designation for prostate cancer research; and one of two centers in the nation to receive NIH funding for neonatal research.

The Methodist Hospital, along with Baylor, is one of the nation's leading research centers in cardiology. The Section of Cardiology, under the direction of Dr. Robert Roberts, has pioneered the application of recombinant DNA techniques to cardiac disorders, and it includes the only National Heart, Lung, and Blood Institute (NHLBI) Center for Molecular Biology of Heart Failure; the NHLBI Training Grant for Molecular Cardiology; a Program Project on cardiac development; as well as numerous clinical studies, such as TIMI (1 to 8), GUSTO and SOLVD for the treatment of heart attacks and strokes.

Dr. Antonio Gotto, Jr., is an internationally recognized researcher and educator in the field of blood lipids and their effects on the development of coronary heart disease. Methodist is a world leader in atherosclerosis research and one of the centers studying the regression, or reversal, of the atherosclerotic lesions of coronary heart disease.

Methodist is also the site of several pioneering cancer treatments being developed under the guidance of Dr. Peter Scardino. New medicines are being studied which may prevent prostate cancer, and new surgical techniques have reduced the side effects and improved the chances of recovery. Dr. Scardino and Baylor College of Medicine have been awarded one of two National Institutes of Health (NIH) grants establishing a Specialized Program of Research Excellence in prostate cancer.

Neurological research performed by Dr. David S. Baskin includes investigation of drugs that can partially reverse paralysis in stroke and spinal cord injury. One such drug, methylprednisolone, has been recently shown to be effective. Another clinical trial, using a drug called tirilizad to lessen damage during brain hemorrhage, is being concluded, and has shown positive results. Dr. Baskin's research also includes the effectiveness of viral techniques for the treatment of brain tumors, and he continues to work with neural tissue transplantation.

ADMISSIONS POLICY

Patients cannot be admitted to Methodist without a physician's referral. The hospital has a patient referral number which anyone can call to make contact with a physician who practices there. The phone number of the physician referral service is (713) 790-3599. Patients who need immediate care, however, may be seen in the emergency room without a private physician referral and without regard to the patient's ability to pay.

The hospital's financial requirements for routine admission are the same for all patients, regardless of income. As part of its pre-admission procedure, the hospital provides patients with an estimate of the cost of the hospitalization so that financial arrangements can be made to cover expenses. For those patients who apply and meet eligibility criteria, financial assistance can be made available for needed medical treatment.

Methodist is a non-profit, private health care institution with no tax support or endowment. In 1994, Methodist provided approximately $18 million in charity care.

ST. LUKE'S EPISCOPAL

HOSPITAL/TEXAS HEART

INSTITUTE

HOUSTON, TEXAS

Since the 1962 chartering of the Texas Heart Institute (THI), St. Luke's Episcopal Hospital and THI have enjoyed a partnership that has brought the hospital international recognition. Under the direction of surgeon-in-chief Dr. Denton A. Cooley, THI's successful cardiovascular surgery record and its advances in the medical management of cardiac disease have brought local, national and international patients to St. Luke's.

St. Luke's and the Texas Heart Institute have reached a number of medical milestones together. More than 550 people have received heart transplants through the Cardiac Transplant Program, which began in July 1982. In addition, 250 kidney transplantations have been performed since 1986, when the Renal Transplant Service at St. Luke's and the Texas Heart Institute joined the Cardiac Transplant Service. And in 1992, St. Luke's performed its first liver transplant, bringing the hospital another step closer to becoming a full organ transplant center. St. Luke's successful cardiovascular program has performed more than 85,000 open heart procedures, more than 145,000 cardiac catheterizations, and over 13,000 coronary balloon angioplasty procedures.

But St. Luke's Episcopal Hospital is more than a cardiac treatment center. At St. Luke's, physicians in 24 clinical services covering more than 41 specialties are supported by some of the most advanced technologies

SINCE THE 1962 CHARTERING OF THE TEXAS HEART INSTITUTE (THI), ST. LUKE'S EPISCOPAL HOSPITAL AND THI HAVE ENJOYED A PARTNERSHIP THAT HAS BROUGHT THE HOSPITAL INTERNATIONAL RECOGNITION.

available. This depth and breadth of medical resources enables St. Luke's to handle a wide spectrum of patients, from the low-risk obstetrics patient who spends 48 hours in the hospital to the patient with multisystem problems requiring the expertise found at an acute-care facility. Last year, St. Luke's handled more than 157,000 patient visits. A staff of nearly 4,000 employees and more than 350 volunteers provided direct patient care and support services for these patients.

St. Luke's Episcopal Hospital is a nonprofit general hospital located in the Texas Medical Center in Houston, the nation's largest health care complex. During the nearly four decades of its existence, St. Luke's has grown from a 180-bed hospital, which accepted its first patient in 1954, into a premier medical facility. The transformation into a modern state-of-the-art facility began with the construction of a 26-story patient tower above the original hospital in 1970. Expansion and modernization continued through 1990 with the opening of the 29-story St. Luke's Medical Tower, which is connected to St. Luke's Hospital via a glass-enclosed skybridge. This expansion of more than one million square feet meant an addition of outpatient facilities with 15 floors of physicians offices and ambulatory care facilities. The Ambulatory Surgery and Endoscopy Department in the tower includes 12 operating rooms, four endoscopy rooms, minor treatment rooms, a large waiting area, separate pediatric areas, and private family consultation rooms.

Through its relationships with Baylor College of Medicine and the University of Texas Medical School at Houston, St. Luke's participates in the training of residents rotating through the hospital. Approximately 60 percent of the 500 members of St. Luke's active medical staff have teaching appointments at one of these two medical schools. St. Luke's dedication to medical education was strengthened in 1992 with the establishment of the Tradition of Excellence Program, inaugurating five new academic chairs—in cardiology, radiology, internal medicine, urology, and surgery.

SPECIAL FACILITIES AND PROGRAMS

St. Luke's offers a number of specialized cardiac services, including the Cardiac Catheterization Laboratories, which are the largest and most fully equipped cath labs in the world. They include one research lab, seven interventional labs, and three double-tabled swing-labs, all equipped with state-of-the-art monitoring and radiographic equipment. Over 10,500 diagnostic and therapeutic cardiac procedures are performed in the cath labs each year.

Heart rhythm problems are evaluated and treated at the Center for Cardiac Arrhythmias and Electrophysiology. Treatment options include medication, electrical therapy, implantation of a defibrillator or pacemaker, radiofrequency ablation, and surgery.

The Heart Failure Treatment Center for patients with advanced-stage heart disease offers the most recent treatment options available, including aggressive medical therapy, drug trials, artificial heart-assist devices, dietary modifications, surgery, and transplantation.

Two Coronary Care Units, nine dedicated cardiovascular surgery suites, and two cardiovascular recovery rooms provide special care units for patients who have suspected heart problems or who are recovering from surgery. The CCUs provide sophisticated central telemetry monitoring, as well as intensive, expert, individualized care. The nurse-to-patient ratio (a major factor in successful outcomes) in both CCUs and the recovery units is either 1:2 or 1:1, or in cases when the patient requires intensive monitoring, 2:1.

The Cardiac Rehabilitation Center in St. Luke's Medical Tower offers a dedicated outpatient facility for medically supervised programs. The multidisciplinary approach practiced at the center includes exercise, nutrition counseling, family therapy, and behavior modification.

In addition to cardiology and cardiovascular surgery, St. Luke's excels in many other areas of care, some of which are mentioned below.

St. Luke's offers a full range of orthopedics programs, including hand and foot surgery and hip and joint replacement. Physicians at St. Luke's Orthopaedic Research Center have developed and refined surgical techniques used around the world.

Approximately 2,000 new patients come to St. Luke's each year for diagnosis and treatment of cancer, including breast and lung cancers. The hospital's Cancer Registry connects the hospital with a national network, enabling staff to track oncology data and compare trends and therapies.

Patients with digestive disorders have access to a broad range of preventive, diagnostic, and therapeutic services, including the most advanced endoscopy procedures.

The Women's Health Service program at St. Luke's Episcopal Hospital is comprehensive, meeting a woman's health needs throughout her life. St. Luke's provides clinical programs in obstetrics, gynecology, cardiology, orthopedics, oncology, urology,

AT A GLANCE

Beds: 949
Occupancy Rate: 69%
Average Patient Count: 655
Annual Admissions: 26,847
Births: 3,928
Outpatient Clinic Visits:
 118,409
Emergency Room/Trauma
 Center Visits: 12,934

HOSPITAL PERSONNEL
Physicians: 1,400+
Residents: 69
Registered Nurses: 987
 BS Degree: 660

ROOM CHARGES (PER DIEM)
Private: $365–$415
ICU: $1,435

ADDRESS
6720 Bertner
Houston, TX 77030

TELEPHONE
(713) 791-2011

internal medicine, and plastic surgery. The Ambulatory Care Center located in St. Luke's Medical Tower provides an excellent outpatient setting for a wide range of diagnostic and treatment procedures, including gynecological laser surgery, fertility testing, urological testing, mammography, and screening for osteoporosis by using bone densitometry. Education is the foundation of Women's Health Services. Through community programs emphasizing wellness and prevention, and through research on women's health, St. Luke's further serves the women of Houston and the surrounding area. In addition, St. Luke's is widely recognized for the medical management of high-risk pregnancy conditions, including premature labor, hypertension, and pregnancy-induced diabetes.

The Stereotactic Radiosurgery Program at St. Luke's is a joint effort with the Methodist Hospital. This collaboration allows the two hospitals to avoid duplication of services while offering a sophisticated noninvasive procedure for patients suffering from brain tumors, blood vessel malformations, and other intracranial conditions. The stereotactic radiosurgery system, called the "XKnife," entails sending high-energy radiation to a precise location of abnormality in the brain, with little risk to the surrounding normal tissue. The XKnife is becoming a preferred treatment for many conditions not easily or adequately treated by conventional means.

St. Luke's offers a full range of therapeutic and diagnostic imaging modalities, including state-of-the-art magnetic resonance imaging (MRI), angiography, computed tomography, echocardiography, electrophysiology mapping, endoscopy, mammography, nuclear medicine procedures, radiography, and ultrasound.

Laparoscopic technology has been successfully employed at St. Luke's to reduce recovery time and enhance patient comfort following such procedures as gallbladder surgery.

Comprehensive urology services have been provided at St. Luke's Episcopal Hospital since the hospital opened in 1954. Today, St. Luke's is a referral center for patients from all over the world. The Urodynamics Laboratory, located on the 10th floor of St. Luke's Medical Tower, is a state-of-the-art center for patients needing diagnostic testing and treatment for urological disorders. The laboratory's setting includes a small, enclosed waiting room which provides privacy. St. Luke's urologists, among the world's best trained and most experienced, include specialists in infertility, prostate disease, impotence, and bladder disorders.

Neuroscience Services include the four disciplines of neurosurgery, neurology, neurophysiology, and psychiatry. Though closely related, these areas are distinct and require the expertise of specialists. A full spectrum of services for neurological conditions is offered, from inpatient emergency care to outpatient rehabilitation. Complex evaluation and surgery for brain tumors and malformations, acute care for stroke patients, neuropsychological evaluation and treatment for cognitive problems (both developmental and acquired), as well as therapy for communication, language, sound, and swallowing problems, are among the many services available.

Psychiatric services, including medical interventions, cognitive rehabilitation, as well as individual, couple, family, and group therapies, are available to patients and their families. In addition, a behavioral medicine program is available to provide people suffering from neurological disorders with information and advice on lifestyle. Patients are taught a variety of strategies that foster medical compliance and coping, enabling them to play an active role in their health and recovery.

In addition to these programs of medical intervention, St. Luke's offers a number of other services to the community. St. Luke's Health Education Channels offer patients informative programs about preventing and treating heart disease, caring for a newborn, women's health, stroke and rehabilitation, relaxation, etc. Programs are shown 24 hours-a-day. St. Luke's Fresh Angles Community Outreach Program disseminates health and wellness information to members of the Houston community through health fairs, presentations by physicians and other health care professionals, and distributions of health materials. Health education is free to companies, churches, community centers, and schools as part of St. Luke's commitment to community education. During 1993, more than 20,000 Houstonians attended either a health fair or an educational presentation sponsored by St. Luke's. The Heart Information Service, a program of the Texas Heart Institute at St. Luke's, is an international hotline that answers questions from the general public about the diagnosis, treatment, and prevention of cardiovascular disease. The toll-free hotline is 1-800-292-2221. An annual Heart Exchange Golf Classic helps support the work of a volunteer organization, the Heart Exchange, whose members supply vital assistance for patients and families awaiting heart transplantation. Now in its fifth year, the golf tournament has been highly successful, with more than $65,000 raised each year for patients and families.

MEDICAL SPECIALTIES

Allergy and Immunology, Anesthesiology, Cardiology, Cardiovascular Anesthesiology, Cardiovascular Surgery, Dentistry, Dermatology, Emergency Medicine, Endocrinology, Family Medicine, Gastroenterology, General Medicine, General Surgery, Hand Surgery, Hematology/Oncology, Infectious Diseases, Nephrology, Neurology, Neurophysiology, Neurosurgery, Newborn and Premature Medicine, Nuclear Medicine, Obstetrics/Gynecology, Ophthalmology, Oral and Maxillofacial Surgery, Orthopaedic Surgery, Otolaryngology, Pathology, Pediatrics, Physical Medicine and Rehabilitation, Podiatry, Psychiatry, Pulmonary Medicine, Radiology, Rheumatology, Transplantation, and Urology.

WELL-KNOWN SPECIALISTS

- Dr. Dale Brown, Jr. *Obstetrics/gynecology; specialist in genital dermatological disease*
- Dr. Denton A. Cooley *Thoracic surgery; specialist in adult cardiovascular surgery*

- Dr. Irving J. Fishman   *Urology; specialist in impotence*
- Dr. O. H. Frazier   *Thoracic surgery; specialist in adult cardiovascular surgery/transplantation*
- Dr. Layne O. Gentry   *Infectious disease; specialist in bone infections/transplantation infections*
- Dr. Robert G. Grossman   *Neurological surgery; specialist in epilepsy surgery*
- Dr. Raymond H. Kaufman   *Obstetrics/gynecology; specialist in genital dermatological disease*
- Dr. John P. Laurent   *Neurological surgery; specialist in pediatric neurological surgery*
- Dr. Eli M. Mizrahi   *Neurology; specialist in epilepsy in children*
- Dr. Joe Leigh Simpson   *Obstetrics/gynecology; specialist in genetics*
- Dr. Rosa A. Tang   *Neurology; specialist in neuro-ophthalmology*

PATIENT SATISFACTION

St. Luke's has implemented the nationally recognized Press, Ganey system to monitor satisfaction by surveying inpatients, outpatients, ambulatory surgery patients, and emergency department patients. Results are generated quarterly and compared with more than 200 hospitals throughout the U.S.

Recent surveys revealed that 96% of St. Luke's inpatients receiving cardiovascular services were satisfied with their quality of care and would recommend St. Luke's to a friend or relative. Surveys of cardiovascular outpatients showed that 98% were satisfied with their quality of care and would recommend St. Luke's.

A comparison of St. Luke's overall hospital score with peer hospitals (of over 600 beds) throughout the United States, and in the first quarter of 1994, showed that St. Luke's ranked in the 91st percentile. St. Luke's results are consistently well above national norms for patient satisfaction.

RESEARCH

Research at St. Luke's Episcopal Hospital and the Texas Heart Institute has flourished for over 25 years. The Cullen Research Laboratories at St. Luke's and Texas Heart Institute were established over 20 years ago to develop new surgical techniques and to improve surgical methods. The laboratories have been involved in such innovations as the ventricular-assist device, the intra-aortic balloon pump, prosthetic cardiac valves, graft materials, and the total artificial heart.

Pioneered by Dr. Cooley and his colleagues, cardiovascular research breakthroughs have led to major milestones of medical history. Among these are the first successful human heart transplantation in the United States, the world's first total artificial heart transplantation, the first successful arterial plaque-removal surgery involving a carotid artery, the first clinical trials of cardiac assist devices, artificial grafts for arterial reconstruction and artificial heart valves, and refinement of the noninvasive procedures of treadmill testing and echocardiography.

Current cardiac research activities include pioneering new applications of lasers in surgery, developing a totally artificial heart, and exploring gene therapy as a treatment for heart disease.

In the field of orthopaedic surgery, physicians at St. Luke's Orthopaedic Research Center have refined surgical techniques used around the world, offering, for example, enhancements in joint replacement and providing new approaches to treating spine disorders.

St. Luke's has taken a leadership role in applying research findings to outcomes management and to patient care in general. Teams of nurses, physicians, and other health care professionals identify outcomes goals for specific patient populations, and then track patient outcomes through examination of length of stay, rate of rehospitalization, complications, morbidity, and patient satisfaction. As a result, researchers are able to measure performance and target areas that require change, providing health care purchasers with accurate quality indicators. St. Luke's has a record of success with outcomes management and has found that it improves hospital-wide performance, cost-effectiveness, and quality.

To broaden its scope of treatment for cancer patients, St. Luke's has established a professional, collaborative relationship with the University of Texas M.D. Anderson Cancer Center through the Texas Community Oncology Network (TCON), a project dedicated to finding new and better treatments for cancer through experimental therapies and research. As one of six sites in the Texas network and the lead institution in the Houston consortium, St. Luke's offers patients a variety of treatment options, including the opportunity to participate in clinical trials involving investigative drugs and new treatments.

ADMISSIONS POLICY

Patients are admitted to St. Luke's by private physicians who have medical staff privileges. St. Luke's accepts private insurance, Medicare, Medicaid, and patients in managed care programs. Also, patients may be evaluated for charity care on the basis of their medical and financial needs.

St. Luke's has two types of express admitting. Individuals with St. Luke's Signature cards have previously supplied the hospital with needed information and therefore proceed directly to their assigned room on arrival. Patients may also be "express admitted" by physicians, who merely fax basic information to the admitting department and request a room assignment.

The amount of charity care provided is not available.

PATIENT/FAMILY ACCOMMODATIONS

Suites are available for family members, but the hospital would not quote charges.

UNIVERSITY OF

UTAH HOSPITAL AND

CLINICS

UNIVERSITY OF UTAH
HEALTH SCIENCES CENTER

SALT LAKE CITY, UTAH

The University of Utah Hospital serves as a major referral center for the 3.5 million residents of Utah, Idaho, Colorado, Nevada, Wyoming and Montana. Patients originating from the five surrounding states represent 16% of the hospital's annual 15,000 admissions; another 8% of admitted patients come from other geographic locations. The hospital is an EMS-designated Level I trauma center and treats patients with multiple injuries or isolated injuries requiring specialty services. It is also Utah's largest provider of services to ambulatory care patients, with 50 general and specialty clinics for outpatients. In addition to clinics within the hospital, services are offered at several other sites.

The hospital and medical staff of the University of Utah gained national recognition in December 1982 when a dentist named Barney Clark received the world's first permanent artificial heart implant. More recently, 52 of the university's doctors were listed in the second edition of *The Best Doctors in America*, a comprehensive survey of physicians on the best practitioners in their fields.

The University Nursing Department was one of the 20 recipients of the Robert Wood Johnson Foundation and Pew Charitable Trusts grants for "Strengthening Hospital Nursing: A Program to Improve Patient Care." The Utah Clinical Practice Model supports excellence in practice and shared

THE UNIVERSITY OF UTAH HOSPITAL SERVES AS A MAJOR REFERRAL CENTER FOR THE 3.5 MILLION RESIDENTS OF UTAH, IDAHO, COLORADO, NEVADA, WYOMING AND MONTANA.

governance and had been adopted to create a practice environment in which staff participate in making decisions which affect patient care and members' professional development. It was one of the first in the country to use nurse practitioners in acute care settings.

Now known as the University of Utah Health Sciences Center, the complex includes the University of Utah School of Medicine; its 395-bed University Hospital; the colleges of pharmacy, nursing, and health; and a major health sciences library, laboratories and outpatient clinics.

SPECIAL FACILITIES AND PROGRAMS

The Intermountain Burn Center is a regional burn treatment and rehabilitation facility. One-third of the total admissions are referred from outside Utah and 50 to 55% of the patients are children. The burn center is a 13-bed, geographically isolated and fully monitored unit with its own operating room, hydrotherapy facilities, skin bank, burn clinic, and physical and occupational rehabilitation areas. In addition to thermal and scald injuries, the center treats electrical, chemical, and other soft tissue injuries or disease processes. The center admits more than 300 burn patients and receives more than 1,800 clinic visits annually. Telephone consultation is available 24 hours-a-day.

The John A. Moran Eye Center is a technologically advanced facility and a crucial resource of eye research, education, clinical care, and community support in the Intermountain United States. Its clinical disciplines include electrophysiology, external and corneal disease, glaucoma, macular and retinal vascular disease, neuro-ophthalmology, ocular pathology, ophthalmic plastic and reconstructive surgery, patient support programs, pediatric ophthalmology and strabismus, refractive surgery, uveitis and ocular inflammatory disease, and vitreo-retinal diseases and surgery.

The Marrow Transplant Program performed 48 transplants in 1993. These included 21 autologous transplants using either marrow or peripheral blood

AT A GLANCE

Beds: 395
Occupancy Rate: 79%
Average Patient Count: 312
Average Patient Stay: 7.6 days
Annual Admissions: 14,855
Births: 2,212
Outpatient Clinic Visits:
   315,268
Emergency Room/Trauma
   Center Visits: 20,351

HOSPITAL PERSONNEL
Physicians: 500
   Board Certified: 450
Residents: 503
Registered Nurses: 645
   BS Degree: 330

ROOM CHARGES (PER DIEM)
Private: $560
Semiprivate: $535
ICU: $560–$1410

ADDRESS
50 North Medical Drive
Salt Lake City, UT 84132

TELEPHONE
(801) 581-2121

stem cells, and 27 allogenic transplants, including 14 from HLA-matched siblings, 9 from matched-unrelated donors, and 4 from HLA-mismatched relatives. Currently there are 10 beds available—soon to be expanded to 12. Other transplantation services are available for heart transplants, kidney transplants (50 to 60 per year), and cornea transplants (450 per year).

The University of Utah's Dialysis Program operates seven dialysis centers, treating approximately 280 patients. Three of the seven facilities are located in rural areas of Utah and Idaho.

The University of Utah Neuropsychiatric Institute operates out of recently expanded facilities. Twenty-four beds for patients with acute mental and physical problems are located at University Hospital. A 99,000-square-foot psychiatric facility with capacity of 90 beds, located in the university's research park, was purchased in March of 1994. This new facility is used primarily for day treatment of psychiatric patients.

The Newborn Intensive Care Unit has treated more than 10,000 critically ill infants since 1968. It provides daily care for an average of 29 babies, focusing on those weighing less than two pounds.

Patients from throughout the world have received cochlear implants since University Hospital began its program for the profoundly deaf in 1984. Intraocular lenses have been implanted in 5,000 patients since the beginning of that service in 1978.

Other specialty clinics offer a variety of services unique to the area. The Sleep Disorders Center treats suspected sleep-disordered breathing, insomnia, and excessive daytime sleepiness. The Pain Management Center offers a comprehensive program of interdisciplinary services. The University Geriatric Clinic provides case management for elderly people and their families. Services offered by the Epilepsy Program are epilepsy patient consultation and EEG laboratory evaluation.

In the Department of Pediatrics, the Intermountain Pediatric-Adolescent Renal Disease Program offers comprehensive care to infants, children, and adolescents with renal disorders and hypertension. Services include diagnostic-therapeutic clinics, acute and chronic peritoneal dialysis and hemodialysis, renal transplantation, and social and nutritional support.

MEDICAL SPECIALTIES

Adolescent Medicine, AIDS, Allergy/Immunology, Anesthesiology, Arthritis, Bone Marrow Transplant, Burn Treatment, Cardiology, Cardiothoracic Surgery, Clinical Pathology, Dermatology, Diabetes, Dialysis, Endocrinology, Family Medicine, Family Planning, Gastroenterology, General Surgery, Headache Treatment, Hematology, Hepatology, High-Risk Maternal Care, Human Genetics, Infertility, Internal Medicine, Laser/Endoscopic Surgery, Metabolism, Mood Disorders, Neurology, Neurocritical Care, Neuromuscular Disease, Newborn Intensive Care, Nuclear Medicine, Neurosurgery, Obstetrics/Gynecology,

Oncology, Ophthalmology, Organ Acquisition and Transplantation, Orthopedic Surgery, Otolaryngology, Pain Clinic, Pediatrics, Perinatal Diagnosis, Physical Medicine and Rehabilitation, Plastic and Reconstructive Surgery, Poison Control, Psychiatry, Pulmonary Function, Radiation Therapy, Radiology, Renal Disease and Kidney Transplantation, Spinal Cord Injury, Sports Medicine, Surgical Pathology, Teen Mother and Child Program, Trauma, Ultrasonography, and Urology.

WELL-KNOWN SPECIALISTS

- Dr. Patrick G. Beatty   *Internal medicine*
- Dr. Merrill T. Dayton   *Surgery*
- Dr. Kathleen B. Digre   *Neurology*
- Dr. M. Peter Heilbrun   *Neurosurgery*
- Dr. Kirtly Parker Jones   *Obstetrics and gynecology*
- Dr. Carl R. Kjeldsberg   *Pathology*
- Dr. Randall J. Olson   *Ophthalmology*
- Dr. Marvin L. Rallison   *Pediatrics*
- Dr. Douglas E. Rollins   *Pharmacology and toxicology*
- Dr. William T. Sause   *Radiology*
- Dr. Paul H. Wender   *Psychiatry*
- Dr. Harry C. Wong   *Anesthesiology*

PATIENT SATISFACTION

University Hospital's 15,000 inpatients per year consistently rate the hospital above 4.0 on a 1-to-5 scale in almost all service categories, according to exit surveys. Physicians, nurses, family experience, quality of care, and meals all rank above 4.

Patient Satisfaction Surveys are mailed to each patient discharged from the hospital. Upon receipt of completed surveys, all information, including verbatim comments, are entered into a database. Survey results are delivered on a daily basis to each patient care unit for corrective action. Quarterly reports including all ratings and verbatim comments are sent to department chairmen and department chiefs.

RESEARCH

The medical education and patient care programs of the University of Utah Health Sciences Center are supported by more than 400 research projects conducted by the faculty members of the School of Medicine. The National Institutes of Health-funded Clinical Research Center provides patient care, laboratory testing, computer data analysis, dietary support, and other necessary resources for clinical investigators studying diseases and disorders such as cancer, diabetes, rheumatoid arthritis, chronic heart failure, and stroke. Significant support also is provided to researchers in the fields of anesthesiology, endocrinology, gastroenterology, genetics, neonatology, and obstetrics/gynecology.

Human genetics research at the medical school is world-renowned. In 1990, the George and Dolores Eccles Institute of Human Genetics, funded jointly by the Howard Hughes Medical Institute and the George and Dolores Eccles Foundation, was completed. In addition to the Department of Human Genetics, the institute houses the Howard Hughes Medical Institute, known for its genetic studies, including gene function, regulation, and expression; the Eccles Program for Human Molecular Biology and Genetics, a consortium of scientists and physicians with a focus on using the tools of molecular biology to discover inherited cell defects that lead to disease; and the Utah Genome Center, one of seven national centers for the Human Genome Project.

The federally-funded Utah Cancer Center involves more than 100 investigators from 20 departments at the university. The Utah Cancer Registry, under the sponsorship of the National Cancer Institute, conducts epidemiological studies in cancer and provides feedback for physicians and hospitals. A $10 million gift from the Jon and Karen Huntsman family has established the Huntsman Cancer Institute at the university to allow development of a world-class center for cancer research and treatment.

Research programs in biomedical engineering and artificial organs bring together scientists from the medical school, College of Engineering, and scholars from other disciplines to work on the development and refinement of artificial limbs and organs, such as the ear and eye. Significant cardiovascular, laser, and diagnostic imaging research also is ongoing. Other prominent Health Sciences Center facilities include the Center for Human Toxicology; Center for Infectious Diseases, Diagnostic Microbiology and Immunology; and the Utah Resource for Genetic and Epidemiologic Research.

ADMISSIONS POLICY

Most patients at University Hospital are referred by their private physicians, although the hospital does contract with several managed care programs for their tertiary care. Individuals may make an appointment to be seen in any of the outpatient clinics and, in some cases, directly by hospital physicians. Patients requiring immediate care can receive treatment and be admitted through the Trauma I-designated Emergency Department.

The hospital operates a toll-free referral and consultation hotline: (800) 453-0122 (outside Utah), (800) 662-0052 (in Utah).

MEDICAL COLLEGE OF

VIRGINIA HOSPITALS

Unlike many of the academic medical centers described in this book, the state-supported Medical College of Virginia Hospitals (MCVH) is not a highly publicized institution. Although MCVH is a major regional referral center and one of the largest and most active teaching hospitals in the nation, its proximity to Duke, Vanderbilt and the University of Virginia seems to have kept it from achieving the widespread recognition it clearly deserves. In fact, what first brought MCVH to our attention were not recommendations from doctors, but the figures, compiled by the people who administer Medicare payments, that convey the complexity of patient care. Historically, MCVH has had one of the highest so-called case-mix indexes in the nation, higher actually than most of the prestigious Boston and New York hospitals. Since this means MCVH is treating very sick people on a continuous basis, we decided to investigate further.

MCV Hospitals serves as a referral center for the southeastern U.S. Almost half a million patients visit its facilities annually. Virtually every form of contemporary medical service is available there, including cardiac intensive care, dentistry, emergency medicine, transplants, newborn intensive care, neurology, obstetrics, oncology, open heart surgery, psychiatry, radiation therapy, and trauma care. An outpatient department with 92 clinics covers a wide range of

RICHMOND, VIRGINIA

ALTHOUGH MCVH IS A MAJOR REGIONAL REFERRAL CENTER AND ONE OF THE LARGEST AND MOST ACTIVE TEACHING HOSPITALS IN THE NATION, ITS PROXIMITY TO DUKE, VANDERBILT AND THE UNIVERSITY OF VIRGINIA SEEMS TO HAVE KEPT IT FROM ACHIEVING THE WIDESPREAD RECOGNITION IT CLEARLY DESERVES.

medical specialties, including allergies, burns, dermatology, genetics, glaucoma, infertility, nutrition, orthopedics, pediatrics, renal dialysis, stroke, and urology. There is a Level I trauma center and a nationally famous neonatal intensive care unit.

Created in 1838 as the Medical Department of Hampden-Sydney College, the Medical College of Virginia became independent in 1854 and state affiliated in 1860. It has since established the only schools of dentistry and pharmacy in Virginia, and its School of Nursing has developed programs at the baccalaureate, masters, and doctoral degree levels. With schools in allied health professions and basic health sciences as well, it has become one of only 20 academic medical centers with a school in every health-related discipline.

Many advances in contemporary diagnosis and treatment have been introduced or refined at the MCV campus, including the isotope lab (1953), renal dialysis (1956), cardiac bypass surgery (1958), maxitron radiotherapy (1961), fiberoptic endoscopy (1968), total parenteral nutrition (1969), CT and ultrasound-guided interventional radiology and fine needle cytology (1974), angioplasty (1979), extracorporeal membrane oxygenation (1981), and magnetic resonance imaging (1986).

The expertise in health care at MCV Hospitals is available to individual healthcare providers and through relationships with the McGuire Veterans Administration Medical Center, St. Mary's Hospital, Metropolitan Hospital, and Children's Hospital. MCV Hospitals responded to more than 18,000 physician consultation calls and 24,000 patient service calls from physicians in 1993.

SPECIAL FACILITIES AND PROGRAMS

The Massey Cancer Center is one of about 60 specialized cancer centers in the U.S. officially designated by the National Cancer Institute. Massey clinicians see about 1,500 new patients yearly, both at the center and in rural outreach locations. The center provides complete consultation and referral services for physicians, and state-of-the-art diagnosis and treatment for patients and families.

The Neuro-Oncology Center is the only center of its kind in the area; it offers a team of physicians specializing in the diagnosis and treatment of brain and spinal cord tumors. The Chest Tumor Center is the only comprehensive diagnostic and treatment center for lung cancer and other chest tumors in the area, and the Breast Health Center offers the same level of expertise in comprehensive diagnostics and treatment for breast cancer and other breast disorders. The Gastrointestinal Tumor Center is a comprehensive center for GI cancers and another unique resource for the region. The Genitourinary Tumor Center offers a diagnostic and treatment program unavailable nearby. These multidisciplinary centers are just one part of the NIH-designated Massey Cancer Center at MCVH. The center also offers expertise in head, neck, and skull-base tumors, and is especially well known for its work in developing anti-cancer drugs.

The Rural Cancer Outreach Program delivers cancer care to underserved rural populations in Virginia located more than 80 miles from a comprehensive cancer treatment facility. Currently, there are community clinics in Kilmarnock, South Hill, Farmville, and Grundy.

The MCV Heart Center provides comprehensive diagnostic and treatment services for patients with cardiovascular disease. Services include general adult and pediatric cardiology, adult and pediatric cardiac catheterization, coronary angioplasty, noninvasive testing, chest pain care, electrophysiology, congestive heart failure/transplantation, adult and pediatric cardiac surgery, adult and pediatric thoracic surgery, and vascular surgery.

Heart Center services at the MCV Children's Medical Center include pediatric cardiac catheterization, cardiac intensive care, noninvasive lab facilities, exercise stress testing, and a preventive cardiology program. There are satellite pediatric cardiology offices in Richmond, Bristol, Newport News, Roanoke, and Fredericksburg.

The Neuroscience Center is comprised of specialists in the areas of neurology, neurosurgery, physical medicine and rehabilitation, psychiatry, pain management, neuroradiology, neuro-ophthalmology, neuropathology, and pediatric neuroscience. Comprehensive diagnostic and treatment services are provided to patients and consultation services to referring physicians. Areas of specialization include epilepsy and epilepsy surgery, neuro-oncology, back and spine, brain and spinal-cord injury, geropsychiatry, and pediatric neuro-oncology.

The adult neuroscience program offers services for epilepsy (including an epilepsy monitoring unit), Alzheimer's disease, neuromuscular disorders, multiple sclerosis, Parkinson's disease and other movement disorders. The stroke unit provides comprehensive treatment programs for acute and chronic conditions and offers special expertise for difficult cases. The pediatric neuroscience program offers comprehensive services, with special interest in neonatal neurological dysfunctions, birth defects, seizure disorders, learning disabilities, and attention deficit disorders.

AT A GLANCE

Beds: 902
Occupancy Rate: 69%
Average Patient Count: 625
Average Patient Stay: 6.5 days
Annual Admissions: 35,194
Births: 3,802
Outpatient Clinic Visits:
 183,870
Emergency Room/Trauma
 Center Visits: 111,123

HOSPITAL PERSONNEL
Physicians: 847
 Board Certified: 706
Residents: 630
Registered Nurses: 1,369
 BS Degree or Higher: 522

ROOM CHARGES (PER DIEM)
Private: $375
Semiprivate: $351
ICU: $1,329

ADDRESS
401 North 12th Street
Richmond, VA 23298

TELEPHONE
(804) 786-4682

The ambulatory and emergency neurology division offers outpatient services and specialized emergency neurology services for strokes, seizures, comas, muscular dystrophy, and other acute neurological conditions.

MCV Hospitals has one of the world's largest organ transplantation programs, including the second oldest and one of the largest heart transplant programs in the U.S. Comprehensive medical and surgical transplantation services are offered for patients with end-stage organ failure and patients with cancers requiring bone marrow transplantation. MCV has earned an international reputation for its work in organ transplantation. In 1993 the bone marrow program became a member of the national marrow registry of over one million donors; the team can now treat adult and pediatric patients who lack a sibling donor.

The Children's Medical Center consolidates all programs related to pediatric patient care, education, and research. Specialized care for children is provided through the Child and Adolescent Emergency Room, the Pediatric Intensive Care unit, the Neonatal Intensive Care Unit, the Virginia Treatment Center for Children, and the Children's Medical Center.

The Department of Radiology at the Medical College of Virginia Hospitals provides diagnostic imaging services using state-of-the-art equipment. The Diagnostic Radiology division has whole-body MRI scanners and spiral CT scanners, as well as digital fluoroscopy and three-dimensional image transmission. The clinical practice is enhanced by the Division of Radiation Physics and Biology through the development and clinical implementation of spiral CT and MRI-based imaging techniques. A newly installed high-field MRI and spectroscopy system is the basis for fundamental research in areas such as head injury, cardiovascular disease, and cancer.

The Department of Radiation Oncology uses the most advanced therapeutic irradiation techniques for the treatment of malignant disease and some benign conditions. The department is equipped with the following therapy machines: three linear accelerators; a treatment-planning computer; two simulators, one CT-interphased; two units for local hyperthermia using microwaves and ultrasound; a remote after-loader; and a linear accelerator equipped for radiosurgery.

Other special services include the Temporomandibular Joint and Facial Pain Clinic which treats patients with facial injuries and those with severe chronic facial pain; the latter are frequently women with stress-related tics. The clinic has developed special heat treatment to relieve pain, but it uses medications as well. Research is also conducted there. The Sleep Disorders Center is a referral center that assists in the diagnosis and treatment of patients with a wide range of sleep disorders. It is the only one of its kind in the state in its ability to conduct research and to deal with these kinds of problems.

The Dementia Clinic is designed as a model for other clinics nationwide. Its multidiscipline team approach is expected to provide a prototype treatment plan for victims of Alzheimer's disease. The clinic provides resources and education to help the patient and the patient's family. Currently, more than 100 patients and their families are seen in the clinic, which is open one morning a week. A backlog of one and a half months indicates that many more people need these services.

A consolidated inpatient and outpatient radiology department with over 30 procedure rooms, 24 operating rooms, two laser rooms, and an entire floor devoted to adult intensive care units, and 64 beds divided into specialty service areas, are all part of the new acute bed facility at MCV.

Another MCVH surgical specialty is in artificial joint replacements; over 3,000 such operations have been performed at this hospital since 1972.

MEDICAL SPECIALTIES

Allergies, Burns, Cardiac Intensive Care, Dentistry, Dermatology, Emergency Medicine, Genetics, Glaucoma, Head and Neck Tumors, Infertility, Neurology, Nutrition, Obstetrics, Oncology, Open Heart Surgery, Orthopedics, Pediatrics, Psychiatry, Radiation Therapy, Renal Dialysis, Stroke, Transplantation Surgery, Trauma, and Urology.

WELL-KNOWN SPECIALISTS

- Dr. James W. Brooks   *Thoracic surgery*
- Dr. Robert DeLorenzo   *Neurology; specialist in epilepsy*
- Dr. Algin B. Garrett   *Dermatology*
- Dr. I. David Goldman   *Hematology and medical oncology*
- Dr. Stephen W. Harkins   *Gerontology; experimental psychology and Dementia Clinic*
- Dr. Hermes A. Kontos   *Internal medicine; specialist in orthostatic hypotension and Raynaud's disease*
- Dr. Walter Lawrence   *Surgery; specialist in surgical oncology*
- Dr. H. M. Lee   *Specialist in vascular and transplantation surgery*
- Dr. Anthony Marmarou   *Neurosurgery*
- Dr. Walter Nance   *Pediatrics; specialist in hereditary diseases and dysmorphology*
- Dr. David Richardson   *Internal medicine; specialist in cardiac arrhythmias, coronary artery disease, and hypertension*
- Dr. Richard M. Schieken   *Pediatrics; specialist in noninvasive and invasive diagnosis of congenital heart disease, hypertension, and hyperlipidemia*
- Dr. Z. Reno Vlahcevic   *Internal medicine and gastroenterology; specialist in liver and biliary tract diseases, pancreatic diseases, and cholesterol metabolism disorders*
- Dr. Harold F. Young   *Neurosurgery; specialist in using body's immune system to fight certain kinds of brain tumors*

PATIENT SATISFACTION

The Medical College of Virginia Hospitals conduct ongoing studies of patients' perception of and satisfaction with MCV Hospitals. The study provides quarterly reports of a random sample of 650 inpatients at MCV Hospitals. The data is collected through a telephone interview with patients and involves 50 interviews per week, an average of 215 a month. There are currently 11 quarters of information available or 7,150 inpatient interviews.

Physician care and nursing care are consistently ranked in the 90th percentile for "very satisfied" responses.

RESEARCH

The Medical College of Virginia Campus of Virginia Commonwealth University receives over $60 million in research grants and support programs annually. Projects cover a broad range of areas, including Alzheimer-type dementia, multiple sclerosis, and sudden infant death syndrome. Most of the clinical research reflects the hospital's strongest medical services—thus cancer, neurology, drug abuse treatment, obstetrics, organ transplantation, and trauma (especially head injuries and burns) are well-funded programs.

In 1985, research scientists at MCV identified a genetic abnormality, biotinidase deficiency, as a major cause of mental retardation. Geneticist Dr. Barry Wolf developed a simple, inexpensive test to identify infants lacking biotinidase, an enzyme that controls the use of the vitamin biotin. Virginia now requires all newborns to be screened for biotinidase deficiency.

Many significant research grants have been awarded recently, including $1.5 million from NIH to study brain swelling and intracranial pressure, and studies of brain microcirculation in relation to stroke and head trauma. Other major grants include studies of the causes of epilepsy, and the National Cancer Institute recently gave $2.5 million for developing anti-cancer drugs. Additional monies were also given to study AIDS reduction in pregnant and nonpregnant addicted women.

ADMISSIONS POLICY

All patients must be admitted by an attending MCVH physician. While many patients are referred by outside physicians, others come through the Emergency Room or through one of the 92 specialty clinics located on campus. For an appointment at one of these clinics, call (804) 786-0500.

Although MCVH does an extraordinary amount of charity care, it does require patients to show they can pay. Only state residents are eligible for financial assistance and this is monitored very carefully. Even those with limited means are asked to pay something and the hospital provides extensive help in financial planning so this can be achieved. In 1992-93, MCV provided an estimated $73 million worth of care to patients who had inadequate health care coverage or resources.

UNIVERSITY OF

VIRGINIA HOSPITAL

In March 1989, the University of Virginia Hospital moved into a new $230 million facility. This move capped a major expansion approved by the state legislature in 1984, and effected the complete replacement of the old University Hospital which opened in 1960. The new facilities alleviated space and physical plant difficulties at the University's Health Sciences Center, thus allowing University Hospital to maintain its place as a nationally recognized teaching and research institution that provides advanced medical services to much of the central part of the state. For instance, the facility is wired with fiber optic equipment that enables the radiology department to expeditiously send x-rays to other departments. This has made UVA Hospital the centerpiece of the University of Virginia Health Sciences Center, which also includes the West Complex, Blue Ridge Hospital, the Children's Medical Center, the Kluge Children's Rehabilitation Center, the Primary Care Center, and the Private Clinics Building. The affiliated Virginia Ambulatory Surgery Center is nearby.

The University of Virginia Health Sciences Center is the major tertiary care center serving central Virginia and the central Shenandoah Valley. Specialized care units include a Medical Intensive Care Unit, a Thoracic-Cardiovascular Surgery Intensive Care Unit, a general Surgical ICU, a Neurological/Neurosurgical Intensive Care Unit, a dedicated,

UNIVERSITY OF VIRGINIA
HEALTH SCIENCES CENTER

**CHARLOTTESVILLE,
VIRGINIA**

THE UVA HEALTH
SCIENCES CENTER HAS A
LONG TRADITION OF
PATIENT-CENTERED CARE. A
NEW ORGANIZATIONAL
STRUCTURE PUTS PATIENT
NEEDS AT THE CENTER OF
THE ORGANIZATION.

self-contained Burn Unit, a General Clinical Research Unit (supported through the National Institutes of Health), a pediatric intensive care, neonatal intensive care, and inpatient and outpatient dialysis units. There are satellite ambulatory care facilities at Northridge, Forest Lakes, Orange, Stoney Brook and Fontaine Park.

At the UVA Health Sciences Center, multidisciplinary teams are organized along service lines so that similar patients are treated in a single area by clinical experts in medicine, nursing, social work, and other therapies. Within this health care complex, individuals and families have all of their medical needs met. Preventive and basic family care are available, along with the wide range of leading specialists you would expect to find only in a major academic medical center, not in a medium-sized town in a rural area. In fact, the UVA Medical Center is one of only six major medical centers in the country currently serving a primarily rural population. It draws patients, however, not only from the contiguous cities and counties, but also from the state's major metropolitan areas, as well as from other states and countries. As such, the UVA Medical Center acts as a health service provider to a population base of some 2.5 million people and more.

The UVA Medical Center is world-renowned for a number of its services, including neurosciences, cardiac care, cancer care, a comprehensive epilepsy program, diabetes research and care, and care of children, including neonatal and pediatric intensive care units, and the Kluge Children's Rehabilitation Center, one of the few of its kind in the nation. It also offers the only burn center in the region; a Level I trauma center; alcohol and drug abuse research and treatment; transplant programs, including the difficult heart-lung transplant; women's services, including prenatal counseling and a menopause clinic; and many others. UVA also offers a number of outreach programs that help physicians throughout the state stay up-to-date in many medical areas.

The UVA Health Sciences Center has a long tradition of patient-centered care. A new organizational structure puts patient needs at the center of the organization. Direct care providers in all disciplines are joined along service lines, reporting to a single administrator to assure that experts in all fields communicate freely and spend as much time as possible in direct patient care. Quality improvement activities are centered at the direct care level, capturing the spirit and intent of continuous quality improvement. All administrative functions are organized to support direct care provision, from personnel support and multidisciplinary continuing education to financial systems support. Fewer administrative levels exist in the "leaner" organization, enabling more direct contact between top administrators and those providing care.

SPECIAL FACILITIES AND PROGRAMS

Specialized services available at the University of Virginia Health Sciences Center include a major regional heart center, an internationally known neurosciences program, oncology services, multidisciplinary pain management, diabetes and endocrinology, and specialized children's services. The Knife Program, providing noninvasive treatment of intracranial conditions, draws patients from all over the world. A unique Stroke Program focuses on prevention and early intervention through the use of educational, medical, and surgical interventions.

Full obstetrical services are provided within the Women's Center, dedicated to the unique needs of women patients. Services available include health screening, health maintenance and educational services for women, as well as the full range of fertility treatments, endocrine specialists, and specialized menopausal clinics. Inpatient and outpatient gynecological oncology services are provided through the Women's Center, bringing patients from a wide area.

The Children's Medical Center includes the Kluge Children's Rehabilitation Center and inpatient and outpatient services provided through facilities on the main university grounds and satellite clinics. The Kluge Children's Rehabilitation Center is a pediatric/orthopedic special care hospital providing evaluation, treatment, habilitation, and rehabilitation using an interdisciplinary approach. The team emphasizes the "whole" child and includes appropriate representation from 17 disciplines and the child's family. Children from birth to 21 years receive inpatient care and outpatient care (10,000 annual visits) for developmental disabilities, chronic illnesses, recent injuries, orthopedic problems, and associated disorders. The KCRC also houses staff training in pediatrics, orthopedics, neurology, radiology, and psychology.

The Surgical Oncology Clinic is an active clinic for the diagnosis and management of cancer, as well as a follow-up clinic for those patients whose cancer is treated primarily by surgery. Problem cases are presented to a weekly multidisciplinary tumor board for discussion and clinical decision. All cases are entered into the Tumor Registry for careful follow-up. A Breast Clinic meets on Tuesday afternoon in the Mammography Department in the Primary Care Center. The University Health Sciences Center, a Level I trauma center, has separate pediatric and adult emergency services covering all specialties, including multiple trauma, and available continuously. The Pegasus Program provides patient transportation

AT A GLANCE

Beds: 683
Occupancy Rate: 78%
Average Patient Count: 534
Average Patient Stay: 7.2 days
Annual Admissions: 27,865
Births: 2,010
Outpatient Clinic Visits:
    336,540
Emergency Room/Trauma
    Center Visits: 58,538

HOSPITAL PERSONNEL
Physicians: 542
    Board Certified: 321
Residents: 637
Registered Nurses: 990

ROOM CHARGES (PER DIEM)
Private: $382
Semiprivate: $360
ICU: $661–$1,655

ADDRESS
Jefferson Park Avenue
Charlottesville, VA 22908

TELEPHONE
(804) 924-0211

via helicopter and fixed wing aircraft. The Regional Burn Center there is one of three in the state that provides care to people suffering serious burns.

Each clinical department offers a wide range of specialized services. Special efforts have been made to simplify surgical admissions for patients with the institution of a Pre-Assessment Center that brings all services to the patient.

The Ambulatory Care Services Department, working with each clinical department, is responsible for the outpatient care delivered at the Health Sciences Center. The 40 outpatient clinics have over 300,000 patient visits per year, with volume increasing at a rate of about 5% annually. The clinics are located in the University Hospital West, the Primary Care Center, the Kluge Children's Rehabilitation Center, the Blue Ridge Hospital, and the Northridge Building. Planning is underway for a major expansion in outpatient clinic facilities.

The Emergency Room, located in University Hospital, handles over 60,000 pediatric and adult patient visits annually. Seven full-time faculty from the Department of Medicine staff the Emergency Room, and the Pediatric Emergency Room is staffed by two faculty members from the Department of Pediatrics. There is an extensive pre-hospital program coordinated with the area rescue squads to provide patient care and transportation to the Emergency Room. In addition, Pegasus, the University of Virginia Health Sciences Center's air medical service, provides rapid transport in emergency situations.

The Blue Ridge Hospital became an integral part of the University of Virginia's Health Sciences Center in 1978. The Blue Ridge Hospital is located three miles southeast of the Health Sciences Center. On the grounds of this complex are a variety of inpatient, outpatient, academic and research programs. Included in the inpatient programs are two Behavioral Medicine and Psychiatry units utilizing 40 beds, including addiction treatment services. The Department of Neurology operates a 13-bed epilepsy unit and the Department of Internal Medicine operates a 10-bed geriatrics unit. The Department of Physical Medicine and Rehabilitation opened an adult rehabilitation program in 1989, utilizing 32 beds.

Among the numerous programs housed on the Blue Ridge Hospital grounds that complement patient activities are the Adult Psychiatry Clinic, the Child and Family Psychiatry Clinic, the Addiction Treatment Center, the Comprehensive Epilepsy Program, and the Physical Medicine and Rehabilitation Clinic. The headquarters of the Institute of Law, Psychiatry, and Public Policy, and their Forensic Clinic; the Institute for Substance Abuse Studies; the Center for the Study of Mind and Human Interaction; the Health Sciences Center Child Care Center; the Medical Information and Referral Service; the Blue Ridge Poison Control Center; and the School of Medicine's Medical Alumni Association and Medical School Foundation are also located on the hospital grounds.

MEDICAL SPECIALTIES

Anesthesiology, Cardiology, Cardiovascular Services, Dentistry, Dermatology, Family Medicine, Endocrinology, Gastroenterology, Geriatrics, General Medicine,

General Surgery, Hematology/Oncology, Infectious Disease and Geographic Medicine, Internal Medicine (Allergy and Clinical), Nephrology, Neurology, Neurosurgery, Obstetrics and Gynecology, Ophthalmology, Orthopaedics, Otolaryngology-Head and Neck Surgery, Pathology, Pediatrics, Physical Medicine and Rehabilitation, Plastic and Maxillofacial Surgery, Psychiatric Medicine, Pulmonary Medicine, Radiology and Radiation Therapy, Rheumatology, Transplantation and Urology.

WELL-KNOWN SPECIALISTS

- Dr. Robert C. Allen *Ophthalmology*
- Dr. George A. Beller *Cardiology*
- Dr. W. Kline Bolton *Nephrology*
- Dr. John S. Davis IV *Rheumatology*
- Dr. Leigh G. Donowitz *Pediatric infectious diseases*
- Dr. Fritz E. Dreifuss *Neurology; specialist in epilepsy*
- Dr. James E. Ferguson II *Obstetrics*
- Dr. Charles W. Gross *Otolaryngology*
- Dr. Richard L. Guerrant *Infectious diseases*
- Dr. Howard P. Gutgesell *Pediatrics*
- Dr. Neal F. Kassell *Neurological surgery*
- Dr. Paul R. Lambert *Otolaryngology*
- Dr. Paul A. Levine *Head and neck surgery*
- Dr. John C. Marshall *Endocrinology and metabolism*
- Dr. Lawrence H. Phillips II *Neurology*
- Dr. Thomas E. Platts-Mills *Allergy and immunology*
- Dr. Bradley Rodgers *Pediatric surgery*
- Dr. Ladislau Steiner *Neurological surgery*
- Dr. Peyton T. Taylor, Jr. *Obstetrics and gynecology*
- Dr. Vamik D. Volkan *Psychiatric medicine*

PATIENT SATISFACTION

The University of Virginia Medical Center participates annually in a patient satisfaction survey through UHC that allows comparisons with other academic medical centers. In the most recent survey, UVA scored significantly above the median in the Discharge Process and Billing Information. High marks were received as well for Admitting Process, Physician Care, Nursing Care, Pain Control, and Surgical Care. As in many hospitals, Food Services was not considered a strength and resulted in UVA changing the food service contract.

In addition to the UHC survey, UVA has contracted to design a highly specific patient satisfaction survey. This survey will provide feedback on a quarterly basis in the second half of 1994. Responses will be tracked by patient diagnosis, thus providing the opportunity to improve specific program parameters.

RESEARCH

For the past year, the University of Virginia had $67.5 million in support of biomedical research from various sources: government, foundation, and industry. The number of "principal investigators" is 374.

In addition to several floors of laboratories, a 13-bed clinical research unit in the University Hospital is the site of a variety of studies under the rigid controls that this type of patient-care facility makes possible. Patients are admitted as volunteer participants in an intensive study of a disease problem, under a research plan or protocol developed by members of the faculty.

Current areas of research at UVA Health Sciences Center include neurosurgery, where one of the few Gamma Units in the United States is used for treatment of patients with malformations of arteries and veins in the brain; a comprehensive epilepsy program; a movement disorders center involved with several clinical drug trials in patients with Parkinson's disease; a comprehensive stroke program involving clinical research in cerebrovascular disease, including stroke intervention, management of cerebral vasospasm following subarachnoid hemorrhage, and noninvasive assessment of cerebral circulation. All of these are available to patients willing to participate. UVA is also investigating the spectrum of acid peptic disorders, including the role of helicobacter pylori in causing ulcers and the pathophysiology of gastroesophageal reflux. The Neurotology Laboratory studies the toxicity of noise and drugs on the cochlea and central nervous system and regeneration of hair cells in the inner ear. In the Gynecology Reproductive Endocrinology Clinic, a whole range of assisted reproductive technologies is offered, including in vitro fertilization (IVF), gamete intrafallopian tube transfer (GIFT), zygote intrafallopian tube transfer (ZIFT), and egg donation.

The Menopause Clinic offers individual and group counseling on changes experienced during menopause, as well as comprehensive gynecological services and bone density screening.

The Sleep Disorders Center treats organic sleep disorders, such as sleep apnea and narcolepsy, diagnosing patients by monitoring sleep overnight or in a series of naps.

ADMISSIONS POLICY

Patients must be admitted by a physician, but may be admitted through the referral of an attending physician (on or off staff) or through an M.D. on duty in the clinics or emergency room.

If a patient lacks insurance, he or she must set up a payment arrangement or pay in advance for elective admission. Urgent/emergency admissions have no pre-admit criteria.

Free care provided per annum runs 16 to 18% of total revenues.

FRED HUTCHINSON

CANCER RESEARCH

CENTER

The Fred Hutchinson Cancer Research Center is devoted solely to cancer research. Its three divisions—Clinical Research, Basic Sciences, and Public Health Sciences—make up one of the best cancer research institutions in the world. The center, affectionately called the "Hutch" by the people who work there, is staffed by an extraordinary collection of biomedical research and clinical talent.

One of 27 National Cancer Institute-designated Comprehensive Cancer Centers, the Hutchinson Center was established under the National Cancer Act of 1971. Opened in 1975, it is the only designated cancer center in the Northwest, and as such serves Washington, Alaska, Montana, Idaho, and Oregon.

Although its primary function is research, the Center is best known to the public for its accomplishments in marrow transplantation, the preferred treatment for several forms of cancer and some other fatal diseases. In fact, more than 5,700 such transplants have been performed at the Center since it began performing them in the late 1960s with a team organized by Dr. E. Donnall Thomas, director emeritus of the Clinical Research Division. Thomas is recognized as the pioneer of marrow transplantation. In 1990, Thomas was awarded the Nobel Prize for his outstanding contributions to medicine. The Hutchinson team now performs approximately 350 transplants

SEATTLE, WASHINGTON

THE FRED HUTCHINSON CANCER RESEARCH CENTER IS DEVOTED SOLELY TO CANCER RESEARCH. ITS THREE DIVISIONS—CLINICAL RESEARCH, BASIC SCIENCES, AND PUBLIC HEALTH SCIENCES—MAKE UP ONE OF THE BEST CANCER RESEARCH INSTITUTIONS IN THE WORLD.

each year, making the Hutchinson Center the largest bone marrow transplant center in the world.

Clinical researchers are working to further develop the use of stem cells in transplant procedures. The ultimate goal is to reduce the risk after transplant by using these specific cells and to decrease the inpatient stay for patients. In all situations, before receiving the healthy marrow or cells, which may come from a patient or donor, the patient's diseased or damaged marrow is destroyed with high-dose chemotherapy and/or total body irradiation. This intensive treatment usually takes seven to nine days. The actual transplant procedure is relatively simple. The marrow is removed from the donor in an operating room environment. Prior to the marrow removal, the donor is given general or local (spinal) anesthesia. With a special needle, marrow is removed from the donor's hip bones, filtered through screens, and placed in a blood bag. (In some cases, the marrow may be treated prior to infusion.) Within several hours, the marrow is given intravenously to the patient, transfused through a catheter (known as a Kickman catheter) implanted in the patient's chest. This procedure is done prior to admission to the transplant unit.

Then begins the wait for the healthy cells—graft—to grow. This takes an average of ten days to three weeks. During this time, the patient has no functioning marrow, which leaves him susceptible to infection and bleeding problems. Patients are kept in semi-sterile to totally-sterile environments (known as laminar-air-flow rooms) for their protection from infection.

There are many risks involved during the course of marrow transplantation. Bacterial, viral, and fungal infections, bleeding, and organ failure can all threaten the patient's chance of survival. Graft-Versus-Host Disease (GVHD) occurs in approximately 50% of all transplant patients. GVHD occurs when the donor marrow (which has a stronger immune system that the patient) attacks the patient's major organs, such as the skin, liver, and stomach. Other possible risks are unsuccessful engraftment, or graft failure, and recurrence of the disease.

The average patient spends between 30 to 40 days as an inpatient on the transplant unit and 60 to 70 days on outpatient care. It takes six months to a year before the immune system is functioning normally.

Many transplant patients come to Hutchinson Center as a last hope. The continued progress at the Center has led to a steady increase in survival rates. Patients come to the Center from all across the United States and from 45 overseas nations.

The Hutchinson Center is one the most-cited institutions in scientific literature, and its researchers are frequently invited to speak at major scientific conferences. These activities ensure the rapid exchange of research findings with biological scientists and cancer specialists around the world, fostering international cooperation in cancer prevention and treatment. In addition, a number of biotechnology companies in the Pacific Northwest have been established by scientists from the Hutchinson Center.

The Hutchinson Center works closely with other health care institutions in the Seattle area, including Children's Hospital and Medical Center, Swedish Hospital and Medical Center, University of Washington Medical Center, Veterans Administration Hospital, and Virginia Mason Medical Center.

A number of the Center's scientific staff have appointments at the University of Washington (UW), and many members of the UW faculty likewise have appointments at the Hutchinson Center. As a nationally recognized research institution, the Center has relationships with major research organizations across the United States and throughout the world.

All Hutchinson nurses are specially trained intensive and cardiac care nurses. They closely coordinate activities with the Center's physicians and are an integral part of the research/transplant team. The Center was named after a Seattle baseball hero, Fred Hutchinson, who died of cancer in 1964 at the age of forty-five. Its funding comes from federal and private grants and contracts, contributions, third-party reimbursement for patient care, dividends, and interest.

MEDICAL SPECIALTIES

Basic Sciences, Bone Marrow Transplantation, Clinical Research, and Public Health Sciences.

WELL-KNOWN SPECIALISTS

- Dr. Frederick Appelbaum *Director of the Center's Clinical Research Division; specialist in marrow transplantation*
- Dr. William Bensinger *Transplantation; specialist in the use of stem cell transplants for breast cancer*
- Dr. Maureen Henderson *Head of the Cancer Prevention Research Unit; developer of the Women's Health Initiative*
- Dr. Paul Neiman *Director of the Center's Basic Sciences Division; specialist in genetics*
- Dr. Jean Sanders *Pediatric oncologist; specialist in marrow transplantation for children*
- Dr. E. Donnall Thomas *Pioneer of marrow transplantation; 1990 Nobel Prize for Medicine recipient*

AT A GLANCE

Beds: 60
Occupancy Rate: 100%
Average Patient Count: 60
Average Patient Stay: 90 days

HOSPITAL PERSONNEL
Physicians/Scientists (MD):
    145
    Board Certified: 68
Physicians/Scientists (PhD):
    288
Physicians/Scientists (Other):
    25
Residents: 195
Registered Nurses: 161
    BS Degree: 100%

ROOM CHARGES (PER DIEM)
Not Applicable

ADDRESS
1124 Columbia Street
Seattle, WA 98104

TELEPHONE
(206) 667-5000

PATIENT SATISFACTION

Due to the critical nature of the cancer cases treated at Hutchinson, patient satisfaction surveys are not applicable. The effectiveness of treatment and service at Hutchinson is measured in terms of the patient survival rates the staff has been able to achieve.

RESEARCH

Scientists at the Center conduct basic, clinical and public health research. These scientists have earned international reputations by achieving excellence in the application of marrow transplantation, in studying cancer prevention, and in training scientists from all over the world. The Center's Division of Public Health Sciences established the first Cancer Prevention Research Unit in the world.

Clinical Research at the Hutchinson Center is devoted primarily to developing effective means of treating a variety of malignant, nonmalignant, and genetically determined diseases—including blood-related cancers such as leukemia and lymphoma. Research studies within this division are primarily funded by the National Cancer Institute. Other funding sources include the American Cancer Society and the Leukemia Society of America, as well as private and public contributions.

Public Health Sciences studies the occurrence of cancer in human populations and the prevention of cancer. It operates a major registration of new cancer cases that serves as a resource for investigations into the causes of cancer. Within this division are national coordinating centers for the Women's Health Initiative, the CARET (beta-carotene and lung cancer study), and the statistical and clinical coordinating center for the HIV Vaccine Efficacy Trials Network. It also houses a site for the National Cancer Information Service program sponsored by the National Cancer Institute.

Basic Sciences is concerned with the study of fundamental life processes to help determine why cells transform from normal to malignant. Researchers study cells and gene structure to find new ways of immunizing against cancer and other diseases. In addition, researchers in this division helped establish a core center for gene therapy, one of nine in the nation.

ADMISSIONS POLICY

People come to the Hutchinson Center through a physician referral process. The Center prefers that the prospective patient's physician call the Center's consulting physician. However, the Hutchinson physician will answer some questions for the patient and will then request that the person's physician call to provide more information.

To be considered for a marrow transplant, the physician must submit a current diagnosis and treatment plan, as well as medical test results. The next step is to identify a donor. Family members are considered first, but if there is no family-member donor, a search of the National Marrow Donor Registry can be done. The Center's physician will work with the prospective patient's physician to obtain information that is used to identify a donor. Sometimes the patient's own marrow can be used.

While the cost of marrow and stem cell transplants have been declining, transplantation remains a complex and expensive procedure, requiring intensive medical care at the Hutchinson Center for a period of one to three months after transplant. For this reason, there are no standard daily room rates at Hutchinson; charges are based on the treatment provided. Patients are responsible for the costs of their care and the Center requires a guarantee of funds, either through insurance or a prepayment of private funds. Once the physicians determine a person is a candidate for transplant, a Center finance specialist works with each patient to identify a financial plan to provide coverage.

Patients are cared for in the Hutchinson outpatient clinic and one of the three Fred Hutchinson and Swedish Medical Center inpatient transplant units. All treatment is coordinated by Hutchinson Center physicians.

UNIVERSITY OF

WASHINGTON

MEDICAL CENTER

Although the University of Washington Medical Center (UWMC) is one of the smallest of all teaching hospitals in the United States, it is rated by many doctors consulted for this book as one of the best. A major tertiary care hospital serving residents of the Pacific Northwest and beyond, UWMC is staffed by faculty of the highly regarded University of Washington School of Medicine, who attract an enormous amount (over $120 million) of research funding.

The University of Washington Medical Center began operations on May 4, 1959 as an integral component of the University of Washington Health Sciences Center. UWMC is the primary teaching hospital for the UW School of Medicine, the only medical school for the Washington, Alaska, Montana, and Idaho region.

Located on the University of Washington campus, UWMC is a 390-bed comprehensive care facility. It is consistently ranked as one of the best hospitals in the nation. Patients benefit from state-of-the-art care, a nursing staff with advanced training, and a commitment to quality and value. The nearly 400 attending physicians on staff are full-time faculty members of the UW School of Medicine. Fifty-eight are listed in the second edition of *The Best Doctors in America*.

ALTHOUGH THE UNIVERSITY OF WASHINGTON MEDICAL CENTER (UWMC) IS ONE OF THE SMALLEST OF ALL TEACHING HOSPITALS IN THE UNITED STATES, IT IS RATED BY MANY DOCTORS CONSULTED FOR THIS BOOK AS ONE OF THE BEST.

UWMC is both a provider of comprehensive primary care services for Greater Seattle residents and a regional referral and treatment center for specialized medical care. There are more than 80 outpatient clinics and multidisciplinary specialty centers. A new primary care facility, UWMC-Roosevelt, will open in Fall 1994 in Seattle's University District, offering expanded services in family medicine, women's health, general internal medicine, pediatrics, a Bone & Joint Center, and a Multidisciplinary Pain Center.

In August 1992, UWMC was accredited with commendation by the Joint Commission on Accreditation of Healthcare Organizations, the highest ranking awarded by the Joint Commission.

SPECIAL FACILITIES AND PROGRAMS

The Cancer Center is a multidisciplinary, internationally recognized referral and treatment center offering neutron irradiation; photon and electron irradiation; chemotherapy; immunotherapy; monoclonal antibody therapy; bone marrow transplants; stereotactic radiosurgery; intraoperative irradiation; interstitial implants; and multiple clinical trial options.

In cardiology and cardiac surgery, UWMC provides integrated services in prevention, diagnosis, management, and surgery, including routine diagnostic evaluation, therapeutic cardiac catheter procedures, electrophysiology service (heart rhythm disturbances), pacemaker placement, coronary artery bypass graft surgery, and heart transplantation. In addition, UWMC is a regional referral center for complex surgery of the aorta, heart valves, and complex coronary disease. It also has active outreach programs for prevention of heart disease.

The Cerebrovascular Diagnostic Laboratory uses non-invasive techniques, such as transcranial Doppler and single photon emission computed tomography, to assess cerebral circulation.

The Diabetes Care Center brings together many resources for people with diabetes, as well as the latest clinical research into the prevention, early de-

AT A GLANCE

Beds: 390
Occupancy Rate: 75%
Average Patient Count: 292
Average Patient Stay: 7.3 days
Annual Admissions: 14,753
Births: 1,764
Outpatient Clinic Visits:
  218,949
Emergency Room/Trauma
  Center Visits: 27,342

HOSPITAL PERSONNEL
Physicians: 385
  Board Certified: 85%+
Residents: 200+
Registered Nurses: 788
  BS Degree: 66%

ROOM CHARGES (PER DIEM)
Private: $425–$726
ICU: $1,726

ADDRESS
1959 Northeast Pacific Street
Seattle, WA 98195

TELEPHONE
(206) 548-3300

tection, diet, and treatment of diabetes and its related complications.

The Eye Center offers comprehensive outpatient ophthalmology diagnosis and treatment, including general services, retina service, cornea service, laser service, cataract service, and neuro-ophthalmology orbit and oculoplastic service.

Specialized services for hearing disorders and other ear problems are provided at the Bloedel Hearing Center.

UWMC-Roosevelt, which opened in October 1994, is a new-model primary care facility located on a major arterial road a few blocks from UWMC. It offers comprehensive care that includes family medicine, adult general internal medicine, pediatrics, and women's health, as well as the Bone & Joint Center, Multidisciplinary Pain Center, and support services.

The Fertility & Endocrine Center is an outpatient service located adjacent to UWMC-Roosevelt and is devoted exclusively to the medical and psychosocial needs of infertile couples, as well as women of all ages with endocrine problems. It offers comprehensive services in general infertility, assisted reproductive technologies, and reproductive endocrinology.

The Center for Anxiety and Depression is a nationally-recognized evaluation, treatment, and research facility in the treatment of anxiety and mood disorders.

Among UWMC's other specialized diagnostic and treatment programs are the Bone & Joint Center, high-risk maternity and newborn intensive care, the Imaging Research Center, the Pain Center, neurosurgery services, psychiatric services, rehabilitation medicine, and multiorgan transplantation services (bone, bone marrow, cornea, heart, heart-lung, kidney, liver, lung, kidney-pancreas).

MEDICAL SPECIALTIES

Allergy and Infectious Diseases, Anesthesiology, Cardiology, Cardiothoracic Surgery, Dentistry, Dermatology, Endocrinology and Nutrition, Family Medicine, Gastroenterology, General Internal Medicine, Gynecologic Oncology, Hematology, Medical Genetics, Metabolism, Nephrology, Neurological Surgery, Neurology, Nuclear Medicine, Obstetrics/Gynecology, Oncology, Ophthalmology, Orthopedics, Otolaryngology, Pediatrics, Perinatal Medicine, Plastic Surgery, Psychiatry, Pulmonary and Critical Care Medicine, Radiation Oncology, Radiology, Rehabilitation Medicine, Reproductive Endocrinology, Rheumatology, Surgery, Transplantation Surgery, Urology, and Vascular Surgery.

WELL-KNOWN SPECIALISTS

- Dr. Suhail Ahmad   *Nephrology*
- Dr. Margaret Allen   *Cardiac surgery*
- Dr. Frederick Appelbaum   *Medical oncology/hematology*
- Dr. Mary Austin-Seymour   *Radiation oncology*
- Dr. William Couser   *Nephrology*

- Dr. David Dunner *Psychiatry*
- Dr. Janet Eary *Nuclear medicine*
- Dr. George Gates *Otolaryngology*
- Dr. Michael Graham *Nuclear medicine*
- Dr. J. Ward Kennedy *Cardiovascular disease*
- Dr. George Kraft *Physical medicine and rehabilitation*
- Dr. George Laramore *Radiation oncology*
- Dr. Robert B. Livingston *Medical oncology/hematology*
- Dr. Hans Ochs *Allergy and immunology*
- Dr. George Ojemann *Neurological surgery*
- Dr. Murray Raskind *Psychiatry Dr. Michael Roy Soules Obstetrics and gynecology*
- Dr. Michael Roy Soules *Obstetrics and gynecology*
- Dr. Ernest Weymuller, Jr. *Otolaryngology*

PATIENT SATISFACTION

Ninety percent of inpatients surveyed rated the quality of care received at UWMC as "excellent" or "very good" (58.8% "excellent," 31.2% "very good"). The vast majority of inpatients (93%) indicate that they would recommend UWMC to their family or friends, or return to UWMC for care and treatment again.

Overall, 87.3% of outpatients rated the quality of care they received as "excellent" or "very good" (54.4% "excellent", 32.9% "very good"). The overwhelming majority of patients (90.4%) indicated that they would recommend UWMC outpatient clinics to family and friends.

RESEARCH

The University of Washington Medical Center is one of two major teaching hospitals of the University of Washington School of Medicine, one of the nation's top research institutions. For the past 20 years, the UW School of Medicine has ranked fifth or higher nearly every year in grants received from the National Institutes of Health. It received more than $171 million in grants from all federal sources in fiscal year 1992-93.

Major current research areas at the UW School of Medicine include hearing, neural signalling, molecular medicine, Alzheimer's disease, cystic fibrosis, AIDS, imaging, epilepsy, vascular biology, embryology, diabetes, reproduction, vision, nutrition, molecular structure, women's health, bioengineering, endocrinology, and the human genome.

The University of Washington School of Medicine has contributed many important discoveries and innovations to medical science and education. The first long-term dialysis for chronic kidney failure and a hormone replacement therapy that reverses the related anemia of kidney failure were developed here. UW researchers developed a multidisciplinary approach to chronic pain, illuminated the origins of atherosclerosis, and designed new methods for testing heart function. Pioneering research in bone marrow transplantation offers the hope of curing leukemia and other blood disorders.

Three School of Medicine faculty members have recently won the Nobel Prize in medicine—Edmond Fischer and Edwin G. Krebs in 1992, and E. Donnall Thomas in 1990.

ADMISSIONS POLICY

Patients may be directly admitted through the emergency room or via a UWMC attending physician at any clinic. Anyone may come to the hospital for care; if an individual does not have a personal physician, he or she may choose a primary care physician or a specialist from the medical staff.

Clinic appointments or referrals can be made by calling (206) 548-4333. Physicians may also call specific departments or University Hospital physicians to arrange referrals for inpatient or specialized tests, such as magnetic resonance imaging.

Patients who enter through the Emergency Department or because of medical necessity are admitted without consideration of their financial resources. Private pay patients scheduled for elective admissions are asked to make a preadmission deposit.

UWMC provided more than $4,650,000 in charity care in fiscal year 1993.

VIRGINIA MASON

MEDICAL CENTER

SEATTLE, WASHINGTON

While the city of Seattle has several first-rate teaching hospitals—Swedish, Harborview, and University Hospital, for example—when Governor Mike Lowry needed a site to sign legislation establishing the most comprehensive health care reform law in the nation, he selected Virginia Mason Medical Center (VMMC). Virginia Mason is a main referral center for the Pacific Northwest and several Western states, including Alaska, Idaho, Montana and Oregon; 30% of its patients live outside the Seattle area. In the world medical community, Virginia Mason has a reputation in league with the Mayo, Scripps, and Cleveland Clinics.

Virginia Mason Medical Center consists of a hospital, a clinic, 13 neighborhood clinics in and outside Seattle, and a research center. It is a tertiary care facility offering acute care services, as well as routine treatment, and is a major referral center for specialized care.

Founded in 1920 by eight doctors under the leadership of Dr. James Tate Mason (who named the facility after his daughter), the hospital was originally to be a place where people from all walks of life could obtain the care they needed. Patients would receive diagnosis and treatment in the clinic, additional care if needed in the hospital, and in extreme cases await with ultimate hope for a cure from the research center. The concept was called "integrated care."

IN THE WORLD MEDICAL COMMUNITY, VIRGINIA MASON HAS A REPUTATION IN LEAGUE WITH THE MAYO, SCRIPPS, AND CLEVELAND CLINICS.

Today, the center functions in somewhat the same way as the Mayo and Cleveland clinics do. Almost 270 doctors representing 58 specialties pool their knowledge to diagnose and treat a wide variety of illnesses. Armed with the most up-to-date diagnostic medical machinery, including MRI scanners and a full service electrophysiology lab, the physicians there treat even the most complex disorders. Modern medical technology pervades the hospital and includes lasers for surgery and a lithotriptor for crushing kidney stones.

The nursing staff at Virginia Mason is exceptional. More than 50% have bachelor's degrees. The turnover rate is extremely low—13% compared to the national average of 20%. Virginia Mason's nursing staff is highly skilled and works with a shared governance model where staff nurses are decision makers. They work in a collaborative practice with the physician to develop critical pathways in the managed care environment. Virginia Mason is also piloting a salary compensation model for registered nurses.

The hospital has its own private hotel—the Mason House—with seven floors of rooms for out-of-town patients and their families. Short Stay Surgery is designed for patients requiring procedures that do not necessitate an overnight hospital stay. This was the first such program in the region. Seattle's first hospital-based midwifery program was initiated here. Virginia Mason was also one of the first hospitals to permit fathers to be present during deliveries.

In the 1920s, Virginia Mason instituted the region's first postgraduate program for doctors. Its highly competitive residency programs in internal medicine, general surgery, radiology, and anesthesiology have historically attracted the best and the brightest. In 1992, there were more than 1,000 applicants for 32 openings. Each year, Virginia Mason trains more than 15 postdoctoral fellows in the latest research technologies in immunology and immunogenetics.

Virginia Mason was one of the first medical centers in the Seattle area to offer continuing education programs to doctors and is a regional provider of accredited continuing education.

SPECIAL FACILITIES AND PROGRAMS

Staffed by nurses trained in cancer care, the N. Peter Canlis Cancer Care Unit has 26 beds. Virginia Mason diagnoses more cancer patients than any other health care institution in the Northwest, treating more than 70 patients a day and 1,600 new cancer patients a year.

Prudential Insurance named Virginia Mason one of its national "centers of excellence" and chose the medical center as their regional heart care referral center. The cardiology program has mortality rates well below the national average. Virginia Mason was one of the first hospitals to use catheters in the treatment of abnormal heart rhythm, enabling patients to avoid open heart surgery or a lifetime of potentially toxic heart medications.

The Benaroya Diabetes Center is the oldest, largest, and most comprehensive of its kind in the Northwest, and includes the region's first comprehensive patient education program. In 1992, a pancreatic transplant program was introduced, allowing some diabetic patients to forgo daily insulin shots. Over the past five years, Virginia Mason scientists have discovered the primary genetic marker for diabetes; methods of determining a person's risk for diabetes; and the "switch mechanism" in the diabetes susceptibility gene that could be triggered to "turn off" the disease.

Virginia Mason's gastroenterology program is pioneering ways to use diagnostic procedures in the treatment of diseases of the stomach and intestines, enabling patients to be treated on an outpatient or overnight basis.

Virginia Mason launched that state's first comprehensive health care facility designed exclusively to meet the medical needs of women. In 1993, the medical center was the first in Seattle to have available a stereotactic core needle breast biopsy machine, the latest nonsurgical procedure for breast biopsy.

Virginia Mason manages and staffs the 35-bed Bailey-Boushay House, the nation's first facility specifically designed to meet the special nursing care needs of people living with AIDS. Opened in 1992, its Adult Day Health Program and 24-hour skilled nursing care program operate at full capacity, serving more than 400 people with HIV/AIDS in the past year.

Virginia Mason has recently enhanced its Fertility and Reproductive Endocrine Center by adding an on-site embryology lab and an expanded andrology lab.

The kidney transplant program is the 17th largest in the nation and the largest in Washington state. Virginia Mason began its pancreas transplant program in 1992. In 1993, 100 actual transplant surgeries were performed—98 kidney and two pancreas. Of these, three were combined kidney-pancreas transplants.

In 1993, 18 bone marrow transplants were performed, including autologous and allogeneic transplants. In addition to performing transplants, Virginia Mason plays a major role in the Blood Marrow Donor Program, the largest unrelated marrow donor program in the United States. Virginia Mason

AT A GLANCE

Beds: 223
Occupancy Rate: 66%
Average Patient Count: 158
Average Patient Stay: 5.1 days
Annual Admissions: 11,844
Births: 1,408
Outpatient Clinic Visits:
  676,000
Emergency Room/Trauma
  Center Visits: 16,181

HOSPITAL PERSONNEL
Physicians: 223
Residents: 105
Registered Nurses: 700

ROOM CHARGES (PER DIEM)
Private: $550
Semiprivate: $550
ICU: $1,560

ADDRESS
925 Seneca Street
Seattle, WA 98111

TELEPHONE
Hospital
(206) 624-1144
Clinic
(206) 223-6600

The Best Hospitals in America   **453**

Medical Center is one of the top three bone marrow collection sites in the nation, performing approximately one bone marrow aspiration per week. Locally, VMMC is the only marrow collection site and works in coordination with the Puget Sound Blood Program. In 1993, it began offering stem cell collection and reinfusion.

Short Stay Surgery is designed for patients requiring procedures that do not necessitate an overnight hospital stay. This was the first such program in the region. Seattle's first hospital-based midwifery program was initiated at VMMC. Other special facilities include the largest hyperbaric chamber and facility in the Northwest; and the Sports Medicine Center, which provides care for athletes with sports injuries, as well as conditioning facilities and educational programs for all athletes. A health promotion service called SENSE provides consulting services to local businesses and offers a range of programs.

MEDICAL SPECIALTIES

Anesthesiology, Cancer, Cardiology, Critical Care, Diabetes,Diagnostic Medicine, Immunology, Infectious Diseases, Intensive Care, Kidney Dialysis and Transplantation, Obstetrics and Midwifery, Oncology, Physical Medicine, and Surgery.

WELL-KNOWN SPECIALISTS

- Dr. Richard P. Anderson   *Cardiothoracic surgery*
- Dr. Robert A. Caplan   *Anesthesiology*
- Dr. L. Frederick Fenster   *Liver and biliary tract disorders*
- Dr. Robert P. Gibbons   *Urology, urologic oncology*
- Dr. Richard O. Gode   *Child and adolescent psychiatry*
- Dr. Mark D. Hafermann   *Radiation oncology, genito-urinary cancer*
- Dr. Richard A. Kozarek   *Gastroenterology, endoscopy*
- Dr. Robert S. Mecklenburg   *Endocrinology and diabetes*
- Dr. Gerald T. Nepom   *Immunology and diabetes research*
- Dr. Gale Thompson   *Anesthesiology*
- Dr. Kenneth R. Wilske   *Immunology, allergy and rheumatic diseases*
- Dr. Richard H. Winterbauer   *Chest and infectious diseases*

PATIENT SATISFACTION

Between June and September of 1992, 6,600 Virginia Mason patients were randomly selected from all patients seen at any VMMC treatment site. Eighty-six percent rated the overall quality of care as "excellent" or "very good."

RESEARCH

Along with the Mayo Clinic, the Cleveland Clinic and the Scripps Clinic, Virginia Mason is one of the few private, nonuniversity medical centers in the nation that operates formal research programs. Research funding from all sources in 1993 amounted to more than $5,200,000. The Hill Repair for hiatal hernia, the Traverso pancreatic resection and the Joel Baker tube for small bowel obstructions are just three of the many now standard surgical procedures invented at Virginia Mason.

VMMC has one of the best immunology programs in the world. Six interrelated laboratories have been established within the Immunology/Diabetes Program. These study such areas as genetic control of the human immune response, selection and usage of antibody genes, and regulation of immune response.

The Williams Reed Laboratory performs projects focused on understanding profound deafness.

The Diabetes Clinical Research Unit was initiated in 1992 under Dr. David McCulloch. He and his staff of six work very closely with the physicians, nurses, and diabetes educators in the diabetes centers to make moving the research from the "bench to bedside" a reality.

A number of clinical research programs address issues aimed at better balancing patient care responsibilities with academic and research interests.

ADMISSIONS POLICY

To be admitted, patients need to be under the care of a Virginia Mason physician at any one of the 13 clinic locations. Virginia Mason does not turn away individuals unable to pay for their care. The cost of indigent care is shared with other area hospitals. In 1992, Virginia Mason provided $16 million in uncompensated care.

PATIENT/FAMILY ACCOMMODATIONS

Room rates at Mason House range from $62 for a standard room to $130 for a king suite. For patient families, these prices reflect a 22–23% discount off the public rate.

UNIVERSITY OF

WISCONSIN HOSPITAL

AND CLINICS

MADISON, WISCONSIN

Situated in a beautiful pastoral setting, the University of Wisconsin Hospital and Clinics (UWHC) provides medical care that rivals many big-city hospitals. With more than 70 inpatient facilities and outpatient clinics, UWHC is a major referral center servicing all of Wisconsin and parts of Illinois, Iowa, Upper Michigan, and Minnesota. As a major teaching institution, UWHC is a leading center for biomedical research, education of health professionals, and public service. All attending physicians who care for patients at UWHC are also faculty members at UW Medical School. The range of medical specialties and services available at UWHC is among the most complete we have come across in writing this book.

UWHC has developed an outstanding reputation for its highly successful organ transplant program, including its kidney, liver, pancreas, lung, heart, and multiple organ transplants. The hospital's transplant center is among the nation's largest, and its associated organ procurement programs have one of the highest per capita rate of donation in the country.

THE RANGE OF
MEDICAL SPECIALTIES
AND SERVICES AVAILABLE
AT UWHC IS AMONG THE
MOST COMPLETE WE
HAVE COME ACROSS IN
WRITING THIS BOOK.

Research at UW Medical School has been used at the hospital to dramatically improve transplant procedures. An organ preservation solution, developed by the UW surgeon Dr. Folkert Belzer, has revolutionized transplant procedures, allowing some transplants to be scheduled ahead of time instead of on an emergency basis. Dr. Belzer and UW surgeon Dr. Hans Sollinger also developed the Wisconsin Technique, a method of connecting a transplanted pancreas to the bladder, reducing infection rates. UW researchers also introduced a four-drug anti-rejection therapy that has markedly improved the success of liver transplantation.

SPECIAL FACILITIES AND PROGRAMS

As the nation's second largest pancreas transplant center, UWHC has performed 357 pancreas transplants since the program began in 1982, with a one-year patient survival rate of 96% and a graft survival rate of 86%. UWHC also claims one of the busiest renal transplant centers (a distinction of special note given the size of the surrounding community). Since 1966, 3,121 kidney transplants have been performed at the center. The hospital's program offers both living-related and cadaveric renal transplants. It is also a leader in non-related living donor transplants, specializing in spousal transplants. The program's success rates are among the best nationally, with a current one-year survival rate for transplant patients, with either living-related or cadaver donors, of between 95 and 98%.

Success rates in other areas of transplantation have also exceeded the national average. For example, 478 liver transplants have been performed, with a success rate of 85% for adults and 90% for children since 1984.

UW Hospital and Clinics also offers one of the world's largest and most successful programs in transplanting bone marrow across HLA histocompatibility barriers (mismatched donor/recipient).

The University of Wisconsin Clinical Cancer Center at UW Hospital and Clinics is one of 27 multidisciplinary comprehensive centers in the U.S. funded by the National Cancer Institute. At any one time, the center provides up to 100 different experimental treatment plans available at only a few other facilities. Specialists in biostatistics, immunology, and microbiology have formulated new treatments for breast, prostate, and bladder cancers. World-renowned

AT A GLANCE

Beds: 503
Occupancy Rate: 76%
Average Patient Count: 376
Average Patient Stay: 7.7 days
Annual Admissions: 18,332
Outpatient Clinic Visits:
    305,880
Emergency Room/Trauma
    Center Visits: 25,050

HOSPITAL PERSONNEL
Physicians: 572
Residents: 374
Fellows: 93
Registered Nurses: 976

ROOM CHARGES (PER DIEM)
Semiprivate: $300–$450
ICU: $1,400

ADDRESS
600 Highland Avenue
Madison, WI 53792

TELEPHONE
(608) 263-6400

for its comprehensive breast cancer program, UW pioneered the use of several hormonal and chemotherapy treatments, including hyperthermia, radiobiology, immune modulators such as interferon and interleukin-2, and hormones such as tamoxifen. The center also has an advanced experimental program in whole body hyperthermia, which involves raising a patient's body temperature to enhance the anti-cancer effect of other therapies.

The center's Cancer Prevention Clinic offers cancer risk assessment, preventive health care counseling and education, and special medical examinations and tests. The Chemosurgery Clinic offers a technique developed and refined at the UW Medical School for the treatment of skin cancer. The chemosurgery removes cancerous growths under plane-by-plane microscopic control, assuring complete removal of the cancer without removing extra skin.

Each year, the center treats more than 300 children with cancer at the UW Children's Hospital. Additionally, the hospital offers advanced pediatric care for problems ranging from allergies to cystic fibrosis. The first formal pediatric bone marrow transplantation protocol in the world for children with brain tumors was developed at UWHC.

One of the largest in the Midwest, UWHC's cardiology department includes 15 full-time cardiologists on staff who specialize in all aspects of adult and pediatric cardiac surgery and transplantation. UWHC is among the few facilities in the country to have developed expertise in the repair of complex thoraco-abdominal aneurysms. It was one of the first hospitals in the state to use the transluminal extraction catheter (TEC) to open blocked bypass grafts. UWHC researchers developed a unique image processing laboratory, combining information from a variety of diagnostic technologies to produce a single, complete picture of the heart.

UWHC ophthalmologists have played leading roles in the National Eye Institute trials demonstrating the effectiveness of lasers in treating diabetic retinopathy, a leading cause of blindness, and macular degeneration, an age-linked eye disease. The department is also known for its program in ophthalmic plastic and reconstructive surgery and maintains clinics in all other subspecialties of ophthalmology, including glaucoma, hereditary retinal disease, low vision, and cornea transplants. Additionally, lasers are being successfully used to halt disease and UW's ophthalmology department acted as a key participant in national studies demonstrating the effectiveness of laser treatment for various eye disorders.

Special areas of the Department of Psychiatry include the Center for Affective Disorders, which treats depression and manic depression; Lithium Information Center; Child and Adolescent Psychiatric Services; Couples/Family Therapy Clinic; and the Anxiety Disorders Clinic, which provides care for patients who suffer from anxiety, phobias, panic attacks, and related disorders.

The Department of Radiology provides complete diagnostic imaging and conducts ambitious research, which has resulted in new applications for MRIs.

Recently, the department developed new methods of measuring the flow in coronary arteries and of detaching brain activation using a echo planar functional MRI. The department is also evaluating new breast imaging techniques as an alternative to breast biopsies for some women.

In addition to its international reputation in organ transplantation, the Department of Surgery specializes in bioengineering, urologic oncology, immunology, and microsurgery. UW surgeons have helped to reduce both costs and recovery time by applying laparoscopic techniques to traditional surgical procedures. UW physicians recently pioneered the nation's first laparoscopic spinal fusion, replacing a damaged spinal disk in the lower back with a stabilizing bone implant without lengthy abdominal surgery. UW surgeons also performed the state's first laparoscopic kidney removal, replacing nonfunctioning kidneys with transplants.

A team of UW neuroradiologists and surgeons also developed a technique to nonsurgically remove abnormal collections of blood vessels in the brain, replacing risky brain surgery in most cases and providing treatment for conditions previously considered inoperable.

The Sports Medicine and Fitness Center offers comprehensive care to improve health fitness and well-being. Diagnosis, treatment, and rehabilitation of sports-related injuries, as well as specialized care for acute and chronic medical problems, are among the services provided by the center's team of sports medicine physicians, athletic trainers, exercise physiologists, and physical therapists. Additionally, a comprehensive Spine Center provides specialized diagnosis and treatment of spinal injuries with orthopedic surgeons specially trained in adult spinal reconstructive surgery.

The Department of Plastic and Reconstructive Surgery offers expert care in all aspects of modern plastic surgery. Major specialty areas include cleft lip and palate anomalies, hand surgery, microsurgery and replantation, cancer surgery, craniofacial and maxillofacial surgery, reconstructive surgery, and cosmetic surgery.

The Rehabilitation Center provides a comprehensive program for patients with spinal cord injuries, head injuries, neuromuscular disabilities and related disabling conditions, and chronic pain. The Center's Neuromuscular Retraining Clinic, one of the first in the nation, offers intensive outpatient rehabilitation therapy for patients with debilitating brain injuries leading to paralysis, muscular spasms, or tremors. The innovative therapy involves retraining portions of the brain to assume functions once controlled by the damaged area. Notable successes have been observed, some in patients chronically disabled for years.

UWHC is rapidly expanding services to the community, and offers several outreach programs to serve patients and health professionals throughout the state and region. The hospital has several clinics in the community and offers extended hours in many primary care clinics. A Women's Health Center focuses on the special health needs of women. All of the major departments at UW run specialty clinics available to the public on an outpatient basis.

MEDICAL SPECIALTIES

Anesthesiology, Cardiology, Emergency Medicine, Family Medicine and Practice, Internal Medicine, Neurology, Neurological Surgery, Obstetrics/Gynecology, Oncology, Ophthalmology, Pathology, Pediatrics, Pediatric Intensive Care, Plastic and Reconstructive Surgery, Psychiatry, Radiology, Rehabilitation Medicine, and Surgery.

WELL-KNOWN SPECIALISTS

- Dr. Daniel M. Albert   *Ophthalmology; specialist in intraocular tumors*
- Dr. Folkert O. Belzer   *Surgery; nationally known transplant surgeon and researcher who developed the UW Solution used for preservation of donor livers and pancreases*
- Dr. Paul P. Carbone   *Oncology; specialist in breast cancer*
- Dr. Timothy Kinsella   *Oncology; specialist in combining treatment approaches*
- Dr. Manucher Javid   *Neurological surgery; nationally known neurosurgeon, pioneered chymopapain injection procedure for slipped disc*
- Dr. Dennis G. Maki   *Infectious diseases; expertise in hospital-acquired infections and AIDS*
- Dr. Elaine Mischler   *Pediatrics; researcher with special recognition in the area of cystic fibrosis*
- Dr. Thomas Zdeblick   *Surgery; pioneering new techniques in spinal surgery*

PATIENT SATISFACTION

In 1993, 90% of the patients who responded to the hospital's questionnaire reported that they would seek care at the hospital again or would recommend the hospital to others.

RESEARCH

With over $78 million in public and private grants coming to the medical school each year, the University of Wisconsin is one of the leading research institutions in the country. Almost 60% of this money is allocated to clinical research, so the hospitals and clinics are able to maintain extensive ongoing research programs.

The largest single research area is oncology, which receives about $18 million in funding a year. Other major research programs exist in pediatrics and ophthalmology. In pediatrics, important research in immunology, cystic fibrosis, and ophthalmology, specifically in diabetic retinopathy, is underway.

Physicians at UW are also working to improve the outcome of transplantation with micro-metabolism research and morphology tests, which may one day assess donor hearts before they are removed. Additionally, UW physicians are researching ways to alter the immunogenicity of organs in order to decrease the amounts of immunosuppressants prescribed after heart, kidney, liver, and pancreas transplantations.

ADMISSIONS POLICY

A doctor's referral is not necessary for admission to UWHC, unless it is required by the patient's health insurance plan. Patients can be admitted without referral through the emergency room or one of the clinics. Any patient may make an appointment at one of UWHC's clinics by calling the hospital. The phone number for general information about the clinics is: (608) 263-8580.

UW Hospital and Clinic does not have a financial requirement for admission, with the exception of certain elected procedures such as cosmetic surgery and in vitro fertilization. In 1993, free care totaled $4.4 million.

CANADA

THE CANADIAN HEALTH

CARE SYSTEM

Some Americans, anxious for a drastic overhaul of their health care system, point to Canada's system of universal coverage as the model. Unlike Americans, no Canadian ever need worry about the prospect of mortgaging his or her life away to pay a five-or six-figure medical bill.

The vast majority of Canadians praise the system, where everyone, rich or poor, is guaranteed all "medically required services," ranging from a routine checkup to heart transplant surgery. But the health care community is now warning Canadians that the system they so dearly love is on the verge of financial collapse.

Universal health care insurance, introduced in 1966, is paid for largely through federal and provincial taxes. In some provinces, employers cover their own employees' health costs.

There is no national health care system per se. Each of the ten provinces, as well as the Yukon and Northwest Territories, administers health care differently in its own region. The federal government foots a portion of the bill through a "transfer" payment. That portion was once as high as 50%, but now is about 30%. The provinces, of course, pay the rest—about a third of their total budgets.

Most provinces do not actually run their hospitals. For instance, in Ontario, hospitals are private, nonprofit organizations. Local district health councils—doctors, nurses, hospital administrators, consumers, and municipal representatives—advise the Ontario health ministry on policy matters, and the ministry in turn dictates to the hospitals.

The vast majority of doctors in Canada are paid according to a "fee-for-service" schedule, negotiated between each province and its provincial medical association. Salary caps are in place to limit what various kinds of doctors earn, long a source of friction in the Canadian medical community.

The disadvantages of the Canadian system, as it now exists, are the salary caps that prevent top Canadian hospitals from keeping their star specialists at home, and the shortage of modern medical equipment, which has led to the rationing of many kinds of elective, specialized surgery.

While primary care physicians in Canada earn close to what their American counterparts do, U.S. specialists are generally paid far better than specialists in Canada. Indeed, Ontario specialists can gross no more than $400,000 per year. As a result, many of Canada's top specialists are successfully wooed by American hospitals. Nearly half of all Canadian specialists who recently moved "south-of-the-border" did so mainly for the money, according to one survey. These same transplanted doctors, however, also complain about the lack of universal care in the United States, the increased paperwork, and the higher costs of malpractice insurance. (In fact, American doctors are 50 times more likely to be sued.)

Because the federal government cut transfer payments to the provinces by about $7 billion in 1993 alone, the provinces have had to reduce coverage and services. All this financial belt-tightening has, of course, had a strong impact on the average Canadian.

American hospitals have long spent considerably more on capital improvements, such as state-of-the-art technology, but in recent years, that discrepancy has increased noticeably. The small number of MRI and CAT scanners in Canadian hospitals shocks American specialists. Not long ago, there were more MRIs in the city of Atlanta, Georgia, than there were in all of Canada. It's not that hospitals don't desire such machines; it's that the provinces, in their desperate attempts to control costs, usually won't allow hospitals to buy them, because more high-tech machines mean more high-tech personnel and more patient visits—all of which sends costs soaring.

Rationing of elective surgery (waiting lists) is the most disturbing trend. While all life-threatening surgery is carried out immediately, other patients must often go on a waiting list. There just aren't enough specialists or high-tech machines to go around anymore.

In early 1994, two of the largest and best hospitals in Canada—The Toronto Hospital and Sunnybrook Health Science Centre, also in Toronto—had long waiting lists for such elective surgeries as hip replacement (three months), gall bladder (eight months), head and neck cancer (four weeks), autologous bone marrow transplants (four to nine months), and cataracts (six months). *Saturday Night* magazine estimated in October 1993 that one percent of the entire Canadian population was on some kind of surgical waiting list.

A small percentage of Canadians arrange to have surgery in American hospitals, either paying for it themselves or with assistance from their provincial government. But now, provinces are drastically cutting "south-of-the-border" coverage. In 1994, Ontario slashed out-of-country hospital coverage from $400 a day to $100, and limited emergency room costs to a flat fee of $50 per visit.

Health Minister Ruth Grier properly advises Ontarians who travel south to buy private insurance before leaving the country.

The Canadian system is indeed ailing. Perhaps, then, it should come as no surprise that in 1993 the Health Action Lobby, a coalition of seven national health care organizations, commissioned a study to suggest ways to define "medically required services." In other words, they want to suggest which services Canadians should get free of charge and which they should pay for.

THE BEST HOSPITALS IN CANADA

Despite the gloomy outlook for Canada's health care system as a whole, there continues to be ground-breaking medicine and revolutionary care practiced at a number of world-renowned Canadian hospitals, and on the standard of overall patient care, Canada still takes a back seat to no other country, including the United States. The 13 Canadian hospitals profiled in this book, then, were selected because they combine advanced medical procedures with first-rate patient care.

Twelve of the 13 institutions are tertiary care hospitals that, not surprisingly, received the highest marks from the Canadian Council on Health Facilities Accreditation (CCHFA). Like the Joint Commission on Accreditation of Healthcare Organizations (JCAHO) in the United States, the CCHFA was incorporated to set standards for Canadian health care facilities and to measure hospitals against these standards. Since 1958, this nonprofit organization has rated hospitals and other facilities that voluntarily participate in an accreditation program. Only one Canadian facility—Mount Sinai Hospital of Toronto—has ever received the highest award. The other 11 tertiary care hospitals listed in this book received awards at the next highest level.

Finally, there are two levels of pediatric hospitals in Canada—the Hospital for Sick Children of Toronto, then everybody else. "Sick Kids," its more common moniker, is also described in the pages that follow. This hospital is clearly in a class of its own. A world leader in many fields, the care it provides is unrivaled.

Certainly, there are outstanding general and specialty hospitals in Canada other than the 13 selected for the second edition of *The Best Hospitals in America.* Montreal alone has the world famous Montreal Neurological Institute, as well as several first-rate tertiary care hospitals. The latter traditionally cater to either the French- or English-speaking community. On the French side, Notre Dame Hospital provides the broadest range of first-rate patient care; but considering overall scientific advancements, level of care, and affiliation with one of the top medical schools in the world at McGill University, the two "English" teaching hospitals, which have entries in this book—Montreal General Hospital and Royal Victoria Hospital—are probably even more prominent. These two hospitals, along with three other McGill-affiliated "English" hospitals—Children's Hospital, Neurological Institute, and Chest Hospital Centre—have collectively endorsed the construction of a single, new complex that would amalgamate their services—to be called the McGill University Hospital Centre. In mid-1994, they were still awaiting approval from the Quebec government.

In Ontario, St. Michael's Hospital in Toronto and the University of Ottawa Heart Institute at Ottawa Civic Hospital are among Canada's premier heart care facilities. Ottawa General Hospital, meanwhile, is one of the most medically advanced in the country, and the Ontario Cancer Institute at Princess Margaret Hospital in Toronto is one of the nation's best cancer care facilities. Toronto also boasts the Shouldice Hernia Hospital, which handles thousands of cases a year and attracts patients from around the world; and Chedoke-McMaster Hospitals in Hamilton is affiliated with the McMaster University Medical School, home of one of the premier multicentered clinical research programs in North America.

In addition to the outstanding services available at "Sick Kids," world class procedures are also being performed at other children's hospitals in Canada, including the Izaak Walton Killam Children's Hospital (IWK) in Halifax, Nova Scotia. IWK, founded in 1909, is the referral center for pediatric care in the Maritimes and is at the forefront of pediatric cardiovascular surgery. In May 1994, IWK doctors performed successful open heart surgery on a four pound baby—the smallest patient ever to survive such an operation.

In 1907, Hospital Sainte-Justine (HSJ) of Montreal became the nation's first French-Canadian children's hospital. Today, it is the largest children's hospital in eastern Canada. HSJ is best known for being the most extensive mother-child center in North America. Since 1928, with the establishment of an obstetrics department, HSJ has provided first-rate care for mothers, children, and adolescents alike. Its research center is the only one in North America to conduct fundamental and clinical research on children and maternal diseases under the same roof. Affiliated with Laval University of Montreal, HSJ is also renowned for successfully performing the world's first separation, in 1978, of Siamese twins joined at the pelvis and abdomen; for transplanting a heart into a 16-year-old boy in 1984 (the youngest patient in Canada to undergo this procedure); and for reattaching an eight-year-old boy's severed arm in 1986. In addition, HSJ has an ultra-specialized pediatric ophthalmology unit and is the provincial center for children's kidney transplants and craniofacial surgery. So, it's no surprise that HSJ attracts almost half of its patients from outside the Montreal/Laval area.

Across town is another world class facility—the Montreal Children's Hospital (MCH). Since opening in 1904, MCH has also compiled an impressive list of "firsts," including the design of the world's first respirator—the forerunner of the "Iron Lung"—in 1932. MCH was the first pediatric hospital in Canada to establish a psychiatry department (1950), the first to establish a center for learning disorders (1960), the first with a multicultural program (1985), and the first to open a center to evaluate, diagnose, and treat potentially fatal sleep disorders (1986). Affiliated with McGill University, MCH's fields of particular expertise include specialized surgery (heart, neurosurgery, transplantation, and reconstruction), critical care of infants and children, and the assessment and short term management of atypical development.

The Children's Hospital of Eastern Ontario (CHEO), located in Ottawa, is the regional center for pediatric care. Founded in 1974, it serves as the primary pediatric teaching hospital for the University of Ottawa. CHEO specializes in open and closed heart surgery, neonatal intensive care, treatment and prevention of child abuse and neglect, poisoning, the surgical repair of cleft palates, and treatment of spinal deformities.

The Alberta Children's Hospital (ACH) in Calgary is the only freestanding pediatric hospital between Winnipeg and Vancouver. Founded in 1922 as an orthopedic specialty hospital, ACH is the regional pediatric center for all of southern Alberta, southwestern Saskatchewan, and southeastern British Columbia. ACH boasts the shortest average length of stay of any children's hospital in Canada—5.1 days. This is due largely to ACH's strong focus on ambulatory care and on parent teaching. Indeed, parents are encouraged to stay with their child during their hospital stay and to participate in his or her care and treatment as much as possible.

The Children's Health Centre of Northern Alberta (CHC) is an organization of children's health services provided at various hospitals in the Edmonton area. The CHC network includes the Grey Nuns and Misericordia Hospitals, the Royal Alexandra Health Care Corporation, Sturgeon General Hospital, and the University of Alberta Hospitals. Most of the advanced procedures are performed at the University of Alberta Hospitals site, covering such pediatric fields as oncology, seizure disorders (one of only two Canadian children's hospitals performing seizure surgery), infectious diseases, solid organ transplantation, and hereditary diseases.

British Columbia Children's Hospital (BCCH), located in Vancouver, is internationally known for its forays into pediatric surgery. As the province's major treatment, teaching, and research facility for pediatric care, BCCH offers many programs and procedures not available anywhere else in British Columbia. It provides the only pediatric MRI service in the province and is the only British Columbia hospital to perform pediatric organ transplants, open heart surgery, and bone marrow transplantation. Through affiliation with the University of British Columbia and other teaching institutions, BCCH has pioneered a neurosurgery technique to reduce spasticity in the limbs of children with cerebral palsy, as well as a new device to measure brain blood volume and levels of oxygen in high-risk newborns. It has also helped perform a heart-lung transplant on the youngest recipient ever in western Canada—a 12-year-old girl. In cooperation with the provincial Ambulance Service, BCCH also designed and implemented, in 1974, the Infant Transport Team—a program that ensures that all newborn babies born in the province have access to BCCH's outstanding services. This model for the delivery of prenatal health care was the first of its kind in the world on this scale.

The Best Hospitals in America

A SPECIAL NOTE ON HOSPITAL CHARGES

Thanks to a national policy of universal coverage, Canadian residents are not billed directly for health care. Instead, hospitals and doctors bill the provincial government for all services, ranging from routine checkups to major surgery. Visitors to Canada, however, including Americans, must arrange for payment at the time of hospitalization.

The Canadian entries that follow include costs for non-Canadian patients, when the information was available from the hospitals. Because those costs are sometimes complicated to describe, though, they are discussed under the "Admissions Policy" heading within the entries, rather than listed with the "At A Glance" data, as in the U.S. entries.

FOOTHILLS PROVINCIAL

GENERAL HOSPITAL

Since it opened in 1966, Foothills Provincial General Hospital (FPGH) has quickly grown from an ambitious community hospital to the principal referral, teaching, and research center in the region—a region encompassing not only southern Alberta, but southeastern British Columbia and southwestern Saskatchewan as well.

FPGH is the primary care facility of the larger Foothill Medical Centre complex, which also includes the closely affiliated University of Calgary Faculty of Medicine and the Tom Baker Cancer Centre.

Most FPGH physicians hold joint appointments with the University of Calgary Faculty of Medicine, and all staff are expected to be both teachers and learners. The philosophy behind this mandate is that patient needs are best served when clinicians, educators, and researchers participate together in the health care process, so that patients receive the most up-to-date care, students receive a more relevant education, and researchers maintain a close relationship with the patients who ultimately benefit from their work.

SPECIAL FACILITIES AND PROGRAMS

The Tom Baker Cancer Centre is at the forefront of cancer research and treatment in North America. It offers advanced screening programs and outpatient care, while FPGH provides surgery, diagnostic services, and in-hospital treatments.

To become the regional leader in heart surgery and research, Foothills spent more than $15 million in the late 1980s on building and equipping the necessary diagnostic laboratories and cardiovascular surgery facilities. The Foothills cardiovascular surgery and angioplasty program has since become one of the best in Canada. In 1987, Foothills was one of only 27 facilities in the world to receive a $1 million grant from the National Heart, Lung, and Blood Institute of the United States to test new heart drugs.

In 1993, Foothills launched the Alberta Stroke Program, whose mandate is to educate, treat, and rehabilitate stroke patients from across Alberta. An intensive public education campaign hopes to not only teach Albertans to quickly recognize symptoms of stroke, but to underscore the importance of immediate treatment. A 24-hour Stroke Hotline offers help, as does the Outpatient Stroke Prevention and Follow-up Clinic.

Since 1975, FPGH has treated burn victims from the tri-province area, as well as from northern Montana. The opening of the $1.2 million Burn Treatment Centre in 1987 extended the boundaries of Foothills' advanced care.

In 1983, FPGH and the University of Calgary pioneered the ovulation induction technique of conception (George Aaron Wiggan's birth that December was dubbed a medical miracle). For more than 20 years, Foothills has been the regional leader in maternal care.

Bone marrow, kidney, corneal, and tissue transplants are performed at FPGH. The hospital also operates the Human Organ Procurement and Exchange (HOPE) program, which coordinates all organ and tissue retrievals in southern Alberta.

MEDICAL SPECIALTIES

Body Injury, Cancer, Cardiovascular Diagnostics, Cataract Surgery, Clinical Neurosciences, Gastrointestinal Disease, Geriatric Assessment, Hand Clinic, Heart Disease, High-Risk Maternal and Newborn Care, HIV Clinic, Joint Injuries and Disease, Kidney and Bladder Surgery, Oral Surgery, Stroke, Substance Abuse, Toxicology, Transplantation, and Trauma.

WELL-KNOWN SPECIALISTS

FPGH chose not to provide a list.

PATIENT SATISFACTION

About 70% of former FPGH patients respond to detailed questionnaires sent by the hospital. In a survey conducted from January to March 1994, 80% of respondents indicated they were "very satisfied" with the overall care provided at FPGH.

RESEARCH

Research scientists and scholars from around the world are attracted to Foothills, one of the most well-endowed research facilities in Canada, with more than $38 million awarded annually in grants. FPGH physicians also have access to the Alberta Heritage Medical Research Building, one of the most modern research facilities in North America, so it's no wonder Foothills has made such significant inroads in many research areas.

In 1990, Foothill neurosurgeons were the first to develop the revolutionary technique of recording human brain activity and mapping brain function through the use of optical signals generated by nerve cells. It was predicted that this optical imaging technique would significantly advance the treatment of epilepsy and stroke.

Cryosurgery, the latest addition to Foothills' arsenal against cancer, was tested on 12 liver-cancer patients in September 1993. During the trial, a team of experts used liquid nitrogen to freeze cancerous tumors found in the liver. Once dead, the tumors were reabsorbed by the body. This procedure is not a guaranteed cure for liver cancer, but the trial illustrated that reoccurrence was suppressed for about two years.

ADMISSIONS POLICY

Patients must be referred by an Alberta physician with admitting privileges to Foothills. Patients without Canadian health care coverage are advised of the approximate cost of services. The daily rate for out-of-country residents is $2,283.75 for a private room, $2,247.75 for a semiprivate room, and $2,283.75 for the ICU.

AT A GLANCE

Beds: 606
Occupancy Rate: 81.6%
Average Patient Count: 494
Average Patient Stay: 8.0 days
Annual Admissions: 23,955
Births: 3,251
Outpatient Clinic Visits:
 272,555
Emergency Room/Trauma
 Center Visits: 57,472

HOSPITAL PERSONNEL
Physicians: 606
 Board Certified: 606
Residents: 267
Registered Nurses: 966
 (FT & PT)

ADDRESS
1403 29th Street, N.W.
Calgary, Alberta T2N 2T9

TELEPHONE
(403) 670-1110

UNIVERSITY OF

ALBERTA HOSPITALS

EDMONTON, ALBERTA

University of Alberta Hospitals (UAH) is one of the most medically ambitious and technologically advanced hospitals in Canada. Clearly, it is the top hospital in an area covering one-third of Canada's land mass and encompassing northern and central Alberta, northeastern British Columbia, northwestern Saskatchewan, and the vast Yukon and Northwest Territories.

UAH began as the 15-bed Strathcona Cottage Hospital in 1906. Eight years later it moved to its current site on the University of Alberta campus and immediately became a teaching hospital. Today, University of Alberta Hospitals complex is comprised of seven buildings, including the Walter C. Mackenzie Health Sciences Centre. Adjacent are the Cross Cancer Institute and University of Alberta facilities, including the Newton Research Building and the Alberta Heritage Medical Research Building.

The University of Alberta medical school is among the very best in Canada. In 1991 and 1992 its medical students ranked first in the country on the Canadian licensure exams.

UNIVERSITY OF
ALBERTA HOSPITALS
(UAH) IS ONE OF THE MOST
MEDICALLY AMBITIOUS AND
TECHNOLOGICALLY
ADVANCED HOSPITALS
IN CANADA.

SPECIAL FACILITIES AND PROGRAMS

UAH's many specialties include multiorgan transplantation, specialized trauma care, hematology, cardiovascular and thoracic surgery, obstetrics and gynecology, psychiatry, ophthalmology and neurology. UAH also has the latest imaging technology, is a leading Canadian academic research institute, and is the referral center for all of Alberta in several medical areas.

UAH performed the first successful open heart surgery in Canada in 1956. Today, the cardiology program has a wide scope of services, including an intensive care unit, cardiac catheterization, angioplasty, and electrophysiology of the heart. Another area of clinical expertise is the laser treatment of atherosclerosis. UAH is the heart surgery referral center for central and northern Alberta.

UAH has a nationally recognized transplantation program. It was the first hospital in Alberta to perform a kidney transplant, in 1967, and the first to perform a heart transplant, in 1985. By May 1994, more than 800 kidneys, 100 livers, 134 hearts, 20 single lungs, four double lungs and eight heart/lungs had been transplanted at UAH, now the provincial referral center for all heart, heart/lung, lung and liver transplants.

Leukemia, blood cell function, and diseases of the bone marrow are among the blood disorders UAH treats.

In neurosurgery, UAH performs functional stereotactic surgery associated with movement disorders, pain, and epilepsy. Other specialties include spinal surgery, cranial and spinal trauma, neuro-oncology, and cerebral vascular surgery.

UAH was the second hospital in North America to establish a chronic renal dialysis program. In addition to its inpatient program that cares for more than 130 patients, UAH's renal dialysis program caters to more than 160 chronic ambulatory peritoneal dialysis patients, 17 home dialysis patients and 90 chronic renal failure patients on hemodialysis in satellite units.

A Geriatric Assessment Team helps UAH staff provide better care for the elderly. Any patient admitted over the age of 65 receives consultation from a team that includes a general practitioner, a nurse-clinician, a physiotherapist, an occupational therapist, and a social worker.

AT A GLANCE

Beds: 699
Occupancy Rate: 81.5%
Average Patient Count: 594
Average Patient Stay: 6.8 days
Annual Admissions: 30,154
Births: 2,721
Outpatient Clinic Visits:
340,816
Emergency Room/Trauma
Center Visits: 56,740

HOSPITAL PERSONNEL
Physicians: 550
Residents: 393
Registered Nurses: 2,107
(FT & PT)
BS Degree: 625

ADDRESS
8440 114 Street
Edmonton, Alberta T6G 2B7

TELEPHONE
(403) 492-8822

The Alberta Asthma Centre opened at UAH in March 1993. Up to 200,000 Albertans suffer from asthma, which costs the province about $50 million annually in job and school absenteeism alone. UAH is heavily involved with asthma treatment and research.

Some of UAH's other special facilities include the Firefighters Burn Treatment Unit, and cardiovascular and neurosurgical intensive care units.

Sophisticated imaging equipment includes an MRI scanner, CT units with helical scanning, multihead nuclear medicine cameras, digital subtraction angiography equipment, and cardiac catheterization units.

In 1992, the Patient Care Design Project was established for the purpose of identifying and implementing breakthrough change in patient care.

Additionally, UAH is a Canadian leader in financial management. At least two layers of management have been removed from all departments and support staffs have been reduced. Aggressive clinical management has reduced the average length of stay for inpatients from 8.9 days in fiscal 1990 to 6.8 days in 1994. UAH has served as an implementation role model in financial restraint for dozens of health care organizations across Canada.

MEDICAL SPECIALTIES

Cardiology, Cardiovascular and Thoracic Surgery, Dentistry, Dermatology and Cutaneous Sciences, Emergency, Endocrinology, Gastroenterology, General Surgery, Gynaecology (General, Oncology, Reproductive Endocrinology), Haematology, Infectious Diseases, Internal Medicine, Neonatology, Nephrology, Neurology, Neurosurgery, Obstetrics (General, Maternal-Fetal Medicine), Ophthalmology, Orthopedic Surgery, Otolaryngology, Physical Medicine and Rehabilitation, Plastic Surgery, Psychiatry, Pulmonary Medicine, Rheumatology, Trauma, and Urology.

WELL-KNOWN SPECIALISTS

- Dr. P. Armstrong *Cardiology*
- Dr. Robert Ashforth *Radiology and diagnostic imaging*
- Dr. M. Brooke *Neurology*
- Dr. Valerie Capstick *Gynecologic oncology*
- Dr. D. C. Cumming *Obstetrics and gynecology*
- Dr. J. M. Findlay *Neurosurgery*
- Dr. Finegan *Anaesthesia*
- Dr. Finucane *Anaesthesia*
- Dr. Gregg *Anaesthesia*
- Dr. P. Halloran *Nephrology*
- Dr. K. Jimbrow *Dermatology*
- Dr. Mary Ann Johnson *Radiology and diagnostic imaging*
- Dr. Kneteman *General surgery*
- Dr. A. Koshal *Cardiovascular surgery*

- Dr. G. Lobay   *Plastic surgery*
- Dr. G. Machin   *Laboratory medicine and pathology*
- Dr. P. Man   *Pulmonary medicine*
- Dr. A. J. B. McEwan   *Radiology and diagnostic imaging*
- Dr. D. Modry   *Cardiovascular surgery*
- Dr. T. Montague   *Cardiology*
- Dr. D. Oldring   *Otolaryngology*
- Dr. A. Penn   *Neurology*
- Dr. A. Rabinovitch   *Diabetes*
- Dr. Alexandra Schepansky   *Gynecologic oncology*
- Dr. J. Z. Scott   *Obstetrics and gynecology*
- Dr. K. Solez   *Laboratory medicine and pathology*
- Dr. D. K. Still   *Obstetrics and gynecology*
- Dr. A. Thomson   *Gastroenterology*
- Dr. T. Tredget   *Plastic surgery*
- Dr. L. J. Tyrrell   *Medical microbiology and infectious diseases*
- Dr. Warnock   *General surgery*
- Dr. R. Yatscoff   *Laboratory medicine and pathology*

PATIENT SATISFACTION

A Patient Satisfaction Committee was established in 1991, and between 1992 and 1993 four patient surveys were conducted. For each survey, 500 randomly selected patients over a three-week period were routinely queried about nine areas of patient care. Volunteers, trained by the Patient Ombudsperson, delivered the surveys to selected patients, who were requested to answer the survey no earlier than the third day of their stay. In 1993, 61% of respondents rated the care at UAH as "excellent." More significantly, more than half of the respondents rated the care they received as "better than expected."

RESEARCH

UAH researchers are among the best funded in Canada. The faculty at UAH medical school generated about $45 million in research grants in fiscal 1993, an attractive carrot for UAH to dangle before world-renowned researchers on the move.

Working primarily out of the University of Alberta's Newton Research Building and Heritage Medical Research Building, medical explorers at UAH are making significant forays in many fields.

UAH is deeply involved in research and treatment of key infectious diseases. The GLAXO Canada Inc. Institute, within the Heritage Building, is the only center in Alberta dedicated solely to basic and clinical research into the AIDS and hepatitis viruses. Dr. L. J. Tyrrell and his team have been working on agents to combat the deadly virus hepatitis B, and this work may lead to research of the hepatitis C virus identified in 1990.

A variety of research projects on heart disease are ongoing. The Epidemiology Coordinating and Research Centre and the Heritage Cardiovascular Research Group review and synthesize data from research done at UAH and abroad.

Other areas of research include bioethics (ethical problems of health care); endocrinology, including islet cell transplantation; neurology; gynecology; ophthalmology, with particular expertise in ophthalmic genetics; and neonatology, including sudden infant death syndrome (SIDS).

ADMISSIONS POLICY

Patients are referred to UAH physicians by their doctors or through the Emergency Department. A deposit is required for non-Canadians and for those requesting private accommodations. Non-Canadians are asked for a seven-day deposit and promissory note. When prearranged by authority of the UAH president or vice-president, charges are waived for a patient from a foreign country as a charity case.

For non-insured, non-Canadian inpatients, there is a charge of $2,756 per day; $2,846 with a private room. Per diem visitor residence rates are $30 for a single room and $20 per person for a double room (each additional person $15). Outpatients and medical escorts receive a 50% discount off these rates.

ST. PAUL'S HOSPITAL

St. Paul's Hospital (SPH) is affiliated with the University of British Columbia Medical School and, as such, is one of the leading teaching hospitals in western Canada. The hospital was founded in 1894 by the Sisters of Providence, a Catholic religious order of women dedicated to caring for the poor and sick. Situated only blocks from Vancouver's downtown, SPH continues to be a Catholic institution run by the Sisters of Providence.

SPH is probably best known for its compassionate patient care. A friendly working atmosphere helps sustain this compassionate care. Healthy Hospitals, a joint union-management project, allows employees at all levels to share control of decisions that affect them. In addition, nurses of all levels participate in decision-making and development.

SPECIAL FACILITIES AND PROGRAMS

SPH is the Canadian leader in AIDS treatment. Since accepting its first AIDS patient in 1984, SPH has gone to great lengths to become a model hospital in this field. It has the only formalized AIDS care team in the country, which includes family physicians, nurses, pharmacists, home care liaison nurses, social workers, psychiatrists, and specialists in infectious diseases, respirology, gastroenterology, and dermatology. SPH has also devoted 50% of its

VANCOUVER, BRITISH COLUMBIA

ST. PAUL'S HOSPITAL (SPH) IS AFFILIATED WITH THE UNIVERSITY OF BRITISH COLUMBIA MEDICAL SCHOOL AND, AS SUCH, IS ONE OF THE LEADING TEACHING HOSPITALS IN WESTERN CANADA.

beds in the terminally ill unit to AIDS patients, the only hospital in Canada to do so.

SPH has long been a regional leader in heart care. In 1958, Dr. Harold Rice built British Columbia's first heart/lung machine. In February 1994, SPH was established as the province's center for comprehensive heart care, including cardiology, critical care, and pulmonary care. With two catheterization laboratories, SPH performs more than 700 balloon dilation, coronary, and valvular surgeries per year.

In 1991, SPH's gastrointestinal unit became a provincial center of excellence in the area of digestive and nutritional disorders. A new endoscopic video information system provides detailed, accurate information that is easily understood by patients and, therefore, allows patients to participate in the planning of their own treatment. New treatment techniques for biliary and pancreatic duct dysfunction or obstructions are being developed at SPH, as well as for inflammatory bowel disease.

St. Paul's renal unit is the provincial referral center for patients with kidney failure. A 15-bed hemodialysis unit performs more than 260 in-hospital treatments per week for both chronic and acute renal failure. A 15-bed nephrology unit cares for those in various phases of renal failure. Additionally, more than 300 patients are treated by the Nephrology Outpatient Clinic and kidney transplants have been performed at SPH since 1986.

The Geriatrics Department focuses on "reactivation," enabling the patient to return to as normal and independent a life as possible. A multidisciplinary team approach provides treatment for such problems as heart disease, incontinence, dementia, diabetes, and broken bones sustained from falls. A 35-bed discharge planning unit cares for elderly patients awaiting placement in other care facilities. The Invisible Seniors project helps link the elderly to other existing health and community services in the Vancouver area.

The third phase of a major reconstruction plan at SPH will add new facilities for emergency, outpatient, and other services, and is expected to be completed by the year 2000.

MEDICAL SPECIALTIES

Cardiac Surgery, Cardiology, Critical Care, Drug and Poison Information Centre, Eating Disorders, Emergency Medicine, General Medicine, HIV/AIDS, Nephrology and Transplantation, and Respirology.

WELL-KNOWN SPECIALISTS

- Dr. Alan Belzberg   *Nuclear medicine*
- Dr. Graham Copeland   *Pulmonary diseases*
- Dr. James Hogg   *Pulmonary research*
- Dr. Samuel Lichtenstein   *Cardiovascular surgery*
- Dr. Hilton Ling   *Cardiovascular surgery*

- Dr. Bruce McManus *Cardiovascular pathology and pathophysiology*
- Dr. Michael O'Shaughnessy *HIV pathogenesis*
- Dr. Peter Pare *Pulmonary research*
- Dr. Angus Rae *Nephrology and renal transplantation*
- Dr. Christopher Thompson *Echocardiography*
- Dr. Keith Walley *Intensivist, circulatory shock*
- Dr. Joanne Wright *Pulmonary pathology, surgical pathology*

PATIENT SATISFACTION

No formal patient satisfaction surveys were done at SPH until 1994, when it joined the group of 14 Canadian hospitals that is measuring and comparing patient satisfaction through a detailed survey.

RESEARCH

With a modest $7 million in research grants in 1994, SPH is not a leading Canadian research hospital; however, it is making huge strides to become one. With the establishment of Research Services in 1992, SPH hopes to develop excellent basic and clinical research programs in the hospital's major specialties.

SPH is already at the forefront of HIV and AIDS research in Canada. Research focuses on experimental drugs, therapeutic treatments, and vaccines. Designated by the province as a center of excellence in this field, SPH works closely with University of British Columbia researchers and is one of a handful of hospitals nationwide involved in a clinical HIV trials network that uses computer tracking to monitor treatment regimes.

The major thrust in cardiovascular research involves understanding how viruses lead to heart infection and heart failure. Other projects study why a lack of oxygen causes heart muscle injury and coronary artery disease in transplanted hearts.

ADMISSIONS POLICY

Patients must be admitted by a staff doctor, except maternity and palliative care patients, who can be referred to SPH specialists and then admitted.

AT A GLANCE

Beds: 560
Occupancy Rate: N/A
Average Patient Count: N/A
Average Patient Stay: 8.7 days
Annual Admissions: 17,381
Births: 1,863
Outpatient Clinic Visits:
    108,108
Emergency Room/Trauma
    Center Visits: 49,951

HOSPITAL PERSONNEL
Physicians: 430
Residents: 85
Registered Nurses: 1,096
    (FT & PT)

ADDRESS
1081 Burrard Street
Vancouver, British Columbia
    V6Z 1Y6

TELEPHONE
(604) 682-2344

Patients without provincial health care coverage must pay either by personal check or VISA. Inpatient care costs $1,800 per day, excluding doctors' fees. For out-of-province patients without health care coverage, a private room is an additional $90 per day, a semiprivate room is an additional $65, and acute care is an additional $900. For non-Canadians, additional per diem charges are: private room—$90, semiprivate room—$65, and acute care—$1,800.

VANCOUVER HOSPITAL

AND HEALTH

SCIENCES CENTRE

VANCOUVER,
BRITISH COLUMBIA

Vancouver Hospital and Health Sciences Centre (VHHSC) serves as a regional referral center in many specialties, and provides some services that are either unique to, or the best offered in, the entire province. The major referral, teaching, and research hospital in British Columbia, VHHSC provides a wide range of medical, surgical and psychiatric services covering virtually everything except pediatrics and obstetrics.

Originally established in 1886 as a nine-bed infirmary for railway workers, VHHSC was long known, until 1993, as Vancouver General Hospital. It adopted the new name following the merger with University Hospital, located on a University of British Columbia (UBC) site. Vancouver General/VHHSC has long been the principal affiliate of the UBC Medical School.

SPECIAL FACILITIES AND PROGRAMS

The provincial leader in trauma care, VHHSC also provides a level of orthopaedic trauma care unequaled anywhere in Canada. Any patient in the province with multiple or difficult injuries, such as displaced pelvis or hip fractures, is referred to VHHSC. A helipad was recently constructed on the roof of the Critical Care Pavilion to assist in the rapid transportation of critically ill or injured patients.

The Department of Ophthalmology is likely the best in the country and is famous worldwide. It has

VANCOUVER HOSPITAL AND HEALTH SCIENCES CENTRE (VHHSC) SERVES AS A REGIONAL REFERRAL CENTER IN MANY SPECIALTIES, AND PROVIDES SOME SERVICES THAT ARE EITHER UNIQUE TO, OR THE BEST OFFERED IN, THE ENTIRE PROVINCE.

been actively involved in providing care in developing countries, and recently established the first Third World Fellowship Program in ophthalmology, with a direction toward developing teaching and research in these emerging nations.

VHHSC is the only hospital in British Columbia providing transplantation services for heart, lungs, liver, and pancreas. Annually, VHHSC performs 12 heart, 2 heart/lung, 12 lung, 20 liver, 64 kidney and 4 pancreas transplant surgeries. The hospital's bone marrow transplant (BMT) service began in 1985. Twenty percent of the 75 annual BMT patients are from outside the province.

VHHSC provides a full range of services in its renal program, including hemodialysis, peritoneal dialysis, home dialysis training, and inpatient/outpatient clinics. In fiscal 1993-94, VHHSC provided more than 15,500 visits for dialysis and 700 visits for home dialysis training.

Advanced procedures in cardiac surgery are also regularly performed at VHHSC. Each year, more than 1,000 cardiac surgeries, 750 angioplasty procedures, and 2,000 diagnostic catheterizations are performed.

The Division of Anatomical Pathology provides a consultation service for other hospitals across British Columbia and provides the only ophthalmologic pathology service in western Canada. The joint U.S./Canada Mesothelioma Panel is housed at VHHSC.

VHHSC is the base hospital for a large tissue bank that provides bone tissue for orthopedic reconstruction work and banked skin tissue for burn patients.

The hospital is also part of the provincial center in neurosciences, including seizure investigation, neurodegenerative disorders (Alzheimer's disease, Parkinson's disease), neuroimmunological disorders (multiple sclerosis and myasthenia gravis), and developmental and genetic disorders (such as muscular dystrophy).

Additionally, VHHSC operates a 475-bed extended care facility that functions mainly as a nursing home. Special equipment at VHHSC includes two CT scans, a renal lithotriptor, a biliary lithotriptor, and two MRI scanners.

Realizing a few years ago that its administrative structure focused on budgeting and other concerns, rather than the most efficient delivery of patient care, VHHSC has reorganized so that accountability, efficiency, and patient outcomes are the primary concern. In fact, for the first time, medical staff now are formally playing key roles in hospital management. The new Medical Quality of Practice Committee has representatives from each clinical department, and is responsible for both overseeing and improving patient care.

MEDICAL SPECIALTIES

Anaesthesia (General, Cardiac, Neuro, Thoracic), Cardiology, Critical Care, Dermatology, Emergency Medicine, Endocrinology, Family Practice, Gastroenterology, Geriatric Medicine, Gynecology (General, Oncology), Medicine (Allergy/Immunology, Haematology/Bone-marrow Transplantation, Infectious Diseases, Internal Medicine, Medical Oncology, Nephrology, Neurology, Rehabilitation Medicine/Physiatry, Respirology and Rheumatology), Ophthalmology,

Orthopedic Surgery (Reconstructive Orthopedics, Orthopedic Trauma, Spinal Services, General Orthopedics), Pathology (Anatomical, Chemistry, Hematology, Microbiology), Psychiatry (Mood Disorders, Schizophrenia, Neuropsychiatry, Personality Disorders, Gender Dysphoria, Sexual Medicine), Radiology (General, Abdominal, Neuro, Nuclear Medicine), and Surgery (Cardiac, General, Neuro, Otolaryngology, Plastic, Radiation Oncology, Thoracic, Urology and Vascular).

WELL-KNOWN SPECIALISTS

- Dr. J. Lou Benedet   *Gynaecology*
- Dr. Donald Calne   *Neurology*
- Dr. Andrew Churg   *Pathology*
- Dr. P. Clement   *Gynaecologic pathology*
- Dr. Max Cynader   *Ophthalmology*
- Dr. Gordon Douglas   *Ophthalmology*
- Dr. Stephen Drance   *Ophthalmology*
- Dr. Richard Finley   *Thoracic surgery*
- Dr. W. Godolphin   *Pathology*
- Dr. M. Kelly   *Pathology*
- Dr. Paul Keown   *Nephrology*
- Dr. Charles Kerr   *Cardiology*
- Dr. Alan Maberly   *Ophthalmology*
- Dr. G. B. John Mancini   *Medicine/cardiology*
- Dr. Robert McGraw   *Orthopaedics*
- Dr. Robert Meek   *Orthopaedics*
- Dr. D. Owen   *Gastrointestinal pathology*
- Dr. Don Paty   *Neurology*
- Dr. Gordon Phillips   *Haematology*
- Dr. Jerrilyn Prior   *Endocrinology*
- Dr. Don Ricci   *Cardiology*
- Dr. Jack Rootman   *Ophthalmology*
- Dr. Urs Steinbrecher   *Lipidology*
- Dr. Joseph Tsui   *Neurology*
- Dr. Peter Wing   *Orthopaedics*

PATIENT SATISFACTION

No formal patient satisfaction surveys were done at VHHSC until 1994, when it joined the group of 14 Canadian hospitals that is measuring and comparing patient satisfaction through a detailed survey.

AT A GLANCE

Beds: 1,153
Occupancy Rate: 90%
Average Patient Count: 1,037
Average Patient Stay: 8.3 days
Annual Admissions: 39,505
Outpatient Clinic Visits: 400,000
Emergency Room/Trauma Center Visits: 75,819

HOSPITAL PERSONNEL
Physicians: 683
Residents: 250
Registered Nurses: 2,233 (FT & PT)

ADDRESS
855 West 12th Avenue
Vancouver, British Columbia
V5Z 1M9

TELEPHONE
(604) 875-4111

RESEARCH

VHHSC is one of Canada's premier research facilities, with its physicians receiving $50 million per year in funding.

Hundreds of research projects are ongoing in many fields at the hospital, but the most renowned forays have been in neurological disorders, transplantation immunobiology, pathogenesis of atherosclerosis, AIDS, ophthalmology, pathology, psychiatry, nursing, and the Drug Use Evaluation (DUE) program.

DUE was the first program of its kind to be implemented at an acute care hospital in Canada. Coordinators in the pharmacy department are responsible for innovative cost containment strategies, which have been routinely adopted by hospitals across North America and around the world. Results of the DUE's research efforts have been presented at more than 75 regional, national, and international conferences.

VHHSC was a principal investigator in a three-year clinical trial involving the use of the cholesterol-lowering drug, pravastatin. A study released in 1994 found that when this drug was taken once a day, the risk of heart attack or other cardiac complications was reduced by 54% among patients with heart disease and elevated cholesterol.

The Department of Ophthalmology has, for decades, been recognized both nationally and abroad for its clinical and basic science research into such eye disorders as glaucoma, orbital disease, cancer, and retina disease. The group of basic scientists under the leadership of Dr. Max Cynader is considered one of the top neurophysiology and visual physiology groups in the world.

In psychiatry, researchers are investigating the biological mechanisms underlying symptom development in schizophrenia.

Among the neurological disorders extensively researched are Parkinson's disease and multiple sclerosis.

Nursing research includes care and management of the chemically dependent, the elderly hip-fracture patient, and the elderly cardiac patient.

ADMISSIONS POLICY

Patients are admitted by hospital physicians only. If an unreferred patient comes through emergency, the appropriate physician on call is assigned. Uninsured patients who require emergency care are treated as if they were insured, with the hospital then attempting to recover costs. Elective admissions for uninsured patients occur only on exceptional occasions, by prior arrangement with hospital administration.

For those without provincial health insurance, per diem costs are $1,851 for a private room, $1,801 for a semiprivate room, and $1,776 for ICU care.

VICTORIA GENERAL

HOSPITAL

Victoria General (VG) is the principal tertiary care hospital in the provinces of Nova Scotia, New Brunswick, Prince Edward Island, and Newfoundland, making it one of the busiest hospitals in the country.

VG was established in 1859 and renamed for Queen Victoria in 1887. Since the nineteenth century, VG has been owned and operated by the province of Nova Scotia, but presently is negotiating to become self-governed. VG is affiliated with the Dalhousie University Medical School and has long been the main teaching hospital in the Maritimes.

SPECIAL FACILITIES AND PROGRAMS

The most technologically advanced hospital in the region, VG is the regional referral center in such specialized areas as AIDS care and transplant surgery. It operates the largest multitissue bank in Canada, processing and storing bone, bone marrow, skin, cardiac tissues, and tissue for neurological procedures. It also operates the largest hospital microbiology laboratory in the country (with 800,000 annual tests) and performs more radiological exams per year (210,000) than any other center in Canada. It is the only hospital in the Maritimes with an MRI scanner, and was only the second in Canada to install an extracorporeal shock wave lithotriptor. Its psychiatric unit specializes in treatment of eating disorders

HALIFAX, NOVA SCOTIA

VICTORIA GENERAL (VG) IS THE PRINCIPAL TERTIARY CARE HOSPITAL IN THE PROVINCES OF NOVA SCOTIA, NEW BRUNSWICK, PRINCE EDWARD ISLAND, AND NEWFOUNDLAND, MAKING IT ONE OF THE BUSIEST HOSPITALS IN THE COUNTRY.

and neuropsychiatric problems. In addition, VG is one of the busiest transplant centers in Canada, transplanting livers since 1985, hearts since 1988, and bone marrow since 1992.

In cardiology, VG performs all invasive and investigative heart procedures for Nova Scotia and Prince Edward Island. Every year it performs some 900 open heart procedures, 3,000 diagnostic cardiac catheterizations, and more than 800 angioplasties and atherectomies. The department has also begun a new program in ablative treatment of uncontrolled cardiac rhythm disorders.

VG houses the Nova Scotia Cancer Treatment and Research Foundation, the sole site for radiotherapy in Nova Scotia. It is the provincial referral center for treatment of gynaecologic and urologic cancer.

All kidney dialysis throughout Nova Scotia and Prince Edward Island is coordinated through VG, which itself had more than 10,000 visits in fiscal 1992-93. Sunshine Retreat was established in 1985 as a summer renal dialysis program operating during July and August at Marco Polo Land on Prince Edward Island. Patients from as far away as Japan have been able to enjoy a visit to the Maritimes by reporting to this portable facility every few days for dialysis treatments.

Through its continuous quality improvement initiative, VG is working hard to improve the morale and patient care knowledge of the entire staff—the idea being that a happier, more informed staff leads directly to better patient care.

VG was the only Canadian hospital, selected for inclusion in this book, to release its infection and mortality rates. VG's surgical-site infection rates are well below accepted standards.

MEDICAL SPECIALTIES

Cancer, Cardiovascular Sciences, Clinical Neurosciences, Hepatobiliary Disorders, Infectious Diseases, Multisystem Trauma, Musculoskeletal Disorders, Oral and Maxillofacial Surgery, Renal and Genitourinary Sciences, and Transplantation.

WELL-KNOWN SPECIALISTS

- Dr. S. Awad   *Urology*
- Dr. P. Belitsky   *Transplantation*
- Dr. S. G. Carruthers   *Clinical pharmacology*
- Dr. D. Fraser   *Diagnostic imaging*
- Dr. M. Gardner   *Cardiology*
- Dr. R. Holness   *Neurosurgery*
- Dr. D. Janigan   *Anatomical pathology*
- Dr. D. Johnstone   *Cardiology*
- Dr. J. V. Jones   *Rheumatology*
- Dr. A. S. MacDonald   *Transplantation*
- Dr. T. Marrie   *Infectious diseases*
- Dr. M. Moss   *Clinical chemistry*
- Dr. D. Precious   *Oral and maxillofacial surgery*

- Dr. W. Schlech *Infectious diseases*
- Dr. W. Stanish *Orthopedics*
- Dr. J. Sullivan *Cardiac surgery*
- Dr. S. VanZanten *Gastroenterology*
- Dr. R. Yabsley *Orthopedics*
- Dr. I. Zayid *Anatomical pathology*

PATIENT SATISFACTION

The VG Hospital Foundation has extensively surveyed former patients. In a recent survey, almost 12,000 patients rated the care they received on a scale of 1 to 5—37% rated it as a "4," 38% as "5."

Before 1984, VG itself did not conduct hospital-wide surveys; individual departments merely surveyed patients about treatment received in their particular areas. But this year, VG is collaborating with a group of 13 other Canadian hospitals that will compare results of their respective hospital-wide patients surveys.

RESEARCH

As the premier research facility in the Maritimes, VG opened the Centre for Clinical Research in 1992. Research grants in 1993 exceeded $3 million and contracts and grants running to 1996 equal about $10 million.

Already, the center has attracted international attention. In 1993, it concluded its Fetal Neural Transplantation Clinical Trials—the injections of fetal tissue into brains of Parkinson's disease patients in an effort to stimulate production of the chemical messenger, dopamine, which is necessary for normal movement of the limbs. Five patients took part in this trial, the first of its kind in Canada and one of the first conducted outside Europe. Results are being evaluated as to its usefulness.

The *New England Journal of Medicine* published results of the Study of Left Ventricular Dysfunction (SOLVD), a clinical trial involving 7,000 heart patients around the world, including 350 at VG. The study suggested mortality rates and hospital admission rates for patients with congestive heart failure could be significantly reduced with the new drug

AT A GLANCE

Beds: 798
Occupancy Rate: 85.1%
Average Patient Count: 680
Average Patient Stay: 9.2 days
Annual Admissions: 23,240
Outpatient Clinic Visits:
    90,248
Emergency Room/Trauma
    Center Visits: 48,016

HOSPITAL PERSONNEL
Physicians: 227
Residents: 100
Registered Nurses: 1,395
    (FT & PT)

ADDRESS
1278 Tower Road
Halifax, Nova Scotia B3H 2Y9

TELEPHONE
(902) 428-2110

enalapril. Sub-studies were spawned and VG ranked first among all 23 participating centres in design, enrollment, analysis, and reporting.

Other projects are underway at VG in gastroenterology, dermatology, oncology, nephrology, neurology, radiology, rheumatology, anesthesia, cardiology, cardiovascular surgery, hematology, respirology, and infectious diseases.

ADMISSIONS POLICY

Elective patients are referred by family physicians to a physician with VG admitting privileges. An emergency patient is seen by the resident and staff physician, who will admit that patient if necessary.

For those without provincial health insurance, per diem charges are $2,204 for a private room, $2,187 for a semiprivate room, and $2,132 for ICU care. Those rates include all drugs, diagnostic tests, and treatments; they do not include physicians' fees. High cost procedures, such as transplantation, are billed at a fixed rate.

HOSPITAL FOR SICK

CHILDREN

If there's one Canadian hospital of any kind renowned the world over, it's Toronto's Hospital for Sick Children. For decades, Sick Kids (as it's commonly called) has been one of the most advanced children's hospitals anywhere, a far cry from its humble beginnings—a six-room downtown house that opened in 1875.

The hospital boasts many impressive achievements over the years. Pablum was invented at Sick Kids in 1930. Two world-renowned surgical developments were pioneered there as well—the Salter operation (in 1957) to repair dislocation of the hip, and the Mustard operation (in 1961) to correct transposition of the great arteries, a heart defect that was often fatal. Canada's first bone marrow transplant program began at Sick Kids in 1972. Up to 50 such operations are now performed annually. Continuous passive motion, an improved method of treating patients with damaged cartilage, was developed at Sick Kids in 1979. A highly successful treatment for near-drowning victims was developed in the 1970s. Four surgical separations of Siamese twins—two sets from Canada and one each from Burma and Trinidad—were performed between 1966 and 1985. Advances in genetics in the 1980s led to the identification of genes responsible for a number of hereditary diseases, including Duchenne muscular dystrophy, Tay-Sachs disease, cystic fibrosis, and Fanconi's anemia.

TORONTO, ONTARIO

IF THERE'S ONE CANADIAN HOSPITAL OF ANY KIND RENOWNED THE WORLD OVER, IT'S TORONTO'S HOSPITAL FOR SICK CHILDREN.

Today, the most complex cases in every area of pediatric medicine and surgery are diagnosed and treated at Sick Kids. That explains why, in 1993, 47 patients came from 14 states in the U.S. and another 136 patients came from 36 other countries around the globe. Since 1979, the Herbie Fund has brought more than 220 children from 63 countries to Sick Kids for treatment they could not obtain at home. In fact, less than half of the total number of patients admitted to Sick Kids come from the metropolitan Toronto area.

With its move to an adjacent, entirely new $232 million facility in 1993, Sick Kids now has a state-of-the-art environment for its state-of-the-art care. A playful feeling pervades the new building. Even the gears of several elevators are exposed and painted in bright colors, so that children and parents can see how they work. The biggest change, though, was the move to single-bed rooms, each containing a daybed for parents, storage space, private telephone, television, and a full private bathroom. In addition, each floor features several large playrooms that look out onto the bustling main floor atrium below. These playrooms are located across from nursing stations for monitoring purposes. The largest cafeteria in downtown Toronto is also located within the new building.

SPECIAL FACILITIES AND PROGRAMS

The new Bone Marrow Transplant Unit features 12 specially ventilated rooms to keep the environment sterile, which is important because children can't receive new bone marrow until their own is first destroyed by radiation, which temporarily wipes out their immune system.

About 800 heart operations are carried out every year at Sick Kids by the cardiovascular surgery team. More than half of these are open heart procedures.

Children born with deformities of the head and neck are helped by a team from the Craniofacial Program.

The Pediatric Intensive Care Unit treats critically ill and injured children, as well as patients recovering from complex surgery.

In the Neonatal Intensive Care Unit, the staff cares for newborns who are ill or premature. Some come from all corners of the province. A transport team of highly trained nurses travels by road or air ambulance to stabilize sick babies and accompany them to Sick Kids or another appropriate nursery.

An expanding day surgery program means many children needing minor operations don't even have to stay overnight. Sick Kids also has outpatient services for sports medicine, breastfeeding advice, children with HIV or AIDS, and mothers exposed to drugs and medication during pregnancy and breastfeeding.

The nursing care at Sick Kids is also leading edge and among the best offered in Canada.

MEDICAL SPECIALTIES

Burns/Plastic Surgery, Cardiology/Cardiovascular Surgery, Critical Care, General Pediatrics, General Surgery, Hematology/Oncology, Infectious Diseases, Medical Specialties, Nephrology, Neurology, Neurosurgery, Orthopedics, Otolaryngology/Ophthalmology, Psychiatry, and Urology.

WELL-KNOWN SPECIALISTS

- Dr. Gerald Stanley Arbus   *Pediatric nephrology*
- Dr. Michael A. Baker   *Medical oncology/hematology*
- Dr. J. Williamson Balfe   *Pediatric nephrology*
- Dr. Laurence E. Becker   *Neuropathology*
- Dr. Leland Nathan Benson   *Pediatric cardiology*
- Dr. Desmond J. Bohn   *Pediatric critical care*
- Dr. Bernard Churchill   *Pediatric urology*
- Dr. William G. Cole   *Orthopedic surgery*
- Dr. William S. Crysdale   *Pediatric otolaryngology*
- Dr. Denis Daneman   *Pediatric endocrinology*
- Dr. Peter Durie   *Pediatric gastroenterology*
- Dr. Allison A. Eddy   *Pediatric nephrology*
- Dr. Robert M. Ehrlich   *Pediatric endocrinology*
- Dr. Robert M. Filler   *Pediatric and thoracic surgery*
- Dr. Robert M. Freedom   *Pediatric cardiology*
- Dr. Jacob Friedberg   *Pediatric otolaryngology*
- Dr. Brenda Gallie   *Ocular oncology*
- Dr. David L. Gilday   *General nuclear medicine*
- Dr. Anne M. Griffiths   *Pediatric gastroenterology*
- Dr. Robert H. A. Haslam   *General child neurology*
- Dr. Diane Hebert   *Pediatric nephrology*
- Dr. Harold J. Hoffman   *Pediatric neurological surgery*
- Dr. Robin P. Humphreys   *Pediatric neurological surgery*
- Dr. Miriam Kaufman   *Adolescent and young adult medicine*
- Dr. Bernice Krafchik   *Pediatric dermatology*
- Dr. William J. Logan   *General child neurology*
- Dr. Gordon A. McLorie   *Pediatric urology*
- Dr. Hugh Mervyn O'Brodovich   *Pediatric pulmonology*
- Dr. Mercer Rang   *Pediatric orthopedic surgery*
- Dr. Eve A. Roberts   *Pediatric gastroenterology*

- Dr. Robert B. Salter   *Pediatric orthopedic surgery*
- Dr. Alma J. Smitheringale   *Pediatric otolaryngology*
- Dr. George A. Trusler   *Pediatric cardiac surgery*
- Dr. John W. Wedge   *Pediatric orthopedic surgery*
- Dr. Bill G. Williams   *Pediatric cardiac surgery*
- Dr. Ronald M. Zucker   *Microsurgery and peripheral nerve surgery*

PATIENT SATISFACTION

Patient satisfaction ratings were not available from the hospital.

RESEARCH

The Sick Kids Research Institute was founded in 1954. Today, more than 821 staff members carry out research, including 73 senior scientists and 98 doctors who direct projects. Altogether, more than 400 research projects are ongoing in 75 fields. About two-thirds of all funding comes from the Medical Research Council and more than 80 other granting agencies. This funding exceeded $25 million in fiscal 1991-92.

In the last three years alone, Sick Kids researchers have made the following groundbreaking discoveries: the protein that is the cystic fibrosis gene product, which made it possible to begin testing replacement therapy; the gene responsible for one form of Fanconi's anemia; human stem cells were successfully grown in mice, paving the way to study the development of the human blood system; cow's milk was identified as a possible causative agent of juvenile diabetes in genetically susceptible children; a drug treatment for Menke's disease was developed; and a new drug, L-1, was successfully given as the first oral therapy for thalassemia major.

ADMISSIONS POLICY

Admissions information, including costs, was not available from the hospital.

KINGSTON GENERAL

HOSPITAL

The city of Kingston sits on the mouth of the St. Lawrence River, across from New York state, about 40 miles northwest of Watertown. When Kingston General Hospital (KGH) opened in 1838, its first patients were 20 wounded Americans taken prisoner in the Battle of the Windmill, during the Rebellion of 1837. Two patients died and the rest were later discharged. Because of its affiliation with the Queen's University Medical School—one of the best in Canada—KGH is a major Canadian teaching hospital. It offers the most advanced care in southeastern Ontario (the expansive area east of greater Toronto and south of greater Ottawa) in such specialties as cardiology, trauma, cancer, perinatal, neurosciences, respiratory diseases, and transplantation. Indeed, KGH is the major referral center in the region. What's more, KGH has found a way to provide these services at lower costs than other comparably sized hospitals in the province, without compromising its first rate personal care.

KINGSTON, ONTARIO

SPECIAL FACILITIES AND PROGRAMS

KGH's Fraser Armstrong Patient Centre was the first outpatient clinic of its type affiliated with a major Canadian teaching hospital. The hospital's astute planning in this area has been justified with the increasing shift of health care to ambulatory facilities.

BECAUSE OF ITS AFFILIATION WITH THE QUEEN'S UNIVERSITY MEDICAL SCHOOL—ONE OF THE BEST IN CANADA—KGH IS A MAJOR CANADIAN TEACHING HOSPITAL.

With the introduction of its own Computed Tomography (CT) HiSpeed Advantage system, and its own MRI scanner in April 1994, KGH has become one of Ontario's top regional diagnostic imaging centers. It also provides a genetic testing service for hemophilia clinics across Ontario.

The Auxiliary (formerly Women's Aid) was founded in 1905 and is an integral part of KGH's care program. The Auxiliary lobbied for the creation of accommodations for families of critically ill patients from out of town, and, in 1992, nine rooms were indeed set aside for this purpose. This "family service area" now has an 85% occupancy rate.

MEDICAL SPECIALTIES

Allergy, Anesthesia, Cancer, Cardiology, Family Medicine, Genetics, Human Sexual Dysfunction, Imaging Services, Infectious Diseases and Medical Microbiology, Joint Disease, Medicine, Neurosciences (including pediatric neurosurgery), Obstetrics and Gynecology, Oncology, Ophthalmology, Otolaryngology, Pathology, Pediatrics, Perinatal, Psychiatry, Rehabilitation Medicine (Occupational Therapy, Physiotherapy, Prosthetics/Orthotics, Transitional Living Centre, Vocational Services, and Speech Pathology), Renal Disease and Nephrology, Respiratory Diseases, Surgery, Trauma, and Urology.

WELL-KNOWN SPECIALISTS

- Dr. Henry B. Dinsdale *Neurologist*
- Dr. Alvaro Morales *Urologist*
- Dr. John O. Parker *Cardiologist*
- Dr. Charles Sorbie *Orthopaedic surgeon*

PATIENT SATISFACTION

KGH annually determines patient satisfaction through an ambitious telephone survey of more than 200 former patients. In 1992, 88% of those interviewed rated the overall care they received at KGH as either "excellent" or "good." In 1993, that percentage was 85%, and 90% were willing to recommend KGH to others. The majority of those interviewed were extremely impressed with the strong interpersonal skills of the KGH staff.

RESEARCH

The Syl and Molly Apps Medical Research Centre is an integral part of KGH, with annual research grants totaling approximately $12 million. Areas of research include Alzheimer's disease, neural regeneration, biomechanics, health outcomes research in oncology and nephrology, reproductive technology, urology, and computer-assisted drug development.

Various bleeding diseases, including hemophilia A, hemophilia B, and von Willebrand's disease, are being researched in the Department of Pathology. The feasibility of treating hemophilia by gene therapy is one area of study.

Research in the neurosciences is extensive at KGH as well. Perhaps the main focus is the attempt to decipher and manipulate those factors responsible for neuronal growth and its failure following injury to the nervous system.

The Department of Urology has, for several years, investigated penile erectile problems. Dr. Michael A. Adams has helped evolve a new understanding of the importance of vascular reactivity and the sympathetic nervous system in the control of erectile function.

The Division of Allergy, within the Department of Medicine, was probably the first to develop a system to evaluate up to 60 patients at once under controlled antigen exposure. This division has also undertaken work on risk assessment of fatal anaphylactic reactions resulting from honey bee stings.

Additionally, KGH now evaluates the effectiveness and outcomes of particular clinical procedures and methods of health care delivery—an important area in such times of economic restraint.

ADMISSIONS POLICY

Any patient can be admitted by a physician with admitting privileges to KGH. Those without provincial health care coverage are billed later at a per diem rate of $836 for a private room and $798 for a semi-private room. (An ICU charge was not available.) In addition to those room charges, the daily rate for "standard" care is $2,520. The daily rate for "critical" care is $3,470.

AT A GLANCE

Beds: 379
Occupancy Rate: 85.6%
Average Patient Count: N/A
Average Patient Stay: 7.71
  days
Annual Admissions: 14,677
Births: 2,419
Outpatient Clinic Visits:
  144,121
Emergency Room/Trauma
  Center Visits: 39,162

HOSPITAL PERSONNEL
Physicians: 257
Residents: 220
Registered Nurses: 783
  (FT & PT)
  BS Degree: 86

ADDRESS
76 Stuart Street
Kingston, Ontario K7L 2V7

TELEPHONE
(613) 548-3232

MOUNT SINAI

HOSPITAL

TORONTO, ONTARIO

In October 1992, Mount Sinai Hospital (MSH) was awarded Canada's first four-year accreditation award from the Canadian Council on Health Facilities Accreditation (CCHFA)—the highest honor ever bestowed on any of the nation's 1,260 health care facilities. This did not come as a surprise to most Canadian health care professionals, as Mount Sinai is regarded as probably the best all-around hospital in the country.

A group of women founded Mount Sinai in 1923 to serve the Jewish community and to provide a strong teaching center. Originally a 30-bed maternity and convalescent hospital, Mount Sinai grew rapidly in both size and stature. It is now a major teaching center affiliated with the prestigious University of Toronto Medical School. The CCHFA's four-year award was the hospital's crowning achievement.

Among its many outstanding attributes, the quality of nursing care is what places Mount Sinai above its peers. MSH is a world leader in nursing, maintaining the highest of standards by relying solely on nursing professionals. One approach that MSH and other hospitals are now adopting is "primary" nursing—a nurse is assigned to every patient and family; the same nurse then coordinates round-the-clock care for the patient.

IN OCTOBER 1992, MOUNT SINAI HOSPITAL (MSH) WAS AWARDED CANADA'S FIRST FOUR-YEAR ACCREDITATION AWARD FROM THE CANADIAN COUNCIL ON HEALTH FACILITIES ACCREDITATION (CCHFA)—THE HIGHEST HONOR EVER BESTOWED ON ANY OF THE NATION'S 1,260 HEALTH CARE FACILITIES.

SPECIAL FACILITIES AND PROGRAMS

Two years ago, the World Health Organization designated Mount Sinai's Gerald P. Turner Department of Nursing a collaborating center—the only nursing service department in the world to hold such a distinction. MSH has since been working in conjunction with other international health service groups to strengthen nursing practices worldwide.

MSH is also a world leader in various fields of medicine. The Orthopaedic Oncology Program is the largest of its kind in North America, featuring Canada's only multidisciplinary sarcoma (bone and soft tissue) unit. The Rachel and David Rubinoff Bone and Tissue Bank is accredited with the American Association of Tissue Banks, supplying medical centers across North America.

Mount Sinai's Cardiovascular Clinical Research Laboratory, which opened in May 1992, is a unique North American human research lab dedicated to cardiovascular research. The hospital received international attention when the *New England Journal of Medicine* and the *The New York Times* publicized a study done at Mount Sinai that found the newer method of artery blockage removal, directional coronary atherectomy, was no more effective than conventional balloon angioplasty.

Mount Sinai's team of obstetricians and gynecologists has broken ground with forays into fetal therapy, helping women with high-risk pregnancies. In 1992, a successful pleuro-amniotic shunt (chest shunt) procedure was performed on a 22-week-old fetus. This is believed to be the first such procedure ever performed on a fetus so young and so ill.

Ophthalmology is another of Mount Sinai's specialties. More tear duct reconstructions are done at Mount Sinai than at any other center in the world, and it handles more oculoplastic cases than any center in North America. Physicians have come from as far away as Scotland, Finland, and Hong Kong to observe Mount Sinai's work in oculoplastics and retinal surgery.

Laparoscopic surgery, delicate operations performed with tiny, sophisticated instrumentation

AT A GLANCE

Beds: 446
Occupancy Rate: 80.5%
Average Patient Count: 422
Average Patient Stay: 6.14
 days
Annual Admissions: 18,874
Births: 5,098
Outpatient Clinic Visits:
 533,836
Emergency Room/Trauma
 Center Visits: 27,985

HOSPITAL PERSONNEL
Physicians: 646
Residents: 100
Registered Nurses: 919
 (FT & PT)

ADDRESS
600 University Avenue
Toronto, Ontario M5G 1X5

TELEPHONE
(416) 586-4200

inserted through ports, holes, or tubes in the body, is an area in which Mount Sinai plans to take a leadership role. Already, MSH has been a Canadian leader in this field.

MSH has long had a firm commitment to quality care. Its Patient Relations Program began in 1974 and was followed in 1983 with the Quality Assurance Program, both of which served as models for other health care facilities. The current "Total Quality Management" program involves teams of staff members at all levels, from janitors to the highest specialists, working in conjunction to review and improve patient care.

It should come as no surprise that MSH is also on the cutting edge of perhaps the most important nonclinical task facing Canadian hospitals in the 1990s—fundraising. Mount Sinai's "Friends For Life" campaign, the most ambitious in the history of Canadian health care, hopes to raise $75 million in private funds—$20 million to go to research, $35 million to upgrade diagnostic and research equipment, and $20 million to construct new space for research and ambulatory care programs.

Despite this impressive resume, Mount Sinai, like most Canadian hospitals, does not have its own MRI scanner or lithotriptor; it shares this machinery with other hospitals. Mount Sinai does have its own CAT scanner.

MEDICAL SPECIALTIES

Anaesthetic Perinatology, Clinical Biochemistry, Dentistry (including Oral Pathology, Oral and Maxillofacial Surgery, Periodontics, Prosthodontics and Restoration Dentistry, Orthodontics, Dentistry for the Disabled, and Endodontics), Family and Community Medicine (including Family Practice Unit-Ambulatory, In-patient Family Practice Unit, Palliative Care Program, Emergency Services, and Sports Medicine), Medicine (including Cardiology, Gastroenterology, Rheumatology, Neurology, Haematology/Oncology, Nephrology, Infectious Diseases, Endocrinology, Geriatrics, and Respiratory Diseases), Microbiology, Obstetrics and Gynaecology (including Obstetrical Perinatology), Ophthalmology (including Oculoplastics), Otolaryngology (including Audiology), Paediatrics (including Neonatal Intensive Care Unit), Pathology (including Hematopathology and Blood Bank), Psychiatry (including Psychoanalysis and HIV Clinic), Radiological Sciences (including Nuclear Medicine, Diagnostic Radiology, and Diagnostic Ultrasound), Rehabilitation Medicine, and Surgery (including General Surgery, Neurosurgery, Orthopedics/Sarcoma, Thoracic Surgery, and Urology).

WELL-KNOWN SPECIALISTS

- Dr. Allan Adelman   *Cardiovascular surgery*
- Dr. Zane Cohen   *Colon and rectal surgery*
- Dr. Ronald Feld   *Medical oncology/hematology*
- Dr. Jeffrey J. Hurwitz   *Ophthalmology*
- Dr. Demetrius Litwin   *Laparoscopic surgery*

- Dr. J. W. Knox Ritchie   *Obstetrics and gynaecology*
- Dr. Joel Sadavoy   *Psychiatry*
- Dr. Bernard Zinman   *Endocrinology and metabolism*

PATIENT SATISFACTION

Patient surveys reflect Mount Sinai's excellent nursing care and overall commitment to quality care. Fifty of 58 patients surveyed in June 1993 indicated hospital staff were "always" caring.

RESEARCH

The Samuel Lunenfeld Research Institute, established in 1985, is one of Canada's premier research facilities, with more than 80,000 square feet of laboratory space and a budget of $20 million. More than 100 ongoing research projects, covering a wide spectrum of patient care, are ongoing. Institute divisions include Perinatology, Molecular Immunology and Neurobiology, Molecular and Developmental Biology, and Clinical Epidemiology. The Lunenfeld Institute will soon be adding an additional 5,000 square feet, to create more workspace for its scientists and to attract others.

In 1993, Dr. Andras Nagy spent two weeks in Israel teaching aspects of cloning mice using embryonic stem cells. The technique, now used by scientists around the world, was pioneered at the Lunenfeld Institute.

The Diabetes Clinical Research Unit opened in 1990 and is devoted to the treatment of diabetics and to the research of causes, and long-term complications, of diabetes. About 1,800 diabetes patients are monitored at least once every three months.

Mount Sinai's Cardiovascular Clinical Research Laboratory is devoted to heart and lung research. It is equipped with specialized X-ray, ultrasound, and catheterization monitoring systems, in addition to other essential technology.

ADMISSIONS POLICY

Any patient can be admitted through Mount Sinai's Emergency Department or referred by a family physician. For more information, call (416) 586-4618 regarding admitting, or (416) 586-4873 regarding pre-admissions.

Nonresidents of Canada are billed directly on a daily basis. Without provincial health insurance, costs are room rate plus $215 per day for a private room, and room rate plus $170 per day for a semiprivate room. ICU care is $2,600 per day. All hospital services, such as food, drugs, supplies, social work, etc. are included in these prices; but room charges do not include physician fees or any extraordinary items not in stock (e.g, bone marrow, prothesis).

SUNNYBROOK

HEALTH SCIENCE

CENTRE

NORTH YORK, ONTARIO

When someone in central Ontario requires specialized emergency treatment, he or she will likely be rushed by air or by ambulance to Sunnybrook Health Science Centre. Without question, Sunnybrook houses the premier regional trauma unit in Canada, and perhaps one of the best in the world. More than 60 hospitals in Ontario refer patients to Sunnybrook, located in the heart of metropolitan Toronto on 100 acres of parkland, and only minutes from the congested downtown area. Sunnybrook's trauma unit treats more than 38,000 patients each year and serves as a base hospital for the Land Paramedic Program and the Air Ambulance Program.

Sunnybrook opened in 1946 as a hospital for World War II veterans. By the 1960s, it began developing a community orientation and became the first university teaching complex in Ontario. Affiliated with the prestigious University of Toronto Medical School, Sunnybrook annually trains more than 1,300 U of T students, as well as 500 from other medical schools.

SPECIAL FACILITIES AND PROGRAMS

WITHOUT QUESTION, SUNNYBROOK HOUSES THE PREMIER REGIONAL TRAUMA UNIT IN CANADA, AND PERHAPS ONE OF THE BEST IN THE WORLD.

Through the Toronto Bayview Regional Cancer Centre, Sunnybrook is Toronto's regional cancer center and serves thousands of outpatients a year. A full range of care is available, from early detection and diagnosis through treatment, palliative care, and supportive care. A home chemotherapy program is offered to some patients.

Sunnybrook is also part of the Regional Geriatric Program and provides specialized care to frail older patients with 100 beds in the new George Hees Wing.

The Departments of Cardiology and Cardiovascular Surgery have their own operating room, intensive care and recovery areas, cardiac catheterization lab, and angioplasty facilities for a wide range of cardiovascular and vascular diseases.

Those with psychiatric disorders aren't the only patients treated in the Department of Psychiatry. Indeed, any patient admitted to Sunnybrook may be referred to a mental health professional. Some specialized clinics address depression and anxiety disorders, sleep disorders, schizophrenia, and Alzheimer's and other neurocognitive disorders of aging.

Other Sunnybrook clinics help those who suffer from back problems, dizziness, headaches, female infertility, sexually transmitted diseases, and AIDS. The hospital also operates a 670-bed long-term care facility that functions mainly as a nursing home, and has a state-of-the-art diagnostic imaging department, with X-ray, ultrasound, CT scan, and an MRI scanner.

To ensure that funding cutbacks don't affect Sunnybrook's services, the hospital has begun a major restructuring. Sunnybrook is decentralizing the hospital into units revolving around the needs of specific groups of patients, instead of around professional departments.

AT A GLANCE

Beds: 649
Occupancy Rate: 88.6%
Average Patient Count: N/A
Average Patient Stay: 10.1
    days
Annual Admissions: 17,220
Births: N/A
Outpatient Clinic Visits:
    286,862
Emergency Room/Trauma
    Center Visits: 36,778

HOSPITAL PERSONNEL
Physicians: 561
    Board Certified: 561
Residents: 145
Registered Nurses: 1,200
    (FT & PT)

ADDRESS
2075 Bayview Ave
North York, Ontario
    M4N 3M5

TELEPHONE
(416) 480-6100

MEDICAL SPECIALTIES

Acute Spinal Cord Injuries, Aging, Arthritis/Rheumatology, Cardiology, Diabetes Education, Dentistry, Dermatology, Gynaecology, Immunology, Oncology (including Gynaecologic, Breast, Genitourinary, Paediatric, Skin, Lymphoma, and Head and Neck Cancers), Ophthalmology, Orthotic and Prosthetic Services, Physiotherapy, Psychiatry (Adult, Adolescent, and Geriatric), Rehabilitation, and Trauma.

WELL-KNOWN SPECIALISTS

- Dr. Bernard Boulanger *Trauma, surgery*
- Dr. John Edmeads *Medicine*
- Dr. Stephen Fremes *Heart and circulation*
- Dr. Bernard Goldman *Cardiovascular surgery*
- Dr. Stanley Kutcher *Adolescent psychiatry*
- Dr. Barry McLellan *Trauma*
- Dr. Christopher Morgan *Cardiology*
- Dr. Kathleen Pritchard *Medical oncology*
- Dr. Duncan Robertson *Geriatric program*
- Dr. Joseph Schatzker *Orthopaedics*
- Dr. Ken Shulman *Geriatric psychiatry*
- Dr. Donald Sutherland *Radiation oncology*
- Dr. Marvin Tile *Surgery*

PATIENT SATISFACTION

The hospital's first patient survey in 1993 indicated that 93% of its patients rate the care they received as either good or excellent—a score that ranked Sunnybrook 14% higher than the average American hospital.

RESEARCH

Sunnybrook's intention to make research a primary mission was boosted in 1991 with the opening of the new Reichmann Research Building, which has 160,000 square feet of lab space. Annual funding for Sunnybrook's research programs has reached $17 million, with an ever-increasing amount coming from U.S. sources.

The six major research programs are aging, cancer, clinical epidemiology (study of disease patterns), medical physics (methods used to take images inside the body), general research (including dermatology, pharmacology, orthopaedics, psychology, and nursing), and trauma.

The Institute for Clinical Evaluative Sciences (ICES) in Ontario grew out of Sunnybrook's clinical epidemiology research program. ICES scientists investigate how health services are delivered in Ontario and suggest means of increasing efficiency and effectiveness.

ADMISSIONS POLICY

Any patient can be admitted through Sunnybrook's Emergency Department or referral by a family physician. Nonresidents of Canada are billed directly on a daily basis. Rates for those without provincial health insurance are $2,600 per day for a private or semiprivate room and $2,864 per day for ICU care. Doctors' fees are not included in these rates.

THE TORONTO HOSPITAL

TORONTO, ONTARIO

No hospital in Canada can claim more "world firsts" than The Toronto Hospital, one of the nation's largest acute care teaching facilities and, overall, the most medically advanced. Some 8% of its patients are nonresidents of Canada—another 11% come from other provinces.

TTH was formed in 1986 with the merger of the Toronto General and Toronto Western Hospitals. So, TTH actually has two facilities located about a half-mile apart in downtown Toronto. Together, they form the premier hospital affiliated with the University of Toronto Medical School.

Toronto General opened in 1829 and established an international reputation almost immediately. Toronto Western opened in 1896 and within five years established specialty departments. Among the impressive, collective world firsts established at the TTH hospitals since then are: establishment of the first psychiatric unit in a general hospital (1906); development and first clinical use of insulin in the treatment of diabetes (1922); invention of the heart pacemaker (1936); design and use of North America's first artificial kidney (1946); first use of hypothermia (cooling of the body) for open heart surgery (1950); establishment of the world's first coronary intensive care unit (1962); first successful single-lung transplant (1983); first successful double-lung transplant (1986); first test for the diagnosis of

NO HOSPITAL IN CANADA CAN CLAIM MORE "WORLD FIRSTS" THAN THE TORONTO HOSPITAL, ONE OF THE NATION'S LARGEST ACUTE CARE TEACHING FACILITIES AND, OVERALL, THE MOST MEDICALLY ADVANCED.

viral heart disease (1990); first to crack the genetic code for myosin, a major structural and functional heart protein (TTH is now the world center for the complete analysis of genes expressed by the heart) (1990); and first hospital to have performed 100 lung transplants (1991).

SPECIAL FACILITIES AND PROGRAMS

Today, TTH continues its exemplary traditions. It is one of the leading centers in North America for both the research and treatment of cardiovascular diseases. More open heart operations are performed here than anywhere else in Canada—some 2,000 annually.

TTH is also a Canadian leader in transplant surgery. It annually performs some 57 autologous bone marrow, 366 corneal, 2 liver/kidney, 62 liver, 90 kidney, 19 heart, 30 double-lung, and 2 single-lung transplants. The bone marrow transplant program, established in 1986, was the first in Ontario.

One of the largest centers for neurosciences in North America is housed at TTH. It is the referral center for neurological disease, both provincially and nationally.

TTH's cancer programs have grown in stature in recent years. In fact, TTH now has one of the largest ambulatory oncology centers in Canada, and is the provincial tertiary referral center for patients with complex diseases.

In early 1994, TTH opened Canada's largest HIV/AIDS clinic. Among its other special programs and facilities are a prostate center, a hand program, an in vitro fertility program, an eating disorders clinic, and a sleep disorders clinic. TTH's special equipment includes a hyperbaric oxygen chamber, an MRI scanner, and CAT scanners.

MEDICAL SPECIALTIES

Cardiovascular Sciences, Dentistry, Eating Disorders, Endocrinology, Family and Community Medicine, General Internal Medicine, Geriatric Medicine, Hand Program, Hematology, Nephrology, Neurosciences (including brain and spinal cord injuries), Obstetrics and Gynecology, Oncology, Ophthalmology, Orthopaedics, Otolaryngology, Psychiatry, Respirology, Rheumatology, Sleep Disorders, Transplantation, Urology, and Women's Mental Health.

WELL-KNOWN SPECIALISTS

- Dr. Michael Baker   *Hematology/Oncology*
- Dr. Mark Bernstein   *Neurosurgery*
- Dr. Carl Cardella   *Nephrology*
- Dr. Alan Chapman   *Respirology*
- Dr. Tyrone David   *Cardiovascular surgery*
- Dr. Alan Detsky   *Internal Medicine and Clinical Epidemiology*
- Dr. Chris Feindel   *Cardiovascular surgery*

- Dr. Bill Francombe   *Hematology*
- Dr. Paul Goss   *Medical oncology*
- Dr. Paul Grieg   *Gastroenterology*
- Dr. Jenny Heathcote   *Gastroenterology*
- Dr. Robert Inman   *Rheumatology*
- Dr. Michael Jewett   *Urology*
- Dr. Wayne Johnston   *Vascular surgery*
- Dr. Armand Keating   *Oncology/Hematology*
- Dr. Gary Levy   *Gastroenterology*
- Dr. Ron Livingstone   *Obstetrics and Gynecology*
- Dr. Don Mickle   *Biochemistry*
- Dr. Harry Moldofsky   *Psychiatry*
- Dr. Darrel Ogilvie-Harris   *Orthopedic surgery*
- Dr. Gary Rodin   *Psychiatry*
- Dr. Alan Sandler   *Anaesthesiology*
- Dr. Brian Shaw   *Psychology*
- Dr. Michael Sole   *Cardiology*
- Dr. Charles Tator   *Neurosurgery*
- Dr. John Trachtenberg   *Urology*
- Dr. Graeme Trope   *Ophthalmology*
- Dr. Sharon Walmsley   *Infectious diseases*
- Dr. Gary Webb   *Cardiology*
- Dr. Bernard Zinman   *Endocrinology*

AT A GLANCE

Beds: 1,173
Occupancy Rate: 85%
Average Patient Count: N/A
Average Patient Stay: 9.0 days
Annual Admissions: 42,000
Births: 2,649
Outpatient Clinic Visits:
    450,000
Emergency Room/Trauma
    Center Visits: 70,000

HOSPITAL PERSONNEL
Physicians: 1,185
Residents: 403
Registered Nurses: 2,200
    (FT & PT)
    BS Degree: 354

ADDRESS
585 University Avenue
Toronto, Ontario M5G 2C4

TELEPHONE
(416) 340-3111

PATIENT SATISFACTION

TTH does not conduct hospital-wide patient surveys. Individual departments, such as the Medical Directorate or Surgical Directorate, routinely survey former patients. In 1994, TTH began to send out surveys to those who have called the hospital to either complain or compliment.

RESEARCH

The Toronto Hospital Research Institute (TTHRI) is the umbrella for all the world-class research being done at TTH. TTHRI annually receives $30 million in grants.

TTH prides itself on a research environment encompassing "bench-to-bedside integration" of basic and clinical research. More than 250 principal investigators, physicians, and scientists are pushing the boundaries of research in four priority areas: cardiovascular disease, cancer, neurological disorders, and transplantation. There are also special research programs for arthritis, reproductive biology, diabetes, clinical epidemiology, and eating disorders.

Ongoing cardiovascular projects include the study of underlying viral and molecular causes of heart failure; studies of atherosclerosis and the influence of hemodynamic forces on the development and remodeling of arteries; and advancement of diagnosis and treatment without surgery.

Studies in cancer include genetic predisposition to breast and ovarian cancer; basic research on cancer cell growth and differentiation, hopefully leading to new approaches to treatment; bone marrow transplantation and genetic therapy; and clinical trials in lung, breast, and prostate cancer.

In the neurosciences, research includes molecular and cellular neurobiology to understand the basis of neurological disorders; clinical research on new therapeutic innovations; and use of the MRI scanner and image-guided invasive therapy.

Transplantation research includes cell preservation to improve surgery strategies; molecular-biological approaches to study immune mechanisms; and clinical and surgical advances in heart, lung, liver, and kidney transplants.

ADMISSIONS POLICY

Any patient can be referred by a physician or admitted through the Emergency Department. Those without provincial health care coverage are billed later, but emergency care is provided immediately, regardless of coverage. Per diem rates for those without provincial health insurance are $2,760 for a private room, $2,705 for a semiprivate room, and $3,120 for ICU care.

UNIVERSITY HOSPITAL

University Hospital (UH) is one of the most famous transplant centers in the world. "Finding a
Better Way" has long been the hospital's guiding
philosophy.

LONDON, ONTARIO

UH truly excels in transplantation. Through the
establishment of the Walter J. Blackburn Multi-Organ
Transplant Unit, UH brings all transplant patients
together in one area, centralizing and improving patient care.

Almost 2,000 organ transplants have been performed at UH since the hospital opened in 1972,
including some 900 kidneys, 500 livers, 300 hearts,
12 lungs, 75 bone marrow, and 2 small bowels.
Heart/ lung, small bowel/liver, and cluster and islet cell transplants have also been performed. In
1993 alone, 22 hearts, 66 kidneys, and 62 livers were
transplanted.

UH is a major referral center for the Ontario region, but patients also come from across Canada,
North America, and around the globe. Affiliated with
the University of Western Ontario Medical School,
UH became a world leader immediately after opening in 1972, when an operating technique for cerebral
aneurysms was pioneered. A year later, the hospital's
first liver transplant was performed. Other UH world
firsts include: a heart operation to correct life-threatening right ventricular dysplasia (1981); implantation
of the first pacemaker cardioverter defibrillator (PCD)

UNIVERSITY HOSPITAL (UH) IS
ONE OF THE MOST FAMOUS
TRANSPLANT CENTERS IN THE
WORLD. "FINDING A BETTER
WAY" HAS LONG BEEN THE
HOSPITAL'S GUIDING
PHILOSOPHY.

(1987); and the world's first successful liver/small bowel transplant (1988).

SPECIAL FACILITIES AND PROGRAMS

UH is the only center in Canada where bowel transplants are performed, and was one of the first in the world to report that adding a segment of the large bowel to the small bowel improves its function, without increasing morbidity or the risk of rejection. In 1992, UH transplanted the world's oldest donor liver (86 years) into a patient with cirrhosis. The liver was accepted from a hospital in Florida, after all American programs refused to transplant it. UH extended this age limit in 1993 by transplanting a 92-year-old liver. In 1993, UH performed a small bowel/kidney transplantation on a seven month old girl, and a mother donated one-sixth of her liver for successful transplantation into her one year old boy.

In addition to transplants, patients from around the world are referred to UH for treatment of cardiac arrhythmias—short-circuits in the heart's electrical system which can be fatal if left untreated. UH has helped develop a sophisticated cardiac mapping device which enables cardiologists to destroy the tiny area of a patient's heart that causes the electrical abnormality. Those with the most common form of cardiac arrhythmia—Wolff-Parkinson-White syndrome—and those with heart attack scars benefit the most from UH's procedures.

UH has long been recognized an international leader in the area of stroke prevention and treatment. One recent UH study indicated that the use of aspirin can reduce the risk of stroke in men by as much as 50%. Furthermore, UH was involved in an international study that found commonly performed arterial bypass operations have absolutely no value in preventing stroke.

On other fronts, some 8,000 kidney dialysis treatments are handled each year at UH, and some 2,500 patients are registered in UH's Multiple Sclerosis Program. The hospital also provides special services in such areas as diabetes, epilepsy, artificial insemination, and orthopaedic athletic injuries.

Special equipment available at UH includes two MRIs (one high-field, one mid-field); laser angioplasty equipment; stereostatic neurosurgery equipment; and an eight-bed, computerized cable telemetry system for localizing epileptic seizures.

Nurses in UH's Emergency, Urology, and Orthopaedics Departments have received national commendation. There are six advanced-nurse practitioners at UH.

UH reviews all patient-oriented services on a weekly basis. Areas reviewed quarterly include: infection control rates, in-hospital accidents, medication incidents, mortality rates, admissions waiting lists, and admissions delays.

MEDICAL SPECIALTIES

Anaesthesia, Clinical Biochemistry, Clinical Neurological Sciences (Neurology, Neurosurgery), Dentistry, Diagnostic Radiology, Emergency, Gynaecology/Reproductive Medicine, Medicine (Cardiology, Clinical Immunology/Allergy, Endocrinology, Gastroenterology, General Internal Medicine, Haematology/Oncology, Nephrology & Transplantation, Respiratory Diseases, Rheumatology), Microbiology, Nuclear Medicine, Ophthalmology, Otolaryngology, Paediatrics, Pathology, Psychiatry, Physical Medicine and Rehabilitation, and Surgery (Cardiovascular and Thoracic, General, Orthopedic, Plastic and Reconstructive, and Urology).

WELL-KNOWN SPECIALISTS

- Dr. H. J. M. Barnett *Neurology*
- Dr. W. T. Blume *Neurology*
- Dr. D. R. Boughner *Cardiology*
- Dr. R. B. Bourne *Orthopedics*
- Dr. C. G. Drake *Neurosurgery*
- Dr. J. Dupre *Endocrinology*
- Dr. G. C. Ebers *Neurology*
- Dr. P. J. Fowler *Orthopedics*
- Dr. A. J. Fox *Neuroradiology*
- Dr. A. W. Gelb *Anesthesia*
- Dr. J. P. Girvin *Neurosurgery*
- Dr. D. R. Grant *General surgery and transplantation*
- Dr. G. M. Guiraudon *Cardiovascular and thoracic surgery*
- Dr. V. C. Hachinski *Neurology*
- Dr. M. D. Haust *Pathology*
- Dr. G. J. Klein *Cardiology*
- Dr. J. W. D. McDonald *Gastroenterology*
- Dr. T. J. McDonald *Endocrinology*
- Dr. W. K. C. Morgan *Respiratory diseases*
- Dr. R. Novick *Cardiovascular and thoracic surgery*
- Dr. M. R. Roach *General internal medicine/biophysics*
- Dr. R. C. Rorabeck *Orthopedics*
- Dr. C. R. Stiller *Nephrology and transplantation*
- Dr. W. J. Wall *General surgery and transplantation*
- Dr. A. A. Yuzpe *Gynaecology/reproductive endocrinology*

AT A GLANCE

Beds: 388
Occupancy Rate: 88%
Average Number of Patients: 321
Average Patient Stay: 10.0 days
Annual Admissions: 11,624
Outpatient Clinic Visits: 143,961
Emergency Room/Trauma Center Visits: 24,572

HOSPITAL PERSONNEL
Physicians: 142
    Board Certified: 142
Residents: 67.5
Registered Nurses: 926 (FT & PT)
    BS Degree: 18%

ADDRESS
339 Windermere Road
London, Ontario N6A 5A5

TELEPHONE
(519) 663-3000

PATIENT SATISFACTION

The hospital monitors quality assurance through various means, including patient surveys. UH's Social Work Department mails a survey to all released patients—about 50% are returned. All patient complaints or serious issues that require prompt follow-up are forwarded immediately to the manager of the area in question.

RESEARCH

More than 200 people, in addition to many support staff, are involved exclusively in research at UH. Virtually all major causes of death and disability are being studied.

Not surprisingly, transplantation research is state-of-the-art, thanks in part to research specialists. UH is studying the effectiveness and side effects of new immunosuppressant drugs. Liver and kidney transplantation between nonhuman primates (baboon to monkey) has been one means of investigating the characteristics of these various drugs. A safe, effective combination of such drugs must be found, however, before nonhuman primates would be used as donors for human recipients. UH is also continuing to explore the possibility of pig-to-human transplants, by either preparing a mixed-marrow infusion to establish a chimeric state or developing a genetically-manipulated ("transgenic") pig. In addition, the Cellular Immunology Laboratory is researching xenotransplantation of microencapsulated human pancreatic islet cells into diabetic mice to study how well these encapsulated cells release insulin.

UH is also exploring the plausibility of using recently deceased humans as donors, in the hope of increasing the number of kidneys for transplantation. Unlike "brain-dead" donors, these would be declared dead by traditional criteria and would include trauma patients who died soon after admission or patients for whom life-sustaining treatment had been deemed futile. Methods that can rapidly cool the organs of such donors are being explored at UH in a joint project with the Critical Care Trauma Unit at London's Victoria Hospital. Before clinical application would ever be undertaken, UH awaits consensus regarding the ethical issues, technical aspects, and required expertise.

Other prominent areas of research at UH, in close collaboration with the University of Western Ontario and the Robarts Research Institute, are: stroke, multiple sclerosis, epilepsy, interventional neuroradiology, diabetes, cardiac electrophysiology, molecular genetics, reproductive endocrinology, orthopaedic implants, cardiac and neuro-anesthesia; and MRI and three-dimensional imagery.

Research projects at UH totaled almost $20 million in 1993, supported by a large variety of agencies, including charitable societies, federal and provincial grants, industrial grants, and private donations. By far, the largest supporters were the National Institutes of Health in the U.S. ($4,546,233), the Medical Research Council of Canada ($3,552,786), and the Heart and Stroke Foundation of Ontario ($1,170,933).

ADMISSIONS POLICY

All patients are referred by family physicians, other specialists, or Emergency Department physicians. Out-of-country travelers requiring emergency care are treated and billed directly. Per diem room rates for those without provincial health insurance are not applicable at University Hospital. Charges are instead based on diagnoses/level of care (i.e., ICU, ORs). For more information phone (519) 663-3000, ext. 5845.

MONTREAL GENERAL

HOSPITAL

MONTREAL, QUEBEC

Montreal General Hospital (MGH) opened in 1819 to serve the rapidly growing English-speaking population of Montreal. In 1955, the hospital moved into a new $20 million building on the island of Montreal, its current home.

Today, MGH continues to evolve with Montreal's ethnic base. The city has become more multiculturally diversified, so the hospital provides services in more than 20 languages. Since 35% of all MGH patients are now francophone, its "English hospital" tag is indeed antiquated.

SPECIAL FACILITIES AND PROGRAMS

MGH is renowned for its work in neurology, including peripheral nerve injury and repair. It is the province's leading center in neural regeneration. Most recently, the MGH Research Institute was the site of the discovery of the linkage of a gene causing amyotrophic lateral sclerosis (Lou Gehrig's disease), and collaborated with teams in Boston and Paris to discover the gene causing the neurological disease neurofibromatosis II.

MGH IS RENOWNED FOR ITS WORK IN NEUROLOGY, INCLUDING PERIPHERAL NERVE INJURY AND REPAIR. IT IS THE PROVINCE'S LEADING CENTER IN NEURAL REGENERATION.

Rheumatic diseases, including rheumatoid arthritis, osteoarthritis, osteoporosis, and systemic lupus, are extensively researched at MGH. Under Dr. John Esdaile, the hospital provides internationally recognized clinical care in these fields.

Cardiology is another specialty. MGH was the first hospital in Canada, and only the second in North America, to perform cardiomyoplasty surgery as an alternative to heart transplant surgery. More than 6,000 nonemergency outpatients are seen annually in the Cardiology Department. In spring 1994, a state-of-the-art cardiac catheterization laboratory was installed.

MGH also regularly performs lung, kidney, pancreas, and bone marrow transplants, and is one of only four trauma centers in Quebec.

Because of the outstanding level of its services, MGH has treated more than 1,000 patients from outside Canada in the past year.

Family-centered patient care is a staple at MGH. In recent years, the Department of Nursing has pushed ahead in other fields, greatly improving trauma care and developing palliative care service for the dying.

MEDICAL SPECIALTIES

Cardiology, Clinical Pharmacology, Dermatology, Diagnostic Radiology (Nuclear Medicine, Ultrasound), Endocrinology, Epidemiology, Family Medicine, Gastroenterology, Geriatric Medicine, Gynaecology, Haematology, Immunology and Allergy, Infectious Diseases, Internal Medicine, Medical Biochemistry, Medical Genetics, Medical Microbiology, Medical Oncology, Medicine (Bone Metabolism), Nephrology, Neurology, Oncology (Medical Physics), Ophthalmology, Orthopaedic Surgery, Otolaryngology, Pathology, Physical Medicine and Rehabilitation, Psychiatry, Radiation Respiratory Diseases, Rheumatology, Surgery (Cardiovascular Thoracic, General Surgery, Plastic Surgery, and Neurosurgery), Tropical Medicine, and Urology.

WELL-KNOWN SPECIALISTS

- Dr. Albert Aguayo *Neurology*
- Dr. P. Bret *Radiologist*
- Dr. Rea Brown *Trauma*
- Dr. Ray Chiu *Cardiology*
- Dr. John Esdaile *Rheumatology*

AT A GLANCE

MONTREAL GENERAL HOSPITAL

Beds: 672
Occupancy Rate: 83.1%
Average Patient Count: 559
Average Patient Stay: 12.5
  days
Annual Admissions: 14,367
Outpatient Clinic Visits:
  248,576
Emergency Room/Trauma
  Center Visits: 32,379

HOSPITAL PERSONNEL
Physicians: 435
Residents: 160
Registered Nurses: 920
  (FT & PT)
  BS Degree: 277

ADDRESS
1650 Cedar Avenue
Montreal, Quebec H3G 1A4

TELEPHONE
(514) 937-6011

- Dr. Denise Figlewicz   *Neurology*
- Dr. Phil Gold   *Cancer research*
- Dr. Carl Goresky   *Gastroenterology*
- Dr. Steven Grover   *Epidemiology*
- Dr. J. P. Julien   *Neurology*
- Dr. David Mulder   *Cardiovascular thoracic surgery*
- Dr. Steve Narod   *Breast cancer research*
- Dr. Peter Richardson   *Neurosurgery*
- Dr. G. Rouleau   *Neurology*
- Dr. Emil Skamene   *Immunology*
- Dr. Christos Tsoukas   *AIDS research*
- Dr. Blair Whittemore   *Haematology*
- Dr. Bruce Williams   *Microvascular surgery*

PATIENT SATISFACTION

Recently, MGH developed a detailed, 28-item questionnaire to measure patient satisfaction. More than half of a sample of respondents rated MGH services as either "excellent" or "very good."

RESEARCH

The Montreal General Hospital Research Institute is annually awarded about $15 million in funding.

In 1992, three new laboratories were built for the Host Resistance and Neurosciences research teams. It is in these fields that MGH has received the most acclaim. Dr. Albert Aguayo is internationally known for his research on the regeneration of nerve cells after injury, and was awarded the 1993 Ameritec Prize at the Neurotrauma Symposium for his significant accomplishments toward a cure for paralysis. Additionally, Dr. Steven Narod is collaborating with American researchers to isolate the gene causing breast cancer, and the Centre for Host Resistance discovered and isolated a mouse gene that confers resistance to infectious diseases such as tuberculosis and leprosy.

ADMISSIONS POLICY

All patients are admitted by a staff doctor, unless entering through the Emergency Department. Per diem rates for those without provincial health insurance are $2,110.44 for a large private room, $2,082.64 for a small private room, $2,042.18 for a semiprivate room, and $2,001.00 for ICU care. A physician's fee may be charged according to Quebec tariffs. Any testing involving high-tech machinery costs extra as well.

ROYAL VICTORIA

HOSPITAL

Royal Victoria Hospital, the "hospital on the mountain," first opened in 1894 on the slopes of Mount Royal. Originally a 260-bed facility, the Vic, as it is commonly known, is now one of the largest hospitals in Canada. From the outset, it has been affiliated with McGill University's world-renowned medical school. In fact, the Vic is the cornerstone of the university's network of 11 teaching hospitals.

The hospital has long been in the forefront with medical advances. It performed the first kidney transplant in Canada in 1958 and one of the nation's first heart transplants in 1968. It was also the first hospital anywhere to offer a training program in emergency medicine.

Its Department of Psychiatry developed the main treatment for Parkinson's disease and, in the 1980s, discovered that adding lithium to antidepressants increases their effectiveness—a treatment now used throughout the world.

Its Department of Radiation Oncology developed a new strategy for treating gynaecological cancer, a method now used to treat respiratory and gastrointestinal tumors as well.

Its endocrinology researchers were the first to isolate estrogen, the basic female hormone; and prolactin, a hormone produced by the female body to stimulate lactation, was discovered at the Vic in 1967.

MONTREAL, QUEBEC

ORIGINALLY A 260-BED FACILITY, THE VIC, AS IT IS COMMONLY KNOWN, IS NOW ONE OF THE LARGEST HOSPITALS IN CANADA.

SPECIAL FACILITIES AND PROGRAMS

Today, the Vic is the regional referral center for greater Montreal in many specialized services and is among the leading hospitals in Canada in AIDS treatment, research, and especially care. In conjunction with the McGill AIDS Centre, Vic researchers have participated in numerous collaborative projects on treatments, outcomes, costs and psychological issues of the HIV epidemic. Research has also been conducted on the related political, sociological, and ethical concerns. On the care side, the Vic has collaborated with the Montreal Chest Hospital Centre to form a joint AIDS care program, in which nursing staff at the Vic closely follows the progress of patients admitted to either hospital.

In cardiology, the Vic continues to offer state-of-the-art procedures, including directional coronary atherectomies (the technique of removing fatty deposits from diseased vessels) and angioplasty.

The Vic also excels in spinal surgery. The implantation of spinal fixation systems—screws and plates to stabilize the spine—is an advanced procedure offered at the Vic by such specialists as Dr. Max Aebi, an internationally-renowned expert and former chief of spinal surgery at the University of Bern in Switzerland.

Among its special equipment, the Vic has gamma cameras and computers, a CT scan, and two lithotriptors.

While detractors point out that the Vic is an aging, crowded facility, the care provided there is nonetheless first rate. The Vic was one of the first hospitals in Canada to appoint a patient ombudsman; it established Canada's first palliative care unit in 1975; and, as at Montreal General Hospital, the Vic now employs a multiethnic staff to best serve Montreal's multicultural community. Moreover, nursing is exceptional at the Vic—it is the only Quebec hospital to offer specialty courses in critical care, intensive care, psychiatric, gerontology, and oncology nursing.

MEDICAL SPECIALTIES

Anesthesia, Cardiology, Cardiothoracic Surgery, Clinical Immunology and Allergy, Dermatology, Diagnostic Radiology, Emergency Medicine, Endocrinology and Metabolism, Gastroenterology, General Surgery, Geriatric Medicine, Hemaetology, Infectious Diseases, Internal Medicine, Maternal-Fetal Medicine, Medical Biochemistry, Medical Microbiology, Medical Obstetrics and Gynaecology, Nephrology, Neonatal-Perinatal Medicine, Nuclear Medicine, Oncology, Ophthalmology, Orthopedic Surgery, Otolaryngology, Pathology (Anatomical, General, Hemaetological), Plastic Surgery, Psychiatry, Radiation Oncology, Respiratory Medicine, Rheumatology, Thoracic Surgery, Urology, and Vascular Surgery.

WELL-KNOWN SPECIALISTS

- Dr. Max Aebi *Spinal surgery*
- Dr. Miguel Bernier *Ophthalmic pathology*
- Dr. Guy Chouinard *Psychopharmacology*

- Dr. N. Christou   *Surgical infection*
- Dr. Mostafa Elhilali   *Urology*
- Dr. David Goltzman   *Calcium metabolism*
- Dr. Herta Guttman   *Psychiatry*
- Dr. Carolyn Kerrigan   *Hand surgery*
- Dr. Brian Little   *Obstetrician/gynaecologist*
- Dr. Peter Macklem   *Respiratory medicine*
- Dr. L. D. Maclean   *Surgery in sepsis, gastroplasty, and nutrition*
- Dr. Jonathan L. Meakins   *Surgical infection and sepsis*
- Dr. Balfour Mount   *Palliative care*
- Dr. Y. Patel   *Gastroenterology*
- Dr. Barry Posner   *Endocrinology*
- Dr. Allan Sniderman   *Cardiology research*
- Dr. Robert Usher   *Neonatologist*

PATIENT SATISFACTION

In a recent patient satisfaction survey, 63% of respondents indicated they were either "very satisfied" or "extremely satisfied" with the care they received.

RESEARCH

The Vic has long been the most active research hospital, French or English, in all of Quebec, as well as one of the nation's most ambitious research facilities. The Vic also leads the way provincially in research grants, with $11 million in 1992-93.

Most of the Vic's practicing doctors and surgeons are also researchers at the Vic's Research Institute—more than 270 in all. The hospital's history of groundbreaking research continues today in many fields.

Dr. Morag Park is doing research on a new gene, called the Met gene, to help identify whether breast cancer is likely to spread in certain women. She was the first researcher to characterize this gene some 10 years ago. Studies suggest the Met gene is lost in about 40% of cases of breast tumors.

The Anesthesia Department is the leading Canadian center in research on the clinical pharmacology and physiology of neuromuscular drugs. This expertise was developed in the last 12 years at the Vic.

AT A GLANCE

Beds: 581
Occupancy Rate: 91.1%
Average Patient Count: 529
Average Patient Stay: 10.9 days
Annual Admissions: 21,509
Births: 3,864
Outpatient Clinic Visits: 301,761
Emergency Room/Trauma Center Visits: 38,260

HOSPITAL PERSONNEL
Physicians: 340
   Board Certified: 278
Residents: 115
Registered Nurses: 1,022 (FT & PT)
   BS Degree: 374

ADDRESS
687 Pine Avenue West
Montreal, Quebec H3A 1A1

TELEPHONE
(514) 842-1231

The Endocrinology Division is focusing on cell biological phenomena related to diabetes, and has identified a new class of compounds in the vanadate family that appears to have powerful hypoglycemia effects. This pioneering work has led to a number of patents.

The Ophthalmology Department is actively involved in a Collaborative Ocular Melanoma Study funded by the National Institutes of Health in the U.S., with the Vic designated as the center to study the DNA pattern of these tumors.

The Department of Obstetrics and Gynaecology has developed 3-D ultrasound methodology for the assessment of fetal weight and organ size, which promises to have important clinical applications in the assessment of intrauterine fetal development and is especially important for the assessment of fetal growth retardation.

The Molecular Oncology Group is studying various aspects of development and cancer at the molecular level. In addition, Dr. Vincent Giguere is continuing his pioneering work on the characterization of the many forms of the retinoic acid receptors.

Among the many forays into other fields, cardiology researchers are conducting extensive clinical trials on anti-arrhythmia agents, and nephrology researchers are continuing extensive experimental studies on the pathogenesis of cirrhosis and sodium retention in chronic liver disease.

ADMISSIONS POLICY

Patients must be admitted under the care of an attending physician with admitting privileges. Non-Canadians must pay, in advance, a daily rate of $1,962, which does not include physician fees and room rates. A private room ranges from $81.64 to $136.62 extra, and a semiprivate room ranges from $48.03 to $55.08 extra. Additional charges for ICU care were not available.

APPENDIXES

U.S. HOSPITALS COMMENDED BY

THE JCAHO

Over any three year period, the Joint Commission on Accreditation of Health-care Organizations (JCAHO) thoroughly evaluates over 5,300 hospitals. Fewer than 5 percent of them earn the commission's "Accreditation with Commendation" award. This recognition is given only if a hospital has achieved very high scores in 28 areas of patient care and administration, covering 700 standards. Everything is included, from medical staff qualifications, medication use, and infection control to plant safety and patients' rights.

Most of the hospitals that follow are not tertiary care centers, and so do not qualify for inclusion in this book; but we believe this list provides an excellent resource for anyone seeking good hospital care in every region of the country. We are grateful to the commission for granting us permission to reprint it. (For more information on the JCAHO, see the Introduction.)

Please note that we have included some nonhospital settings in this list, such as clinics and hospices, that have also received the commission's highest rating.

STATE	LOCATION	HOSPITAL
Alabama	Fort Rucker	Lyster US Army Community Hospital
Alaska	Anchorage	Alaska Regional Hospital
Arizona	Phoenix	Maricopa Medical Center
	Phoenix	Phoenix Memorial Hospital
	Tucson	El Dorado Hospital and Medical Center
California	Anaheim	Kaiser Foundation Hospital
	Atascadero	Atascadero State Hospital
	Bellflower	Kaiser Foundation Hospital
	Chico	Enloe Hospital
	Chula Vista	Scripps Memorial Hospital
	Davis	Sutter Davis Hospital
	Folsom	Vencor Hospital-Sacramento
	Fontana	CPC Rancho Lindo Hospital
	Fresno	Cedar Vista Hospital
	La Jolla	Green Hospital of Scripps
	Monterey	Community Hospital of the Monterey Peninsula
	Oakland	Naval Medical Center
	Panorama City	Kaiser Foundation Hospital
	Sacramento	Sutter Memorial Hospital
	San Diego	Kaiser Foundation Hospital
	San Francisco	Kaiser Foundation Hospital
	Santa Rosa	Kaiser Foundation Hospital
	Travis AFB	David Grant USAF Medical Center
	Vallejo	Kaiser Foundation Hospital
	Walnut Creek	Kaiser Foundation Hospital
	West Hills	West Hills Medical Center
	Whittier	Whittier Hospital Medical Center
	Woodland Hills	Kaiser Foundation Hospital
Colorado	Aurora	Rocky Mountain Rehabilitation Institute
	Englewood	Craig Hospital
	Grand Junction	St. Mary's Hospital and Medical Center
	Grand Junction	VA Medical Center
	Pueblo	Parkview Episcopal Medical Center
Connecticut	Branford	The Connecticut Hospice, Inc.
	Bridgeport	St. Vincent's Medical Center

STATE	LOCATION	HOSPITAL
Connecticut (cont'd)	New Britain	New Britain Memorial Hospital
	New Canaan	Silver Hill Hospital
Florida	Aventura	Aventura Hospital and Medical Center
	Boynton Beach	Bethesda Memorial Hospital
	Bradenton	HCA L.W. Blake Hospital
	Brandon	Brandon Hospital
	Dade City	Dade City Hospital
	Destin	Destin Hospital
	Fort Lauderdale	Vencor Hospital-Fort Lauderdale
	Fort Walton Beach	Fort Walton Beach Medical Center
	Hollywood	Memorial Hospital of Hollywood
	Hudson	HCA Bayonet Point-Hudson Medical Center
	Kissimmee	Osceola Regional Hospital
	Plantation	Plantation General Hospital
	Pompano Beach	Pompano Beach Medical Center
	St. Petersburg	St. Petersburg General Hospital
	Sarasota	Rehabilitation Institute of Sarasota
	Tamarac	Universty Pavilion Hospital
	Tampa	Shriners Hospitals for Crippled Children
	Tarpon Springs	Helen Ellis Memorial Hospital
Georgia	Atlanta	Charter Brook Hospital
	Atlanta	Crawford Long Hospital of Emory University
	Atlanta	Northlake Regional Medical Center
	Atlanta	Scottish Rite Children's Center
	Atlanta	West Paces Medical Center
	Augusta	Augusta Regional Medical Center
	Austell	Cobb Hospital, Inc.
	Cartersville	Cartersville Medical Center
	Dalton	Hamilton Medical Center
	Decatur	Georgia Regional Hospital at Savannah
	Dunwoody	Dunwoody Medical Center
	Fort Benning	Martin Army Community Hospital
	Macon	HCA Coliseum Medical Centers
	Newnan	Peachtree Regional Hospital
	Savannah	Candler Hospital, Inc.

STATE	LOCATION	HOSPITAL
Georgia (cont'd)	Savannah	Georgia Regional Hospital
	Savannah	St. Joseph's Hospital
Illinois	Arlington Heights	Northwest Community Hospital
	Elgin	Elgin Mental Health Center
	Evanston	Evanston Hospital
	Hazel Crest	South Suburban Hospital
	Lemont	The Rock Creek Center
	McHenry	Northern Illinois Medical Center
	Park Ridge	Lutheran General Hospital
	Wheaton	Marianjoy Rehabilitation Hospital and Clinics
Indiana	Evansville	Tri-State Regional Rehabilitation Hospital
	Fort Wayne	VA Medical Center
Iowa	Cedar Rapids	St. Luke's Methodist Hospital
	Davenport	Mercy Hospital
	Davenport	St. Luke's Hospital
	Iowa City	VA Medical Center
	Muscatine	Muscatine General Hospital
	Sioux City	Marian Health Center
Kansas	Overland Park	Overland Park Regional Medical Center
	Wichita	VA Medical Center
Kentucky	Covington	St. Elizabeth Medical Center
	Fort Knox	Ireland Army Community Hospital
	Lexington	Eastern State Hospital
	Lexington	Humana Hospital-Lexington
	Louisa	Three Rivers Medical Center
	Louisville	Southwest Hospital
	Louisville	Suburban Medical Center
	Louisville	University of Louisville Hospital
	Princeton	Caldwell County Hospital, Inc.
Louisiana	Alexandria	PHC of Louisiana
	Bogalusa	Washington-St. Tammany Regional Medical Center
	Houma	Bayou Oaks Hospital
	Marksville	Avoyelles Hospital
	New Orleans	Alton Ochsner Foundation Hospital
	New Orleans	Eye, Ear, and Throat Hospital

STATE	LOCATION	HOSPITAL
Louisiana (cont'd)	New Orleans	Tulane University Hospital
	Oakdale	Oakdale Community Hospital
	Ville Platte	Ville Platte Medical Center
Maine	Togus	VA Medical Center
Maryland	Baltimore	Church Hospital
	Bethesda	National Naval Medical Center
	Bethesda	Suburban Hospital, Inc.
	Bethesda	Warren Grant Magnuson Clinical Center
	Prince Frederick	Calvert Memorial Hospital
Massachusetts	Beverly	Beverly Hospital
	Boston	Massachusetts Eye and Ear Infirmary
	Boston	New England Baptist Hospital
	Boston	New England Deaconess Hospital
	Burlington	Mary and Arthur Clapham Hospital
	Cambridge	Massachusetts Institute of Technology Medical Department
	Holyoke	Holyoke Hospital, Inc.
	Palmer	Wing Memorial Hospital
	South Weymouth	South Shore Hospital, Inc.
	Woburn	New England Rehabilitation Hospital
	Worcester	AdCare Hospital of Worcester
Michigan	Grand Rapids	Pine Rest Christian Hospital
	Lansing	St. Lawrence Hospital and Health Care Services
	Sault Ste. Marie	Chippewa County War Memorial Hospital
Minnesota	Minneapolis	Shriners Hospitals for Crippled Children
	St. Paul	Gillette Children's Hospital
Mississippi	Keesler AFB	Keesler Medical Center
Missouri	Cape Girardeau	St. Francis Medical Center
	Lee's Summit	Lee's Summit Hospital
	Nevada	Heartland Hospital
	St. Louis	Bethesda General Hospital
	St. Louis	St. Louis University Hospital
	Warrensburg	Western Missouri Medical Center
Nebraska	Omaha	Childrens Memorial Hospital
	Omaha	VA Medical Center
New Jersey	Chester	Welkind Rehabilitation Hospital

The Best Hospitals in America

STATE	LOCATION	HOSPITAL
New Jersey (cont'd)	Denville	St. Clares-Riverside Medical Center
	Lawrenceville	St. Lawrence Rehabilitation Center
	Mountainside	Children's Specialized Hospital
	New Brunswick	St. Peter's Medical Center
	Wayne	Wayne General Hospital
New Mexico	Crownpoint	Crownpoint Healthcare Facility
	Zuni	Zuni Comprehensive Community Health Care
New York	Bronx	Calvary Hospital, Inc.
	Bronx	VA Medical Center
	Canandaigua	VA Medical Center
	Long Beach	Long Beach Memorial Hospital
	Roslyn	St. Francis Hospital
	West Point	Keller Army Community Hospital
North Carolina	Greensboro	Charter Hospital of Greensboro
	Roanoke Rapids	Halifax Memorial Hospital
	Winston-Salem	North Carolina Baptist Hospital
North Dakota	Minot	Trinity Hospital
Ohio	Cincinnati	Bethesda Hospital, Inc.
	Cincinnati	Deaconess Hospital
	Cincinnati	Jewish Hospital of Cincinnati
	Columbus	Central Ohio Psychiatric Hospital
	Dayton	Children's Medical Center
	Dayton	Miami Valley Hospital
	Mayfield Heights	Meridia Hillcrest Hospital
	Middletown	Middletown Regional Hospital
	Norwalk	Fisher-Titus Medical Center
	Oregon	St. Charles Hospital
	Troy	Stouder Memorial Hospital
	Westerville	St. Ann's Hospital of Columbus
	Worthington	Harding Hospital
	Zanesville	Bethesda Hospital
Oklahoma	Claremore	PHS Comprehensive Indian Health Facility
	Enid	St. Mary's Hospital
	Oklahoma City	Presbyterian Hospital
	Oklahoma City	Southwest Medical Center of Oklahoma
	Sapulpa	Bartlett Memorial Medical Center

STATE	LOCATION	HOSPITAL
Oregon	Portland	Bess Kaiser Medical Center
Pennsylvania	Abington	Abington Memorial Hospital
	Bethlehem	Muhlenberg Hospital Center
	Bloomsburg	Bloomsburg Hospital
	Center Hall	Meadows Psychiatric Center
	Chambersburg	Chambersburg Hospital
	Danville	Danville State Hospital
	Erie	Lake Erie Institute of Rehabilitation
	Erie	Shriners Hospitals for Crippled Children
	Latrobe	Latrobe Area Hospital
	Malvern	Bryn Mawr Rehabilitation Hospital
	McKees Rocks	Ohio Valley General Hospital
	Monroeville	Greater Pittsburgh Rehabilitation Hospital
	Mount Gretna	Philhaven Hospital
	Philadelphia	Chestnut Hill Hospital
	Philadelphia	Fox Chase Cancer Center
	Philadelphia	Germantown Hospital and Medical Center
	Philadelphia	Magee Rehabilitation Hospital
	Philadelphia	Naval Medical Clinic
	Pittsburgh	Jefferson Health Services
	Scranton	Moses Taylor Hospital
	Wilkes-Barre	First Hospital Wyoming Valley
	Wilkes-Barre	Geisinger Wyoming Valley Medical Center
	Wilkes-Barre	Wilkes-Barre General Hospital
Puerto Rico	Bayamon	Hospital San Pablo, Inc.
Rhode Island	Newport	Newport Hospital
	Providence	VA Medical Center
	Wakefield	South County Hospital, Inc.
South Carolina	Anderson	Anderson Area Medical Center
	Charleston	Trident Regional Medical Center
	Columbia	HealthSouth Rehabilitation Hospital
	Columbia	Providence Hospital
	Greenville	Shriners Hospitals for Crippled Children
	West Columbia	Lexington Medical Center West
South Dakota	Ellsworth AFB	28th Medical Group/SGAM
	Forte Meade	VA Medical Center
Tennessee	Chattanooga	East Ridge Hospital

STATE	LOCATION	HOSPITAL
Tennessee (cont'd)	Kingsport	Indian Path Medical Center
	Kingsport	Indian Path Pavillion
	Millington	Naval Hospital
	Morristown	Lakeway Regional Hospital
Texas	Alvin	Alvin Community Hospital, Inc.
	Beaumont	Beaumont Regional Medical Center
	College Station	Brazos Valley Medical Center
	College Station	HCA Greenleaf Hospital
	Corpus Christi	Doctors Regional Medical Center
	Corsicana	Navarro Regional Hospital
	Dallas	Dallas Rehabilitation Institute
	Dallas	Medical Arts Hospital
	Dallas	Medical City Dallas Hospital
	El Paso	Columbia Medical Center-East
	El Paso	R. E. Thomason General Hospital
	El Paso	Rio Vista Rehabilitation Hospital
	El Paso	Sierra Medical Center
	El Paso	William Beaumont Army Medical Center
	Harlingen	South Texas Hospital
	Harlingen	Valley Baptist Medical Center
	Houston	Diagnostic Center Hospital
	Houston	HCA West Houston Medical Center
	Houston	Texas Children's Hospital
	Houston	University of Texas M.D. Anderson Cancer Center
	Houston	Vencor Hospital-Houston
	Nacogdoches	Pinelands Hospital
	North Richland Hills	Richland Hospital
	Rusk	Rusk State Hospital
	San Antonio	San Antonio Regional Hospital
	San Antonio	Wilford Hall USAF Medical Center
	San Antonio	Women's and Children's Hospital
	Stafford	Fountain Brook Behavioral Health Center
	Texas City	Danforth Hospital
	Waco	Hillcrest Baptist Medical Center

STATE	LOCATION	HOSPITAL
Texas (cont'd)	Wichita Falls	Wichita Falls State Hospital
	Wylie	Physicians Regional Hospital
Utah	Layton	Davis Hospital and Medical Center
	Salt Lake City	Wasatch Canyons Hospital
	Woods Cross	Benchmark Regional Hospital
Virginia	Portsmouth	Maryview Medical Center
	Reston	HCA Reston Hospital Center
	Richlands	Clinch Valley Medical Center
	Richmond	Chippenham Medical Center
	Richmond	HealthSouth Medical Center
	Richmond	Johnston-Willis Hospital
	Richmond	Sheltering Arms Rehabilitation Hospital
	Rocky Mount	Franklin Memorial Hospital
	Salem	Lewis-Gale Hospital, Inc.
	Salem	Lewis-Gale Psychiatric Center
	Virginia Beach	Virginia Beach General Hospital
	Williamsburg	Williamsburg Community Hospital
	Woodbridge	Potomac Hospital
Washington	Kirkland	CPC Fairfax Hospital
	Pasco	Our Lady of Lourdes Health Center
	Seattle	University of Washington Medical Center
Wisconsin	Brookfield	Elmbrook Memorial Hospital
	Kenosha	Kenosha Hospital and Medical Center
	Portage	Divine Savior Hospital and Nursing Home
West Virginia	Bluefield	St. Luke's Hospital

U.S. NEWS & WORLD REPORT

SURVEY OF BEST HOSPITALS, 1994

Because many of our readers will be searching for care in specific medical areas, we have included the results of the only significant survey that asked a large number of doctors to name the best hospitals in their own particular specialties. We believe that the raw results of this survey accurately reflect the medical community's collective opinion about where one can find top quality care in specific fields.

According to the magazine, "the fifth annual U.S. News ranking of America's best hospitals draws on a groundbreaking mathematical model that combines three years' worth of U.S. News reputational surveys, federal death-rate statistics and nine categories of hard data. The model was developed by senior analysts Craig Hill and Barbara Rudolph of the National Opinion Research Center (NORC), a social-science research group at the University of Chicago.

"The reputational results are based on a mail survey of a geographic cross section of 150 board-certified specialists in the 16 specialties ranked, or 2,400 doctors. The physicians were asked to name the top five hospitals in their specialty without considering location or expense. Each hospital was then matched against a master list, assembled by NORC, of the nation's major academic hospitals and specialized medical centers.

"Qualifying hospitals must be affiliated with a medical school, be a member of the Council of Teaching Hospitals, have a ratio of interns and residents to beds of .25 or more, or score 9 or higher on a technology index that represents one of the nine objective indicators of quality.

"In 12 of the 16 specialties, reputation counted for one third of the total score. The death rate, based on pooled 1988-91 data from the federal Health Care Financing Administration, counted for another third. The final third came from a specialty-specific combination of the nine quality indicators, which range from the ratio of registered nurses to beds to the number of geriatric services.

"In the four remaining specialties, rankings are based solely on reputation; death rates and other indicators of quality are inapplicable, unavailable or unreliable."

AIDS

RANK	HOSPITAL	LOCATION
1.	San Francisco General Hospital Medical Center	San Francisco, CA
2.	Johns Hopkins Hospital	Baltimore, MD
3.	Massachusetts General Hospital	Boston, MA
4.	University of California San Francisco Medical Center	San Francisco, CA
5.	Memorial Sloan-Kettering Cancer Center	New York, NY
6.	UCLA Medical Center	Los Angeles, CA
7.	New York University Medical Center	New York, NY
8.	University of Miami Hospital and Clinics	Miami, FL
9.	New York Hospital-Cornell Medical Center	New York, NY
10.	Mayo Clinic	Rochester, MN
11.	Columbia-Presbyterian Medical Center	New York, NY
12.	University of Washington Medical Center	Seattle, WA
13.	Deaconess Hospital	Boston, MA
14.	Mount Sinai Hospital Center	New York, NY
15.	Beth Israel Hospital	Boston, MA
16.	Duke University Medical Center	Durham, NC
17.	Barnes Hospital	St. Louis, MO
18.	Rush-Presbyterian-St. Luke's Medical Center	Chicago, IL
19.	Stanford University Medical Center	Stanford, CA
20.	Indiana University Medical Center	Indianapolis, IN
21.	University of Illinois Hospital and Clinics	Chicago, IL
22.	Northwestern Memorial Hospital	Chicago, IL
23.	Georgetown University Medical Center	Washington, DC
24.	Roswell Park Cancer Institute	Buffalo, NY
25.	Thomas Jefferson University Hospital	Philadelphia, PA
26.	UCSD Medical Center	San Diego, CA
27.	Cleveland Clinic	Cleveland, OH
28.	Montefiore Medical Center	New York, NY
29.	University of Wisconsin Hospital and Clinics	Madison, WI
30.	Ohio State University Medical Center	Columbus, OH
31.	New England Medical Center	Boston, MA
32.	Cook County Hospital	Chicago, IL
33.	Brigham and Women's Hospital	Boston, MA
34.	Cedars-Sinai Medical Center	Los Angeles, CA
35.	Mount Sinai Medical Center	Cleveland, OH
36.	George Washington University Medical Center	Washington, DC
37.	Long Island Jewish Medical Center	New Hyde Park, NY
38.	Presbyterian University Hospital	Pittsburgh, PA
39.	Hospital of the University of Pennsylvania	Philadelphia, PA
40.	Green Hospital of Scripps Clinic	La Jolla, CA

CANCER

RANK HOSPITAL   **LOCATION**

Rank	Hospital	Location
1.	Memorial Sloan-Kettering Cancer Center	New York, NY
2.	University of Texas M.D. Anderson Cancer Center	Houston, TX
3.	Dana-Farber Cancer Institute	Boston, MA
4.	Mayo Clinic	Rochester, MN
5.	Roswell Park Cancer Institute	Buffalo, NY
6.	Fred Hutchinson Cancer Research Center	Seattle, WA
7.	Johns Hopkins Hospital	Baltimore, MD
8.	University of Washington Medical Center	Seattle, WA
9.	Stanford University Medical Center	Stanford, CA
10.	Duke University Medical Center	Durham, NC
11.	Indiana University Medical Center	Indianapolis, IN
12.	Massachusetts General Hospital	Boston, MA
13.	University of California San Francisco Medical Center	San Francisco, CA
14.	University of Wisconsin Hospital and Clinics	Madison, WI
15.	New York University Medical Center	New York, NY
16.	UCLA Medical Center	Los Angeles, CA
17.	Cleveland Clinic	Cleveland, OH
18.	Thomas Jefferson University Hospital	Philadelphia, PA
19.	University of Illinois Hospital and Clinics	Chicago, IL
20.	Deaconess Hospital	Boston, MA
21.	Green Hospital of Scripps Clinic	La Jolla, CA
22.	Lahey Clinic	Burlington, MA
23.	Brigham and Women's Hospital	Boston, MA
24.	Virginia Mason Medical Center	Seattle, WA
25.	Mount Sinai Medical Center	Cleveland, OH
26.	Beth Israel Hospital	Boston, MA
27.	New England Baptist Hospital	Boston, MA
28.	Lenox Hill Hospital	New York, NY
29.	Kaiser Foundation Hospital	Los Angeles, CA
30.	New England Medical Center	Boston, MA
31.	Hospital of the University of Pennsylvania	Philadelphia, PA
32.	University of Chicago Hospitals	Chicago, IL
33.	Barnes Hospital	St. Louis, MO
34.	Presbyterian University Hospital	Pittsburgh, PA
35.	University of Minnesota Hospital and Clinic	Minneapolis, MN
36.	Georgetown University Medical Center	Washington, DC
37.	New York Hospital-Cornell Medical Center	New York, NY
38.	Boston University Medical Center Hospital	Boston, MA
39.	University Medical Center	Tucson, AZ
40.	Rush-Presbyterian-St. Luke's Medical Center	Chicago, IL

CARDIOLOGY

RANK HOSPITAL   **LOCATION**

1.	Mayo Clinic	Rochester, MN
2.	Cleveland Clinic	Cleveland, OH
3.	Massachusetts General Hospital	Boston, MA
4.	Stanford University Medical Center	Stanford, CA
5.	Duke University Medical Center	Durham, NC
6.	Brigham and Women's Hospital	Boston, MA
7.	Emory University Hospital	Atlanta, GA
8.	Johns Hopkins Hospital	Baltimore, MD
9.	University of California San Francisco Medical Center	San Francisco, CA
10.	Texas Heart Institute (St. Luke's Episcopal Hospital)	Houston, TX
11.	New York University Medical Center	New York, NY
12.	Barnes Hospital	St. Louis, MO
13.	Indiana University Medical Center	Indianapolis, IN
14.	Columbia-Presbyterian Medical Center	New York, NY
15.	Cedars-Sinai Medical Center	Los Angeles, CA
16.	Beth Israel Hospital	Boston, MA
17.	New York Hospital-Cornell Medical Center	New York, NY
18.	UCLA Medical Center	Los Angeles, CA
19.	University of Illinois Hospital and Clinics	Chicago, IL
20.	Thomas Jefferson University Hospital	Philadelphia, PA
21.	Deaconess Hospital	Boston, MA
22.	Green Hospital of Scripps Clinic	La Jolla, CA
23.	University of Washington Medical Center	Seattle, WA
24.	University of Wisconsin Hospital and Clinics	Madison, WI
25.	Mount Sinai Medical Center	Cleveland, OH
26.	University of Minnesota Hospital and Clinic	Minneapolis, MN
27.	Presbyterian University Hospital	Pittsburgh, PA
28.	Lahey Clinic	Burlington, MA
29.	Rush-Presbyterian-St. Luke's Medical Center	Chicago, IL
30.	Mount Sinai Medical Center	New York, NY
31.	University of Alabama Hospital at Birmingham	Birmingham, AL
32.	Methodist Hospital	Houston, TX
33.	Ohio State University Medical Center	Columbus, OH
34.	Georgetown University Medical Center	Washington, DC
35.	New England Medical Center	Boston, MA
36.	University of Michigan Medical Center	Ann Arbor, MI
37.	Foster G. McGaw Hospital at Loyola Medical Center	Maywood, IL
38.	New England Baptist Hospital	Boston, MA
39.	George Washington University Medical Center	Washington, DC
40.	Long Island Jewish Medical Center	New Hyde Park, NY

ENDOCRINOLOGY

RANK HOSPITAL   **LOCATION**

1.	Mayo Clinic.	Rochester, MN
2.	Massachusetts General Hospital	Boston, MA
3.	University of California San Francisco Medical Center	San Francisco, CA
4.	UCLA Medical Center.	Los Angeles, CA
5.	University of Washington Medical Center	Seattle, WA
6.	Barnes Hospital	St. Louis, MO
7.	Johns Hopkins Hospital	Baltimore, MD
8.	University of Chicago Hospitals.	Chicago, IL
9.	Deaconess Hospital	Boston, MA
10.	University of Michigan Medical Center	Ann Arbor, MI
11.	Brigham and Women's Hospital.	Boston, MA
12.	Clinical Center, National Institutes of Health	Bethesda, MD
13.	Beth Israel Hospital.	Boston, MA
14.	New York University Medical Center	New York, NY
15.	University of Minnesota Hospital and Clinic.	Minneapolis, MN
16.	Columbia-Presbyterian Medical Center.	New York, NY
17.	University of Illinois Hospital and Clinics	Chicago, IL
18.	Cleveland Clinic.	Cleveland, OH
19.	Vanderbilt University Medical Center	Nashville, TN
20.	Thomas Jefferson University Hospital.	Philadelphia, PA
21.	Duke University Medical Center	Durham, NC
22.	Indiana University Medical Center	Indianapolis, IN
23.	Presbyterian University Hospital	Pittsburgh, PA
24.	University of Wisconsin Hospital and Clinics	Madison, WI
25.	Stanford University Medical Center.	Stanford, CA
26.	Ohio State University Medical Center.	Columbus, OH
27.	Mount Sinai Medical Center	Cleveland, OH
28.	New York Hospital-Cornell Medical Center.	New York, NY
29.	University of Virginia Health Sciences Center	Charlottesville, VA
30.	George Washington University Medical Center.	Washington, DC
31.	Green Hospital of Scripps Clinic	La Jolla, CA
32.	Georgetown University Medical Center	Washington, DC
33.	Mount Sinai Medical Center	New York, NY
34.	University of Texas M.D. Anderson Cancer Center	Houston, TX
35.	Lahey Clinic	Burlington, MA
36.	New England Medical Center.	Boston, MA
37.	Rush-Presbyterian-St. Luke's Medical Center	Chicago, IL
38.	UCSD Medical Center.	San Diego, CA
39.	Long Island Jewish Medical Center	New Hyde Park, NY
40.	Hospital of the University of Pennsylvania	Philadephia, PA

GASTROENTEROLOGY

RANK HOSPITAL   **LOCATION**

1.	Mayo Clinic	Rochester, MN
2.	Johns Hopkins Hospital	Baltimore, MD
3.	Massachusetts General Hospital	Boston, MA
4.	Cleveland Clinic	Cleveland, OH
5.	UCLA Medical Center	Los Angeles, CA
6.	Duke University Medical Center	Durham, NC
7.	University of California San Francisco Medical Center	San Francisco, CA
8.	Mount Sinai Medical Center	New York, NY
9.	Brigham and Women's Hospital	Boston, MA
10.	University of Chicago Hospitals	Chicago, IL
11.	Beth Israel Hospital	Boston, MA
12.	Presbyterian University Hospital	Pittsburgh, PA
13.	Indiana University Medical Center	Indianapolis, IN
14.	Memorial Sloan-Kettering Cancer Center	New York, NY
15.	New York University Medical Center	New York, NY
16.	Lahey Clinic	Burlington, MA
17.	Hospital of the University of Pennsylvania	Philadelphia, PA
18.	Mount Sinai Medical Center	Cleveland, OH
19.	Thomas Jefferson University Hospital	Philadelphia, PA
20.	University of Wisconsin Hospital and Clinics	Madison, WI
21.	Deaconess Hospital	Boston, MA
22.	New York Hospital-Cornell Medical Center	New York, NY
23.	Barnes Hospital	St. Louis, MO
24.	Rush-Presbyterian-St. Luke's Medical Center	Chicago, IL
25.	Georgetown University Medical Center	Washington, DC
26.	New England Medical Center	Boston, MA
27.	University of Minnesota Hospital and Clinic	Minneapolis, MN
28.	Yale-New Haven Hospital	New Haven, CT
29.	University of Michigan Medical Center	Ann Arbor, MI
30.	Green Hospital of Scripps Center	La Jolla, CA
31.	Lenox Hill Hospital	New York, NY
32.	Boston University Medical Center Hospital	Boston, MA
33.	Montefiore Medical Center	New York, NY
34.	Long Island Jewish Medical Center	New Hyde Park, NY
35.	University of Virginia Health Sciences Center	Charlottesville, VA
36.	Virginia Mason Medical Center	Seattle, WA
37.	Columbia-Presbyterian Medical Center	New York, NY
38.	George Washington University Medical Center	Washington, DC
39.	New England Baptist Hospital	Boston, MA
40.	University of Texas M.D. Anderson Cancer Center	Houston, TX

GERIATRICS

RANK HOSPITAL   LOCATION

1.	UCLA Medical Center	Los Angeles, CA
2.	Mount Sinai Medical Center	New York, NY
3.	Duke University Medical Center	Durham, NC
4.	Beth Israel Hospital	Boston, MA
5.	Johns Hopkins Hospital	Baltimore, MD
6.	Massachusetts General Hospital	Boston, MA
7.	University of Michigan Medical Center	Ann Arbor, MI
8.	University of Washington Medical Center	Seattle, WA
9.	Mayo Clinic	Rochester, MN
10.	New York University Medical Center	New York, NY
11.	Cleveland Clinic	Cleveland, OH
12.	Brigham and Women's Hospital	Boston, MA
13.	University of Wisconsin Hospital and Clinic	Madison, WI
14.	University of California San Francisco Medical Center	San Francisco, CA
15.	University of Chicago Hospitals	Chicago, IL
16.	New York Hospital-Cornell Medical Center	New York, NY
17.	Barnes Hospital	St. Louis, MO
18.	University of Minnesota Hospital and Clinic	Minneapolis, MN
19.	Rush-Presbyterian-St. Luke's Medical Center	Chicago, IL
20.	Mount Sinai Medical Center	Cleveland, OH
21.	Montefiore Medical Center	New York, NY
22.	Thomas Jefferson University Hospital	Philadelphia, PA
23.	Long Island Jewish Medical Center	New Hyde Park, NY
24.	Deaconess Hospital	Boston, MA
25.	University of Illinois Hospital and Clinics	Chicago, IL
26.	Yale-New Haven Hospital	New Haven, CT
27.	Stanford University Medical Center	Stanford, CA
28.	Indiana University Medical Center	Indianapolis, IN
29.	Hospital of the University of Pennsylvania	Philadelphia, PA
30.	Georgetown University Medical Center	Washington, DC
31.	Boston University Medical Center Hospital	Boston, MA
32.	UCSD Medical Center	San Diego, CA
33.	Columbia-Presbyterian Medical Center	New York, NY
34.	New England Medical Center	Boston, MA
35.	University of Miami Hospital and Clinics	Miami, FL
36.	University Hospitals of Cleveland	Cleveland, OH
37.	North Carolina Baptist Hospital	Wiston-Salem, NC
38.	George Washington University Medical Center	Washington, DC
39.	Ohio State University Medical Center	Columbus, OH
40.	Presbyterian University Hospital	Pittsburgh, PA

GYNECOLOGY

RANK HOSPITAL   LOCATION

1. Johns Hopkins Hospital .... Baltimore, MD
2. Mayo Clinic.. Rochester, MN
3. University of Texas M.D. Anderson Cancer Center................ Houston, TX
4. Brigham and Women's Hospital............................... Boston, MA
5. Massachusetts General Hospital .... Boston, MA
6. Duke University Medical Center.............................. Durham, NC
7. Memorial Sloan-Kettering Cancer Center .... New York, NY
8. Los Angeles County-USC Medical Center..................... Los Angeles, CA
9. University of Chicago Hospitals .... Chicago, IL
10. UCLA Medical Center .... Los Angeles, CA
11. Cleveland Clinic.. Cleveland, OH
12. University of California San Francisco Medical Center .... San Francisco, CA
13. Stanford University Medical Center........................... Stanford, CA
14. Yale-New Haven Hospital .... New Haven, CT
15. Northwestern Memorial Hospital.............................. Chicago, IL
16. University of North Carolina Hospitals....................... Chapel Hill, NC
17. New York Hospital-Cornell Medical Center .... New York, NY
18. Beth Israel Hospital .... Boston, MA
19. Roswell Park Cancer Institute .... Buffalo, NY
20. University of Virginia Health Sciences Center .... Charlottesville, VA
21. Hospital of the University of Pennsylvania .... Philadelphia, PA
22. University of Washington Medical Center .... Seattle, WA
23. Cedars-Sinai Medical Center .... Los Angeles, CA
24. Parkland Memorial Hospital .... Dallas, TX
25. Foster G. McGaw Hospital at Loyola Medical Center .... Maywood, IL
26. UCSD Medical Center....................................... San Diego, CA
27. Columbia-Presbyterian Medical Center........................ New York, NY
28. University of California, Davis Medical Center................. Sacramento, CA
29. Emory University Hospital .... Atlanta, GA
30. Barnes Hospital .... St. Louis, MO
31. University of Utah Hospital................................. Salt Lake City, UT
32. Vanderbilt University Medical Center .... Nashville, TN
33. University Hospital .... Portland, OR
34. Rush-Presbyterian-St. Luke's Medical Center................... Chicago, IL
35. Thomas Jefferson University Hospital .... Philadelphia, PA
36. Georgetown University Medical Center .... Washington, DC
37. Penn State University's Milton S. Hershey Medical Center.......... Hershey, PA
38. Presbyterian University Hospital .... Pittsburgh, PA
39. Medical College of Virginia Hospitals .... Richmond, VA
40. Scott and White Memorial Hospital........................... Temple, TX

NEUROLOGY

RANK HOSPITAL   LOCATION

1.   Mayo Clinic. . . . . Rochester, MN
2.   Massachusetts General Hospital. . . . . Boston, MA
3.   Johns Hopkins Hospital . . . . Baltimore, MD
4.   Columbia-Presbyterian Medical Center. . . . . New York, NY
5.   University of California San Francisco Medical Center . . . . San Francisco, CA
6.   New York Hospital-Cornell Medical Center. . . . . New York, NY
7.   Cleveland Clinic. . . . . Cleveland, OH
8.   Barnes Hospital . . . . St. Louis, MO
9.   Hospital of the University of Pennsylvania . . . . Philadelphia, PA
10. UCLA Medical Center. . . . . Los Angeles, CA
11. New York University Medical Center . . . . New York, NY
12. Duke University Medical Center . . . . Durham, NC
13. University of Illinois Hospital and Clinics . . . . Chicago, IL
14. Thomas Jefferson University Hospital. . . . . Philadelphia, PA
15. Beth Israel Hospital. . . . . Boston, MA
16. Brigham and Women's Hospital. . . . . Boston, MA
17. University of Washington Medical Center . . . . Seattle, WA
18. University of Wisconsin Hospital and Clinics . . . . Madison, WI
19. Indiana University Medical Center . . . . Indianapolis, IN
20. New England Medical Center. . . . . Boston, MA
21. Deaconess Hospital . . . . Boston, MA
22. Memorial Sloan-Kettering Cancer Center . . . . New York, NY
23. Rush-Presbyterian-St. Luke's Medical Center . . . . Chicago, IL
24. University of Michigan Medical Center . . . . Ann Arbor, MI
25. Georgetown University Medical Center . . . . Washington, DC
26. Green Hospital of Scripps Clinic . . . . La Jolla, CA
27. Presbyterian University Hospital . . . . Pittsburgh, PA
28. Lahey Clinic . . . . Burlington, MA
29. University of Minnesota Hospital and Clinic. . . . . Minneapolis, MN
30. George Washington University Medical Center. . . . . Washington, DC
31. University of Iowa Hospitals and Clinics. . . . . Iowa City, IA
32. Mount Sinai Medical Center . . . . Cleveland, OH
33. Cook County Hospital . . . . Chicago, IL
34. University of Chicago Hospitals. . . . . Chicago, IL
35. New England Baptist Hospital . . . . Boston, MA
36. Long Island Jewish Medical Center . . . . New Hyde Park, NY
37. Mount Sinai Medical Center . . . . New York, NY
38. University of Virginia Health Sciences Center . . . . Charlottesville, VA
39. Lenox Hill Hospital. . . . . New York, NY
40. Boston University Medical Center Hospital. . . . . Boston, MA

The Best Hospitals in America   **537**

OPHTHALMOLOGY

RANK HOSPITAL   **LOCATION**

1.	University of Miami (Bascom Palmer Eye Institute)	Miami, FL
2.	Johns Hopkins Hospital (Wilmer Eye Institute)	Baltimore, MD
3.	Wills Eye Hospital	Philadephia, PA
4.	Massachusetts Eye and Ear Infirmary	Boston, MA
5.	UCLA Medical Center (Jules Stein Eye Institute)	Los Angeles, CA
6.	University of Iowa Hospitals and Clinics	Iowa City, IA
7.	Doheny Eye Hospital	Los Angeles, CA
8.	Barnes Hospital	St. Louis, MO
9.	Duke University Medical Center	Durham; NC
10.	University of California San Francisco Medical Center	San Francisco, CA
11.	Mayo Clinic	Rochester, MN
12.	Manhattan Eye, Ear and Throat Hospital	New York, NY
13.	New York Eye and Ear Infirmary	New York, NY
14.	Emory University Hospital	Atlanta, GA
15.	University of Michigan Medical Center	Ann Arbor, MI

ORTHOPEDICS

RANK HOSPITAL   LOCATION

1.	Hospital for Special Surgery	New York, NY
2.	Mayo Clinic	Rochester, MN
3.	Massachusetts General Hospital	Boston, MA
4.	Johns Hopkins Hospital	Baltimore, MD
5.	Duke University Medical Center	Durham, NC
6.	University of Washington Medical Center	Seattle, WA
7.	Cleveland Clinic	Cleveland, OH
8.	UCLA Medical Center	Los Angeles, CA
9.	Hospital for Joint Diseases Orthopedic Institute	New York, NY
10.	University of Iowa Hospitals and Clinics	Iowa City, IA
11.	University of Tennessee Medical Center	Memphis, TN
12.	Brigham and Women's Hospital	Boston, MA
13.	Presbyterian University Hospital	Pittsburgh, PA
14.	Hospital of the University of Pennsylvania	Philadelphia, PA
15.	James Lawrence Kernan Hospital	Baltimore, MD
16.	University of Michigan Medical Center	Ann Arbor, MI
17.	New York University Medical Center	New York, NY
18.	Thomas Jefferson University Hospital	Philadelphia, PA
19.	Beth Israel Hospital	Boston, MA
20.	Columbia-Presbyterian Medical Center	New York, NY
21.	University of Illinois Hospital and Clinics	Chicago, IL
22.	University of Miami Hospital and Clinics	Miami, FL
23.	Rush-Presbyterian-St. Luke's Medical Center	Chicago, IL
24.	Georgetown University Medical Center	Washington, DC
25.	New England Baptist Hospital	Boston, MA
26.	Indiana University Medical Center	Indianapolis, IN
27.	Vanderbilt University Medical Center	Nashville, TN
28.	University of Wisconsin Hospital and Clinics	Madison, WI
29.	Stanford University Medical Center	Stanford, CA
30.	Ohio State University Medical Center	Columbus, OH
31.	Deaconess Hospital	Boston, MA
32.	Harborview Medical Center	Seattle, WA
33.	University of Texas M.D. Anderson Cancer Center	Houston, TX
34.	Emory University Hospital	Atlanta, GA
35.	Memorial Sloan-Kettering Cancer Center	New York, NY
36.	Hughston Sports Medicine Hospital	Columbus, GA
37.	University of California San Francisco Medical Center	San Francisco, CA
38.	Cook County Hospital	Chicago, IL
39.	University of Minnesota Hospital and Clinic	Minneapolis, MN
40.	Barnes Hospital	St. Louis, MO

The Best Hospitals in America

OTOLARYNGOLOGY

RANK HOSPITAL   **LOCATION**

Rank	Hospital	Location
1.	Massachusetts Eye and Ear Infirmary	Boston, MA
2.	Johns Hopkins Hospital	Baltimore, MD
3.	New York Eye and Ear Infirmary	New York, NY
4.	University of Iowa Hospitals and Clinics	Iowa City, IA
5.	Manhattan Eye, Ear and Throat Hospital	New York, NY
6.	Mayo Clinic	Rochester, MN
7.	UCLA Medical Center	Los Angeles, CA
8.	University of Michigan Medical Center	Ann Arbor, MI
9.	Barnes Hospital	St. Louis, MO
10.	University of Texas M.D. Anderson Cancer Center	Houston, TX
11.	Presbyterian University Hospital	Pittsburgh, PA
12.	Cleveland Clinic	Cleveland, OH
13.	Stanford University Medical Center	Stanford, CA
14.	New York University Medical Center	New York, NY
15.	Mount Sinai Medical Center	New York, NY
16.	University of Virginia Health Sciences Center	Charlottesville, VA
17.	University of Washington Medical Center	Seattle, WA
18.	University of Illinois Hospital and Clinics	Chicago, IL
19.	University of California San Francisco Medical Center	San Francisco, CA
20.	University of Minnesota Hospital and Clinic	Minneapolis, MN
21.	Vanderbilt University Medical Center	Nashville, TN
22.	Memorial Sloan-Kettering Cancer Center	New York, NY
23.	Indiana University Medical Center	Indianapolis, IN
24.	Beth Israel Hospital	Boston, MA
25.	Thomas Jefferson University Hospital	Philadelphia, PA
26.	Northwestern Memorial Hospital	Chicago, IL
27.	Hospital of the University of Pennsylvania	Philadelphia, PA
28.	University of Miami Hospital and Clinics	Miami, FL
29.	Deaconess Hospital	Boston, MA
30.	New England Medical Center	Boston, MA
31.	University of Wisconsin Hospital and Clinics	Madison, WI
32.	University of North Carolina Hospitals	Chapel Hill, NC
33.	Lahey Clinic	Burlington, MA
34.	Ohio State University Medical Center	Columbus, OH
35.	University Hospital	Portland, OR
36.	University Hospitals of Cleveland	Cleveland, OH
37.	Brigham and Women's Hospital	Boston, MA
38.	George Washington University Medical Center	Washington, DC
39.	Mount Sinai Medical Center	Cleveland, OH
40.	New York Hospital-Cornell Medical Center	New York, NY

PEDIATRICS

RANK HOSPITAL   **LOCATION**

1.	Children's Hospital	Boston, MA
2.	Children's Hospital of Philadelphia	Philadelphia, PA
3.	John's Hopkins Hospital	Baltimore, MD
4.	University Hospitals of Cleveland (Rainbow Babies and Childrens Hospital)	Cleveland, OH
5.	Children's Hospital Los Angeles	Los Angeles, CA
6.	Children's Hospital of Pittsburgh	Pittsburgh, PA
7.	Children's National Medical Center	Washington, DC
8.	Children's Hospital Medical Center	Cincinnati, OH
9.	Children's Hospital	Denver, CO
10.	Children's Memorial Hospital	Chicago, IL
11.	Stanford University Medical Center	Stanford, CA
12.	Columbia-Presbyterian Medical Center	New York, NY
13.	Children's Hospital and Medical Center	Seattle, WA
14.	Miami Children's Hospital	Miami, FL
15.	Texas Children's Hospital	Houston, TX
16.	University of California San Francisco Medical Center	San Francisco, CA
17.	St. Jude Children's Research Hospital	Memphis, TN
18.	St. Louis Children's Hospital	St. Louis, MO
19.	UCLA Medical Center	Los Angeles, CA

PSYCHIATRY

RANK HOSPITAL   **LOCATION**

1. McLean Hospital .... Belmont, MA
2. Menninger Clinic .... Topeka, KS
3. Johns Hopkins Hospital .... Baltimore, MD
4. New York Hospital-Cornell Medical Center .... New York, NY
5. UCLA Medical Center....................................... Los Angeles, CA
6. Sheppard and Enoch Pratt Hospital........................... Baltimore, MD
7. Massachusetts General Hospital .... Boston, MA
8. Institute of Living.. Hartford, CT
9. Columbia-Presbyterian Medical Center........................ New York, NY
10. Mayo Clinic... Rochester, MN
11. Yale-New Haven Hospital .... New Haven, CT
12. Duke University Medical Center.............................. Durham, NC
13. Chestnut Lodge Hospital .... Rockville, MD
14. Timberlawn Mental Health System .... Dallas, TX

REHABILITATION

RANK HOSPITAL   **LOCATION**

1.   Rehabilitation Institute of Chicago............................... Chicago, IL
2.   University of Washington Medical Center .... Seattle, WA
3.   Craig Hospital .... Englewood, CO
4.   The Institute for Rehabilitation and Research .... Houston, TX
5.   New York University Medical Center
     (Rusk Institute for Rehabilitation Medicine) .... New York, NY
6.   Mayo Clinic.. Rochester, MN
7.   Los Angeles County-Rancho Los Amigos Medical Center ...... Los Angeles, CA
8.   Ohio State University Medical Center........................ Columbus, OH
9.   Thomas Jefferson University Hospital...................... Philadelphia, PA
10. Baylor University Medical Center .... Dallas, TX
11. Kessler Institute for Rehabilitation......................... West Orange, NJ
12. University of Michigan Medical Center .... Ann Arbor, MI
13. Moss Rehab Hospital .... Philadelphia, PA

RHEUMATOLOGY

RANK	HOSPITAL	LOCATION
1.	Hospital for Special Surgery	New York, NY
2.	Mayo Clinic	Rochester, MN
3.	Brigham and Women's Hospital	Boston, MA
4.	UCLA Medical Center	Los Angeles, CA
5.	Johns Hopkins Hospital	Baltimore, MD
6.	Massachusetts General Hospital	Boston, MA
7.	University of Alabama Hospital at Birmingham	Birmingham, AL
8.	Duke University Medical Center	Durham, NC
9.	Cleveland Clinic	Cleveland, OH
10.	New York University Medical Center	New York, NY
11.	University of Michigan Medical Center	Ann Arbor, MI
12.	Presbyterian University Hospital	Pittsburgh, PA
13.	Stanford University Medical Center	Stanford, CA
14.	University of Washington Medical Center	Seattle, WA
15.	Green Hospital of Scripps Clinic	La Jolla, CA
16.	University of California San Francisco Medical Center	San Francisco, CA
17.	Indiana University Medical Center	Indianapolis, IN
18.	Beth Israel Hospital	Boston, MA
19.	University of Illinois Hospital and Clinics	Chicago, IL
20.	Hospital of the University of Pennsylvania	Philadelphia, PA
21.	Hospital for Joint Diseases Orthopedic Institute	New York, NY
22.	Yale-New Haven Hospital	New Haven, CT
23.	Thomas Jefferson University Hospital	Philadephia, PA
24.	Barnes Hospital	St. Louis, MO
25.	Deaconess Hospital	Boston, MA
26.	UCSD Medical Center	San Diego, CA
27.	University of Minnesota Hospital and Clinic	Minneapolis, MN
28.	Clinical Center, National Institutes of Health	Bethesda, MD
29.	University of Wisconsin Hospital and Clinics	Madison, WI
30.	George Washington University Medical Center	Washington, DC
31.	New England Medical Center	Boston, MA
32.	University of Chicago Hospitals	Chicago, IL
33.	Medical University of South Carolina	Charleston, SC
34.	University Hospitals of Cleveland	Cleveland, OH
35.	Rush-Presbyterian-St. Luke's Medical Center	Chicago, IL
36.	Long Island Jewish Medical Center	New Hyde Park, NY
37.	Georgetown University Medical Center	Washington, DC
38.	Ohio State University Medical Center	Columbus, OH
39.	New York Hospital-Cornell Medical Center	New York, NY
40.	University of Virginia Health Sciences Center	Charlottesville, VA

UROLOGY

RANK HOSPITAL   **LOCATION**

1.	Mayo Clinic.	Rochester, MN
2.	Johns Hopkins Hospital	Baltimore, MD
3.	Cleveland Clinic.	Cleveland, OH
4.	UCLA Medical Center.	Los Angeles, CA
5.	Memorial Sloan-Kettering Cancer Center	New York, NY
6.	Stanford University Medical Center.	Stanford, CA
7.	Barnes Hospital	St. Louis, MO
8.	University of Texas M.D. Anderson Cancer Center	Houston, TX
9.	Massachusetts General Hospital.	Boston, MA
10.	Duke University Medical Center	Durham, NC
11.	Indiana University Medical Center	Indianapolis, IN
12.	University of Washington Medical Center	Seattle, WA
13.	University of California San Francisco Medical Center	San Francisco, CA
14.	Roswell Park Cancer Institute	Buffalo, NY
15.	Lahey Clinic	Burlington, MA
16.	New York University Medical Center	New York, NY
17.	New York Hospital-Cornell Medical Center.	New York, NY
18.	Thomas Jefferson University Hospital.	Philadelphia, PA
19.	Brigham and Women's Hospital.	Boston, MA
20.	University of Illinois Hospital and Clinics	Chicago, IL
21.	Columbia-Presbyterian Medical Center.	New York, NY
22.	Deaconess Hospital.	Boston, MA
23.	Beth Israel Hospital.	Boston, MA
24.	University of Wisconsin Hospital and Clinics	Madison, WI
25.	University of Minnesota Hospital and Clinic.	Minneapolis, MN
26.	Baylor University Medical Center	Dallas, TX
27.	Georgetown University Medical Center	Washington, DC
28.	Green Hospital of Scripps Clinic	La Jolla, CA
29.	Hospital of the University of Pennsylvania	Philadelphia, PA
30.	University of Virgina Health Sciences Center	Charlottesville, VA
31.	Presbyterian University Hospital	Pittsburgh, PA
32.	Mount Sinai Medical Center	Cleveland, OH
33.	University of Iowa Hospitals and Clinics.	Iowa City, IA
34.	New England Medical Center.	Boston, MA
35.	Rush-Presbyterian-St. Luke's Medical Center	Chicago, IL
36.	Boston University Medical Center Hospital.	Boston, MA
37.	New England Baptist Hospital	Boston, MA
38.	Ohio State University Medical Center.	Columbus, OH
39.	Mount Sinai Medical Center	New York, NY
40.	Emory University Hospital	Atlanta, GA

NATIONAL CANCER INSTITUTE

CANCER CENTERS IN THE U.S.

Finding the best place for cancer care is the serious concern of millions of Americans. Over 1.2 million new cancer cases are diagnosed in the U.S. each year, and cancer remains the nation's second leading cause of death—in 1992, over 500,000 cancer deaths were reported in the U.S. Over the last decade, however, enormous progress has been made in the development of new therapies and improved treatments that have relieved suffering and increased life expectancies for a large number of cancer patients.

Since the passage of the National Cancer Act in 1971, the federal government has funded medical research largely through the National Cancer Institute (NCI). The NCI's comprehensive and clinical cancer centers conduct multidisciplinary research to reduce the incidence of cancer, as well as the morbidity and mortality rates of cancer patients. This program provides any patient ready access to the most advanced forms of cancer care in every region of the country.

Comprehensive Cancer Centers. There are 27 Comprehensive Cancer Centers across the country—up from 19 in 1990. Each must meet eight strict requirements, including a strong core of basic lab research in several scientific fields, such as biology and molecular genetics; a strong program of clinical research; a record of innovative clinical research studies in the community it serves; and an ability to transfer research findings into clinical practice. In addition, comprehensive centers must participate in NCI-designated high priority clinical trials and be able to organize multidisciplinary research to exploit important new findings or address timely research questions.

Clinical Cancer Centers. Numbering 13 nationwide, these centers focus on clinical research. They frequently incorporate nearby affiliated research institutions into their overall research programs.

COMPREHENSIVE CANCER CENTERS

STATE	LOCATION	CENTER
Alabama	Birmingham	University of Alabama at Birmingham Comprehensive Cancer Center
Arizona	Tucson	Arizona Cancer Center University of Arizona
California	Los Angeles	Jonsson Comprehensive Cancer Center University of California at Los Angeles
	Los Angeles	Kenneth Norris, Jr. Comprehensive Cancer Center University of Southern California
Connecticut	New Haven	Yale Comprehensive Cancer Center
District of Columbia	Washington, DC	Lombardi Cancer Center Georgetown University Medical Center
Florida	Miami	Sylvester Comprehensive Cancer Center University of Miami Medical School
Maryland	Baltimore	Johns Hopkins Oncology Center
Massachusetts	Boston	Dana-Farber Cancer Institute
Michigan	Ann Arbor	University of Michigan Cancer Center
	Detroit	Meyer L. Prentis Comprehensive Cancer Center of Metropolitan Detroit
New Hampshire	Hanover	Norris Cotton Cancer Center
New York	Buffalo	Roswell Park Cancer Institute
	New York	Kaplan Comprehensive Cancer Center New York University Medical Center
	New York	Memorial Sloan-Kettering Cancer Center
North Carolina	Chapel Hill	Lineberger Comprehensive Cancer Center University of North Carolina
	Durham	Duke Comprehensive Cancer Center
	Winston-Salem	Bowman Gray School of Medicine Wake Forest University
Ohio	Columbus	Ohio State University Comprehensive Cancer Center
Pennsylvania	Philadelphia	Fox Chase Cancer Center
	Philadelphia	University of Pennsylvania Cancer Center
	Pittsburgh	Pittsburgh Cancer Institute
Texas	Houston	M.D. Anderson Cancer Center University of Texas
Vermont	Burlington	Vermont Cancer Center University of Vermont
Washington	Seattle	Fred Hutchinson Cancer Research Center

| Wisconsin | Madison | University of Wisconsin Comprehensive Cancer Center |

CLINICAL CANCER CENTERS

STATE	LOCATION	CENTER
California	Duarte	City of Hope National Medical Center/Beckman Research Institute
	San Diego	University of California San Diego Cancer Center
Colorado	Denver	University of Colorado Cancer Center
Illinois	Chicago	Lurie Cancer Center Northwestern University
	Chicago	University of Chicago Cancer Research Center
New York	Bronx	Albert Einstein College of Medicine
	New York	Columbia-Presbyterian Cancer Center
	Rochester	University of Rochester Cancer Center
Ohio	Cleveland	Ireland Cancer Center Case Western Reserve University
Tennessee	Memphis	St. Jude Children's Research Hospital
Texas	San Antonio	San Antonio Cancer Institute
Utah	Salt Lake City	Utah Cancer Center University of Utah Medical Center
Virginia	Richmond	Massey Cancer Center Medical College of Virginia

INDEXES

SPECIALISTS INDEX

This index lists, alphabetically, by last names, all medical professionals included in the "Well-Known Specialists" section of each entry, as well as those mentioned elsewhere in entry text.

GENERAL INDEX

This index is an alphabetical listing of diseases, disorders, conditions, and subject specialties mentioned in the text for each entry, with references to the hospitals that provide treatment for or conduct research in, and the medical professionals who specialize in, those areas. Also included are medical procedures and special programs/facilities named in the entries. Names of the hospitals described in this book are listed as well. They appear in boldface type for easy access.

Anxiety disorders (*See also*
Obsessive-compulsive disorder;
Panic disorder; Phobias;
Post-traumatic stress disorder)
specialists 197, 228
treatment 67, 115, 194, 212, 351, 448,
458, 501
Aortic aneurysms *See* Aneurysms, aortic
Aplastic anemia *See* Anemia, aplastic
Apnea
treatment 130
Apnea/snoring
specialists 235
Arrhythmia
research 172, 284
specialists 203
treatment 83, 104, 122, 202, 208, 227,
281, 325, 356, 486, 508
Arrhythmias, cardiac 418
specialists 433
treatment 16, 171
Arrhythmias, pediatric cardiac
treatment 77
Arrhythmias, shock ablation of
treatment 9
Arterial restenosis
research 138
Arterial switch procedure
specialists 45
Arteriography, coronary 44, 338
Arteriosclerosis
research 53, 59, 223, 322
specialists 101
Arteriovenous malformations (AVMs)
treatment 128
Arthritis (*See also* Osteoarthritis;
Rheumatology)
research 26, 210, 216, 312, 506
specialists 27, 222
treatment 4, 11, 25, 67, 109, 115, 129,
170, 187, 202, 214, 251–252, 282, 309,
314, 333, 369, 378, 393, 400
Arthritis, pediatric
treatment 282
Arthritis, rheumatoid
research 20, 167, 396, 427
treatment 130, 252, 256, 512
Arthroscopic surgery *See* Surgery,
arthroscopic
Arthroscopy 45
Arthur G. James Cancer Hospital and
Research Institute 325

Arthur M. Fishberg Research Center in
Neurobiology 271
Articular cartilage damage
research 229
Artificial heart 367, 424
research 8, 88, 322, 422
Artificial heart, CardioWest 8
Artificial heart, Jarvik-7 8
Artificial heart-assist devices 419
Artificial insemination 202, 296, 508
Artificial joints
research 11, 259
Artificial kidney 318
Artificial knee 157
Artificial limbs
research 428
Artificial lung
specialists 364
Artificial organs
research 428
Artificial surfactant
research 59
Artificial tendon 372
Asthma
research 162, 167, 474
specialists 72, 342, 364
treatment 24, 37, 130, 141, 171, 282,
414, 474
Asthma, pediatric
treatment 276, 378
Astigmatism
treatment 386
Atherectomy 246, 274, 347, 486, 516
research 31, 497
Atherosclerosis
research 143, 238, 284, 415, 450, 484, 506
specialists 414
treatment 189, 282, 473
Atherosclerosis in African-Americans
research 85
Attention deficit disorder (*See also*
Hyperactivity)
treatment 195, 394, 431
Audiology 130
Autism
specialists 124
treatment 314, 361, 394
Autoimmune disease (*See also* Arthritis,
rheumatoid; Dermatomyostis;
Lupus erythematosus; Scleroderma;
Vasculitis)
research 26
treatment 122, 267

The Best Hospitals in America

Memory
  research 162
Memory disorders
  treatment 282, 295
Menke's disease
  research 492
The Menninger Foundation 145
Menopause (*See also* Estrogen
      replacement therapy; Hormone
      replacement therapy)
  research 440
  specialists 335
  treatment 105, 117, 166, 170, 226, 270,
      282, 332, 349, 361, 436
Menstrual disorders
  treatment 332
Mental disorders, geriatric
  treatment 247
Mental health 500
  specialists 248
Mental health, child and adolescent
  research 115
Mental illness
  research 197
  treatment 145, 193
Mental retardation
  research 7, 434
  specialists 248
  treatment 394
Met gene
  research 517
Metabolic bone disease *See* Bone disease,
      metabolic
Metabolic disease (*See also* Cushing's
      disease; Diabetes; Gaucher's
      disease)
  specialists 90, 131
  treatment 82, 208, 376
Metabolism
  research 69
  specialists 123, 229, 342, 414, 439, 499
Metabolism, pediatric
  specialists 311
Methadone Maintenance Treatment 295
Methodist Hospital 411
Methylprednisolone
  research 416
Miami shunt
  specialists 96
Michigan Alzheimer's Disease Research
      Center 216
Microbiology
  research 132, 268

  specialists 277, 304, 457
Microbiology, medical
  research 41
  specialists 475
Microsurgery 105, 302, 308, 459
  research 59
  specialists 311, 492
Microsurgery, urologic 130
Microvascular surgery *See* Surgery,
      microvascular
Migraine
  research 149
  treatment 208
**Milton S. Hershey Medical Center of
      Pennsylvania State University 359**
Miscarriage
  specialists 235
Mitral valve replacement
  research 88
Moffitt and Long Hospitals 56
Mohs surgery *See* Surgery, Mohs
Molecular and experimental medicine
  research 26
Molecular biology 121
  research 85, 132, 178, 220, 238, 329,
      335, 343
Molecular biology, structural
  research 178
Molecular genetics
  research 154, 178, 220, 311, 358, 510
Molecular medicine 374
  research 79, 449
Molecular neurobiology
  research 506
Molecular pathogenesis
  research 305
Molecular structure
  research 449
Molecular virology
  research 335
Moles (*See also* Dysplastic nevi)
  treatment 356
Monoclonal antibodies
  research 6, 40, 399
Monoclonal antibody therapy 447
Montreal Chest Hospital Centre 516
Montreal Children's Hospital 466
Montreal General Hospital 512
Montreal Neurological Institute 465
Mood disorders (*See also* Bipolar
      disorder; Depression)
  research 198
  specialists 197, 228